THOUGHT AND CHARACTER OF
WILLIAM JAMES

VOLUME II. PHILOSOPHY AND PSYCHOLOGY

WILLIAM JAMES

Portrait by Mrs. Ellen Emmet Rand, Presented by Friends and Former Pupils to Harvard University on January 18, 1910, and Hung in the Faculty Room, University Hall

THE
THOUGHT AND CHARACTER OF
WILLIAM JAMES

*As revealed in unpublished correspondence and
notes, together with his published writings*

By

RALPH BARTON PERRY

VOLUME II
PHILOSOPHY AND PSYCHOLOGY

With Illustrations

An Atlantic Monthly Press Book

LITTLE, BROWN AND COMPANY
BOSTON   TORONTO

Copyright, 1935,
BY HENRY JAMES

All rights reserved

ATLANTIC–LITTLE, BROWN BOOKS
ARE PUBLISHED BY
LITTLE, BROWN AND COMPANY
IN ASSOCIATION WITH
THE ATLANTIC MONTHLY PRESS

PRINTED IN THE UNITED STATES OF AMERICA

TABLE OF CONTENTS

PART IV. PSYCHOLOGY

and Difficulties, 36. Beginnings of the Work —
Turning Point in 1883, 38. Ups and Downs, 39.
Articles Sent to Croom Robertson, 40. Nearing
Completion — Author *vs*. Publisher, 44. Finished
at Last — Correcting Proof, 48

Letters: —

Functionalism, 51. The Preface to the Italian
Translation, 52. The Wide Range of James's
Sources — Wundt, Helmholtz, and Bain, 54.
James and Ward — Ward's *Britannica* Article, 56.
James and Stumpf — Beginnings of Their Friend-
ship, 59. The *Tonpsychologie,* 61. Comparison
of Views on Psychology and Psychologists, 64.
Common Antipathies — Spencer and Wundt, 66

Letters: —

Unpublished Notes, etc.

Positivism — Epistemological Dualism, 72. Con-

CONTENTS

PART V. ETHICS AND RELIGION

James's Moral Earnestness — Relations with Holmes, 250. Distaste for Decadence — Switzerland As an Ideal, 251. Moralist vs. Artist — Art vs. Æsthetics, 253. The Relativity of Æsthetic Values, 255. Art Associated with Tradition, 257. Subordination of Feeling to Moral Will, 258. Ethics vs. Psychology of Moral Experience, 260. Historical Sources — Spencer and Mill, 261

Letters: —

Unpublished Notes, etc.

Philosophy 4, and "The Moral Philosopher," 263. Individualism the Fundamental Principle, 265. Tolerance — to the Mass and to Individuals — Peabody, Münsterberg, and Santayana, 267. Antagonistic Motives — The Gospel of Heroism, 270. Its Psychology, 272. Kipling, 274. Reconciliation of Martial and Humanitarian Motives, 277

Letters: —

Unpublished Notes, etc.

PART VI. THE ULTIMATE PHILOSOPHICAL SYSTEM

CONTENTS

Early Influence, 406. James and Peirce on Pragmatism, 407. James and Peirce on Pluralism, 411. Correspondence of Peirce and James, 412. Peirce's "Prospectus," 413. Peirce and Schelling, 415. James Presses Peirce's Appointment, 416. Arranges His Cambridge Lectures, 418

The National Academy of Science and the Carnegie Corporation, 422. The Philosophy 3 Syllabus, 425. More Lectures at Cambridge and Boston, 426. Peirce Explains His Views — Pragmatism, 430. Radical Empiricism, 430. Both Doctrines Discussed, 432. The Limits of Logic, 437

CONTENTS

CONTENTS

Their Differences, 514. Early Correspondence —
Dewey's *Ethics,* 516. The "Chicago School," 519.
The *Studies in Logical Theory,* 523. Instrumen-
talism, 524. Radical Empiricism, 526. Dewey
Interprets *Pragmatism,* 528. James's *Meaning of
Truth* and Dewey's Suggested Amendments, 531

Letters: —

General Relations, 534. Pragmatism and God,
534. Strong's Manuscript on "Substitutionalism,"
535. Truth: Confluence *vs.* Similarity, 537.
James Insists on Being a Realist! 543. Approaching an Understanding, 551

Letters: —

From Pragmatism to Metaphysics — Revival of Correspondence with Blood, 553. Blood's Criticism of Pragmatism — He Harps upon Mysticism, 555. James and Émile Boutroux, 560. Pragmatism, Pluralism, and Religion, 561. Boutroux at Harvard, 566. The Last Weeks, 568

Letters: —

Papini and His Circle, 570. James's Enthusiasm, 571. Political Pragmatism — James and Mussolini, 574. Influence of Sorel — Sorel, Lenin, and Pragmatism, 575. Fascism and Pragmatism, Their Common Ground, 577. Pragmatism in Germany — Mach, 579. Jerusalem and Goldstein, 580. From Pragmatism to Metaphysics, 581

Letters: —

The Hibbert Lectures, 583. Criticism of the Monists, Lotze, Bradley, Royce, and Hegel, 584. From Pragmatism to Pluralism, 585. James and Fechner, 586. The Compounding of Consciousness, 588. Abandoning Logic, 589. The Continuum of Experience — Realism, 590. Pluralism

James and Bradley — Pure Experience and *A Pluralistic Universe,* 637. Bradley Criticizes James's Realism, 640. "Bradley or Bergson?" 642. James and Ward — Agreement and Difference, 644. Ward's *Naturalism and Agnosticism,* 645. Religion and the Subconscious, 648. Bergson and the *Pluralistic Universe* — Attempts at *Rapprochement,* 650

Letters: —

Interest in Mysticism — James and Blood, 658. "A Pluralistic Mystic," 659. The Last Book — Turning to Technical Philosophy, 661. The Problem of Novelty, 663. The Unfinished Task and Its Implications, 665. The Manifoldness and Permanence of James's Influence, 668

ILLUSTRATIONS

PART IV

PSYCHOLOGY

LII

EARLY STUDY AND TEACHING OF PSYCHOLOGY

THE first of James's major works was the *Principles of Psychology,* which appeared in 1890 when the author was forty-eight years old. It was a work of first importance, not only for James but for the history of psychology — the fruit of over twenty years of study and writing, carried on during a crucial period in the development of the subject to which it was devoted. For whether or no James be regarded as one of the founders of modern psychology, in any case he was present while it was being founded, and experienced in himself the motives which led to its founding. In 1867 and 1868 he was in Germany — ostensibly pursuing his medical studies, in reality studying the science of physiology, combating ill-health, inviting his soul, and observing the life and monuments about him. What was the state of psychology at this time? Writing from Berlin to Thomas W. Ward in the autumn of 1867, he said : —

"It seems to me that perhaps the time has come for psychology to begin to be a science — some measurements have already been made in the region lying between the physical changes in the nerves and the appearance of consciousness-at (in the shape of sense perceptions), and more may come of it. I am going on to study what is already known, and perhaps may be able to do some work at it. Helmholtz and a man named Wundt at Heidelberg are working at it, and I hope I live through this winter to go to them in the summer." [1]

James here alludes to the most important signs of the new "experimental psychology." In 1860 Fechner [2] had published his *Elemente der Psychophysik,* in which he had formulated the law which had been envisaged by E. H. Weber as early as 1846,[3] and which became known as the Weber-Fechner Law. This law stated the relations between intensities of stimulus and intensities of sensation,

[1] *L.W J.,* I, 118–9.
[2] *Cf.* below, 19, 586–8.
[3] In his *Tastsinn und Gemeingefühl.*

and promised to qualify psychology (as "psychophysics") for membership in the select circle of the quantitative and experimental sciences. Helmholtz, on the other hand, continuing the work of Johannes Müller,[4] had approached psychology by way of the physiology of the senses. The first complete edition of his great *Handbuch der physiologischen Optik* appeared in 1867, while he was professor of philosophy at Heidelberg. Wilhelm Wundt was the man in whom experimental psychology was weaned from this physical and physiological parentage. He was James's senior by ten years — in age, in academic status, and in his command of the subject of psychology. Trained in physiology under Müller and Helmholtz, and *Dozent* in physiology at Heidelberg from 1857, he had already, in 1862, published a volume of experimental studies on sense perception[5] and begun to lecture on "psychology as a natural science."

James underwent in the development of his own interests a change similar to that represented by the emergence of Wundt from Müller and Helmholtz. There was in James, as in Wundt, that breadth of interest or concern with the whole of life which distinguishes the philosopher, so that if he was to be scientific it must be from a new centre. Man, for him, could not constitute a mere chapter of physics or physiology. Thus in 1868 James described himself as "wading his way" *towards* the field of psychology, through the physiology of the senses; and spoke of his possible studies as helping to prepare the way for the appearance of psychology.[6] After his return to America in the same year, and during his ensuing illness, he followed with keen interest the work of the German physiologists with whom his more fortunate friend and correspondent, Bowditch, was carrying on his studies.[7] But he never confused or identified psychology with physiology.

There was another similarity between James and Wundt: both men, like Lotze and Helmholtz before them, qualified themselves for the practice of medicine. It is safe to assume that this professional aspect of their studies influenced all four of these men in the direction of psychology, for medicine deals with the human individual, and takes him centrally rather than as a mere proliferation of his physical environment. Among the earliest books which James read

[4] *Handbuch der Physiologie des Menschen* (1833–40).
[5] *Beiträge zur Theorie der Sinneswahrnehmung.*
[6] *L.W.J.*, I, 126–7; and above, I, 274–6.
[7] Notably K. F. W. Ludwig of Leipzig; *cf. L.W.J.*, I, 158–63.

having an immediate bearing on his psychological interest was Lotze's *Medizinische Psychologie,* which he bought in Berlin in 1867 and carried with him during this European sojourn. His copy is interleaved and summarized throughout, in a manner that suggests the conscientious, acquisitive mind of the beginner.

James's medical training, together with his own personal experiences, implanted in him a deep interest in psychopathology. It must have been on his way home in 1868, during his sojourn in Paris, that he bought Wilhelm Griesinger's *Pathologie und Therapie der psychischen Krankheiten.* This he read shortly after his return and pronounced a "noble book." [8] The same interest drew him in the direction of the French school of Charcot.[9] Hypnosis received scientific recognition in France about 1860, and Charcot, who had begun his career at the Salpêtrière in 1862, began giving public clinical demonstrations in this field of study in 1878. There was no sharp dividing line between psychopathology, so considered, and psychical research. They both belonged broadly to the field of abnormal mentality, and constituted a considerable part of what James regarded as the domain of psychology.

James's psychological cosmopolitanism was completed by his direct inheritance of the British tradition. Although Taine in France resembled the British school, and Henry Maudsley in England manifested the French fondness for psychopathology,[10] French and English psychology on the whole ran in different grooves. In the year 1867 John Stuart Mill and Herbert Spencer were approaching the summit of their influence. The former's *Examination of Sir William Hamilton's Philosophy* appeared in 1865, and his edition of his father's *Analysis of the Phenomena of the Human Mind* in 1869. The definitive edition of Spencer's *Principles of Psychology* appeared in 1870. The one concluded the orthodox associationist movement, and the other diverted this movement into biological channels. At their side stood Alexander Bain, an offshoot of the associationistic school. His *Senses and Intellect* in 1855, and *Emotions and Will* in 1859, became in their successive revisions the standard treatises of British psychology and embodied to an ever-increas-

---

[8] James had heard Griesinger lecture in Berlin. Several of James's earliest reviews were of books on psychopathology. *Cf. Bg.,* 1873–1; 1874–1; 1874–5.

[9] James was attending Charcot's lectures in Paris in 1882 when he received news of his father's last illness.

[10] *The Physiology and Pathology of Mind,* 1867.

ing extent the results of the psychophysical and physiological studies which were developing contemporaneously in Germany. With the work of Mill, Maudsley, Taine, Spencer, and Bain, James was thoroughly familiar.[11]

The fact that James was an American accounts for the peculiar catholicism of his psychology. He benefited by the new movements in German, French, and English psychology without surrendering himself wholly to any of them. His wide acquaintance and mobility, both of person and of mind, enabled him to sit at all of these feasts and combine their several nutritive values. That he lost something by this cosmopolitanism is perhaps true — but it is certain that he gained. He was a more complete psychologist, and more fertile in happy anticipations of future development, than Stumpf, Ebbinghaus, Brentano, and others who were nourished on a German diet; than Richet, Janet, Ribot, or Binet, who preferred their own national food; or than Sully and Ward, the Englishmen. It might be added that most of James's American contemporaries, such as Hall, Cattell, Ladd, and Titchener, lost the same opportunity through surrendering themselves too completely to their German masters.

Having imbibed the newer tendencies in Europe, and having followed them up with physiological and empirical studies of his own, James became one of the first American teachers to recognize the existence of psychology as an independent science. Although it was not characteristic of him to make claims for himself, he was drawn into a public controversy over the question of priority by the extravagant counterclaims of one who had been his pupil.

In April 1890, President G. Stanley Hall, having received a letter from James promising coöperation with the Clark University Laboratory, replied as follows: "Your note is certainly satisfactory and even gratifying, except your supposition that we may want you to turn away all men who want experimental psychology. No such thought ever entered my head. . . . It distressed me to know that you have even moments of discouragement. To this you have no right. You started this whole movement yourself and are the very best man, in my opinion, in the world at the present time in your own lines, and I only fear that you are working too hard on your book.

---

[11] Bain was influenced in the physiological direction by W. B. Carpenter, whose *Principles of Mental Physiology* James reviewed for the *Atlantic* in 1874, and from whom he derived much, especially on the topic of habit.

The cause of psychology in this country is more dependent upon you and your safe delivery of that book than upon anything else whatever."

Apparently something happened between 1890 and 1894 to affect Hall's memory or the state of his feelings. In an article written in the latter year, he distinguished three types of modern psychology in America — the British empirical, the German transcendental, and, lastly, the type to which he gave no name, but which he described as follows : —

"The last psychological departure . . . began with the establishment of the first laboratory for experimental psychology in Baltimore in 1881. Something had been done in these lines previously in Germany, but the time was ripe and the soil fertile. . . . It reduces introspection to a perfectly controlled system by means of suitable apparatus. . . . In the opinion of many of its more sanguine devotees, [it] is showing itself not only to be the long hoped for, long delayed science of man, to which all other sciences are bringing their ripest and best thoughts, but is introducing a period that will be known hereafter as the psychological era of scientific thought, even more than a few recent decades have been marked by evolution. . . . It is asking the old question, what is man, in many new ways, and giving, bit by bit, new and deeper answers in a way that I deem it not too much to say makes every prospect of our own national future and of the republican type of government generally, brighter ; and promises to be a realization of all that the old professors of logic, ethics, and religion, in their best days, dimly strove for, — and more." [12]

It will be noted that in this account of the beginnings of experimental psychology even Germany came off a poor second. Then, in October 1895, Hall published in his *American Journal of Psychology* an editorial in which, having referred to the establishment of that *Journal* in 1887 under the auspices of the department of psychology (namely, himself) at the Johns Hopkins University, as "one of the boldest and most sagacious as well as one of the most successful and beneficent steps ever taken by this leader of the new academic movement," he went on to speak of his own transfer to Clark University. Giving a long list of men who had at one time

[12] "On the History of American College Text-Books," etc., *American Antiquarian Soc.*, IX (1893–4), 160–1. As to the date "1881," cf. below, 9, 22.

or another been associated with him at Johns Hopkins or Clark, he then said: "Under the influence of these men departments of experimental psychology and laboratories were founded at Harvard, Yale, Philadelphia, Columbia, Toronto, Wisconsin and many other higher institutions of learning."

This was too much! In the following month there appeared simultaneously in *Science* [13] letters from James, George Trumbull Ladd, James McKeen Cattell, and James Mark Baldwin denying the allegation altogether so far as concerned three of these institutions, and correcting it as regards the others. Hall replied a few weeks later [14] in an aggrieved and conciliatory tone, and explained that what he really meant was that "in the development of a new academic 'department' a crucial point is reached . . . when an instructor is appointed whose central work and interest is in that line" — a formula skillfully designed to cover the appointments of Herbert Nichols at Harvard, E. W. Scripture at Yale, Cattell at Pennsylvania and Columbia, Joseph Jastrow at Wisconsin, and himself at Johns Hopkins. Toronto he withdrew altogether, with apologies.

Such was the famous public controversy over the beginnings of experimental psychology in America. While it proved the folly of boasting, it served a useful purpose in bringing to light certain major facts regarding the question at issue. Baldwin, having studied at Princeton with McCosh, who had given a course in physiological psychology (with "practical work" by William B. Scott and Harry F. Osborn) as early as 1883, began the teaching of experimental psychology at Toronto in 1889. Ladd, having begun his studies of physiological psychology in 1879 (apparently with the reading of Wundt's work on that subject) [15] while professor at Bowdoin, continued them after 1881 in James K. Thatcher's physiological laboratory at the Yale Medical School, began teaching the subject in 1884, and published his own *Elements of Physiological Psychology* in 1887. When Hall began laboratory instruction at Johns Hopkins in the fall of 1882, Cattell and Jastrow were members of his class. The former studied for two years with Lotze and Wundt, and after his return to this country introduced the new psychology at Pennsyl-

[13] *N.S.*, II (1895), 626.
[14] *Ibid.*, 735.
[15] *Grundzüge der physiologischen Psychologie,* 1874; "the most important book in the history of modern psychology" (Boring, *History of Experimental Psychology,* 1929, 317).

vania in 1888, and at Columbia in 1891.   Jastrow took his degree
at Johns Hopkins in 1886 and began laboratory teaching at the
University of Wisconsin in 1888.   But he had begun experimental
studies in psychology under Charles Peirce, as is indicated by his
own statement, as follows: "Though I promptly took to the laboratory of psychology when that was established by Stanley Hall, it
was Peirce who gave me my first training in the handling of a
psychological problem, and at the same time stimulated my self-
esteem by entrusting me, then fairly innocent of any laboratory
habits, with a real bit of research.   He borrowed the apparatus
for me, which I took to my room, installed at my window, and
with which, when conditions of illuminations were right, I took the
observations.   The results were published over our joint names in
the *Proceedings of the National Academy of Science.*" [16]

Let us now consider the question of priority as it relates to
James.   When he read Hall's extraordinary editorial he at once
(October 12, 1895) wrote the latter a long letter, in which he said:
"As an arm-chair professor, I frankly admit my great inferiority
as a laboratory-teacher and investigator.   But some little regard
should be paid to the good will with which I have tried to force my
nature, and to the actual things I have done.   One of them, for
example, was inducting you into experimental investigation, with
very naïve methods, it is true, but you may remember that there was
no other place but Harvard where during those years you could
get even that.   I remember also giving a short course of psychological
lectures at the Johns Hopkins years before you went there.[17]   They
were exclusively experimental, and, I have been told, made an
'epoch' there in determining opinion.

"I well recognize how contemptible these beginnings were, and
that you and your pupils have in these latter years left them far
behind.   But you are now professing to state history; beginnings
are a part thereof, and should not be written down in inverted
order. . . .   In this world we all owe to each other.   My debt to you
and to Clark is great, and if only my own person was concerned,
I should let you say what you like and not object, for the bystanders

---

[16] "Charles S. Peirce As a Teacher," *Jour. of Philos.*, XIII (1916), 724.   The
experimental work, "On Small Differences of Sensation," was reported Oct. 17,
1884, and published in *Memoirs* of the National Academy of Sciences, III (1884–6),
75.
[17] In 1878; *cf.* below, 27.

generally see truly. In this case, however, the misstatement concerns the credit of my university."

The early history of James's teaching of psychology is briefly as follows. Beginning in 1872 and for the next few years, he gave courses in anatomy and physiology in Harvard College. These subjects were taught by the comparative method, and were grouped with geology under natural history, indicating, as we have seen, the preoccupation at this time with the topic of evolution. In these courses James devoted considerable attention to the physiology of the nervous system and some to psychophysics. In 1875 he announced a course for graduates on "The Relations between Physiology and Psychology," and thereafter this course or some equivalent course of advanced grade was given regularly.[18] James began his undergraduate instruction in psychology in 1876–1877 with a course announced as "Natural History 2" and described as "Physiological Psychology — Herbert Spencer's Principles of Psychology." In the following year his psychological teaching was transferred to the department of philosophy, though he remained until 1880 assistant professor of physiology.[19] Instead of Natural History 2, he now announced his undergraduate course as: "Philosophy 4. Psychology. — Taine on Intelligence." The scope of this earliest undergraduate course was very broad, including physiological psychology, the traditional topics of the associationists, and such philosophical problems as knowledge of the external world and freedom of the will. Indeed its scope corresponds fairly closely to the contents of the *Principles of Psychology,* and most of the author's characteristic views were worked out in his lectures and in his criticisms of the texts which were assigned. The following letter, written to President Eliot the year before the course was inaugurated, contains James's idea of the intermediate place of psychology between philosophy and the biological sciences: —

Cambridge, Dec. 2, 1875

Dear Sir, —

Since you are about to confer with the Corporation about my general position in the College program, it may not be improper

---

[18] The scope of this graduate course can be gathered from the examination paper set at the end of the year 1879–80, and printed below as Appendix VII.

[19] In other words, for five years psychology was taught at Harvard by one who at the same time taught biology! This was fifty years ago. Can we say that psychology is to-day any closer to biology or any remoter from philosophy than it was then?

for me to give you on paper my notion of the way in which my proposed teaching would fit in without stretching unduly the canvas. . . .

As I understand it, the object of multiplying the courses is two-fold: (1) to let the student progressively advance in the subject for three years, if he wish; and (2) to make the "divisions" of manageable size. . . . The new course in psychology which I propose would, of course, be partly judged by the importance of this condition. But the principal claim I should make for it is its intrinsic importance at the present day, when on every side naturalists and physiologists are publishing extremely crude and pretentious psychological speculations under the name of "science"; and when professors whose education has been exclusively literary or philosophical, are too apt to show a real inaptitude for estimating the force and bearing of physiological arguments when used to help define the nature of man. A real science of man is now being built up out of the theory of evolution and the facts of archæology, the nervous system and the senses. It has already a vast material extent, the papers and magazines are full of essays and articles having more or less to do with it. The question is shall the students be left to the magazines, on the one hand, and to what languid attention professors educated in the exclusively literary way can pay to the subject? Or shall the College employ a man whose scientific training fits him fully to realize the force of all the natural history arguments, whilst his concomitant familiarity with writers of a more introspective kind preserves him from certain crudities of reasoning which are extremely common in men of the laboratory pure and simple?

Apart from all reference to myself, it is my firm belief that the College cannot possibly have psychology taught as a living science by anyone who has not a first-hand acquaintance with the facts of nervous physiology. On the other hand, no mere physiologist can adequately realize the subtlety and difficulty of the psychologic portions of his own subject until he has tried to teach, or at least to study, psychology in its entirety. A union of the two "disciplines" in one man, seems then the most natural thing in the world, if not the most traditional. But if tradition be required, Göttingen with Lotze, and Heidelberg and Zürich with Wundt would serve as most honorable precedents for Harvard College, in the path I propose. . . . I remain, very truly yours,

WM. JAMES

James was clearly advocating the recognition of the new psychology — "new" in the sense of allying itself with science as well as with philosophy, and in combining the methods of observation and experiment with those of speculation and reflection. This was a distinct innovation. Psychology as then taught in the United States was indistinguishable from the philosophy of the soul, embracing a brief account of the senses and of association, but devoted mainly to the higher moral and logical processes. In doctrine it was usually a blend of common-sense realism of the Scottish school with traces of Kantian influence and such drafts upon the major philosophers as might serve the purpose of protecting religion and morals against the menace of materialism.[20] The psychology taught at Harvard had been in this Scottish tradition, with Thomas Reid's *Intellectual Powers of Man* and Dugald Stewart's *Active and Moral Powers* as texts.[21] In 1871 a committee of the Harvard Overseers reported: "Psychological studies cannot be said to rank very high among us. They are neither taught by as many teachers nor studied by as many students as they might be; — nor do they seem to excite that interest among those engaged in them which should be felt in questions interesting to every generation of educated men."[22] The following year Professor Francis Bowen announced an elective course on "Psychology" (so called for the first time), but his texts, Porter, Locke, Cousin, and Mill, did not differ from those which he had previously used, and the course was distinctly less psychological than a course on "Philosophy" offered in 1873–1874 by Palmer, who used Bain's *Mental Science*. In any case neither of these teachers had "a first-hand acquaintance with the facts of nervous physiology."

Thus it is not surprising that James's early teaching of physiological psychology at Harvard attracted considerable attention. The very expression "physiological psychology" was just coined. Wundt had lectured on a subject so designated since 1867 and had published a book bearing that title in 1874; but in America both

[20] The most important book of this type was N. Porter's *Human Intellect,* 1868. James McCosh, originally representing the same tendency, veered definitely in the direction of a more scientific and physiological psychology, in his teaching and in his works — *Psychology, the Cognitive Powers,* 1886; *The Motive Powers,* 1888.
[21] *Cf.* B. Rand, "Philosophical Instruction in Harvard University," *Harvard Graduates' Magazine,* XXXVII (1928–9).
[22] Report of Committee on Resolutions, Dec. 19, 1871, 3.

the label and the contents were new.   Stanley Hall, writing from Cambridge in 1878, spoke of James's undergraduate course as follows: "[It] has been organized only two years, and is conducted by the assistant professor of physiology.   It was admitted not without some opposition into the department of philosophy, and is up to the present time the only course in the country where students can be made familiar with the methods and results of recent German researches in physiological psychology." [23]   J. E. Cabot, the watchful and candid Chairman of the Overseers' "Committee to Visit the Academic Department," welcomed the innovation on the ground that "the ignoring by philosophers of the physical side of mental phenomena has had the natural effect of exaggerating the importance of materialistic views." [24]   Two years later he wrote: —

"The course in psychology offers a great deal of interest and stimulus to thought, which cannot fail to be of great advantage to those of the students who are sufficiently grounded in the matter to be able to test for themselves the methods of investigation and the fundamental assumptions which prevail in the 'scientific' school of philosophy at the present day. . . .   The application of physiology to the explanation of the phenomena of thought must presuppose a sufficient apprehension of the distinctive character of these phenomena, and, without that, is liable to become merely the substitution of facts of one order for the facts of another order, to the confusion of all right thinking.   We do not think, however, that, with the eminently liberal and inspiring method pursued in this course, the danger in our case is a serious one." [25]

The undergraduates were a little vague as to what the new course meant, but they wrote letters to the *Crimson* about it; and evidently expected to learn about "evolution," and at the same time be initiated into recent discoveries about the relations between the mind and the body.[26]

In his published reply to Stanley Hall's famous claim of priority, James said that the psychological laboratory at Harvard grew up in connection with these new courses: "I, myself, 'founded' the instruction in experimental psychology at Harvard in 1874–5, or 1876, I forget which.   For a long series of years the laboratory

---

[23] "Philosophy in the United States," *Mind*, IV (1879), 97.
[24] *Report*, 1875–6, 4.
[25] *Report*, 1877–8, 5–6.
[26] *Cf.* the letters printed above, I, 475–6.

was in two rooms of the Scientific School building, which at last became choked with apparatus, so that a change was necessary. I then, in 1890, resolved on an altogether new departure, raised several thousand dollars, fitted up Dane Hall, and introduced laboratory exercises as a regular part of the undergraduate psychology-course." [27]

Just when a psychological laboratory can be said to begin is a question which is incapable of definite settlement, because it is impossible to determine just when a physical or physiological laboratory becomes a *psychological* laboratory; and just when a set of instruments collected and used for demonstration or research in psychology becomes a *laboratory*. James's undergraduate teaching was in the main from texts, such as Spencer, Bain, and Taine, but he made use of apparatus for classroom demonstrations, gave his advanced students experimental problems, and carried on a certain amount of experimental research of his own. It was for these purposes that he fitted up two rooms on the ground floor of Lawrence Hall, then occupied by the Lawrence Scientific School. The exact date of the installation is doubtful, and in any case it was not his first place for experiments of the sort. G. Stanley Hall, referring apparently to the middle '70s, wrote: "In a tiny room under the stairway of the Agassiz Museum he [James] had a metronome, a device for whirling a frog, a horopter chart and one or two bits of apparatus." [28]   There was also the physiological laboratory of Dr. H. P. Bowditch at the Medical School, North Grove Street, Boston, of which James made frequent use as early as 1872. It is said to have been the first laboratory for experimental medicine in the United States, and, under the liberal policy of its director, border problems, such as those of physiological psychology, readily found a place. The installation in Lawrence Hall must have taken place either in 1875–1876, when graduate instruction was first offered in "The Relations between Physiology and Psychology"; or in 1876–1877, when the undergraduate course in "Physiological Psychology" (Natural History 2) was inaugurated; or, perhaps, in the

    [27] *Science, N.S.,* II (1895), 626.
    [28] *Life and Confessions of a Psychologist,* 1923, 218. Prof. E. L. Mark tells me that in connection with the instruction which James gave in "Physiology" and afterwards in the "Comparative Anatomy and Physiology of Vertebrates," he used what had formerly been Prof. Agassiz's private room in the University Museum. This laboratory in the Museum would date from the removal from Boylston Hall in 1875; *cf.* above I, 359–60.

following year, when James was transferred to the department of philosophy.

This laboratory remained in existence for many years, though it appears to have been used intermittently. It was here, probably, that James experimented on "the sense of dizziness" in 1880–1881. There are references in James's correspondence to "two or three little mustard seeds of mental investigations" in 1883, and to a "laboratory for psychophysics" in 1885. In any case, during the year 1890–1891, finding these quarters overcrowded, James raised $4300 for the new equipment and facilities, and in the autumn of 1891 moved into Dane Hall. The improved laboratory there was in good running order, with Dr. Herbert Nichols installed as laboratory assistant, when Hugo Münsterberg arrived to take charge in September 1892.

As for Stanley Hall, he had begun his advanced studies in 1869 in Germany, but had then been chiefly concerned with philosophy and theology. After teaching miscellaneous subjects for four years at Antioch College, he came in 1876 to Harvard, where he was registered for two years, and was closely associated with James in the study of physiological psychology. The work for his thesis, on "The Muscular Perception of Space," was done in Dr. Bowditch's laboratory, but the degree of Ph.D., which he received in 1878, was awarded in the subject of "psychology," by recommendation of the department of philosophy, and upon examination by a committee consisting of Bowen, Hedge, Bowditch, Everett, Palmer, and James. Having obtained his degree, Hall then repaired to Leipzig, whence he wrote to James and Bowditch describing his scientific adventures and projects. James replied: —

Prout's Neck, Maine, Sept. 3, 1879

My dear Hall, —

I have long been silent towards you, on account mostly of my eyes, but partly of various domestic cares which drove correspondence out of my head. . . . I . . . got your copy of Wundt, whose polished irony places him in quite a new light. I wish some other German polemic writers would learn the lesson from him. The college year ended satisfactorily. Poor Palmer has gone abroad to steep himself I suppose still more deeply in that priggish English Hegelism. Much good may it do him. He is an extraordinarily

able man, but associating with him is like being in a dentist's chair
the whole while. . . .   I am composing a chapter on space for my
psychology and find I have to re-read about all I ever read on that
driest of subjects, which seems an awful waste of precious time.
However, once that is done, I 'm free to browse on other fields.   In
fact already this summer I 've read about half of Lotze's *Metaphysik*.   He is the most delectable, certainly, of all German writers
— a pure genius.   But how I wish you were back, — I fairly pine
for psychologic intercourse.   Our club is about talked out. . . .

You don't know, my dear fellow, what great advantages you are
enjoying over the rest of us in being able at your mature age to
pump the German founts of wisdom.   You are bound to return
and let us pump you.   When are we going to spend that month in
Ashfield together?   I feel conscious of any amount of thirst, and
of a good deal of digestive and assimilative power, but the supplies of
material are to me so small.   However, it gratified and at the same
time disgusted me to see how many choice pages of my everlasting
psychology had been anticipated by Lotze.   It is a great boon to
have some long cud like that to keep chewing on. . . .   Pray
write soon a good long letter and believe me, yours always,

                                                     WM. JAMES

                                         Cambridge, Oct. 10 [1879]
My dear Hall, —
Receive my heartfelt congratulations! may you be as happy as I
have been in the past year and a half!   I can say no more. . . .
It 's great fun keeping house.

College has begun.   I have three rather lowly graduates in
"Physiological Psychology," five seniors in Renouvier, about thirty
juniors etc., in Spencer's *First Principles,* and a lecture a week on
Physiology.   Enough to do!   My psychology hangs fire awfully,
and my ideas are stagnant from want of friction.   Palmer is back
from Caird in splendid condition and (I fear me) fully *aufgegangen*
into the great arcanum of the identity of contradictories.   Of all
mental turpitudes and rottennesses, that may claim the prize.   But
the delicious bewilderment it engenders will always attract certain
poetic and priggish natures.   The worst of it is, it makes an absolute
sterility where it comes.   If Palmer does n't recover, good-bye to
him.   His ability strikes me more and more.   For a non-original

G. STANLEY HALL, 1881

HUGO MÜNSTERBERG, ABOUT 1900

(Reproduced, by special permission, from Hall's "Life and Confessions of a Psychologist," published by D. Appleton-Century Co.)

man, he seems to me the ablest I know.   He has three students to
my one now, but I 'm not afraid of him at all in a fair field. . . .

If you can send me a photograph of Wundt I shall esteem it a great
favor.   I thank you very much for Lotze's.   I read your letter
on him in the *Nation* with great interest.[29]   I must say I feel rather
more kindly than you to his type of man.   He keeps flying the
standard of a *rounded* mental character, the very notion of which
would be forgotten if the laboratory blackguards all had their way.
I 'm glad you write to Bowditch about Wundt as you do.   He certainly is *not* a first-class *ingenium,* but only a rather ordinary man
who has "worked up" certain things uncommonly well.   Write
soon. . . .   Yours ever,

WM. JAMES

Leipzig, Oct. 26 [1879]
My dear Dr. James, —

Yours [of Sept. 3] was received about a month ago, just after
I was married and had left Berlin. . . .   I now hear Ludwig,
Flechsig, Kries [30] and Wundt, and attend Wundt's psychological
society — all of which by a fortunate arrangement of hours I am able
to do after 4.00 P.M., so all the day before is free for writing and
a little laboratory work.   I have been drifting by my own inward
impulse for a long time, to try to gather my hobbies together, and at
the same time collect all the lore I could from experimental records
and write a physiological psychology; but have been hindered by
the consideration that you were already ahead of me in the field, and
also by the vastness of the undertaking — but the impulse has grown
too strong, and I am already hard at it.   It will be more than a year,
perhaps two, before I can have anything finished of the sort I want,
but I have come to the point where it *must* be tried, if I am to have
a restful grave at last.   Yours will be the fame of opening the
field in the United States, and I shall very likely be given a modest
place — and not altogether unjustly — as your disciple and at best
amplifier, but I shall have the great advantage of seeing your work
first.

I am on the whole disappointed in Wundt.   He opened this week

[29] "Hermann Lotze," *Nation,* XXIX (1879).
[30] Paul Flechsig and Johannes von Kries were "psychological physiologists"
and professors at Leipzig.

with great cheering, to a class of 300, on the history of philosophy. I had his *famulus* read me all his lecture notes — anthropology, psychology, ethics, logic, history of philosophy, each a course. He is about writing an enlarged edition of the *Psychology,* is very accessible, free to talk about everything, and I am very much indebted to him and he is the big man here — but still I am disappointed. On the contrary I am amazingly lifted and impelled by Helmholtz, though I saw comparatively little of him personally. My work with him is unfinished because new instruments had to be made. I spend a few weeks there in December.[31] . . .   Very truly yours,

G. STANLEY HALL

Leipzig, Dec. 27 [1879]

Dear Dr. James, —

Hope you received my card about Wundt's [*Logic*] in time to be of service. I have read with pleasure your articles on Rood, Clifford, and Spencer in the *Nation,* all of them books which I have *not* read. I envy you immensely in the satisfaction you must feel in housekeeping, — more and more every day in this dreary *pension* life. My wife, I think, is likely to be reconciled to my plan of going back to *farming* next fall, provided, as I hope, we can also keep house. . . .

I have lately seen something of . . . Schneider who is an enthusiast for studying the habits of ants, dogs, fish, etc., and who writes for Avenarius's review occasionally about animal psychology. . . . Avenarius was lately here. He is publishing Göring's papers, who grew pessimistic and drowned himself last summer near here. . . . Fechner is a curiosity. His eyelids are strangely fringed and he has had a number of holes, square and round, cut, Heaven knows why, in the iris of each eye — and is altogether a bundle of oddities in person and manners. He has forgotten all the details of his *Psychophysik;* and is chiefly interested in theorizing how knots can be tied in endless strings, and how words can be written on the inner side of two slates sealed together. [He] . . . wants me to go to Zöllner and talk to him about American spiritualism, but I have not been. Fechner is tedious enough, and I hear Zöllner is more so.[32] . . . I am drifting

---

[31] Helmholtz was at this time in Berlin.
[32] G. H. Schneider was a private lecturer in philosophy at the University of Leipzig, devoting most of his time to the study of experimental psychology. It was upon him that James drew for data regarding habit and instinct in animals.

into laboratory work more than I expected, sometimes dig at it all day except when in lectures. Am hearing special courses — one each in zoölogy and chemistry — more for diversion than anything else, and two or three times a week doing a bit of microscope work on nervous centres; but at present all my interest centres in *reflex action,* on which I am working with Ludwig — my first work alone. I think — though it is really too soon to say it — that I can disprove some essential points of Wundt's elaborate theory in the *Mechanik.* . . . Very truly yours,

G. S. HALL

Cambridge, Jan. 16, 1880

My dear Hall, —

The sight of your familiar crabbed hand transported me with joy two days ago. I fancied I perceived also the subtle influence of matrimony in making your letter more expansive, more communicative of your emotions on the subject of Fechner, Wundt & Co., less statistic and cognitive; and the reference to the present *pension* and the future farm brought in a waft of mundane air which was as refreshing as it was surprising in your epistles, usually *inhaltsreich* in such a different direction. The only thing lacking is a photograph of Mrs. G. S. H., to gain which in the next letter I send you herewith a similar self-objectivation of my own family. My plan of spending a year in Europe is quite unfeasible but replaced by a very probable one of spending the summer vacation there. If you and I can only manage to be together a part of the time, we can make psychological feathers fly at a great rate and no part of the prospect attracts me so much as being with you. . . .

Your description of Fechner is entertaining enough. You know I always thought his psycho-physic as moonshiny as any of his other writings, fundamentally valuable only for its rich details. I have n't seen, still less read, Wundt's *Logic,* and shall be satisfied with your account of it for some time to come. I confess I have not found him prolix hitherto, so much as singularly dry. . . .

Richard Avenarius was professor of philosophy at Zürich and editor of the *Vierteljahrsschrift für wissenschaftliche Philosophie.* Carl Göring had been professor of philosophy in the University of Leipzig and one of the editors of Avenarius's review. G. T. Fechner, physicist, philosopher, mystic, psychophysicist, occultist, and æsthetician, was at this time seventy-eight years old, residing in Leipzig, where he spent his entire life. J. K. F. Zöllner was professor of physical astronomy at the University of Leipzig.

I don't see how he can ever be a great philosopher for the lack of that personal, unitary, all-fusing point of view which the great ones have. I tend to work more and more deeply into my pure phenomenalistic standpoint — provisionally, at any rate, so as to see how far it can carry one. . . . But . . . I long to talk it over with you. How lonesome psychologists are in this world of matter!

I did n't know poor Göring had drowned himself. He was always repugnant to me as a writer. What a *burschikos* swagger Avenarius's *Nachruf* had![33] *He* also repels me singularly. How men who are neither gentlemen nor men of the world, but live swathed in the thick atmosphere of a particular technical calling, writing for each other and quarreling with each other, and senseless clods to all outside, can claim to give voice to the spirit of Universal Being is more than I can understand. I may misapprehend them, but such fellows as Göring and Avenarius seem to me, personally considered, mere cads, or university blackguards. Schneider, on the contrary, fills me with the liveliest admiration and gratitude. His paper on the feeling of motion is really exquisite. . . .

Palmer is fully enrolled in the white-winged band of seraphim *illuminati*. Caird has done the business for him. I fear my turn will come next. Nothing but the thought of you keeps my head straight. Our Club does n't meet this winter. Davidson is trying to make a living by lecturing on Hellas with a magic lantern. Fiske *ditto* on American history without. Howison has five students (private) in Hegel, and lectures on Ethics in our Divinity School. . . . I seem to myself to do nothing at all in the way of work. . . . I 'm glad for my sake your "Psychology" is so little advanced. But I 'm sure we 'll help, not hurt, each other's success. Your book of articles will give you a good reputation and the farming will, I 'm sure, not last long. . . . Farewell! . . . My spirit bounds at the chance of rejoining you. Yours ever,

WM. JAMES

Feb. 15 [1880]

My dear Dr. James, —

Your letter both delights and alarms me. First, of the latter. Transported as I am at its prospect of seeing you in the summer I am *very* solicitous about *your* part of the "happiness." If you

---

[33] What a free-and-easy swagger Avenarius's obituary notice had!

thought me dry before, what will you think to find me pretty well *aufgegangen* in empiricism? . . . But what alarms me most is the fear which has somehow arisen within me that you are going the other way. Forgive me if I am wrong, as I trust, for my fear rests only on a waft or two of gossip and your saying you *may* follow Palmer, which Heaven forfend. I think Hegelism unsurpassed for helping men easily and without agony or crisis over any part of the long way from Rome to reason, but to rest in it as a finality is arrested development, and to go back to it seems to me mystic and retrogressive. . . . My ideal of a philosopher is not a laboratory man who does n't rely much on books, but studies mind in the twitch of a frog's muscle, and yet just this independent look at nature is what has opened new impulses and enthusiasm for me such as nothing else has. . . .

You fancy marriage has changed me perhaps. . . . But what has had more influence than anything else is the growing hope and prospect that I may earn my own bread, somehow, without filling a position which would limit my freedom in any way; the prospect of sometime having *my own* experience about some of the great interests of life at home, as they look *to me,* without considering how Eliot will like it. . . . I may have no influence at all, but I do believe I have some things in my head and note-books to say which are so true to *me* that it will be the supremest intellectual luxury to work and hunt around till I can get them said somehow. . . . Ever yours,

G. S. HALL

Cambridge, March 16 [1880]

My dear Hall, —

Yours of the 15th received. It did me good to see your photograph. I was greatly amused at the "alarm" with which you looked to our meeting, on account of your being sunk in "empiricism." I always thought I was the empiricist of the two, and you were seeking an ultra-phenomenal Identity. If by empiricism you now mean the negation even of a systematic unity in thinking, and a "fragmentarianism" (!?) of study, I should not go so far. But I do not suppose you mean that, nor can I well imagine what you do mean, unless my seeming sterility, the news of my bad eyes, and I know not what . . . engendered the baseless suspicion in your mind that I had reached mental equilibrium already and become ossified.   As for Hegel, there is not a fibre in my being which is not ready to swear him humbug; but not having achieved the reading of one of his works yet, I still give him the benefit of the general doubt which we are all heirs to, of possibly not being unmixed villains. . . .

Perhaps we can have the pleasure of harboring you and Mrs. Hall as guests here next fall, for I think of building a house behind my father's.   Yours in great haste,

W. J.

In the summer of 1880 James went to Europe for a short rest, but before he set sail he had entertained the idea of spending a whole year abroad.   On May 30, writing in a semi-jocular vein to his friend Henry Bowditch, he said: "I 'm to sail on Wednesday for Berlin, where I hope Helmholtz's lectures, Munk's vivisections in the veterinary school, *and a year of laboratory work under Hall* will bring peace to my distracted soul."   He was joined by Hall at Heidelberg, where they carried on much verbal psychologizing together.   To Bowditch, who had been expected to join the group, James wrote that Hall was a *"herrlicher Mensch,"* and "singularly solidified" by his "recent studies."   Hall returned to America this same summer, and after giving public lectures at Williams and Harvard was invited, in January 1882, to Johns Hopkins, where he began giving regular instruction (including experimental laboratory psychology) in the following autumn — first as lecturer and then, in 1884, as professor.

In view of these facts, what shall we say of the relative priority of James's laboratory and Hall's?   Professor Boring has made a statement which seems to me to constitute the sum of wisdom on the matter.   "Nothing," he says, "that is called 'first' is ever literally first; there always turn out to have been 'anticipations.'"   Such anticipations, he adds, are not "founded," they simply occur and exist.   James's laboratory was such an anticipation.   It was earlier, but it "came into being, whereas Hall founded his.   The difference between *having* and *founding* is a difference between the temperaments of the two men." [34]   About five years after this "founding" (or ten years after the "anticipation"), owing to the influence of

[34] E. G. Boring, *History of Experimental Psychology*, 1929, 318, 507.

Harvard and Hopkins, and to the independent studies of American psychologists in Germany, laboratories began to multiply rapidly. By 1900 there were twenty-five or more in American universities. In 1905 the Harvard Laboratory was removed from Dane to Emerson Hall, where it has since occupied the entire third and fourth floors of the building, being one of the first, if not the first, psychological laboratory originally designed and built for the purpose.

In judging of James's relations to experimental psychology in general, it is to be remembered that there is more than one sense of the term "experimental." In the broad sense of testing hypotheses by experience, James's mind was instinctively and profoundly experimental. It is characteristic of him to "try" and "see." His self-imposed nitrous-oxide-gas experiment is a case in point,[35] also the studies of attention, memory, and imagination which he set as tasks to his students.[36] His work in psychical research may be said to be altogether experimental. He had a large correspondence, and in this way collected a great deal of material from amateur observers. He also made use of the questionnaire, as, for example, in the study of consciousness of lost limbs.[37] This method he distrusted, unless the questionnaire was filled out by an expert. The latter was the case with the observations on "The Sense of Dizziness in Deaf Mutes," compiled by James chiefly from reports of trained physicians and attendants; and the information which he collected from ophthalmologists, on the effects of paralysis of the muscles of the eye. In order to obtain a basis of comparison for these cases, nearly two hundred students and instructors in Harvard College were also examined, which meant being "whirled rapidly around with the head in different positions."[38] Even earlier than this James had performed similar experiments on frogs, experiments

[35] W.B. 294; and above, I, 728. "The Spatial Quale," published in the Jour. of Specul. Philos. in 1879, also throws a light on his procedure. He tested the alternative hypotheses regarding the perception of space by submitting himself to the conditions called for by the hypotheses, and observing the results.

[36] To determine, e.g., whether there is any general improvement of memory from practice. The records of these experimental classroom exercises are preserved among James's papers.

[37] The results were published in the Proc. of the Amer. Soc. for Psychical Research, I (1887), and reprinted in C.E.R. For W.J.'s comments on the method, cf. C.E.R., 286, note.

[38] The results were published in Bg., 1881–2 and 1882–3. James's "Suggestion for the Prevention of Seasickness" grew out of this research, and has its place in the history of medicine. Cf. the note to Bg., 1887–7.

which were never published, and "which others with better eye-sight may be able to complete." [39]

But when such scanty data as these have been compiled, the fact remains, and it is only the more striking, that James did not him-self contribute experimental results of importance. Not more than a fifth of his *Principles of Psychology* can be said to relate even to the experimental work of others. That he could not en-dure long hours in a laboratory was due to physical reasons. That he did not incline to the use of quantitative methods was due to his non-mathematical cast of mind. That he did not organize ex-periments and carry them on through years of sustained diligence was due to his impatience. To this threefold incapacity was joined an opinion that the new laboratory method had not yielded significant results.[40]

Whether psychology lost or gained by this incapacity and dis-inclination, who shall say? That the peculiar quality of James's influence is in some measure due to it seems clear. He could not stand in the laboratory, but he *could* move about outside. Just as he was bound to no national movement, so he was restricted to no technique. He was an exceptionally acute observer of the natural man in all the varied aspects of his life. He had a lively and veracious imagination. He used whatever facts he could thus find for himself or gather from other observers, interpreted them freely, and constructed an image of human nature which after forty years is not yet obsolete.

[39] The experiments were described in *Amer. Jour. of Otology,* II (1880).

[40] Nevertheless he admired and envied experimental capacity in other psy-chologists; *cf.* his comment on H. Ebbinghaus's "heroic" experimentation on mem-ory, in *Science,* VI (1885).

LIII

THE AUTOMATON THEORY

UP to 1878, when James began to prepare his systematic treatise, the psychological problem which interested him most deeply was that of the relation between mind and body. This problem stood at the crossroads where science met religion and where physiology met psychology. James's scientific studies disposed him to accept the view that man is a "conscious automaton." Human behavior, according to this view, is wholly determined by the train of physical events which pass from stimuli through sense organs to the central nervous system and out again through the muscles. Consciousness is present, but has no vote; it supervenes but does not intervene. James's first idea was to adhere to this view more strictly than many of its avowed proponents. In the *Principles* (1890) we read : —

"The present writer recalls how in 1869, when still a medical student, he began to write an essay showing how almost every one who speculated about brain-processes illicitly interpolated into his account of them links derived from the entirely heterogeneous universe of feeling. Spencer, Hodgson (in his *Time and Space*), Maudsley, Lockhart, Clarke, Bain, Dr. Carpenter, and other authors were cited as having been guilty of the confusion. The writing was soon stopped because he perceived that the view which he was upholding against these authors was a pure conception, with no proofs to be adduced of its reality. Later it seemed to him that whatever *proofs* existed really told in favor of their view." [1]

How James and Hodgson exchanged positions in this subject, James crossing from automatism to interactionism at the same time that Hodgson was moving in the reverse direction, has already been narrated. The following letter to Charles A. Strong refers to the

[1] *Principles*, I, 130, note.

same topic, and indicates that James began at an early date to distrust the automaton theory even on scientific grounds: —

Cambridge, Oct. 21 [1889]

My dear Strong, —

. . . As for the conscious automaton theory, I excogitated it all by myself, and began to write an article about it (my first) whilst still in the Medical School. But I ere long saw grounds to doubt it. Clifford, in his lecture "Body and Mind," has given the most radical English presentation of it, and Münsterberg the latest I know of in his *Willenshandlung*. I tried to criticize it in an article called "Are We Automata?" in Volume IV of *Mind*. I confess I am a little startled at your enthusiasm over it as a *novelty*. Of course it is a grandly simple conception, and like all such tends to sweep one to affirmation; but really we know so little, so *ultra* little, about these last crannies and recesses of things, that I feel very reluctant to deny all causality to consciousness with so little positive proof. It may be so; but if so, it will only become clearly so when some great metaphysical theory has so shown us the relations of feeling and motion as to give all activity to the latter without surrendering to materialism in a crude way. As now held, the theory is *crudely* materialistic. Materialism may be *aufgehoben* in something completed, and then this theory will seem more rational to me. I advise you to read some articles by Delbœuf, Renouvier, Fouillée, Tannery, etc., in the *Revue philosophique* and the *Critique philosophique* about seven or eight years ago, — free will is the title.[2] They brought out the difficulties of conceiving the relations of body and mind very strongly. I can't send exact references, for I'm only just camping in my new house on the Norton land, and books are not unpacked. The only news is Bowen's resignation, and Santayana's taking his course as well as mine! A stiff job, but I trust he'll do it. No more tonight from yours always,

WM. JAMES

James never forgot the claims of man's moral and religious nature even when expounding those doctrines of science which seemed most contrary to them. On March 1, 1877, he gave a public lecture in Sanders Theatre in which he discussed "Recent Investigations

2 *Cf.* above, I, 688.

on the Brain," and pointed out that current physiology tended to construe all human behavior, even so-called "rational acts," in terms of specific and determined processes in the nervous system. It was characteristic of him that he should have concluded by "deprecating any anxiety about materialistic consequences." "If the spiritualistic faith of to-day finds central physiology a stumbling-block," he said, "that of to-morrow will be all the stouter from successful contact with it. The human mind always has and always will be able to interpret facts in accordance with its moral interests." [3]

In the year 1878 (in February at the Johns Hopkins University in Baltimore, and in October at the Lowell Institute in Boston) James gave a series of lectures on "The Brain and the Mind." In these lectures he summarized recent developments in psychophysics, in the physiology of sensation, memory, habit and association, and in brain localization, urging his hearers to regard them as provisional, and indecisive in their bearing on the fundamental question of the causal efficacy of consciousness. The Baltimore lectures were attended by a class of about sixty. An interesting side light is contained in the following letter of the time addressed by Francis J. Child to James Russell Lowell: —

"I had William James with me a fortnight in Baltimore. He gave ten lectures on the brain as the organ of the mind, and made a decided impression. I heard the last, in which he offered reasons for not accepting the theory that we are automatons unreservedly. At that lecture [I met] your friend Mrs. Thomas and her daughter, and Miss Bessie King, whom you did not see, I think — a sweet little demi-Quakeress that is fond of Greek and pictures — wears a grey dress and a peachy cheek — not a girl to be explained as an automaton. Mrs. Thomas was delighted with the lecture. She enjoyed being explained as a machine, as she said — *when you know just how it is.* . . .

"William James was sleepless and restless, and, as it turned out, not because the lectures troubled him, but because his fate was in the scales and Miss Alice Gibbens would not say the word he wanted. But she did in June, and in July they were married, and

---

[3] This was one of a series of scientific lectures under the auspices of the Harvard Natural History Society, of which James was corresponding secretary and Theodore Roosevelt a member. The citations are from a contemporary newspaper report. The lectures were attended by an average audience of one thousand.

now they are happy together at the Adirondack Mountains. She serves as eyes to him, and as she has a low, sweet voice truth comes mended from her lips. William has already begun a Manual of Psychology — in the honeymoon — but they are both writing it."

The lectures of 1878 reflected very clearly James's growing dissent from automatism. He argued that we know mind better than we do the nervous system, and cannot, therefore, argue psychology from physiology: "We have seen an *a priori* notion of physiological necessity give rise to a fictitious anatomy. But in just the same way our notions of psychological necessity may give rise to an imaginary physiology. The whole theory of different local habitations in the brain for different classes of ideas with fibres connecting the localities together — so that when one locality is excited the excitement may travel along the fibres and waken up the other locality — this whole theory, I say, was originally derived from our introspective knowledge of the way in which our feelings awaken each other. . . . In a word, psychology with its associations went first and from it physiology took its cue. . . . There is nothing, then, more ludicrously false than the assertions so loudly made by some authors that the only sound psychological science is that founded on physiology. Page after page of Maudsley's book, for instance, are filled with denunciation of the subjective method in psychology — the truth really being that the subjective method has not only given us almost all of our fundamentally secure psychological knowledge, but has also suggested all our interpretations of the facts of brain-physiology."

The remarks delivered at the opening lecture before the Lowell Institute [4] admirably convey James's persistent conviction that no theory which slights *either* mind or body can possibly be the last word on the matter : —

"In these recent days we hear a great deal of the marvelous achievements of science, how Darwinism has made us understand so much about animal and vegetable forms, and how in particular the physiologists by the deep insight they have been acquiring into the nervous system and the brain, have to a great extent banished the mystery which used to hang about the action of the mind, and constituted a new psychology which explodes and renders obsolete

[4] Six lectures, beginning Oct. 15, 1878.

the old views of mental action — all based on *a priori* speculation and metaphysics. Whilst this is triumphantly repeated by the sectaries of physical science, it is as indignantly denied by another class of persons. The latter fancy that they see the most brutal materialism lurking behind what the former call enlightenment and scientific progress, like some hideous heathen idol whose form is dimly seen through the glare of fireworks and golden dust and dazzling vapors of incense with which its followers continually fill the air before it. Both sides alike are confident and often bitter. . . . The worst of it is that in this matter of the brain and the mind people are ready to become very eager partisans on a very slender basis of study. Those whose highest flights are articles in the *Popular Science Monthly* will talk of the exploded superstitions of introspective psychology, and those who have hardly opened a treatise on physiology will declaim against the degrading sophistries of medical materialists.

"It has seemed to me that the six hours which the trustees of the Lowell Fund have done me the honor to place at my disposal, could not be better spent than in taking a single subject, the brain, and in seeing exactly how much recent investigations have explained its action, and in particular how much they may be said to have cleared up or made less mysterious the action of consciousness in each one of us. A sober review of this kind ought to do good to the overhasty partisans of both sides. . . . I have for some years past, in thinking of my duties as teacher in Cambridge, been inclined to deplore the rather wide surface over which my instruction had to be spread. I have been obliged to teach a little anatomy, a little physiology, a little psychology; and I have felt that where one's wisdom tried to cover so much ground it must needs be thin at any given spot. But in standing before you now I feel that my misfortune has had its good side. A teacher must form responsible opinions; a reader need not. But the difficulties of deciding a question are not often felt by one who is not responsible for his decision. The judge feels them more than the two lawyers. A physiologist may form the most careless opinions in psychology and keep a good conscience. The only thoroughness obligatory on *him* is physiological. The philosopher, on the other hand, who follows the subjective method, may in like manner scorn the crudities of the physiologist's. . . . Each owns a lot in the field of human knowledge, and each, provided he cultivates his own lot conscientiously, feels tolerably indifferent about what happens in his neighbor's. . . . I think we ought tonight to aspire to the attitude of one who should own both lots. He does not care where the fence stands and, being master of all the land, tries to cultivate every square foot of it impartially. We are each alike proprietors of a body and a mind. We are . . . interested in having [as] sound a science of the one as of the other. . . . I confess that in the past few years, owing to the divided duties I have alluded to, I have felt most acutely the difficulties of understanding either the brain without the mind, or the mind without the brain. I have almost concluded in my moments of depression that we know hardly anything."

In the closing lecture James presented the sober arguments which he thought made interactionism more probable than automatism, even on scientific grounds. In concluding he uttered a blast against the dogmatic negations of science. It is evident that for James the question of automatism transcended any narrow psychological application, and was pregnant with moral and religious significance: —

"Many persons nowadays seem to think that any conclusion must be very scientific if the arguments in favor of it are all derived from twitching of frogs' legs — especially if the frogs are decapitated — and that, on the other hand, any doctrine chiefly vouched for by the feelings of human beings — with heads on their shoulders — must be benighted and superstitious. They seem to think too, that any vagary or whim, however unverified, of a scientific man must needs form an integral part of science itself; that when Huxley, for example, has ruled feeling out of the game of life, and called it a mere bystander, supernumerary, the matter is settled. The lecturer knows nothing more deplorable than this indiscriminating gulping down of everything materialistic as peculiarly scientific. Nothing is scientific but what is clearly formulated, reasoned and verified. An opinion signed by the Pope, if it have these merits, will be a thoroughly scientific opinion. On the other hand, an opinion signed by Professor Huxley, if it violate these requirements, will be unscientific. To talk of science as many persons do whose mental type is best represented by the *Popular Science Monthly* is ridiculous. With these persons it is forever Science against Philosophy, Science against Metaphysics, Science against Religion,

Science against Poetry, Science against Sentiment, Science against
all that makes life worth living.

"The truth is that science and all these other functions of the
human mind are alike the results of man's thinking about the phenomena life offers him.   No mode of thinking is *against* any other,
except false thinking and illogical thinking.   If we think clearly
and consistently in theology or philosophy we are good men of
science too.   If we think logically in science we are good theologians and philosophers.   If, on the contrary, our thought is
muddled in one field, it is worthless in all the rest.   It must be that
truth is one, and thought woven in one piece.   I, for one, as a scientific man and a practical man alike, deny utterly that science compels me to believe that my conscience is an *ignis fatuus* or outcast,
and I trust that you too, after the evidence of this evening, will go
away strengthened in the natural faith that your delights and sor-
rows, your loves and hates, your aspirations and efforts are real
combatants in life's arena, and not impotent, paralytic spectators
of the game."

In the following year, 1879, James published in *Mind* an article
entitled "Are We Automata?" in which he attacked Helmholtz and
Clifford, and presented empirical evidence for the efficacy of consciousness.[5]   The cerebrum, he said, is distinguished from the spinal
cord by its instability and indeterminateness of action.   Viewed
merely as a mechanism, it appears to be characterized by the great
diversity of the actions which it conditions.   If it is not to be a mere
field of disordered happenings, under the impact of casual stimuli
and subject to fluctuating organic changes, there is need of guidance.
With guidance the cerebrum is admirably suited to the exigencies of
life, since it may then by its very flexibility adapt the organism to
external changes and to remote contingencies.   When we turn to
consciousness, on the other hand, we find that it is marked on all
its levels, from sensation and perception through reason to the moral
will and the æsthetic preferences, by discrimination and choice.
Adding the general consideration that because consciousness has
evolved it may be assumed to be useful, we reach the probable conclusion that consciousness affirms and expresses the organism's
interest, and regulates the action of the brain accordingly.   In other
words, the function of the upper brain can only be understood tele-

[5] This article was never reprinted in full, and will repay careful study.

ologically, and "teleology is an exclusively conscious function." [6]
Here, at any rate, is a hypothesis that fits many of the facts; and
"fragmentary probabilities supported by the study of details are
more worthy of trust than any mere universal conceptions, however
tempting their simplicity." The theory that consciousness is in-
efficacious is a dogma, formulated in order to preserve the ideal
rationality of the realm of molecular physics, as a refuge whither
"science may retreat and hump her strong back against the mockeries and phantasms that people the waste of Being around." [7]

James thus had his scientific as well as moral and religious motives
for espousing interactionism. One of the chief grounds of his dissatisfaction with experimental psychology was its evasion of *causal
explanation* through the hypothesis of psychophysical parallelism.
It was in accordance with his principles to prefer a physiological
laboratory or medical clinic, in which physiological or physiochem-
ical causes were invoked, to a psychological laboratory in which
apparatus was used as a means of arousing states of mind, which,
being discriminated and labeled, were thereupon merely added to the
collection. He was willing himself to accept the principle of "corre-
lation" as a provisional working method, but felt that until somewhere, sooner or later, the psychophysical bridge was crossed, the
job of science was not done. He wanted to regard consciousness
and nervous system, mind and body, as both parts of nature, so
connected that one could be controlled through the other. It was,
I think, the laws of their connection, by which they could be thus
brought into one dynamic system, for which he looked to that
Galileo or Lavoisier whose advent would mark the beginning of a
really scientific psychology.

It will be noted that although James somewhat hesitatingly rejected the automatist theory, he did not question the conception of
the so-called "reflex arc," which was in his day so closely associated
with automatism. According to James the reflex arc may be given
either an automatist or an interactionist interpretation. It is the
function of a "central" process to mediate between the incoming
sensory message that traverses the so-called "afferent" nerves, and
the outgoing response that takes effect through the "efferent" nerves
and the muscles. The possibilities which James considered all

[6] *Mind*, IV (1879), 7, note.
[7] *Ibid.*, 21–2.

lay within this general framework. He denied, only, that this central process merely repeats or transmits the message from without: it takes initiatives and makes important contributions of its own. And he denied (though less unqualifiedly) that the central process can be construed wholly in cerebral terms — to the exclusion of consciousness. But in either case the central process was a phase of action, and its intellectual functions (or their cerebral equivalents) were subordinated to their motor functions. This was the nub of his "Reflex Action and Theism," written in 1881 : —

"The willing department of our nature . . . dominates both the conceiving department and the feeling department; or, in plainer English, perception and thinking are only there for behavior's sake. I am sure I am not wrong in stating this result as one of the fundamental conclusions to which the entire drift of modern physiological investigation sweeps us. If asked what great contribution physiology has made to psychology of late years, I am sure every competent authority will reply that her influence has in no way been so weighty as in the copious illustration, verification, and consolidation of this broad, general point of view." [8]

[8] *W.B.*, 114.

LIV

THE WRITING OF THE "PRINCIPLES"

In June 1878, at the close of the year in which he had transferred his undergraduate course to the department of philosophy, and a month before his marriage, James contracted to write a *Psychology* for Henry Holt's "American Science Series." He declined to promise the manuscript in one year, but thought he might have it ready in two. Holt began as early as the autumn of 1878 to have misgivings, and to allude to the possibility of turning to Hall or some other rival author. As a matter of fact, however, the composition of the book took twelve years — and Holt waited!

James's relations with Henry Holt were not merely professional and commercial. They *were* professional and commercial — and, as both men spoke plainly, how a publisher annoys an author and an author a publisher, appears very plainly in their long correspondence extending over a period of twenty-five years. Holt was a man who had intellectual interests of his own, enabling him to meet his author on his own ground, and he was capable of a humor and pungency of statement which his correspondent greatly relished.

James had just published his first three articles [1] attacking Spencer's one-sided emphasis on the environment and on the standard of survival — insisting upon the mind's "subjective interests," and its right to obey them. These he sent to Holt, who defended his favorite author, and argued that the cultural values and admired ways of life *could* all be subsumed under the standard of survival. Here is James's reply: —

Cambridge, Nov. 22, 1878

My dear Sir, —

Many thanks for your letter. I will keep dribbling away at the work, and trust to providence and to your inability to find anyone else, to leave me sole master of the field.

[1] *Bg.*, 1878–1; 1878–2; 1878–4.

I sent you my articles, not to inflict on you the duty of reading them, but simply that you might know what I had been doing. I think you have somewhat misapprehended the scope of my criticism of Spencer. . . . So far am I from leaving out the environment, that I shall call my textbook "Psychology, as a Natural Science," and have already in the introduction explained that the constitution of our mind is incomprehensible without reference to the external circumstances in the midst of which it grew up. My quarrel with Spencer is not that he makes much of the environment, but that he makes *nothing* of the glaring and patent fact of subjective interests which coöperate with the environment in moulding intelligence. These interests form a true spontaneity and justify the refusal of *a priori* schools to admit that mind was pure, passive receptivity. Very truly yours,

WM. JAMES

Holt having returned to the attack, James again replied: —

Cambridge, Nov. 25, 1878

My dear Sir, —

I am sorry that my optical condition vetoes a correspondence on the interesting questions between us, and indeed I despair of ever expressing myself more clearly than I did in my article. As for the first point of your present letter, whether the race best fitted to survive be one which should make that its exclusive conscious purpose, and have intellect enough to discern whatever means helped that purpose, or one whose attention was equally interested in other ends — that I admit is a question about which opinions may fairly differ, for we have never had an example in history of a highly intellectual race in which prudence was the ruling passion. Such individuals as have shown this type, *e.g.*, Franklin, would certainly have an admirable chance of survival. Their only weakness would lie in the fact of their social environment not recognizing this as the ultimate interest, and of their consequent liability to occasionally arouse antipathies which would be fatal. *A priori,* however, I think you would have a hard case to demonstrate that, cognitive powers being supposed at a maximum (the insight into *means*), that race was most likely to survive which least powerfully wished to. But, as I said, this question is a mere side incident.

By "subjective interests" I mean all interests whatever. Objectively considered I can correspond to my environment either by assimilating roast beef and surviving, or by dying and feeding the worms. Which of these adjustments will you choose? If the former, you take your stand on one subjective interest, that commonly called egoistic; if the latter, on another, that called sympathetic in that it identified itself with a foreign egoistic interest, that of the worm. Remove the conscious desire both of ego and worm and in heaven's name what interest of any sort remains, objectively? All is equally fatal, equally indifferent. As for Spencer's assertion that the mind is not pure receptivity, I should like to see a single passage in which he explicitly makes it. The elementary *qualia* of sensibility he may of course call original, since their nature is unlike the objective reality. But the form and order which these *qualia* take in evolved intelligence is solely and absolutely the work of environment. I think he hardly mentioned the word "interest" once in his work.

Regretting again to be unable to pursue this discussion any farther but hoping my *Psychology* may yet convert you, I am very truly yours,

WM. JAMES

Between 1878 and 1890 James was teaching psychology continuously, and the book, as he tells us in the Preface, grew up "in connection with the author's class-room instruction." [2] James's animated and polemical method of teaching is largely accountable for the style of the book — its persuasiveness, its profusion of illustration, and its liberal citation of authors. Although the work as a whole did not appear for many years, it *began* to appear in installments at once. The prior publication of these numerous articles, sixteen in all, gave rise to the mistaken supposition that the *Principles* was a mere compilation.[3] This was not the case — it was as near an approach to a systematic treatise as James could permit himself to write. His peculiar genius compelled him to be interesting, to be absorbed by each topic in turn, and to present it concretely and vividly. Any elaborate scientific schematism, furthermore, he

[2] *Principles.* v.
[3] This was James Sully's chief complaint; cf. *Mind,* XVI (1891), 393.

would have thought specious and pretentious in view of the transitional, and therefore provisional, character of all psychological knowledge.

Why did he put his psychological work out in the form of articles? Partly for a very mundane reason — some of the articles were sold to popular magazines in order to augment the teacher's meagre income. Furthermore, James applied to himself as well as to his juniors the Harvard policy of basing appointments and promotions on published work. In 1878 he was assistant professor of physiology, but had, as we have seen, already begun the teaching of psychology in the department of philosophy. He was evidently anxious to be transferred altogether, and hoped that his published articles might help. A further and more psychological reason for putting the psychology out topic by topic was the relief he felt at getting each topic off his mind, with the power to return to it later and view it with critical detachment.

No one who knows James can be surprised to learn from his letters that he was heartily sick of the *Principles* before he got through. When he was in America he longed for Europe, when he was in Europe he longed for America — and so it was with philosophy and psychology. His weariness was always associated with the present and communicated a rosy and seductive quality to the absent. Perhaps philosophy was really James's deeper vocation. One often has the feeling that psychology was his legal wife and philosophy his preferred mistress. In any case, twelve years was a long time to live with the same task and to be cut off from other allurements by the obligations of fidelity.

The composition of the *Principles* was, like all of James's writing, laborious. He was easily fatigued; and — having diverse interests, an eager mind, a driving creative impulse, and a generous heart — there was much to fatigue him. If genius implies continuous, frictionless, outpouring spontaneity, then James was not a genius. Periods of outpouring alternated with periods of painful effort. He struggled, and he suffered; and though he achieved much, he always seemed to himself to be achieving little, and extravagantly admired what he took to be the greater fecundity of more gifted contemporaries. The letters and excerpts that follow will throw light on the slow but steady progress of James's great psychological enterprise. Despite his other burdens, his ill-health, his discouragement, his repining and occasional backsliding, he nevertheless steadily added chapter to chapter.

Up to the year 1882–1883, which James spent abroad, he had published six articles that may be said to have contributed to the making of the *Principles,* but only one of them, "The Association of Ideas," was incorporated as it stood. The others were either, like "Are We Automata?" discussions of fundamental and quasi-philosophical problems, or, like "The Spatial Quale" and "The Feeling of Effort," preliminary studies superseded by later articles. Thus by this date James's general view of the nature of mind and of its relation to the body, his theory of the perception of space and of the will, were thought out; but of the final draft of his book very little was as yet written, and many problems were as yet untouched. One of the principal objects of this year abroad was to obtain an opportunity for the uninterrupted writing of his book. But in December 1882 he was compelled to confess that, though he had "hoped to begin writing about November 1," he had "written as yet *six pages!*" Early after the new year the tide turned. On January 22 and 23, 1883, he had "written some psychology." The following paragraph is from a letter to his wife, written from London on February 10, 1883: —

"Yesterday I was parturient of psychological truth, being in one of my fevered states you wot of, when ideas are shooting together and I can think of no finite things. I wrote a lot at headlong speed, and in the evening, having been appointed, gave an account of it — the difference between feeling and thought — at the Scratch Eight. Unluckily neither Sully nor Robertson, the two men most capable of understanding and seeing the truth of it, were present. Hodgson is constitutionally incapable of understanding any thoughts but those that grow up in his own mind, — with all the desire in the world to do justice to them, he simply can't reproduce them in himself. But there was a fair amount of discussion afterwards, and the thing passed off well. I am sure the things I said were highly important scientifically."

What was the "psychological truth" of which James was parturient on February 9, 1883? If, as seems probable, this was the meeting "at Carveth Read's" mentioned in Hodgson's letter of September 2,[4] then the substance of James's remarks was the same as that

[4] *Cf.* above, I, 624.

of "the three lectures" delivered at the "rather absurd little" Concord School of Philosophy in the summer of 1883; and afterwards written out "in six days" for *Mind*, where they appeared under the title, "On Some Omissions of Introspective Psychology." If there is doubt of this identity, it is because of the statement above that on February 9 he was discussing "the difference between feeling and thought"; whereas the famous article deals mainly with feelings of relation. There is, however, no inconsistency. The article deals with the "halo" or "fringe" which surrounds every substantive state of consciousness and links it to its neighbors in the conscious stream, and the author declares that "the difference between thought and feeling reduces itself . . . to the presence or absence of 'fringe.' " This is the same as the doctrine of the *Principles* that there is *no* difference between feeling and thought, except an extraneous or functional difference.[5]

In this same period James was floundering around in "the morasses of the theory of cognition," and finding it impossible to do anything with the "much meditated subject of the Object and the Ego." In other words, while his mind had become clear as to the interrelations of the parts of the stream of consciousness, — their transitional and functional continuity, — he was greatly troubled by the question of the relation of consciousness to the external world which it purports to know. In order to get on with his psychology, therefore, he made up his mind to shelve this question by *assuming* the position of *dualism*. These two questions, together with that of the teleology of mind and its relations with the body, being thus provisionally settled, the foundations were laid.

The progress of the work was very uneven, owing to two causes. The first was personal — his limited time and capacity for work, as recorded in such passages as these from letters to his brother : —

Oct. 18, 1884

College work has begun never for me with so little strain. . . . I hope this will permit me to do something towards my psychology. My working day is sadly short, however — do what I will with my eyes I can't get them to do anything by lamplight without having to pay the piper for it afterwards, and the hunger that arises in me for reading in the evening is sometimes most poignantly severe.

[5] *Mind*, IX (1884), 18; *Principles*, I, vi, 186, 222.

April 1, 1885

I am running along quite smoothly, and my eyes, — you never knew such an improvement! . . . I have made a start with my psychology which I shall work at, temperately, through the vacation and hope to get finished a year from next fall, *sans faute*. Then shall the star of your romances be eclipst![6]

The second impediment to steady progress was the difficulty of the task. He had undertaken, not a summary of existing psychological knowledge, but its extension and revision. Every problem, he found, "bristles with obstructions" requiring years for their "mitigation." Every sentence had to be forged "in the teeth of irreducible and stubborn facts." He had to overcome not only "the resistance of facts," but "the resistance of other philosophers." It was "no joke slaying the Helmholtzes as well as the Spencers." The "science" of psychology was "in such a confused and imperfect state" that every paragraph presented "some unforeseen snag." In other words, between 1878 and 1890 James was not only *composing* a systematic work on psychology, but making observations, searching out acceptable hypotheses, and waging a vigorous polemical warfare.

The year 1884 saw the publication of the famous "James-Lange theory" of emotion.[7] In 1885 he wrote the important discussion of "Necessary Truths and the Effects of Experience," which became the concluding chapter of the *Principles*. The winter of 1886–1887 found him doing his work "easily," writing with more "continuity," the book "two-thirds done," and hopeful of finishing it in a year. Of the chapters which now flew thick and fast many were sent to Croom Robertson for publication in *Mind,* so that the following letters to that editor convey a good impression of the accelerated growth of James's enterprise. In 1886 he sent his long manuscript on "The Perception of Space," which Robertson published in the following year in four articles. It will be remembered that on September 25 of that year Robertson had written jocularly that their addressing letters to one another on the same day (August 29) had converted him to telepathy (his skeptical attitude to such matters being well known to his friends) : —

[6] Reprinted from *L.W.J.,* I, 242–3
[7] "What Is an Emotion?" *Mind,* IX.

Oct. 4, 1886

My dear Robertson, —

Yours of the 25th of last month has just arrived. I again lament your ill estate, and wish I could help in some other way than by sending you "copy." I'm glad you're so good a convert to telepathy. I always felt that at bottom your mind was candid, and that the prejudices of a bad education were alone to blame for your disbelief! I expect now to see *Mind* become the chief of wonder-mongering periodicals, leading off with our strange experience under the head of "experimental research." . . .

In looking at my "Space" I found it would take up certainly more than one hundred of *Mind's* pages, — how much more I can't say. So since you seemed dependent on something, I looked over my other manuscript, and after first choosing, and then rejecting on account of its length and lack of novelty, a very *readable* paper on "Instinct," [8] concluded to send you the first half — the second will be a little shorter by my computations — of a chapter on the "Ego." Much of it is altogether *banal* and hackneyed, but there is no time to change. In the second part I review the "theories" of the ego, and strive to give a clearer statement than any yet published of the purely phenomenalistic conception thereof. This second part is the more important, but it leaned on the first so that I could not, without much reëditing, send it alone. I regard the whole treatment (so far as not merely descriptive) as provisional. . . . I am tempted to ask you to publish it anonymously, but conclude on the whole to leave my name. Having got the thing once into print in this shape, I can start to revise it far better than if it were not thus objectified. I find that printing a thing *dispossesses* me of it in a surprising way, and leaves me free to go against it as I otherwise should not be. . . . But please return me the manuscript as soon as you have done with it. I may need it for my class before January arrives. . . .

I mailed you t'other day Part II of the *Proceedings* of the American Society for Psychical Research, a rather sorry "exhibit," from the "President's" address down.[9] There is no one in the Society

---

[8] This paper appeared in *Scribner's* in the same year.
[9] These *Proceedings* contained a "Report of the Committee on Hypnotism," James being one of the two members.

who can give any time to it, and I suspect it will die by the new year. Farewell! keep a stout heart, and a stiff upper lip. Time and the hour run through the roughest day! Yours ever,

WM. JAMES

The discussions of the "Ego" did not see the light until they appeared as Chapter X of the *Principles,* but Robertson accepted the manuscript on "Space" with enthusiasm, in spite of its bulk. Of this James wrote six months later: "I felt in reading the last proof how much a great deal of it would gain in clearness by being all written over again. That's the advantage of seeing a thing in print, — it *exteriorates,* and you can judge it as a foreign body."

Robertson was interested in the articles on space not only as an editor but as a psychologist. Being of an opposite school of thought, he published a criticism which evoked a reply from James: —

Chocorua, Oct. 7, 1888 [10]

My dear Robertson, —

Here goes at you with as fatal a series of remarks as I could muster! [11] Why couldn't you let me lie in peace? I should so gladly have forgotten space and all its contents, and left my articles as a prey to the wolves and the ravening vultures, without stirring a finger in their defense. I *'spise* the subject, now that I've said my say about it, and verily fear (so quickly reached are the limits of our mental growth) that I am incapable of learning anything more about it than I have there expressed. You shall have your fling hereafter all over it, with never another word of objection from me.

Your news of yourself interested me hugely, and sorry I am that it is no better than it is. Poor Gurney! He is a terrible loss to me. I didn't know till the news came how much I mentally referred to him as a critic and sympathizer, or how much I counted on seeing more of him hereafter. He had both quantity and quality, and was certainly only at the threshold of his productive activity. It is a dire calamity for all the interests concerned, and one that makes the course of the world seem strangely stupid in its brutality. . . . I

[10] A part of this letter has been printed in *L.W.J.,* I, 283.
[11] "The Psychological Theory of Extension," published in *Mind,* XIV (1889), in reply to the editor's critical remarks in *ibid.,* XIII (1888).

don't know well how the Society for Psychical Research can keep agoing without his aid.

I hope Sully may get your place if your resignation does become a reality, but I also hope very much that another year may give you ease. . . . I myself have had a wonderfully well summer, and so, I am glad to say, has my whole family. College has begun, and I am only up here for this Sunday and Monday. Royce is back from his voyage round the world, as fresh as a new-born babe, and as full of promise. I am teaching ethics and the philosophy of religion for the first time, with that dear old duffer Martineau's works as a text. It gives me lots to do, as I only began my systematic reading in that line three weeks ago, having wasted the summer in farming (if such it can be called) and psychologizing. My *Psychology* will therefore have to be postponed another year; for with as much college work as I have this year, I can't expect to write a line of it. — But I must stop! I've been all day at this sorry performance, and must send the manuscript as it is, without copying or more revision. With warmest regards and sympathy for both yourself and Mrs. R., believe me, ever yours,

WM. JAMES

P.S. Oct. 9. I got home last night and found the October *Mind* awaiting me with your obituary on Edmund Gurney, — as good and heartfelt a thing of that sort as I ever read, and true and beautifully said, every word of it. I thank you, and so must all his friends, for writing it.

Cambridge, Nov. 4, 1888

My dear Robertson, —

Before I sent you "Space," you remember you wrote me that you wanted articles more lively and popular than you often got for *Mind*. I venture to send you part of a chapter on "Belief" which I wrote last [summer?] as possibly less technical than the common run of contributions. It is, as you will readily see, quite unoriginal, and yet I cleared up my own ideas a little in writing it. . . .

My college work so takes me *in Anspruch* that I don't expect to be able to write a single page this year. Meanwhile a considerable psychologic manuscript is rotting on my desk and growing obsolete for mere lack of its complement. Most of the chapters are too long for articles, but by working a few of them off in this way I relieve myself of the burden of so much dead or dying matter, once a part of myself. A published thing is something which one no longer appropriates. Trusting you may find this fit for your pages, I am, with heartiest regards, yours ever,

WM. JAMES

P.S. The "Ego" business is unfinished still, and had better be left to the very last, when my wisdom shall be at its unsurpassable climax!

As the book neared completion James's correspondence with his publisher became frequent, voluminous, and intense. Holt was quite alive to the unbusinesslike habits of his authors. He gave and took rebuke indulgently. Thus he once wrote to James that "dear old Royce" had been in the office "professing that the one effort of his life was 'to keep free from the business virtues.' I kind of love the wambling cuss, nevertheless." Holt's authors not only had their own code, which differed from that of the publisher, but felt quite sure that theirs was a loftier code. This feeling was only partially concealed by a mask of pleasantry: —

Cambridge, March 21, 1890

My dear Holt, —

Publishers are demons, there's no doubt about it. How silly it is to fly in the face of the accumulated wisdom of mankind, and think just because one of them appears genial socially that the great natural law is broken and that he is also a human being in his professional capacity. Fie upon such weakness! I shall ne'er be guilty of it again. . . .

As for the manuscript, I confess I don't know why you need the whole of it *en bloc* in your own hands, before printing begins. After this week of recess I shall write a chapter which may take three weeks at the outside and complete the book. Some 1700 pages of manuscript will then be ready for the printer without another touch from me. There will remain five or six chapters, some of which need slight retouches and additions, which can be added by me perfectly well in the intervals of correcting proofs, thereby enabling the latter to begin about the first of May. The *whole* work,

as I said, will then be *written,* only those few chapters not *revised.*
Time is so precious now that I don't see what possible thing is
risked by proceeding to press with the revised manuscript. The
rest *could* be printed without revision, but it will be better to go
over it again. Write and tell me what is your decree. I want to
get forward now with the least possible delay. . . .

We will debit you with one dinner for some future day. I find
that I have lost the contract you sent me last spring. I did not even
examine it then. Pray send another that I may see what to do.
Yours always,

WM. JAMES

New York, April 2, 1890

My dear James, —

If "publishers are not demons," it is a striking instance of long-
suffering. I have illustrations here made years ago for manuscript
that has never appeared. Your letter makes plain what I took for
granted, — that your manuscript will not be ready as early as May 1.
Of course you "don't know why I need the whole of the manuscript
before printing begins." It's not in your line to know. If you
were gradually being converted into a demon, however, by the dis-
appointments occasioned by authors, you would know all about it.
I *never* began printing an instalment of a manuscript, so far as I
can remember, without having to stop work before the book was
finished, thus forcing the printer to put away the apparatus in place
for it, and giving him excuses (which they always avail themselves
of to the full) for dilly-dallying with the rest of the work when
it came, and eventually getting out the work later and after vastly
more friction than would have been the case if it had not been
begun till the manuscript was all ready. . . . One of the things
that makes me a demon, is to have to go over this weary explanation
again and again. I'm glad that you "want to get forward now
with the least possible delay." To accomplish that, believe that I
do too; put some faith in my experience; and complete your manuscript before doing anything else.

My demoniacal character has not been developed so much by
authors failing to look at contracts and losing them, as by the other
thing; so I'm angelic enough to send you duplicates, of which please
sign both and return us one. I have just seen a contract signed

by you to give us that manuscript June 12, 1880, and yet, you, you, you, Brute (two syllables) revile me for being a demon! I'm awfully sorry, all the same, that you're not coming here and to dine with us, but that all must be in due time. Yours ever,

> H. HOLT, Professional Demon,
> which being correctly interpreted
> meaneth Δαίμων

Cambridge, April 5, 1890

My dear Holt, —

Your letter awaits me on my return from Newport. Poor publisher, poor fellow, poor human being, ex-demon! How those vermin of authors must have caused you to suffer in your time to wring from you such a tirade! Well, it has been very instructive to me to grasp the publisher's point of view. Your fatal error, however, has been in not perceiving that I was an entirely *different kind* of author from any of those whom you had been in the habit of meeting, and that *celerity,* celerity incarnate, is the motive and result of all my plans and deeds. It is not fair to throw that former contract into my face, when you know, or ought to know, that when the ten years or a little more from the time of its signature had elapsed I wrote to you that you must get another man to write this book for you, and that, as things were then going, I didn't see how I could ever finish it.

I would return these contracts signed, herewith, but for two points. First, the provision that the author "shall prepare" matter for new editions "whenever called on" by publishers. I should naturally hope to do that, but certainly can't pledge myself. . . . Secondly, I find in the former contract a manuscript addition to the effect that on publication you deliver me twenty copies free of charge. That seems fair enough. I was calculating the other day that I should have in all to give away at least seventy-five copies of the book, most of them to professors here and abroad. . . . Let me know about these points and I will sign. Yours always,

WM. JAMES

New York, April 7, 1890

My dear James, —

"Celerity" is good. I don't want to "throw anything into your face," but upon my soul I don't see how after agreeing to do a thing, a suggestion that somebody else should do it is to be accounted a valid substitute for doing it; but your sins which are many are forgiven, as you know. Now, don't you be afraid of that provision about new editions. Experience has shown me that it is necessary to have that point settled in advance, and you are not going to be abused on the strength of it. . . . Yours ever,

H. Holt

Cambridge, April 8, 1890

My dear Holt, —

Here goes a copy of the contract signed by me. Your copy found again. I add as you suggest, the clause about twenty copies; and I leave the clause about new matter for new editions; but I warn you clearly that I shall only consent to furnish such new matter in case it involves no great sacrifice. I can easily imagine myself engrossed in some other work hereafter, and having grown into such a state of disgust for my old psychology book as to find the rehandling of it an intellectually impossible task. In that case I should calmly fold my arms and say, "the book has had its day — let it be republished if at all as an historical monument, not as a show exhibition of my present opinions." There comes a time in all books when a man can't tinker them; he must write a new work altogether. . . . Ever truly yours,

Wm. James

Cambridge, May 9, 1890 [12]

My dear Holt, —

I was in hopes that you would propose to break away from the famous "Series" and publish the book independently, in two volumes. An abridgment could then be prepared for the Series. If there be anything which I loathe it is a mean overgrown page in small type, and I think the author's feeings ought to go for a good deal in the case of the enormous *rat* which his ten years' gestation has brought forth. In any event, I dread the summer and the next year, with two new courses to teach, and, I fear, no vacation. What I wrote you, if you remember, was to send you the *heft* of the MS. by May 1st, the rest to be done in the intervals of proof-correcting. You however insisted on having the entire MS.

---

[12] Reprinted from *L.W.J.*, I, 293–4.

in your hands before anything should be done. It seems to me that this delay is, *now* at any rate, absurd. There is certainly less than two weeks' work on the MS. undone. And every day got behind us now means a day of travel and vacation for me next September. I really think, considering the sort of risk I am running by the delay, that I must *insist* on getting to press now as soon as the page is decided on.

No one could be more disgusted than I at the sight of the book. *No* subject is worth being treated of in 1000 pages! Had I ten years more, I could rewrite it in 500; but as it stands it is this or nothing — a loathsome, distended, tumefied, bloated, dropsical mass, testifying to nothing but two facts: *1st,* that there is no such thing as a *science* of psychology, and *2nd,* that W. J. is an incapable. Yours provided you hurry up things,

WM. JAMES

The writing of the *Principles* was completed in May and the book appeared in the autumn. The interval between these dates James spent in Cambridge, correcting proof. A letter to his sister affords a glimpse of him: —

Cambridge, July 23, 1890

Dearest Alice, —

I snatch a breathing space between two batches of proofs to send you a word which I have long meant to write, and which I ought to have sent you long ago had I been physically able to get to it. I don't mean any particular word, but just something in the way of a letter. . . . I, as you doubtless know, found it necessary to come here a couple of weeks since and correct my proofs. The printers are bent on overwhelming me and making me cry mercy now (I having complained of slowness at first), so that every mail, four times a day, is apt to bring a big bundle. I have stood it so far, but it's bad for head and stomach. I carry the last ones in at night to mail in the Boston Post Office and often don't get at my dinner till 9 o'clock. My breakfasts I usually take in our old home on Quincy St., whose brand-new bright surface together with certain structural alterations have entirely wiped away all old associations. The outlook from the windows, however, is the same, only the trees about the back and sides have grown and closed in the view. I have it pretty much to myself there just now — Jim Myers [13] being the only person whom I am likely ever to meet — and I confess it is pleasant to have that spot again recognizing my tread. Its walls are saturated with my groans and tears, as well as with yours! But the new wallpapers lie close, and let none of them transpire. . . .

But here comes the postman with the proofs, which I've just opened — forty pages in galley and fifty-six of page-proof! I ought to get it all mailed tonight — it's now half past three — but of course I can't. Anyhow, no more dalliance with the likes of *you!* . . . I'm so glad Harry is enjoying the Tyrol. He ought to get more of that salubrious element. How *good* the *Tragic Muse* is! He can rest his reputation on that. *Adieu. Mille baisers!*

W. J.

And here are two softer paragraphs to Holt, the second to "Dearest Holt": —

July 27, 1890

The proofs go on bravely now and the first volume is all in page. I suppose you'll be going to press with it any day, and wish to ask whether 100 copies or so may not be printed in *black* ink, I mean real black, not the gray substance which is usual nowadays. . . . I enjoy this life very much, all alone here with only one thing to think of, and daily a great stride of achievement. Quite unlike the usual state of things, with fifty things to think of and no achievement at all!

Aug. 12, 1890

Nothing remains now but the Index — hallelujah! The printing office did nobly, and so (though I say it as should not) did I, for I rarely got my dinner before 9 P.M. when I took the stuff into Boston to the late mail. My fears about not getting through before September were grounded on what you had told me in the winter, that the printers could not be expected to do more than fifteen or sixteen pages a day. What do you mean to ask for the book? I get a good many notes inquiring about it.

[13] The house at 20 Quincy St. had become the Colonial Club, where one of the most familiar figures was Hon. James J. Myers, Harvard '69, Speaker of the Massachusetts House of Representatives.

In short, while James's first feeling had been one of weariness and disgust, this soon gave way, as the summer wore on, to a happy sense of completed achievement. He was conscious that an epoch was closed. Of course most of the book was "unreadable from any human point of view," but seeing it "as a unit" he felt, nevertheless, "as if it might be rather a vigorous and richly colored chunk." He who had always considered himself "a thing of glimpses, a discontinuity, of *aperçus*," had written a *big book* on psychology — "a good one, as psychologies go." [14]

[14] *L.W.J.*, I, 295–8.

GENERAL SOURCES OF THE "PRINCIPLES"

No one who considers the sources of James's *Psychology* can fail to be impressed by their number and variety. This plenitude of tributary streams was not an accident, nor does it imply any lack of originality on the part of the author. It goes with his conception of the scope of psychology — the conception which he described as "functional" or "clinical": "We habitually hear much nowadays of the difference between structural and functional psychology. I am not sure that I understand the difference, but it probably has something to do with what I have privately been accustomed to distinguish as the analytical and the clinical points of view in psychological observation. . . . The clinical conceptions, though they may be vaguer than the analytic ones, are certainly more adequate, give the concreter picture of the way the whole mind works, and are of far more urgent practical importance. So the 'physician's attitude,' the 'functional psychology,' is assuredly the thing most worthy of general study today."[1] For James, in other words, functionalism meant keeping constantly in view the total concrete individual, conceived as active and as occupying an environment. Functionalism so conceived accounts for James's promiscuousness and catholicity.

He saw man in the round — as he presents himself to the clinician, the biologist, the traveler, the artist, or the novelist.[2] He was willing to learn about man from any source, however disesteemed by orthodox scientists. His more or less shady excursions in psychical research are well known. He "believed there was much truth in phrenology."[3] He had a strong interest in physiognomy, and

[1] "The Energies of Men," *Philos. Rev.*, XVI (1907), 1, 2.

[2] *Cf.* on this and the topics immediately following, D. S. Miller's admirable article on "Some Tendencies of Prof. James's Work," *Jour. of Philos.*, VII (1910). The influence of Spencer's biological approach to psychology coincided with these other influences in the direction of functionalism.

[3] T. A. Hyde, *How to Study Character*, 1884, 8. This book grew out of an essay on "Phrenology and Analysis of Types of Character," prepared for James in 1881 when the author was a member of the senior class at Harvard.

made a large collection of photographs both of friends and of strangers. Thus a letter from the elder Holmes written in 1888 advises him to examine Edmund Calamy's *Nonconformist's Memorial* for portraits suggestive of "pious and painful preachers of the orthodox persuasion" — "faces worth looking over to verify or dispute the resemblances of type." As soon as James became known he received a flood of letters from obscure or queer people, relating incidents that had come under their observation. He invited such letters and replied to them. He had the old-fashioned attitude of the "naturalist" who collects facts out of doors instead of in a laboratory. He did not scorn even the literary psychologists — when they were not too "scientific!" Thus, writing to his brother about Paul Bourget, he said: —

"The man has so much ability as a writer and such perception that it seems a ten-fold shame that he should be poisoned by the contemptible and pedantic Parisian ideal of materialism and of being scientific. How can men so deep in one way be so shallow in another, as if to turn living flesh and blood into abstract formulas were to be scientific. Sainte-Beuve's method of giving you the whole of an individual is far more scientific than this dissecting out of his abstract essence, which turns out after all only a couple of his bones."

James quite consciously intended to draw into his psychology not only information gathered from miscellaneous and extra-scientific sources, but also the several *schools* of psychological inquiry which flourished in his day. In 1900 he consented with much reluctance to write a preface to the Italian translation of the *Principles*. It contains a statement of the purpose of the book, and especially emphasizes the diversity of the streams which the author hoped to unite: —

"We live at a time of transition and confusion in psychology as in many other things. The classic spiritualistic psychology using the soul and a definite number of distinct ready-made faculties as its principles of explanation, was long ago superseded by the school of association. But it still lingers. . . . The older associationism itself retained a half-scholastic character. Recognizing no general evolution of the human species, it took the mind too statically, as something whose peculiarities were absolute and not to be explained. Moreover, it was purely intellectualist, and did justice neither to our impulses and passions nor to the coöperation of our will with our intellectual life. Within our generation Darwinism has come and added its new insights to these older tendencies. It has cast a flood of light upon our instinctive and passional constitution, and has brought innumerable attempts at explaining psychological facts genetically, in its train. Later still, exact and ingenious studies of sense-perception and illusion began to be made in physiological laboratories, higher intellectual operations themselves were compared experimentally and their duration measured, the modern physiology of the brain fêted its triumphs, and finally the study of mental defects and aberrations and other abnormal states of consciousness began to be carried on in an intelligent and psychological way.

"All these different tendencies — the classic tradition, the associationist analysis, the psychogenetic speculations, the experimental methods, the biological conceptions, and the pathological extensions of the field, have introduced a period of chaotic fermentation from which some writers have profited by developing one-sided crudities in a very confident way. . . . Such being the general condition of the time in which my book has been written, I fear that it may bear some traces of the prevalent confusion. I confess, however, that my aim in writing it, was to help to make the confusion less. I thought that by frankly putting psychology in the position of a natural science, eliminating certain metaphysical questions from its scope altogether, and confining myself to what could be immediately verified by everyone's own consciousness, a central mass of experience could be described which everyone might accept as certain no matter what the differing ulterior philosophic interpretations of it might be. . . . On this . . . basis . . . I tried to reach a harmony by giving to each of the different tendencies of which I have spoken its just voice in the result. The harmony involves some compromise, and possibly no one will be absolutely contented. My hopes lie with the unprejudiced reader and the newer generation. . . .

"I have expressly avoided the outward appearance of doctrine and system, the definitions, classifications, subdivisions and multiplication of technical terms, because I know that these things tend to substitute an artificial schematism for the living reality with which I wished to bring my reader into direct concrete acquaintance, whether he should have technical names to call its parts by or not.

So instead of starting with the mind's supposed elements (which are always abstractions) and gradually building up, I have tried to keep the reader in contact throughout as many chapters as possible, with the actual conscious unity which each of us at all times feels himself to be. . . .

"In sum, then, my effort has been to offer in a 'natural science' of the mind a *modus vivendi* in which the most various schools may meet harmoniously on the common basis of fact. . . ." [4]

It must not be supposed, therefore, that James's promiscuousness implied any neglect of "scientific psychology." He was an omnivorous reader and diligent student of the "authorities" of his day. The psychologists of whose writings James made the largest use, as judged by citations and references in the *Principles*, were Spencer, Helmholtz, Wundt, and Bain. Spencer and Wundt he both used and rejected — using them as reservoirs of facts and as texts for discussion, rejecting their characteristic and dominating ideas.

James's views on Spencer have already been set forth. [5] In 1875 James greeted the publication of Wundt's epoch-making *Physiological Psychology* with a qualified respect. He praised the book for its usefulness as a "cyclopedia of reference," and for its at least partial recognition of the mind's *active* nature. On the other hand, he found in Wundt's notion of "synthesis" the equivalent of the "mental chemistry" of the British school, and felt that neither had solved the problem as to how new qualities are generated out of old. Wundt was "perhaps the paragon" of the new experimental psychologists, illustrating virtues which James commends, though without enthusiasm: "The method of patience, starving out, and harassing to death is tried; Nature must submit to a regular *siege,* in which minute advantages gained night and day by the forces that hem her in must sum themselves up at last into her overthrow. There is little of the grand style about these new prism, pendulum, and galvanometer philosophers. They mean business, not chivalry. What generous divination, and that superiority in virtue which was thought by Cicero to give a man the best insight into nature, failed to do, their spying and scraping, their deadly tenacity and almost diabolic cunning, must some day accomplish." [6]

[4] From the English original of the Preface to W. James, *Principii di psicologia,* edited by Dr. G. C. Ferrari, Milan, 1901.
[5] Above, Ch. XXVIII.
[6] *North Amer. Rev.,* CXXI (1875), 196.

James continued during the '90s to read Wundt's works, psychological and philosophical — with unflagging attention and growing dissatisfaction. The following comment on Wundt's *System der Philosophie* was written in Florence in 1892: "This book is intolerable from its manner of licking everything so smooth, and pretending to *deduce* all results from previous ones by continuous necessity, without jolt or abrupt hypothesis. As the results are of such different degrees of solidity, this uniform manner has a terrible flavor of humbug, which might have been easily eliminated by a different style of exposition." [7] Citing chapter and verse, this note then proceeds to charge the author with looseness, vagueness, obscurity, paradox, unexplained conceptions, and unproved assertions.

Finally, in 1894, in reviewing Wundt's latest work,[8] James gently chided him for paying too little attention to other writers. He had, it was true, at length abandoned "feelings of innervation," but if he had only read James's "Feeling of Effort" in 1880, he would have been saved fourteen years of error! There was also unquestionably a lack of personal warmth on Wundt's side, which prevented their early acquaintance from ripening into friendship; and James's intimacy with Carl Stumpf did not tend to mend matters.[9]

Helmholtz was not only the source from which James learned physiological psychology in his youth, — the authority whose *Physiological Optics, Sensations of Tone,* and *Popular Lectures on Scientific Subjects* [10] were taken as his points of departure in this field, — but also one of his scientific idols. He represented the rare capacity to combine "experimental patience" with "skill and fresh ways of observation." James did not succeed in making any personal contact with him, — even when he took tea with the Jameses in Chocorua, he was a "monumental example of benign calm and speechlessness," — but he was "the great Helmholtz" none the less.[11]

Alexander Bain was an older contemporary whom, in psychology as in philosophy, James regarded with mingled deference and disagreement. It is evident that James was not impressed by his

[7] From flyleaf of James's personal copy.
[8] *Bg.*, 1894–1.
[9] *Cf.* below, 59–71, Ch. LXII.
[10] The original German works were: *Handbuch der physiologischen Optik,* 1856; *Die Lehre von den Tonempfindungen,* 1863; and *Populäre wissenschaftliche Vorträge,* 1873. Helmholtz's *Die Erhaltung der Kraft* (1847), one of the first proofs of the conservation of energy, was to James, as to his contemporaries, one of the great classics of science (*cf. Principles,* II, 668).
[11] *L.W.J.,* I, 266, 347.

critical powers, for in 1886 he wrote to Robertson: "It's too bad
about poor old Bain and Ward, — but when I saw Bain waddling
about over the surface of Ward's beautiful *Psychology* I could n't
help calling him duck-legs." [12]   Nevertheless James drew upon him
very heavily.   He treated him as the standard psychologist of
English-speaking countries, and used him both as a compendium
of existing knowledge and as a point of departure for innovation.
He acquired *The Senses and the Intellect* in Paris in 1868, the year
of its appearance, and read it with his customary thoroughness and
critical independence.   The *Emotions and the Will* he reviewed in
1876, with the remark that "the thoroughness of the descriptive
part of Bain's treatises, and the truly admirable sagacity of many of
the psychological analyses and reductions they contain, has made
them deservedly classical." [13]

Next in importance among James's psychological sources come
E. Hering, J. Delbœuf, and G. T. Fechner, followed by Carl Stumpf,
W. B. Carpenter, H. Ebbinghaus, S. Exner, T. Lipps, G. E. Müller, G. H. Schneider, James Ward, Ernst Mach, and Hugo Münsterberg.[14]   There were two among these writers, Ward and Stumpf,
whom he felt to be in a peculiar sense his collaborators.   They were,
like himself, promoting the new psychology, and their aims, methods, and genius were such as to win his cordial sympathy.

James Ward of Cambridge University was only a year younger
than James, and there is a close parallel between their careers —
both of them studying in Germany in the late '6os, teaching and
promoting experimental psychology in the late '7os, writing psychology in the '8os, and shifting the focus of their activities from
psychology to philosophy in the '9os.   There was much to bind
James to Ward.   The latter, like himself, was of British extraction,
developing out of the school of Locke and never moving wholly
away from it.   Like James, Ward believed in experimental psychology, especially in his youth, but practised it little.   Hence both
devoted themselves to introspection, and to the discussion of the
problems lying on the border between psychology and philosophy.

[12] The reference is to Bain's article on "Mr. Ward's Psychology," *Mind*, XI
(1886) ; *cf. Principles*, I, 162, note.
[13] "Bain and Renouvier," *Nation*, XXII (1876) ; reprinted in *C.E.R.*
[14] Delbœuf, Fechner, and Mach have been introduced above.   For Münsterberg,
cf. below, Ch. LX.   James also read extensively in German and other periodicals —
e.g., the *Vierteljahrsschrift für wissenschaftliche Philosophie* and the *Zeitschrift für
Psychologie*.

Both conceived of the mind as a motor response to cognitive presentations, and thus emphasized its personality and activity. Here, however, the parallel ceases. James was expansive, brilliant, and colorful, while Ward was concise, analytical, and systematic. Ward wholly lacked the radical temper of mind essential to James, and in his *Psychological Principles,* published eight years after James's death, he found little to say in the latter's favor and much to say against his "absurdities." [15]

The two men appear to have met for the first time when James went to Europe in the summer of 1880. Upon his return to America he sent Ward reprints of his recent articles, which the latter acknowledged as follows: —

Cambridge [Eng.], Dec. 20, 1880

Dear Sir, —

I have to thank you for three of your papers received in the thick of work and hence so tardily acknowledged. The paper on "Great Men and the Environment," I enjoyed immensely, and a friend of mine, George Darwin, whose opinion is worth having, was particularly enthusiastic about it. The paper on "Association" I have not yet read — that on "Feeling of Effort" I have in my hands now, and if it were only possible I should ask you to come and have a good long talk about it. . . .

What I chiefly object to is your method: you start from the physiological side, or, at least, you mingle physiological and psychological. Can you, for example, really make clear such terms as "efferent feeling" or "afferent feeling"? My humble contention is that we ought to ascertain: (1) such facts as can be expressed in psychological terms — efferent and afferent are not such terms and never will be; (2) such facts as can be expressed in physiological terms — feeling can never be among these; (3) to compare the two as respects complexity, in time, intensity, etc. On the psychical side the fact, as it seems to me, of cardinal importance is the one you mention almost casually. . . . "The outer force seems in no wise constrained to back the mind's adoptions, except in one single kind

[15] He declares James's treatment of the self and of the emotions to be absurd, and these are the only doctrines of James which he treats at length. (*Cf. Psychological Principles,* 1918, 270, 379.) The same thing is true of the philosophical relations of the two men. They were both "pluralists," but James meant his pluralism in a radical sense that could not fail to scandalize Ward. For the correspondence on philosophical matters, *cf.* below, 644–56.

of case, — where the idea is that of bodily movement." It is this dependence in normal circumstances upon subjective initiation that makes psychologically all the difference between sensory and motor presentations. That the presentation is in both cases preceded by afferent "nerve currents" is, so far as I can see, neither here nor there. . . .

I take the liberty of sending you copies of some papers written from my lecture notes and printed for private discussion last term. I shall be at all times glad to hear from you and regret I saw you for so short a time. Yours very truly,

JAMES WARD

Cambridge, Feb. 27, 1881

Dear Mr. Ward, —

. . . The sheets you sent me proved most important and stimulating, although in spite of several re-readings the meaning of certain parts remains, owing to extreme concision, obscure. Psychology is evidently plastic in your hands in a degree hardly met with hitherto. I applaud most heartily your attempt to speak in subjective terms exclusively at one time, and in objective at another, and am full of curiosity to see how you carry it through. Your use of certain words, as *object* for *feeling, continuum,* etc., really puts a new power into our hands. . . . As for your letter and its criticisms on my feeble production, I will only say this: that the mingling of psychological with physiological statements does not ever, I think, proceed in me from confusion. My problem was relative to the *connection* between the two aspects; and "afferent-feeling" was only an abridgment for "feeling linked with afferent process." . . . I hope you will not fail to send me anything else you may print. I shall prize it exceedingly. Faithfully yours,

WILLIAM JAMES

In 1885 James called the attention of his students approvingly to articles in which Ward had stressed the subjective or Berkeleyan standpoint and had affirmed the "continuity" of consciousness as against the associationist school.[16] In 1886 appeared Ward's fa-

[16] Ward's articles entitled "Psychological Principles" appeared in *Mind* in April and Oct., 1883. For James's recognition of Ward as an ally against associationism, *cf. Principles,* I, 162, note. I suspect that James owes more to Ward on this than on any other topic.

mous article on "Psychology" in the *Encyclopædia Britannica.*
James asked Ward for an offprint, and acknowledged it as follows: —

Cambridge, July 29, 1886

My dear Mr. Ward, —

I got the article on "Psychology," which you so kindly sent me,
a month ago, and have just read it carefully and with extreme interest. You have packed away so much in its short compass, and
made such a vast number of original and suggestive remarks, that
I think I will make no attempt at comment on its details. I trust
you may some day or other receive from me something which will
show that it has not been without effect of one sort or other, in
the formation of my own opinions. I shall have to do a good deal
of re-reading and assimilating yet, before I definitively settle my
accounts with what you say. I rejoice to find that in the greater
number of your innovations I either follow you, or have already
anticipated you in my own less incisive and pregnant way. Your
treatment is so very condensed in this article that I fear you will
not have many understanding readers. I believe I have, in places,
missed your full sense myself from lack of expansion and illustration. I trust that you may be able to spread out and fill in this
framework ere long, in a book that may serve for college students.
But though this should never happen, I think no competent person
will deny that this article, by itself, marks the transition of English psychology from one epoch to another. It will be impossible
after it to discuss things from the meagre and superficial standpoint
of the classical English school and its critics.

Thanking you again for the article — which I don't see how I
could have done without, I am faithfully yours,

WM. JAMES

James's favorite experimental psychologist was Carl Stumpf, of
Würzburg, Prague, Halle, Munich, and finally Berlin. Stumpf
had the kind of versatility that James liked. Though he was six
years James's junior, he was more precocious, and received his
Doctor's degree in 1868 at the age of twenty; so that the '70s and
'80s found the two men at the same stage of their scientific and
academic development. Stumpf received a thorough philosophical

training and has remained a philosopher throughout his entire career.[17]   His first psychological work was on the perception of space, and took the "nativistic" position which James afterwards adopted. In writing his acknowledgments to those who had preceded him in this field, James said, "Stumpf seems to me the most philosophical and profound of all the writers; and I owe him much." [18]   It was owing to his authorship of this work on space that James looked up "the good and sharp-nosed Stumpf" in Prague at the end of October, 1882, and, after talking with him for twelve hours in three days, came away resolved to engage him in correspondence.[19]   The following letter was written by James shortly after this meeting: —

Paris, Nov. 26, 1882

My dear Stumpf, —

(I 'm sure you will allow me to drop titles of ceremony with a colleague with whose person and whose ideas alike I feel so warm a sympathy; and I trust that when you write to me you will give the same token that you regard me in the light of an old friend.)

I mailed you the papers you were kind enough to lend me the day before yesterday.   I hope they will reach you safely.   When I say that I actually had not time to finish reading them before I got to Paris, which was three days ago, it will give you an idea of the busy character of my life since leaving Prague.   Both in Leipzig and Berlin I found a host of old American friends, many of them former students.   I stayed in Berlin a week, in Leipzig five days, in Liége two and a half days with Delbœuf.   In each place I heard all the university lectures I could, and spoke with several of the professors.   From some I got very good hints as to how *not* to lecture.   Helmholtz, for example, gave me the very worst lecture I ever heard in my life except one (that one was by our most distinguished American mathematician).   The lecture I heard in Prague from Mach was on the same elementary subject as Helmholtz's, and one of the most artistic lectures I ever heard.   Wundt in Leipzig impressed me very agreeably personally.   He has a ready smile and is entirely unaffected and unpretending in his man-

---

[17] At this writing, 1935, he is engaged, in retirement in Berlin, on a systematic treatise on epistemology.

[18] *Principles*, II, 282.   Stumpf's work was *Ueber den psychologischen Ursprung der Raumvorstellung, 1873.*

[19] *L.W.J.*, I, 211–2, 216.

ner. I heard him twice, and was twice in his laboratory, he was
very polite but showed no desire for a further acquaintance. *Überhaupt* I must say that the hospitality of Prague towards wandering
philosophers much surpasses that of Berlin and Leipzig. In great
capitals it is more difficult to give one's time to strangers. I found
M. Delbœuf a most delightful man, full of spirits and originality;
and altogether I enjoyed extremely my sojourn in Liége. . . .

I read your *Aus der vierten Dimension* with lively interest and
admiration. Where did it appear? [20] I should like the reference
for the use of my students. I make a couple of them work up that
subject in an essay every year. I hope that this will find you, the
Frau Professorin and the youthful Rudi all well. It will be long
ere I forget those pleasant days in old Prague — pleasant chiefly
on account of you. . . . Believe me, always faithfully yours,

WM. JAMES

In 1883 Stumpf published the first volume of his *Tonpsychologie,*
in which he drew upon his musical knowledge and dealt with various problems of psychology and psychophysics in their bearing on
auditory sensation. This volume, as well as the second volume
which appeared in 1890, James read with his usual painstaking care
and with more than his usual sympathy. He found Stumpf disposed to the "nativistic" view wherever the issue arose, and to be
relatively free from the usual psychological vices and fallacies. He
applauded Stumpf for arguing, against the relativists, that sensations have their own intrinsic qualities not dependent on effects of
difference and contrast; and he drew copiously from Stumpf when
he came to treat the subject of "Discrimination and Comparison." [21]
But a full statement of his indebtedness is contained in his letter of
acknowledgment : —

Cambridge, Nov. 15, 1884

My dear Stumpf, —
Thank Heaven that I can at last write to you that I have read your
Tonpsychologie, and like and admire it as it deserves. It will give
you an idea of how my studies are hindered by poor health, bad

[20] *Philos. Monatshefte,* 1878.
[21] *Principles,* II, 11; Ch. XIII. For another reference to Stumpf's soundness on
the matter of relativity, *cf. Mind,* X (1885), 28, note.

eyes, and other necessary occupations, when I tell you that although from the first moment your book came into my hands, I hungered to devour it, it was only a few days ago that I was able to close it, read. I had an attack of fever during the summer vacation, that spoilt a good two months for me; and as my eyes are never good for more than about four hours a day, and I have eight hours of lecturing a week to get ready for — besides having during the past few months to get through the press a volume of my father's literary remains — you see how near I am to being left high and dry and abandoned by the advancing tide of psychological literature.

But enough of groaning! Your book is masterly through and through; and I feel quite proud, now that everyone must rank you among the first psychologists, that I long ago discovered in your space-book the same merits that are here so conspicuous — exhaustive thoroughness, subtlety of discrimination, firmness and clearness of style, and incorruptible good sense, not to speak of great learning. Your German brains are built after another fashion from those of the rest of us, you can carry a heavier freight of facts, and handle them in a freer way. What I *care for* most in the book is, of course, its general theoretic tendency — away from "psycho-mythology" and logicalism, and towards a truly empirical and sensationalistic point of view, which I am persuaded is the only practical and solid basis for psychological science. Your opening pages about the doctrine of relativity did my very heart good, — I had been longing for years for something like that. It seems to me that what you have said is final. *We* are especially pestered just now by the relativity doctrine in its most extreme form, from the side of the Anglo- and Americano-Hegelians, who are getting very active. The best proof that there is something absolute and positive in our "simple ideas" (as Locke calls them), has already seemed to me to be the existence of *problems*. A problem is a *quaesitum* of which one knows the *relations,* but which one ignores as a *term,* with an intrinsic quality of content. Who, if asked to furnish a sound which should be both higher and yet the same in quality with a given sound, would think of the *octave,* unless he had already *felt* it? etc., etc.

For similar reasons I enjoyed immensely your treatment of *Aehnlichkeit,* of *Distanz,* and of *Tonhöhe,*[22] as immediate percep-

[22] "Similarity," "distance," and "the height of tones."

tions of sense, and not logical inferences from other related facts. Most psychologists, and what is worse, ordinary people, seem to think that if you can *develop* a thing's relations, and *define* it in terms of those relations, then it can never have had any other *status* in the mind than as a perception of those relations. Thus motion is a synthesis of *terminus a quo* and *terminus ad quem,* with earlier and later moments of time, and cannot be a simple feeling; space is a synthesis of *positions,* and no feeling; action, because happiness is an incident of its successful performance, must have been *motivated* by that happiness, — everywhere confusion of the worst sort, to which you, in this noble book, have dealt one of the very heaviest of blows. I wish very much you might continue in this same line for a good while to come.

There is but one matter in relation to which it seems to me that the psychology of the future may find something to correct in your pages. In your treatment of *Subjective Zuverlässigkeit,*[23] you speak as if the sensation to be judged were an unvarying and permanent bit of content, no matter what its concomitants. In *Mind,* for January last, I gave some reasons for thinking that we never have the same subjective modification twice. When we judge, name or estimate a sensation, just as when we judge an outward thing, we are dealing with an *object.* What we mean by c^3 for example is an *ideal* note abstracted from several sensible experiences, never *felt* except as entering into some total consciousness of the moment; tinging, to be sure, that consciousness, but also tinged by it, and *judged* by us in a unitary mental state that probably never recurs in just the same way. . . . When the attention discriminates an overtone which a moment before it did not notice, I don't think we ought to say the overtone was already there *as a sensation.* It surely was *not* there as the sensation *we now get out of it;* and I think the more rational way of considering the matter is to say that the *sound* was there as an object — that with our brain in one state and our consciousness in the corresponding state we defined that object in one way, but that with our brain and consciousness in a better, more active state, we now define the *same* sound in *another* way, namely, as having an overtone. Sully has something to the

[23] Subjective reliability. The passage referred to is *Tonpsychologie,* 1883, I, 186–7, and it is criticized by W.J. in *Principles,* I, 522–3, note. The article in *Mind* referred to below is "Some Omissions of Introspective Psychology."

same effect in his review of you in *Mind,* but I 'm not sure it is from the same point of view.[24]   Still less am I sure I have made my own point of view clear to you.   But enough.   Your book is solid, and will be a model for the future.   I expect with great interest the æsthetic part, and only wish my own organization were not so unmusical. . . .

As for me, we are all getting on fairly well in the family, and I am thinking of building a house of my own ere long, to lodge my three boys in.   My "psychology" makes *no* progress, literally.   But whilst there 's life there 's hope.   I always think with the keenest sympathy of you, and with the keenest pleasure of the days I spent in Prague.   Please give my very best regards to Mrs. Stumpf, and tell her my wife sends the same. . . .   Let me hear from you soon and believe me, faithfully yours,

WM. JAMES

Cambridge, Jan. 1, 1886 [25]

My dear Stumpf, —

The first of January is a good day for sending you my annual letter, with a hearty New Year's Greeting to yourself and all your family. . . .   I was reminded of you only a week or so since, as I accidentally fell upon a number of the *Deutsche Literaturzeitung* which contained a review of Lipps's *Psychologische Studien* (if that is the title) which I had just read and admired for their originality and acuteness, — although his argument against the *Tiefendimension* had failed to convince me as much as it failed to convince you. Your rallying to the fight strengthened my own steadfastness in the faith.   The feeling of distance *is* a feeling, or nothing is a feeling. That immediate simple fact of introspection cannot be overthrown by any amount of argument. . . .   I have got Lipps's larger book, but not yet had a chance to read a page of it.   He is evidently a very able writer, with whom one must reckon in psychology.[26] . . .

[24] J. Sully's critical notice of Stumpf's *Tonpsychologie* appeared in *Mind,* IX (1884).
[25] Reprinted in part from *L.W.J.,* I, 247–9.
[26] T. Lipps was on the whole an advocate of the geneticist or empiristic view as against nativism.   The dimension of depth (*Tiefendimension*) could not, he thought, be sensed, but only inferred.   On the other hand, he criticized the attempt to explain the sense of extension in terms of the sense of movement, and so far James welcomed him as an ally against the prevailing fashion to substitute genesis for innateness everywhere in our explanations. Lipps's *Psychologische Studien* appeared in 1885, and was reviewed approvingly by James in *Science,* VI (1885).

I don't know whether you have heard of the London "Society for Psychical Research," which is seriously and laboriously investigating all sorts of "supernatural" matters, clairvoyance, apparitions, etc. . . . It is a field in which the sources of deception are extremely numerous. But I believe there is no source of deception in the investigation of nature which can compare with a fixed belief that certain kinds of phenomena are *impossible*.

My teaching is much the same as it was — a little better in quality, I hope. I enjoy very much a new philosophic colleague, Josiah Royce, from California, who is just thirty years old and a perfect little Socrates for wisdom and humor. I still try to write a little psychology, but it is exceedingly slow work. No sooner do I get interested than bang! goes my sleep, and I have to stop a week or ten days, during which my ideas get all cold again. Nothing so fatiguing as the eternal hanging on of an uncompleted task. Apropos to which let me hope that your second volume is soon to see the light and leave you with *that* fatigue relieved. If it is as good as Vol. I, the whole will form a great book, whose fame will always endure. I have just received from Professor Mach, that truly *genialer* man, the bare announcement of a new theory of sensations of sound, which reads as if it might be very important. His book, too, he writes me is about to appear.[27] I am thirsty to read it, although my reading goes on very slowly. I try to spend two hours a day in a laboratory for psycho-physics which I started last year, but of which I fear the *fruits* will be slow in ripening, as my experimental aptitude is but small. But I am convinced that one must guard in some such way as that against the growing tendency to *subjectivism* in one's thinking, as life goes on. I am *hypnotizing*, on a large scale, the students, and have hit upon one or two rather pretty unpublished things of which some day I hope I may send you an account. Spending a number of hours a week in a laboratory is not, however, a sure remedy for subjectivism, as the case of Stricker proves. I have just read your note about him in the *Revue philosophique*.[28] Was there ever such an ass, such an intellectual barbarian as that man! . . .

Bah! Well, this is all the news. I hope you still like Halle, and

---

[27] The *Analyse der Empfindungen.*
[28] "Sur la Représentation des mélodies," XX (1885). S. Stricker of Vienna, whom W.J. nevertheless read and used (*cf. Principles,* II, 62 ff.).

are well, and in good working condition. I don't yet see my way clearly to another trip abroad within five years. Many changes may occur in both of us before then. Let me hear how things go with you ere long. Meanwhile, once more the heartiest of *Gluckwünsche zum neuen Jahre* to both yourself and Frau Stumpf from both of us! Ever faithfully yours,

WM. JAMES

James and Stumpf were united by their antipathies as well as by their sympathies, Spencer and Wundt being the most notable cases in point.[29]

Sassnitz (Rügen), Sept. 8, 1886 [30]

Dear James, —

Forgive me for not having answered your pleasant and full letter of the first of January. I postponed this, among other things that have remained undone, until the long vacation. . . . I probably do not think quite so highly of Lipps as you do; he seems to me talented, it is true, but still very immature. It would be better for him if he consorted with scholars for several years, and did not give his studies to the public. But our younger generation is very ambitious. Mach's work gave me much pleasure; but upon closer examination much of it is seen to contain *aperçus* that are more ingenious than true. In my review in the *Deutsche Literaturzeitung* [31] I ventured to indicate this conviction as politely as possible, and was delighted to hear that Mach took no offence at my criticism. Instead he expressed his thanks to me. I also reviewed Spencer's *Psychology* in the same paper recently, and while doing so got a real insight into the essential nature of Spencer's thought; he is fundamentally a modernized Hegel. Do you concur in this? . . .

Agreement on the principles and purposes of research becomes more valuable to me in proportion as I see men whom one would once have classed as of the same tendency and opinion, straying from them. Thus it seems to me that Sully, for example, no longer makes the right use of his great talents; he seems to me to be tending more and more toward voluminousness and popularization. . . . Perhaps his position as examiner offers the occasion for this. But

---

[29] For the long and painful Wundt-Stumpf controversy, *cf.* E. G. Boring, *History of Experimental Psychology*, 1929, 355.

[30] The German originals of Stumpf's letters will be found in Appendix VIII.

[31] A review of E. Mach's *Beiträge zur Analyse der Empfindungen*, VII (1886).

science suffers when students laugh. . . . Wundt leads students and some others to believe that the ever-repeated measurement of reaction-time marks the beginning of an entirely new "experimental psychology" from which one can look back upon the old psychology only with scorn and derision. Look at his essays on this point — note the claims of his pupils in the *Literarisches Centralblatt.* As though anything important at all could follow from time measurements as such; as though these themselves did not have to be interpreted by inner observation; as though finally, numbers, rather than clear concepts, were the chief thing! And what a bad example the teacher gives his pupils in respect of clear and acute thinking! Like his doctrine of relativity, so also his doctrine of apperception, and almost everything of more general significance, is full of ambiguity and contradiction. . . . My dear Marty [32] has just subjected Wundt's doctrine of apperception to a keen critique in the latter's own *Vierteljahrsschrift,* and this appears to have put Wundt so badly out of humor, that the editor, Avenarius, has temporarily suppressed it. But Wundt will not be able to come back with anything cogent; he will attempt superciliously to dispose of it with a few general phrases in the hope of rehabilitating himself at least with his blind admirers.

My inclinations are too little in the direction of mere polemic, — otherwise I should indeed compile a register of Wundt's sins, and attempt to direct attention again to what is truly significant in research, on which the younger generation has in many respects been so confused by Wundt. But people will return to it of their own accord. How often already has not psychology been made "exact" in this way, only to be led back again into the path — into "psychological" psychology!

But enough, yes, too much even, of these complaints, my dear James! Let us rather admire what is admirable both in the world and in man, and above all let us attempt to realize this in ourselves. And I beg that you remain well disposed to your Carl Stumpf, who, with his wife, greets you and your wife most heartily.

In his missing reply to the last letter James evidently gave expression to his growing impatience with Spencer, which evoked in

[32] Anton Marty was head of the department of psychology at the University of Prague.

January the following comment from Stumpf: "Your judgment concerning Spencer interests me since one seldom hears such sharp comment on this thinker, especially on the part of English and American philosophers. Each of us sees more clearly the failings and the insolidity of that which is nearer to him: you see those of Spencer, I those of Wundt."

Cambridge, Feb. 6, 1887 [33]

My dear Stumpf, —

Your two letters from Rügen of Sept. 8th, and from Halle of Jan. 2, came duly, and I can assure you that their content was most heartily appreciated, and not by me alone. I fairly squealed with pleasure over the first one and its rich combination of good counsel and humorous commentary, and read the greater part of it to my friend Royce, assistant professor of philosophy here, who enjoyed it almost as much as I. There is a heartiness and solidity about your letters which is truly German, and makes them as nutritious as they are refreshing to receive. Your *Kater-Gefühl* however, in your second letter about your *Auslassungen* [34] on the subject of Wundt, amused me by its speedy evolution into *Auslassungen* more animated still. I can well understand why Wundt should make his compatriots impatient. Foreigners can afford to be indifferent for he does n't *crowd* them so much. He aims at being a sort of Napoleon of the intellectual world. Unfortunately he will never have a Waterloo, for he is a Napoleon without genius and with no central idea which, if defeated, brings down the whole fabric in ruin. You remember what Victor Hugo says of Napoleon in the *Misérables* — *"Il gênait Dieu"*; Wundt only *gêners* his *confrères;* and whilst they make mincemeat of some one of his views by their criticism, he is meanwhile writing a book on an entirely different subject. Cut him up like a worm, and each fragment crawls; there is no *nœud vital* in his mental medulla oblongata, so that you can't kill him all at once.

But surely you must admit that, since there must be professors in the world, Wundt is the most praiseworthy and never-too-much-to-be-respected type of the species. He is n't a genius, he is a *professor* — a being whose duty is to know everything, and have his

[33] Reprinted, with omissions and additions, from *L.W.J.*, I, 262–7.
[34] An *Auslassung* is a tirade. *Katergefühl* combines the idea of unhappiness and self-reproach.

own opinion about everything, connected with his *Fach*. Wundt has
the most prodigious faculty of appropriating and preserving knowl-
edge, and as for opinions, he takes *au grand sérieux* his duties there.
He says of each possible subject, "Here I must have an opinion.
Let's see! What shall it be? How many possible opinions are
there? three? four? Yes! just four! Shall I take one of these?
It will seem more original to take a higher position, a sort of
Vermittelungsansicht [35] between them all. That I will do, etc., etc."
So he acquires a complete assortment of opinions of his own; and,
as his memory is so good, he seldom forgets which they are! But
this is not reprehensible; it is admirable — from the professorial
point of view. To be sure, one gets tired of that point of view
after a while. But was there ever, since Christian Wolff's time,
such a model of the German professor? He has utilized to the ut-
termost fibre every gift that Heaven endowed him with at his birth,
and made of it all that mortal pertinacity could make. He is the
finished example of how much mere *education* can do for a man.
Beside him, Spencer is an ignoramus as well as a charlatan. I admit that Spencer is occasionally more *amusing* than Wundt. His
Data of Ethics seems to me incomparably his best book, because it
is a more or less frank expression of the man's personal *ideal of
living* — which has of course little to do with science, and which, in
Spencer's case, is full of definiteness and vigor. Wundt's *Ethics*
I have not yet seen, and probably shall not "tackle" it for a good
while to come. . . .

I found to my surprise and pleasure that Robertson was willing
to print my chapter on Space in *Mind*, even though it should run
through all four numbers of the year. So I sent it to him. Most of
it was written six or even seven years ago. To tell the truth, I am
off of space now, and can probably carry my little private ingenuity
concerning it no farther than I have already done in this essay; and
fearing that some evil fiend might put it into Helmholtz's mind to
correct all his errors and tell the full truth in the new edition of his
Optics, I felt it was high time that what I had written should see
the light and not be lost. It is dry stuff to read, and I hardly
dare to recommend it to you; but if you do read it, there is no one
whose favorable opinion I should more rejoice to hear; for, as you
know, you seem to me, of all writers on space, the one who, on the

[35] Mediatory attitude (view).

whole, has thought out the subject most *philosophically*.   Of course,
the experimental patience, and skill and freshness of observation of
the Helmholtzes and Herings are altogether admirable, and perhaps
at bottom *worth* more than philosophic ability.   Space is really a
direfully difficult subject!   The third dimension bothers me very
much still.

I have this very day corrected the proofs of an essay on the Perception of Time, which I will send you when it shall appear in the
Journal of Speculative Philosophy for October last.   (The number
of "July, 1886" is not yet out!)   I rather enjoyed the writing of it.
I have just begun a chapter on "Discrimination and Comparison,"
subjects which have been long stumbling-blocks in my path.   Yesterday it seemed to me that I could perhaps do nothing better than
just translate §§6 and 7 of the first *Abschnitt* of your *Tonpsychologie,* which is worth more than everything else put together which
has been written on the subject.   But I will stumble on and try to
give it a more personal form.   I shall, however, borrow largely
from you.

What you say of Sully is true.   But poor man!   The anxieties
of his life are enough to take the quality out of any man's work.
His *Outlines of Psychology* was written *merely* to sell.   He is very
poor, without a professorship, and in poor health, bad sleep, morbid
sensitiveness to sounds, etc.   He is a beautiful, reasonable, unselfish
character, and the *Objectivität* of which you speak, in his notice of
your *Musikpsychologie* in England, is the natural result of this.   I
wish he could have had more money many years ago.   But after all,
there is no *nerve* in his mind, — it vacillates.

Have you seen [Edmund] Gurney's two bulky tomes, *Phantasms
of the Living,* an amazingly patient and thorough piece of work?
I should not at all wonder if it were the beginning of a new department of natural history.   But even if not, it is an important chapter
in the statistics of *Völkerpsychologie,* and I think Gurney worthy
of the highest praise for his devotion to this unfashionable work.
He is not the kind of stuff which the ordinary pachydermatous
fanatic and mystic is made of. . . .

I bought last summer a bit of land on a lovely lake in New Hampshire with a mountain 3500 feet high just behind it, and ninety acres
of land, oaks, pines, etc., brook, splendid spring of water, house,
etc., for $750.00 (!)   I wish you could come and spend a sum-

mer there with us! We would conspire against the philosophic world. Why, ah why, is it that "Freiheit liegt nur in dem Reich der Träume"? Well, since 't is so, good night! Thank you again for your splendid letters. Pray give my warmest greetings, and my wife's, too, to the Frau Professorin, and believe me faithfully yours,

WM. JAMES

It will be recalled that James spent the summer of 1889 in Europe and that he attended the International Congress of Physiological Psychology in Paris. Stumpf's hope of seeing him was disappointed, but on August 15, as he was about to sail for home, James wrote a letter of which the following is a paragraph: —

"The Congress in Paris was delightful. I have written a very short account of it for *Mind* [36] . . . which you will see, so I say nothing of it now, except this, that the courtesy of the Frenchmen was beyond all praise, and that the sight of 120 men all actively interested in psychology has made me feel much less lonely in the world, and ready to finish my book this year with a great deal more *entrain*. A book hanging so long on one's hands at last gets outgrown, and even disgusting to one. The Congress has remedied that. . . . I am . . . very glad that your second volume is so forward.[37] Being the musical barbarian that I am, I very much fear that I cannot assimilate it as well as I did the first."

Although James's relations with Stumpf were based on their common psychological interests, they continued after James had shifted his emphasis to philosophy. This was possible because Stumpf, too, was a philosopher, and because by that time their personal friendship had become too strong to be broken by a divergence of occupation.

[36] *Mind*, XIV (1889).
[37] The second volume of Stumpf's *Tonpsychologie* appeared in 1890.

LVI

SOURCES OF SPECIAL PSYCHOLOGICAL DOCTRINES

SPEAKING of his book as avoiding spiritualistic, associationist, or other metaphysical theories of explanation, James wrote: "In this strictly positivistic point of view consists the only feature of it for which I . . . claim originality." [1] Notwithstanding this claim, a comparison of the *Principles* with any subsequent or even contemporary treatise professing to deal with the *science* of psychology reveals James's liberal use of philosophical literature. The pages of the book abound in such names as Locke, Berkeley, Hume, Kant, Mill, Lewes, Taine, Bradley, Hodgson, and Renouvier, to say nothing of Spencer. This is to be accounted for in part by the fact that James's philosophers were also, as a rule, psychologists; but mainly by the fact that he believed philosophy to be the only means of attaining that very emancipation of psychology from philosophy which he sought. Instead of attaining this emancipation in advance, James introduced it into the *Principles,* the result being that his psychology as it stands is inseparable from his philosophy — in its sources, its conclusions, and its inconclusiveness.

Thus "dualism" was a provisional doctrine by which James the psychologist hoped to eliminate and postpone a question on which James the philosopher had not made up his mind. But this question — namely, of the relation between "the state of mind" and its "object" — *refused* to be eliminated, as James himself realized immediately after the publication of the *Principles,* and more and more strongly as the years passed. In the *Principles* we are told that "the dualism of Object and Subject and their preëstablished harmony are what the psychologist as such must assume, whatever ulterior monistic philosophy he may, as an individual who has the right also to be a metaphysician, have in reserve." [2] James, of course, *had* his monistic solution in reserve. In 1882–1883, when

[1] *Principles,* vi.
[2] *Principles,* I, 220.

he was "floundering in the morasses of the theory of cognition," he was evidently trying to formulate a "phenomenistic" philosophy which might serve as the basis for his psychology.   Thus he wrote, in an unpublished note: "As regards the 'object' known, some call it a mere locus upon which the mind projects its own affections; some, on the contrary, say the mind is a mere locus into which the objective qualities wander and are known.   Some say there is no locus of either sort, nothing but a stream, for which 'phenomena' is the neutral name, and which according to one way of viewing it may be called 'feeling,' according to another way 'objective fact.' Others again try to discriminate, and call part of the stream 'feeling,' and the remainder 'fact.' "

Although James steadily adhered to a view of this type, he did not yet feel that it afforded a secure foundation for his psychological superstructure.   Instead, therefore, of *reducing ultimate distinctions,* as a phenomenistic philosophy undertook to do, he *multiplied provisional distinctions,* in the interest of noncommittal scientific description.   But here the consistency of his empirical method betrayed him.   His distinctions being construed in terms of experience, and experience yielding conjunctions as well as disjunctions, the distinctions were reduced in the very act of describing them; and James was perpetually being led, despite his profession of dualism and of metaphysical abstinence, to the disclosure of a homogeneous and continuous world.

The profession of dualism, combined with an inner tendency to monism, led to confusion and ambiguity.   Thus, in discussing the relative merits of the terms "thought" and "feeling" to represent the mental state, he says that the former has the merit of suggesting "the omnipresence of cognition (or reference to an object other than the mental state itself), which we . . . see to be of the mental life's essence." [3]   But just what is the difference between the "thought" and the thought's "object"?   "The *Object* of your thought," says James, "is really its entire content or deliverance, neither more nor less . . . all that the thought thinks, exactly as the thought thinks it, however complicated the matter, and however symbolic the manner of the thinking may be."   If I think that Columbus discovered America in 1492, then the object of my thought is the complex "Columbus-discovered-America-in-1492."   "Noth-

[3] *Principles,* I, 186.

ing but this can possibly name its delicate idiosyncrasy. And if we wish to *feel* that idiosyncrasy we must reproduce the thought as it was uttered, with every word fringed and the whole sentence bathed in that original halo of obscure relations, which, like an horizon, then spread about its meaning." What then, is the *difference* between the thought and the thought's object? [4]

The question becomes the more embarrassing when it is recalled that the uniqueness and organic unity of the thought are ascribed to its cerebral conditions. James tells us that "whilst we think, our brain changes, and . . . like the aurora borealis, its whole internal equilibrium shifts with every pulse of change." "The *knower* is in every case a unique pulse of thought corresponding to a unique reaction of the brain upon its conditions." [5] If it be asked, then, what room there is for thought as a separate item between the cerebral pulsation and the thought's object, there appears to be no clear answer in the *Principles*.

Or, consider the distinction between the thought's object and the ulterior reality. The reason for the distinction lies in the fact that the latter is repeated when the former is not. Thus, although the thinking that Columbus-discovered-America-in-1492 is an indivisible whole, Columbus may be thought of in other thoughts. Hence we need to distinguish between the object and what may be called the "kernel" or "topic" or "grammatical subject" of the thought: the latter being what the thought is "about," [6] the former what is thought about it. Unless two or more thoughts can be about a common thing, rational discourse is impossible. *"The mind can always intend, and know when it intends, to think of the Same"* — this is "the very keel and backbone of our thinking." [7] But the thought's term of intentional reference, like its object, tends to be assimilated to one homogeneous and continuous stream with the thought itself: becoming either the thought's felt tendency or the sensation in which the tendency terminates. In his own characteristic thinking, [8] as distinguished from his Lockean inheritance, James tended to attach diminishing importance to the external relation of "resemblance" between ideas and reality, and to emphasize their functional relation;

[4] *Ibid.*, I, 275–6.
[5] *Ibid.*, I, 234; II, 28.   *Cf.* also I, 232, 242, 246, 252, 257.
[6] *Ibid.*, I, 275–6.
[7] *Ibid.*, I, 459–60.   *Cf.* the slightly different statement on pp. 271–2.
[8] *Ibid.*, I, 471.

the one leading to or toward the other, and both lying on the same plane of experience or line of action.[9] This was later James's "radical empiricism," that ulterior monistic philosophy which he intended to "hold in reserve" but constantly betrayed.

The composition of the *Principles* thus found James with a half-finished theory of knowledge. If he was not to carry on his philosophizing in the *Principles,* he must arrange a truce. In other words, his dualism was not a completely thought-out set of presuppositions for psychology, but a half-thought-out compromise designed to give him a temporary respite from philosophizing. This explains his saying in 1900: "I confess that during the years which have elapsed since the publication of the book, I have become more and more convinced of the difficulty of treating psychology without introducing some true and suitable philosophical doctrine." [10]

James's psychological positivism had a constructive and not a merely negative sense; it was a professed avoidance of metaphysics, but also a leaning toward natural science. This was not a mere accident of training and approach. He sought an integral view of mind that would throw light on man's place in nature, and he found this in biology. He sought for a non-metaphysical explanation of mental events, sequences, and concurrences, and he believed that the physiology of the nervous system offered the most likely prospect. Both motives inclined him, for example, to the acceptance of the theory of the reflex arc. An essay published in 1888 contains this significant passage: "The only conception at the same time renovating and fundamental with which biology has enriched psychology, the only *essential* point in which 'the new psychology' is an advance upon the old, is, it seems to me, the very general, and by this time very familiar notion, that all our activity belongs at bottom to the type of reflex action, and that all our consciousness accompanies a chain of events of which the first was an incoming current in some sensory nerve, and of which the last will be a discharge into some muscle, blood-vessel, or gland. . . . Viewed in this light the thinking and feeling portions of our life seem little more than half-way houses towards behavior; and recent Psychology accordingly tends to treat consciousness more and more as if it

---

[9] *M.T.,* 41, note; an important passage as bearing on James's historical development.
[10] Preface to Italian translation of *Principles,* xi.

existed only for the sake of the conduct which it seems to introduce, and tries to explain its peculiarities (so far as they can be
explained at all) by their practical utility." [11]

James accepted the physiological implications of this theory most
scrupulously. He recognized an obligation to find a physiological
correlate for every state or function of mind, and to confine psychological speculation within the bounds of physiological probability. Nothing is more striking than the fidelity with which James
carried out this method, in his treatment of association, habit, emotion, will, perception, and other topics. Furthermore, he used
physiological hypotheses to extend and supplement, as well as to
explain, the processes of consciousness. He supposed physiological
processes to lie below the conscious threshold, around the outskirts
of attention, and in the interstices of sensory and ideational states.

The theory of the reflex arc commended itself to James because,
while it introduces mind into the context of nature, it nevertheless recognizes that character of *interestedness* which distinguishes
mind: "The mind's relations to other objects than the brain are
cognitive and emotional relations exclusively, so far as we know.
It *knows* them, and it inwardly *welcomes or rejects* them, but it has
no other dealings with them." This welcoming or rejecting is felt
in the fringe of consciousness, as a "sense of furtherance" or "sense
of hindrance." "Every actually existing consciousness seems to
itself at any rate to be a *fighter for ends,* of which many, but for its
presence, would not be ends at all. Its powers of cognition are
mainly subservient to these ends, discerning which facts further
them and which do not." In short, the teleological interpretation
of mind does not contradict either its cognitive or its biological rôle
— it explains them both. The *use* of the mind, which accounts
biologically for its existence, consists in its taking cognizance of the
environment in behalf of the interests of an organism. [12]

Turning to James's more specifically *psychological* doctrines, the
first place must be given to the "stream of thought." The most
signal "omission of introspective psychology," as James saw it,
was the relational or transitive state, which, when adequately rec-

[11] "What the Will Effects," *Scribner's,* III (1888), 240.
[12] *Principles,* I, 216, 259, 141. *Cf. W.B.,* 114; E. G. Boring, *A History of Experimental Psychology,* 1929, 501. James's teleology forms a part of "functionalism" as sometimes conceived.

ognized, gives to consciousness an aspect of streamlike continuity. Except possibly for the dependence of knowledge on will, this was James's most important insight.[13]

The doctrine of the stream of thought implied the rejection of "associationism," and signified a sharp break with the tradition. Associationism in the accepted sense meant the association of *ideas*. These were simple or complex, and it was possible to obtain the simple by analyzing the complex, or the complex by combining the simple. The same idea could retain its identity in different combinations, and had a power to call up or inhibit other ideas, thus determining the order of the mental life. This James rejected *in toto*. It was based, he believed, on confusing the objects of thought with the thoughts themselves — on supposing that one is analyzing the thought when one is only analyzing the object; and on neglecting the feelings of relation, which not only unite ideas but so *qualify* them that they can never be twice the same. There are mental units of a sort in James's view, but they are total pulses or waves, each having an indivisible unity, a transitory existence, and a unique identity. And these units are neither simple themselves nor analyzable into simple constituents. In short, James rejected the fundamental presupposition of associationism, namely, its psychic atomism or "elementarism." [14]

This doctrine pervades the whole work. It determines James's view both of qualitative fusion and of comparative intensities in the psychology of sensation: the feeling of pink is not *in* the feeling of scarlet; sensations that feel greater are not multiples of sensations that feel smaller. The treatment of the "self" provides another notable example. "Personal form" is a dominant characteristic of "the stream of thought." [15] The sameness of the self is either the unity of the momentary state, as it is felt all at once by the "passing thought"; or the continuity of such states, whose unifying thoughts inherit and appropriate the content of their predecessors. The stream of thought, in other words, presents the self empirically, and contains among its own aspects or phases all those

[13] It dates from 1882, and James seems to have been sensible of its importance. His "experientialism" and radical empiricism is a *philosophical* application of this doctrine.
[14] *Cf.* Boring, *op. cit.*, 499.
[15] For James's debt to Locke here, *cf.* above, I, 548–9.

functions and distinctions which are ordinarily supposed to require a "soul" or a "transcendental ego." [16]

The same doctrine constituted the foremost objection to that pan-psychistic theory which otherwise made so strong an appeal to him. Mind cannot be treated as so much "stuff" or "dust" which grows by accretion from lesser to greater units. It is this same doctrine, again, which for many years stood in the way of a satisfactory completion of James's religious philosophy. He wanted an immanent rather than a transcendent God, but God could not be a compound of terrestrial minds. How James wrestled with this question, and how at the end he abandoned or modified the doctrine which he had laid down in the *Principles,* constitute one of the central themes of his final metaphysics. [17]

James's doctrine of the stream of thought was essentially his own. Such acknowledgments as he had to make were not to a "scientific" psychologist, but to the philosopher Hodgson. [18] It may be pointed out that Spencer had recognized the existence of "feelings of relation." [19] This is true, but when James did point it out he did so not from gratitude, but as credit given where it was due — to one who needed it. John Stuart Mill, it is true, had recognized that the properties of psychic compounds *differ* from those of their elementary constituents. This was his famous notion of mental chemistry, stated in the Preface to his edition of his father's *Analysis of the Phenomena of the Human Mind.* [20] But this was a refinement, rather than an abandonment, of the associationist view, and in no sense an anticipation of James. Nor must James's view be confused, on the other hand, with that of the "relativists," who went so far in their emphasis on the relations of conscious states that they denied intrinsic qualities altogether. [21] There can, James insisted, be no relations without terms, no transitives without substantives.

When James wrote "On Some Omissions of Introspective Psychology," he wrote exuberantly out of a mind that had been filled from its own underground springs. He was not, in general,

[16] *Principles,* I, 225, 336 ff.
[17] *Ibid.,* 145–182; *P.U.,* 185 ff.
[18] *Cf.* above I, 613. Some influence may also be credited to Ward; *cf.* above, 58–9.
[19] *Principles,* I, 247, note, and ff.
[20] Edition of 1869. *Cf.* also the *Logic,* II (1872), 441.
[21] *Principles,* II, 9 ff. For James's approval of Stumpf here, *cf.* above, 61–2.

disposed to claim originality, but in this case he very explicitly distinguished his own from the doctrines of the reigning schools, believing it to afford an as yet undiscovered *via media.* He was an associationist, who nevertheless affirmed the "indecomposable unity of every pulse of thought"; and a substantialist or transcendentalist, who nevertheless affirmed that all the necessary identities and syntheses could be supplied by these same pulses of thought without resort to any realm behind or above the stream of conscious human experience.[22]

Although, in denying the atomistic conception of ideas, James departed radically from the classic associationism, he did not, of course, deny association. His functional units are interconnected not directly, but through their objects or central conditions. Paradoxical as it may seem, the association that does occur, and forms the theme of James's chapter on that subject, is not an association of "ideas" at all: "Association, so far as the word stands for an effect, is between things thought of — it is things, not ideas, which are associated in the mind. We ought to talk of the association of objects, not of the association of ideas. And so far as association stands for a cause, it is between processes in the brain — it is these which, by being associated in certain ways, determine what successive objects shall be thought." [23]

Governed by his naturalistic propensity, and following Hartley, James explained the mechanism of association by a fundamental law of general habit: "When two elementary brain-processes have been active together or in immediate succession, one of them, on recurring, tends to propagate its excitement into the other." When there are several such others, then which shall be reëxcited depends on the comparative frequency and intensity of the original excitements. But at this point James again departed from tradition. For over and above this he recognized a force of *interest,* which determines what part of the present mental state shall survive, and, surviving, introduce its associates.[24] In other words, mechanical association provides a range of possibilities from which *selection* is made, in behalf of whatever purpose, theoretical or practical,

[22] *Principles,* I, 371. James's anti-atomism is closely related to the contemporary *Gestalt* movement. *Cf.* Boring, *op. cit.,* 499, and Index under "*Gestalt* Psychology." Among the passages in James that suggest this movement, *cf. Bg.,* 1880–1, 577–81; and 1884–1, 12–3.
[23] *Principles,* I, 554 (italics omitted).
[24] *Ibid.,* 566–7, 572.

dominates the subject at the moment. This view James ascribed
to "Mr. Hodgson, ablest of recent (if not of all) English philosophers"; [25] but it is unnecessary at this stage to point out that if
James had not found such a view in Hodgson, he would have found
it in himself.

Next, James's *nativism.* I am using this term broadly to mean
his general tendency to emphasize what is original rather than what
is acquired. This took two forms. In the first place, influenced
by Darwin, he credited the human mind with a liberal share of
inborn traits and aptitudes. This appears in his long list of human
instincts, and his apparent readiness to add to the list, as well as in
his recognition of innate categories which predetermine the human
modes of thinking and even of experience.[26] In the second place,
he believed in the diversity and fecundity of first experience. He
was skeptical of the possibility of generating one experience out of
another, because he was so keenly alive to the unique *qualia* of each
experience; and he did not feel the need of such a genetic account,
because he was confident of finding the derived experience among the
originals. As early as 1878 James recorded in a notebook his
belief in the limitless possibility of introspective *discovery,* and
pointed out that such discoveries immediately settle theoretical disputes: —

"The strange thing about these quarrels over incomplete data has
been that whereas the sensationalists were all the while very proud
of their acuteness about facts and the *a priorists* rather plumed
themselves upon their sense for the logical totality, it generally
turned out that the men of facts had been right in their theory, and
the men of theory right in their facts. For the former said: all
mental facts are feelings, these so-called facts are not feelings, therefore they don't exist at all; whilst the latter said: these facts certainly exist, but they are not feelings, therefore the mind is not
composed of feelings — it being true all the while that the facts
both existed, and existed *as* feelings. Generic images, inborn
associations between sensation and motion, will be remembered
as further instances of facts persistently denied by empiricists until
expressed in such form as to fit into their general theory. . . .

[25] *Popular Sc. Mo.,* XVI (1880), 580.
[26] *Principles,* Chs. XXIV, XXVII.

If our analytic discrimination has been carried to so little distance into the mind's operations, that an entirely distinct special sense which we have all of us used every day of our lives (that of the semicircular canals) was only discovered yesterday; if the entire class of feelings of innervation was ignored until a few years ago, and muscular sensibility was unknown to Hume, Berkeley and James Mill; it is palpable enough that our own differences of opinion now may still be due to ignorance of fundamental data and incapacity to make elementary distinctions."

The most important application of the doctrine of nativism was to the perception of space, James taking the view that all three dimensions of space are directly sensed, and not constructed or inferred. While James's nativism was no doubt itself native, he found confirmation of its spatial application in the writings of Stumpf and Hodgson. The support of the former has already been cited. When James's articles appeared in *Mind* in 1887, Hodgson hailed them as "working out in detail and with psychological proofs my very conception of space." To which James replied that he had always supposed that they were but a "filling out" of Hodgson's *"Time and Space* framework." [27]

The following from Hodgson and the reply from James indicate that the former, though he started first, advanced less boldly: —

Dec. 10, 1887

I have read, and also re-read, your four articles on space, in *Mind*. I cannot say I am quite convinced that sight alone, without the aid of touch, would ever arrive at *discriminating* what we call depth from superficial extension. Of course I understand, and have long thought, that we see *extension,* indiscriminated into the three dimensions, which are our reasoning way of understanding what we see. We see superficial extension *at least,* but *not* defined against or contrasted with the third dimension. In order to discriminate the latter, in order to see things solid, I think we require the aid of touch. However, I am quite open to conviction, and have no *philosophical* reasons for not welcoming your *psychological* view of the immediateness of our perception of solids or depth.

Do tell me whether you know of any writer prior to my *Time and Space* who maintained an immediate perception of spatial ex-

[27] Above, I, 564–5, 641–3. *Time and Space* had appeared in 1865.

tension as part ("formal element" is my phrase) of the visual perceptum, while at the same time rejecting the Kantian doctrine that the "form," the *spatial* element, in the perceptum was supplied by the subject? I should really be glad to know this, as I think the view I take, or rather took in *Time and Space,* is of some importance and certainly occurred to me independently of any other writer; but I do not know whether I was actually the first to say it; I may have been anticipated.

Dec. 25, 1887

You make me blush at my poor stuff about space being read twice over by such learned eyes. As for your question about who first made visual perception immediately spatial and yet not subjective *à la Kant,* I can *think* of no one prior to your *Time and Space.* I won't swear there was no one, for my memory lapses when a subject has been out of my mind, and my reading also has been limited to the more strictly psychological literature of the subject.

While James was undoubtedly encouraged by Hodgson to seek a nativistic solution of the problem of space, he obtained no help from Hodgson on the questions of detail which created its real difficulty. This problem occupied more of James's time and more pages of his *Principles* than any other, partly, no doubt, owing to the emphasis which it received among the psychologists who had influenced him in his early years, such as Lotze and Helmholtz. But it was a subject on which he felt that he had some little "private ingenuity" of his own, for which he hoped to obtain credit. "It has struck me," he wrote to Robertson in 1886, "that if the foul fiend should enter into Helmholtz during the preparation of this new edition of his *Physiological Optics,* and lead him to abandon his old errors and publish a true space-doctrine just to spite me, it would be an awful thing for my 'reputation.' The world would, it is true, be rid of the duty of reading my stuff, but where should *I* be? . . . The thing seems to me decidedly solid; but of course I am no judge."

In the article of 1879 on "The Spatial Quale," and in unpublished notes of the same period, James distinguishes his own peculiar position. He first sets aside, as least worthy of attention, his old friends Mill, Bain, and Spencer, who "seem all to have gone astray, like lost sheep." Their failure is the failure of associationism. They deny space to be an attribute of elementary sensations, try in vain to identify it with the coexistence or succession of these, and hint indecisively at the Kantian view, though this is opposed to their fundamental professions. The Kantian view James calls the "intellectualistic" view. While it has the merit of recognizing that there *is* an irreducible "spatial quale," this view supposes it to be produced from within and applied to the data *ab extra* — as though there were two moments of experience, one before and one after its being spatialized. "I repudiate this view," says James, "because it appears to me thoroughly mythological. I have no direct experience of any such mental act of creation or production." [28] With this view, broadly interpreted, he associates not only Kant, but Helmholtz, Lotze, and Wundt. These two views, the associationistic and the Kantian, are allied through their common denial of the "nativistic" position. Space is not given, therefore it has to be constructed out of non-spatial data, or added to them from another dimension of the mind. At some point something new magically appears.[29] James calls his own position, on the other hand, "sensationalistic" — meaning that the spatial quale is a sensory quality *having the same status as color*. This does not mean that it is not *a priori,* for sensory qualia are for James as a rule *a priori;* but that spatiality, like color, "comes *to* the intellect, not from it." [30]

Finally, however, James distinguishes two groups among the sensationalists: those two, like Hering, hold that space is given completely from the first; and those who, like Stumpf and himself, hold that it is given dimly and then developed and articulated by experience. It is, perhaps, not irrelevant that his own spatial experience should have been qualitative rather than articulated: "There is no doubt," he once wrote, "that individuals differ amazingly in the degree to which they are sensible of their space-coördinates. I, *e.g.,* have no 'bump,' and no sense of anything in the way of

[28] *Jour. of Specul. Philos.,* XIII (1879), 85, 86.
[29] Some of the "geneticists," such as Delbœuf, Zöllner, Münsterberg, Helmholtz, and Wundt, take the indefensible course of appealing to an act of "unconscious inference." *Cf.* above, I, 686; and *Principles,* II, 189, 248.
[30] *Jour. of Specul. Philos.,* XIII (1879), 86; *Principles,* II, 618. Among the sensationalists from whom he derived aid and comfort, James names J. Le Conte, A. W. Volkmann, W. Schön (*Mind,* XII, 1887, 548).

space common to remote localities. Boston and New York, *e.g.*, occupy two entirely unrelated spaces, and the different quarters of Cambridge have no frontage in relation to each other. I can't tell you now what sort of an angle Kirkland Street makes to Brattle Street."

Croom Robertson, the friendly editor of *Mind,* served in a double capacity, as a medium of publication and as a critic. James's articles on "The Perception of Space" appeared in 1887, and Robertson's reply (deriving spatial experience from the tactual or muscular sense of resistance) was published in the same periodical in 1888.

Cambridge, Nov. 9, 1887

My dear Robertson, —

The "off-prints" came a fortnight ago, following close upon your letter. I was grieved again to hear of the threatenings of your enemy. I dare say you may even now be in his infernal grasp. I have neither exhortations nor consolations to offer. I can only say that your misfortunes make one love and admire you all the more. . . . The saddest blow I've received is *your* sententious and obdurate refusal to be converted by my space views! Two friends have written me words of adhesion to the first of the four articles — one of them no less a personage than Hodgson. One has praised the whole lot. Three eulogists in all — nay four — for Royce also read and praised the first article. But what are the four against the still outstanding *one,* who won't even tell me *which* are the points to be condemned? Pray don't think I wish to challenge you to set to work and specify. To tell the sober truth about the matter, I fancy I have done all about space that my poor powers are capable of, in that little essay. Now that I have "extradited" it, I feel no longer any personal connection with it, and am willing to let it drift and take its chances in the literary ocean. If it have merit it will probably float. If it sink 't is that it will deserve to. And others may see to it if they will.

I published a paper on "The Perception of Time" in the last *Journal of Speculative Philosophy* (the one yclept October, 1886) which possibly you may be interested to read. Much of it is mere compilation; but the core of the thing is a view I have nowhere seen, that our *intuited* time is only a few seconds long, and is a genuine sensation, due to a nerve-process which I try to adumbrate hypothetically. . . .

Hall is a wonderful creature.   Never an articulate conception comes out of him, but instead of it a sort of palpitating influence making all men believe that the way to save their souls psychologically lies through the infinite assimilation of jaw-breaking German laboratory-articles.   If you try to draw any expressible theoretic conclusion from any of them, he won't hear it; what you ought to do is to pass on to a lot more of them; and so *in infinitum*.   His devotion to the cause is admirable, and I must say he has produced a very creditable first number.[31]   He writes me that the second and third will be better still.   Heaven send you patience and a stout heart with your trials. . . .   Your affectionate

WM. JAMES

Chocorua, Aug. 22, 1888 [32]

My dear Robertson, —

I ought to have written you about your space criticisms long since, but I only got my *Mind* ten days ago when I went to Cambridge, and have been so preoccupied since then and busy with other things, that this is my first morning of leisure.   In the first place, it "warms the innermost cockles of my heart," as Darwin says, to see you a-writing again; for it makes me trust that you are getting into better condition as regards the enemy within.   Drop me a card and tell me it is so!   Of course you have respect enough for the genuineness of fibre of my philosophic character to know in advance that I shall oppose steadfast resistance to your opinions, clear as is their expression, and reasonable as is their tone!   Seriously speaking, it seems to me that you have made such concessions, and *zugespitzt* the question so, that the issue is now very narrow and distinct, and I don't see how it can help being decided in *my* way, when once thus stated.   For either this sense of a resisting object is of a *big* object or not; and if of a big object, then my contention is granted as to the "muscular sense," — only the question comes,

[31] The first number of Stanley Hall's *American Journal of Psychology* had appeared in Nov. 1887.
[32] For the remainder of this letter *cf.* above, I, 609, and below, 279.

why the deuce are our muscles the only sense-organs whose objects are big? — a question not easy to answer either *a priori* or *a posteriori,* methinks. But if this resisting "base" of objectivity, be *not* itself immediately given as big, I'm blest if I can see how "intensive time-clusters" can "take on the new character" of bigness by being "experienced in connection with" it. In short, it is the old dilemma back again: either space is given immediately, or it is made by the mind. If given, it must be given in some ·sensation. If made, it must be made out of non-spatial elements. *In abstracto* you seem to relinquish this latter idea. But *in concreto* you retain it.

I'm not sure that we mean the same thing by the "Kantian" view. *I* mean the doctrine of a *supersensational* construction. For Kant there is a non-spatial sensational chaos before there is space in the mind. For me there is no mental object not already spatial. I don't know what you mean by supposing us to have in mind an "extension that is extension of nothing at all," when we assume experience of non-resistant extension. Experiences of colors are not of nothing at all. Insects crawling over the skin do not give a feeling of nothing at all, etc. These experiences seem to me to have just as much and just as little of space in them as our experiences of resistance. And have you thought how queer it is on your view that our experiences of resistance, if they are the "psychological basis" of our space-perception, should be among the least spatially *discriminative* of all our experiences?

Lastly, as to your last half-page, — thanks for the concession to the eye! I also concede that in the concrete individual all these experiences come abreast and are inextricably entwined. In a sense the tactile ones are "basal," *i.e.,* we choose them as the *reals;* but if you have ever seen a blind man (as I have) trying to tell with his fingers which of two angles cut out of paste board is the larger . . . and compared his slowness and inaccuracy with the instantaneous certainty of the eye dealing with the same objects, I don't see how you can doubt the entire *independence* of our eye-space-measurements of those of touch. . . . But hold! enough! I did n't mean to reopen a controversy on the subject of which I am already pretty sick, and I hope you won't have the burden laid upon you, either by the pugnacious instinct or anything else, of issuing a rejoinder. . . . Believe me, always your friend,

WM. JAMES

James's views of time constitute a further application of his nativism.   There is an intuition or sensation of extensity in the one case as in the other.   In the case of time extensity is duration, distinguished from the mathematical instant as the spread of space is distinguished from the mathematical point.   Here, as in the case of space, although such a view was the almost inevitable expression of deep-seated tendencies, James acknowledged specific obligations. The first of these was again to Shadworth Hodgson, the second to a comparatively unknown Irish-American writer, E. R. Clay, from whom he borrowed the now famous expression "specious present," as the name for the present moment, which is not *strictly* present, since it unites present and past in an act which perceives them both at once.   But though others had preceded James in his general conception, he claimed originality for fixing the amount of temporal duration directly intuited, and for developing (characteristically) a neural hypothesis to account for it.[33]

James's nativism was as deep-seated and constitutional as it was all-pervasive.   Whatever the topic, James was always ready with some peculiar nuance or pattern of original experience to match it. He was above all a *qualitative* psychologist.   He saw with a sensitive eye, and his differences always outran his unities.   He established an equation between experience and being not by reducing the varieties of being, but by multiplying the varieties of experience.

James's psychology of the will is a combination of two factors, a doctrine concerning "the feeling of effort," and a doctrine of "ideo-motor action."   Both doctrines were set forth in one of his earliest papers, "The Feeling of Effort," which was published in 1880[34] and at once attracted attention to him among European psychologists.   Delbœuf's enthusiasm has already been recorded. Later, in 1888, James republished his views under the title of "What the Will Effects," in more popular form and with less stress on their physiological aspects.   Of this article James said that it excited more comment than all of his others put together.[35]

[33] For Hodgson, cf. C.E.R., 380.   Clay's book, *The Alternative*, was published anonymously in 1882 (cf. pp. 167–8), and was reviewed by Renouvier in *Critique philos.*, II, 1888.   For James's views, cf. *Principles*, I, Ch. XV, especially 632 ff.; above, 84.
[34] In the *Anniversary Memoirs of the Boston Society of Natural History*, and reprinted in C.E.R.
[35] Cf. above, I, 702.

As regards the feeling of effort James reversed a judgment which he had himself formerly held, that the feeling of effort accompanies the efferent (outgoing) current which innervates the muscle. He was struck with the fact that the "feeling of muscular exertion consists of an immense number of in-coming sensations, due to the contraction of the muscles of our glottis, chest, jaws, body and limbs, and to our strained joints and ligaments and squeezed or twisted skin." [36]   In other words, he rejected the feeling of innervation because he *found no feeling* that was not sensory, and hence afferent (ingoing) rather than efferent on its neural side. He took this position quite independently, and conscious of the fact that the leading authorities, such as Wundt and Bain, were against him.[37]   Ward wrote, it will be remembered, that the question whether the current is afferent or efferent was "immaterial," the important point being that volition is initiated centrally through ideas rather than peripherally through outer stimuli. This difference of emphasis was characteristic of the two men, and illustrates the obligation which James felt to think the physiological and psychological aspects of his subject together.

In adopting the theory of "ideo-motor action," James claimed no originality. He had found the theory in Lotze before 1870, and he found it again soon after in Renouvier.[38]   According to this doctrine, an idea once in full possession of the mind translates itself into action. The work of conscious volition is done when the idea is instated. In order thus to perform any specific act such as *a,* it is necessary to instate the idea of *a* which is left in the mind as the result of a previous performance of *a;* and, feelings of innervation having been dismissed, this idea is held to consist of a reproduction of the (kinæsthetic) sensations aroused by the original bodily movements.

When in 1888 Renouvier published a translation of "What the Will Effects," he appended "Quelques Remarques," in which he called attention to the "fundamental identity" of his view and that of James. But in commenting further he expressed his doubt

---

[36] "What the Will Effects," *Scribner's,* III (1888), 247.
[37] *C.E.R.,* 153.
[38] *Cf.* Lotze's *Medicinische Psychologie,* §§266–8, and *Critique philos.,* II, 1882, 401. James prefixed a citation from Renouvier to his "Feeling of Effort," and repeatedly ascribed his doctrine of ideo-motor action to that master. (*C.E.R.,* 31, 151, 193–4.)

whether their common view of will agreed with the principles of psychophysiological parallelism and reflex action which James professed. James replied that the will may select within the field of reflex possibilities, but Renouvier, in more "Quelques Remarques," argued that then the action would cease to be a reflex. It is clear, in other words, that James was inclined to go much further than Renouvier in the naturalistic direction. This is only one of the consequences of their differences of origin and destiny.[39]

The seed of James's famous theory that emotions are fusions of organic sensations aroused by bodily expression — that "we feel sorry because we cry, angry because we strike, afraid because we tremble"[40] — was evidently planted in his mind at a very early date. The flyleaf of his copy of Lotze's *Medicinische Psychologie* which he was reading in 1867–1868 contains the reference, "Emotions due to bodily reverberation, §438."[41] Lotze did not take James's radical view of the matter, and retained feelings as distinct mental elements over and above sensations, but he attached great importance to organic sensation and to the effects of bodily posture.

James's view was more explicitly anticipated by the anthropologist Henle, of Göttingen, in published form in 1876 and in lectures twenty years earlier.[42] James cites illustrative passages from this as from many other antecedent works, but there is no reason to suppose that Henle any more than Lotze was primarily responsible for the theory. There were two deeper and more general influences, both of which led in this direction. One was the influence of Darwin, which inclined James to link the emotions with the instincts, and to stress the biological aspect of emotional expression. The other was the influence of British empiricism, inclining him to stress the receptive and cognitive aspect of mental content. In one of his letters to Renouvier he wrote that his theory had reference only to "the nerve process which emotion accompanies." It cannot be accidental that James took the same view

[39] *Critique philos.*, II, 1888, 117, 401.
[40] *Principles*, II, 450. This theory is now commonly called the "James-Lange Theory," because the Danish physiologist C. Lange published a similar view in 1887. James first published his view in *Mind* in 1884 ("What Is an Emotion?").
[41] James's copy was the edition of 1852. The flyleaf note gives "§538," which I assume to be a slip of the pen.
[42] J. Henle: *Anthropologische Vorträge*, 1876. For a thorough discussion of the anticipation of James and Lange by earlier writers, *cf.* E. B. Titchener, "Historical Note on the James-Lange Theory of Emotion," *Amer. Jour. of Psych.*, XXV (1914).

here that he took in connection with the alleged "feelings of innervation." It was not that he neglected the importance of the central
and outgoing nerve currents, but that he believed it to be *their* function to preserve, select, and act, while it was the function of the
incoming or afferent currents to supply the material and to report
the outer occasion. This was the British empiricism of the orthodox variety. James's rejection of affective and conational states,
as distinct from and coördinate with sensory states, requires no
special explanation. If he had not earned this position by formidable arguments, he would have inherited it.

Many chapters and passages of the *Principles* attracted attention. Often they were noteworthy and influential, not because of
any psychological originality, but because of the brilliancy of style
and richness of concrete illustration with which an old theme was
given new life. Such was the case, for example, with the discussions of belief and instinct. But the most signal case of this was
the chapter on habit. In a letter to Robertson he referred slight-
ingly to the article which first treated this subject: "A mere pot-
boiler, which I had long had, written, in my drawer. No new
thing in it, so I hardly advise you to read it." [43] Its ideas, even its
moral precepts, were gathered from Carpenter and Bain.[44] But
James, the artist and teacher, combining vividness with moral conviction, created a popular classic. It is not without bearing on its
success that it should have sprung from an early and lifelong faith
of his own in the benign effect of routine and the cumulative significance of little acts. At the head of the chapter on habit in
his *Briefer Course* he wrote with his own hand: "Sow an action,
and you reap a habit; sow a habit and you reap a character; sow a
character and you reap a destiny."

[43] The article, entitled "The Laws of Habit," was published in *Pop. Science Mo.,*
XXX (1887).
[44] *Cf.* James's personal copy of W. B. Carpenter's *Principles of Mental Physiology* (1874), which contains a note indicating that James saw Carpenter in London
in 1883. The famous remark that "we learn to swim during the winter and to skate
during the summer" was originally made by "a German writer." (*Principles,* I,
110.) James had a genius for collecting remarks of this sort, and then for making
them *stick!* For the present validity of James's maxims, *cf.* W. H. Gantt, "Conditioned Reflexes and Habit Formation," *British Medical Jour.,* 1932, I, No. 3715.

LVII

THE RECEPTION OF THE "PRINCIPLES"

JAMES's *Principles of Psychology* was successful in a sense that is unusual for a book of science — it was widely read, not only by other psychologists, or by students of psychology, but by people who were under no obligation to read it. It was read because it was readable, and it was read by people of all sorts because of the very qualities which condemned it in the eyes of some professional psychologists. Because it did not substitute the artifacts of analysis for the concrete, living mind, the reader constantly recognized *himself* in its descriptions and illustrations. It was, as we have seen, unsystematic — exploring and depicting human nature in all its dimensions, gathering facts from any quarter and by any method, and theorizing as the spirit moved, undismayed by the prospect of starting something that could not be completed. It was a tolerant, curious book; and because its author saw so wide a range of possibilities, and was so promiscuously hospitable to them, almost any recent development in psychology can trace a line of ancestry there. The size of the psychological family has become so notorious that their census is itself now a recognized task of psychology.[1] One recent writer says that there are three schools of psychology, "the conscious, the unconscious and the anti-conscious,"[2] referring to the introspective, the psychoanalytical, and the behavioristic schools. It is easy to find all three in James. The same may be said of the *"Gestalt"* school, or the *"Akt"* school, or the "Functional" school.[3] James promoted the method of introspection traditional in the British school, and imported the results and technique of the experimental school from Germany. He was interested in applied psychology and comparative psychology. His chapter on instinct gave a great impetus to social psychology, and his medical approach and emphasis

[1] *Cf., e.g.,* C. A. Murchison, *Psychologies of 1925* and *Psychologies of 1930.*
[2] Grace Adams, "The Babel of the Psyche," *American Mercury,* XX (1930), 463.
[3] A brief statement of James's relations to these movements will be found in E. G. Boring, *History of Experimental Psychology,* 1929, 494–504.

on "exceptional mental states" gave him a place in the development of abnormal psychology and psychopathology. The result is that the *Principles* was acclaimed by laymen and beginners, by students of other subjects who looked for some special application of psychology to their own problems, and by philosophical or nonsectarian students of psychology who had not yet become addicted to any special method of investigation; while at the same time it was viewed with some shade of disapproval by laboratory experimentalists and by systematizers.

When the *Principles* appeared in 1890, most of its doctrines had already been presented in articles and received their baptism of critical fire. The theory of emotion had proved peculiarly challenging. Writing in June 1884, two months after his original article had appeared, he said, "I find that of my friends, the only ones to whom it seems plausible are the physiologists, and that is not *necessarily* a point in its favor. I must confess, however, that it grows rather more plausible to my own mind, the more I think it over." The article on habit, in the *Popular Science Monthly* for February 1887, had evoked the following sprightly criticism from the erstwhile admiring Delbœuf : —

"Tell me, then, whether Robert Houdin's balls did not acquire the habit of leaping into the air of their own accord and falling back into his hand? For this ought to be the consequence of the comparisons and analogies which, at the opening of your article, and following Wundt and Léon Dumont, you make between dead and living matters. As for me, these channels hollowed out by flowing water, these folds of the garment, these keys and locks, communicate nothing clear to my mind, and to me fail entirely to explain habits either bodily or mental. I know *Popular Science* well, but is n't it a bit too popular ?" [4]

The articles on space and time had been greeted by Howison as a consistent application of James's reprehensible empiricism. The following was written in 1888 in reply to a letter from James setting forth the complexities of the problem: "You own two *pièces de résistance* — the 'Perception of Time' and, above all, the 'Perception of Space' — I have as yet done no justice to, though I have read them enough to catch your leading point. Of course I can't

[4] May 5, 1887. The originals of Delbœuf's letters will be found in Appendix IV.

quite agree with you, though there are lots of things in the discussions in regard to which I should be in most hearty accord. In the 'Perception of Space' I consider that you have really, at last, taken the empirical bull by the horns. If there really is anything to be made out of the fundamental theory of empiricism for philosophy, it has got to be proved that there are *perceptions of relation;* it has got to be shown that space, *e.g.,* is itself *sensible.* You've done wonders in the effort to make this out; but, naturally, I still look on them all as failures. But I can't help feeling, that, leaving Hume always out of the question, nothing from the empirical standpoint I have ever yet noticed goes so far as your papers toward bringing the bottom difficulties to light."

When the *Principles* appeared, James heard from friends whom he had named among his benefactors, but who did not always recognize their ideas in Jamesian dress. Hodgson, for example, had made a great point of distinguishing between philosophy as the preliminary analysis of experience in general, and psychology as the ulterior explanation of mental states in terms of their bodily accompaniments. James, on the other hand, proposed to postpone philosophy until the task of psychology should be completed, and in practice carried on the two together.[5] It is not strange, therefore, that Hodgson should have complained at such procedure on the part of one who professed to be his disciple!

West Malvern, Aug. 19, 1891

Dear James, —

I am remorseful at owing you a letter for so long, which shall be something more than a mere reply, as my last was, to your kind present of your *Principles of Psychology.* I have long ago finished reading it, and have found it the most valuable and instructive book on the subject that I ever came across. This is chiefly because you make us see the reality of things, the real common-sense of the questions and problems at issue, while you go into full details on the moot points, and argue the whole out with the utmost fairness. I think the points which struck me most were two, your speculation of the tissues covering the joints being the real seat or rather origin of the so-called muscular sensations of motor di-

[5] Hence the *Principles* had its philosophical as well as psychological influence. *Cf., e.g.,* the influence on J. Dewey, below, 516. For Hodgson's recognition of the *philosophy* in James's *psychology, cf.* above, I, 644.

rections; and that of the emotions being primarily and essentially
due, owing, that is, their specially *emotive* character, to their being
a record of organic or systemic disturbances, and depending on the
sympathetic or ganglionic system of nerves for their incorporation
into the general cerebral system. . . .

By the way, I must say I think your whole book contributes
powerfully to the support of the so-called conscious automaton
theory. The more you explain, the less room do you leave for
transcendental agency, since none of your explanations make any
use of the latter. It is like an article in a creed which we may
believe if we please, because beyond the reach of positive disproof.
This is logical in the case of a religious creed, because (to quote
from a revered but antiquated authority — the old Eton Latin
Grammar) *"fides* religionis nostrae *fundamentum* habetur." I
think you will acknowledge, if ever I complete my long-worked-at
big book, that I can make quite as good use of my hypothesis of
matter being the only positively known real condition of consciousness, I mean in the direction of religion and morals, as has ever
yet been made of the hypothesis of an immaterial soul or transcendental ego.

Few things have given me greater pleasure than your kind mention of me among those four or five stars of high magnitudes, at
the end of your Preface, especially followed up as it was by such
frequent and full citation from my poor writings. I have certainly
never before found myself in such distinguished company. But,
my dear fellow, the impression I have *really* made on you must
be small indeed! My fundamental position you entirely ignore,
and without mentioning it adopt unhesitatingly, in your Preface
and obviously throughout the whole book, the opposite and old
traditional view of the relation between philosophical and psychological enquiry. My view is, that this relation itself, including of
course the scope and limits of psychology, must be learnt from a
previous philosophical analysis of experience in the widest sense.
The old view I take to be, that the positive sciences come first, discover all the laws, and truths of every sort they can, and then, whatever they find insoluble, including all their own false starts, that
they dub "metaphysics," and relegate to philosophy. Much in the
same sort of way as the old materialistic atheists used to push God
out of this, out of that, out of matter altogether, and leave him

hovering in dim uncertainty, outside the whole dominion of laws of nature. God forbid that philosophy should share his unenviable position! . . . Ever sincerely yours,

SHADWORTH H. HODGSON

James Ward's comment on the *Principles* was for several years the chief theme of the correspondence between these two friends: —

Cambridge [Eng.], Jan. 12, 1891

Dear Professor James, —

Many thanks for your two bulky volumes; they have been continually refreshing my soul and stirring me up ever since I got them. I don't think I am overmuch given to hero-worship, but certainly you have been my one hero this Christmas vacation. The geniality, the incisiveness, the trenchant vigor of your book mark you out as — well, as unique among psychologists. I have just begun to lecture again upon psychology, after an interval of three years. Your book will thus naturally be continually in my hands, and in the hands of our more advanced students; so that I expect by degrees to find myself at home in it and perhaps, if I find it does not bore you or affront you too much, I shall venture to ask for enlightenment on sundry points.

At this moment the thing in your book that impresses me the most is your exposition of will: there is a real "heaven ahead" in this. The thing that puzzles me the most is your treatment of the causal relation of mind and body. I happened to be busy with this question as a question in metaphysics when your book came; but up to the present I can't say you have resolved my difficulties, nor can I as yet acquiesce in your proposal — as matter of method to stick to common sense so long as we are only psychologists. But this is an old difference between us; I think I wrote to you about it once before apropos of your article on "Automatism" in *Mind*. Finally, your *penchant* for spiritualism in the new sense amazes me. . . . Yours sincerely,

J. WARD

Criticizing James's *Briefer Course* in 1892, Ward gave high praise to the author's treatment of "Will" and "The Stream of Consciousness," but condemned the book as unsystematic, over-physiological, and defective in its treatment of such topics as pleasure and pain and the self. Here is James's acknowledgment: —

Florence, Nov. 1, 1892

My dear Ward, —

I must thank you for your very "handsome" review of my *Briefer Course* in the October *Mind,* which only reached me a few days since. I ought to apologize or in some way "make it up" to you for giving out so much of your precious self on so unworthy an occasion, but it's all in the line of our trade, so I won't waste time on humility. Your heartily expressed objections give to the cordiality of the praise all the more solidity of flavor; and feeling as I do the desperate character of all psychologizing, that you should find any merit at all in the book is enough for the notice to seem to me in the main highly flattering.

Yes, I *am* too unsystematic and loose! But in this case I permitted myself to remain so deliberately, on account of the strong aversion with which I am filled for the humbugging pretense of exactitude in the way of definition of terms and description of states that has prevailed in psychological literature. What does a human being really learn from it all beyond what he knew already by the light of nature? *But* — I doubtless have carried my reaction too far, so I won't defend myself. I admit that the best pedagogic order would be a general analysis followed by a detailed synthesis (only the analysis seems to me to be one of the things we need no book for); but when you contend for *genetic* treatment, I must say that you seem to me impractical. What *light* is shed by enumerating the *order* in which terms (themselves unexplained) make their appearance? For I shouldn't suppose that for *you* the namby-pamby baby-lore of M. B. Perez would have any instructiveness, nor that even such careful genetic description as Sully's account of the growth of space perception in his last book, would really appear explanatory.[6] The real thing to aim at is a *causal* account; and I must say that that appears to lie (provisionally at least) in the region of the laws as yet unknown of the connection of the mind with the body. There is *the* subject for a "science" of psychology!

[6] For Perez, *cf.* "Le Caractère et les mouvements," *Revue philos.,* XXXI (1891). Sully's last book was *The Human Mind,* 1892.

As for what you say of the relation of feeling to emotion and action, I will admit that what one may call *elementary* feeling may be an integral part of all consciousness.   What you, Külpe, and lately Fouillée have written on that seems to me pretty conclusive.[7] Only in developed states, the elements grow so magnified out of all proportion to each other that the state is called by the name of one or the other exclusively.   As I discussed the hedonistic contention, it was the doctrine that states of feeling in the developed sense are the only conceivable springs of action, that I combatted. If you fall back on the germinal infinitesimal element of feeling, which all consciousness must have, to save psychological hedonism, it seems to me you have given up the case as commonly held and raised another question altogether — of an interesting theoretic kind, it is true, and essential to psychology, but disconnected with the old historic battle.   It is only in this transcendental sense that I should be disposed to admit that *thought of pleasure* is a pleasure. I have taken things too coarsely, however, I dare say, so I bow my head.   As regards the self, I can't bow my head, and I feel really discouraged at the difference that subsists between us.   It makes me suspect misunderstanding, especially since you protest against sensations knowing sensible qualities.   It is surely the sensational "element" in a mental state by means of which that state knows a sensible fact.

But here we come upon elements versus states, and the whole problem of synthesis, concerning which all that has been written (either by you or by me I feel like saying) is as naught.   There can be no psychology worth the paper it is written on (*except* the science of the correlations of brain states with objects known) until something sound in epistemology is done.   *Pray* go ahead and do it!   Yours always, fraternally and teachably,

WM. JAMES

P.S.   Your *boutade* on the S. P. R., since it touched others, I have just written a short note about to the Editor.[8]

---

[7] *Cf.* Oswald Külpe, *Zur Theorie der sinnlichen Gefühle,* 1887.   A. Fouillée's views are to be found in *Revue philos.*, under the titles of "Existence et développement de la volonté," XXXIII (1892) ; and "Le Développement de la volonté," XXXIV (1892).

[8] James's letter to the editor appeared in *Mind, N.S.,* II (1893).

Cambridge [Eng.], Nov. 10, 1892

My dear James, —

I was fearfully glad to get your letter and find that I had not for ever alienated you by that "critical" notice. The fact is I did mean to wind up with a humble sentence or two, but Stout,[9] though I asked him specially to let me have the proof in page, printed the thing off as it was. I do feel it is great cheek in me to sit in judgment upon you, but of course I forgot that while I was at it. As you have let me off so mildly this time I think I may promise to shew due gratitude for the future. But don't suppose — indeed you can't suppose it, — that I set up to teach you or anybody. I am all in a fog, God knows, but I only don't keep for ever saying so because the fact is so hideously palpable. I don't believe that anybody could have more serious misgivings as to the truth of the opinions I have ventured to put out than I have myself. I spend a good deal of time refuting myself: and if there really were any chance of the said opinions finding general favour, I should probably imitate Master Hartmann and anonymously demolish myself.[10] You won't mistake this for cynicism. No, I honestly feel that the best thing I can do is to go on: even an erroneous view worked out will help things on by lessening the *minus,* though not by adding to the *plus.*

One part of my craze is precisely this straining after exactitude that you say you cannot abide. Now, there has been plenty of barren defining in the world, — witness the scholastics; still I fancy a strong general presumption in favor of the attempt in psychology could be made out from the history of science as a whole. And a history of psychology — a "critical" history, let us say — would shew that "appropriate conceptions," to use Whewell's phrase, have been the great want, and the few that have been so far hammered out the great help and the great stay.

I won't defend the genetic method if the procedure of Perez & Co. is to be meant by it. All that I found puzzling in your exposition was the detail into which you carried your analysis without any subsequent synthesis. After such analysis, of course, synthesis would have entailed serious repetition. To avoid this I should vote for: (1) an analysis after your model, full enough to be im-

---

[9] G. F. Stout, the new editor of *Mind,* who succeeded Robertson in 1892.
[10] Presumably E. von Hartmann.

pressive; (2) a statement of clearly ascertained generalizations —
habit, association, etc.; (3) a synthesis in which perception would
precede imagination, and that precede conception, and in which,
in particular, reasoning and self-consciousness would come late.
I have tried this plan myself in my lectures, and perhaps that is
why I believe in it.

The position that you (and Bradley) take about self (=subject)
is absolutely incomprehensible to me. I have pored over Bradley
and cannot make him out. As to you, I find it hard to believe
that the same man has written such opposite and seemingly incompatible statements as some of yours on this topic are to me. I
should apply to you the words of Goethe: "Es sind zwei Menschen
in dieser Brust," *u.s.w.* I shall some day perhaps play off James
the psychologist against James the metaphysician, moralist and
human.

In your letter to me, *e.g.,* you say: "It is surely the sensational
'element' in a mental state by means of which *that* state knows a
sensible fact." Now I can't understand this at all. If state A
know a fact (x) and state B knows a fact (y) either they have a
common part or they have n't. If they have, is n't it that common part that enables you to say A and B are my states? And
when the like can be said of a continuity of state A-B-C-D-, is not
that common part the Knower in *all* those states? And if it is
common to all the states, how, according to ordinary psychological
theories of knowledge, can it be *known* in any? On the other
hand, if the conception of knowledge requires a knower as well as
a known, is not the common and unknown part of all states the
being that has them all — that is active in them all? But what a
fool I am to pester you with these raw giblets — my knowledge,
I call it; my organic sensation, it will seem to you. For verily
temperament has much to do with these things: a *Melancholiker*
like me, with a good stable base in that imposing viscus the liver,
is bound to make much of the "I"; while a *Sanguiniker* like you
is impressed only by the "Me."

No doubt psychophysics is the business of the hour: *is,* whether
it ought to be or not, and *will be,* spite of all the protests of me
and those like me. But for all that I regard it as a needless and
wasteful detour. And yet I say this much as I might commend a
canal as a model to a river. Nature is everywhere zigzaggy, and

the straightening out is artificial. Still, however picturesque the
course of knowledge in the making, all this turning aside from the
straight and narrow way is, like sin, a thing to transcend and correct from the point of view of the ideal. And so I stick to my
jeremiad, and lament over transgressors. But it is an odd position for me, who has worked for two years in physiological laboratories and of whom it has been said that he is a "physiologist
spoiled."

My reference to the "S. P. R." (those potent symbols of bygone
glory — pity they could n't squeeze a "Q" in) was no "boutade."
I think you are a most arrogant set of people. You have spoiled
two good words, "psychical" and "spiritual," and made us no wiser.
I have always let you alone, and always mean to; but then I expect
to be let alone myself.

Are you likely to be coming to England in the summer? If
so, perhaps you would come and stay with us a little while if you
can put up with cottage life for a bit; or I might meet you in
Scotland or somewhere, where the atmosphere has less azote than
here. Believe me, ever truly and admiringly yours,

JAMES WARD

Florence, Nov. 15, 1892

My dear Ward, —

You are a man with a soul, so creatures such as I must needs
take delight in your existence, in spite of the hardness of your
heart towards S's. P. R. and other humble and struggling forms of
life, and of your sins generally. I mean seriously that your letter
touches me, and I should like just to say so. I don't wish *reno-
vare dolorem* about the self, but a passage in your letter shoots a
gleam that looks as if there might really be misunderstanding.
You say we need a part that is *common* in states *A* and *B*, to account for their identification as *my* states. I grant it; only
whereas you give what seems to me the merely nominal definition
of "ego" to the common something, I attempt to determine it more
concretely and really, by saying that it is the *actually experienced
relation* which these states have to state *M* which calls them "mine."
That common relation *constitutes* practically what we *mean* by being part of an ego; and I say: "What need of reduplicating it by
an abstract ego as its *ground?*" This is what you seem to me to

do. So if *A* and *B* both know a common object *O,* there is again something common to them. But what? Why, what but the fact of that determinate relation to a third thing? No need of any *antecedent* commonness before the fact — no need, at any rate, for descriptive purposes! Pardon my pertinacity, and believe me, ever gratefully yours,

WM. JAMES

From Stumpf James received the warm and impulsive praise of a friend. He had written the *best* of all psychologies, such as would make the German envious, were envy admitted to "these sacred halls!" The following is James's reply: —

Cambridge, Dec. 1, 1890

My dear Stumpf, —

It gave me the greatest pleasure to get your letter today. There is a solidity of heartiness, so to call it, in the tone of your letters, of which you of course are not aware yourself as a peculiar quality, but which *is* altogether personal, and which makes me especially rejoice in the possession of you as a friend and correspondent. It is partly *deutsch;* but not all the *Deutschen* have it; so I make the most of it. Besides, so far off, you are the ideal *homo* or *vir,* and when you speak kindly, as now of my book, it is as if I were being approved by "the Absolute!" — an Absolute, moreover, who can write a *Tonpsychologie!* The second volume [11] is still on my shelf waiting to have its leaves cut. It is the great trial of my life to have to move so slowly from point to point, and postpone what I most want to do till the things I least want are finished. I know that I shall learn endless things from that volume, but as I am giving this year a course in Metaphysics and one in the History of Philosophy, neither of which I have ever given before, all psychological reading is at at standstill. — The publication of my two volumes has cleared my mind for *receiving;* and I feel now as if I might *learn* something about psychology, had I plenty of time to give to it. But life seems sometimes to consist of pure interruptions; and day after day often passes here without my finding an hour in which to *read. Sonst,* things go well. . . . Yours ever,

WM. JAMES

[11] Published in 1890.

For the *Revue philosophique* L. Marillier wrote a series of four long articles on "La Psychologie de W. James," in which the author referred to the *Principles* as *"une œuvre glorieuse"* that deserved a place between the works of Taine and Stuart Mill, but argued at length in support of associationism.[12] These articles provoked the following reply from James: —

"The passing thought, which I propose that psychologists should adopt as their ultimate datum on the mental side, is expressly intended to make psychology more positivistic and free from subtle disputes than she has been. Practically all schools agree with common sense that we do have thoughts which pass, although they differ as to the genesis and constitution of such thoughts. Now I contend that all the facts of our experience are *formulable* in terms of these undecomposed thoughts, on the one hand, and of the 'objects' which they 'know' on the other, quite as simply and more naturally than by the theory of ideas. Formulating them thus gives us a good honest empirical body of science, which does not of course go to the bottom of all mysteries, but which, as far as it does go, is sound, and as free as possible from containing paradoxes and stumbling-blocks in its terms. The further questions that remain (as to the genesis and constitution of these thoughts, etc.) seem to me so subtle that they had best be relegated to 'metaphysics'; and it is the misfortune of the age in which I write quite as much as my personal fault, that in trying to show how to make a psychology which shall be 'positivistic' I have to exert myself also to show the metaphysical difficulties that the current theories involve, and of which their supporters seem so profoundly unconscious. I cannot, however, [see] why you should *object* to my formulation, for even if our thoughts *are* compounds of 'ideas,' they are at least superficially and practically also all that I say they are, namely, integral pulses of consciousness with respect to the multitude of facts of which they may take cognizance in a single passing moment of time. All you ought to accuse me of is *insufficiency,* not error. But I freely admit that in the vehemence of my argumentation in the chapter on the 'Stream of Thought,' I seem to be contending for the unity more as an ultimate and definitive truth than as a peculiarly advantageous method-

[12] *Revue philos.,* XXXIV (1892); XXXV (1893). Marillier was later professor of morals and psychology at Sèvres.

ological assumption. That chapter was really written as a bit of popular description, to show (first) the natural way in which our mental life would appear to a man who has no theories, and (second) to show certain omissions and difficulties involved in the account given by the theory of ideas. I should be sorry to have it taken as a 'theory' of my own; and in particular . . . I have no definite theory whatever as to just how the consciousness of relations may arise.

"I protest heartily against what you say on page 627, that I 'superpose upon states of consciousness thoughts which think them.' The thoughts are the states of consciousness; and since common sense and natural science think that the things of which we are conscious do exist *extra mentem,* I prefer to say that the thoughts think *those things.* Now it is quite true that some of these things are *sensible qualities,* and that in this case there is no distinction between the feeling and its object. At this point, then, to my mind, the whole *problem of cognition* opens. The dualistic views of common sense and science, that the thought is one thing and the object another, breaks down, the object appearing as what you call the *'sensation objectivée.'* [13] But to trace the consequences of this idea involves one in the most diabolically subtle and insoluble of all the higher metaphysical problems; and a straightforward psychology can never be written in consistent terms in any but dualistic language. Therefore I exclude all this consideration from psychology, and talk of sensation's 'object' just as I do of conception's or perception's objects. If *Erkenntnistheorie* is ever thought out (and I confess that its problems are what for some years past have weighed most heavily on my own mind) there will probably be a reconciliation between the notions of states of mind compounding themselves and of objects being combined in thoughts. Meanwhile why should you insist on keeping the more paradoxical form of statement? Why protest against the other, in which no one ever has found or ever will find cause of offense?" [14]

James Sully, writing in *Mind,* said that James had done "the big thing," and expressed agreement and approval on many points, *but* — and there were many "buts"! He was particularly troubled

---

[13] *Op. cit.,* XXXIV, 469.
[14] The original of the letter is not available. What is here reproduced is a copy in James's hand bearing the heading "Letter to Marillier."

by what Henry James once alluded to as his brother's "intellectual larking." Sully was not harsh in his judgment — it was rather as though he felt uncomfortable and mildly scandalized. In the first place, he complained that the book was made up of articles independently composed and having no general plan,[15] and beyond this there was its questionable style. Nobody could be less disposed than he to resent "the introduction into psychology of a little imagination, or, for that matter, a spice of humor"; and yet there may be too much of it — so much of "dazzling effect" as to blur "the sharp boundaries of scientific thought." Professor James "sets aside the crudities of a reigning English philosopher with all the delightful *insouciance,* the naïve egoism, of a boy. For this ingredient of rollicking defiance of the authorities, again, the reader of many dull psychologies may well be thankful, and yet he may wish here and there for just a *soupçon* of the old spirit which has prompted mankind at all stages of culture to pay reverence to ancestors." [16]

The Gallic sensibility, on the other hand, was not offended by the fact that a writer of psychology should have been *"malicieusement bonhomme";* [17] and the American stomach was stronger than Sully's. "One of my friends," wrote John Dewey, "summed up Sully's review in *Mind* for me as follows: 'A good book, but too lively to make a good corpse and every scientific book ought to be a corpse.' If we were n't indebted to you for any specific things, we should be indebted to you for what you did to break down this superstition." [18]

The New York *Nation* contained a review by Charles Peirce which, despite its opening remark that the *Principles* was probably "the most important contribution that has been made to the subject for many years," was so unsympathetic in tone as to arouse the brotherly partisanship of Henry, who wrote from Ireland: "I am unspeakably disgusted to hear of the *Nation* on William (the paper has n't come yet). Its behaviour is utterly incomprehensible to me save on the ground of a vicious *parti-pris* of Garrison's. But it alienates me from Godkin." The reviewer charged that James indulged in "idiosyncrasies of diction and tricks of language

---

[15] In this he was quite mistaken. *Cf. P.B.C.,* iii–v.
[16] *Mind,* XVI (1891), 393, 394 ff.
[17] E. Baudin's Préface to the French translation of the *Briefer Course,* 1912.
[18] It is to be noted, however, that J. M. Baldwin found the *Principles* to be too personal, unsystematic, etc., — too "unlike the ordinary textbook," — to be valuable for students. *Science,* XVI (1890), 208.

such as usually spring up in households of great talent." Although professing to treat psychology scientifically, he had ignored the example of science; confining himself to superficial and untested data, whereas physics and chemistry pass beyond experience to theories which are logically coherent and methodically verified. It is not strange that fraternal indignation should have been stirred by such comments as these: —

"Of course, he [James] is materialistic to the core — that is to say, in a methodical sense, but not religiously, since he does not deny a separable soul nor a future life; for materialism is that form of philosophy which may safely be relied upon to leave the universe as incomprehensible as it finds it. . . . Brought up under the guidance of an eloquent apostle of a form of Swedenborgianism, which is materialism driven deep and clinched on the inside, and educated to the materialistic profession, it can only be by great natural breadth of mind that he can know what materialism is, by having experienced some thoughts that are not materialistic. . . . It is his *métier* to subject to severe investigation any doctrine whatever which smells of intelligibility. . . . The principle of the uncritical acceptance of data, to which Professor James clings, practically amounts to a claim to a new kind of liberty of thought, which would make a complete rupture with accepted methods of psychology and of science in general. . . . And into the enterprise of thus revolutionizing scientific method he enters with a light heart, without any exhaustive scrutiny of his new logic in its generality, relying only on the resources of the moment." [19]

There is also an unpublished manuscript of Charles Peirce entitled "Questions on William James's *Principles of Psychology*." There are forty-five questions in all, relating to the first half of the first volume of the *Principles*. The following are selected for the light they throw on Peirce's own thoughts as well as his manner of criticizing James. The first two questions cited deal with James's theory of the physiology of habit, according to which repeated action breaks out a line of lowered resistance which subsequent action tends to follow: —

"Qu. 8, p. 108. Is it a sufficient explanation to say there 'seems

[19] *Nation*, LIII (1891), 15. Wendell Phillips Garrison was at this time literary editor of the *Nation*.

no reason why it should not happen,' when there certainly seems no reason why it *should?*

"Qu. 9, p. 109. Is anything *harder* than to imagine how, when a current has once traversed a path, it should traverse it more readily a second time, *consistently with the conservation of energy?* How does water wear a channel? Is it not by lifting a grain of sand from a state of rest and depositing it in a state of rest? Can a differential equation be produced, consistent with the law of energy, which would have such a solution? . . . Is it sufficient to explain psychical action by saying it is like something else which is utterly inexplicable?"

On James's argument (against automatism) for the teleological efficacy of consciousness, Peirce comments as follows: —

"Qu. 13, p. 141. I cannot understand this argument. When we are 'darwinizing' all we are saying is that variations in reproduction cannot be carried in certain directions beyond certain limits without bringing the race to an end, while in *opposite* directions they are not so narrowly limited. I do not see how this treats survival as an absolute end, in the sense of a 'should be.' I cannot see how consciousness is going to alter the case. We are all aware that this country has a . . . disease of government which must prove fatal in the end. But for all that we can do nothing about it."

To James's provisional and somewhat lame defense of the soul, Peirce replies: —

"Qu. 18, p. 182. Does it give any value to a hypothesis which 'explains nothing,' and is therefore destitute of all logical support, to say that it is not open to objections that some other hypotheses are open to? It seems to me like a man who, being on trial for vagrancy, answers that he doesn't sport a loud waistcoat nor eat sugar on his salad."

The next questions deal with James's provisional dualism between the knowing state and its object: —

"Qu. 28, p. 220. So the psychologist must further accept preestablished harmony. He seems to be in a pitiable condition. I should think it would be far better to abandon a study which, for the present, can only be built on such foundations. But how can a 'thorough-going dualist' entertain an 'ulterior monistic philosophy'? This general point is anything but clear. All that is clear is the very strenuous metaphysicism. . . . There is too much 'will to believe,' here. . . .

"Qu. 29, p. 222. 'Through feelings we become acquainted with things.' This seems to me to be at the root of a good deal of bad metaphysics. On the contrary, the feelings are matters of indifference (in their qualities). It is by the *reactions* of ourselves upon things and of their parts on one another that we become acquainted with things, as it seems to me."

The remaining questions deal with James's chapter on "The Stream of Thought" — its personality, continuity, and passage through transitive to substantive states: —

"Qu. 32, p. 226. Everybody will admit a personal self exists in the same sense in which a snark exists; that is, there is a phenomenon to which that name is given. It is an illusory phenomenon; but still it is a phenomenon. It is not quite purely illusory, but only mainly so. It is true, for instance, that men are *selfish,* that is, that they are really deluded into supposing themselves to have some isolated existence; and in so far, they *have* it. . . . It is true that there are certain phenomena, really quite slight and insignificant, but exaggerated because they are connected with the tongue, which may be described as personality. The agility of the tongue is shown in its insisting that the world depends upon it. The phenomena of personality consist mainly in ability to hold the tongue. This is what the tongue brags so about. . . . Meantime, physicians are highly privileged that they can ask to see people's tongues; for this is inspecting the very organ of personality. It is largely because this organ is so sensitive that personality is so vivid. But it is more because it is so agile and complex a muscle. . . .

"The cases of double personality show that the cunning right hand can in a measure replace the tongue. But till a personality can control the tongue, it is very obscure. The principal personality resides there. Its superiority is shown by this, that if cut out the person soon gets along and talks very well, with the remaining fragments. Farmers sometimes slit the tongue of self-milking cows. But they soon learn to make use of the slit tongue just the same. So if a man's right hand is cut off, it is marvellous how much he can do with the stump. But the hand altogether lacks the extreme subtlety of the tongue. The school-boy writes with his tongue. That is the tongue teaching the fingers language. Some people roll up their tongues, or bite them, or shove them down when they do something sly or tricky. Some people stick them into their cheeks. These are the gesture of pure egotism. The tobacco chewer shifts his quid when he betrays his vanity. All animals capable of domestication have good tongues.

"Qu. 39, p. 237. To say that consciousness feels as if it were continuous, — that is, as if *it had been* continuous (for all experience relates exclusively to the past), is a very different proposition from saying that it *is* continuous. The fact is there is an utter want of understanding of continuity here, as well as of the kind of evidence required to establish it. It is most important to know whether consciousness is in time distributed like the values of the rational fractions, that is, like an infinitely fine powder, or in fluid continuity, or in some intermediate way."

James's distinction between the "transitive" and "substantive" parts of the stream of thought Peirce commends as "one of the finest, if not the finest, passage in the whole book"; but he proceeds at once to condemn James's use of terms and to propose better ones of his own. To this topic, as well as to other issues raised in the *Principles,* Peirce recurs in his later correspondence.[20]

The most effective of the negative criticisms which the *Principles* received was contained in a review by his old friend, pupil, and colleague, Stanley Hall. On the whole, with allowance made for personal factors, it represents the protest of the "scientific" man against James's methods and style. The reviewer deprecates James's mixture of science and metaphysics, and his lack of the experimental spirit — says that a yearning for the traditional soul (*Seelensucht*) is James's fundamental motive, and defends associationism and the psychophysical law against his attacks. His commendation, on the other hand, is so shrewd that I cannot forbear a few citations: —

"Passing now to *the work as a whole,* the author might be described as an *impressionist* in psychology. His portfolio contains sketches old and new, ethical, literary, scientific and metaphysical, some exquisite and charming in detail and even color, others rough charcoal outlines, but all together stimulating and suggestive, and showing great industry and great versatility. . . . This is

[20] *Principles,* I, 243; *cf.* below, 413–4.

through and through a 'tendence' book. Its very inconsistencies and incoherencies not only reflect but greatly magnify all the unrest, distraction and conflicts of the present hour. The author is a veritable storm-bird, fascinated by problems most impossible of solution, and surest where specialists and experts in his own field are most in doubt, and finding it very hard to get up interest in the most important matters, if settled and agreed to, even to state them well. . . . The ripeness, repose and perfect mental digestion of Lotze, who abhorred every flavor of rococo, eclecticism or extravagance of expression; or of our own Charles Peirce, who burns his own smoke, and talks with the rifle rather than with the shot gun or water hose, are most contrasted with this author, and most desired in this confused and distracting field. . . . It is on the whole and after all the best work in any language, and we earnestly advise every one with the least interest in psychology to own and study it." [21]

The very traits which offended the scientific scruples of Sully, Peirce, and Hall, delighted the tolerant humor and artistic taste of Howells, who wrote about the book in the "Editor's Study" of *Harper's Magazine:* —

"We suppose it would be rather damaging to Professor William James with other scientists to show that in his volumes on *The Principles of Psychology* he writes with a poetic sense of his facts, and with an artistic pleasure in their presentation. We must content ourselves with a far less positive recognition of the charming spirit, the delightful manner, and the flavorous and characteristic style of the work. . . . It must be admitted that he has come dangerously near writing a 'popular' book. It is not exactly 'summer reading'; the two vast volumes, aggregating some fourteen hundred octavo pages, would not go easily into the pocket or the hand-bag . . . we could not imagine their being 'lapped out' by the train-boy. But there is no doubt that several of the chapters . . . can appeal successfully to people of average culture; and that throughout the work there are passages which may be read aloud to the tenderest female, so lightly and agreeably are some of the most difficult problems of the soul handled in them. . . . Nothing could be more winning than the informality of his discourse;

[21] *Amer. Jour. of Psych.*, III (1891), 585, 589–91. For James's comment on this charge of "self-evisceration," *cf. L.W.J.*, I, 306–7.

it captivates the average human being to find that the study of his mind is not necessarily allied to a frigid decorum. Those who know the rich and cordial properties of the philosophical writings of Henry James the elder, will find a kindred heartiness in the speculations of his son, and will be directly at home with him. . . . If Psychology in this work is treated philosophically rather than scientifically, there can be no question but it is treated profoundly and subtly, and with a never-failing, absolute devotion to the truth." [22]

It was evidently this appreciation which evoked the following from James to Howells: "Surely never before did a work on mental science get so judged at the court of letters. I only wish you were not a friend of the family, so that my astonished eyes might read it as a tribute wrested by invincible evidence from an originally reluctant judge. It is a great deal too handsome for the book, that is all I can say."

An admirably penetrating review of the *Principles* appeared in the *Atlantic Monthly* from the pen of George Santayana. Some of its paragraphs are worthy of being rescued from obscurity and reprinted here. The writer has understood the method in James's apparent madness: —

"Individuality is here more than a charm, more than a human warmth and personal flavor pervading the discussions; it is a safeguard against pretension and hollowness. Those who deal with the abstract and general, who think impersonally and along the lines of a universal system, are almost sure to ignore their own ignorance. They acquire what has been called the architectonic instinct; their conceptions of things are bound to be symmetrical and balanced, and to fit into one another with perfect precision. . . . Their cold breath congeals the surface of truth into some system; and on that thin ice they glide merrily over all the chasms in their knowledge. But Professor James's simplicity and genuineness have saved him from this danger. He is eager for discovery, and conscious that too little is known for any final or comprehensive statements. The result is that in his book, more than in many books of philosophy, that which is known is set down, and the rest is omitted."

[22] *Harper's,* LXXXIII (1891), 314–6. It should be stated that there is no record establishing the authorship of this review, but Howells was in charge of the "Editor's Study" at this time, and the internal evidence is overwhelming.

This reviewer is peculiarly perspicacious in grasping the essence of James's polemic against associationism. The mental state is an indecomposable intermediary between a decomposable nervous system and a decomposable object. The mind sums up the body, and orients it to its environment. "In fact," writes Santayana, "Professor James's conception may, perhaps, be best expressed by saying that the human mind is a series of single sensations, each of which has the whole brain for its cause and the whole world for its object."

The following judgment by the same writer flows from friendly indulgence as well as from the liberal mind: "His treatment of every subject is not equally radical and incisive; where his sympathies are engaged the edge of his criticism is blunted. . . . In regard to these matters Professor James is cautious, puzzled, apologetic; and in making his final decision he is avowedly guided by his æsthetic and moral bias. Such procedure is not unphilosophic for one who believes, with Lotze, that our moral and emotional instincts are the best guides to ultimate truth. Of course the sceptic will smile at such convictions, and murmur something about mysticism and superstition. . . . But it would be pedantry to regret the loss of logical unity in a book so rich and living, in which a generous nature breaks out at every point, and the perennial problems of the human mind are discussed so modestly, so solidly, with such a deep and pathetic sincerity." [23]

[23] *Atlantic,* LXVII (1891), 553, 555–6.

LVIII

JAMES'S OPINION OF PSYCHOLOGY

JAMES'S fluctuations of mood about his own book were such as might have been expected. There is a time of surfeit or ennui when all writers loathe their books, and James was peculiarly subject to such reactions. Thus he wrote to his brother, two days after the book had appeared: "Most of it is quite unreadable, but you may find some pages in the second volume that will go. Also the earlier pages of the chapter on 'Consciousness of Self.' The infernal thing is too long to sell well, I 'm afraid." In more buoyant moods, on the other hand, he thought well of his achievement and enjoyed a sense of successful delivery.[1]

But the completion of the *Principles* in 1890 moved James to expressions of opinion not only about his own book in particular, but about psychology in general. One of the most interesting of these judgments was written in the summer of 1890 to James Sully, whose disapproving tone toward the *Principles* has already been noted. Sully's paler efforts in psychology had the misfortune to be contemporaneous with those of James's colorful genius. The fact that Sully's sense of failure and inferiority were in part due to this unavoidable comparison enhanced the loyalty of James's friendship.

The two men had met in 1882–1883 as fellow members of the Scratch Eight and there had been an intermittent correspondence. Sully's *Outlines of Psychology* had appeared in 1884, and the author was now undertaking its revision. This was at James's suggestion, and it was James who chose the title, *The Human Mind*.[2] In June 1890, Sully wrote to James, saying that he had heard of the latter's forthcoming work, and wished to refer to it in his own. The following is James's reply: —

[1] *Cf.* letters of this period in *L.W.J.* and above, 49–50.
[2] J. Sully, *My Life and Friends*, 1918, 228. The publication of *The Human Mind* in 1892 led to Sully's appointment to the Grote Professorship in the University of London, as Croom Robertson's successor.

Cambridge, July 8, 1890

My dear Sully, —

Surely two such laborers can drop honorific titles! I am much flattered by your letter, and especially glad to hear that you are working your book over again; not that it needs it in my eyes, but it shows that you are still "energizing" at the old tasks. I learned that you were, in still another way, last week when I got a proof from the Editor of *Brain* of your paper on "Attention," with request for comment. I agreed with it so entirely that I could say nothing hostile, and had no time for mere compliments, so have contributed nothing.

My book ought to be out in October, but the printers are dawdling fearfully with the proofs and I fear it may not be out till the new year. I'm sorry to say that my manuscript table of titles of chapters is in the country. But I will copy it and send it to you when I go back. It is a very different affair from yours, — each of us is pushed fatally along in his own orbit; and mine has resolved itself into a mixture of critical discussion of principles on the one hand, and raw physiological facts on the other, with almost none of the descriptive psychologizing in the old sense, in which your book abounds to such good purpose. I had marked a whole page-full of places of passages in your book which I meant to quote, but as the writing proceeded I found that I could not weave in quotations from other authors in anything like the abundance which I originally had in mind, so at present your book is hardly used at all.

It seems to me that psychology is like physics before Galileo's time, — not a single *elementary* law yet caught a glimpse of. A great chance for some future psychologue to make a greater name than Newton's, but who then will read the books of this generation? Not many, I trow. Meanwhile they must be written. I will send you mine as soon as it appears, and I hope you'll do the same by me. I should have sent you many things in these last years, but knew that you had moved, without knowing whither. Cordially yours,

WM. JAMES

James's judgment that his own psychology would be, and de-served to be, superseded by a more "scientific" psychology had

already been made in a letter to his brother and was evidently much
in his mind at this time: "As 'Psychologies' go, it is a good one,
but psychology is in such an ante-scientific condition that the
whole present generation of them is predestined to become unreadable old mediæval lumber, as soon as the first genuine tracks of
insight are made.   The sooner the better, for me!" [3]

It is clear that James did not, like Hall, accept the experimental
psychology of his day as marking the advent of the new era.   This
was clearly not what he was looking for!   It is true that he had
from the beginning, and never lost, a respect for facts.   He distrusted speculation *in vacuo,* abstract dialetic, and learning from
books.   He felt that such methods tended to fill the mind with secondary products — fancies, conventions, and verbalisms.   Science,
with all its dogmatism and hard-heartedness, had the merit of being close to the originals of things.   It should be, he believed, a part
of the discipline even of the philosopher to come into the direct
presence of nature — to observe, touch, and handle the reality
which was unquestionably *there,* and to which all significant thinking must refer.   But James felt, as we have seen, a growing distaste for experimental psychology owing to physical and temperamental reasons.   He lacked the strength to spend long hours in a
laboratory; a recurrent lumbago prevented his standing, and trouble
with his eyes interfered with his use of the microscope.   With his
precarious health there went a fitfulness of mood that incapacitated
him for continuous routine.   And then James had a romantic
mind, eager for new adventure and repelled by detail and repetition.
The psychological laboratory frankly bored him, not because of
its instruments, but because of its measurements.   This appears
politely but unmistakably in a passage of the *Principles* on "The
Experimental Method": —

"Within a few years what one may call a microscopic psychology
has arisen in Germany, carried on by experimental methods, asking
of course every moment for introspective data, but eliminating their
uncertainty by operating on a large scale and taking statistical means.
This method taxes patience to the utmost, and could hardly have
arisen in a country whose natives could be *bored*.   Such Germans as
Weber, Fechner, Vierordt, and Wundt obviously cannot; and their
success has brought into the field an array of younger experimental

[3] *L.W.J.,* I, 296.

psychologists, bent on studying the *elements* of the mental life, dissecting them out from the gross results in which they are embedded, and as far as possible reducing them to quantitative scales." [4]

From distaste to disesteem the transition is easy and natural. In such a passage as the following it is impossible to say which of these attitudes dominates: "The results that come from all this laboratory work seem to me to grow more and more disappointing and trivial.   What is most needed is new ideas.   For every man who has one of them one may find a hundred who are willing to drudge patiently at some unimportant experiment." [5]   In short, James not only disliked the psychological laboratory, but came to disbelieve in any fruitfulness commensurable with the effort expended.   In 1887, writing to Robertson about *Mind* and its circulation in America, he said: "I must confess that the lack of concrete psychological work in England is rather a surprise.   France is going ahead famously meanwhile.   I'm afraid your *psychical researchers* really are the holders of the torch at present among you! Humiliating confession! eh?   Still, I think it is a great thing for a country, a thing to put all readers in its debt, that it should *not* produce certain kinds of things, and force innocent people to read them.   The whole 'psychophysic law' business in Germany, for example, what is it but an idol of the cave, fit only to be kept in an intellectual pathological museum? a sheer injury, on the whole, to the philosophy of the age."

In 1893 Howison wrote to James from California asking the latter's advice on the question of a laboratory, and James replied: "As for your laboratory, I don't think that the *results* ground out of all the labor have so far been important; so you can easily console yourself on that score.   But of course it is a healthy and cheerful thing for the young to be in touch with the concrete facts of the human organism, as well as with the abstract products of its intellectual functioning, so you had better get a laboratory when you can, and stock it well with apparatus illustrating the senses, if with nothing else."

The following letter pursues the same topic apropos of George Malcolm Stratton, who had just been appointed instructor in philoso-

[4] *Principles*, I, 192.
[5] Written in 1896; *L.W.J.*, II, 54.

phy at the University of California; and is also interesting for its reference to Charles Peirce, concerning whom Howison had been making inquiries: —

Cambridge, April 2, 1894

My dear Howison, —

. . . As for Mr. Stratton, I can answer an abstract question, but how can I know whether he is the concrete man who realizes the concept. My impression is that a man of twenty-seven, already caught with metaphysical fever, would hardly be likely to grow into a successful laboratory psychologist *in the long run* unless he happened to be also an individual of a lively mechanical and experimental turn of mind originally. I should fear otherwise that he would drift away from the laboratory and find it quiddling and irksome, and that book work would absorb his attention more and more as he grew older. . . . Perhaps I am influenced too much by my own career; but unless he loves to tinker *anyhow,* I should n't hope a great deal. There are, to be sure, tinkers and metaphysicians in one, but the combination is rarer than is either separate element. Münsterberg and Wundt are such. . . . Give up the notion of having a laboratory of *original research.* My private impression is that that business is being overstocked in America, and that the results are not proportionate to the money expended. I refer especially to "exact" work like that of Wundt's laboratory. I fear that in a few years, if nothing more significant in the way of ideas emerges from it all, there may be a reaction which will make trustees repent of their enterprise in founding laboratories. . . . At any rate we have now as many laboratories as America needs. And with the natural experimenter Angell at Palo Alto,[6] the Pacific Slope ought to be satisfied, I should think, with a man at Berkeley who should be a competent psychologist and exhibiter of classic experiments without having to torture his brain to devise new varieties of insipidity for publication, as he would have to do if appointed on the basis lately fashionable. If Stratton has any psychology at all in him, two years would be ample to teach him what has been acquired and to enable him to teach, and show his pupils the physiology of brain, senses, and psychophysic methods in

[6] Frank Angell, professor of psychology at Leland Stanford University, had been a pupil of Wundt's.

general. *I* always enjoyed that much of psychology, but I was bowed down with weight of woe that I could n't invent original investigations or find the patience to carry them out. . . .

As for Charles Peirce, it 's the most curious instance of talents not making a career. He dished himself at Harvard by inspiring dislike in Eliot. . . . He is now so mature in character, with rather fixed half-bohemian habits, and no habit of teaching, that it would be risky to appoint him. I yield to no one in admiration of his genius, but he is paradoxical and unsociable of intellect, and hates to *make connection* with anyone he is with. With all this curious misanthropy, he has a genuine vein of sentiment and soft-ness running through him, but so narrow a vein that it always sur-prises me when I meet it. Anyhow he 's a genius, and I look for-ward with avidity to his work. When shall we have your work, into which you cast the quintessential extract of all your untiring labors? Good-bye! Affectionate regards from

WM. JAMES

P.S. Thos. Davidson has been staying with us for a week. Matured and improved by the good years. As a visiting lecturer Peirce might be really inspiring.

Such being the unsatisfactory state of psychology, James prized the flexible and inventive mind, hoping that some such mind might happily hit upon a new and more fruitful theory. Thus in 1891 he wrote to Münsterberg, defending him against his elders: —

Chocorua, July 8, 1891 [7]

Dear Dr. Münsterberg, —

I have just read Professor G. E. Müller's review of you in the *G. G. A.*,[8] and find it in many respects so brutal that I am impelled to send you a word of "consolation" if such a thing be possible. German polemics in general are not distinguished by mansuetude; but there is something peculiarly hideous in the business when an established authority like Müller, instead of administering fatherly and kindly admonition to a youngster like yourself, shows a malign

[7] Printed in part in M. Münsterberg, *Hugo Münsterberg*, D. Appleton–Century Co., 1922, 31–2.
[8] *Göttingische gelehrte Anzeigen*, June 1891. Münsterberg's restrained reply appears in his *Beiträge*, 1892, 40.

pleasure in knocking him down and jumping up and down upon his body. All your merits he passes by parenthetically as *selbstver-ständlich;* your sins he enlarges upon with unction. Don't mind it! Don't be angry! Turn the other cheek! Make no ill-mannered reply! — and great will be your credit and reward! Answer by continuing your work and making it more and more irreproachable. I can't myself agree in some of your theories. *A priori,* your muscular sense-theory of psychic measurements seems to me incredible in many ways. Your general mechanical *Weltanschauung* is too abstract and simple for my mind. But I find in you just what is lacking in this critique of Müller's, a sense for the perspective and proportion of things (so that for instance you *don't* make experiments and quote figures to the thousandth decimal, where a coarse qualitative result is all that the question needs). Whose theories in psychology have any definitive value to-day? No one's! Their only use is to sharpen further reflection and observation. The man who throws out most new ideas and immediately seeks to subject them to experimental control is the most useful psychologist in the present state of the science. *No one* has done this as yet as well as you. If you are only *flexible* towards your theories, and as ingenious in testing them hereafter as you have been hitherto, I will back you to beat the whole army of your critics before you are forty years old. Too much ambition and too much rashness are marks of a certain type of genius in its youth. The *destiny* of that genius depends on its power or inability to assimilate and get good out of such criticisms as Müller's. Get the good! forget the bad! — and Müller will live to feel ashamed of his tone.

I was very much grieved to learn . . . lately that the doctor had found some weakness in your heart! What a wasteful thing is nature, to produce a fellow like you, and then play such a trick with him! Bah! — But I prefer to think that it will be no serious impediment, if you only go *piano piano.* You will do the better work doubtless for doing it a little more slowly. — Not long ago I was dining with some old gentlemen, and one of them asked, "What is the best assurance a man can have of a long and active life?" He was a doctor; and presently replied to his own question: "To be entirely broken down in health before one is thirty-five!" — There is much truth in it; and though it applies more to nervous than to other diseases, we all can take our comfort in it. *I* was entirely broken down before I was thirty. Yours cordially,

WM. JAMES

Did James offer anything in place of the experimental laboratory psychology which he esteemed so lightly? Did he have any intimations of the direction in which a Galileo or Lavoisier of psychology would advance? [9] There is, I think, a clue. Among the most notable reviews of the *Principles* was that contained in an article by George T. Ladd, entitled "Psychology As a So-called 'Natural Science,' " [10] in which the writer attacked James's cerebralism. In reply James wrote "A Plea for Psychology as a 'Natural Science' "; and he afterwards reviewed Ladd's own work, *Psychology: Descriptive and Explanatory.*" [11] This controversy establishes beyond any doubt the fact that James was looking for a psychology that *explained*. As he wrote to Ward, "the real thing to aim at is a *causal* account." The best prospect of a causal explanation is afforded by the connections of mind and body. There, then, is "*the* subject for a 'science' of psychology." [12] When James read such psychology as Ladd's he found it *tedious* — "tedious not as really hard things, like physics and chemistry, are tedious, but tedious as the throwing of feathers hour after hour is tedious." [13] He was dissatisfied with such psychology, in other words, because it was too easy; and its easiness lay in the fact that it evaded the problem of causal explanation. This same method which made a purely introspective psychology easy also made it useless, since prediction and control depended on the discovery of dynamic laws: —

"To me this lack of craving for insight into causes is most strange. Here is a flagrant mystery, that of the union of mind with brain, and we are apparently told that we must seek no reasons for it in a deeper insight into either factor! . . . To me, on the other hand, it seems as if 'methodologically' the crudest cerebralistic

[9] "Psychology . . . is to-day hardly more than what physics was before Galileo, what chemistry was before Lavoisier." (*C.E.R.*, 316.)
[10] *Philos. Rev.*, I (1892).
[11] The former in *Philos. Rev.*, I (1892); the latter in *Psychol. Rev.*, I (1894). Both are reprinted in *C.E.R.* In his *Philosophy of Mind*, 1895, Ladd again returns to the attack.
[12] Above, 96.
[13] *C.E.R.*, 343.

theories, or the wildest theosophic ones about the seven principles of human nature, lead in a more healthy direction than this contented resignation. And as the theories of inheritance have killed the taxonomic and biographic view of natural history by merely superseding it, and reduced the older books of classification to mere indexes, so will the descriptive psychologies be similarly superseded the moment some genuinely causal psycho-physic theory comes upon the stage."

Causal laws, then, for the sake of prediction and control — in mental science, as in physical science! "As constituting the inner life of individual persons who are born and die, our conscious states are temporal *events* arising in the ordinary course of nature, — events, moreover, the conditions of whose happening or non-happening from one moment to another, lie certainly in large part in the physical world. Not only this; they are events of such tremendous practical moment to us that the control of these conditions on a large scale would be an achievement compared with which the control of the rest of physical nature would appear comparatively insignificant. . . . If the hard alternative were to arise of a choice between 'theories' and 'facts' in psychology, between a merely rational and a merely practical science of the mind, I do not see how any man could hesitate in his decision. The kind of psychology which could cure a case of melancholy, or charm a chronic insane delusion away, ought certainly to be preferred to the most seraphic insight into the nature of the soul. And that is the sort of psychology which the men who care little or nothing for ultimate rationality, the biologists, nerve-doctors, and psychical researchers, namely, are surely tending, whether we help them or not, to bring it about." [14]

It was because of his emphasis on causal explanation, then, that James insisted on relating mind to the corporeal world. In his address as president of the Third International Congress of Philosophy held in Munich in 1896, Stumpf criticized parallelism as being contrary to the general presumption of the causal unity of nature, and predicted that "in the future we shall continue to regard our sense perceptions as the effects of the external world, and our wills as the cause of our actions, without being compelled to look upon this manner of expression . . . as a figure of speech." [15] To this

[14] C.E.R., 344–5, 318–9, 327.
[15] Psychol. Rev., III (1896), 593.

declaration, James gave his most hearty assent, and there can be no doubt that he adhered throughout to the view that psychology should consider the whole man, physical and mental, as a system of interacting parts.

The same idea dictated James's attitude to those forms of psychology which his contemporaries were accustomed to condemn as unscientific. The "nerve-doctors," though they invoke causes whose precise nature remains obscure, at any rate proceed on the hypothesis that the mind may be controlled through the body and the body through the mind. Psychopathology is a kind of "functional" psychology, because it treats mind as a function having its place in that system of interdependent functions which constitutes a living individual. Writing to Stumpf in 1894, James said that Janet's *État mental des hystériques* was worth more than "all 'exact' laboratory measurements put together." In his presidential address before the American Psychological Association in the following year he said that the phenomena of dissociation (hypnosis, hysteria, the trance, and so forth) threw more light on human nature than did the psychophysical laboratories.[16] When he wrote in 1900: "I have read Dumas's *Tristesse et joie* with much interest. I think the French are doing perhaps the best psychological work in these days," he was moved by the same considerations. Georges Dumas was a doctor of medicine, working in the French psychiatric tradition. James praised the book because it dealt with concrete human states and moods, in their dependence on bodily conditions, as well as on the mind as a whole.

The *Varieties of Religious Experience* contains a paragraph in which James refers to Myer's discovery of an extramarginal or subliminal consciousness as "the most important step forward that has occurred in psychology since I have been a student of that science." Its importance lies in its revealing "an entirely unsuspected peculiarity in the constitution of human nature," through which one may *explain* both abnormal and normal phenomena.[17] In 1906 James addressed the Psychology Club at Harvard. "When a student of psychology," he said, "I always regarded it as but a part of the larger science of living beings. . . . Official psychology is a very *small* part!" He then went on to outline a "concrete" or "functional psychology," which, having discovered the forces

[16] Below, 2184; *C.E.R.*, 384–5.
[17] *V.R.E.*, 233.

hat govern the moral and religious life, should develop a technique for their control. "Laboratory psychology," he concluded, "may be more accurate at present, but this program makes it look *small!*"

In the same year James again advocated the study of "dynamogenesis" — in his presidential address on "The Energies of Men" delivered before the American Philosophical Association: "We ought somehow to get a topographic survey made of the limits of human power in every conceivable direction, something like an opthalmologist's chart of the limits of the human field of vision; and we ought then to construct a methodical inventory of the paths of access, or keys, differing with the diverse types of individual, to the different kinds of power. This would be an absolutely concrete study, to be carried on by using historical and biographical material mainly. The limits of power must be limits that have been realized in actual persons, and the various ways of unlocking the reserves of power must have been exemplified in individual lives. Laboratory experimentation can play but a small part. . . . Here is a program of concrete individual psychology, at which anyone in some measure may work. It is replete with interesting facts, and points to practical issues superior in importance to anything we know. I urge it therefore upon your consideration." [18]

Finally, a year before his death, James welcomed psychoanalysis, applauding its aims even when he distrusted its individual exponents: " 'Functional psychology,' and the twilight region that surrounds the clearly lighted centre of experience! Speaking of 'functional' psychology, Clark University, of which Stanley Hall is president, had a little international congress the other day in honor of the twentieth year of its existence. I went there for one day in order to see what Freud was like, and met also Jung of Zürich, who . . . made a very pleasant impression. I hope that Freud and his pupils will push their ideas to their utmost limits, so that we may learn what they are. They can't fail to throw light on human nature; but I confess that he made on me personally the impression of a man obsessed with fixed ideas. I can make nothing in my own case with his dream theories, and obviously 'symbolism' is a most dangerous method. A newspaper report of the congress said that Freud had condemned the American religious therapy (which has

[18] *Philos. Rev.,* XVI (1907), 19.

such extensive results) as very 'dangerous' because so 'unscientific.' Bah!" [19]

A similar judgment found expression in a letter to Professor Mary W. Calkins: —

Chocorua, Sept. 19, 1909

Dear Miss Calkins, —

. . . My day at Clark University was very enjoyable, not only in meeting you, but in seeing new faces; especially Titchener's,[20] whom I had never yet met, and who made on me a very pleasant impression. I strongly suspect Freud, with his dream-theory, of being a regular *halluciné*. But I hope that he and his disciples will push it to its limits, as undoubtedly it covers some facts, and will add to our understanding of "functional" psychology, which is the real psychology. The "function" of Titchener's "scientific" psychology (which, "structurally" considered, is a pure will-of-the-wisp) is to keep the laboratory instruments going, and to provide platforms for certain professors. Apart from that it seems to me more unreal than any scholasticism. "Is 'affection' an entity or an attribute?" "Has it three 'dimensions' or one?" *Can* serious men take facts in these verbal ways? Bah!! I hope that your new book will disdain to discuss such questions. Always faithfully yours,

WILLIAM JAMES

That which he approved in others is what James undertook to do himself, in the limited time which, after 1890, he devoted to psychology. He continued to interest himself in psychical research and in abnormal psychology. The "transmission" theory applied to the question of immortality was the hypothesis of a cerebralist. In his "Energies of Men" he set forth the power of the mind to resist bodily fatigue and overcome physical obstacles.[21] He was interested in types of mentality, in all their fullness, such as those

[19] *L.W.J.*, II, 327-8. In one of his Lowell Lectures of 1896 on psychopathology, James had said: "In the relief of certain hysterias by handling the buried idea, whether as in Freud or in Janet, we see a portent of the possible usefulness of these new discoveries. The awful becomes relatively trivial."

[20] E. B. Titchener was a rigorous Wundtian — a "structuralist" in the sense that he emphasized the analysis of states of mind into their elementary parts. His strict adherence to introspection and Wundtian experimentalism distinguished him and at the same time isolated him. It will be noted that although Titchener had been teaching psychology at Cornell since 1892, he and James did not meet until a year before the latter's death.

[21] Below, 272-3.

exemplified in religion and war.   And he was interested in applied psychology, especially in ethical and educational applications.   In all of these essays he kept in view the integral man, and sought for causal explanations through taking account of the body and the environment.   He never felt confident that he had found such an explanation, but he practised his own psychological creed.

LIX

THE AFTERMATH OF THE "PRINCIPLES"

Upon the publication of the *Principles* James undoubtedly experienced a profound sense of relief and a desire to disport himself in other pastures. It is also true that he never afterwards produced any considerable article or book on the standard problems of psychology. To this extent he bore out his own judgment, written in 1894: "There is n't a page more of psychological literature in this child's mental organism. . . . Our reputation first begins as our talent commences to decay." But it would be a mistake to suppose that he abandoned psychology, now or later. He continued his reading, both of treatises and of periodical literature.[1] He wrote a large number of psychological reviews, in fact some fifty-five between 1891 and 1898; with the result that when, in the latter year, he was asked to review Henry Rutgers Marshall's *Instinct and Reason,* he wrote to the author: "I have been forced by instinct and reason, working together to protect and save my own body and soul, to forswear and renounce book-reviewing forever. I 've served my time and bought my freedom, and must employ my ebbing sands of life for things parasitic, insolent, and inconclusive."

In 1892 James published his so-called *Briefer Course,* a short textbook, of which two fifths was new or rewritten — the rest "scissors and paste." [2] In particular, much to his distaste, he added chapters on the psychology of the several senses. His motives were quite frankly commercial, and his expectations were fully justified when the book became and remained for some years the most widely used English text in the subject. The following letter was written to his publisher, Holt, as this task of bookmaking was nearing completion : —

[1] As, *e.g.,* the *Zeitschrift für Psychologie.*
[2] *P.B.C.,* iii.

Oct. 25, 1891

My impression is that the proof corrections will be comparatively slight, after we get through all this wretched twaddle about the senses which I am correcting now, and which had to be put in to satisfy the market. But *how* sorry I am we can't have a book of 350 pages! The fact is that the subject can't possibly be treated concisely and interestingly at the same time. And I think that as things go, the most interesting book will be the one that sells best. When I got through the job last summer I had a rather distinct impression that this work would kill most of its competitors for the reason that they are all (except Taine) so uninterestingly written. We shall see. . . . I am curious for Baldwin's second volume.[3] It will doubtless be better than his first one, he is such a growing man. I acquire more and more respect for him.

Neither of James's psychologies was ever revised, in spite of strong pressure brought to bear on the author from several quarters. He adhered to the advice he so often gave to others,[4] to write new books instead of revising old ones.

After the publication of the *Principles,* James continued his psychological studies in connection with his teaching. In his undergraduate course he usually taught from his own book, but in connection with his "Psychological Seminary" he applied himself to unsolved problems and to topics which he felt that he had hitherto neglected. Thus in the Preface to the *Briefer Course* he had regretted his inability "to supply chapters on pleasure and pain, æsthetics and the moral sense"; [5] and his seminary of 1890–1891 was accordingly devoted to the topic of "Pleasure and Pain." In 1893–1894, 1894–1895, and 1896–1897, he took up "Questions in Mental Pathology." In 1895–1896 the subject for the first half of the seminary was "The Feelings," and he returned again to his studies of pleasures and pain with special reference to æsthetics; while in the second half he discussed "Certain Theoretic Problems, as Consciousness, Knowledge, the Self, the relation of Mind and Body, etc."

[3] The work referred to is J. M. Baldwin's *Feeling and Will,* 1891.
[4] Apparently James *considered* revising both books. There is an interleaved copy of the *Principles* on which proposed changes have been noted; and a copy of the *Briefer Course* in which similar notations have been made on margin and flyleaf. There are letters from Prof. E. L. Thorndike indicating that at one time (1902–5) he offered to assist James in a revision.
[5] *P.B.C.,* iii.

In the autumn of 1891, when he was reading extensively in the literature of the subject of pleasure and pain, James entered into correspondence with Henry Rutgers Marshall, whose articles on this subject had begun to appear in *Mind*.[6] Writing on November 18, 1891, he said: "The upshot of my reading this fall is to make me realize how few *ideas* there are in the literature of this subject, and how we still wait for an entrance to the method of treatment which is to prove really scientific.   So far I confess you are ahead of any one."   In 1894 he was still of the opinion that the psychology of feeling was peculiarly inadequate.   This opinion was in no small measure due to the vast discrepancy between his own vivid and colorful experiences and the abstract schematisms of science.   Thus in reviewing Marshall's *Pain, Pleasure and Æsthetics,* he said: —

"The feelings of pleasure and displeasure form a truly immense portion of the life of man, but man's attempts to give to himself some intimate account of their conditions, whether inside or out-side of his organism, form a very shabby episode of his achieve-ments in the theoretic line — so shabby, indeed, that one's first impulse is to shy away from any book with the word 'æsthetics' in its title, with the confident expectation that, if read, it could only emphasize once more the gaping contrast between the richness of life and the poverty of all possible formulas. . . .   Everything that is subtle in our preferences escapes from the accounts that are given; the nature of the pleasure and pain-processes in the nerve-centres still remains unknown; and the student concludes that the experience of a single strain of melody or verse of poetry, of a single square foot of genuine color, is more important to the soul than the reading of all the books on beauty ever composed." [7]

In presenting the topic of feeling to his seminary in 1895, James was still discontented with existing theories.   He was especially concerned to expose the common confusion between the "rational ground" of feeling — that is, the ideal object which would be held to justify it — and the actual "course" of feeling; and it was char-acteristic of him both to emphasize the second of these problems and to look for its solution in the physiology of the nervous system. He went into the subject with his customary thoroughness, read extensively, prepared an exhaustive bibliography, drew up fifteen

[6] Marshall was an architect, living in New York City. He later published a book on the same subject as his articles — *Pain, Pleasure and Æsthetics,* 1894.
[7] *Nation,* LIX (1894), 49–50.

"facts which every theory must keep account of," corresponded with dentists regarding the painfulness of teeth and gums, and collected pamphlets.

Bringing together notes, letters, and published statements, including the article entitled "The Physical Basis of Emotion," in which James replied to his critics, it is possible to formulate a fairly systematic, though always provisional, view of feeling. Though he sharply criticized Marshall's view *qua* physiology, and felt that it only concealed an ignorance of details, he inclined to believe with Marshall that the tone of pleasantness and unpleasantness which is "beaten up with" the qualitative content of sensation is due to the relatively efficient or inefficient form of afferent nerve action. He argued this theory against the more complicated and far-fetched theory that pleasure and pain have special nerves of their own. At the same time it seemed to him "more and more as if pain proper were a specific sensation," and that Marshall was wrong "in lumping it with all the other displeasures." Beyond these sensory factors James also recognized factors of a secondary order, arising from a response to the first. There are the milder feelings of welcome and intolerability, and there are the more powerful "seizures" which constitute the major emotions. Since both are reflex organic "irradiations" reported back to the central nervous system, James thus brought the whole class of affective phenomena into accord with his basic idea that the original conscious experiences are conditioned by afferent and not efferent nerve currents.[8]

In the decades of the '90s James capitalized his rising fame by giving a large number of popular addresses. He was much in demand, and was glad to take advantage of this means of increasing his income at a time when his children were being educated. Many of these addresses were on ethical and philosophical subjects and appeared in his *Will to Believe and Other Essays* and his *Talks to Students*. These will receive attention elsewhere. There were two sets of lectures on psychology. The first, published under the title of *Talks to Teachers on Psychology*, was originally delivered in Cambridge in 1892, and afterwards repeated in various parts of the country.[9] The second set was entitled "Exceptional Mental

[8] *C.E.R.*, 358–60. It is interesting to note that James found support for his theory in Kant's *Critique of Judgment*, which he was reading at this time.
[9] The *Talks* appeared in 1899, first in installments in the *Atlantic*, and then in book form.

States." They were first delivered before the Lowell Institute in 1896, and were never published.[10] In 1897 James conceived the idea of giving one or both of these sets of lectures in California, and wrote to Howison to sound him out on the subject. Howison responded warmly to the suggestion, but proposed that James postpone his trip until 1898 and give a lecture at the same time before the Philosophical Union. After a more ambitious programme had first been discussed, Howison submitted a second plan more consistent with James's limitations of strength and time. This plan was adopted, and led to James's first California visit and to the famous lecture on "Philosophical Results" in which "pragmatism" was first proclaimed to the world. The following letters, written to Howison in the course of the negotiations, throw light on James's methods as a public lecturer and on his judgment of the audience to which he was addressing himself : —

Cambridge, April 5, 1897

Dear Howison, —

. . . I am afraid you are thinking of a larger program for me than my health or inclination craves. It is always better for me to have a vacation without nervous wear and tear, and starring it on a great scale is the most expensive process one's organism can be subjected to. My own idea was *to pay my traveling expenses* to and from the Pacific with as many dollars more as might be conveniently earned; but the latter condition is by no means imperative. I do not want great publicity, and I want as few lectures as are compatible with the above mentioned need. I can give from five to eight lectures (according to the degree of expansion or condensation) on "Psychology Applied to Teaching," in your Summer School, practically the same lectures that I give here. My regular price for lecturing outside has been fifty dollars a lecture. Now I never take less, though I sometimes lecture gratis. I have another course of eight lectures given here at the Lowell Institute last winter, on "Exceptional Mental Phenomena." . . . They were a real success here, the hall seating 900 people being crowded till the end. In these lectures I did not go into psychical research so-called, and although the subjects were decidedly morbid, I tried to shape them towards optimistic and hygienic conclusions, and the

[10] *Cf.* below, 168–9.

audience regarded them as decidedly anti-morbid in their tone.

If the Leland Stanford University should care for these lectures, or if Berkeley will pay me fifty dollars apiece for them (of course I should not refuse more if more were urged upon me), I should like to limit my entire lecturing activity to these two courses — with the exception of one sublime and transcendental lecture on Heaven and Hell and all that lies between, which I make a free gift to your Philosophical Union, and after delivering which, and receiving your treatment, my remains may be gathered up and sent home by freight to my wife with what money remains in my pocket from the experience.

Of course I make you impresario of the whole affair. You hear my preferences; but I am open to any suggestions from you that do not require the preparation of entirely new lectures for that vacation summer. The two mentioned courses have proved themselves attractive to audiences, and as I can give them with a minimum of preparation, they are obviously what my self-regarding virtues require me to put forward first. I am really hungry for California scenery, and for all that lies between. The spectacle of your single-handed activity over there is something really heroic, and your nervous system must be strong in an extraordinary degree. It comes after all, though, from a man's belief that there is truth, and that he is on the track of it; and *that* virtue you have in a most extraordinary degree, and I think your earnestness is what accounts for your success.

I am afraid that Mrs. James in any case will have to stay at home, unless the emoluments should reach a figure for which in this wicked world it is impossible to hope. Believe me, with warmest and most sympathetic regards, yours always affectionately,

WM. JAMES

April 5 . . . I hope you don't think my course too short. It is all I can give, to teachers; and I find it serves the purpose best for them, since but few need *much* psychology; and in trying to dispel their mystifications from others, I ought not to mystify them myself as I should do if I lectured too often. . . . My great desire is not to be *lionized,* but as soon as possible after the lecture is over to get into the country and see the face of nature. . . .

Cambridge, Oct. 27, 1897

Dear Howison, —

Your second plan pleases me much better, only I am sorry to be giving you so much trouble. . . . I prefer it egotistically for these following reasons: (1) It lets me rest in June; (2) it lets me give my eight Summer School lectures here in July; (3) not least, it does n't offer the morbid mental phenomena to teachers.

Experience has taught me that teachers have less freedom of intellect than any class of people I know, and these lectures not only are not pedagogic, but they demand a certain philosophic flexibility of mind, and easy look at life. A teacher wrings his very soul out to understand you, and if he does ever understand anything you say, he lies down on it with his whole weight like a cow on a doorstep so that you can neither get out or in with him. He never forgets it or can reconcile anything else you say with it, and carries it to the grave like a scar. Let us hope that all these institutes will help them — I 'm afraid the normal schools do not, much. . . . Thank you for all the trouble you are taking and for the niceness of your letter. . . . Yours always,

WM. JAMES

It is evident that James did not find the collective pedagogical mind as alert and critical as he would have liked, nor did he have a very high opinion of the organs and institutions designed to improve it. Writing in 1871 to Henry Holt, who had asked him to give his opinion of the *Educational Review,* he said: "I suppose the fault is less with the editing than with the subject, which must perforce deal with mighty and aspiring generalities and puerile concretes, with nothing between to fill the gap. Harris and the schoolmarm!" His own lectures were evidently designed to "fill the gap." The Preface and the contents of the *Talks* as it finally appeared make clear how James thought a psychologist could best serve teachers — not by expounding the science of psychology in its technicalities, but by enabling them to "conceive, and, if possible, reproduce sympathetically in their imagination, the mental life of their pupil as the sort of active unity which he himself feels it to be." [11] In this there is not only an echo of the *Principles,* but perhaps a memory

[11] *T.T.,* iv.

of those far-off days when he was the pupil and had learned something about the mental life of his teachers.

In spite of all James took a genuine and sympathetic interest in the work of the teacher and contributed substantially to the development of educational psychology. His rejection of the possibility of the transfer of training in memory — his belief, namely, that general retentiveness was unalterable and that one could only improve one's memory in specific fields by one's method of dealing with their materials — exercised a notable influence. More important, because of its wider bearing, was James's emphasis upon interest and action. The pupil, like other human beings, is essentially a reacting organism, which can be affected only by stimuli appropriate to its existing propensities, and which must as a result of its reactions inevitably form habits that will condition its future reactions.[12]

In 1898 James was asked to give the "Ingersoll Lecture on the Immortality of Man." This lecture, published under the title of *Human Immortality: Two Supposed Objections,* was related both to his ethical and to his psychological interests. The second of the "supposed objections" took the ground that a future life which provided for mankind at large would be too crowded and promiscuous. James's reply was an appeal to that sympathetic imagination which knows how to find an inward significance behind the external appearances of life. The first objection was the argument of science that the mind was dependent on the body and could not, therefore, outlive it. James replied that the facts of physiological psychology require only a "functional" dependence of mind on body. Such a dependence does not necessarily imply that the brain *produces* the mind; it may merely release it, or *let it through.*[13] In that case the larger reservoir or "mother-sea" of consciousness would remain intact after the dissolution of the brain and might retain traces of the life history of its individual emanation.

This idea that the brain, instead of creating mind, merely strains and canalizes it was an idea that James had long entertained, and an idea which seemed to him entirely congruent with the alleged

---

[12] This has come to be known as the "situation-response psychology." For this brief estimate of James's influence in educational psychology I am indebted to Prof. E. L. Thorndike of Teachers College, Columbia University.

[13] *Human Immortality,* 1899, 16, 50–2.

phenomena of psychical research. It was here formulated in dualistic terms, as though body and mind were different stuffs or substances. He was still holding in reserve that "phenomenism" in which this dualism was to be overcome. But the transmission theory was clearly an anticipation of the hypothesis developed in his later metaphysics and philosophy of religion, in which the mystical and similar experiences were interpreted as an overflow of superhuman mentality through a lowering of the normal threshold. In 1898, as later, James was influenced by Fechner and quoted him at length.[14]

Many years before, in the letter to his sister Alice written eight months before her death, and when hope of recovery had been abandoned, he had already broached the same theory — and given it a very practical and personal meaning: "These inhibitions, these split-up selves, all these new facts that are gradually coming to light about our organization, these enlargements of the self in trance, etc., are bringing me to turn for light in the direction of all sorts of despised spiritualistic and unscientific ideas. . . . And what a queer contradiction comes to the ordinary scientific argument against immortality (based on body being mind's condition and mind going *out* when body is gone), when one must believe (as now, in these neurotic cases) that some infernality in the body *prevents* really existing parts of the mind from coming to their effective rights at all, suppresses them, and blots them out from participation in this world's experiences, although they are *there* all the time. When that which is *you* passes out of the body, I am sure that there will be an explosion of liberated force and life till then eclipsed and kept down." [15]

A paragraph from a letter to Schiller affords evidence on the question of James's originality: "I write in haste for the practical purpose of asking you what *history* (so far as you know) the idea may have which you propound in *Riddles of the Sphinx* of the brain acting not as producer of consciousness but as sifter, limiter and individualizer thereof. Kant somewhere in the latter part of the *Kritik der reinen Vernunft* expresses the hypothesis very clearly, but gives no references to previous opinion. For several years past I have defended the view to my students, and was accordingly

14 *Ibid.*, 24–5, 50–1, 59–60.
15 *L.W.J.*, I, 310–1.

pleased to find it in your book, and last year in Kant. I supposed myself to have had the thought spontaneously, but it may have been sown in my mind by Kant years ago, and then become subliminal. Do you know any forerunners? If, *without research,* you can merely name them, I shall be obliged." [16]

The same hypothesis is somewhat playfully stated in a letter written in reply to the objections of Thomas Davidson. Among the metaphors which James commonly used (and occasionally mixed!) were those of light — "the white radiance of eternity" stained by "a dome of many-colored glass" — and the mother-sea divided by channels or overflowing its barriers.

Cambridge, Oct. 20, 1898 [17]

Dear Thomas, —

If you had the slightest spark of scientific imagination you would see that the mother-sea is of a glutinous consistency, and when she strains off portions of her being through the dome of many-colored glass, they stick so tenaciously that she must shake herself hard to get rid of them. Then, as there is no action without re-action, the shake is felt by both members, and remains registered in the mother-sea, like a "stub" in a check book, preserving memory of the transaction. These stubs form the basis of the immortal account, which we begin when the prismatic dome is shattered. These matters, you see, are ultra simple, and would be revealed to you if you had a more humble and teachable heart. Your whole lot of idle and captious questions proceed so obviously from intellectual pride, and are so empty of all true desire for instruction that I will not pretend to reply to them at all. I am glad that my poor little book took them out of you, though. You must feel the better for having expressed them. . . . In great haste. Yours affectionately,

W. J.

How the doctrine was received by James's psycho-philosophical colleagues is illustrated by an exchange of letters with Ward: —

[16] Written Aug. 19, 1897. *Cf.* F. C. S. Schiller, *Riddles of the Sphinx,* 1891, 293 ff.; Kant's *Critique of Pure Reason,* Max Müller's translation, 1881, II, 667. For another reference to Schiller's "conception of the brain as a sifting agency," cf. *L.W.J.,* II, 65–6.

[17] This letter has also been printed in J. S. Bixler's *Religion in the Philosophy of William James,* Marshall Jones Co., 1926, 152.

Cambridge [Eng.], Dec. 11, 1898

My dear James, —

Many thanks for the copy of your lecture on *Human Immortality*. It reached me in the thick of term, which only ended yesterday. I have only just read the book and here are my first impressions.

Of the two points you take up, I like the handling of the second best: there you seem to me very effective. Of your treatment of the first and more important I do not feel that I can say this. You might, I fancy, have done better to stick to it and work it out more. For the nonce you seem, more than you have done elsewhere, to admit the validity of the Cartesian dualism that still possesses the scientific mind, and of "psycho-physical parallelism," the logical outcome of that dualism. The question, what is the relation of the "white radiance" or, may be, its source, "the super-solar blaze," to the subjects that receive it as a kaleidoscopic show — this, the main point, as it seems to me — does not come clearly to the fore. And moreover the whole figure tends to drop out of sight the *active* side of life. Life implies not only windows, but doors: what is the meaning of matter, the equivalent of transparency on this side? And what is the process of differentiation continually going on, and, so to say, never going off? Does not evil call for annihilation, does not the survival of the fittest imply it? Death and oblivescence are teleologically important in the natural sphere — have they none in the realm of ends itself?

Prior to any very profitable discussion of this question of immortality comes, I am strongly of opinion, this tremendous problem of the relation of the One to the Many. Lotze, among the comparatively sane thinkers known to me, is the man who has wrestled with this riddle with most persistence. I wish I could say he has made the answer clear. My own notion is that the true solution lies on another tack. When one can't answer a question it is a point scored to show that the question ought never to have been asked. So here: "our wills are ours we know not how." And perhaps, even with Lotze, this is the last word. We can never in thought construe *how* reality is *made*. Well for us, if when it is there we know what it is well enough to clear our thinking of contradictions, and to find satisfaction in it for our spiritual needs. The understanding which can always ask one question more, just as it can always add one number more, can never be satisfied. But this *progressus ad indefinitum* is really a limitation and an excellence. Reason alone, which is not merely logical, but moral and æsthetic too, has an idea of complete unity, — not a continuum or a sum, but a consensus and a system. From any point of view in which such a system implies beginnings it seems to me to imply endings too. The only immortality I can think of is not "remerging in the general Soul," but an abiding consciousness of being an abiding idea there, in place of sinking into the Divine Oblivion. This may be eternal life but it is not immortality. Yours ever,

JAMES WARD

Cambridge, Jan. 28, 1899

My dear Ward, —

Yours of December 11th was very welcome. I hardly expected you to send me a letter in return for that poor little lecture of mine. You won't expect me to reply to all the points raised. You seem to take my intention in the lecture to have had a wider *portée* than I ever thought of. The first part was a mere *argumentum ad hominem* to the materialists. Admit, I say, the duality of mind and matter, and the functional relation — still, the individual's consciousness may survive the brain, for in the mother-sea the scars of cerebral operations may remain as records of the transaction, like stubs in a check book, and form the basis of an eternally remembered account. I should have said more explicitly that there is no objection to considering the mother-sea in as individualistic a form as you like. We should then (doubtless for wise purposes) be filtered into this world's experiences, and then be reunited to our deeper, truer selves; which would, doubtless, be all the better for the fact. It is needless to say that the dualistic view is far from satisfying me, but one nail is good enough to drive out another, and that is all I meant.

I long to get your Gifford Lectures. I fear that it will be hard for me to come up to the scratch with mine, I am kept so busy with other things, and my working power is very small. Believe me, with warm regards, yours truly,

WM. JAMES

The provision for a more "individualistic" form of the mother-sea grew out of James's correspondence with Howison. The latter had objected that even though the mother-sea were conceived as "many minds behind the scene," there would be no assurance of their identity with the mortals who perish.   James now, in a second edition of *Human Immortality,* revised his hypothesis, making the mother-sea consist of a collection of individual spirits, each existing there in a completer and truer form than in what filters through to this phenomenal life.[18]

[18] *H.I.,* v–ix.

LX

JAMES AND MÜNSTERBERG

IN the autumn of 1892, Hugo Münsterberg, formerly a pupil of Wundt, came from the University of Freiburg to relieve James of the directorship of the Harvard Psychological Laboratory. He remained for three years, and then after a two years' interruption returned to remain at Harvard until his death in 1916. Münsterberg's *Willenshandlung* appeared in 1888, after James had already written his chapter on "Will," but the latter at once read it, and proclaimed it "a little masterpiece." [1] The *Beiträge*, or "Contributions to Experimental Psychology," which represented Münsterberg's work in his Freiburg laboratory and appeared in installments from 1889 to 1892, impressed James as "masterly," and convinced him of Münsterberg's competence as an experimentalist. The latter opposed James's nativistic view of space, and supported his rejection of feelings of innervation, but, regardless of doctrinal agreement, James admired the quality of Münsterberg's work and thought him to be "the ablest experimental psychologist in Germany, allowance made for his being only twenty-eight years old." He also admired the boldness and flexibility of his mind and the vigor of his style. Thus it came about that when in 1892 James looked for a man who might become both his temporary substitute as a teacher and his permanent substitute as director of the psychological laboratory, he turned to "that vigorous young psychologist," "the irrepressible young Münsterberg." [2]

Cambridge, Feb. 21, 1892 [3]

Dear Dr. Münsterberg, —

Is it conceivable that if you should be invited, you might agree to come and take charge of the Psychological Laboratory and the higher instruction in that subject in Harvard University for three years at a salary of say $3000 (12,000 marks)? This is a private

[1] *Principles*, II, 505, note.
[2] *L.W.J.*, I, 318; *Principles*, II, 189, 590.
[3] Printed also in M. Münsterberg, *op. cit.*, 33.

question of my own, and not an inquiry on the part of our University authorities. My mind is in travail with plans for regenerating our philosophical department, and the importation of you has come to figure amongst the hypothetical elements of the case. I cannot of course go on with the combinations till I know whether or not that particular feature is impossible. So pray tell me.

The situation is this: We are the best university in America, and we must lead in psychology. I, at the age of fifty, disliking laboratory work naturally, and accustomed to teach philosophy at large, although I *could, tant bien que mal,* make the laboratory run, yet am certainly not the kind of stuff to make a first-rate director thereof. We could get younger men here who would be *safe* enough, but we need something more than a safe man, we need a man of genius if possible. Meanwhile there is no additional money at the disposal of our philosophical department, and if you were to come, it would be necessary to raise money for three years expressly by appealing to friends of the cause. Such a thing might *possibly* succeed. After three years (if it did succeed), you would know us, we should know you, and it *might* be possible to make the arrangement permanent. You would have to contemplate, in deciding to accept such an invitation, the possibility of going back to Germany after an experiment of three years. Of course we should hope for permanence. Our university is one you need not be ashamed of. I got a fund of $4300 last year to start a laboratory, of which some $1600 still remains unspent. You would have an assistant (or two if needful) and of actual *teaching* would not be called to do more than six hours a week, or less.

Once more, this is a private question from me to you, and you will oblige me by not making it public. The scheme will require much labor to carry it into effect, and I cannot begin the work at all unless I have something definite to go upon on your side. At your age and with your facility I am sure the language won't trouble you after the first year. Faithfully yours

WM. JAMES

P.S. Of course you understand that an affirmative answer to me now will not pledge you to say yes hereafter, in case additional details should then come up, which might make you change your mind.

Münsterberg's prompt acceptance evoked the following outburst from James: —

Cambridge, May 3, 1892

My dear Münsterberg, —

A telegram arrives from you "joyfully accepting the call." *Gottlob!* I believe that this has been the best stroke I ever did for our University! Not that I deem you infallible, far from it; but I have the greatest confidence in your combined originality and sanity, and in the solidity of your future career — in spite of the Müllers and the Titcheners! It is an enormous relief to me to see the responsibility for experimental psychology in Harvard transferred from my feeble and unworthy shoulders to those of a man as competent as you. I shall proceed immediately to proclaim the news, as an early ventilation and publication of it will decide many wavering students to come to us next year.

No more today! I forgot in my last to say that nothing could please me more than the dedication to me of anything that you might write, and I am much gratified that you should have had the thought.[4] Go to work immediately upon English so that your ears and tongue, if possible, may be expert when you arrive. Greetings to your *gnädige Frau* from both myself and my wife. Always truly yours,

WM. JAMES

At the end of May James sailed for Europe, and went to see Münsterberg at Freiburg. His impressions are described in the following letter to Royce: —

Luzern, June 22, 1892

My dear Royce and verehrteste Herr Kollege, —

Agreeably to the promises I made on the eve of my departure, I take pen in hand to inform you of our prosperous voyage and safe arrival and to hope that yourself and family are the same. We have been ten days in the deliciously pretty little Freiburg (days for the most part rainy, unfortunately) and I am now here as scout for a "pension" to bring the family to, the weather having glo-

---

[4] Münsterberg had apparently asked permission to dedicate to James a work on "*Der Ausdruck der Gemüthsbewegungen,*" which was never published.

riously cleared up and nature's full orchestra going it on this extraordinarily operatic lake. . . .

My great purpose in writing is to speak of Münsterberg, whom I have seen a good deal of — he came on here with me and we spent the whole of the next day scouring the shores together for boarding places and talking all the time, so that I feel as if I knew him pretty well. He is an extraordinarily engaging fellow, not of the heroic type, but of the sensitive and refined type, big, inclined to softness and fatness, poor voice, vain, loquacious, personally rather formal and fastidious I think, desiring to please and to shine, liberal of money, quick to forgive . . . fond of traveling and of all kinds of experience, interested in many intellectual directions, and talking anything rather than "shop" when he gets out of harness. I imagine him to be a man of the truest moral refinement and idealism, with probably a certain superficiality in his cleverness, and lack of the deeper metaphysical humor (such as the Harvard philosophical department possesses in such unwonted measure). But he is gentlemanly through and through, so far as one can be a gentleman without ferocity, and is a man to whom I should suppose one might easily become deeply attached. It is in the laboratory that he appears at his best, and that best is *very* good. His indefatigable love of experimental labor has led him to an extraordinarily wide range of experience, he has invented a lot of elegant and simple apparatus, his students all seem delighted with him, and so far as I can make out, everyone recognizes him to be, as a *teacher,* far ahead of everyone else in the field, whatever they may think of his published results. His brain never tires; he is essentially a man of big ideas in all directions, a real genius; and I feel more than ever, since I have been here, how great an addition he will be to our strength, *if only he gets along with our language.* . . . With Münsterberg's torrential flow of eloquence in his own tongue, he will have a fearful *Hemmungsgefühl*[5] when he tries ours. You must all try to help him out next year! I don't know how quickly he will learn, — he is timid about trying now, and Cambridge will probably teem with anecdotes about him before he has been there a month. . . .

[5] Sense of inhibition.

Riehl[6] is a disappointed man with a morbid expression of contraction on his face, whom I heard deliver a very well-composed lecture on Hegel's *Naturphilosophie*, and with whom I spent two very agreeable evenings and had an afternoon's walk in the rain. He is extraordinarily well read, and prompt of memory, talks like a man of the world, and we got on well together, though I confess I rather shrink from a long winter's *tête-à-tête* with one who is as sensitive as he evidently is. . . . Best love to you both,

W. J.

At the same time James wrote to Stumpf of the new appointment: —

Luzern, June 24, 1892

My dear Stumpf, —

. . . You will have heard of our calling Münsterberg to Harvard University. We have there now a first-rate laboratory and a lot of students, and we ought to have the best experimental teacher; and when all is said that can be said against Münsterberg (and much has been said that is very unjust) it remains true that he is a great *force* in psychology, a wonderfully active thinker who tries to test all his ideas by experiments, and a man so amiable and liberal minded that he is sure to grow riper with the years. I have seen a good deal of him and like him thoroughly. I should think one might grow to love him very much. Meanwhile he is, by the unanimous confession of all his students, a *teacher* whom it is impossible to surpass. . . . Always cordially,

Wm. James

The following letter from James in Florence to Münsterberg in Cambridge will throw light on their intellectual relations at this period. Münsterberg had sent a full account of his activities, enclosing his plans for the laboratory and a copy of the opening speech (*Antrittsrede*) which he had addressed to his students.

Florence, Nov. 24, 1892

My dear Münsterberg, —

I am in your debt for two letters and the fourth part of your *Beiträge*. The first letter, of Oct. 9th, was a fairly encyclopædic

---

[6] Alois Riehl, at this time professor of philosophy at Freiburg.

document, with its *Antrittsrede* and list of subjects for possible investigation. I congratulate you heartily on the fact that your English goes so well. If you composed those remarks without assistance or correction, it shows that your progress has been very rapid, and that you have nothing to fear, for there are no mistakes. . . . I am delighted to find, from both of your letters, how well the University, and America in general, seem to agree with you. Your program of occupations in your last letter indicates what is called "a full life." The excitement of novelty won't last forever, so keep it up whilst the mood continues! Only I 'm afraid that by spring time you may experience a sort of fatigue which you have n't been accustomed to feel in Germany. Overstimulation and depressive reaction are the great evils of our otherwise interesting and on the whole, it seems to me, beautiful climate. You are experiencing one great exemption, which if you stay much longer, you will hardly escape — I mean serving on various committees of the Faculty. They eat the very soul out of one with their tediousness and consumption of time. Keep clear of them and of the Faculty as long as you can! . . .

Your *Beiträge* came some weeks ago, but owing to occupation with other things, I did n't get to reading them till a few days ago. They are simply *charming;* and I don't see what your worst enemy can say, except with reference to the last few pages, which seem to me a speculation in rather too simplified a form. If your record of Harvard work at the end of the year results in a volume at all comparable with this, it will be magnificent. . . . In the [*Mitbewegungen*] [7] you quote me. The fact I had in mind when I explained Loeb's results as due to an automatic reversion to an infantile type, was the symmetrical movements of both arms which I had noticed in my own babies towards the end of their first year, when for many weeks together (I think) they manifested all emotional excitement by alternate flexions and extensions of the trunk, with symmetrical rising and falling of both arms. Their movements during the first months are certainly most unsymmetrical, according to my observation; and the period I noticed, of symmetrical movements, is transient. I was too little explicit in my book. [8] . . . As regards the pleasure-pain business, your frank

[7] Simultaneous movements.
[8] *Principles*, II, 516–7, note. The discussion interested James as bearing on "feelings of innervation," for which Prof. Jacques Loeb had argued.

distinction between *Schmerz* and the *Gefühl* which it awakens
is important, and starts a new era of discussion.[9] . . . All I hope
is that you may have more ideas and opportunities to work them
out in this fashion! It is a great pity that Angell, Hodder,[10] and
Bakewell are not with you this year — they were three splendidly
strong fellows out of whom you would infallibly have got good
assistance, both in the way of discussion and criticism, and of experiment.

Our winter comes on well. The boys are contented at their
school, and I am beginning to do a little serious reading. I have
just got through Lasswitz's *Geschichte der Atomismus,*[11] and am
about to attack Wundt's *System der Philosophie.* The pictures are
delicious. Unfortunately I have no visual images whereby to enjoy them when my back is turned. One can buy old pictures here
so easily, that I wish I had a little money to spend upon them. We
have only lighted fires today, the thermometer having hardly
varied from sixteen degrees centigrade during the past month.
Good-bye! Pray give the best regards of both of us to your wife,
be industrious and cheerful! and believe me, always yours affectionately,

                                                    WM. JAMES

The appointment of Münsterberg relieved James of all responsibility for the laboratory, but he continued to devote a large part
of his time to the teaching of psychology, elementary and advanced
— and with special attention, as we have seen, to abnormal psychology and to the problem of feeling. The three years during
which Harvard was trying Münsterberg and Münsterberg was trying Harvard expired in the spring of 1895, and he returned to
Freiburg. Meanwhile the place was kept open for him. James
was nominally in charge of the laboratory during the year 1895–
1896, and Edmund B. Delabarre of Brown University during the
year 1896–1897, but Münsterberg was supposed to "maintain ad-
visory relations by correspondence." [12] James kept him informed

---

[9] The distinction was between pain as a sensation, and dislike or unpleasantness
as a reaction to the sensation.
[10] James R. Angell, president of Yale University; the late Alfred Hodder, associate in English literature for two years at Bryn Mawr College.
[11] James made extensive use of this book in his course on "cosmology" (Philos.
3); *cf.* above, 482–3.
[12] He sent James lists of problems for the laboratory. When the question of his

of developments, including Bryan's sensational campaign for the
Presidency : —

Chicago, Sept. 2, 1896

Dear Münsterberg, —

I don't remember whether I wrote you a letter at the end of the
term in Cambridge.   I am afraid I may not have done so, because
I was as usual very much overworked and in arrears with everything.
I have not had much rest since, having been starring about the country giving lectures to teachers on psychology, — some at Cambridge,
some at Buffalo, one at Chautauqua and now a course at Chicago.
Fortunately in two days I can go to the Adirondacks and have
some hygienic vacation.   The year was, on the whole, a satisfactory
one in Cambridge, although my own part at the Harvard laboratory was of the humblest.   We are going to suffer more and more,
I think, from the new fellowships which are being founded in
other institutions.   We shall get fewer good graduate students.
What the prospect is next year no one knows.   I have just had
a few words about the Congress from . . . Strong and Baldwin.[13]
Baldwin speaks of having met you but says nothing more about
you.   A Berlin paper has been sent me with a letter from Munich,
which said that the "psychological pope of the old world, Wundt,
and the psychological pope of the new world, James, were both
distinguished by their absence."   I am becoming illustrious!   I
am also becoming possessed of the Chicago spirit, for I am writing
letters for the first time in my life by dictating to a stenographer.
I hope you sympathize.

I lunched with Loeb yesterday, who seems on the whole well
contented here and who (I think with great sincerity) expressed
the opinion that he thought you would make a mistake not to return
to this country.   The conditions strike him as so much healthier
than those of Germany; and truly enough, going around among
the teachers as I have lately done, seeing the magnificent development of the university here and feeling the fermentation that everywhere exists in education, one cannot doubt that learning has a great

return was open he advised James as to a successor.   Edward W. Scripture, Joseph
Jastrow, and E. C. Sanford, he said, were experimentalists, but not psychologists;
J. M. Baldwin was a psychologist, but not an experimentalist; E. B. Delabarre and
Lightner Witmer, he thought, struck "the right middle."
[13] The third International Congress of Psychology was held in Munich, Aug. 4-7.

future in America. If a few men of genius spring up in the next generation, fifty years will see us perhaps in the very first rank.

I hope you enjoyed and profited by the Congress. I extremely regret not having been there, but it was pecuniarily impossible. I have not the least idea how many pages you have written of your *magnum opus*, but I sincerely hope you have not experienced the usual disappointment of finding that to plan a book is one thing and to write it something quite different. It almost always turns out so, but for many reasons I want your book out early. I regret to say that my brain has been so bad that after agreeing to review Stout's book for *Mind* and keeping the volumes two months, I had to back out and hand the job over to Royce who is ready for everything in this world or the next. He seems in splendid condition and has been reading and writing vigorously all summer in Cambridge. Titchener's book is out, but I have not read that either. I am just beginning to read a little for my Kant course next winter. You see my *jämmerliches* condition more or less continues, but I did get on to some new thoughts in my seminary last year, which I may be able to work out, and which give me some small consolation.[14] . . .

The political campaign goes on admirably — splendid speeches and documents on both sides. It seems difficult to doubt the essential soundness of people where such a serious mass of discussion, pursued on the whole in such a dignified tone, is a regular incident of life. Of course, the silver party must be beaten, but they have much that is ideal on their side.

Good-bye, dear old Münsterberg. Keep in good health. Write like a steam-engine through next winter and be ready to resume your old place a year from now. Cordialest greetings to the *gnädige Frau* and the children, who have probably forgotten me, and best wishes to yourself from yours always truly,

WM. JAMES

Cambridge, Jan. 14, 1897

My dear Münsterberg, —

The President will be writing you in these days to make your definitive decision about returning. You see it would be practically intolerable for the University to let things hang over a

[14] G. F. Stout's book was his *Analytic Psychology;* Titchener's, his *Outline of Psychology.* For James's seminary of 1895–6, *cf.* above, 126.

third year, losing continuity and all that goes with it. So I hope
you will say yes and appear here next September, taking entire
charge of psychology except so far as you wish me to continue
Philosophy 1, or occasionally to take a seminary. I shall never
again take an intermediary general course as I consented to before.
I see that my future interests will lie with philosophy, and I am
more harmoniously occupied this year with Kant and the philosophy
of nature than I have been for a long time back. . . . Yours
always,   Wm. James

After some hesitation, and the rejection by Harvard of several
proposed compromises, Münsterberg returned to Harvard as a
permanent and full-time professor in the autumn of 1897. The
magnum opus, the *Grundzüge der Psychologie,* which was dedicated
to James, did not appear until 1900. Although Münsterberg actively fomented experimentalism among his students in the laboratory, he, like James, had heard the siren voice of philosophy and
was rapidly becoming more interested in the "principles" of psychology than in the discovery of new facts. Indeed between his
philosophical interest on the one hand, and his social and political
interests on the other, Münsterberg almost wholly defeated James's
hope of acquiring for Harvard a great leader and exponent of
experimental research. He became famous in America for his
promotion of science, rather than for his contributions to it — for
his personal brilliancy, his participation in public affairs, his voluminous popular writings, and his innovating applications of psychology to industry, jurisprudence, and medicine. Though James
retained both affection and esteem for Münsterberg, he was unquestionably disappointed. At the same time, as the years passed,
there emerged the total and irreconcilable difference between their
philosophies.[15]

In the spring of 1900 James was in Europe seeking to recover
his health, and Münsterberg was on his way to Europe to spend
his summer vacation in Germany : —

                                                Ouchy, June 18, 1900
Dear Münsterberg, —
    Your jolly good letter of six weeks ago with all its Cambridge
news and gossip, came duly, along with the *Atlantic.* You must

[15] *Cf.* below, 469–72.

now be approaching this side, if not actually landed, and I trust that
the voyage has been a comfortable one. Is any *rest* comparable to
that of the steamer, for the first three or four days of change to it,
if the sea is smooth? I hope everything was prosperous at the end
of the year, and that you both are in the best condition to enjoy
the things of home. *I* never touch Germany without delight. The
beauty and order; the speech and voices; the smiles of the chamber-
maids; the splendid carriage of the men, taught to walk in the
army; the wholesome animality; the moral earnestness and readiness to take you seriously; the loquacity; the simplicity; everything,
in short, that is audible and visible is a real refreshment to one's
soul; and when the "uncivilized" parts of the world would be as
safe as in the hands of Germany they certainly would be, I don't
see why England should still insist on the Anglo-Saxon race as the
sole providential vehicle of "colonial" salvation. But Germany has
greatly changed superficially since I lived there in the later sixties
— changed for the better, too. Better clothes, better, or at least
smarter and more worldly, manners; a more energetic and enter-
prising expression on the faces, similar to what is so characteristic
of the English. You certainly *ought* to return through England.
You would find that a great many peculiarities that you have hitherto
taken to be American are English as well. But I don't mean to
write a treatise on ethnography!

I continue to be greatly flattered at the notion of your dedicating
your new volume to me. My "reputation" needs all the contributions it can get from benevolent well-wishers, in the present state .
of decay of my organism. I feel a certain compunction, however,
on the score of imperfect sympathy with some of your theoretic
conclusions. The rule in dedications is that they should express
either intellectual indebtedness or indicate *Geistesverwandtschaft;* [16]
yet, as it turns out, there is hardly a distinction made in your *Psychology and Life,* of which I would n't make a different systematic
use from what you do. If, as I suppose, this book is a more technical statement of the main theses of that one, it may find in me one
of its worst enemies. And how will that comport with the dedication? Can I then criticize it openly, if the devil tempts me so to
do? And if I do, won't you feel as if you had thrown a good
dedication away? — pearls before swine, etc? I state this frankly,

[16] Spiritual kinship.

because now is the time to make sure there shall be no misunderstanding. For my own part, dear Münsterberg, I am as much pleased by your *desire* to dedicate the book to me, as I should be by the dedication — for the most precious thing about it is the manifestation of personal regard. Whether the more intellectual aspect of the matter ought not, however, to prevail, is a thing which I think you ought now at the last moment to reconsider, and possibly to conclude not to carry out a plan made many years ago in a less evolved state of the cosmos, merely in order that you may remain *unerschütterlich consequent*.[17] You see my main object is to set you entirely free from the past, and to have you act in the light of purely present conditions. If *then,* as a new-born resolve, you still think me to be the worthiest being now living on the surface of the globe, for the honor of such a dedication, in spite of the unaccountable hardening of my heart towards many of your beliefs, Heaven knows I shall be gratified enough. But I shall not be in any way made miserable, or accuse you of being a promise-breaker, if on opening the volume, I see no dedication, or else some entirely unknown name! Don't write anything about this now, but let me wait to see what I *shall* see! — when the volume comes out. It will be a riddle, and communicate a zest to life. In any case, I hope that you will succeed in getting the proofs corrected this summer, though it will doubtless be hard work. . . .

I much enjoyed reading the *Atlantic* article.[18] I think it is the cleverest thing you have written so far, and the English *absolutely* idiomatic. It will doubtless have a great effect. It is possible to interpret it as a document in favor of the elective system. If a curriculum which so many persons condemn can produce such good results merely because it is well-taught, why attribute such importance to the curriculum? *Anything* will suffice, if only the teaching be in good hands — I must say that that is largely my own opinion. . . .

With best regards from both of us, and wishes for a happy German summer to you all, especially to the girls, I am as ever, affectionately yours,

WM. JAMES

[17] Unshakably consistent.
[18] The *Atlantic* for May 1900 contained an article entitled "School Reform" in which Münsterberg described his own schooling and explained the more rapid

The *Grundzüge* was published in the autumn with its dedication to James and sent to him in Europe. Meanwhile the latter had written to Schiller, on September 30: "I have become a mere clothes-horse on which to hang literary distinctions. 'La renommée vient à ceux qui ont la patience d'attendre, et s'accroît à raison de leur imbécillité!' Münsterberg's book is announced to be out in a few days. It will probably be better than the rude rehearsal in English. Anyhow, the dedication saves it! Think kindly of him hereafter, yoked together in a common personal devotion! He has his faults, as who has not, but he is not as bad as you think him, and may yet be a ministering angel when you lie howling."

Although James did not receive his copy of the *Grundzüge* until October, he had read it by December. He wrote to Münsterberg on December 29 that he had finished it "some days ago." "My fundamental objection to your philosophy," he went on to say, "is that I still believe the immediate living moment of experience to be as 'describable' as any 'scientific' substitute therefor can be." That James read his *Grundzüge* thoroughly is proved by its annotated and heavily scored pages. It was in James's judgment a good example of a bad kind of philosophizing — the worst kind, in fact. It was ingenious, but excessively conceptual and schematic. It assigned to psychology the task of describing unrealities of a peculiar sort created for the purpose. All such methodological barriers, especially that between philosophy and psychology, were odious to James. Some of his marginal comments, selected at random, will convey his reactions: —

"*Erkenntnistheoretische etiquette* gives poor God no chance to get recognized even if he exist. . . . Exquisite example of Münsterberg's fluent ingenuity along unreal lines of artificial obstruction. . . . *How* Münsterberg must have been pleased when this self-extrication from a self-imposed difficulty was safely invented and written out!! . . . This seems a most unnatural and violent distinction. . . . Awfully cleanly said. . . . How *slickly* does he skip from every trap! . . . Oh! Oh! such plausibility is worthy of a better cause."

When James discussed Münsterberg's *Grundzüge* with his seminary in 1903–1904 he made the following note: "Shall the direct

progress of German boys by the superior quality of the teachers, greater coöperation at home, and a prescribed programme.

dealings of our minds with life, descriptive or non-descriptive, passively consent to be first falsified and mutilated and then handed over to certain professionals called psycho-physicists, who claim to be the only persons licensed to give any account? — at the behest of another set of beings who say that they are 'epistemologists,' that the universe in its entirety is their property, that life in its immediacy must never be removed from their back-shop, or ever talked about by anyone except the aforesaid psycho-physicists? . . . Bah!"

It was this same artificiality of psychological procedure that gave rise to the following interchange of comments between James and Ward. The latter had come to America to attend the Congress of Arts and Sciences held in 1904 as a part of the St. Louis Exposition. The plan of the Congress followed Münsterberg's systematic classification of human knowledge, and he was largely responsible for its promotion and success. Ward wrote from Berkeley on July 24: —

"What tries me most is Münsterberg's own psychology. He reminds me of an old story: — A physician from the East arrived in these parts and a child in high fever was brought to him by its parents for advice. He could make nothing of the case; but at length he said, 'Put his feet in cold water.' The mother protested that that was no way to cure fever. 'Ah, well,' was the reply, 'you do it and he will have fits, and I can always cure fits!' I cannot describe or explain the actual realities of mental life, says Münsterberg, but let me substitute psycho-physical atoms — which to be sure are quite different — and I *can* describe and explain these."

To which James replied on July 31: "I pity you at Saint Louis, but you'll doubtless meet some men worth meeting. To me the whole Münsterbergian Circus seems a case of the pure love of schematization running mad. Your story of the fits-doctor applies so absolutely to his general philosophy that I don't know why I never thought of it myself. *Pray use it soon,* it will be an unparalleled *Denkmittel* for handling that theory succinctly. Münsterberg's labors over the Congress have been enormous, and he may have the laugh yet on us scoffers."

On December 27, 1905, Emerson Hall was dedicated to the uses of the Harvard department of philosophy at a ceremony held in conjunction with the annual meeting of the American Philosophical

Assocation. Münsterberg had played an important part in launching the enterprise and raising the money. He was a member of the Philosophical Association and had a place on its programme. He was also chairman of the department, and it was natural that he should preside. But there were persons who thought that he was excessively prominent, and James wrote to Eliot complaining that Münsterberg had made five speeches in the course of an hour. In his reply Eliot said: "Of course Münsterberg has a German way of doing things, which is different from our Yankee way. For instance, his introduction of me on that occasion would have been absolutely impossible for any born Yankee, and it grated on the ears of all the Yankees. But when you recommended Münsterberg for an appointment you must have expected that he would be different from us, and doubtless reckoned on those very differences as part of the profit to the University."

To Münsterberg Eliot wrote a soothing letter, in which he said: "I venture to add that I do not at all sympathize with Professor James's feeling that a Yankee would have been better than a German to guide the very simple ceremony of Wednesday last. If philosophy is not cosmopolitan or universal, what subject can be?"

Meanwhile James concluded that he had judged Münsterberg too hastily. "I learned today," he wrote to Marshall, "that [Münsterberg] had not jumped in . . . to boss the show yesterday; but that Palmer, Dewey and the President had all urged him to preside. So I did him injustice and take back my blame. It is our own fault. If we are too lazy to do any work ourselves and put it all on him, we are estopped from carping at the way in which he does it."

In consequence of Eliot's letter and a cordial note from James, Münsterberg withdrew the resignation which he had submitted, and the incident was over. But the friendship between the two men was further strained by their sharp differences of opinion on psychical research. Although Münsterberg had at one time been a member of the Society for Psychical Research and had manifested a benevolent, if somewhat remote, interest in its work, in 1899 he wrote an article on "Psychology and Mysticism" in which he definitely joined the opposing party, taking the ground that he was "only a psychologist, not a detective." [19] "Have you read Münster-

[19] *Atlantic*, LXXXIII (1899), 78.

berg's article?" James asked a friend. "How clever! but how essentially childish. The insolence of these fellows, sure of the applause of Scientism whatever they say, is amusing!"

As late as 1909, however, Münsterberg had occasion to prove his undiminished loyalty to his colleague. Professor Lightner Witmer, whom Münsterberg had a dozen years before singled out as one of the men best qualified to succeed him at Harvard, had in January criticized Münsterberg for his psychotherapeutic activities, and for his application of psychology to the testimony of witnesses in the Orchard trial.[20] In February he published an article in which he attacked, with considerable ferocity, both psychical research in general and James in particular. James was admirable as a *"littérateur,"* and excusable on account of his "Swedenborgian parentage," but he was no psychologist, as was proved by the fact that Wundt's *Physiological Psychology* referred to him only nine times. "In this issue," he said, "it is William James *versus* science." Professor Witmer was on the side of science: —

"William James deliberately opens a campaign for occultism. . . . A philosopher-psychologist, temperamentally interested in mysticism, professionally engaged in philosophy, and temporarily assuming the rôle of a psychologist, Professor James represents to-day the survival of an academic tradition. . . . The spoiled child of American psychology, exempt from all serious criticism, and the beau ideal of a large and cultured circle, Professor James, since the publication of his *Principles of Psychology,* has apparently relaxed the intellectual inhibition which every man should exert over his desires. . . . Professor Royce has been more guarded in indicating the popular implications of his obscurantist attitude than James has been in exploiting the occult and mystical elements of his psycho-philosophical theories, or than Münsterberg in the application of psychological methods and results to law, medicine, and every day affairs."[21]

Münsterberg wished the American Psychological Association to take cognizance of this assault upon "the greatest living American scholar"; whereas James himself, who had not even known of the affair until Münsterberg called his attention to it, took it quite light-heartedly, thought it a good sign that psychologists expressed

[20] For Münsterberg's account of the Orchard trial, *cf.* his *On the Witness Stand,* 1908.
[21] *Psychological Clinic,* II (1909), 289–99.

their differences of opinion so freely, and persuaded Münsterberg to withdraw his protest. Writing to Münsterberg, he said, "I take such things very calmly myself, but am curious to see what can so have raised your ire, and converted you into such an eloquent laudator of my greatness!" [22]   To which Münsterberg replied : —

Cambridge, March 17, 1909

You know that I am always in perfect agreement with you, if you do not by chance talk pragmatism. But your last letter contains a word with which I cannot agree at all. You say that I have been "converted" into a laudator of your greatness. I feel sure that if you would undertake a philological inquiry into my collected writings, you would find exactly the same statement about your psychological work on a dozen occasions in most public print. It is a fact that my whole conflict with Wundt which went on for years, originated, as he has delightfully described it himself, with my putting you publicly at the head of the profession. There was no Witmer needed to convert me.

[22] For James's final judgment on the matter *cf. L.W.J.*, II, 320–1.

LXI

PSYCHICAL RESEARCH

JAMES's interest in "psychical research" was not one of his vagaries, but was central and typical. He grew up in a circle in which heresies were more gladly tolerated than orthodoxies. Men like his father and his father's friends, who were attracted to Fourierism, communism, homœopathy, women's rights, abolition, and spiritism, were not likely to have any prejudices against mediumship, clairvoyance, mesmerism, automatic writing, and crystal gazing. From his youth James contemplated such "phenomena" without repulsion and with an open mind.[1]

Psychical research was only one of many examples of James's fondness for excursions to the scientific underworld. This general sympathy with every line of inquiry, however speculative or irregular, that might by any chance throw light on the nature of man is illustrated by his early interest in phrenology. In the *Principles* he rejected phrenology as a theory, but admitted it as an art.[2] He had also, as has been noted, a passion for physiognomy, collected portraits of his friends and of celebrities, and attempted to read the character from the face.[3] Symptomatic of this same intellectual bohemianism was his interest in "the Welsh fasting girl," reported in 1870 and called to his attention by Garth Wilkinson. And when, in 1897, he prepared a course of lectures on "Exceptional Mental States," he devoted considerable time to a study of demoniacal possession and witchcraft.

James's freedom from prejudice against theories or sects of dubious repute was converted into something more positive by his chivalry. He not only tolerated, but *preferred,* the despised and rejected — in movements as well as in men. Orthodox science was a symbol of arrogance and vulgar success, disposed to exaggerate

[1] *Cf.* his early book review of E. Sargent's *Planchette, Bg.,* 1869-1.
[2] *Principles,* I, 28. This passage appears in notes that date from 1878, written for the Baltimore and Lowell Lectures; *cf.* above, 27–31.
[3] *Cf.* above, 51.

its claims and to abuse its power. In any dispute between science and a weaker brother in which it appeared that science was the aggressor, James would invariably be found intervening. Hence he proposed as a suitable motto to Myers's posthumous work the scriptural passage, "And base things of the world and things which are despised hath God chosen, yes, and things which are not, to bring to naught things that are."[4]

A number of reasons accumulated to confirm this early and general predisposition in favor of psychical research. As one who approached psychology from the side of medicine he gave attention to the pathology of mind. Then, during the memorable winter of 1882–1883, he met the Englishmen who were the founders of the new Society for Psychical Research. Gurney, Myers, and Sidgwick became his intimate friends, and loyalty to them implied loyalty to their cause. He thus became a partisan of psychical research, both as officer and as soldier in the ranks. Passing on to more important reasons, there was a relish for the non-normal which was deeply rooted in James's genius and philosophy. He was confident that orthodoxies, respectabilities, schematisms, unities, architectural symmetries, always missed the native quality of existence. One cannot be at the same time fastidious and profound. His was the philosophy of the strong stomach and the thick skin, capable of encountering the untamed, unrefined, and unselected. Not only did James refuse to disparage any doctrine because of the "abnormality" of the channel by which it was communicated,[5] but he inclined to regard normality in the hygienic or social sense as tending to shallowness and conventionality of opinion. In any case, it generated an intellectual prejudice. The following paragraph was written in 1897 as part of a lecture on "Hysteria": —

"There is a deep and laudable desire of the intellect to think of the world as existing in a clean and regular shape. The mass of literature, growing more abundant daily, from which I have gathered my examples — consisting as it does almost exclusively of oddities and eccentricities, of grotesqueries and masqueradings, incoherent, fitful, personal — is certainly ill-calculated to bring satisfaction either to the ordinary medical mind or to the ordinary psychological mind. . . . Everything here is so lawless and individualized that it is chaos come again; and the dramatic and humoring and hum-

---

[4] L.W.J., II, 157. The motto was not adopted.
[5] Cf. V.R.E., 15.

bugging relation of operator to patient in the whole business is profoundly distasteful to the orderly characters who fortunately in every profession most abound. Such persons don't wish a *wild* world; a world where tomfoolery seems as if it were among the elemental and primal forces. . . . So the universe of fact starts with the simplest of all divisions; the respectable and academic system, and the mere delusions. Thus is the orderliness which is the great desideratum, gained for contemplation."

James felt that the critics of psychical research, like Stanley Hall,[6] were obeying the dictates of a "theoretic creed," while he, on the other hand, was "baldly empirical." The rejection of phenomena for methodological reasons is an inversion of the rightful priority. We should never regard phenomena as "impossible." Furthermore, as we have seen, James hoped that psychical research, like other studies of abnormal phenomena, might throw light on the central constitution and deeper causes of human nature. Instead of being rejected as unscientific it should be welcomed as affording promise of a psychology that might be really scientific.

James also saw in psychical research the possibility of a more kindly treatment of suffering humanity. It puts a more benign interpretation on certain phenomena, such as possession, witchcraft, hysteria, or disorders of personality. They are no longer punished or reprobated, or held to signify moral evil. "Looking directly at the facts makes the Devil's sphere seem less broad and deep." Unquestionably, too, psychical research was connected in James's mind with the possibility of mental healing, and this, in turn, with his own personal sufferings and recoveries.[7] He frequently attempted such cures himself. The following exchange of letters with Myers is interesting on several accounts, but it is introduced here because it reveals a connection between James's interest in psychical research and his own therapeutic experiences. James has been invited to become president of the Society for the year 1894, and has begged off on the score of ill-health: —

Cambridge [Eng.], Nov. 16, 1893

My dear James, —

I am very sorry that you are feeling ill; but a touch of something is mixed with my sympathy that I may as well have out. It seems

[6] *Amer. Jour. of Psych.*, I (1887).
[7] *Cf. L.W.J.*, I, 170.

to me that your mental and physical disorganisation and decay is never by any chance perceptible to anyone but *yourself;* and, moreover, that when you are actually in the presence of friends you are able to make an effort (if such it be) which presents you to them as a source of wisdom and delight — "as light and life communicable"; which makes them rather wish that they were even as you, than grieve over any hidden malaise within you — and yet it seems to me that you lack one touch more of *doggedness* which would render you of even more helpfulness in the world than you are. Why on earth should you not in *public* matters act upon other people's view of you and not on your own? We all wanted you to place your name at our head — we should have been satisfied, however little you had actually *done;* why not have let us have our way? To *underrate* one's own importance in the eyes of others may be (though rarer) as great a nuisance to them as it is to *overrate* it. We must not push you further now; but I warn you that we shall ask you again another year, and that unless we have evidence to your decrepitude from someone besides yourself, we shall then take it somewhat unkind if you won't oblige us!

Mrs. Piper [8] is all right — and the universe is all right — and people will soon pay up more money to S. P. R. — and an eternity of happiness and glory awaits you — and I am sure Mrs. James would agree to much in this letter — and the dear spirits are hovering around us in the Summer Land. Yours always,

F. W. H. MYERS

Cambridge, Dec. 17, 1893

My dear Myers, —

I telegraphed you this morning "James accepts" — the Presidency of the S. P. R. being understood. This is in consequence of a letter from Pearsall Smith informing me that the Council still desire it and regard it as a matter of importance. They are bent on having a King Log, so they shall be humored. I had no idea, when I got your first invitation, that it was a matter of the slightest real *importance,* or so regarded by any of you; and I much regretted to perceive, from your reply to my own letter of declination, that the latter, so far as you were concerned, had been a genuine disappoint-

---

[8] Mrs. William J. Piper, the famous Boston medium whom James had discovered in 1885.

CARL STUMPF, 1896

F. W. H. MYERS, ABOUT 1893

ment. Since however in that reply you treated the refusal as definitive and implied that its consequences were then evolving, I have let the matter drop from my own attention. . . . To tell the truth I supposed the true inwardness of the offer to lie in your friendly wish, yours and the Sidgwicks', to pay me a compliment; which friendly wish I thought almost as well acknowledged by "declined with thanks" as by "accepted."

My state of mind is also revolutionized since that time. I had a pretty bad spell, and know now a new kind of melancholy. It is barely possible that the recovery may be due to a mind-curer with whom I tried eighteen sittings. What makes me think so is that I am enjoying an altogether new kind of *sleep,* or rather an old kind which I have been bereft of for so many years that I had forgotten its existence, and considered myself sleeping as well as I ought to, and told her so, when I went to her, saying my only trouble was my mind. . . . Two . . . other cases of brain-trouble, intimate friends of mine, treated simultaneously with me, have entirely recovered. It is a good deal of a puzzle. I should like to get this woman into a lunatic asylum for two months, and have every case of chronic delusional insanity in the house tried by her. That would be a real test, and if successful would *have* to produce some effect. I may possibly bring it about yet!

My college work is all-engrossing, as ever. For a presidential address, even, I should be at a loss for matter. When, by the way, is such a thing due? Here nothing goes on but Mrs. Piper — *toujours* Piper! I wish we could unearth a little variety. I appreciate your strictures . . . as to the absence of doggedness in me, but you must remember that tenacity like *yours* is what puts you in the *immortal galaxy* which I have already previously enumerated, and that if it were a common possession, you would lose your distinction! . . . Yours ever,

WM. JAMES

The ultimate results of James's treatments were almost invariably negative,[9] and the theories by which mental healers supported their practices were entirely repugnant to his mind; but belief that help for suffering mankind *might* be hoped for in that direction was to

[9] For an early experiment of this sort, *cf. L.W.J.,* I, 261.

him a sufficient reason for giving psychotherapy of every sort a fair opportunity to prove itself.[10]

Finally, we have to note that for James the idea of consciousness "beyond the margin" or "below the threshold" was a metaphysical hypothesis of the first importance. This hypothesis afforded an experimental approach to religion, and constituted the only hopeful possibility of giving scientific support to a supernaturalistic faith.

The Society for Psychical Research was founded in 1882, the year of James's residence in London and of his close contact with those who, like Gurney, Myers, and the Sidgwicks, were primarily responsible for its success. James became a member in 1884, and remained a member until his death. He was a vice president for eighteen years, and president in 1894–1895 and 1895–1896. The American Society was founded in 1884, and like the parent society it borrowed repute from the distinguished names of its officers and members. In 1884 James wrote: "We are founding here a 'Society for Psychical Research,' under which innocent sounding name ghosts, second sight, spiritualism and all sorts of hobgoblins are going to be 'investigated' by the most high-toned and 'cultured' members of the community."[11] Such men as Stanley Hall, E. C. Pickering, H. P. Bowditch, C. S. Minot, W. Watson, J. M. Peirce, Asa Gray, W. T. Harris, Simon Newcomb, G. S. Fullerton, and Josiah Royce,[12] as well as James himself, were among the early supporters and workers. It published its *Proceedings* once a year and continued to do so through 1899.

James's idea of the policy which should govern a Society for Psychical Research is stated in a letter of 1885: "I take it the urgent thing . . . is to ascertain in a manner so thorough as to constitute *evidence* that will be accepted by outsiders, just what the *phenomenal conditions of certain* concrete phenomenal occurrences are. Not till that is done, can spiritualistic or anti-spiritualistic theories be even mooted. I'm sure that the more we can steer clear of theories at first, the better. . . . '*Facts*' are what are wanted."[13]

During the next few years James himself investigated and reported on such topics as hypnosis, mediumistic phenomena, and automatic

[10] For a full statement of James's relations to unorthodox medicine, cf. *L.W.J.*, II, 67–72.
[11] Bixler, *op. cit.*, 159.
[12] Cf. his review of "Recent Psychical Research," *Nation*, XLV (1887).
[13] *L.W.J.*, II, 250.

writing. In 1889 he became the American representative of the committee formed by the International Congress of Experimental Psychology to make a census of hallucinations.[14]   Early in 1887 Richard Hodgson came over from England as permanent secretary of the American Society.   But the burden upon James continued to be heavy, — a burden upon his purse as well as upon his time, — and in 1890 it was decided to unite the American with the British Society, Hodgson to maintain an office as that Society's representative in Boston.   It was in this mood of retrenchment that James heard from Davidson of steps taken to promote the work in New York: —

Cambridge, Dec. 13, 1890

My dear Davidson, —

I have just seen Hodgson who gives an account of what seems to have been a very enthusiastic meeting, and shows me your proposed circular — telling me with some disappointment, which I confess that I share, that you seem rather to be forming an independent New York organization. I beg you to do nothing conclusive until you have carefully weighed the following reasons. . . .

(1) The only Society worth lifting one's finger for must be one for *investigation of cases,* not for theoretic discussion — for *facts,* and not yet for *philosophy.* The name of "S. P. R." has been sadly discredited by certain literary and spiritualistic societies in western cities.

(2) Investigation demands someone who will give his whole time to what is mainly drudgery. Hodgson now gives all his time, and employs a clerk in addition. . . .

(3) Suppose that in New York you could find a worker of the sort required, it would be a sheer waste of his power to work *independently* of Hodgson, — they ought to share their materials and divide their labor. . . .   The great use of the English Society in my eyes is that it is a central bureau in charge of proved experts, towards which all threads converge, thereby providing for a maximum of facts behind conclusions.

(4) A *separate society* in New York would . . . be a sort of fire in the rear, competing with us for evidence, and interfering in other ways. . . .

[14] *Cf. Proc. of Soc. for Psychical Research,* VI (Dec. 1889). The final report was submitted by Sidgwick and others in *Proc.,* X (Aug. 1894), the result being, in James's judgment, indecisive.

(5) But you don't mean a separate society of course. You mean, I suppose, a branch coördinate with what you supposed to be the Boston branch, and founded as a concession to local pride, with a view to rousing more New York enthusiasm.

(6) To this I say, "there *is* now no Boston branch." When the *American* Society for Psychical Research was founded, local branches were formed in New York, Philadelphia and Boston (the Society was organized in *Philadelphia,* as a matter of history). The Philadelphia branch died first, then the New York branch, and a year ago the Boston branch died, leaving its members all over the country to join the London S. P. R. if they would. The London Council simply continued to keep their *office* in Boston. I am sure they would be too happy to move it and Hodgson to New York, if some-one else there proved a genuine investigator, or if money were forthcoming. . . . You must remember that *every* considerable donation which we have had since the beginning has been from Boston, with one exception from Philadelphia.

(7) If the New Yorkers are willing to give money there is one way, and only one, in which *at present* it seems to me to be likely to do much scientific good, and that is paying for experimental or observational work to be done by Hodgson on people at a distance, covering, *inter alia,* his traveling expenses.

(8) It seems to me quite absurd, when our existing organization just as it stands is crippled for this (its *most* important work) for lack of funds, to rally a crowd of people to the cause, and then divert their funds into any other channel.

I trust therefore, in conclusion, that your committee will not think of recommending anything but an enlargement of the American branch as it stands, and a disbursement of donations thereto. . . . Don't, for Heaven's sake, get people to subscribe the precious dollars, and then go to work to reduplicate machinery which already costs far too much. . . . You could n't inflict a worse blow on the cause. . . .

Please read this letter to your committee. I cannot but think that what I say ought to carry a good deal of weight. I care nothing myself for either Boston or New York, but I do care to make psychic research *effective*. For that, there is but one way, strengthen the existing organization. . . . Too busy for more! beloved Tomasso! Yours ever,

                                        W. J.

James's correspondence with Myers during this period reveals the pressure of his duties and the somewhat ruthless demands made upon him from across the water. Thus Myers wrote on January 12, 1891 : —

"I have read Vol. I and part of Vol. II of your *Psychology* with deep interest, and much admiration. I am extremely glad that you have written this big and good book, and I trust that it will become both bigger and better in many a future edition. . . . I believe that with a view (*a*) to the good of mankind (*b*) even to your own ultimate fame, it is essential that a main part of your energy shall henceforth be devoted to these S. P. R. inquiries. As a professional psychologist you can work them in with admittedly orthodox speculation far more easily than (say) a physiologist like Richet. You can take things in your psychological stride at which the physiological horse will shy for many a year to come. . . . I do not regret your efforts — I don't mind your having to speak constantly at meetings, to interview informants, to write letters, etc. . . . You may not *like* it, but I am sure it is the right thing ! And far more important than teaching students ordinary textbook facts. Don't kill yourself — lay as many golden eggs as you can — but never mind if the S. P. R. does give you a great deal of trouble. It is out of that trouble that your main usefulness and fame will spring. . . .

"Not one single member of our small group (Richet and I count up less than twenty in all the world) — the group who are going for *the* discovery of this century, *viz.,* scientific proof of man's survival — not one single member, I say, is on the whole so well situated as you for the successful pushing of the inquiry. Remember that in spite of our individual inferiority to Darwin, our collective work is far more important than Darwin's : more important in so far as the evolution of a boundless spiritual future is more important than the evolution of a finite terrene past."

In the margin of this letter James wrote : "Myers is the stuff out of which world-renewers are made. What a despot !" His reply indicates that while he could admire Myers's single-minded devotion to the cause he could not emulate it : —

"I always feel guilty in your presence, and am, on the whole, glad that the broad ocean rolls between us for most of the days of the year. . . . I find . . . that *narratives* are a weariness, and I must confess that the *reading* of narratives for which I have no personal responsibility is almost intolerable to me. . . . Of course I wholly

agree with you in regard to the *ultimate* future of the business, and
fame which will be the portion of him' who may succeed in natural-
izing it as a branch of legitimate science.   I think it quite on the
cards that you, with your singular tenacity of purpose, and wide
look at all the intellectual relations of the thing, may live to be the
ultra-Darwin yourself.   Only the facts are *so* discontinuous so far
that possibly all our generation can do may be to get 'em called
'facts.'   I'm a bad fellow to investigate on account of my bad
memory for anecdotes and other disjointed details.   Teaching of
students will have to fill most of my time, I foresee; but of course
my weather eye will remain open upon the occult world." [15]

The vicissitudes of the American Branch of the Society, and
James's responsibilities and discouragements, appear in a letter to
Sidgwick: —

Cambridge, Nov. 8, 1895

My dear Sidgwick, —

I wrote Myers a hurried line two days ago to say that Hodgson
had arrived here without funds, and that the treasury of the branch
was empty.   I wrote Myers in the early summer that the estimated
deficit for 1895 would be $1000. . . .   I can advance money for
pressing needs.   The circular for a "fund" will be issued after the
Piper *Proceedings* appears.   I myself hope little or nothing from
it — but miracles sometimes happen and the only thing is to try.   I
still believe that you will have to decide finally whether to stop the
branch here or contribute at least $1000 a year.   I fear the Eusapia [16]
business may prove a blow to our prosperity for a while, even though
Hodgson's withers are unwrung thereby.   It has been a bad blow
to my own faith in expertness and the effects of education in these
matters, to see Lodge and Myers so precipitate in publication, not to
say conclusion.   You, as usual, have saved yourself by holding your
tongue, and nobody, not even I, knows what you thought, and I have
understood all along that Mrs. Sidgwick was in doubt.   The worst
of it is that the rabble that now catch up the laugh would have been
the first to be deceived had they seen the phenomena. . . .   I shall
try to get out some remarks that may serve as a presidential address,
and have them in your hands early in January.   This is a somewhat

---

[15] *L.W J.,* I, 305–6.   In 1895, when James announced his intention of lecturing
in Colorado, Myers wrote, "O my friend, let us labour onwards in the narrow path!
Even in far Colorado there must be tasks for the pious soul to do."
[16] Eusapia Palladino; *cf.* below, 170.

autumnal letter. The November wind rustles the dead leaves, and the springtide is far away!!! If only we could get up here some variation upon Piper! Best regards to you both, from yours always truly

WM. JAMES

How unfailing was the enthusiasm of Frederic Myers, and how difficult it must have been for any friend to fall away so long as *he* was alive, appear from the pair of letters which follow. Myers was at work on the volumes which appeared in 1903 under the title of *Human Personality and Its Survival of Bodily Death.* His mind naturally reverted to the autumn of 1893 when he had visited James in his Cambridge house for the study of Mrs. Piper, that "insipid Prophetess" who played so important a part in the unrolling "drama" of psychical research.

Cambridge, Jan. 19, 1897

Dear Myers, —

It is long since I have written you a word of friendliness. The struggle for existence seems to reduce all of articulation to the mechanical expression of immediate wants. But now that the New Year is beginning, I feel moved to waft toward you a sentimental greeting. How goes on the book? The great book, I mean, on "Subliminal Consciousness"? I can warrant an immense sale for it in this country. Not a week passes that I don't get either a verbal or written inquiry as to what I think of Hudson's *Law of Psychic Phenomena.* That wretched abortion seems to have had the greatest literary success since *Trilby.* It evidently supplies a need which must be supplied in some way, and which your forthcoming book will supply in a worthy way. I am more and more persuaded that times are ripe for you to make a great impression. But publish the volumes separately, tone down your transmundane enthusiasm in the first one, and reserve all lyrical outbursts for the last pages of the second; where they will crash in with full effect, the reader having been unsuspectingly led up from one step to another until at last the full view bursts upon his vision, and he finds that he must take it in. Hodgson's devotion to Mrs. Piper is a real monstrosity of patience. From the neuro-pathological point of view I should say that he was now in the stage of complete systematization of his delusion concerning Phinuit, George & Co.[17] It is now a scaffolding

[17] Among Mrs. Piper's "controls" were "Dr. Phinuit" and "George Pelham."

of interlinked hypotheses, and speaking seriously, there is no doubt but on his ordinary friends he makes this impression. In strict science I imagine the work now being done is the most important that yet has been done by him. But it is fearfully tedious to a mere hearer, and I am much afraid will get few readers careful enough to do justice to all the points it covers. . . .

I am in better accord with my duties this year than for many a year past, have got rid of all practical psychology and am having a seminary in Kant for the first time, which I enjoy. I have just finished correcting the proofs of a little volume of collected essays, which I will send you as soon as it appears to put upon your shelves.[18] You have probably read them all already. I groan constantly at my inability to read much or to remember anything. But what's the use of complaining? Schiller spent the Christmas holidays with us, and I find him a most peculiarly delightful fellow. His philosophy and mine run abreast in an altogether gratifying way to me. Good-bye, old boy. . . . Please give my very best regards to Mrs. Myers, to whom my wife would send hers if she were in the house, and believe me, *cher maître,* always affectionately your disciple and friend,

WM. JAMES

Cambridge [Eng.], Feb. 3, 1897

My dear James, —

All your words are stimulating and delightful: — all your advice is good! I wish that there were more people like you, and that I were one of them! I like to think of you as untired and unworried, and sailing smoothly along the current of your blest Eternity. I also am happy; — too happy, I fear! — in danger of losing strength and fibre among soft affections and prosperities of earth, and a too luxurious and contented hope of heaven. I feel in myself the growth of the characteristic vices of the new era of revelation — a tendency to a quietism without sanctity, and a gnosticism without intellectual effort. As the great deliverance approaches me, I find myself already watching with a sombre exaltation the symptoms of decay, and saying inwardly: —

> But since the longed-for day is nigh,
> And scarce a God could stay us now;

[18] *The Will to Believe and Other Essays.*

till the anticipation takes me prematurely from labour into a land of dreams. . . .

I have had [two] pleasures lately connected with America. One, a delightful time with your brother at Aston Clinton, where in a long walk together I seemed to be allowed somewhat nearer to him than heretofore. Another, the appointment of Lyman Gage, whom I really *loved* when at Chicago, to the Secretaryship of the Treasury. . . . And meantime the great Piper drama unrolls itself, now not without responsive psychical contribution (as Hodgson will tell you) from this side of the Atlantic also; and we hear from the mouths of sucklings, and in broken stammer, the first authentic message from outside the sphere of earthly air. Beneath a strange disguising these are mighty days; remember them well! for we shall be called upon to tell the story long hence in an unimaginable world.

Kindest, warmest remembrances from us both to your wife! I shall not forget her gracious welcome on September 9, 1893, when in the midst of all her fatigue and her settling down after long absence, she accepted as guests not only Richard Hodgson and myself, but also that insipid Prophetess, that tiresome channel of communication between the human and the divine. . . . Yours always,

F. W. H. Myers

During Myers's last illness the two friends were much together. In 1900 they were fellow guests in Richet's château at Carqueiranne in the French Riviera. When Myers died on January 17, 1901, in Rome, James and his wife were staying at the Hotel Primavera with him.[19] After Myers's death James's first thought was to exalt his memory. He regarded Myers's speculations as "fragmentary and conjectural," but "laborious and praiseworthy"; and "knowing how much psychologists as a rule have counted him out from their profession," he felt the more impelled to offer his personal tribute.[20] Thereupon he prepared one of his characteristic memorials, entitled "Frederic Myers' Services to Psychology," in which he both praised

[19] Dr. Axel Munthe, who was also present and describes the scene, says that James sat just outside the door, overwhelmed with grief, but waiting with notebook and pencil to receive the message that Myers had promised to send after his death. *Story of San Michele*, 1931, 371–3. The reader who would like to form his impression of "spirit return" as applied to James himself may read "From William James," in *Unpopular Review*, IV (1915).
[20] *L.W.J.*, II, 141.

Myers and at the same time restated his views of psychology. Myers, he said, was a leader in the new "romantic" school of psychology: "The menagerie and the madhouse, the nursery, the prison, and
the hospital have been made to deliver up their material. The
world of mind is shown as something infinitely more complex than
was suspected; and whatever beauties it may still possess, it has lost
at any rate the beauty of academic neatness."

Myers not only was a representative of this new and freer spirit
in psychology, but created a bold hypothesis, that of a wider subliminal and extra-liminal consciousness, of which "the whole system
of consciousness studied by the classical psychology is only an extract." He had shown great power of generalization in bringing
under this unifying conception a wide range of phenomena, including "unconscious cerebration, dreams, hypnotism, hysteria, inspirations of genius, the willing-game, planchette, crystal-gazing,
hallucinatory voices, clairvoyance, thought-transference, even ghosts
and other facts more doubtful." But while James felt the liveliest
sympathy with this hypothesis, which was so like his own, and with
its author's promiscuous and robust interest in living nature, he was
nevertheless quite aware that the foundations were insecure. As he
remarked, apropos of the posthumous work on *Human Personality
and Its Survival,* "the piles driven into the quicksand are too few
for such a structure." [21]

James never abandoned psychical research. In 1909 he published
the most ambitious of all his investigations in this field, a voluminous report on "Mrs. Piper's Hodgson-Control"; and later in
the same year, and less than a year before his death, he published a
popular article entitled "The Confidences of a 'Psychical Re-
searcher.'" [22] Such, in brief, is the history of James's participation
in physical research. What was his conclusion?

In the first place, it is important to remember that for James this
more or less extra-scientific domain of investigation was continuous
with psychopathology and abnormal psychology. He had seen
phenomena such as hypnotism, hysteria, and multiple personality
removed from the realm of charlatanry and superstition and brought
within the pale of science; and he saw no reason why the phenomena
that were still outlawed should not undergo a like change. In the

[21] *M.S.,* 149, 158, 168–9.
[22] *Proc. of the Soc. for Psychical Research,* XXIII (1909); and *American
Magazine,* Oct. 1909. Richard Hodgson had died in 1905.

late autumn of 1896 he began a course of eight lectures on "Abnormal Mental States" before the Lowell Institute in Boston. The subjects of the lectures were: "Dreams and Hypnotism," "Hysteria," "Automatisms," "Multiple Personality," Demoniacal Possession," "Witchcraft," "Degeneration," and "Genius." These lectures were never written out, but the notes that remain indicate the wealth of their material and the profusion of concrete illustration with which they were made palatable to the audience. He made the following allusion to the field that lay beyond: —

"[I am] at the portal of psychical research, into which I said I would not enter. But I suppose that it would be over-cautious in me, and disappoint some of my hearers if I did not say here frankly what I think of the relations of the cases I have dwelt on to these supernormal cases. I put forth my impression merely as such, and with great diffidence; the only thing I am absolutely sure of, being the extreme complication of the facts.

"Some minds would see a marvel in the simplest hypnosis — others would refuse to admit that there was anything new even if one rose from the dead. They would either deny the apparition, or say you could find a full explanation of it in Foster's [23] *Physiology*. Of these minds one pursues idols of the tribe, another of the cave. Both may be right in respect to a portion of the fact. I myself have no question that the formula of dissociated personality will account for the phenomena I have brought before you. Hypnotism is sleep. Hysteria is obsession, not by demons, but by a fixed idea of the person that has dropt down — Janet's phrase suffices here. But to say that is one thing and to *deny any other range of phenomena* is another. Whether supernormal powers of cognition in certain persons may occur, is a matter to be decided by evidence. If they can occur, it may be that there must be a chink. The hypnotic condition is not *in itself* clairvoyant, but is *more favorable* to the cause of clairvoyance or thought transference than the waking state. So alternate personality, the tendency for the self to break up, may, if there be spirit influences, yield them their opportunity . . . and if there were real demons, they might possess only hysterics. Thus each side may see a portion of the truth."

What he had to say on this subject in the *Principles* is contained in the chapters on "Hypnotism" and on "The Consciousness of

[23] Presumably Sir Michael Foster.

Self." Hypnotism he treats as an acknowledged fact. ¹Here James argues that the explanation by suggestion will not suffice, and defends the Salpêtrière theory of a specific state of trance as necessary to account for the subject's hyper-suggestibility. In connection with "The Consciousness of Self" he discusses dissociation, somnambulism, hysteric anæsthesia and amnesia, multiple and alternating personality, subconsciousness, and trance phenomena. It is in this context that he declares himself persuaded that the mediumistic control may be "different from any *possible* waking self of the person." [24] Here is the breach or "chink" through which such hypotheses as telepathy, clairvoyance, and spiritism may enter. It is thus essential to the understanding of James's interest in psychical research to bear in mind that he regarded it as an extension of abnormal psychology and psychopathology.

There remains the question of James's final verdict on the residual, the "supernormal," phenomena. As compared with the average man he was rather more than less sensitive to the vulgarity and scandal which frequently attended mediumistic and spiritistic "manifestations." He was perfectly aware of the imposture that was commonly practised, and regarded the greater part of the alleged revelations as "rubbish." He was especially disgusted and disillusioned by the séances held with Eusapia Palladino, the Italian medium who visited New York in 1909.[25] Writing the following year to his friend Theodore Flournoy, James said: "Eusapia's visit to America has not been a success from the point of view of investigation. Poor Carrington had to promise her enormous pay, and to raise the money he had to give sittings to every idle rich person who asked for them, hoping to invite some serious experts gratis with the surplus. But the experts became suspicious of him, and six or eight of them raised money elsewhere and [had] some sittings by themselves, which in the end ceased without producing any unanimous results. They disagreed as to methods, and made Eusapia angry, and the whole thing 'fell through.' . . . Eusapia's type of performance is detestable — if it be not fraud simulating reality, it is reality simulating fraud." [26]

Among his friends of the Society James was perpetually ex-

---

[24] *Principles,* I, 396.
[25] Brought by Hereward Carrington. James had become interested in her through Richet when he occupied the latter's château in 1900.
[26] This case brought to a head James's disagreement with Münsterberg over the

pressing not only his weariness of the whole business, but his skepticism. He was especially insistent that the Society should accumulate authentic data and reserve judgment as to their interpretation. Writing to Myers in 1892, he said: "Yours of the 10th received, bristling as usual with 'points' and applications of the spur. This galled jade, however, will not wince. The good years shall devour me, flesh and fell, or ere I write a paper of an expository and historical nature for that Chicago Congress. What we want is *facts*, not popular papers, it seems to me; and until the facts thicken, papers may do more harm than good. 'Professional' opinion won't be conciliated by popular expositions, but only by S. P. R. *Proceedings,* and my feeling is that you and the Sidgwicks might as well save your thunder." [27]

In 1906, when James was at work preparing his report on the "Piper Hodgson-Control," he felt only doubt, which he expressed to Flournoy: "I have undertaken to coördinate a lot of stuff that is now coming out through Mrs. Piper, purporting to be from Hodgson, in order to make a report. There is a great amount of subliminal automatism involved, but I suspect that the residual doubt will always remain as to whether it may not be a very amnesic extract of the real Hodgson trying to communicate. It will be sad indeed if this undecided verdict will be all that I can reach after so many years. *Ars longa,* indeed!"

And yet, in spite of all, James believed. He committed himself quite flatly both in the *Report* and in the "Confidences." It was a belief without proof — the cumulative effect of experiences no one of which was altogether cleared of doubt. "Theoretically" he was, like Sidgwick, no "further" than he had been at the beginning, twenty-five years before.[28] But after long experience, in spite of having become more skilled in the detection of fraud and more apt to suspect it, he "found himself believing" that there was

issue of psychical research. James regarded Münsterberg as representing the closed mind of science, while Münsterberg retaliated with the charge of mysticism. Münsterberg's "exposure" of Eusapia appeared in the *Metropolitan Magazine* for Feb. 1910. Royce derived a certain mischievous joy from the spectacle, and circulated the following verses among his friends: —

> "Eeny, meeny, miney, mo,
> Catch Eusapia by the toe,
> If she hollers that will show
> That James's theories are not so."

[27] Apparently an International Congress was planned, to be held at Chicago.
[28] *M.S.*, 175.

"something in it" — a residuum of supernormal knowledge, a pattern of mentality not admitted by orthodox science; or, if one prefers, a form of "fraud" and "bosh" so voluminous and so characteristic that even under that name it requires an explanation which would violate the categories of established psychology.

Furthermore, James had a hypothesis for which he claimed a "dramatic probability" — an impression of things, left upon his mind by his familiarity with the phenomena. He tended "instinctively to picture the situation as an interaction between slumbering faculties in the automatist's mind and a cosmic environment of *other consciousness* of some sort which is able to work upon them." There is on the subject's side a "will to personate," so that the revelations from his subconscious mind assume the form of a "control" or "possession." Whether there is from without a corresponding "will to communicate," as the spiritists maintain, James hesitated to say. He suggested, following Fechner, that the individual might survive in traces of his action left in the outer world, and that the so-called "spirit" might be a revival of the individual through a systematic excitation of these traces, as memory is revived from an excitation of cerebral traces. This speculation was at best an aid to the imagination. Out of James's experience with psychical research only "one fixed conclusion dogmatically" emerged, namely, that "there is a continuum of cosmic consciousness, against which our individuality builds but accidental fences, and into which our several minds plunge as into a mother-sea or reservoir." [29]

This theory was unverified in any sense that would be acceptable to science. It was unsupported by experiment, and afforded no basis for control or prediction. It left many questions unanswered. But it was the same theory which he had broached in dealing with the topic of immortality, and to this theory he again returned in his final metaphysical and religious conclusions. James accepted it, in short, as a generalization which most nearly satisfied all the manifold requirements of a philosophy, providing both for the facts of experience and for the subjective demands of the moral subject.

[29] *Ibid.*, 196–200, 201–2, 204.

LXII

JAMES AND STUMPF: FROM PSYCHOLOGY TO PHILOSOPHY

ALTHOUGH James never ceased to be a psychologist and was apt to exaggerate the fluctuations of his interest, there was on the whole a veering towards philosophy during the decade of the '90s. This change can best be perceived in a series of letters written mainly to Carl Stumpf. The latter, like Renouvier, Hodgson, Delbœuf, Croom Robertson, James Ward, and Theodore Flournoy, was a philosopher and a psychologist combined. Early in their acquaintance he had written to James: "I consider all the detailed work which I carry on as unimportant in comparison with the great questions which will for all time constitute the heart and soul of philosophy." From Stumpf James could count upon a sympathetic interest in psychology and in philosophy, and in a disposition to forsake the first for the second.

On April 25, 1891, James wrote: "I am perplexed about translations of my book. . . . [It] is so unclassic in form, that I confess it seems not altogether right to inflict the whole of it on a foreign nation with whom my country is at peace. Yet, on the other hand, I can see that the unconventionality and excursiveness of the style may have something to do with making it more readable than most of its rivals. I write with great difficulty, and aim at brevity, hating too many words. Yet although I may succeed with my *sentences* I don't succeed with my pages, of which there are far too many. . . . Alas! I have n't yet had a chance to look into your second volume. But vacation comes in two months, and ere the summer is gone I shall have read every word. Next year, by way of variety, I am to be allowed to teach nothing but psychology, and hope to be able to do some reading on that profoundly unsatisfactory subject." A long and revealing letter followed five months later : —

London, Sept. 21, 1891

My dear Stumpf, —

Do not be too much surprised by this superscription — I am only here for a week, having been suddenly called over by the alarming illness of my only sister. . . . On the ship, coming over, I finished the second volume of your *Tonpsychologie* which one frustration after another has prevented my attacking at all until about three weeks ago. And truly it is not a morsel to be taken up when one's mind is occupied with other things, but a book to be studied with all the liberty of one's attention. You have done a monumental piece of work, which will be a model to all time of the way in which general views and the minute study of details can be combined. My interest in the reading lay more with the general views, for although I know a little more of music than I did when I was with you at Prague I am still an exiled spirit kept outside the walls of that paradise. Of course for you, and for such readers as are truly worthy of you, the culmination of the work will be the æsthetical part, and as the only effects you can there treat will be simple effects, I do not despair, by the time the next volumes are out, of being able to some degree to "catch on" to their significance also. But my powers of *Analyse und Heraushören* [1] will always, I fear, be minimal. The way in which you squeeze the last drops of formulable truth out of the facts is admirable, but of course your strong point is your incorruptible critical clear-headedness. It is certainly not the clear-headedness of a purely and drily logical mind which always seems negative and shallow, but that of a mind whose dissatisfaction with vague and facile formulas proceeds from its own sense of the presence of profounder sources of truth. What a strange thing an intellectual *atmosphere* is! To many of your "popular scientist" readers you must seem displeasingly cold-blooded, but it was a constant delight to me to feel the firm and close-knit *texture* of your thought. It is a strange fact — for your positive and constructive ideas seem to have no great similarity to mine — that I feel you, perhaps more than any other psychologist whom I read today, to be a *gleichgesinnter Mensch* [2] with myself. I am sure that if fate had allowed us to grow up side by side we could have worked out many things together — a thing now probably impossible even if we *were* side by side, on account of the difficulties

[1] Analysis and auditory selection.
[2] Like-minded.

which increasing age brings to the irresponsible interchange of un-matured ideas. Of one thing I am sure: the quality of your book will give it a *permanent* place in the history of psychology.

I am so overwhelmed with the thought of . . . things to do during these few days (I hope in the midst of it all to be able to run over to Paris for twenty-four hours) that I am in no mood for going into details in regard to the book. . . . I confess that what wor-ries me most is the sense of similarity and the metaphysics thereto appertaining, concerning which I have found your previous writ-ings most instructive. It seems to me an almost irresistible *postulate* that resemblance should be analyzable into partial identity. May we be here before one of the antinomies of the infinite, — to be treated no differently from the others?

Your whole doctrine of *Mehrheitslehre*[3] and of existent sensa-tions not discriminated, is at variance with the formulas I have used in my book, and seems to me hard to keep clear of entangle-ment with psychic chemistry, etc. I believe that there will be no satisfactory solution of that whole matter except on some *erkenntnis-theoretische*[4] basis, which will succeed in clearing up the relations between the "state of mind" and its "object." This is an obscure matter about which I have aspirations to write something which shall do away with the contradictions which occur so much on the psychological plane. I mean no ontological theory of knowledge, but an analysis of the way in which we come to treat the phenomenon or datum of experience sometimes as a thing, sometimes as a mental representation of a thing, etc. But this is unintelligible! . . . Cordial greetings to Frau Stumpf. I hope that you both are well. Always yours,

WM. JAMES

P.S. I have n't read your controversy with Wundt yet — I see it has reached the dangerous stage. Poor Wundt! He is only a make-believe strong man in his powers of execution, but his *program* is so noble that I feel kindly towards him, and don't wonder at his having been irritated by the references in your book.

But James was already planning a longer sojourn abroad. He had written to his brother on June 1, 1891: "Next year . . . is a bright year, for we shall take our 'leave of absence' when it is over,

[3] Theory of manifolds.
[4] Epistemological, *i.e.,* relating to theory of knowledge.

and as at present minded, will go abroad, every soul of us. A sweet and peaceful thought. Incessant 'productive activity' needs intervals of reception. 'The heart must pause to breathe, and love itself must rest.'"

This fond anticipation was only partially realized. It was a period of broken and scattered activities, of domestic cares, of social distractions, of indulgence in art and literature, and of philosophical reading and thinking, during which, after a long immersion in psychology, he lifted his head above water and looked around. On March 28, 1892, he started a letter to Hodgson in which he said, "I imagine that all I need is a good solid holiday; and *that* I am about to take by bringing my whole family to the continent." On July 13 he finished the letter in Gryon, Switzerland, as follows: —

"This sheet lay on my table for some days and then it became impossible to finish it — but I brought it with me to Europe as a monument of my intentions, and hurl it now at your head. I am amused as I read the phrase . . . about getting a 'solid holiday' by bringing the 'whole family' to the continent. The wear and tear of continuous exposure to infancy in the narrow quarters with which one has to put up in hotels is something not to be imagined without actual trial. But with the two boys soon to be domiciled in families to learn French, and certain perplexities decided which have harassed my mind, I fancy the solid holiday will soon begin. But I shall not get to England for the Congress.[5] It costs too much, for one thing; and the grassy slopes are too delicious for another. I saw the menagerie, essentially, three summers ago, and though I would fain see some of the English *men* this time, *you* particularly, yet I hold out against the temptation. Besides, I doubt whether I can leave the neighborhood of the 'family' just yet. You write of inviting Pillon — he is the best of men, but of that catlike French domesticity that I doubt whether he would dare to enter a foreign land. They buy their perfection in their own French line by a singular incapacity for everything else. I am glad that *you* will attend the Congress. . . .

"I have fifteen months' furlough on half pay, and *ought* to make a good thing of it. After the stubble of psychology on which I have spent a good deal of my working force for the last ten years

[5] The Second International Congress of Psychology.

I have a sort of longing for *Erkenntnistheorie,* and even cosmology; and the prospect of the possibility of a little unimpeded *reading* next winter is most sweet. We shall probably go to Paris or its immediate neighborhood, and put the boys to school there. *Then,* of course, I will pay a visit to London. I spent ten days in Freiburg, and saw quite intimately Münsterberg whom I heartily rejoice to say that we have secured for Harvard — a charming human being and a genius for psychological work, whether some of his theories be true or false."

Theodore Flournoy, professor of experimental psychology at the University of Geneva, was one of the most intimate friends of William James's later years.[6] The acquaintance began at the International Congress of Physiological Psychology in Paris in 1889. Flournoy, however, had read James before that date and had felt especially drawn to him: "I often have occasion to say, in speaking of you, 'There is a man after my own heart.' " He reviewed the *Principles* with warm approval in the *Journal de Genève,* and the two men afterwards corresponded on their common personal and professional interests.

[Lake Maggiore], Sept. 19, 1892

My dear Flournoy, —

. . . I am *much* obliged to you for the paper by Secrétan,[7] and (unless you deny me the permission) I propose to keep it, and let you get a new one, which you can do more easily than I. . . . I entirely agree that Renouvier's system fails to satisfy, but it seems to me the classical and consistent expression of *one* of the great attitudes, that of insisting on logically intelligible formulas. If one goes beyond, one must abandon the hope of *formulas* altogether, which is what all pious sentimentalists do; and with them M. Secrétan, since he fails to give any articulate substitute for the "Criticism" he finds so unsatisfactory. . . . I have been reading with much interest the articles on the will by Fouillée in the *Revue philosophique* for June and August. There are admirable descriptive pages, though the final philosophy fails to impress me much. . . .

[6] *Cf.* his *La Philosophie de William James,* 1911.
[7] Charles Secrétan (1815–95), influenced by Schelling, was the most distinguished Swiss philosopher of the second half of the nineteenth century. The article referred to is probably "Le Néo-criticisme," later published in *Essais de philosophie et de littérature,* 1896. This letter is reprinted in part from *L.W.J.,* II, 323–6.

You and I are strangely contrasted as regards our professorial responsibilities, you are becoming entangled in laboratory research and demonstration just as I am getting emancipated. As regards *demonstrations* I think you will not find much difficulty in concocting a program of classical observations on the senses, etc., for students to verify; it worked much more easily at Harvard than I supposed it would when we applied it to the whole class, and it improved the spirit of the work very much. As regards *research,* I advise you not to take that duty too conscientiously, if you find that ideas and projects do not abound. As long as man is working at anything, he must give up other things at which he might be working, and the best thing he can work at is usually the thing he does most spontaneously. You philosophize, according to your own account, more spontaneously than you work in the laboratory. So do I, and I always felt that the occupation of philosophizing was with me a valid excuse for neglecting laboratory work, since there is not time for both. Your work as a philosopher will be more *irreplaceable* than what results you might get in the laboratory out of the same number of hours. . . . Always affectionately yours,

WM. JAMES

From Lake Maggiore the family went to Florence, whence James made a short trip to Padua and Venice before settling down for the winter. The following paragraphs are from letters to his wife and brother: —

Padua, Nov. 2, 1892

I have rarely in my life passed a day of greater contentment. . . . The contentment does n't come from your absence (far from it, for I 've done little else but wish that you were by my side), but from the extraordinary satisfaction which this place yields to the age. It soothes it as stillness soothes the ear or lukewarm water the skin. I surrender to Italy, and I should think that a painter would almost go out of his skin to wander about from town to town. One wants to paint everything that one sees in a place like this — as a *town* Florence can't hold a candle to it. She has her galleries, her palaces and her bridges, but the rest is incumbrance, here it is the entire town that speaks to one in the most charming unpretending way. . . . I understand Giotto's eminence now. It started tht tears in my eyes to see the way the little old fellow had gone to work with such joyousness and spirit . . . and it is an honor to human nature that so many people feel under his quaintness that he is a *moral* painter.

Venice, Nov. 6 [1892]

I left Florence on Wednesday for Padova to transact some psychical research at the instigation of the fell Myers.   The psychical research amounted to but little, the main thing being that I spent an evening with six Italians and found that I practically understood every word they said so long as they spoke directly to me or gave narrative, which was gratifying.   But dear little Padova!   How can I ever sufficiently express my gratitude and delight?   I kept going over and over it for all three days as long as daylight lasted as if I could n't possibly drink it in enough. . . .   I spent four hours in the Academy yesterday, and went into some churches, and am presently about to start for the Ducal palace.   I find the Academy less splendid than I had remembered it, and altogether get a sort of impression that the Venetian pictures wear less well than those of the Florentine sort.   Giovanni Bellini and the earlier ones are the most immortal — the trail of the world, flesh, devil, chic, and conscious ability lying too thick over the others.   Moreover too luscious!   No matter, they *possess* one's eyes.   The odd thing about it is that although my appetite to see them is ravenous, I have practically *no* recollection of how they look an hour after my back is turned.   No visual images — a nice equipment for a would-be connoisseur!   However, the great thing is to be able to use one's eyes at all. . . .   I really enjoy this furiously.

James was less boastful of his linguistic accomplishments in the following paragraph written soon after his return to Florence: "Our Italian is of the bottom most-infernal quality; and the pathetic resignation of the natives to the like of it, which they get from all us foreigners, is a touching sight.   Centuries of servitude have bred in them a spirit very different from that noble mirth and scorn with which the free Anglo-Saxon meets the attacks of outsiders on his mother tongue!"

Letters to Stumpf afford a clear view both of James's varied activities during the decade of the '90s, and of the persistence of his psychological interests despite a growing preoccupation with philosophy: —

Florence, Dec. 20, 1892

My dear Stumpf, —

I really cannot remember now whether I ever wrote to you since leaving Luzern. . . . I can only assure you that there is no one in Europe of whom I have *thought* more often . . . and there is no one the loss of whose neighborhood I have so much regretted in coming to Italy. . . . I sometimes think that you may turn up in Florence before I do in Munich. If you did we could re-visit the monuments together and soften Philosophy with Art. Does n't the idea tempt you at all?

We are settled here in a furnished apartment, with an ultra-conscientious and cheap man-cook, and save that our rooms are uncomfortably cold, the winter is passing pleasantly away. We could devise no entirely satisfactory school-plan for our boys, so, tired of the problem, we said, "Old age has its rights as well as youth, let 's make sure of a light and entertaining winter for our-selves, which shall be a real holiday, and go to Florence." We have not regretted it. The city is both small and *important,* a very rare combination. You go from one end of it to another in an ordinary afternoon walk, and yet you feel as if in a *Weltstadt.* The streets are endlessly entertaining and the art-treasures divine. The boys are at a school which, though English, seems really good, and are kept hard at work; and I, after months of absolute intel-lectual lethargy am beginning to wake up again, and feel as if there might be some powers of production left in me yet. . . .

I hear excellent news of the way in which Münsterberg is taking hold of the work at Harvard, and he in turn seems delighted with the place. I don't know whether you have yet looked into the fourth volume of his *Beiträge,* but they seem to me charming, and I don't see what fault his worst enemy can find there. He *is* rash, oversweeping and shallow in his generalizations; — but who is not, in psychology? A psychologist's merit seems to me, in the *present* condition of that science, to consist much less in the *definitiveness* of his conclusions than in his suggestiveness and fertility. Crea-tures like G. E. Müller are up so high on horseback on their mathe-matical and logical criticism of experimental methods that they

make experimentation simply impossible. They are sterile themselves (I confess, however, that I have n't read Müller's *Theorie
der Muskelcontraktion*), and almost the entire upshot of the work
of the exact school of psycho-physic experiment, including especially
the work of Wundt's laboratory, tends to show that *no* experimentation can be exact enough to be of any value. The result will be to
abandon experimentation altogether, as a false and fruitless direction of activity!

I am now in the midst of Wundt's *System der Philosophie* which
interests me a good deal, though he irritates me more and more by
his strange mania for appearing *smooth*. He oils his transitions
and *soaps* all his conclusions on to you by plausible *a priori* introductions that make you sick. It is the subtlest sort of mental dishonesty, born rather in the sphere of an abominably false æsthetic ideal
than in that of will, but it is turning him fast into a humbug. Moreover, this everlasting search for *unoccupied ground* on which he
may plant a new theory!

I went last week to Padua to a Galileo tercentenary at the University. I represented Harvard, and it was great fun. . . . I
hope that you, Mrs. Stumpf, and the children are all well, and that
the year's work is going bravely. How comes on Vol. III of
the *Tonpsychologie?* We both send to both of you our heartiest
Christmas wishes, and beg you to believe me your sincere and faithful friend,

WM. JAMES

Meggen, April 24 [1893]

My dear Stumpf, —

I ought to have written to you some time since to tell you of our
decisions, which were still inchoate when I was at Munich. If
you could have seen the confusion in which my last six weeks have
been spent, however, you would excuse any derelictions on my part.
Incessant sociability in Florence, pushed to such an extreme that one
pair of young American friends came and *had a baby!!!* in our apartment, there being no other convenient place for the event to take
place in. Fortunately my wife came away three days ago, and
left them in possession — "mother and child well." I have also
done a little traveling in Italy, and for a week past have been in
Switzerland putting my second boy in a family at Vevey, seeing

some sick cousins at Geneva, and finding this paradise for the rest of the family here. When it became evident that Harry could not be fitted for the Gymnasium in April, we concluded that the whole family had better return together in the summer to America. It is the *comfortable* decision, and we have been happy in it ever since. I believe that from the point of view of education, the best possible thing for American boys would be to pass the years from *six to ten* in German schools. At Harry's age, however, the advantages of only one single year are doubtful. . . .

We are going to spend most of the summer in England, and have taken the road through Switzerland rather than through Tyrol for economical reasons. This means that my wife, and possibly I, will not have the chance of meeting you and Mrs. Stumpf this summer, which we both regret — but of regrets life seems to be made up! We are in this heavenly spot, with the trees all in bloom about us, and shall stay a fortnight at least, before going farther. . . . I am glad to have said good-bye to the sweet rottenness of Italy, of which I shall always preserve the tenderest memories, but in which I shall always feel a foreigner. The ugly Swiss faces, costume and speech seem to me delicious, primeval, pure, and full of human soundness and moral good. And the air! the air! there can be nothing like it in the world. I was hardly able to read a line in the past six weeks in Italy; but in the last few days in Switzerland I have read 250 pages of Paulsen's *Einleitung in die Philosophie.* I don't know on what account you spoke so disparagingly of it in Munich, but our tone about a book always depends on what we expect of it. To me it seems a wonderful book for the human sympathy that is in it, for the fairness and candor that it breathes, and for its admirable artistic composition. It will probably be a classic translated into all languages, a means of enlarging the narrowness of mind of many scientific materialists, and an adequate expression of the naturalistic pantheism that is in the air today. It is the work of a thoroughly cultivated man; and although I am not satisfied with the standpoint that satisfies Paulsen, I have learned much both morally and intellectually from the pages which I have read, and expect to learn much more from those that remain. It seems to me that if there ever is a *true* philosophy it must be susceptible of an expression as popular and untechnical as this. The man is a *good* man, through and through!

I am sorry that those days, those not easily to be forgotten days, that I spent in dear old Munich, are likely to be the last ones of our seeing each other for a long time to come. My boy has enjoyed much his visits to your house, and I thank you for inviting him. My love to you both. . . . Yours ever,

WM. JAMES

Stumpf's reply revealed his feelings towards James and touched a responsive chord. It was written from Munich on May 17: "You have been in Europe a whole year — a year to which I have been looking forward for ten years — and out of this year only a few hours were spared for our reunion; during which, to make matters worse, your thoughts and emotions were preoccupied with pressing matters. Naturally I cannot blame you for this, but it makes me very sad; and so much the sadder, to speak frankly, because I have the vague feeling that your friendship for me has lost some of its liveliness in the course of the years — that you, perhaps, have not found in it what you at first promised yourself, or that something in me has struck you as estranging or uncongenial. Perhaps my opposition to Wundt? We have both become more serious, much more serious, in these ten years; life is so short, too, and the world in which we live so small. But only so much the more firmly would I hold to those whom I heartily esteem and love." [8]

Meggen, May 26, 1893

My dear Stumpf, —

Your letter of the 17th, just received, touches me very much, and confirms me in my habitual belief that your heart is as strong and active an organ as your head. But how *could* I have conveyed to you the impression that my feeling of personal affection for you, and satisfaction in being able to count you as a friend, had grown less in the past ten years? Older I am indeed, and probably much duller, but I speak sincerely when I say that during my last visit I felt more intimately and closely the charm of your character and our intellectual kinship than when we were together ten years ago in Prague. That was relatively superficial. I only wish it were possible for my wife to repeat to you all the things I said about

[8] For the German text of this and other letters from Stumpf, *cf.* below, Appendix VIII.

the impression I had of you, when I got back to Florence.   I was,
as I now see, a little too afraid, when in Munich, of encroaching on
your time and appealing to your hospitality.   My own experience of
the visits of English people to Cambridge who expect entertainment
when I am hard pressed with work, has perhaps made me too sensitive in that regard towards others.   You were busy and I was
relatively idle.   I did n't wish to make it possible that you should
think me a bore.   But with *you,* I see now that the thought of such
possibilities ought to have been absent from my mind.   Over and
above that, however, most men's friendships are too inarticulate.
As our Emerson says: "There is more kindness than is ever spoken."
And in the beautiful verses of an old friend and neighbor of mine,

> Thought is deeper than all speech,
> Feeling deeper than all thought.
> Heart to heart can never teach
> What unto itself was taught. . . .

> We are spirits clad in veils,
> Soul with soul can never meet;
> We are columns left alone,
> Of a temple once complete.[9] . . .

Alas!   I find that I have forgotten the words, which sadly express
the "dialectic contradictoriness" that is to be found in finite individuality.   Will a "higher synthesis" ever come to give relief?
Your letter, meanwhile, shall be one of my most cherished possessions, and makes me feel freer with you than ever before.   I feel
free now to express my amusement at your suggestion that the tone
of your polemics with Wundt should have made my love turn cold.
I confess that that sentence gave me a good long laugh, and makes
me laugh again now!   Wundt seems to be "getting himself generally disliked."   In this pension we have had a Herr Carl Hauptmann, author of a book called *Die Metaphysik in der Physiologie*[10]
(which you perhaps know) and his friend Professor Avenarius,
both with their wives.   Hauptmann is a charming modest man,
and his wife an angel, and Avenarius a very good natured creature

[9] Quoted (inaccurately) from "Gnosis" by Christopher P. Cranch, *Poems,*
1844.
[10] Hauptmann was a private scholar.   His work referred to is *Die Metaphysik
in der modernen Physiologie,* 1893.   Richard Avenarius was author of *Kritik der
reinen Erfahrung.*

(superficially, at any rate), but they both seem to have Wundt "on the brain" and can hardly talk for five minutes about any subject without some groaning reference to him. Victor Hugo says of Bonaparte that he fell because *"il gênait Dieu."* Is that to be also Wundt's fate? He certainly begins to encroach on God's omniscience. If only he could show a spark of creative genius *dabei!* As for Hauptmann, the book does not seem to me as good as the man. I have not yet read a page of Avenarius's books, but have an *a priori* distrust of all attempts at making philosophy systematically exact just now. The frequency with which a man loves to use the words *streng wissenschaftlich* [11] is beginning to be for me a measure of the shallowness of his sense of the truth. Altogether, the less we have to say about *Strenge* the better, I think, in the present condition of our speculations. That is one reason for which I enjoy Paulsen's book. There is no pretense of *Strenge* about it; and yet the most pedantically written works have no *more* solid *stuff* to give you than he gives in this absolutely popular and unpretending way. To me the stuff is theoretically quite unsatisfying, but it is so fundamental and uncomplicated that it admits of addition, possibly without much alteration; and I cannot but esteem it a great gain for the truth to have such deep matters treated so absolutely without technical apparatus. It makes one realize the alternatives in their natural nakedness, unveiled by what I must call the humbug which a would-be-*streng wissenschaftlich* treatment generally disguises them in.

On the matter of resemblance, there is a reply from me to Bradley in the April *Mind*. . . . I agree with you that a multitude of qualitatively identical coexistent elements of consciousness is an unintelligible conception; but still, *if* one chooses to adopt it (as Spencer and Taine, *e.g.*, adopt it) it affords a refuge from the infinite regress of composition, it seems to me.

The dinner bell rings, and I must stop. My wife has been saying all the morning that we *must* come over to the Munich "Congress" in 1895, we two without the children! *Perhaps* the Gods will provide the means! but I have no very strong hopes. Meanwhile I enclose a sheet from her, written yesterday, and am with warmest regards to you all, your faithful friend,

Wm. James

[11] Strictly scientific.

Cambridge, Sept. 12, 1893

My dear Stumpf, —

Let me announce to you that we have arrived safely at home after an admirably smooth voyage, and that after fifteen months of *pensions* and hotels the comforts of our house are most enjoyable. It has been a costly, but on the whole a profitable year to all, especially to the children who have been made much more perceptive and intelligent than they would have been without all the travel they have had.

I also have a business matter to propound to you. The *American Journal of Psychology* edited by G. Stanley Hall has always left much to be desired. Its field is very narrow and much of its work ill-done. During the past year Professors Baldwin, Cattell and Münsterberg have been negotiating with Hall to see if some arrangement might not be made for improving the *Journal,* but everything has failed; and the result is that a new journal is to be started, under the title (probably) of *The Psychological Review* with Baldwin and Cattell as chief editors, and all the professors of psychology in the American universities (except Jastrow and Hall) as coöperating editors. . . . I cannot but hope that the new *Review* will prove good. . . . The Editorial Committee now request you (through my hand) to permit your name to be placed on the title page as coöperating editor. Binet has already allowed his name to be so used for France. I feel quite sure that the *character* of the *Review* will be such that you need have no mistrust about your name being connected with it. On the other hand, what the editors particularly desire is that your name figuring on the title should be a guarantee to other Germans of your own confidence in the capacity of the other editors. We do not expect that you should take your *duties* very seriously, but should be exceedingly grateful for anything you may be able to send. . . . I will undertake either myself to translate or to guarantee a good translation of any manuscript, long or short, which you may send for publication. Pray think favorably of this. We all, including Münsterberg, think that there is no German psychologist whose name would so honor and adorn the new journal as yours. And I earnestly hope that you may yield to our desire. I hope that you are having a good vacation in the Tyrol. Nothing agrees with *me* as well as the mountains. With affectionate regards to all your family I am as ever, yours faithfully,

WM. JAMES

Cambridge, Jan. 24, 1894

My dear Stumpf, —

. . . First of all, let me congratulate you on the Berlin professorship,[12] for which you were, of course, the most suitable candidate, and your appointment to which made Baldwin, Cattell, Münsterberg and myself all very glad. I only feared that Berlin might prove a rasping, fatiguing and *ungemüthlich* place to live in, and that you might be buying honor, if you accepted the appointment at the price of peace of soul. But Münsterberg tells me that they have exempted you from responsibility about a laboratory; and that is a great point gained. I may say that I myself enjoy inward peace and a good professorial conscience for the first time, now that Münsterberg has taken charge of the entire experimental field. Needless to say that if I had lived a thousand years I should not have done what he has been doing in the past two years here. He is a wonderful organizer, methodical to the last degree, our laboratory being a picture to look upon since he has taken hold; and he is, moreover, a most high-minded and lovable human being, so that I can only be thankful for the inspiration that led me to tempt him away from Freiburg. My only fear now is that his stay with us may be short, for although he likes America so far, and perhaps sees it in too ideal a light, his ambition, of course, would be better fulfilled by a German professorship. But the future will decide. We have a three weeks' holiday from lecturing at present, and with characteristic energy he has gone to California in order to visit the educational institutions there, and the principal colleges on the way. Some 13,000 kilometers of railroad in three weeks seems to me a bit too much! . . .

I found it very hard to begin teaching again. I had been rather melancholy all summer, but it grew acute with my lectures. *I shrank to nothing, psychology shrank to nothing,* — etc. It passed away, however, and now not a trace of it is left. But it has taught

[12] Stumpf was elected in 1894 to the professorship of philosophy and directorship of the psychological laboratory at the University of Berlin, where he remained until his retirement in 1921.

me the lesson that fifteen months is too long a vacation for a man like me to take. Teaching is such an artificial discipline that one loses the habit of it almost immediately, and seems to forget all that one ever knew. At present I have "Cosmology" and "Mental Pathology" (taken in a wide sense), three and two hours a week throughout the year, and "Psychology" (three hours a week) until the middle of March.

Our new *Psychological Review,* of which your name adorns the cover, promises well. I think that Baldwin and Cattell will be good editors, and if you will only occasionally write a few pages, or give them timely advice about German books or news, the thing will succeed. It is a bad time to start such an enterprise, for the country is groaning under the worst financial depression it has ever known. With the passage of the bill reducing the tariff, and with the beginning of the spring, business will probably revive. Meanwhile everyone is trying to save money, and the poor are in a sad condition of distress. Fortunately the winter so far has been a mild one. Our University has even had to dismiss instructors; but our *own* income is, so far, not reduced, although we are trying to spend as little as possible in order to repair the frightful ravages left by our European year.

Ladd is just out with a new and heavy-looking *Psychology.*[13] From all the new psychologies either published or about to appear, there *ought* to be *some* sedimentary deposit of truth, — I devoutly hope that it may be clearly discernible by all! To me the sort of thing that Pierre Janet has just done in his *État mental des hystériques* seems to outweigh in importance all the "exact" laboratory measurements put together. For of what laboratory experiments made with brass instruments can one say that they have opened an entirely new chapter in human nature and led to a new method of relieving human suffering? Not even of the ophthalmoscope can *all* that be said. We had Helmholtz here, by the bye, in the autumn. A fine looking old fellow, but with formidable powers of holding his tongue, and answering you by a friendly inclination of the head. His wife was a *femme du monde,* however, and fully made up for his lack of conversation. Another countryman of yours, Hagen from Königsberg, for many years Professor of Entomology

---

[13] *Psychology: Descriptive and Explanatory.*

at Harvard, died here this winter after a sad illness of nearly three years. Also a *herrlicher Mensch*.

I think of the strong good air, the horizontal spaces, the noble architecture both German and Greek, of Munich — the beer, the pictures, the whole civilization there — as an *el Dorado* to which I wish I could return. I should think that you and Mrs. Stumpf would hate to leave so good a dwelling place. I fear I never may return. One should not be a cosmopolitan — one's soul becomes "disaggregated," as Janet would say. Parts of it remain in different places, and the whole of it is nowhere. One's native land seems foreign. It is not a wholly good thing, and I think I suffer from it. But it is a danger that menaces not *you*. Please take the heartiest wishes from both of us for your continued prosperity in 1894. . . . I am as ever, your most affectionate

WM. JAMES

James was urged to attend the International Congress of Psychology held in Munich in the summer of 1896, but he felt obliged to decline. Stumpf was president of the Congress.

Cambridge, Dec. 18, 1895

My dear Stumpf, —

It did my eyes good to see your handwriting once more, and I was gladder still to hear the pleasant words in which you urge me not to be absent from Munich next summer.

I wish for many reasons I could go. Such things keep one from fossilizing and prolong one's possibilities of "adaptation." Nevertheless I have little hope. I ruined myself financially by my last excursion *en famille* to Europe, and nothing but the need of foreign travel for my health could justify so speedy a repetition of the process. Moreover, it unsettles my Americanism (that tender plant) to go too often abroad, and that must be weighed against the intellectual and social advantages of the Congress. It is no light matter to feel foreign in one's native land. I am just beginning to feel American again, when this temptation comes! I should like to see you, and a very few others. I should like to see Munich, and then spend a month in Tyrol, but I don't think I can or shall, and *my name must on no account be announced*. I am heavily worked this year, but doing nothing original. As I grow older I get impatient (and incompetent) of details and turn to broad abstractions. I wish to get relieved of psychology as soon as possible, but am trying at present to keep Münsterberg's nest warm for him ere his return, which we all pray for; for he proved an efficient, and in fact an invaluable man here. There are many valuable attributes, even in a professor, besides infallibility, and taking one man with another, Münsterberg is about as infallible as anyone who takes as broad a field. I am glad Dr. Schumann [14] has charge of most of your laboratory operations. There are two classes of men, and the regular routine of the laboratory can only be well carried on by those trained from youth *ad hoc*. I also reëcho your groans about Berlin. Your going there was a case of obedience to the army maxim of accepting promotion "though it lead to hell." And meanwhile you are publishing hardly at all. Does the *Aesthetik* come on? . . . Always truly yours,

WM. JAMES

Stumpf took the above letter to mean that James had avoided Europe to keep his superior American ways untainted; and that he resented the fact that Münsterberg had not been properly appreciated in Germany. He explained at length the peculiar circumstances which had made it impossible at that time to call Münsterberg as *Privatdozent* to the University of Berlin.

Cambridge, Nov. 24–28, 1896

My dear Stumpf, —

. . . Your account of the Congress was highly interesting, and the most complete account I had received except from Sidgwick. . . . Many of the leaflets which were sent to me were full of interest, and I confess that the quantity of material astonished me. As for myself, I have given up trying to keep abreast of the progress of experimental psychology. Communications succeed each other so abundantly, and what they contain is usually so much a matter of hair-splitting, that the experimental ones make no impression upon my memory at all; though this, I know, is, in part, a symptom of senile degeneration. I feel (though) as if I had bought the right to say good-bye to psychology for the present, and turn myself to more speculative directions. For instance, as long as I have been

[14] Dr. Friedrich Schumann was a lecturer in psychology in the University of Berlin and assistant in the Institute of Experimental Psychology.

teaching, I have never had an opportunity until this year to teach Kant, and you may imagine that I enjoy it very much.   Next year I have some hopes of a course in Hegel, and who knows if I live long enough whether I may not get out a system of metaphysics before you have finished your *Tonpsychologie?*   I should think that from the hardness and confusion of Berlin, you would look back with occasional regrets to the relative simplicity of Munich. I found Munich so sympathetic, that if three years hence I take another sabbatical year, I imagine that I shall spend the winter in that place. . . .

I am really amused at what you say of my *"Verstimmung über die deutschen Psychologen."* [15]   I did not know that I had expressed any, and can't now remember the passage in my letter to which you refer.   It must have been some general pessimism.   But I am still more amused that you should ascribe it to Münsterberg's influence. My fear of losing my Americanism if I went abroad again was entirely complimentary to your side of the Atlantic.   Civilization is so much more advanced in many ways with you, and the American so quickly catches the European tone, that when he comes back he finds his own country in many ways foreign and displeasing, and it takes him a long time to resume his old, simple-minded relations with it.   I have suffered from this discord many times, particularly after my last return home; I am now on thoroughly good terms with my native land, and dread very much to throw myself out of tune again.   Like all ideal things, harmony of this kind must be worked for and bought by certain renunciations.   We have many ideal things here, and the best thing an American can do is to stay at home as much as possible, and try to increase them.   Therefore, I am making an effort not to go to Europe again until 1900, when my regular leave of absence from the University falls due. Münsterberg, so far from appearing "disgruntled," at not being able to go to Berlin, explained to me the situation as you have just explained it, agreeing entirely with its reasonableness. . . .

I read the [presidential] address [16] with extreme satisfaction. I think it is high time that someone in such an authoritative position should raise a voice against the excessively shallow dogmatism of the parallelists, who simply affirm the truth of a conception that

[15] Disaffection towards German psychologists.
[16] *Dritter Internationaler Congress für Psychologie,* 1897.

they conceive as neat and pretty. You did the business in a perfectly masterly way. I especially admired the breadth of the treatment and the skill with which you avoided entering into any minute or secondary considerations. I can't help thinking that the day of the cruder parallelisms, as the last word of scientific philosophy, is passed. That thistle needs only to be firmly grasped to show its feebleness! . . . I am putting a book through the press now, a collection of essays, of which I will send you a copy as soon as it appears.[17] . . . My wife sends her best regards, and I am, as always, dear Stumpf, yours affectionately,

WM. JAMES

The later correspondence with Stumpf throws light on the decline of James's psychological interests, and at the same time serves as an introduction to the successive chapters of his philosophical productivity. Intellectual coöperation between the two scholars inevitably declined, but the warmth of their personal friendship was undiminished, and as James moved on to ethics, religion, and metaphysics he tried with characteristic ardor to carry Stumpf with him.

Bad-Nauheim, Aug. 30, 1899

My dear Stumpf, —

It will doubtless surprise you to get a letter from me with the above dating — but here I am and have been here for a month. . . . Last June I went to my beloved Adirondack hills, and got lost in the woods one day, converting what was to have been a walk of a few hours into a thirteen hours' scramble, etc. This produced a bad dilatation with severe chest-symptoms, and for that I am now under treatment. . . . Meanwhile my doctor expresses himself as satisfied with my progress as revealed to the stethoscope. We are all mortal! and the trees don't grow into the sky. . . . In any case my mountain climbing days (such as they were) are over. To continue on the chapter of the ego, I have leave of absence from work for the next academic year, and have also an appointment to give the "Gifford Lectures" for this year and next, at the University of Edinburgh. There are two courses of ten lectures each on "Natural Religion," public, and very well paid, so that it is both an honor and a profit to receive the appointment. But I am terribly

---

[17] *The Will to Believe*, etc., 1897.

unprepared. . . . I may possibly be at the Paris "Congress." [18] Is it likely that you shall be there? I detest congresses, but the American Psychological Association appointed me as delegate, and I did n't like to say no.

It seems impossible injustice that Dreyfus should not be acquitted. France will have turned a very bad corner, and everything will probably go well. If not, no one knows what will happen! Does Berlin better agree with you? or is the life there still too *aufreibend?* [19] Have you a new book, or some more *Tonpsychologie* in preparation? I find myself growing less psychological — I have nowadays a perfect horror of experimental psychology, for which fortunately Münsterberg is exclusively responsible — and more metaphysical. I have certain glimmerings of new ideas, but they are very hard to make clear, and nothing will ever come of them, probably. The writing and printing of these Gifford Lectures will fully occupy me for the next three years. Write and give me good news of yourself, of Mrs. Stumpf and of all the family! Always faithfully yours,

WM. JAMES

Wengen, Sept. 8, 1899

Dear Friend, —

Your letter certainly surprised me very much, and however glad I would otherwise be over a stay of yours in Germany, this sojourn grieves me immeasurably. I have confidence in the baths of Nauheim, which have benefited many of my acquaintances, and I hope that you will come out strengthened. But these Gifford Lectures! . . . Would you not do better at this important moment, so critical for the remaining years of your life, to subordinate everything to the recovery of your physical strength? I am prompted by true friendship and concern to ask these questions.

In all probability I shall not get to Paris in 1900. I am even less fitted for congresses than you are, and for my part would rather see Paris without any congress. Besides, the tumult of a world fair — even the thought of it makes me nervous! As for the French, I must confess, alas! that this nation — naturally, excepting certain individuals — commands less and less respect. Even if the truth about Dreyfus does come to light, is it not immeasurably

[18] The Fourth International Congress of Psychology took place at Paris in Aug. 1900. Münsterberg apparently took James's place.
[19] Upsetting.

sad that such obstacles should be put in its way? . . . Could one show more clearly that the truth is not wanted? In that respect, my dear James, you and I are better men, since we do at least desire the truth. Whether we find it, is another question. And this I say with special reference to a disagreement which has arisen between us — without your being aware of it, apparently. It seems that you have not yet received the last article which I sent you, "Über den Begriff der Gemütsbewegung." [20] Since I there took a position in opposition to your theory, I originally intended to send an accompanying letter; but I did not get around to it before my departure, and consoled myself with the thought that you, more than any living philosopher, would be able to combine personal friendship and scientific opposition. . . .

Between [Franz] Brentano and me things have taken a curious turn. I thought that I was rather in agreement with him in respect of the emotions, and now I receive a letter from him, seven pages long, in which he definitely declares himself for your views and against mine. A rather humiliating effect of my arguments! If he ever gets to the point of publishing his works you will have in him a not inconsiderable support for your doctrine. . . . But what is truth? Of one thing I am certain, that in case I become convinced of the opposite it will cost me no inner struggle to make a frank confession and retract all former statements, *sans phrase,* following your noble example in other cases. With heartiest greetings, your devoted

STUMPF

Bad-Nauheim, Sept. 10, 1899

My dear Stumpf, —

Your letter, so full of the truest sympathy and friendship, gave both me and my wife acute pleasure. Affectionate recognition by men like you is surely to be counted among the prizes of life. Friendships of personal intimacy grow up in youth, through propinquity. A friendship like ours, based on higher mental affinities and sympathy of character, is the fruit of years and of work. I greatly repent now that I did n't write to you earlier, for I have been here now for just six weeks. . . . In case I have to stay here

---

[20] Concerning the Conception of Emotion: *Zeitschrift für Psychologie und Physiologie der Sinnesorgane,* XXI (1899). The article contains a criticism of the James-Lange theory.

longer, I think we must put off the meeting till next summer. I shall unconditionally return here next April and very likely once more next August, and a *Zusammenkunft* with plenty of time to arrange it will be easily brought about. And who knows? We may both yield to the temptations of the Devil and find ourselves in Paris, in spite of all our good resolutions!

No! I have not received your essay on the emotions, and shall be too delighted to read it, whatever its conclusions may be. I think the question is introspectively an exceedingly difficult one to solve, as soon as one takes the less excited *Stimmungen*[21] as the object of investigation. Everyone seems to admit that the feeling is from the body so far as there is violent affect. . . . Have you received a little volume of mine, called *Talks to Teachers,* etc. — very popular? The only thing I care to have you read in it is the last two articles, especially the one before the last.[22]

I fear I am ceasing to be a psychologist, and becoming exclusively a moralist and metaphysician. I have surrendered all psychological teaching to Münsterberg and his assistant, and the thought of psycho-physical experimentation, and altogether of brass-instrument and algebraic-formula psychology fills me with horror. All my future activity will probably be metaphysical — that is, if I have any future activity, which I sometimes doubt. The Gifford Lectures (which have to result in two volumes of 300 pages each) are a fine opportunity were I only able to meet it. Don't be afraid, I shall not risk my life; the conditions are fortunately elastic enough to permit of postponement in case my health should imperatively require it. Are you not also growing cold towards the details of psychology, and turning more and more towards those widest views of life which seem the proper occupation of one's latter years?

What dreadful news is this from Rennes![23] It *did* seem as if the French Republic were about to turn successfully round the most dangerous corner in her history; and that after the crisis a new evolution might slowly begin. It will do so yet, I believe. *Les intellectuels* have not become militant in France for nothing. But meanwhile all the difficulties are a hundred-fold increased by this slip into the hell-ward direction. This verdict proves that the spirit

[21] Attitudes.
[22] "On a Certain Blindness in Human Beings" and "What Makes a Life Significant?"
[23] Capt. Dreyfus had the day before been recondemned.

of caste is the strongest force in society.   I am glad I belong to a
republic. . . .   Affectionately yours,

WM. JAMES

In December 1899, Stumpf wrote announcing that James had
been nominated as a corresponding member of the Prussian Academy of Science.   James promptly accepted: "Your letter was a
most agreeable surprise to me this morning, both as a reminder of
you, and for its interesting content. . . .   My health has run down
very much since I wrote you last September! in fact I am in a deplorable condition of imbecility. . . .   I have given up my Edinburgh lectures, and shall probably not be able to do any more teaching at Harvard.   If I can live long enough to get a couple of things
written I shall only be too thankful.   Under these circumstances
the compliment of the Berlin Academy is unusually valuable to me.
If I never write anything more, it may be my children's chief title
to hereditary respectability, to be able to point to their father as a
correspondent of the Academy of Sciences of Berlin!" [24]

Carqueiranne, March 17, 1900

My dear Friend, —
   It is a long time since I have given you any account of myself,
and in the meantime I have received your address on the *Entwicke-
lungsgedanke* [25] and an invitation from Professor Auwers [26] to be
present at the festival of the Academy.   As that takes place in a
few days, I feel a certain enlivening of the Berlin department of my
soul, and it seems natural to take my pen and write a little to you.
First, as regards my own condition, I have good news to report.
We left England the 10th of January, and came straight down to
Costebelle, near Hyères.   After a week at the hotel we got a cook
and chambermaid and took possession of Charles Richet's empty
château, where we have been very comfortable ever since. . . .   I
am now *much* better . . . and am, as you see, able to do each day
a little writing.   I have finished *one* (!) lecture for Edinburgh, and
hope to begin the second tomorrow. . . .   I still am unable to walk
except for a *very* short distance once daily; but I am mending fast,

[24] From Rye, Jan. 2, 1900.
[25] Thoughts on evolution.
[26] Prof. Arthur Auwers, director of the Observatory of Potsdam, and permanent
secretary of the Prussian Academy.

and despair has given way to hope and new aggressive projects upon life. . . .

I read your [Address] with great interest. . . . You have a Roman severity of style, in all this kind of work, which makes you very impressive — monumental as it were — and one can make use of you for "texts." I got much *Anregung* from this address. But I won't tire myself with commenting upon it now, except to call your attention to the logical possibility that out of a world of *complete* chance at the origin, during infinite time systems of coherent order were sure to have developed, of which our world may be one; all the chance facts disconnected and ununified with that world having long since disappeared, either from existence, or from observation from that world's point of view. In my second course of Gifford Lectures I am going to defend *radical* pluralism and tychism, and I hope to make a convert of you.

You don't know how pleased I feel at this honor from Berlin. The world at large will never know that it is really an honor from Professor Carl Stumpf! I suppose that Herr Auwers . . . will send me the official programs, etc., but perhaps you will send me some newspaper with a report. It is a *tremendous* disappointment to me not to be able to go in person — not my only disappointment this year! . . . With best regards . . . to both of you, I am, always faithfully yours,

WM. JAMES

James continued to manifest much pleasure in his election to the Prussian Academy. He learned from Stumpf that Wundt and Heinze [27] were the only philosophers who had been honored at the same time with himself, though many had been proposed.

Montreux, June 8, 1900

My dear Stumpf, —

Your card reached me duly at Nauheim a fortnight ago. I should probably have written to you earlier, but the baths, although four doctors conspired in recommending me to go at them again, threw me once more into such a formidable state of nervous prostration that all letter writing had to stop and the only thing left to me for a couple of weeks seemed to be the contemplation of the

[27] Max Heinze, retired professor of philosophy and editor of Ueberweg's *Grundriss der Geschichte der Philosophie.*

vanity of human wishes. . . . Of course philosophy is at a stand-still and so are my Edinburgh lectures. But I don't despair of attacking the latter very slowly after a few weeks. One so quickly adapts himself to new conditions that my active life of only a year ago seems almost as if it were a fiction. . . .

I was much interested to learn from you that these recent three elections are the only three "correspondents" yet named in Philosophy. I don't exactly understand why the Academy should preserve so many places vacant. Is the world so unworthy? To tell the unvarnished truth, it seems to me that if any one living foreign philosopher be entitled to such an honor, it is the veteran Charles Renouvier. He is a *chef d'école* in the complete sense of the term (as very few philosophers nowadays are), although he holds no academic place and hardly ever leaves his country house near Avignon; his technical equipment and erudition are immense; the moral and civic aspects both of his system and of his life are elevated and influential, and now at the age of eighty his activity as a writer is undiminished. It seems to me there have been few such careers and that the Academy would honor itself in honoring him, whilst at the same time it would be a graceful international act. You see I am already taking seriously my privileges and duties as "Corresponding Member"! If you wish me to nominate an English Correspondent I am also ready to do that! Cuba and the Philippine Islands I will hold in reserve.

How are you feeling about all this war and international savagery?[28] Yet the world does advance, but oh! how slowly. I am afraid of what the French people may do during the *Katzenjammer* which will inevitably succeed the Exhibition. Keep well, dear Stumpf. . . . With best regards to all of you, in which my wife joins, I am, ever affectionately yours,

WM. JAMES

Bad-Nauheim, July 10, 1901

My dear Stumpf, —

It is high time that I should once more send you *de mes nouvelles*. You see where I am. . . . I have come back more as a routine precaution than anything. . . . My wife and I spent the winter very happily in Rome. If you ever gain a winter of holiday or take *ein*

[28] South African War, the Boxer Rebellion, etc. The Paris "Exposition Universelle" was opened in May and closed in Oct. 1900.

Urlaub, I recommend that place. Its climate is excellent, and its intellectual climate wonderfully tranquillizing and yet nourishing. In April we went to my brother's in England, and in May I went with some trembling to give my lectures on the "Varieties of Religious Experience" at Edinburgh. They turned out a perfect success, both as regards the size and interest of the audience, and as regards their effect on my health. They made me tougher, and of course the effect on my *morale* of being able to earn my bread again is unspeakably good. Next year I give ten more lectures on the same subject, which completes my appointment there, and I hope to publish the two courses together, soon after. The matter is treated psychologically and descriptively, and illustrated by as many documents as possible, and will doubtless be a popular book — too biological for the religious, too religious for the biologists, I fear! . . . We sail for home on the 31st of August, and shall feel like kissing the walls of our own house, etc. Two years is too long a time away. I shall only keep up a half nominal connection with my university duties, giving but one hour a week of instruction ("Psychology of Religion") next year, until I find out whether or not my aorta will permit me to give more. . . .

Do you feel as sad as I do, at the savagery of "empire" that is pouring itself over the world? The good ancient soul of my own native country is, I fear, dead beyond resurrection. Man is essentially an adventurous and warlike animal, and one might as well preach against the intercourse of the sexes as against national aggrandizement by piracy. I hope to get good news of you. With affectionate regards both to yourself and Mrs. Stumpf. . . . I am, ever faithfully yours,

WM. JAMES

Bad-Nauheim, Aug. 6, 1901

My dear Stumpf, —

My fate is at last decided. We leave here on Saturday next in all probability, and take the after-cure in the Vosges, starting from Strassburg. . . . As your destination is Munich, Bayreuth and Tyrol, I begin to fear that we must put off the date of our meeting to some watering place in "another and a better world." . . . I confess that after my next spring's course of Edinburgh lectures (which finishes my engagement there) I should like to return to

America with the certainty that I might finish my days there and never be obliged to leave it again.   These absences from one's native country break up the adhesions of the rootlets of one's being in the soil, and I have made too many absences, first and last.   I should like to stay at home, and see my children grow up successfully and establish themselves in life; and *write*, myself, in a way which, if possible, might slightly help to influence American ideals. But successfully to do so one must live very close to them.   Otherwise one's voice sounds foreign.   There are splendid things about America, but the old human leaven of national adventure and aggrandizement is threatening to substitute its brute instinctive power for our historic and hereditary principles, and liberal Americans will have a hard fight to keep the country on the happier and more beneficent traditional track.   Münsterberg is to publish next year in German a book on the Americans, which will be brilliant certainly, and contain much true observation.   I shall be very curious to see it.   I think Münsterberg has by various articles of his done a good deal towards helping the two nations towards mutual understanding.

After my lectures on religious experience are published, I hope to write a more systematic attempt at a *Weltanschauung* on a radical empiricist and pluralist basis, seeking to destroy the notion of a monistic absolute of any sort.   Of course I shall fail; but I can say a few things differently from others, and I am sure that in the general organization of philosophical literature some far more radical expression than pluralism has yet received will be useful, even though in the end pluralism were not the true philosophy.   Just try *seriously* to conceive the world as a finite collection of many original facts, — I think you will lose some of your prejudices in favor of an absolute.   But few people ever try seriously enough. Good-bye! my dear friend.   That you may remain active and well and as productive of truth as ever, is my wish.   My wife and I both send our love to you and yours.   I will write to you again within the year.   Affectionately,

                                                                WM. JAMES

                                                        Cambridge, Jan. 1, 1904

My dear Stumpf, —

It is years, it seems to me, since a word has passed between us in either direction.   I sent you my *Varieties of Religious Experience* when it appeared, but did not get from you any acknowledgment of reception.[29]   I hope you got it all the same.   I have heard of you occasionally from passing students, but I have read nothing from your pen for two or three years, and I feel that if I let the year 1904 begin without anything in the way of an electric current pass- ing, the way from your heart to mine is in danger of becoming obliterated by the growth of distance and time.

For the last two years I have been regaining my health which is now, although not exactly vigorous, satisfactory enough.   At the same time I am letting go of much of my academic work.   As one grows older one is appealed to in so many different ways to write articles, make speeches and the like, that it becomes a terrible corvée,[30] and I am thinking very seriously of withdrawing entirely from teaching and spending the rest of my life more or less in the country and as a free man.   I ought to be writing a big book on metaphysics; but with my abridged working power and the interrup- tions I speak of, it does not get ahead at all.

I don't know whether you saw Münsterberg this summer, who seems to have had great success in enlisting German lecturers for his great scheme at the St. Louis Exhibition.   I confess I felt re- lieved at not seeing your name.   It will be frightfully hot and fa- tiguing, and I personally take no interest either in the form or the content of the whole enterprise.   But Münsterberg has the most extraordinary power of schematization and program-making and so far has succeeded, as he always does succeed, in a remarkable way. For his sake I trust that the thing will not be a failure.   It will give me, I hope, an opportunity of seeing at our own little country place some of the foreigners who come here, among whom Bergson of Paris, Ostwald, Windelband and Lipps are perhaps the more excit- ing to my imagination.   I wish that you were coming merely as a visitor, although I confess that America does not offer the agré- ments to a tourist which almost any part of Europe offers.   I sup- pose that by this time you feel like one of the aboriginal Ber- liners; but life in a capital, unless a man is made of iron and India rubber (and you are not!), is too aufreibend for anyone whose main interest is contemplation and the pursuit of truth.   I wish you would write to me soon after receiving this and tell me

[29] The further exchange of letters on the *Varieties* is printed below, 342–6.
[30] Enforced labor.

just how it is with yourself and all your family. . . . Yours ever affectionately,

WM. JAMES

James's feeling that he and Stumpf were drifting apart owing to their lack of contact was reiterated in his infrequent letters. There was also a philosophical difference, to which Stumpf testifies in the following reply: —

Berlin, May 8, 1907

Dear Friend, —

At last I am getting around to answering your good card of January which has lain continually in my desk. Yes, it is true "we lead a life of non-communication," and it is no less a matter of regret to me than it is to you. But how can it be otherwise so long as this Berlin machine holds me bound? You give up your teaching in order to live wholly for science. I have not yet been able to make this resolve. . . .

Unfortunately, dear and respected friend, a growing divergence seems to have arisen between our views. I cannot reconcile myself to pragmatism and humanism. The positivistic theory of knowledge, in which you approach Mach, seems to me to be impossible and unfruitful. In the two articles which you will receive at about the same time with the present letter, I attempt to prove this.[31] You will characterize my standpoint as one which you yourself have abandoned; I agree with the earlier more than I do with the present James. But the man himself is withal just as close to me as ever, and I hope that you feel the same towards me. Have I sent you also the *Gefühlsempfindungen?*[32] This would be much more to your taste than the two Academy articles. Remember us cordially to all, and please do not forget your devoted

STUMPF

Cambridge, May 20, 1907

My dear Stumpf, —

You have enriched me in three days with two *Abhandlungen* . . . and with your most welcome letter of the 8th. . . . I cannot attack

[31] "Erscheinungen und psychische Funktionen" and "Zur Eintheilung der Wissenschaften," *Abhandlungen der Königlich Preussichen Akademie der Wissenschaften,* 1906, Abh. IV, V.
[32] *Zeitschrift für Psychologie,* XLIV (1907).

the *Abhandlungen* immediately, as I should like to, but I shall devour them in a month's time, and let you know of my reaction. They both look *exciting;* and it rejoices me that you too are working more and more into metaphysics, which is the only study worthy of Man! Music and metaphysics! You will receive from me in a week or two the sole product of *my* muse this winter, namely, a little popular book called *Pragmatism.* In spite of what you say so gravely and even sorrowfully in this letter, I shall be surprised if, when I have read your quarto pages, and you my much smaller ones, we seem to each other as far apart in our thinking as you now suppose us to be. What staggers me in the recent controversial literature of pragmatism and humanism is the colossal amount of mutual *misunderstanding* that can exist in men brought up in the same language and with almost identical educations. It is hard to believe! Language is the most imperfect and expensive means yet discovered for communicating thought.

I see, dear Stumpf, from the way in which you speak of Berlin, that you are one of the victims of life in a modern "great capital." *Simplification* is the *summum bonum* for a certain type of man, to which I, and (I fancy) you belong. Great capitals make it impossible. I, having resigned my professorship, shall be able from next autumn onwards to simplify *my* life far more than heretofore, and the thought of being free from all those "adaptations" to other human beings, unintelligible and unassimilable as most of them are, fills me with extraordinary elation. Alone with God! with truth! what a prospect!!! Join me!! . . . Warmest regards *von Haus zu Haus.* Yours affectionately,

WM. JAMES

In 1909 Stumpf acknowledged *The Pluralistic Universe* with a hope of agreement: "It stimulated me . . . very considerably, and I intend now to occupy myself more closely with your Bergson. Regarding the 'last things' I believe my position is closer to yours than in regard to the pragmatic concept of truth, although I do not fail to see some force in this latter. . . . Could n't we see each other again some time? There is such a meagre intercourse with the pen, and I am a bad letter writer."

The last of this series of letters, written by James in the closing years of his life, reveals the persistence of his interest in psychology and the indefatigable eagerness of his mind: "I thank you heartily for your new book. I shall be glad to read some of the essays a second time. We seem to be growing asunder in our pursuits; the various finite minds, buried under the infinite mountain of problems to follow and books to be read, cannot follow the same directions, and get out of sight of one another's operations. I believe that if you and I were near each other, and could see each other frequently, we should work very well together, but at present we inhabit somewhat different fields of view. The thing of yours that has most interested me of late is the *Erscheinungen und psychische Funktionen*,[33] wherein you differ from things that I have printed in a way to make me take notice and revise. I have got very far away from psychology in my recent work, but I hope to get back again and to pick at the dropped threads."

[33] *Cf.* above, 202. The author distinguishes sharply between "phenomena" and "relations" on the one hand, and on the other hand the psychic "functions" or acts which are the proper subject matter of psychology.

PART V

ETHICS AND RELIGION

LXIII

THE WILL TO BELIEVE

ALTHOUGH during the decade between 1890 and 1900 James turned
with relief from psychology to philosophy, there were rhythms
within rhythms, and moments when philosophy was even more
repugnant than psychology. A letter to Howison written on June
29, 1895, contained a postscript apropos of the latter's philosophy:[1]
"The pluralistic idealism is very pregnant — of course it needs development in order to be assented to or denied, especially the un-
changeable aspect as distinguished from the phenomenal one of the
finite spirits. I vow I am getting a little discouraged about metaphysics. The triviality *in abstracto,* and also the sublimity, and the
urgency, *in concreto."*

Howison took this to be James's indirect and kindly way of
criticizing his "pluralistic idealism." James replied as follows: —

Cambridge, July 17, 1895

My dear Howison, —

. . . How you *have* misunderstood the application of my word
"trivial" as being discriminatively applied to your pluralistic idealism! Quite the reverse, — if there be a philosophy that I believe
in, it 's that. The word came out of one who is unfit to be a philosopher because at bottom he hates philosophy, especially at the beginning of a vacation, with the fragrance of the spruces and sweet
ferns all soaking him through with the conviction that it is better
to *be* than to define your being. I am a victim of neurasthenia,
and of the sense of hollowness and unreality that goes with it. And
philosophic literature *will* often seem to me the hollowest thing.
My word "trivial" was a general reflection exhaling from this mood,
vile indeed in a supposed professor. When it will end with me I
do not know. I wish I could give it all up. But perhaps it is a

---

[1] Howison's views were published in 1897, in reply to Royce, in *The Conception
of God,* and in 1901 in *The Limits of Evolution.*

grand climacteric and will pass away. At present I am philosophizing as little as possible in order to do it the better next year, if
I can do it at all. And I envy you your stalwart and steadfast
enthusiasm and faith. Always devotedly yours,

WM. JAMES

In this very summer James delivered the famous address on
"The Will to Believe" [2] which was to give the name to his volume
of essays, and a few months later he delivered the scarcely less
famous essay entitled "Is Life Worth Living?"

We have already traced the fitful prolongation through this period of the psychological interest which had so preoccupied and
taxed him during the previous decade. We have seen that the
middle '90s were a time of browsing, of travel, and of popular
lectures; the compass needle pointing, though with many oscillations, in the direction of the deeper problems of philosophy. These
problems presented themselves as problems of life rather than of theory. Such an antithesis can in the case of James have only a very
limited meaning, but nevertheless as we pass from the '90s to the
next and last decade of James's life we shall witness a growing
scientific and professional zeal. In the '90s James was often moved
to reaffirm and amplify the faith of his youth. Release from the
pressure and discipline imposed by the writing of the *Principles*
rendered him again vulnerable to brooding melancholy; and he
again felt the need of a saving gospel. At the same time there was
a great expansion of his human sympathies and of his political and
social activities. This was the decade of the Spanish War and of
the Dreyfus case, both of which deeply stirred his moral emotions.
His activities in psychical research revived his old sympathy with
religious mysticism, and gave him a new hope of justifying it. All
of these reasons conspired to make the decade from 1890 to 1900,
or more precisely from 1892 to 1902, James's period of reform and
evangelism.[3]

The volume entitled *The Will to Believe,* published in 1897, was
made up of articles and addresses which had been written at inter-

[2] At a "Summer School of Ethics" in Plymouth, Mass., sponsored by Felix
Adler. The address was repeated at Yale in April 1896.
[3] James said of one of the essays in *The Will to Believe* that scientific rigor
had been sacrificed to "effectiveness in composition" (above, I, 620). The style of
the essays is governed not so much by literary taste as by a desire both to express and
to induce *conviction.*

vals from 1879 to 1896. Its doctrines go back to his early examination of "the motives of philosophizing," and are pervaded
throughout by the influence of Renouvier — "cribbed from Renouvier," James once wrote to Peirce.[4] They fall naturally into three
groups, those, namely, which deal with fideism, with pluralism, and
with individualism. Fideism touches theory of knowledge, pluralism metaphysics, and individualism ethics, but in all three cases the
personal and practical accent predominates.

In the older treatment of fideism James had both brought to
light and also justified the motives which govern human philosophizing. Such revisions and additions as appear in *The Will to
Believe* differ only in breathing a more confident and downright
air. The writer is sure enough of his gospel to be willing to preach
it and convert the unbeliever. The "motives of philosophizing,"
as we have seen, are "theoretical" and "practical." The intellect
fashions theories in accordance with its innate taste for clarity
and unity, and reaches some sort of compromise between them.
The data presumably lend themselves to either emphasis. Fideism,
however, has to do with the extra-theoretical motives which express
man's "active powers" and carry belief beyond the data of experience. There are two specific senses of it, both of which have
already appeared in the early beginnings of James's thought: the
fideism which goes beyond all possible facts, and thus supplements
a necessary agnosticism; and the fideism which supplements an accidental ignorance.

There is a necessary agnosticism owing to the ultimate intractability of data. It is a part of James's empiricism to hold that after
the intellect has done all that it can the world remains a brute
fact — baffling to reason. But if reason cannot be satisfied, it can
at least be silenced — by the representation of a world which satisfies the will. This is fideism in the first sense.

The second mode of fideism is that which compensates for the
accidental insufficiency of evidence. Thought occurs in the mid-
section of the reflex arc. Action, stimulated from without, is on
its way back to the periphery. It tarries at the centre for counsel,
but it cannot tarry long, lest the occasion pass and the opportunity
be lost. The action proceeds to its consummation before the de-

---

[4] The influence of S. Hodgson is also apparent, as, *e.g.*, in the contention that all
thinking is inspired by a voluntary faith in truth. (*Cf. W.B.*, 10, note; and Hodgson's *Time and Space*, 1865, 310, read and marked by James about 1875.)

liberations at the centre have exhausted the pros and cons and arrived at an incontrovertible conclusion. To act more or less ignorantly (as judged by the strictest canons) is thus a law of life. Extreme intellectual scrupulosity paralyzes action and annuls the very function of the intellect itself, which is to facilitate and fructify action. If one is to believe at all one must believe with some degree of "vital heat," having the courage to make the plunge despite the imperfect visibility.

But if belief thus requires a "will to believe," it is of the utmost importance to examine the *canons* by which such a will should be guided. It is this critique of faith with which James was primarily concerned in the leading essay of the volume of 1897. When is it proper that the will should determine belief? James gives two answers. First, when abstinence from belief or suspension of judgment means losing the chance of truth, or is equivalent to a disbelief which is no better proved by sensible fact than the positive and more fruitful belief. Second, when the effect of conviction is to bring about the very facts which will verify it. This holds of all beliefs regarding the future when that future depends in some measure on the will. Belief in this case is confidence, and confidence often justifies *itself*. "The thought becomes literally father to the fact, as the wish was father to the thought." [5] But there is a deeper and more comprehensive logic of faith which asserts the priority of will over intellect. It is the practical rather than the theoretical motive that has the last word, for the question between them is a practical question. This is the gist of his *argumentum ad hominem* against the Huxleys and the Cliffords — the censors of faith, who are unaware of their own faithful "aspiration to be scientific." [6] Indeed, to be an *earnest* positivist is self-contradictory. For so heroic an abstinence from belief could only be justified in a world which assigned a place of eminence to the moral will.

All of this is a plea for conviction and confidence as opposed to skepticism and doubt. That this plea expressed the ardor of James's personal temperament, he himself would have been the last to deny. There is an indubitable connection, also, with James's upbringing. Having committed no excesses of credulity in his

[5] *W.B.*, 103.
[6] *Principles*, II, 640.

youth, there was nothing to repent in his maturity or old age. There was nothing to drive him by reaction into intellectual asceticism. But while he craved belief, he indulged that craving with restraint and moderation. He urged the case for belief with a certain vehemence, because he was addressing himself to "academic audiences"[7] who lived in the unnatural atmosphere of scientific pursuits. He was also addressing himself. He was not credulous, but *suffered from incredulity*. He was deeply concerned with the need of belief and with the right to believe, but made no considerable use of that right. He was not a dogmatist. He was essentially a critic of the intellect, for he doubted that much could be proved.[8] He claimed less than either the rationalist or the mystic. As compared with the latter, he considered himself an exponent of intellectual sobriety. "There may be an *Infinite One*," he wrote to a reviewer, "but the apprehension of it must be by mystical channels, and it seems to me that if we are to pursue intellectual methods we must take our stand by moralism and pluralism and real vicissitude. But I feel the antinomy, the crux, the doubt, and respect the mystic so long as he does not articulately philosophize."

The same spirit of unpretentious empiricism prompted James to chill the ardor of friends who took his fideism too seriously: "As for faith, don't treat it as a technical word. It simply means the kind of belief a person may have in a doubtful case — and may carry a sense of 'heat in your throat,' readytobackoutness, or a sort of passionate refusal to give up, or anything between; and is the same state, when applied to some practical affair of your own, or to a theological creed."[9]

Assuming that belief may be dictated by the preferences of our practical nature, what do these preferences dictate? The answer is to be found in "pluralism." This doctrine, in turn, has to be interpreted in the light of its moving appeal. It is not a mere doctrine of plurality, but plurality in its bearing on human feelings and resolves. Thus pluralism means a finite God, who evokes a passionate allegiance because he is in some measure hampered

---

[7] *W.B.*, x.

[8] *Cf., e.g., Varieties*, 455, where "in sad sincerity" he concludes that the deliverances of religion are indemonstrable.

[9] In the same letter (to Mrs. Glendower Evans, July 29, 1897) he wrote: "Let me thank you for all the pleasant things you say of the book — only *don't* take it too damned serious." For other letters to Mrs. Evans, *cf.* "William James and His Wife," *Atlantic*, CXLIV (1929).

by circumstances, and dependent on the aid of others; or because, the evil of the world being external to him, he may be loved without reserve.[10]   Freedom is here approached from the same angle. James was, no doubt, an indeterminist, accepting the doctrine of chance as a way of providing for alternative possibilities under identical conditions; but in the brilliant essay on "The Dilemma of Determinism" which forms a part of the present volume, he is concerned not so much to reject determinism in general as to reject a *monistic* determinism, in which the world, being all of one piece, must be approved or condemned as a unit.   The moral will is essentially partisan — recognizing and promoting what ought to be, in a context of things that were better not, and which it seeks with all its might to make as though they had never been.

But the moral will needs a pluralistic environment for another reason: not only because good must be free from any compromise with evil, but also because one moral will must not be compromised by another.   The very goodness of life is inseparable from its aspect of privacy.   The world is "a sort of republican banquet . . . where all the qualities of being respect one another's personal sacredness, yet sit at the common table of space and time." [11]   Pluralism is thus united with individualism to constitute a metaphysics commonly known as "ethical idealism."

There may be said to be two motives in James's pluralism, representing the two deeper motives of his empiricism.   The experimental and voluntaristic motive inclined him to affirm the world as a society of moral wills, while the experiential motive inclined him to picture it as an irreducible variety of qualitative differences. *The Will to Believe* is dominated by the first of these motives, while his later pluralism is dominated by the second.   James's unwillingness to surrender himself wholly to the first affords a key to his philosophical method.   Ethical idealism was too formalistic, too much tainted with the apriorism of Kant.   James's philosophical conscience was never satisfied with the affirmation of principles, even ethical principles.   To affirm the freedom and priority of the individual, or the plurality and immortality of souls, or the finitude and moral purity of God, was much — but it was not enough.

---

[10] Goethe once told Jacobi that "as a poet he was a polytheist, as a student of nature a pantheist, and as a moral being a monotheist."   (Quoted by W. Fliedner, *Goethe und Christentum*, 1930, 10.)

[11] *W.B.*, 270.

Something very deep in the constitution of James's mind impelled him to search out the *meanings* of these principles, and to translate them into terms of actual experience.

The first or voluntaristic phase of James's pluralism gave him a sense of kinship with Davidson, Howison, Bowne, Lutoslawski, and with the English writers who contributed to the volume entitled *Personal Idealism*. The encounter with Davidson has already been recorded, and relations with Bowne and with Personal Idealism belong to later chapters. Two representatives of the group remain — the old friend Howison, and a new friend Lutoslawski.

Wincenty Lutoslawski, Platonic scholar, linguist, reformer, exponent of Yoga, Polish patriot, and latterly professor at Wilno, came to America in 1893 to attend the Congress of Religions at the Chicago World's Fair and took the occasion to visit James in Cambridge. This year marked the beginning of a correspondence, personal and philosophical, which continued until 1909. Its volume may be gauged by the fact that the records show over seventy items from James, whereas (according to James's estimate) the letters written in reply were in the ratio of eight sheets to one post card! James took a warm interest in his friend's career and personal affairs. He entertained him at his home, endeavored with varying success to obtain lectureships and other appointments for him in America,[12] read and promoted his writings. He applauded both his individualistic-pluralistic philosophy and his heroic moralism. "A perfect passion of friendship, love, brotherhood and loyalty sings through his pages." [13] But Lutoslawski's zeal was a little too much — even for James. "These Slavs," he said, "seem to be the great radical livers-out of their theories"; [14] besides which, the theories themselves lost plausibility through their extravagance.

On January 10, 1898, James wrote, in reply to Lutoslawski's comments on *The Will to Believe:* "I will just say that I thoroughly believe in suicide for certain situations; that I believe in a finite God, if in any; that I use 'reflex action' in the broadest possible way, including postponed reactions; that I still doubt the mental influence of the parents on their offspring, etc.; and that I am considerable less of a 'rationalist' or gnostic than you. But we are

[12] Lutoslawski lectured at Harvard in Oct. 1907.
[13] Lutoslawski's *World of Souls,* 1924, James's Preface, 8.
[14] *L.W.J.,* II, 103.

both pluralists, and *par le temps qui court* that ought to be a bond of union." In the same year Lutoslawski published his thesis, submitted for the Doctor's degree at Helsingfors, and entitled *Über die Grundvoraussetzungen und Consequenzen der individualistischen Weltanschauung.* This and the *Seelenmacht,*[15] published in the following year, excited James's enthusiastic admiration. Of the former he wrote to an inquirer that he "owed much" to it, while to the author he said: "If I live to write my metaphysical treatise I may possibly translate and print it as an appendix to the book." In 1899, Lutoslawski visited James at Nauheim and "read to him in improvised English translation many masterpieces of Polish literature." James's description of this visit gives a summary both of the philosophy and of the philosopher: —

"We have been having a visit from an extraordinary Pole named Lutoslawski, 36 years old, author of philosophical writings in seven different languages . . . and knower of several more, handsome, and to the last degree genial. He has a singular philosophy — the philosophy of friendship. He takes in dead seriousness what most people admit, but only half-believe, *viz.,* that we are *Souls* (Zoolss, he pronounces it), that souls are immortal, and agents of the world's destinies, and that the chief concern of a soul is to get ahead by the help of other souls with whom it can establish confidential relations. . . . He is a *wunderlicher Mensch:* abstractly his scheme is divine, but there is something on which I can't yet just lay my defining finger that makes one feel that there is some need of the corrective and critical and arresting judgment in his manner of carrying it out."[16]

It was in this same year, 1899, that James wrote a Preface for an English edition of Lutoslawski's *Seelenmacht* which did not find a publisher until many years after James's death. It finally appeared in 1924, under the title of *The World of Souls,* and with the Preface which had been prepared twenty-five years before. In a paper on "Eleutherisme"[17] presented to the Academy of Cracow in 1900, Lutoslawski paid his respects to James and Renouvier: —

[15] *Fundamental Presuppositions and Consequences of the Individualistic View of the World;* and *The Soul's Power.*
[16] *L.W.J.,* II, 103.
[17] From the Greek word ἐλεύθερος (free). "Eleutheria" was the ideal society, and its members "Eleutherians."

"The great majority of philosophers have always recognized the unity of the universe as a real fact prior to its common origin. The author considers this unity as an ideal which we approach indefinitely without ever attaining. In this he finds himself peculiarly in agreement with the recent writings of the eminent American thinker William James, who has reached his pluralism by an entirely different route. This conception of the universe, as forming a plurality of free substances or monads acting directly on one another, is a still more radical pluralism than that of M. Renouvier, who, in his *Nouvelle Monadologie,* accepts almost completely the doctrine of preëstablished harmony.[18]

James read this paper in manuscript and returned it with marginal notes and an accompanying letter : —

Bad-Nauheim, May 16, 1900

Dear Lutoslawski, —

. . . I read the sketch of the Eleutherians with great interest. . . . My general complaint is that you express the thing as if there were *so much* freedom. I believe it to exist, but to have very narrow play. However, your description as an *ideal* makes the scheme all the more beautiful. I have in detail found nothing *à redire* except what this general objection would cover. . . . As regards your reference to Renouvier, I believe him to have become a little less pluralistic in the recent book which you quote, but I *can't* believe that he admits the details of the harmony in which nature's "laws" consist to be *all* preëstablished, so pray modify that passage slightly. . . . Now, *leb'wohl,* and *go slow!* . . . Affectionately,

WM. JAMES

P.S. You do too much honor to my name in .mentioning it, for although you represent my opinions rightly, I have hardly ever expressed them in print as yet — and fear that, as things are going with me, I never shall.

Another letter of the same year reveals James's effort to induce restraint and theoretical detachment : "I hope your holiday did you good and that you are moderating the transports of your revolution-

[18] Translated from the French, *Bulletin de l'Académie des Sciences de Cracovie,* May 1900, 170.

ary ardor on your return. Division of labor is the great thing. You belong to the theoretic life as few men do, and you do not belong to the practical sphere. Work out the abstract theory of freedom, and let the close-lipped, iron-willed, hard-hearted men of affairs who exist for that purpose, translate it into action. Thus shall it best succeed! . . . I mean, if I ever live to work again, to translate and republish your Helsingfors thesis."

In 1904 James declined to ally himself actively with Lutoslawski's political activities: "Your Polish University in London interests me very much, but when you ask me to become its honorary president I have to say no. . . . My name is already identified with so many unorthodox things, such as psychical research, anti-imperialism, mind-cure medicine, etc., that if I were now to begin to figure as a Polish patriot the only place left for me in public esteem here would be the lunatic asylum! For your sake I would do a great deal, but you can see yourself how little reality the mixing of my name with your patriotic purposes would have. . . . Believe me, my dear friend, your wondering but always affectionate Wm. James." And then, as though overtaken with doubts — "I consider you, now and always, a man in charge of his own destiny, who *may* be wiser than ordinary prudential maxims would make him."

James sent his own publications to Lutoslawski, and the latter approved — with misgivings which were precisely the reverse of James's. Thus, for example, in 1904: "I want to thank you for three pamphlets on 'Pure Experience.' I think all you say is quite right — but I have the impression that your *Self,* whose pure experience you relate, disappears amidst its own productions; and I see not the slightest allusion to your eternal, substantial existence as a Being, a thing, a reality, a source of power. Thus I am afraid that you would deprive me of the certainty I enjoy that I shall meet you, yourself, your own soul, in a better life amidst new experiences. . . . I am struggling with many difficulties, inside my body and outside even more — but after all I believe I am progressing somewhere towards my ultimate aims. God bless you!"

The later correspondence between Lutoslawski and James dealt largely with the system of Hatha Yoga, which the former had learned to practise and to which he was eager to convert James, but which the latter accepted not as a cult but as experimental evidence of the existence of "deeper levels of will-power than are habitually used." He printed extracts from Lutoslawski's letters in his "Energies of Men," and hailed him as one of those who are privileged to tap reservoirs of life inaccessible to the "healthy philistine." [19]

The early correspondence between James and Howison touched on doctrines which were later incorporated in *The Will to Believe,* and the appearance of this volume seems to have received no special comment. But in 1901 Howison published his *Limits of Evolution and Other Essays,* in which, though a pluralist, he dissented from the radical pluralism of James: "I confess . . . that I am almost ashamed to record, here and elsewhere in these pages, this dissent from Professor James, — a writer for whose genius I feel so warm an admiration, and with whom, on the great main matter, pluralism, I am in such hearty accord. Only, I cannot consent to put our common metaphysics at such risk and disadvantage, in comparison with monism, as a confessed and despairing ultimate irrationalism involves." [20] The writer then proceeded to defend a cosmology in accord with "the ideal of reason"; and in later chapters, after discussing James's view of immortality, expounded "The Harmony of Determinism and Freedom" as a substitute for the latter's "Dilemma of Determinism." Having read the book and a letter which followed it, James acknowledged them both from the scene of his Gifford Lectures: —

Edinburgh, June 17, 1901

Dear Howison, —

Your letter of May 29th came yesterday. I should in any case be writing to you about this time to tell you of the successful completion of my lectures, and to acknowledge reception of your *Limits of Evolution.* It grieves me sore that you give so poor an account of your health, *und zwar* without telling me what the matter is. I hope it may be "nerves" which is greatly what's the matter with me, and that the summer's vacation may give you a different view of yourself, though we are mortal men and these betterments are after all only reprieves, pending the final execution of our sentence. Happy you, with such a confident assurance of more life beyond! I find that I myself am growing more and more into a feeling of the probability of the same.

[19] *Philos. Rev.,* XVI (1907), 9 ff.; *L.W.J.,* II, 252–5.
[20] Preface, xii.

I have been so crowded here and at the same time so trammeled as hardly to have read a page of anything. But I threw myself upon your book and have read the Preface, the first two, and the last two essays. First of all, the style is a delight and a refresher, in this vulgar world, by its elevation and distinction, along with its rare perspicuity. The book is a gentleman (— or a lady?)! What seems to me its strength is the radical and direct and uncompromising way in which it lays down a conception of the world on lines of *rational fitness.* Few today dare to be so aggressively and positively teleological; and as each age has to alter its mode of expression, I don't see why your mode might not become the standard text for reference and attack. It will if you ever write the systematic book. The weakness of this book seems to me to lie in the *purity* with which the considerations of teleological fitness disport themselves. You seem almost unconscious of the *prima facie* rebelliousness of the world of facts. You simply *override* them, strong in your conviction of the ultimate ideality, whereas with most of us their brutality and madness are the principal stimulus to thought; and *untying* the knot, not *cutting* it, is what we want help in doing, from teachers like yourself. I must say that for my mind your deduction of evil from the logical necessity of some *defect,* in the definition of every finite, does n't meet the want; and I find myself more and more disposed to believe in irrationality as the *prius,* out of which ideality slowly and empirically emerges by a *de facto* process of evolution — or, if you wish, of improvement by alteration. *But* — I can't write on the book! — merely this word as I lie in bed, to give you a summary sense of the way it impresses me. I apprehend your thought far better than I ever did, in its consistent totality. I always felt baffled and puzzled by you; now I realize, as it were, your centre, and recognize its importance.

I must forthwith spring up and dress and give my *last* lecture (*Gobb lob!*), which is due at 12. Will write more when the agony is over. . . . 3.30 P.M. The lecture is over, and the course has been a great success judging by the audience, unparalleled in numbers in Gifford history (about 300) and undiminished to the end. Thank heaven the strain is over. . . .

You have treated me *most* handsome in your book. I have already warded off the accusation you (very naturally) make against my suggestion of the *modus operandi* of immortality, in a preface to the second edition of that lecture. . . . As regards the essay on determinism and freedom, I "note" that you are what I call a thorough-going indeterminist [21] . . . and so am naturally displeased at your talking of "reconciliation," the reconciliation being by taking a meaning of the term "determinism" absolutely alien to that over which the controversy rages. Who ever denied that whatever once is, is "determined" in your logical sense, by its genus and differentia? The question is whether, the rest of the universe being posited (and determined also in that sense), this thing is *ambiguously* or *unequivocally* determined. You and I say "ambiguously," the determinists in the usual sense of the word say "unequivocally," — so you don't reconcile! But no matter! I won't cavil, for the book is a noble book; and you on the right flank and I on the left flank will execute one of Kitchener's sweeping movements, and clear the country of all boors, monists, fatalists, and annex it in the name of the pluralistic philosophy. Good-bye! and *pray* get well. Give my love to Mrs. Howison, and take plenty for your self. Yours always,

WM. JAMES

Shasta Springs, July 21, 1901

Dear James, —

Your most welcome and generous letter from Edinburgh of June 17th I at length get to the answering of. I 've been in a *welter* of letters as well as of weakness, and I little thought that seventeen days would pass before I came to reply. I had yours on our "glorious 4th," and it was much the best thing I had that day. Glad am I, glad are we both, that you not only survived the great strain of the Edinburgh lectures, but came out of them even improved in tone and strength. . . . May you get back to Harvard in good trim, able to take hold without risks, — where they will justly be prouder of you than ever, as all we Americans are. . . . As for myself, I think the summer up here in these lovely wilds, in full sight of grand old Shasta, and glorified by the numberless bright waterfalls that he sends forth, has done me perceptible good. I did not tell you of my trouble in detail, because it is at bottom too much like your own. . . . I must try to be content. I shall not

[21] *Limits of Evolution,* 376 ff.

have had a *very* short life anyhow, as our human lives go, as I am now in my sixty-seventh year. Now, let this matter be finally laid aside.

As to the *Book*. I am glad it is well off my hands. Yours is the least unconsoling letter I have had about it. I am pleased at your praise, proud that you can say anything good about the style of it, and yet (so perverse is our appetite for glory!) rather disappointed that you do not mention (and therefore I must suppose do not find) other qualities of a good style than "elevation," "distinction," and "perspicuity." As for your criticism, that the book *overrides* or ignores the horrid irrationality and evil in the world, instead of facing and explaining it, and capers away in a fatuous confidence in an ultimate idealism, I must say that I do not think it is correct. *You* feel that it is so, because you have so dead-set a confidence in your "radical empiricism" that arguments however careful and however emphasized for *a priori* certainties make no impression on you at all. Yet such arguments form the most important parts of my book, and all the "overriding of evil" is simply the application to the matters, of the straight corollaries from those arguments.

Your later objection, that my "attempt to deduce evil from the logically necessary presence of *defect* in every finite" is to your mind insufficient, I can readily appreciate, if by "evil" you mean moral evil or wickedness, as I suppose you do. *That* kind of evil, the only *real* evil, I do not suppose *can* be "deduced." If it could, it would cease to be moral evil; for then it would be necessitated upon the agent, whereas its very nature is that the agent himself originates it. All it behooves any system to show, is how the *risk* of it inheres in the nature of existence; to show, in short, that it is a *real* possibility, lying in the nature of real existence itself; and to show, furthermore, that even in introducing this irrational and horrid fact into the temporal world, the self-active person, as wicked, still obeys reason in one of its functions, and never passes out of the profoundest control of reason, which is eventually to redeem him. And all this, which is all I undertook, and all that any moral thinker ought to undertake, I still believe I have done something toward explaining. . . . The question is not whether I have answered every possible dark question, but whether I have not gone some distance in advance, upon a new and significant path, in answering such questions, or in making their answer possible.

Then I must put in a *caveat* to your being "displeased" at my essaying to harmonize freedom and determinism. *Of course* I don't reconcile predestinationism and capricious free-will. I *proclaim* I don't, — at the very start; and I proclaim that no man *can*. But I call attention to the great fact, that there is no such thing as *ultimate* predestination, and no such thing as *capricious* free-will; and that the trouble in the discussion has been that the two maddened parties have supposed these two impossible facts to be realities. Also, my object is to show what determinism and freedom *really* mean. Freedom is nearly the opposite of caprice; and determinism *can't* mean predestination, in a moral world. Nevertheless, there is a *real* fact, corresponding to the *real* meaning of determinism, just as there is a real freedom. *My* object is to point these out, and thus to show that the old dispute, while in *itself* insoluble, need not have arisen. What you wrote in this connection convinces me that you read my last essay too hurriedly to take its real position in. I do not doubt that we are in main agreement, but your own phrases, frequently repeated, about freedom's being "caprice," etc. — if your readers wanted to take it so — and the constant verging to the point of making "indeterminism" have its *absolute* meaning, led me to make more of our seeming differences than I otherwise would. Nor do I agree with you that *my* meaning of determinism is "merely logical definition by genus and species." I intend to say that the *whole* being of each self is *self*-determined, in the sense that its logical self-definition carries a rational *law* out upon its entire temporal life. But I must spare you, — I can't go into detail about this without wearing you out. May we sometime meet again, dear James, and in a stormless hour compare notes verbally!

We go home next Friday, 26th. Were you ever at this lovely spot? If not, save it for some future summer! Mrs. Howison sends great wishes to you both. Yours always,

G. H. H.

The Will to Believe was dedicated "To My Old Friend, CHARLES SANDERS PEIRCE, to whose philosophic comradeship in old times and to whose writings in more recent years I owe more incitement and help than I can express or repay." From Peirce came a prompt response which throws a clear light on his difference-in-agreement.

New York, March 13, 1897

My dear William, —

Your letter and the dedication and the book gave me more delight than you would be apt to believe. . . . I got the book last night. I have read the first essay, which is of great value; and I don't see that it is so very "elementary," as you say, unless you mean that it is very easy to read and comprehend, — and it is a master-piece in that respect. That everything is to be tested by its practical results was the great text of my early papers; so, as far as I get your general aim in so much of the book as I have looked at, I am quite with you in the main. In my later papers, I have seen more thoroughly than I used to do that it is not mere action as brute exercise of strength that is the purpose of all, but, say, generalization, — such action as tends toward regularization, and the actualization of the thought which without action remains unthought. . . . Much have I learned of life and of the world, throwing strong lights upon philosophy, in these years. Undoubtedly its tendency is to make one value the spiritual more, but not an abstract spirituality. . . . This is not so aside from the subject of your book as it might seem at first blush, because it implies that much has led me to rate higher than ever the individual deed as the only real meaning there is in the concept; and yet at the same time to see more sharply than ever that it is not the mere arbitrary force in the deed, but the life it gives to the idea, that is valuable.

As to "belief" and "making up one's mind," if they mean anything more than this, that we have a plan of procedure, and that according to that plan we will try a given description of behavior, I am inclined to think they do more harm than good. "Faith," and the sense that one will adhere consistently to a given line of conduct, is highly necessary in affairs. But if it means you are not going to be alert for indications that the moment has come to change your tactics, I think it ruinous in practice.[22] If an opportunity occurs to do business with a man, and the success of it depends on

---

[22] For Peirce's criticism of "tenacity" in belief, cf. "Fixation of Belief," *Popular Science Mo.*, XII (1877-8).

his integrity, then if I decide to go into the transaction, I must go on the hypothesis he is an honest man, and there is no sense at all in halting between two lines of conduct. But that won't prevent my collecting further evidence with haste and energy, because it may show me it is time to change my plan. That is the sort of "faith" that seems useful. . . .

I am much encouraged at your thinking well of "tychism." But tychism is only a part and corollary of the general principle of "synechism." [23] That is what I have been studying these last fifteen years, and I become more and more encouraged and delighted with the way it seems to fit all the wards of your lock. It was a truly sweet thing, my dear William, to dedicate your book to me.

C. S. Peirce

New York, March 18, 1897

My dear William, —

I have been much struck with the "Dilemma of Determinism." I do not mean that there was any new thought to me in it, because this matter has been the subject of a very serious analysis on my part, a work much more elaborate than anybody would suppose from anything I have printed. But I was surprised to see how far you had penetrated into the logical analysis so long ago as 1884. Two points particularly struck me. One was your resolving the matter altogether into a question of plurality, which is another name for my "variety" of nature. . . . The other was your remark that the question is, Is possibility a mode of being? Good. Precisely so. . . . I reached this truth by studying the question of possible grades of multitude, where I found myself arrested until I could form a whole logic of possibility, — a very difficult and laborious task. You would not have reached it that way. You must have some short cut, which I am curious to know more about. . . . I have never read the *Logique* of Charles Renouvier. Do you possess a copy of it; and if so could you spare it long enough for me to read it? [24] . . . In my opinion the scholastics were right in holding that, putting God into time, there is no contradiction be-

---

[23] Tychism, the doctrine that there is real chance in the world; synechism, the doctrine of continuity (*cf.* below, 411–2).

[24] James sent his copy, and Peirce wrote this impression of Renouvier: "Although there are some of his conclusions I like, I do not think his method of reaching them is up to the requirements of today."

tween foreknowledge and free will. I forget what your father said about it, but I remember being much struck with it. Your father saw a long way in a certain direction. Very faithfully

C. S. PEIRCE

These letters were never properly answered, but they were *acknowledged* as follows: —

Cambridge, March 27, 1897

Dear Charles, —

Your two inspiring letters have been received duly "and contents noted," though you will excuse me if the laziness of my epistolary nature and the general dislocation of my wits in the multiplicity of different interests that I am supposed to attend to, make me disinclined just now to making animadversions in detail on their contents. . . . You *shall* have a course of lectures here next year, long or short. I know it can be done, and I will see to it. We all want to hear you, and our graduates *ought* to. But why has the first volume of your book so vanished into the kingdom of mere possibles? I thought that the subscriptions had panned out adequately. Your intensely mathematical mind keeps my non-mathematical one at a distance. But so many of our categories are the same that your existence and philosophizing give me the greatest comfort. Ever faithfully yours,

WM. JAMES

LXIV

A CHAPTER OF CRITICISMS

AMONG the most vigorous and sympathetic critics of *The Will to Believe* was Benjamin Paul Blood of Amsterdam, New York — who had heard James's father preach fifty or sixty years before, and had then already acquired a "fancy for the family name." He was born in 1832 and lived for eighty-six years. During that time he wrote much, but unsystematically. His favorite form of publication was letters to newspapers, mainly local newspapers with a small circulation. These letters "dealt with an astonishing diversity of subjects, from local petty politics or the tricks of spiritualistic mediums to principles of industry and finance and profundities of metaphysics." [1]

Blood was a man after James's own heart, in temperament and style as well as in the substance of his thought. He was an unacademic philosopher who wrote from the depths or shallows of his own experience, and fitted his vehicle to this content. He was a mystic, which in itself would have commended him to James. But, wondrous to relate, he was also a man of exceptional physical vigor, and sufficiently affected by the diversity and particularity of this world to lean to pluralism rather than to monism. *Mens mystica in corpore sano!*

We know that James's partiality for mysticism was innate, if not ancestral. It coincided with his neurasthenia, his religiosity, and even with his empiricism — that is, his reliance on original experience as conveying a more veracious impression of reality than its intellectualized derivatives. But he was suspicious of mysticism for equally good reasons — for its corrupting effect upon the moral will, and for its tendency to monism. In 1874 Blood published his *Anæsthetic Revelation* in which he affirmed, on the basis of his own experiments with anæsthetics, that at the moment of

---

[1] H. M. Kallen's Introduction to Blood's *Pluriverse,* 1920, xxi.

"coming to" there is a revelation of "the genius of being."[2]
James reviewed this pamphlet for the *Atlantic Monthly* in the same
year and said, in expressing his qualified skepticism: "We shall not
howl with the wolves or join the multitude in jeering at it."[3] But
he emphasized his moral misgivings, and these he repeated even more
emphatically in 1880 to Xenos Clark, another exponent of anæsthetic
mysticism.[4] Meanwhile, in 1879, he had cited Blood again as evidence of the fact that "the heart can . . . wall out the ultimate
irrationality which the head ascertains"; and conceded that if mysticism could only be universalized, or erected into a "systematized
method," instead of being left to the unverifiable affirmation of the
individual, it would be of capital philosophic importance.[5] In 1882,
when he scandalized the philosophic world by his flippant observations "On Some Hegelisms," James referred to anæsthetic experiments of his own, prompted by reading Blood's pamphlet, and
which gave him a new understanding of the monistic insight — to
which he did not in the least object so long as it was recognized *as*
insight and not advanced as logic.[6] It was in this same year that
he received a letter from Blood containing the following paragraph:[7]

"Now about the revelation. Mr. Xenos Clark in the letter I
sent you, underscored *one* expression: 'the succession is the thing.'
This comes nearer to me than any of the rest. . . . It is mainly
about succession, the going on of time or life, with an overpowering
sense of the utter unavoidableness of the going on, — with a sense
of initiation into the fact of it as ancient and common (homogeneous) to all intelligence; it is the *old* mystery, the Adamic, the hairy
primogene. There is nothing grotesque in the revelation itself, but
we chuckle at the simplicity and the impregnable certainty of it.
The grin is partly self-gratulation, and partly a shrug at being
necessarily in it and of it. God, reason, religion, philosophy have
nothing to do with it, save as afterthoughts. God especially is
nowhere in it (nor anywhere else perhaps): it is wholly secular, like
common air. The one 'dead certainty' we retain from it is that it
is true, the truth about something which we have been taught to

[2] Pp. 33–4.
[3] *Atlantic*, XXXIV (1874), 628.
[4] *Cf.* above, I, 727. .
[5] "Sentiment of Rationality," *Mind*, IV (1879), 345.
[6] *Mind*, VII (1882), 206–8; *W.B.*, 294–8.
[7] *Cf.* also the paragraph cited above, I, 127.

look for in religious regions — as if one had the multiplication table given him to displace the 'Holy Scriptures.' . . . I always get a hint of the mystery *when the clock stops of itself.*" [8]

After five years there came this more personal letter with its photograph and autobiographical detail. Blood had meanwhile become known to the philosophic world through the publication of his "Philosophical Reveries" in the *Journal of Speculative Philosophy.*[9]

Amsterdam, June 11, 1887

My dear Sir, —

Your welcome and encouraging letter enhances the cheer of my return home, and I must say you could not have done a nicer thing for me than sending your picture in it. It is a head for anything; but if, seeing it, I had been asked, What manner of man is this? I should have said, a soldier in the larger sense, although the dome of the head were rather wasted on a soldier — but a director, engineer, and manager of men. If you will put shoulder straps on it and set it ten feet away, most people would take it for a picture of our Gen. Sherman, though younger, and not so grim and grizzly. . . . I have no picture to send you save, alas, the one I enclose, taken for devilment some fifteen years ago to please some of my men on a day when I had lifted by a chain on my right shoulder and around my right arm, 1160 lbs. You will say of it, with Virgil, *"arma virumque";* it shows more brawn than brains. But I do not look that way now. I weigh about 165, and am five feet ten. My wife has been some time urging me to sit again, and I will replace this with a worn and thoughtful face of fifty-four. There was a popular cut of me in *Frank Leslie's Illustrated News* — in 1860 or 1861 on occasion of a momentary stir over a book of mine from the common sense standpoint, called *Optimism the Lesson of Ages* — published by old man Bela Marsh of . . . Boston. Nice letters I had about it from Mr. Emerson, Wendell Phillips, Mr. Bryant, Fitz-Greene Halleck, and have them yet, but philosophically it was nothing more than good writing. . . .

In mailing you this *outré* picture I have felt that I should give you some definition of my circumstances, lest I seem all sorts of a scapegrace in your apprehension. I was born here in Amsterdam.

---

[8] It is instructive to compare this statement of Blood with the passage cited from Xenos Clark in *V.R.E.*, 389, note.
[9] XX (1886).

My father was a landholder of 700 acres here adjoining the city on both sides of the river, and lived, as I now live, in a large brick house on the south bank of the Mohawk visible as you enter Amsterdam from the east.   I was his only child, and went a good deal my own way.   I ran to machinery, by fancy; patented among other devices a swathing reaper which is very successful.   I was of loose and wandering ways, and was a successful gambler through the Tweed régime — made "bar'ls" of money, and threw it away.   I was a fancy gymnast also, and have had some heavy fights, — notably one of forty minutes with Ed. Mullett, whom I left senseless. This was mere fancy.   I never lifted an angry hand against man, woman, or child — all fun — for me.   My father divided his estate equally between myself, son and daughter. . . .   I do farming in a way, but am much idle.   I have been a sort of pet of the city, and think I should be missed.   In a large vote taken by one of the daily papers here a month or so ago as to who were the twelve leading citizens, I was sixth in the twelve, and sole in my class.   So you see, if Sparta has many a worthier son, I am still boss in the department I prefer.   It may seem foolish — supererogatory — to say all this, yet I think otherwise.   It were different with you people who are known hereditarily.   I have worn out many styles, and am cosmopolitan, liberal to others, and contented with myself. I never could value things at others' rates, — never was respectable or conforming; but truth and honesty are a fashion by themselves, and I have lived to have my ways, once called heterodox, now called merely advanced; the chaff blows off, the grain remains and I could borrow the city treasury if I wanted the money — which (I sometimes think, unfortunately) I never did.

B. P. B.

Cambridge, June 19, 1887

Dear Mr. Blood, —

On my return from a few days' absence on business I find your letter, poems and portrait.   I confess that I did not expect the author of your works to look just like that, and am anxious to see the later edition of the creature.   Your letter does one's heart good. I am so delighted to find that a metaphysician *can* be anything else than a spavined, dyspeptic individual fit for no other use.   Most of them have been invalids.   I am one, can't sleep, can't make a de-

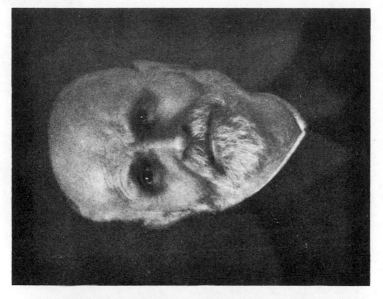

WINCENTY LUTOSLAWSKI, 1904

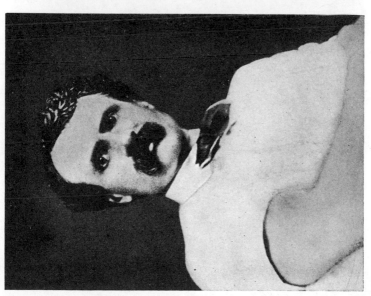

BENJAMIN PAUL BLOOD, 1860

cision, can't buy a horse, can't do anything that befits a man; and yet you say from my photograph that I must be a second General Sherman, only greater and better! All right! I love you for the fond delusion. I enjoy your letters from top to toe. . . . You seem to be a man after Walt Whitman's own heart, — I 've got much good from that man's verse, if such it can be called. As for your verse, I keep it till a more propitious moment — a week hence, perhaps, when I shall be in the country.[10] I am now clean daft, with college examination papers to read, and all the worry of winding up the year's business and getting my family away. Faithfully yours,

WM. JAMES

In June 1895, James went to see Blood in Amsterdam and had his good opinion confirmed.[11] The effects of this visit on Blood are recorded in the letter which he wrote to James almost immediately after: —

Amsterdam, June 20 [1895]

My dear Herr Doctor, —

I have wanted to write to you and have put it off to do it more thoroughly, which at last I don't intend to do, for I should make a book of it; but I have to tell you, however briefly, the impression you left on me and the style of contemplation you entailed — this is what we keep living for, I suppose — and all this in a page or two of the fated perfunction of pounding and punching the chaos into the logos, etc.

I have to laugh to myself thinking how readily people are imposed upon. One difference between you and me (you will pardon the familiarity, for one has to measure with his own ruler) is that you are the professional and compelled reality of which I am an idle, indifferent and amateur fraud. I with my assurance, as well as you with your mastership that "has long digested all," might go through the world and impress it successfully. . . . It is to me memorable that your honored father was the first to impress me with the presence of that transcendent which we call genius, and

---

[10] Blood's verse was usually printed privately or in newspapers, but in 1899, 1900–1, 1904, 1915, and 1919, appeared in *Scribner's Magazine*.
[11] *Cf. L.W.J.*, II, 22.

now from the same strain I am impressed with an all-round expert — not but that also is genius, possibly overwrought. . . .

One gets to like the solemn music of that word *farewell* — a cadence in the immortal procession.   With true love to you!

B. P. B.

Blood's comments on the doctrine of *The Will to Believe* began in 1896 when James sent him the essay "Is Life Worth Living?" first published as a separate pamphlet.

Amsterdam, June 7 [1896]

My dear Doctor, —

If I could have fancied you having any doubts about the quality of your lecture "Is Life Worth Living?" I should not have put off my thanks for it for a month.   When I was a young fellow I used to seek the opinions of literary men on things of mine, and I learned a nice scheme from them: they would "hasten" to acknowledge, etc., and of course had not had time to read, etc., but would at their earliest, etc. — and of course by that time I had ceased to care for the matter myself.   But the fact is that your topic had long been familiar to me, as I told you when you were here, — so much so that last September I felt compelled to go into more active life, and since then I have been in our mills ten hours a day, missing only a day or two.[12]   I am at "condition" pitch, and the weeks fly past me unheeded, and life is worth living.   But I have before now had many thoughts of making an end of it.   I even went so far as to prepare a kind of consolatory farewell to the few who would care anything about it.   I told them not to be sad, but think that this man thought it "nobler in the mind" to knock boldly for admission to the life to come, rather than to be haled shrieking to the dark river, — decrepit, perchance demented — stretching back hands of supplication to the shadows of the past.   It must be that the spirits who shall greet him applaud one who comes of his own brave accord.   What though he fled from trouble or in discouragement, yet like distracted Lear, if they shall say to him, "Is this the King?" he shall answer "Every inch a King," and so the great shade shall enter.   But the thought that I might when I would, left plenty of time for reflection — no hurry about it — and so I

---

[12] Blood worked for a year in the packing room of a mill which belonged to members of his family.

took a better inventory than I had ever taken before of what I was to leave: the long progress of philosophy, the achievements of science and the wonders of astronomy, — especially now when we are advancing so rapidly.   And what with one distraction and another I forgot all about it.   What most detained me was a conscientious scruple that there was something that I ought to say before I went, — something for which I sadly doubted the capacity of the audience as well as of my words.   It is the best effect of your little book upon me that it has increased my faith in the audience. . . . If I were going to the court of Heaven right off I should have to admonish you that there are people who would say that in serious and sustaining discourse you sometimes drop to the colloquial rather too good-naturedly — possibly in old Doctor Nott's [13] animus, that among people who say "cowcumbers" you may say cowcumbers too, but there is a doubt at last about their being thankful for the condescension.   From a writer whose works nobody will buy this criticism should be very rich and nourishing to you!   May I add to my thanks for the book the very extraordinary fact that Mrs. Blood has read it twice through — something that I never knew her to do to any book before, and she has loaned it around; her "dominie" has it now. — As Grover [14] says, — Yours sincerely,

BENJ. PAUL BLOOD

Chatham, June 28, 1896 [15]
My dear Blood, —
    Your letter was an "event," as anything always is from your pen — though of course I never expected any acknowledgment of my booklet.   Fear of life in one form or other is the great thing to exorcise; but it is n't reason that will ever do it.   Impulse without reason is enough, and reason without impulse is a poor makeshift. I take it that no man is educated who has never dallied with the thought of suicide.   Barely more than a year ago I was sitting at your table and dallying with the thought of publishing an anthology of your works.   But, like many other projects, it has been postponed *in indefinitum*.   The hour never came last year, and pretty surely will not come next.   Nevertheless I shall work for your

[13] Presumably the late Dr. Eliphalet Nott, who had been president of Union College, Schenectady.
[14] Grover Cleveland?
[15] Reprinted with omissions from *L.W.J.*, II, 38–40.

fame some time! Count on W. J. I wound up my "seminary" in speculative psychology a month ago by reading some passages from the *Flaw in Supremacy* [16] — "game flavored as a hawk's wing." "Ever not quite" covers a deal of truth — yet it seems a very simple thing to have said. "There is no *Absolute*," were my last words. Whereupon a number of students asked where they could get "that pamphlet," and I distributed nearly all the copies I had from you. I wish you would keep on writing, but I see you are a man of discontinuity and insights, and not a philosophic pack-horse, or pack-mule. . . . Pray thank Mrs. Blood for her appreciation of my "booklet" (such things encourage a writer!), and believe me ever sincerely yours,

WM. JAMES

In the Preface to *The Will to Believe* James had quoted from *The Flaw in Supremacy,* and referred to its author as a "gifted writer" and pluralistic ally.[17]

Amsterdam, April 18, 1897

My dear Doctor, —

Mrs. Blood has gone to church, and I have sat hesitating about longer delay in trying to do some justice to your *Essays,* which I have read and re-read occasionally every day since I received them — for which my cordial thanks, and for the "cotton" in the book for me. Alas! that there should recur to me so often the refrain of the little nun or novice in "Guinevere" — "Late, late — ye cannot enter now." Mrs. Blood says this is the only fame I ever had that was any good. She says the minister of the Second Methodist here quoted you extensively last Sunday, and by name, but she could not locate the matter for me. She is a thinker and a wag. I was telling her of your notion of the "Sentiment of Rationality" as easily flowing thought, etc.: she said there was more of it than that — something *has* to be, to put any go into the world; and she illustrated from what she was doing by saying, "If you have picked-up codfish for dinner on Friday, you have got to have codfish balls for breakfast on Saturday!" There is an apodictic judgment for you.

But it would take as much matter as your book contains to tell

[16] A pamphlet published by Blood in 1893.
[17] *W.B.,* viii–ix.

what I think of it, for it is all ahead of the procession, and all along the lines which interest me most. The style is not perfection. The meanings are all classic, but there is a colloquial insouciance which is not as a man would write for his life, unless indeed he did n't give a continental whether he lived or died. When we think how anything has to be written, re-written, copied, printed, proofed, and criticized, there is no room left for any excuse for carelessness, for lack of judicial selection of terms. As copies of lectures, the essays may perhaps be not liable to stricture; there are several passages which, well delivered, must have had strong oratorical effect — that is, for the right audience, which, possibly, all your work rather too much presumes. You are full of the "literature of the topics" which you treat, and to most people you would be more interesting if you went straight on with your own ideas. And you are the born psychologist: "radical empiricist," indeed. This is all the faultfinding I can do for you.

But about the leading animus of the book: "pluralism." I am a pluralist easily enough, believing only in lower-case gods, and in no grand climacteric results of being; there is no finale, no one lesson to be learned. Everything happens in the middle of eternity. All days are judgment-days and creation-morns, and all the hustle and bustle and hurry and worry of the man who had lost a day! — him who had a charge to keep, a God to glorify, a never-dying soul to save, and other ethical chores pressing — stamped him out of "the caste of Vere de Vere:" [18] "for the slow planets sun themselves in green immortal leisure." The gods recline on asphodel; no sympathy with these our rushing purposes, ruffles the languor of their patrician repose. Yet will it ever do to put pluralism in the place of philosophy? It is still true, though there be no god with the capital G, that "the one remains, the many change and pass. . . ." [19]

"The Dilemma of Determinism" strikes me as the most dramatic "piece of work" in your volume, though possibly "The Sentiment of Rationality" is more original; but all are good and have a future — negative, iconoclastic, perhaps, but powerful. You do not build — how can you build on foundations that run everywhere? and I am not sure that you generalize at all. And does not pluralism

[18] Tennyson's "Lady Clara Vere de Vere."
[19] Shelley's *Adonais*.

"have in it its own negation?" as the many (*per se*) must afford a specimen of the one.   The world has long believed in limited space (subjective), unity of intelligence, community, a home, a heaven, a duty, an order, a chance for fame that is known of all, not *a* world but *the* world, under control — all facts and possibilities known and realized — imperial peace.   Even in pluralism *per se* this must be *sometime;* if we are to have everything we must try the One awhile, however stale it may become, till "there was war in heaven." Pluralism is hard to focus, — it is like sand, or meal.   It is a necessary conception, but so is the One.   I leave to you and to time the reconciliation, very grateful that something compels you to write about it, — and let me read it.   When details shall puzzle you, then turn back to the Anæsthetic Revelation — that antedates all explanations and principles.   Believe that you have afforded a great pleasure to your humble friend,

BENJ. PAUL BLOOD

Cambridge, April 28, 1897

Dear Blood, —

Your letter is delectable.   From your not having yet acknowledged the book, I began to wonder whether you had got it, but this acknowledgment is almost too good.   Your thought is obscure, — lightning flashes, darting gleams — but that's the way truth is. And although I "put pluralism in the place of philosophy," I do it only so far as philosophy means the articulable and the scientific. Life and mysticism exceed the articulable, and if there is a *One* (and surely men will never be weaned from the idea of it) it must remain only mystically expressed.

I have been roaring over and quoting some of the passages of your letter, in which my wife takes as much delight as I do.   As for your strictures on my English, I accept them humbly.   I have a tendency towards too great colloquiality, I know, and I trust your sense of English better than any man's in the country.   I have a fearful job on hand just now: an address on the unveiling of a military statue.[20]   Three thousand people, Governor and troops, etc. Why they fell upon me, God knows, but being challenged, I could not funk.   The task is a mechanical one, and the result somewhat

[20] The monument to Robert Gould Shaw, unveiled in Boston, May 31, 1897; *cf.* below, 277-8.   The address is published in *M.S.*

of a school-boy composition. If I thought it would n't bore you I should send you a copy for you to go carefully over and correct or rewrite as to the English. I should probably adopt every one of your corrections. What do you say to this? Yours ever,

WM. JAMES

Some years later James wrote to Blood: "You have the greatest gift of superior gab since Shakespeare"; but to his request that Blood revise the Shaw Address the latter's reply was prompt and decisive: "Thanks no! I have not the gall to undertake to improve your English, which for ordinary purposes, whether praying or swearing, will probably be understood; and I infer that it has a charm of its own."

Among the critics of *The Will to Believe* there was one, at least, who complained not of James's boldness but of his excessive caution. A faith so generalized, so consciously and punctiliously justified, was not faith at all! John Jay Chapman was at this time practising law in New York City, and had been for many years a friend and kindred spirit.[21]

New York, March 30, 1897

My dear Mr. James, —

I met John Graham Brooks at the Century Club last night and he told me that your first essay on "The Will to Believe" was the best statement of that kind of thing that had ever been made, — so I read the essay. It seemed to me — as you are evidently used to having the ideas seem — the last volley from the last redoubt gallantly discharged and which ought to be attended to with respectful silence. (This sounds well but these two things, respect and silence, are impossible to me — I am sorry — but the words are a mere literary embellishment.) On closer reading, it seemed like the most immoral and dangerous writing, and I was about to write the time-honoured confutations; — and finally an idea occurred to me that I think you might just possibly conceivably agree with, and if you do you will be finished off to all eternity.

[21] This was the only time that Chapman read a philosophic work of James with serious attention, but the impact of James the man on Chapman's own rich temperament produced a most interesting effect, reported in the latter's *Memories and Milestones*, 1915. The content of the present letter was elaborated by Chapman in his highly entertaining but short-lived monthly, *The Political Nursery*, July 1899.

The course of reasoning — or, say, the state of mind of a man who justifies faith by the considerations you mention — is well enough. He makes himself content. His shanty will last his day. He's got some kind of tar or hopes that'll keep faith in him and prevent it from evaporating. But he'll never convey it — arouse it, evoke it — in another. . . . This is a somewhat roundabout way of saying that such a man hasn't got faith at all. The faith you begin to talk about has been so justified and bolstered, and drugged up and down, and ironed and wired — damme if I call that faith! Damned if I call that faith! If I cared about such matters and thought them important, your essay would make me a Roman Catholic. I honestly think the Roman system contains a better statement of spiritual truth than this shy at it.

The question is one of expressiveness. You remember that at the "Swarry" in *Pickwick Papers* the Bath butler, to make conversation, asks Sam Weller whether he has noticed the chalybeate in the Bath waters. "I noticed," says Sam, "a taste of warm flat-irons — but I noticed no chalybeate, and I think chalybeate is a very inexpressive word."

Another thing. . . . I kept wondering, — "But why all this pother — what *difference* does it make whether a man believes or not? Why is this question important enough to be discussed?" — and then I have to wait till page 29, next to the last, to be enlightened. Now I had supposed that the idea of that note — the supposed connection between belief and conduct — was one of the busted ideas of the world, like astrology, or the divining rod — a thing containing some elements of truth worthy perhaps of investigation, but rather (at present) discredited on account of its manifest error. My own studies have led me to believe that there may be men who in some matters are sometimes influenced by the form of their religious tenets, and act and feel as they wouldn't have acted and felt but for some dogma; but this is so rare and so complex, and is of course rapidly disappearing.

There, it is a wicked thing for me to have written you this letter. But I must tell you. I am trying to get an article on Stevenson published as a result of our conversation at Mrs. Whitman's last summer. I kept thinking, — if a man like James thinks this about Stevenson, it's worth while to take an awful lot of trouble to find out about the thing. Sincerely yours,

JOHN JAY CHAPMAN

Cambridge, April 5, 1897

Dear Chapman, —

Pray continue your epistolary explosions. The latter one did my heart real good. You belong to the Salvation Army party; and the poor little razor-like "thin end of the wedge" which your academic personages twiddle between their fingers must indeed seem loathsome to the robuster temperaments at the other end. You remind me of the farmer who said to his bishop, after a sermon proving the existence of God, — "It is a very fine sermon, but I believe there be a God after all."

Faith indeed! Damme if I call that faith, either. It is only calculated for the sickly hotbed atmosphere of the philosophic-positivistically enlightened scientific classroom. To the victims of spinal paralysis which these studies superinduce, the homeopathic treatment, although you might not believe it, really does good. We are getting too refined for anything; altogether out of touch with genuine life. Therefore I tie to you as a piece of water-closet paper might try to tie to a stone, if it were afraid that the wind would blow it away.

All this rubbish is only for public purposes. In my individual heart I fully believe my faith is as robust as yours. The trouble about your robust and full-bodied faiths, however, is, that they begin to cut each other's throats too soon, and for getting on in the world and establishing a *modus vivendi* these pestilential refinements and reasonablenesses and moderations have to creep in. I am sorry for your paragraph about your supposed connection between belief and conduct. It is by no means busted; on the contrary, it is one of the most tremendous forces in the world.

Now send me another letter soon, and read my Preface if you have not yet read it, and believe me, ever devotedly and affectionately yours,

WM. JAMES

P.S. I wish you knew a few of the intellects *at* whom that speech was delivered. Have you read Hoar's article on the Senate in the April *Forum?* Bully! Pity so dear an old boy can't believe that God created also democrats and mugwumps.

For fifteen years or more James carried on an active correspondence with F. H. Bradley, the distinguished neo-Hegelian, whose mind he admired as greatly as he dissented from his doctrines. The most important of Bradley's letters deal with pragmatism and with James's later metaphysics, but there is a letter on *The Will to Believe* which belongs in the present context: —

Oxford, Sept. 21, 1897 [22]

Dear Sir, —

I have been reading some of your *Will to Believe,* and I remember that I have used some expressions about some of the opinions I find there which I should like to tell you had no reference to you, as I had read none of your papers. I feel also perhaps that I can show best that I am not inclined to treat any views of yours with disrespect by writing a few words to you on them, mainly on free will. Please do not think I want to lead you into a discussion. I have always myself found such things useless. One may, where an objection is not a mere mistake, profit by it when one reconsiders the matter as a whole, but otherwise I fancy never. So do not trouble yourself to reply to what I say. If I thought you would I would not inflict this letter on you. On free will I will state very shortly where you fail to satisfy my mind, that is, of course, as I understand you.

First, I am pleased to see you identify freedom openly with chance, but I cannot think you realize the consequences in science or morality. For the first, it seems to me that the whole of our knowledge rests on the assumption that there is no chance. If a thing can happen for no reason, then, so far as I see, there is no truth at all; for at one time A will be $b,$ and at another time something other than $b,$ with no reason whatever for the difference. . . .

Next, for morality. I have always supposed that I am not morally responsible for mere accidents. You seem to tell me that these are all I am responsible for. But you offer me no sort of explanation. I do not understand this at all. . . . All that the ordinary man asks, so far as I see, is that his act should come from himself and not be extraneous. I think this demand is fully satisfied by the view that the self, once in being, is an internal principle and agency — not the same with selfless conditions, nor the same even with what it is

---

[22] "This letter, and the ones which follow from F. H. Bradley, though obviously written in a personal and friendly way and not for publication, appear too valuable to be withheld." (From the authorization for the publication of Bradley's letters.)

conscious of.   But what has all this to do with *chance?*   I cannot
see. . . .

The trouble, I believe, has been mainly caused by the moral (or
immoral) Creator.   Once tell a man that another fellow, however
big, has made him to be and do what he is and does, and of course he
throws it on the other fellow; and his poor morality goes to the
devil, or may do so.   I don't understand a word of what you say
about "possibilities" in connection with this other fellow, unless
you mean to say that he's not a "Creator" at all, but somehow a
limited struggling sort of chap like ourselves only bigger and better,
and loves us and tries to help us, and we ought to stick to him.
That's a moral doctrine if you like, and you may even say, too, he
tried to make us to be like him as well as he could and he knew how
— and that's moral or not *un*-moral, again.   But go further and I
don't think you'll save either the morality of the personal God or
ours either, so far as we take him seriously and look on ourselves
as his pottery. . . .

With the main purpose of your book I am very much in sympathy.
The "primacy of the will" I entirely reject, but I accept the doctrine
that truth is what satisfies the intellect; and if only one could find
the doctrines required to satisfy the rest of our nature, then I think
we might hold them to be true also in some sense or other.   For
no truth we can get is wholly true, and I don't think it could be
shown that these various truths really would in the end clash.   I
should like to have tried to do something on this line, but I don't
see my way.   I cannot, in the first place, make the assumption that
mere morality is our main nature — surely beauty counts for something.   And I cannot connect even morality with certain doctrines
I won't mention again.   What I miss in your work, if I may say so,
is a sufficiently serious enquiry as to what *does* satisfy us all round.
You strike me first as laying a most excessive and I think mistaken
stress on "conduct" taken by itself, and then as not fairly considering all round what it is necessary to postulate even for that. . . .

Of course (to return to the moral Creator) I too believe that it
is natural and necessary in religion to relate oneself to a Will which
desires and wills what is right.   I think this attitude is also justi-
fiable.   It is also true, I believe, that the same Power which appears
as this Will for good, is also that to which our being and the being
of the world is due.   But it is *not* true, I think, that these aspects

can be lumped together, so that you can say: "The God that speaks to my conscience did *as such* make me and the world." . . .

I can't end this letter without a word about Hegel. Pitch into the man how you like, I would say, for anything he has said; only, if so, try to be just to him otherwise. Now *that* you fail to be, it seems to me. . . . Don't you think you might have mentioned that Hegel said just what Carlyle said,[23] and about as brutally; and that that is, in fact, his tone? . . . Again, Hegel does n't, so far as I know, use the phrase "subliminal" self, which is a translation from Herbart, I presume. But is there nothing about it in Hegel's psychology? . . . I think it was pretty common at that time, only I don't know about that, having made no study of it. Every reader of Hegel is familiar with it, and you 'll find it in all Hegel's disciples, I believe. But I have bored you enough. Yours truly,

F. H. BRADLEY

The most important of the discussions stimulated by *The Will to Believe* was that in which the leader of the opposition was Dickinson S. Miller, one of the closest of James's personal friends, and on other issues a powerful ally. After reading the titular essay as separately published in 1896, Miller had written a letter of comment which had evoked from James the following reply: —

"I was greatly relieved to find that you had nothing worse to say about 'The Will to Believe.' You say you are no 'rationalist,' and yet you speak of the 'sharp' distinction between beliefs based on 'inner evidence' and beliefs based on 'craving.' I can find *nothing* sharp (or susceptible of schoolmaster's codification) in the different degrees of 'liveliness' in hypotheses concerning the universe, or distinguish *a priori* between legitimate and illegitimate cravings. And when an hypothesis is once a live one, one *risks* something in one's practical relations towards truth and error, *whichever* of the three positions (affirmation, doubt, or negation) one may take up towards it. *The individual himself is the only rightful chooser of his risk.*"[24]

At the annual meeting of the American Psychological Association held in New York in December 1898, James and Miller were sched-

---

[23] Where James is arguing for Carlyle's gospel of action against "subjectivism"; *W.B.*, 171–4.

[24] *L.W.J.*, II, 48–9.

uled to lead a "Discussion on the Relations of Will and Belief."
They were both prevented from attending, and the discussion took
place in their absence.[25] Prior to the meeting, and in preparation
for it, there had been an exchange of letters between James and
Miller, and selections from the former's letters were read aloud by
one of the members present. Miller's views soon saw the light in
an article entitled " 'The Will to Believe' and the Duty to Doubt,"
in which he expressed his opposition to James by saying: "It does
not follow, because we cannot prove everything, because in the last
resort we can prove nothing, that we are free to assume what we
choose." The writer argued against the exclusive identification of
belief with will, stressing its relations to presentation and habit, to
a sense of evidence, and to instinctive and unconscious influences
that operate independently of volition. But when, he contended,
belief *is* made a matter of volition, it is seen that its purpose is to
correspond to the environment and face the facts.[26]

Preserved among James's papers is a transcript in his hand
of several paragraphs written by F. C. S. Schiller to Charles A.
Strong: "You may remember that D. S. Miller wrote a criticism of
James's *Will to Believe* in 1899, which he wanted answered. Failing James, he applied to me. I replied, 'but you seem wholly to
have mistaken James's doctrine.' Miller appealed to James (whom
at that time I did n't know well). James decided for me. This
made me realize for the first time how James's principle was being
misconstrued (by ignoring its demand for empirical verification)
as an incitement to make-believe, instead of as an analysis of the
psychological process of acquiring beliefs. . . . You really agree
. . . when you admit that a 'will to find out' is an essential preliminary to finding out: in all knowing it is the will which starts the
process, while the final shape of our beliefs is moulded by the results
of our experiments." [27]

Henry Rutgers Marshall also published an article in reply to Miller.[28] He announced his intention to James and sent him a pre-

[25] A summary will be found in *Psychol. Rev.*, VI (1899).
[26] *Inter. Jour. of Ethics*, IX (1898–9), 171, 187, etc. The article appears to have
been circulated in proof at the time of the N. Y. meeting.
[27] Schiller describes the same incident in "William James and the Making of
Pragmatism," *Personalist*, VIII (1927). Miller reiterated his views in *Jour. of
Philos.*, XXIV (1927); and Schiller again replied in *ibid*.
[28] "Belief and Will," *Inter. Jour. of Ethics*, IX (1898–9). Cf. also *L.W.J.*, II,
87–8.

liminary draft of his manuscript, which was acknowledged as follows: —

Cambridge, Feb. 9 [1899]

Dear Marshall, —

I have read your manuscript once rather fast and find it clear, and naturally convincing, so far as it covers my ground, which it does perfectly . . . as against Miller. I therefore find no "misapprehension" whatever of my own position. You do much psychologizing beyond my position, which I find highly instructive. The only thing I strongly doubt is whether the believing impulses which you say come up from the depths of the ego, are in any *general* way to be ascribed to race experience. The kind of fact, I take it, is this: we have a conception which being opposed by another is only *probable*. But we feel, it is so good that it is *fit* to be true, it *ought* to be true, it *must* be true, etc. And then we say it *shall* be true for me; it *is* true. Many of these conceptions are novelties for the race; and you ought to prove in detail how ancestral experiences *can* sum themselves subconsciously into new conclusions. Perhaps they can; but I should like to have it proved. Meanwhile you have written a most valuable essay. I shall write nothing, probably. Always truly yours,

WM. JAMES

Among those who attended the New York discussion was J. Mark Baldwin. Writing to James in January 1899, he referred to the James-Miller correspondence, and discussed the question at issue with special reference to the legitimacy of guessing.[29]

"As to the 'guessing matter' — there lies a point, or one aspect of a point, on which we are at a certain variance; the only point on which you are essentially confused, in my opinion, in your psychological analysis. Miller indicated it in his article; and I think it vitiates much of your development of the *Will to Believe*. It is the confusion of more-or-less-vaguely-grounded-hypothesis with voluntary-guessing-or-throwing-of-dice under the impulse of passion, freedom, and the like. The one, the hypothesis, falls on the side of

---

[29] The discussion grew out of Baldwin's attack on the method of "guessing" as recommended to their pupils by teachers of Latin; *cf.* his *Story of the Mind*, 1898, 198–200. James was also familiar with the discussion of belief in Baldwin's *Feeling and Will* (*Handbook of Psychology*), 1891.

what is really, in so far, belief: the other is, from the word go, a different psychosis — *a voluntary determination to get along without belief.* . . . *Guessing* is deliberate pretension to belief, to knowledge; it is deliberate make-believe, for personal advantage, and so is essentially immoral when employed for social purposes. Also essentially bad in the private life, for it loosens the moorings of real conviction in the world of evidence."

On the margin of Baldwin's letter James wrote the following comment: "When you say to a man, 'don't guess,' it can't mean, 'don't come to a conclusion' — it can only mean, 'be *serious*,' 'don't come to a silly, wanton, conclusion.' The best pledge that my deliberations shall be serious is the participation in them of my passional nature." In his own letter of reply, James said that had he been consulted he would never have allowed his letters to Miller to be read in New York "by themselves" : —

"I don't know what actually *was* read — it must in any case have been quite malapropos and irrelevant. I have had a long correspondence with [Miller] about his article on me. It is a complete *ignoratio elenchi*, and leaves untouched *all* my contentions in the *Will to Believe*. Had I not labeled my article the 'Will to Believe,' had I entitled it a defense of faith, or words to that effect, he would have been without a pretext for most of what he says. And in *your* remarks about guessing . . . you also seem to be fighting a man of straw. In the abstract, one may conceive a man pretending to himself to believe what he does n't believe. There may be such men — the nearest approach I know to them is in those who out of obstinacy stick to a refuted position. The 'will to believe' that I meant, I called the 'passional nature' in the only important passages of the essay. This is essentially a will of complacence, assent, encouragement, towards a belief already there, — not, of course, an *absolute* belief, but such beliefs as any of us have, strong inclinations to believe, but threatened. The inner process is a succession of 'synthetic judgments.' What is so good, *may* be, *ought* to be, *must* be, *shall* be, — so far as I am concerned, I won't admit the opposite.[30]

[30] The final form of this succession of stages was elaborated by James in an address given in 1906 in San Francisco: "Faith's form of argument is something like this: Considering a view of the world: 'It is *fit* to be true,' she feels; 'it would be well if it *were* true; it *might* be true; it *may* be true; it *ought* to be true,' she says; 'it *must* be true,' she continues; 'it *shall* be true,' she concludes, '*for me;* that is, I will treat it as if it *were* true so far as my advocacy and actions are concerned.'" *Jour. of Philos.*, XXIV (1927), 198. For the occasion of this address, cf. above, I, 775.

In all the great hypotheses of life there is this *parti pris,* which from the inside is the completest concrete expression of the individual's life: but what, for the outside observer, is only a 'guess.' My contention is that the outside observer must *keep his hands off and let the thing occur.* Neither *a priori* rationalism nor authoritative scientism have any standard by which in a general precursive way they can divide the legitimate from the illegitimate guesses and say: 'Thus far guess, but no further.' And they have no means of knowing psychologically *how* sincere the guesser is, or *how* adequate or inadequate the 'evidence' to him may seem. . . .

"The only discussion which is of practical importance is discussion of *probable* things; and if any general laws of value can be laid down as binding individuals in their relations to such, I have yet to learn them. 'Don't guess' would abolish three-quarters of life at a stroke; and probably condemn us in advance to lose the truth in most cases. Surely your tabooing of guessing in Latin would kill the whole literary life of the pupil reading the author. The 'guess' must be a 'chance' affair viewed from *without,* and before the fact. *After* the fact, it may be 'sympathetic divination,' the only live thing in literature. . . . We seem to be getting into rather verbal squabble. I am willing to give up the word 'guess' provided you suggest a *tertium quid,* between that and going to the dictionary. . . . What an awful thing it is to *draw* a man, by attacking his opinions. You will probably feel bound to reply, and then I again, etc., *ad infinitum.*" [31]

Baldwin's later proposal that an article be prepared on "The Will to Believe" for his *Dictionary of Philosophy and Psychology* evoked from James an expression of growing dissatisfaction with his famous title: —

Cambridge, Oct. 24, 1901

Dear Baldwin, —

It seems to me absurd to make a technical term of the "Will to Believe." Would God I had never thought of that unhappy title for my essay, but called it a "Critique of Pure Faith!" Why not define the Will-to-swim, or to get rich, or to sit down? . . . What I meant by the title was the state of mind of the man who finds

---

[31] This (in part) and the following letter (in full) have been printed in Baldwin's *Between Two Wars,* 1926, II, 212–4, 217–8, and are here reprinted (with minor corrections) by permission of the publishers, The Stratford Co.

an impulse in him toward a believing attitude, and who resolves not to quench it simply because doubts of its truth are possible. Its opposite would be the maxim: Believe in nothing which you can possibly doubt. Pray leave it out of your dictionary. It can't be treated technically and has been the source of utter misunderstanding of my essay. If *that* could n't explain the title, what could? Ever truly yours,

WM. JAMES

In 1904 L. T. Hobhouse published an article in which he first attacks a doctrine which he says consists of two doctrines: "The first is, that by believing a thing we make it true; the second is, that we can believe in a thing without asking ourselves seriously whether it is true or false." He then affirms his own view that we need not "take the world precisely as reason shows it us," but may "give weight to the element of feeling as well"; for two reasons: because the feeling for belief is sometimes "compelling," and because feeling is the "forerunner of thought." [32] This article led to the following exchange of letters: —

Chocorua, Aug. 12, 1904 [33]

Dear Brother Hobhouse, —

Don't you think it a *tant soit peu* scurvy trick to play on me ('t is true that you don't name me, but to the informed reader the reference is transparent — I say nothing of poor Schiller's case) to print in the *Aristotelian Proceedings* . . . a beautiful duplicate of my own theses in the "Will to Believe" essay (which should have been called by the less unlucky title the *Right* to Believe) in the guise of an *alternative and substitute* for my doctrine, for which latter you, in the earlier pages of your charmingly written essay, *substitute a travesty* for which I defy any candid reader to find a single justification in my text? My essay hedged the license to indulge in private over-beliefs with so many restrictions and signboards of danger that the outlet was narrow enough. It made of tolerance the essence of the situation; it defined the permissible cases; it treated the faith-attitude as a necessity for individuals, because the total "evidence," which only the race can draw, has to

---

[32] "Faith and the Will to Believe," *Proc. of the Aristotelian Soc.,* IV (1904), 91, 104-5, 109.
[33] Reprinted from *L.W.J.,* II, 207-9.

include their experiments among its data. It tended to show only that faith could not be absolutely *vetoed,* as certain champions of "science" (Clifford, Huxley, etc.) had claimed it ought to be. It was a function that might lead, and probably does lead, into a wider world. You say identically the same things; only, from your special polemic point of view, you emphasize more the dangers; while I, from *my* polemic point of view emphasized more the right to run their risk.

Your essay, granting that emphasis and barring the injustice to me, seems to me exquisite, and, taking it as a unit, I subscribe unreservedly to almost every positive word. — I say "positive," for I doubt whether you have seen enough of the extraordinarily invigorating effect of mind-cure-philosophy on certain people to justify your somewhat negative treatment of that subject; and I say "almost" because your distinction between "spurious" and "genuine" courage . . . reminds me a bit too much of "true" and "false" freedom, and other sanctimonious come-offs. — Could you not have made an equally sympathetic reading of *me?*

I should n't have cared a copper for the misrepresentation were it not a "summation of stimuli" affair. I have just been reading Bradley on Schiller in the July *Mind,* and A. E. Taylor on "the will to believe" in the *McGill Quarterly* of Montreal.[34] Both are vastly worse than you; and I cry to Heaven to tell me of what insane root my "leading contemporaries" have eaten, that they are so smitten with blindness as to the meaning of printed texts. Or are we others absolutely incapable of making our meaning clear?

I imagine that there is neither insane root nor unclear writing, but that in these matters each man writes from out of a field of consciousness of which the bogey in the background is the chief object. Your bogey is superstition; my bogey is desiccation; and each, for his contrast-effect, clutches at any text that can be used to represent the enemy, regardless of exegetical proprieties. In my essay the evil shape was a vision of "Science" in the form of abstraction, priggishness and sawdust, lording it over all. Take the sterilest scientific prig and cad you know, compare him with the richest religious intellect you know, and you would not, any more

---

[34] "On Truth and Practice," *Mind,* N.S., XIII (1904) ; and "Some Side Lights on Pragmatism," *The McGill Univ. Magazine,* III ² (1903-4).

than I would, give the former the exclusive right of way. But up to page 104 of your essay he will deem you altogether on his side.

Pardon the familiarity of this epistle. I like and admire your *Theory of Knowledge* so much, and you reduplicate (I *don't* mean *copy*) my views so beautifully in this article, that I hate to let you go unchidden. Believe me, with the highest esteem (plus some indignation, for you ought to know better!) Yours faithfully,

WM. JAMES

Wimbledon, Sept. 8, 1904

Dear Professor James, —

I feel my withers altogether unwrung by your charming letter. Contrite as I am for unintentionally misrepresenting you, I can't but think that some good may have been done, and that through a certain amount of friction we are for once getting a little nearer to a mutual understanding. I certainly attacked what I thought to be the meaning and drift of your essay, and (apart from the personal contrition of which I have spoken) it is a great satisfaction to me to find that I read you wrongly and that the view of faith and reason put up in my paper to be demolished is *not* yours. At the same time, to be honest in self-defence, I must still say that I think my interpretation of your general drift was not an unnatural one. At any rate it represented accurately the impression made on my mind, and therefore I suppose an impression which might be made on other minds as well.

No doubt, as you say, one judges things too much by the particular fear that we bring to the reading of them. I don't think I should describe my "bogey" as superstition, but rather as that kind of scepticism as to the rational — a faith founded on faithlessness — which, especially under the influence of A. J. Balfour, has predominated in England of late years, and is, I am convinced, no mere doctrine of the schools but a real influence making for demoralization in public affairs. That make-believe will do instead of reality is the only thing approaching to a principle which I can find in the fashionable modes of thinking about great affairs practical and speculative, and I have had Schiller writing to me, and asking me as a journalist to accept H. G. Wells's statement that facts which the public will not accept are not facts. This seems to me on one side childish, but on another most tragically serious — a mood pregnant with utter mischief. Schiller's principle is that of our "mafficking" mobs who yell victory where there is no victory, break the head of the journalist or orator who tries to tell them the truth, and are much surprised five years afterwards at finding themselves heavily taxed to pay the costs of the "facts" which they had not recognised. This is the mood which I want to exorcise. Perhaps you do not experience it on your side of the Atlantic. But here it flourishes, carefully fostered by a whole tribe of popularisers (I don't include Schiller) with the Prime Minister at their head. But many thanks for your letter and the Atlantic breeze! Very sincerely yours,

L. T. HOBHOUSE

The ground of James's complaint is quite clear. He was accused of encouraging *willfulness* or *wantonness* of belief, or of advocating belief for belief's sake, whereas his whole purpose had been to *justify* belief. He had affirmed that belief was voluntary, but had naturally assumed that, in this as in other cases, volition would be governed by motives and illuminated by reasons. His critics had accused him of advocating *license* in belief, whereas, on the contrary, his aim had been to formulate rules for belief. And whatever one might think of its extensive religious applications, the thesis had been simple. He had argued that in certain cases where both belief and doubt are possible there is a greater likelihood of getting the truth by believing than by doubting — or at least an equal likelihood, with other advantages besides. Over and above the risk of incurring error, to which science is so acutely alive, there is another risk to be considered, the risk, namely, of losing truth. What truth was, he had not undertaken to show: thus the theme of "the will to believe" and that of "pragmatism" were not the same. This is made quite clear in a letter which James wrote in 1907 to Professor H. M. Kallen. He had made the "satisfactoriness" of the true idea consist in its leading to a specific object or factual context,[35] and his correspondent had applauded the statement that the "will to believe" ought to "play no part in this discussion."

[35] *M.T.*, 156.

South Lincoln, Aug. 1, 1907

Dear Kallen, —

I am glad you think my article clarifying. As regards the "Will to Believe" matter, it should not complicate the question of what we mean by truth. Truth is constituted by verification actual or possible, and beliefs, *however* reached, have to be verified before they can count as true. The question whether we have a right to believe anything before verification concerns not the constitution of truth, but the policy of belief. It is *usually* poor policy to believe what is n't verified; but sometimes the belief produces verification — as when it produces activity creative of the fact believed; and again, it may without altering given facts, be a belief in an altered meaning or value for them. In that case, why is n't it "true," if it *fits* the facts perfectly? It is neither "false" nor "irrelevant" then; and the will to believe in the *better* interpretation, can only be contrasted with the will to believe in a worse one or in none at all. What absurd alternatives for the "truth"-lover to insist on! I think Schiller is quite right in emphasizing (if he does emphasize) this aspect of the relation of our mind to reality. In any case the verification of the individual's will to believe may first occur long after he is dead — yet for him it may be the best policy; and he too must square his will to believe with the facts and truths already verified, in his possession. . . . Yours truly,

WM. JAMES

This letter, while it divides the doctrines of "pragmatism" and the "will to believe," also points the way to their union. For if verification is a sort of "satisfactoriness," then truth becomes in some broad sense commensurable with those subjective values which justify belief in the absence of verification. So the way is paved for the generalized idea of truth as the goodness of ideas on the whole, where agreement with fact, though it may take precedence, is only one value among others.

LXV

ETHICS VERSUS ÆSTHETICS

THERE is an undeniable moral accent in the life as well as in the thought of James. In view of the fact that he subordinated thought to action, and therefore in principle accepted the Kantian doctrine of the "primacy of practical reason," it is surprising that he wrote so little on moral philosophy. But this comparative inattention to the traditional problems and theories of ethics was offset by the strength of his moral convictions. His total expression was infused with moral zeal — his personal code was rigorous and unmistakable.

It was James's moralism that stood in the way of a more perfect sympathy with the most stimulating and congenial of his early friends. On March 7, 1900, Holmes, then Chief Justice of the Supreme Court of Massachusetts, was given a dinner by the Bar Association of Boston. His response was a brief formulation of his philosophy of life: "We cannot live our dreams. We are lucky enough if we can give a sample of our best, and if in our hearts we can feel that it has been nobly done. . . . The joy of life is to put out one's power in some natural and useful or harmless way. . . . The rule of joy and the law of duty seem to me all one. I confess that altruistic and cynically selfish talk seem to me about equally unreal. . . . From the point of view of the world the end of life is life. Life is action, the use of one's powers. As to use them to their height is our joy and duty, so it is the one end that justifies itself. . . . Life is an end in itself, and the only question as to whether it is worth living is whether you have enough of it." [1]

Having read this speech, James wrote to his friend Miss Frances R. Morse: "I thank you for the paper with the Chief Justice's speech to the bar dinner. I must say I 'm disappointed in O.W.H. for being unable to make any other than that one set speech which comes out on every occasion. It 's all right for once, in the ex-

[1] *Speeches by Oliver Wendell Holmes*, 1913, 83–6.

uberance of youth, to celebrate mere vital excitement, *la joie de
vivre,* as a protest against humdrum solemnity. But to make it
systematic, and oppose it, as an ideal and a duty, to the ordinarily
recognized duties, is to pervert it altogether — especially when one
is a Chief Justice. It is curiously childish to me, and Wendell
always forgets that on his own terms the dutiful people also fulfil
his law. Even they live hard, and enjoy the struggle with their
opposing devils! So let them alone! W. reminds me of the verse
of Browning, which Santayana in his new book says Attila or Alaric
might have written: 'Bound dizzily to the wheel of Change, to slake
the thirst of God.' Mere excitement is an immature ideal, unworthy of the Supreme Court's official endorsement." [2]

James's strong attachment to Holmes on other grounds makes
this dissent the more striking. It derives further significance from
the fact that James himself seemed so often to be preaching the
same gospel — of action for the action's sake. But there can be
no doubt whatever of his sensitiveness to any skeptical slur upon
moral earnestness, or to any faint-hearted abandonment of the
cause of righteousness. If there is to be anything inherently
valuable in living, it must be living *of a certain sort,* in which one
both serves a moral ideal and *believes in it.* This note appears in
his comments on the French, whose brilliancy never quite reconciled
him to their seeming capriciousness. By the same token he admired the Germans for their recognition of "discipline in life, of
something external really existing, which it is the duty of a man
to bring his will into harmony with." [3] Whether in this James
was voicing the genius of his ancestry — their Scotch-Irish levity
curbed by their Presbyterian sobriety — I shall not venture to say,
but there is an unmistakable connection with James's personal need
of a stabilizer for his mercurial temperament.

Closely allied to James's moral earnestness was his strong distaste
for anything which he suspected of being decadent. It was not
merely that he disapproved of moral irregularities, but that he felt
an almost physiological repugnance to anything which was over-
refined, overseasoned, or overmature. He applauded Blood's remark that the universe was "game-flavored as a hawk's wing," [4] but
he did not want his game too high. He liked simplicity, purity, and

[2] Other parts of this letter appear in *L.W.J.,* 124–9; and below, 326–7.
[3] Above, I, 296.
[4] *W.B.,* ix.

wholesomeness, in life as well as in nature. That at the same time he was tolerant of difference, addicted to morbid psychology, and catholic in his love of art and literature is not to be denied, but rather recognized as proving how deeply rooted was the plant which could resist these opposing influences. There are many evidences of this "wholesome" side of James's moralism. In its positive form it is illustrated by his fondness for Erckmann-Chatrian, whose *L'Ami Fritz* and *Les Confidences d'un joueur de clarinette* he loved as much in the year of his death as when he first read them in 1867. There is his admiring antipathy of Santayana's philosophy, with its "perfection of rottenness" and "moribund Latinity." [5] Best of all, there is his feeling toward the seduction of Italy — his alternations of yielding and rejecting. When he judged the debility and "sweet decay" [6] of Italy it was usually in contrast with the hygienic "insipidity" of Switzerland. "Switzerland is *good!* Good *people!*" [7] This feeling appears in the two following letters, divided by an interval of eight years. The first was to Charles Ritter, the second to Grace Norton.

Firenze, Oct. 5, 1892

Florence seems to me even more attractive than it was when I was here eighteen years ago. We have taken our apartment for six months. I shall read philosophy, dabble a little in the history of art, and lead a very quiet winter. But how sovereignly *good* is Switzerland! It meets all the major needs of body and soul as no other country does, in summer time. After the æsthetics, the morbidness, the corruptions of Italy, how I shall want again in *ihrem Thau gesund mich zu baden!* You have doubtless been shocked by Renan's death. A true magician, but a man who caused legitimate disappointment by the form which his intellect finally found most congruous. He used the vocabulary of the moral and religious life too sweetly and freely for one whose thought refused to be *bound* by those ideals. Moral ideals go with refusals and sacrifices, and there is something shocking about the merely *musical* function they play in Renan's pages. So I call him *profoundly* superficial! But *what* an artist!

[5] *L.W.J.*, II, 122–3.
[6] *L.W.J.*, I, 342.
[7] *L.W.J.*, 328; *Journal*, May 19, 1905.

July 6, 1900

We are in a glorious situation, looking down on Lucerne and its
Lake, from a glorious hill-top on which there is a good deal of
level walking possible and good *woods,* which I greatly crave.
Unfortunately five of our six days have been cloud-wrapt, cold,
and pouring with rain, or sodden and blanketed with mist.   That
is the worst of Switzerland, which apart from that is surely the
cream of the whole earth.   Prosaic, but oh! so practically intelligent
and so proud and good.   When we are reincarnated, dear Grace,
let us pray to be Swiss, — I a country hotel-keeper, you a "saleslady"
in a "bazaar" for tourists, rather spare and dry in person, but
with such clear truthful eyes, such pink roses in your cheeks, and
such a sweet caressing voice.   We must be born in German Switzerland, so as to have that nerveless nature, and that delightful vocal
intonation; and *if* you prefer it, we shall be mountaineers, rather
than the (possibly too citified) pair I first suggested.   Again, *qui
vivra verra!* . . .

How does the state of the world strike you?   Our children and
perhaps their children are evidently bound to live through another great epoch of savagery.   It seems to me that we ought to
let China alone, too thankful that she is contented to cork herself
up.   When once *she* grows inoculated with restlessness and progress and machinery she is much more likely to pauperize us by
her labor, than enrich us by her purchases.   The Boers of course
must be licked, but also England ought to get out of South Africa,
and leave the Africans to settle their own affairs.   She won't;
and there 'll be endless trouble.   It sickens one to read the stupid
English papers.   Yesterday a *Standard* editorial praising McKinley
for his conduct of the Philippine business, and saying that the
United States is bound to be a big empire.   Today I suppose we
shall get news of the Kansas City Convention.   Bryan has in him
many elements of a very great man, I believe, and I shall vote for
him, whatever happens, if I am at home.   But why has God made
him so obstinate about silver *just now?* . . .   Farewell, dear Grace.
It is Irving Street which is really the hub of the earth, — the
"Norton land."

The strength of the æsthetic motive in James is well known and
abundantly attested.   In his youth he was deeply impressed by

Goethe's amoralism, and this impression was repeated and confirmed as late as 1902. He respected canons of taste, both in his conduct and in his judgment. He recognized the importance of the æsthetic motive in the intellectual life. Our knowledge being so fragmentary, "inconsistent thought is no doubt truer" (in the sense of agreement with fact) than consistent thought; and we must attribute the demand for consistency, therefore, to an independent subjective passion. James had a keen relish for creative originality. His own artistic impulse, transferred from painting, found expression in philosophizing, which involved the same "sacrificial element" and (for James, at least) the same inseparable fusion of style and matter. From time to time, notably in Paris and Dresden in his youth, and again in Florence twenty-five years later, he indulged a ravenous appetite for the visual arts. He often remarked that he had no visual *memory,* but the effect of this was to make him more rather than less dependent upon immediate visual experience. Thus we read in the *Principles:* "I am myself a good draughtsman, and have a very lively interest in pictures, statues, architecture and decoration, and a keen sensibility to artistic effects. But I am an extremely poor visualizer, and find myself often unable to reproduce in my mind's eye pictures which I have most carefully examined." "I envy ye the world of Art," he wrote to his brother in 1872. "Away from it, as we live, we sink into a flatter, blanker kind of consciousness, and indulge in an ostrich-like forgetfulness of all our richest potentialities — and they startle us now and then when by accident some rich human product, pictorial, literary or architectural, slaps us with its tail." [8]

The lack of art in the *environment* made it impossible that James should ever be completely reconciled to the "American scene": "We're a thousand years behindhand in so many things; and the *attained* social character of European civilizations generally is more *erfreulich* than those mere suggestions and possibilities of good, that are perhaps more abundant here. After five months spent mainly in rural England, both my wife and I were sickened by the shock of the scurviness and *decay* which the face of things presented when we landed here. In 500 years we may hope for polish, but hardly in less, with the West wide-open to drain off every rise of the water-level of civilization in the older parts of the country.

[8] *Principles,* II, 53, note; also 61, note; *cf.* above, I, 327.

Tight fit is what shapes things definitely; with a loose fit you get no results, and America is redolent of loose fits everywhere." [9]

If James felt the futility of theoretical æsthetics, it was not, then, for lack of artistic sensibility or owing to any disparagement of the value of art. Nor did he neglect the problem. He returned to it again and again, but always with the same sense of failure. A diary contains the following entry for April 11, 1868: "I went yesterday again to the collection of casts. All I have written or may write about art is nonsense. Perhaps the attempt to translate it into language is absurd — for if that could be done what would be the use of the art itself? I found last night quoted from Goethe a sentence like: 'je incommensurabler und für den Verstand unfasslicher, eine poetische Produktion, je besser.' [10] Yet I feel myself forced to inquire, while standing before the Greek things, what the x is that makes the difference between them and all modern things, and I clutch at straws of suggestions that the next day destroys." He read the standard literature on the subject, but "why," he wrote in 1879, "does the *Aesthetik* of every German philosopher appear to the artist like the abomination of desolation?" [11]

As time went on this feeling of futility was converted into a definite judgment that the æsthetic experience was insuperably personal and subjective. It was not that James regarded this experience as one of undiscriminating emotionality — quite the contrary. In the *Principles* he describes an aged couple who sat for more than an hour before Titian's "Assumption" in Venice, supported by "a glow of spurious sentiment that would have fairly made old Titian sick." They had missed the point. "In every art, in every science, there is the keen perception of certain relations being *right* or not, and there is the emotional flush and thrill consequent thereupon." [12] But it is this "flush" or "thrill" which is the ultimate criterion, and this is too hopelessly relative to the individual observer to permit of any general formulation.

We have seen that in the '90s, realizing that he had slighted the subject of feeling in the *Principles,* James turned to a study of

[9] To C. A. Strong, Dec. 31, 1908.
[10] "The more incommensurable and unintelligible a poetic production, the better." The original, from Eckermann's *Gespräche mit Goethe,* reads "desto besser" instead of "je besser."
[11] "Sentiment of Rationality," *Mind,* IV (1879), 338.
[12] *Principles,* II, 471-2.

this subject and to the allied subject of æsthetics. On both subjects he corresponded with Henry Rutgers Marshall, to whom the
following paragraph was addressed in 1893: "I am entirely converted to the relativity-doctrine which you set forth with such
effect. I don't believe that 'differences of taste' are a provisional
infirmity, to be superseded by more evolved insight into 'the Beautiful.' Any abstract treatment of the 'Æsthetic Ideal' is inadequate
to the innumerable different demands which different men (and
the same man at different moments) are entitled to make upon the
artist. The clash of opinions, and of mutual disdains lavished on
each other by the different dilettantes and experts at Florence had
begun to make me doubt of any 'objectively true' standard of
criticism, and the radicalism of your articles settled my mind entirely."

The "experts" appear again in a letter written to Flournoy
from Florence in the same year: "I see here a couple of young men
who are devoted to Italian painting in a *strengwissenschaftlich*
manner,[13] their principal interest being the renaming of all the
pictures in the galleries. I have also another friend, who is an
entomologist,[14] blessed with a great memory for details and who
has taken *Kunstgeschichte* in an entomological manner. Alongside of their severity there seems little room for a merely loving
relation to the pictures. But the good thing about a work of art
is that it tells all sorts of things to different spectators, of none of
which things the artist ever knew a word."

Though denying any absolute standard, James admitted a felt
æsthetic obligation, based on a regard for consistency or a respect
for authority. In the late '90s he made a careful study of Kant's
æsthetics as presented in the *Critique of Judgment*. The only general comment which he recorded was written on the flyleaf of this
book: "We are quite willing to recognize the value of certain works
of art, provided their lovers make *no* claim of universal validity
for them. . . . Others which (judged by classic standards of
'beauty') are 'ugly,' we nevertheless feel that we 'ought' to admire,
either because the qualities they have are in the *line of prolongation*
of qualities which we do admire, or because we see persons admiring them whose judgment in other ways we emulate, and so

[13] Presumably Bernard Berenson and Charles A. Loeser.
[14] Baron C. R. Osten-Sacken, authority on the *Diptera* of North America, and
fellow member with James of The Club.

would be with them in this way too.   The last standard of 'beauty' is in *someone's feeling;* and we think the beauty objectively valid for *us* when we recognize the authority of its recognizer and feeler, as someone whom we would fain resemble."

Apart from its relativity, the æsthetic experience resists formulation because it consists in *feeling*.   Writing later to Marshall, he said: "The difference between the first- and second-best things in art absolutely seems to escape verbal definition — it is a matter of a hair, a shade, an inward quiver of some kind — yet what miles away in point of preciousness!   Absolutely the same verbal formula applies to the supreme success and to the thing that just misses it, and yet verbal formulas are all that your æsthetics will give." [15] This objection is an application of the most general principle in James's philosophy, the priority, namely, of original experience over representations or descriptions — "the contrast between the richness of life and the poverty of all possible formulas." [16]   He insisted on this priority wherever his own original experience was peculiarly vivid.   There is food for reflection in the fact that while he wrote at length about religious experiences he shrank from any account of æsthetic experiences.   I suspect that the explanation is to be found in the fact that he *had* the æsthetic experience, and borrowed the religious — which was thus, even in his "sources," already verbalized.

So much for James's æsthetics, or his rejection of the "universal," "objective" æsthetics of his day.   This in itself implies no subordination of the æsthetic experience, or of art, in the hierarchy of values. [17]   To account for this subordination we must turn to other considerations, and note, in the first place, that there was in James a *primitivism* which always disputed for possession of his soul. Assuming that art and even landscape imply some regard for form, their enjoyment was opposed in James to his relish for the *unformed* — the raw and crude.   To the same correspondent to whom he complained of the "looseness" of America (and in the same year!) he recorded this opposite judgment: —

"I enjoy an occasional thing when it comes in my way, like York or Durham, but a methodical pursuit of the picturesque — heaven

[15] *L.W.J.,* II, 87.   *Cf.* "What an absolute thing genius is!" (*N.S.B.,* 450.)
[16] Above, 127.
[17] James has been criticized by Schiller, Bradley, and others, for failing to allow a proper place for æsthetic values.

remove me sooner! The only thing that does me real good is the *country* in the American sense, as something that you can go *into*, and lie on the ground with a book all day. *This* [English] country is splendid if one have proper legs and wind, which I have n't. It is full of crags and climbs and possible loneliness, but the entire foreground is cocknified in the extreme, solidly built up and walled round."

In a limited, orderly world, whether made by the hand of man or by his thought and imagination, James felt a sort of claustrophobia. The *historic* aroused a similar feeling. The cult of art lovers was associated in his mind with traditionalism, especially in Italy; whereas James preferred the boundless future or the opportune present. He was an exponent of contemporaneousness. There is something to be done *now* to make the world better. It was in this vein that he wrote to his sister from Rome in 1873: "Italy is a very *delightful* place to dip into but no more. I can't imagine how, unless one is earnestly studying history in some way, it can in the long run help injuring all one's active powers. The weight of the past world here is fatal, — one ends by becoming its mere parasite instead of its equivalent. This worship, this dependence on other men is abnormal. The ancients did things by doing the business of their own day, not by gaping at their grandfathers' tombs, — and the normal man today will do likewise. Better fifty years of Cambridge, than a cycle of Cathay! Adieu. Your brutal and philistine Brother."

We are thus brought back again to the priority of the moral will — over feeling, as well as over thought. He was far from proposing to abolish feeling. He recognized it as composing a large part of that inwardness of life from which the individual derives his uniqueness and dignity. He even advocated intensity of feeling: "It is a consequence of the 'law of stimulation' that, apart from motor effect and *per se,* feeling is reckoned as a good. Which lives most, this orderly man whose life runs on oiled rails of propriety, who never does ill or makes a mistake or has a regret, or a pang, because on every occasion the right *action* presents itself to his mind and he simply does it; or the passionate tumultuous blunderer, whose whole life is an alternation of rapturous excitement, and horrible repentance and longing for the ruined good? He *feels;* the other *does.* If his type should be extinguished, surely would not one of the divinest of human gifts, the gift of intense feeling, be lost from life?"

But James, as he said, was a "motor." [18]   It was an essential feature of his psychology, furthermore, that emotion, being organic and sensory in its nature, was an unnatural terminus of mind.   A completed cycle of conscious life will always culminate in action — feelings merely enjoyed lead to the atrophy of will: "Even the habit of excessive indulgence in music, for those who are neither performers themselves nor musically gifted enough to take it in a purely intellectual way, has probably a relaxing effect upon the character.   One becomes filled with emotions which habitually pass without prompting to any deed, and so the inertly sentimental condition is kept up.   The remedy would be, never to suffer one's self to have an emotion at a concert, without expressing it afterward in *some* active way." [19]

James's subordination of æsthetic feeling to the moral will was not effected without a struggle or without lapses.   When as a youth he was reading Schiller's *Loveliness and Dignity,* he noted in his diary: "My old trouble, and the root of antinomianism in general, seems to be a dissatisfaction with anything less than grace." [20]   In short James shared the romanticist's repugnance to obstructions interposed by duty against the free flow of spontaneity. But so ineradicable was his moralism that he could finally accept no spontaneity save that of the enthusiastic will already pledged to righteousness.

Additional evidence of this characteristic subordination of feeling is provided by a letter of 1882: "I am myself a prosaic wretch, and find myself reading little poetry, especially little that is not lyric, but I must say that when I *do* enjoy it I enjoy it very much.   To you gifted ones who can float and soar and circle through the sky of expression, so freely, our slow hobbling on terra firma must sometimes be a matter of impatience.   I think that the power of *playing* with thought and language such as you possess is the divinest of gifts.   You should not be too much professional artists at it, I mean too exclusively bound to it, — it ought to be the overflowing of a life rich in other ways. . . .   It was very agreeable to hear

[18] *L.W.J.,* II, 163.
[19] *Principles,* I, 125–6.
[20] April 21, 1868 (above, I, 273).

your praise of my article. But I think you undervalued poor
Royce's. . . . I think Royce meant that the doing of outward acts,
as a sort of opaque limit to our life, was something that could never
be healthily transcended. If you try to get beyond their outwardness, and change them from ends to means, means whose end is
emotional, you slide towards corruption inevitably." [21]   In all this
there is an echo of old parental admonitions. In spite of his artistic
calling and the artistic seductions to which he was highly vulnerable,
it was his steadfast opinion that the æsthetic experience is not fit
to be either the whole of life or its highest moment.

James did not subordinate ethics to æsthetics; neither did he
subordinate it to psychology, as he might with equal reason have
done. He might have devoted himself to a description of moral
experiences and moral types; none was better fitted to do so. When
he was a youth of twenty-seven he delivered himself as follows on
the question of women: —

"However he might shrink from expressing it in naked words,
the wife his heart more or less subtly craves is at bottom a dependent
being. In the outer world he can only hold good his position by
dint of reconquering it afresh every day: life is a struggle where
success is only relative, and all sanctity is torn off of him; where
failure and humiliation, the exposure of weaknesses, and the un-
masking of pretense, are assured incidents: and he accordingly
longs for one tranquil spot where he shall be valid absolutely and
once for all; where, having been accepted, he is secure from further
criticism, and where his good aspirations may be respected no less
than if they were accomplished realities. In a word, the elements of
security and repose are essential to his ideal; and the question is,
Are they easily attainable without some feeling of dependence on
the woman's side, — without her relying on him to be her mediator
with the external world, — without his activity overlapping hers
and surrounding it on almost every side, so that he makes as it
were the atmosphere in which she lives?" [22]

Sometime between 1878 and 1880 James noted his reflections

---

[21] To Emma Lazarus, Aug. 26, 1882. This letter will be published in full in
Letters to Emma Lazarus, edited by Prof. R. L. Rusk. James's essay was probably
"Rationality, Activity and Faith"; Royce's, "The Decay of Earnestness," *The
Californian,* III (1881).

[22] From a review of J. S. Mill's "Subjection of Women," *North Amer. Rev.,*
CIX (1869), 563.

on the subject of "sentimentality"; and listed the following "cases where sensations, in becoming ideal, form sentiments stronger than the parent sensation": —

"We do a disagreeable thing now rather than look forward to it. . . . Valuing the potential more than the actual. . . . Rousseau glows with ideal parental love. . . . Enthusiasm for the abstract quality may coexist with perfect insensibility to its particular manifestations, as where the goodness of God is used for denying all goodness in his creatures. . . . The way Carlyle, Ruskin, Kingsley, Froude and all that fry idealize the past and don't see in the present the very qualities they prate about. . . . As where we do a thing now because we shall be glad to have done it. . . . Or where we enjoy a present experience the more for representing the pleasure with which in future we shall look back upon it. . . . A sailor goes to sea for the pleasure of landing. . . . A woman has all her own sound teeth extracted so that she may be relieved of the dread of it for some future day. . . . Rather *deserve* a thing and not have it, than have it as a matter of course. . . . Rather keep the *power* of having or doing a thing and go without the thing, than have the thing 'over' and lose the power."

During the last twenty years of his life James developed his peculiar genius for the psychology of motivation. In his study of religion he discovered by sympathetic divination the value of faith and of mystical insight to those, not himself, who felt them. In his essay on "Energies of Men" he described the emotional and ideal incentives which can prevail over the extremities of physical exhaustion. He studied the mentality of war, of patriotism, of lynching, with the same penetration. He was peculiarly qualified, in short, both by interest and by aptitude, to become intimate with the strange and to enter into the external. It is necessary to be reminded of this if one is to feel the full force of James's moralism. He had every qualification to become a mere pathologist of morals — a recorder of moral symptoms, retaining the detachment of the clinical observer; whereas on the contrary he was a heated moral partisan.

James's ethics was not derived from or profoundly influenced by the ethics of any other philosopher. It was the product of his general philosophical thinking together with his personal traits and attitudes. He admired Spencer's *Data of Ethics* as the best of that writer's works, and a student would have no difficulty in finding a similarity between Spencer's "evolved society" and the "all-enveloping demands" of James's ideal universe.   But James must have more of heat and struggle, and a more realistic recognition of the fatal incompatibility of men's natural desires, than was provided for in Spencer's "lady-like tea-table elysium."   He admired the individualistic strain in Spencer's social philosophy, but took him as his chief polemical opponent on the question of the rôle of the individual in history.   And it was inevitable that James should feel the personal limitations of the man himself.[23]

Something like the reverse is true of James's relations to Mill. He admired the man, and sympathized with the general trend of his liberalism;[24] but he could not accept either of his principal doctrines, — his associationism or his utilitarianism, — though he learned them in early days from Chauncey Wright. He thought that association with pleasure furnished an inadequate explanation of moral ideas, which often require the assumption of "innate preferences," or congenital variations of the Darwinian sort that prove themselves in life.[25]   Pleasure he believed to be only one of many demands — all entitled to consideration, and standing in conflict one with another.   He rejected the doctrine of a uniform motivation, in favor of a multiplicity of instincts and ideals; and his ultimates of value were not felt satisfactions, but claims and heroic deeds.[26]

[23] *Cf.* above I, 478; and *W.B.*, 168, 214, 260.
[24] *Cf.* above, I, 552–4; *W.B.*, 234.
[25] *W.B.*, 187; *Principles*, II, 672–5.
[26] *Principles*, II, 549–59; *W.B.*, 194.

LXVI

MORAL PHILOSOPHY

"WHAT does the moral enthusiast care for philosophical ethics?" asked James in 1879. "The Moral Philosopher and the Moral Life," originally an address given at Yale in 1891, is his answer to this question and his only published discussion of theoretical ethics. He recognized its uniqueness, and was disappointed at its reception.[1] His conclusions grew out of the reading and thinking done for his lectures when he took over Philosophy 4 from Palmer in 1888–1889. The outline of these lectures has been preserved, and the following selections serve to supplement the published address : —

"Man spontaneously *believes* and spontaneously *acts*. But as acts and beliefs multiply they grow inconsistent. To escape *bellum omnium contra omnes*, reasonable principles, fit for all to agree upon, must be sought. The search constitutes philosophy, which has two subdivisions: (1) science, the principles of *fact* or what *is*, whether good or bad; (2) ethics, what is good or bad, whether it *be* or *be not*. The principles of ethics are independent of those of science. . . .

"Things are either immediately admitted to be good, without discussion, or there is discussion. To *prove* a thing good, we must conceive it as belonging to a genus already admitted good. Every ethical proof therefore involves as its major premise an ethical proposition; every argument must end in some such proposition, admitted without proof. . . . How come such ethical propositions to be admitted? . . . There are innumerable ways in which men have been led to their judgments that things are good and bad. The satisfaction of any desire or impulse is good, its frustration bad. From the conflicts and harmonies between our instinctive constitution and the

---

[1] "Sentiment of Rationality," *Mind*, IV (1879), 338. M. Frank Abauzit, French translator of the *Varieties*, informs me that James valued this essay above the others contained in *W.B. Cf.* below, 274–5.

circumstances of our life there must necessarily arise innumerable goods and bads, social and physical. And remote things (either real or imaginary) by association with immediate things come to be esteemed good and bad themselves. Analogy leads us, moreover, to admit that apart from the instinctive preferences and repugnances which are necessary to life, there must be others arising spontaneously or by 'accidental variation.' . . .

"The ulterior proposition usually brought forward is that whatever seems to us *obligatory* is better than what seems not so. . . . But impulses and imperatives run together, and the same act may seem imperative to one man, but not so to another. . . . Moreover there are two sorts of obligation, internal and external, [and] the two obligations may conflict. . . . The feeling of obligation taken alone is thus too wavering and fallible a thing upon which to found a definitive system of ethics. Its data must themselves be compared, discussed and judged. But how? . . .

"So far as I feel anything good, I make it so. It *is* so, for me. . . . *Prima facie,* goods form a multifarious jungle. Must we so leave them, or can they be unified? If there were any quality by participating in which all concrete goods are made good, that would be a unifying and subordinating principle. Of all the proposed *summa genera,* pleasure and perfection have the best claim to be considered. So far as enjoyment is a part of perfection, and so far as the consciousness of perfection brings pleasure, these two standards do not conflict, but involve each other. Inquiry presently shows us that, whether we take a unifying principle or whether we treat goods as irreducibly plural, in either case we practically bring up against problems insoluble by *a priori* rules. The abstract best would be that *all* goods should be realized. That is physically impossible, for many of them exclude each other. The whole difficulty of the moral life consists in deciding, when this is the case, which good to sacrifice and which to save. The difficulty is the *good excluded,* and exists where pleasures and perfections are the goods as much as when these have no common denominator. . . . The solution is by Royce's 'moral insight' — consider *every* good as a real good, and *keep as many as we can.* That act is the best act which *makes for the best whole,* the best whole being that which prevails at least cost, in which the vanquished goods are least completely annulled. . . .

"But how decide conflicts? . . . Follow the common traditions. Sacrifice all wills which are not organizable, and which avowedly go against the whole. No one pretends in the main to revise the decalogue, or to take up offenses against life, property, veracity, or decency into the permanent whole. If those are a man's goods, the man is not a member of the whole we mean to keep, and we sacrifice both him and his goods without a tear. When the rivalry is between real organizable goods, the rule is that the one victorious should so far as possible keep the vanquished somehow represented. Find some innocent way out. Examples: savage virtues preserved by athletics; warlike, by organized warfare . . . aristocratic love of art and splendor, [reconciled] with democratic equality; variety of races, with supremacy of the best; humanity, with Darwinism; romantic love, with breeding. . . . The world's trial better than the *closet solution.*" [2]

The principle is clear: value derives ultimately from the interests of the individual; and the social whole is justified by the inclusion and reconciliation of its individual parts. Individualism is fundamental.

Between 1893 and 1899 James gave a large number of public lectures and addresses in different parts of the United States — Hot Springs (Virginia), Chautauqua, Buffalo, Chicago, Lake Geneva (Wisconsin), Colorado Springs, and California.[3] In the course of his travels he made human as well as geographical discoveries. The exterior unattractiveness and apparent meaninglessness of what he saw was a challenge to his sympathy. One of the addresses which he gave was entitled, "A Certain Blindness in Human Beings," in which he insisted that the view of the outsider should be corrected by an imaginative understanding of the individual's experience and feeling. Then the aggregate life of man, otherwise monstrous, repetitive, and trivial, would take on an aspect of dignity and rich diversity. Writing in 1899 to Mrs. Glendower Evans about the *Talks to Teachers,* which contained this address and which he had just sent to her, James said: "Pray don't wade through the Teacher part, which is incarnate boredom. I sent it to you merely that you might read the essay 'On a Certain Blindness,' which is really the perception on which my whole individualistic philosophy

[2] For the parallel statement in the published essay, cf. *W.B.,* 205–15.
[3] *Cf.* above, 128–9, 145, and below, 371.

is based." [4]   "I care very much," he wrote in the same year to
another friend, "for the truth which it so inadequately tries . . .
to express."   In the Preface to the *Talks with Teachers,* we read: —

"I wish I were able to make the second, 'On a Certain Blindness
in Human Beings,' more impressive.   It is more than the mere piece
of sentimentalism which it may seem to some readers.   It connects
itself with a definite view of the world and of our moral relations to
the same.   Those who have done me the honor of reading my volume of philosophic essays will recognize that I mean the pluralistic
or individualistic philosophy.   According to that philosophy, the
truth is too great for any one actual mind, even though that mind
be dubbed 'the Absolute,' to know the whole of it.   The facts and
worths of life need many cognizers to take them in.   There is no
point of view absolutely public and universal. . . .   The practical
consequence of such a philosophy is the well-known democratic
respect for the sacredness of individuality." [5]

Peirce and Royce, who were lonely souls and more or less disqualified for social and public relations, emphasized the community,
both as a reality and as an ideal; James, the most sociable and ur-
bane of men, — actively, eagerly, almost painfully interested in the
state of his country and the world, — proclaimed the supreme value
of those feelings and strivings which are unique in each individual,
and whose authentic quality is immediately revealed to him alone.
This quality is a *redeeming* quality in so far as it possesses some
flavor of fidelity or courage, and the common "blindness in human
beings" is their failure to discern its inward glow.   James wrote to
his daughter of a dog who was once his housemate: "His tail keeps
wagging *all* the time, and he makes on me the impression of an
angel hid in a cloud.   He longs to do good." [6]   Human beings as
well as dogs usually wagged their tails in James's presence, and
wanted to do good, which no doubt confirmed his gospel that every
man is an angel hid in a cloud.

In proportion as one appreciates the inward significance of other
people's lives one attaches importance to differences: "The obstinate
insisting that tweedledum is *not* tweedledee is the bone and marrow
of life.   Look at the Jews and the Scots, with their miserable fac-

[4] Reprinted from *Atlantic,* CXLIV (1929), 377.
[5] *T.T.,* v.
[6] *L.W.J.,* II, 26.

tions and sectarian disputes, their loyalties and patriotisms and exclusions, — their annals now become a classic heritage, because men
of genius took part and sang in them. A thing is important if
anyone *think* it important." [7]

The institutional life of men must necessarily be based on their
likenesses, but its purpose is to make room for their differences.
It is what slips through the meshes of classification and resists organization that justifies either classification or organization: "The
memory of Davidson," said James, "will always strengthen my
faith in personal freedom and its spontaneities, and make me less unqualifiedly respectful than ever of 'civilization,' with its herding and
branding, licensing and degree-giving, authorizing and appointing,
and in general regulating and administering by system the lives of
human beings. Surely the individual, the person in the singular
number, is the more fundamental phenomenon, and the social institution, of whatever grade, is but secondary and ministerial.
Many as are the interests which social systems satisfy, always un-
satisfied interests remain over, and among them are interests to
which system, as such, does violence whenever it lays its hand upon
us. The best commonwealth will always be the one that most cher-
ishes the men who represent the residual interests, the one that leaves
the largest scope to their peculiarities." [8]

The inward, felt value of a human life is independent of the esteem of the world, or of such standards as fame and importance.
From this insight sprang James's endorsement of democracy.
Whereas, taken wholesale and externally, mankind form an un-
edifying spectacle, taken as individuals, one by one, each with his
own spark of idealism, they may be respected and valued. James's
humanity was not the pity excited by infirmity, but the admiring
regard excited by merit. Men are worth loving, regardless of their
high or low station in the world. And each individual may draw
self-respect from the same source.

Tolerance is an essential part of the same gospel. When one
sees the inward value of other lives one acknowledges their right to
exist, or even exults in their existence. James felt a tolerance of
mankind even in the aggregate — a will that life in its inexhaustible
quantity and irreducibly alien quality should exceed his power to

[7] *Principles,* II, 674–5, note.
[8] *M.S.,* 102–3.

comprehend.   He dealt with this question in the latter part of his lecture on *Human Immortality*.   He had no fear of an overcrowded Heaven: "The Deity that suffers us, we may be sure, can suffer many another queer and wondrous and only half-delightful thing. For my own part . . . I am willing that every leaf that ever grew in this world's forests and rustled in the breeze should become immortal." [9]   By the same token, unless he was fatigued or in the contrary mood, James was quite willing that the earth should be crowded with masses of "only half-delightful" beings, because he attributed to them an inward value which even the wisest sympathy could not measure.

Tolerance was a maxim of James's youth — not only the sympathetic tolerance for what is different, but the intellectual tolerance or humility which arises from a sense of the *limits* of sympathy. Thus he wrote in 1873: "Sight of elephants and tigers at Barnum's menagerie whose existence, so individual and peculiar, yet stands there, so intensely and vividly real, as much so as one's own, so that one feels again poignantly the unfathomableness of ontology, supposing ontology to be at all.   They *are, eodem jure* with myself, and yet I with my pretensions or at least aspirations to adequately represent the world, can never hope to *sympathize* in a genuine sense of the word with their being.   And the want of sympathy is not as in the case of some deformed or loathsome human life, for their being is admirable; so admirable that one yearns to be in some way its sharer, partner or accomplice.   Thus their foreignness confounds one's pretension to comprehend the world, — while their admirableness undermines the stoic or moral frame of mind in which one says the real meaning of life is *my* action.   This great world of life in no relation with my action, is so real!"

In the same period of James's life in which he thus praises the acknowledgment of ignorance, he set himself a standard of liberality in his moral judgment: "The 'man of the world's' scepticism . . . is at its finest in those generous characters who show it with regard to fortune, what she gives and what she withdraws — and with regard to particular misdemeanors and shortcomings of their friends, which are not allowed seriously to alter the general im-

---

[9] *H.I.*, 43–4.   This is a very old motive in James's thought.   In the "Sentiment of Rationality," where, referring to "a too infinite accumulation of population in the heavens," he goes on to say that the real wonder of existence is not that there should be so many, but that there should be *any*.   *Mind*, IV (1879), 344.

pression of their character in the long run. Such people can laugh at fate, are flexible, sympathize with the free flow of things, believe ever in the good, but are willing that it should shift its form. They do not close their hand on their possessions. When they profess a willingness that certain persons should be free they mean it not as most of us do — with a mental reservation, as that the freedom should be well employed and other similar humbug — but in all sincerity, and calling for no guarantee against abuse which, when it happens, they accept without complaint or embitterment as part of the chances of the game. They let their bird fly with no string tied to its leg."

Finally, there was a tolerance felt by James towards particular individuals — peers, fellow members of the élite, but whose beliefs or talents were contrary to his own. This tolerance is best exemplified by his relations with his colleagues, with no one of whom was he wholly in agreement or sympathy. He did not merely suffer their existence, but rejoiced in it, and hoped that each would be strong in his own way, to the greater enrichment of the total sum of life. His friendly disagreements with Palmer and Royce have been abundantly illustrated. The following letters concern Francis G. Peabody, Münsterberg, and Santayana. In each case he singles out for applause that which was most unlike himself. To Peabody he wrote: —

"I have just finished your masterly book,[10] which has both educated me, and filled me with pride in the quality of Harvard Production. It is one of those mature, fine-grained products of long incubation, and careful composition, whose weight is out of all proportion to their bulk, but which, being *wise* in the best sense of the term, are sure of a long lease of use and influence. We must all work like the mischief to keep our Harvard work up to something like that standard! This book of yours seems to me a sort of 'ægis' and guarantee cast over us — it holds the balance so well between 'individualism' which is ethical idealism, and institutionalism which is its deposited shell, and explains their mutual interaction and organic dependence. Hurrah, hurrah!"

And to Münsterberg, who in 1901 had prepared a statement of the needs of the department as a basis for the effort to raise funds for

[10] *Jesus Christ and the Social Question*, 1900. The date of this letter is Feb. 4, 1901.

the building of Emerson Hall: "Your jolly epistle of March 30th with all its enclosures comes this morning, and gives me a sense of the amount of life from which I have been cut off. I admire the talent with which the circulars are written; — like the elephant's trunk which uproots a tree or picks up a pin, your brain produces *Grundzüge der Psychologie* and the paragraph on Emerson Hall with equal ease! Return thanks to God for such an organ! I don't feel very sanguine of many thousands coming in; and to tell the truth, apart from the laboratory, whose need is real, I don't feel very eager to have them do so. Philosophy, of all subjects, can dispense with material wealth, and we seem to be getting along very well as it is. . . . I am not sure that I should n't be personally a little ashamed of a philosophy hall, but of course I shall express no such sentiments in public."

The praise of Santayana was contained in letters written to Eliot in 1896 and 1898: "Santayana is a very honest and unworldly character, a spectator rather than an actor by temperament, but apart from that element of weakness, a man (as I, see him) of thoroughly wholesome mental atmosphere. He is both a 'gentleman' and a 'scholar' in the real sense of the words, an exquisite writer and a finished speaker." "I learn from Professor Royce that the Corporation is making up its mind about the question of Santayana's promotion. I wish to say that I am distinctly in favor of it. . . . Whatever shortcomings may go with the type of mind of which he is a representative, I think it must be admitted to be a rare and precious type, of which Harvard University may well keep a specimen to enrich her concert withal. We shall always have 'hustlers' enough — but we shall not often have a chance at a Santayana, with his style, his subtlety of perception, and his cool-blooded truthfulness."

The inwardness of the individual's passion is precious — but in what consists its preciousness? The sequel to "A Certain Blindness in Human Beings" is addressed to the question, "What Makes a Life Significant?" The answer is that it is courage, struggle, risk — in a word, heroism, that makes life significant, and is revealed to the eye of sympathy. Chautauqua had led James to feel that "the higher heroisms and the old rare flavors are passing out of life," until it suddenly dawned upon him that there were "great fields of heroism lying round about" — "in the daily lives of the laboring classes." [11]   This is a familiar and persistent theme in James.   It is the old gospel of Carlyle, with which James had been impregnated in his childhood.   It is his answer to the question, "Is Life Worth Living?"   Yes, because it can be *made* worth living, by imparting to it the quality of bold and strenuous action.   It provides one of his fundamental norms of criticism: "Literature has no character when full of slack and wandering and superfluity.   Neither does life.   *Character* everywhere demands the stern and sacrificial mood as one of its factors.   *The price must be paid.*"

The martial spirit was implied in James's moral dualism.   Good is good and evil is evil, and it is the part of righteousness to love the one and to hate the other with equal whole-heartedness.   To a "motor," hating can only mean attacking and destroying.   This was James's attitude from early youth: "To hate evil does not mean to indulge in a brooding feeling against particular evils; that is, to be possessed by it.   No, it is to avert the attention, till your chance comes, and then strike home.   My trouble is that its existence has power to haunt me.   I still cling to the idol of the unspeckled, and when evil takes permanent body and actually sits down *in* me to stay, I 'd rather give up all, than go shares with her in existence."

This heroic motive in James was connected with his tendency to neurasthenia.   He would be driven in upon himself by illness, and then with a powerful revulsion of feeling would burst into a plea for action.   An incident of this sort was recorded in his diary in 1868, when he was a youth of twenty-six: "Tonight while listening to Miss Havens' magic playing, and the Doctor and the Italian lady sing, my feelings came to a sort of crisis.   The intuition of something here in a measure absolute gave me . . . an unspeakable disgust for the dead drifting of my own life for some time past. . . . Oh God! an end to the idle, idiotic sinking into *Vorstellungen* disproportionate to the object.   Every good experience ought to be interpreted in practice. . . .   Keep sinewy all the while, — and work at present with a mystical belief in the reality, interpreted somehow, of humanity!"

That James's preaching of the martial spirit reflected his *need* rather than his achievement is admitted with characteristic candor in a letter to Lutoslawski: "Of course I know, as well as anybody

[11] *T.T.*, 265, 273-4; *L.W.J.*, II, 40 ff.

that he who verbally celebrates and glorifies a function writes himself down for the time being as one who does n't exercise it, but aspires towards it rather, and seeks to animate himself and keep his courage up — often merely to *encourager les autres* (*témoin* myself in *re* the function of 'faith'). In so far forth every *writer* is what you call a 'weakling.' But man as man is essentially a weakling. Heroism is always on a precipitous edge, and only keeps alive by running. Every moment is an *escape*. And whoever is sensitive as well as motor well knows this, and ought not to be ashamed of it. One who should pretend to be in *possession* of a *kräftige Seele,* would thereby prove himself a donkey ignorant of the conditions — the thing has to be conquered every minute afresh by an act, and if writing and rhetoric help us to the act, they are also part of the function and we need never be ashamed of them."

James's address on "The Energies of Men" might be considered as his psychology of heroism. There is a limit of power for the everyday life of everyday men. Beyond this lie ranges of activity that are infrequently attained: "the excitements that carry us over the usually effective dam are most often the classic emotional ones, love, anger, crowd-contagion or despair." The history of religion, war, and discovery abounds in cases of extraordinary endurance and sustained effort. The Yoga and other ascetic and spiritual exercises have produced like results methodically. It is not a question of the quantity of muscular work in the strict physical sense, for human work may involve the conversion of energy into more refined forms. Some such broader conception of work is necessary if we are to deal with the invigorating effect of ideas and say that "will-acts register the faith-pressure within." [12]

In obedience to his own appeal for further inquiry in this field, James undertook, beginning about 1904, a study of the military experience. Some of the reading which he did on this subject found expression in his published essays on "The Energies of Men" and "The Moral Equivalent of War." But it was an unfinished project of which only the scaffolding remains in the form of two boxes containing bibliography, pamphlets, and letters written in reply to inquiries. In the great California earthquake of 1906, James found, involuntarily, an opportunity for psychological observation of the same general character, being a direct witness both

[12] *Philos. Rev.,* XVI (1907), 6, 14, 18; above, 122.

of the earthquake itself and of its effects upon the community. Again he discovered that men find within themselves unexpected resources upon which to draw in times of danger or privation.[13] There is thus a common thread running through James's observations on religion, neurasthenia, war, earthquakes, fasting, lynching, patriotism — an interest, namely, in human behavior under high pressure, and the conclusion that exceptional circumstances generate exceptional inner power. These phenomena have a bearing on metaphysics because such exceptional power suggests the sudden removal of a barrier and the tappings of a greater reservoir of consciousness; and they have a bearing on ethics, since this power differs in degree rather than in kind from that moral power — that fighting and adventurous spirit, that heroic quality — which gives to life the color and radiance of value.

It is characteristic of individualism that it should be divisible into two divergent motives which create a tension even when they do not break into open antagonism. There is the motive of self-assertion, and the motive of sympathy: the expression of one's own individuality, and the appreciation of the individuality of others. In the case of James both motives were native and strong. There is, therefore, an oscillation between the ethics of conciliation, peace, and social utility, and the ethics of aggression, militancy, and romanticism. His literary enthusiasm followed these motives — now the one and now the other. He praised poets and writers of fiction for their sensitiveness to the inwardness of nature or their creation of characters that *live*. Tolstoi, Howells, Wordsworth, and Whitman are all cited as witnesses testifying to the worth of life as revealed to an emancipated sympathy. Three new luminaries joined them later — W. H. Hudson, Robert Louis Stevenson, and H. G. Wells. He spoke of Hudson with an almost reverential enthusiasm. Writing in 1901 to a friend through whom he had received Hudson's photograph, he said, "If I could only believe that he had sent it himself! He is no mere dog, but a supernatural being — a reincarnation of the Buddha or something like that. I hope to get nearer him in a future life." To Stevenson's "Lantern-Bearers" James owed the metaphor underlying his whole doctrine of the inward illumination of humble lives. To Wells, "a sunny and healthy-minded Tolstoi," — whose limpid style, moral enthusiasm, "tridimensional

[13] *M.S.*, 225–6.

human heart," melioristic philosophy, and Anglo-empirical method James keenly relished, — he owed in his later years a powerful reënforcement of his wavering optimism.[14] His old loves, Carlyle and Emerson, on the other hand, continued to be the favorite oracles of the opposite gospel, declaring the inalienable right of the individual to be *himself* and his duty to execute his *own* ideal. The strangest occupant of James's literary pantheon was Rudyard Kipling, the prophet of imperialism. The following letter to his brother throws light on the origins of this attachment: —

Cambridge, Feb. 15, 1891

Dear Harry, —

. . . Last Sunday I dined with Howells at the Childs', and was much delighted to hear him say that you were both a friend and an admirer of Rudyard Kipling. I am ashamed to say that I have been ashamed to write of my adoration of that infant phenomenon, not knowing, with your exquisitely refined taste, how you might be affected by him and fearing to *jar*. The more rejoiced am I at this, but why did n't you say so ere now? He 's more of a Shakespeare than anyone yet in this generation of ours, as it strikes me. And seeing the new effects he lately brings in in "The Light That Failed," and that Simla Ball story with Mrs. Hauksbee in the *Illustrated London News,* makes one sure now that he is only at the beginning of a rapidly enlarging career, with indefinite growth before him. Much of his present coarseness and jerkiness is youth only, divine youth. But *what* a youth! Distinctly the biggest literary phenomenon of our time. He has such human entrails, and he takes less time to get under the heartstrings of his personages than anyone I know. On the whole, bless him.

All intellectual work is the same, — the artist feeds the public on his own bleeding insides. Kant's *Kritik* is just like a Strauss waltz, and I felt the other day, finishing "The Light That Failed," and an ethical address to be given at Yale College simultaneously,[15] that there was no *essential* difference between Rudyard Kipling and myself as far as that sacrificial element goes. I gave the address last Monday to an audience of about a hundred, absolutely mute. Professor

---

[14] *T.T.*, 234–40; *L.W.J.*, II, 231, 316. James visited Wells at Sandgate in July 1908.

[15] "The Moral Philosopher and the Moral Life."

Ladd, who was my host, did not by a single syllable allude to the address after it was delivered, either on our walk home or the following morn.   Apparently it was unmentionable.

Speaking of the unmentionable, it may interest Alice to hear that I have had this afternoon a two hours' visit from Mrs. H. of Princeton, Mass., where she and the family boarded in the '60s.   I didn't know it till Mrs. H. reminded me, and asked about Alice and Mrs. Walsh.   Her husband is the victim of one of those hideous mockeries of our civilization, and now serves out a two years' sentence in state prison for sending obscene matter through the mails; the matter consisting in a minute sheet called the *Voice,* which, of all imaginable causes of oppressed things, has taken up that of defending certain Saxon words not usually mentioned in polite society. These few words are martyrs and victims of injustice and prejudice, and one must die to reinstate them! *Grandeur et Néant de l'Homme!*   Could anyone imagine such a crusade?   Mrs. H. is a gifted creature in her way but practically quite mad.   The Almighty must have laughed to see her *aux prises* with Dr. Peabody [16] whilst the trial was going on.   She came out here to get some scholars to stand up for her husband.   Knowing no names she called at a house, and asked who were "liberal" in the college.   "Do you mean in the way of *giving?*"   "No, in the way of thought."   Peabody and C. C. Everett were named.   She goes to Peabody.   He says "Your husband is a *bad,* a very *bad* man.   He deserves to be imprisoned." . . .   She told him she hated to cry, and forgave him. Outside the door the tears rained on the ground. . . .   The two opposite lacks of humor, for her "the words" absolutely good, for Peabo "the words" absolutely bad, — what fools we all are! . . . Love to all. . . .

W. J.

So far Kipling is admired for his divination of character, and if James's mood is to be judged by the last paragraph of the letter, it is humor and kindly tolerance that speak the last word — not fanatical adherence to conviction.   In the summer of 1896, when the recent experience of Chautauqua had repelled James towards the heroic pole of his moral philosophy, he turned to Kipling as his

[16] Dr. Andrew Preston Peabody, former Plummer Professor of Christian Morals.

collaborator and exhorted him to "devote himself to the laboring classes." He wrote from Bagg's Hotel, Utica, New York, — where he stopped overnight en route from the Adirondacks to Chicago, — expounding the high romance of lowly people in the vein of the lecture on "What Makes a Life Significant?" : "Divinity lies all about us, and culture is too hide-bound to even suspect the fact.   Could a Howells or a Kipling be enlisted in this mission?" [17] Kipling, who had recently visited Norton at Ashfield, was about to sail for Europe on the *S.S. Lahn:* —

Morristown, N. Y. [Aug. 31, 1896]

Dear James, —

It was just and luminous (but why, in God's name, Bagg's Hotel of all places?) and the thing that made it more impressive to me mineself was because I have just finished off a long tale wherein I have deliberately travelled on the lines you suggest — *i.e.* I have taken the detail of a laborious and dangerous trade (fishing on the Grand Banks) and used it for all the romance in sight.[18]   Also, I have thought along those lines — *and* also, I have been four days in Chautauqua, seven years ago, when I thought unspeakable things. Half your trouble is the curse of America — sheer, hopeless, well-ordered boredom; and that is going some day to be the curse of the world.   The other races are still scuffling for their three meals a day.   America's got 'em and now she does n't know what she wants but is dimly realizing that extension lectures, hardwood floors, natural gas and trolley-cars don't fill the bill.   The Chautauquan "civilization" is to my mind precisely on the same plane as the laborious, ordered ritual of drum, dance and sacred pollen that the Zuñi (with other races) has evolved to fence off his bored soul from the solitude and loneliness of his own environments (I am not a psychologist, but you are and you 'll see what I mean).   Down below among the men of the trades you get, for proof that there is incident and colour in their lives, the melodramatic form of speech which is always resorted to in moments of stress or passion.   We the bourgeoisie, become inarticulate or inept.   It is a vast and fascinating subject and you 'll see later how I purpose to use it.   Your

[17] *T.T.*, 277.
[18] *Captains Courageous,* which appeared in *McClure's Magazine* in Nov. and Dec., 1896.

wail and "eructation" was delightful to my soul. . . .   Yours ever
sincerely,

RUDYARD KIPLING

In the last analysis James preferred the humanity of peace to the
cruel heroism of war.[19]   The grip of the hand on the sword is
relaxed by the reflection that the other's cause is as real and warm
to him as is mine to me, and has its own inner and equal justification.   If the principle of sympathy be given priority over the
principle of self-assertion it is still possible, however, to save the
militant and heroic qualities.   The principle of sympathy is itself
a cause which calls for moral and even for physical courage.   There
are two enemies which may be fought without inhumanity.   First,
physical nature: "The . . . ideal of the field of ethics being that
of the human interests allied against the material environment, and
the consequent appeal to reasonableness all round, seems to me
unconquerable truth and common-sense."

The second enemy which remains when humanity is enthroned
is inhumanity — whatever weakens, resists, or opposes the moral
will.   The major issue of life is the war of good and evil.   This
war calls for the fighting virtues, such as courage, endurance, fidelity,
energy, and loyalty.   Though literal war provides conditions peculiarly favorable to these virtues, especially in their heroic intensity,
they appear in all life wherever life is dramatized as the bearing of
hardship or the overcoming of resistance.   Darwin was a favorite
instance of heroism.   "I have just been reading Darwin's life . . .
and, whilst his nervous system makes bad nerves respectable, the
tale of it shuts the mouth of all lesser men against complaining." [20]
In his oration at the unveiling of the monument to Robert Gould
Shaw, James took pains to place the emphasis upon *moral* courage,
of the sort that is equally possible in peace and in war: —

"What we really need the poet's and orator's help to keep alive
in us is not, then, the common and gregarious courage which Robert
Shaw showed when he marched with you, men of the Seventh
Regiment.   It is that more lonely courage which he showed when

[19] It was this universalistic motive that stood between James and Nietzsche, who
would otherwise have attracted him greatly and to whom he did turn with growing
interest in his later years.   Cf. *L.W.J.*, II, 340.
[20] W.J. to Croom Robertson, Aug. 22, 1888.   Other parts of this letter are used
above, I, 609, II, 85.

he dropped his warm commission in the glorious Second to head your dubious fortunes, Negroes of the Fifty-fourth. That lonely kind of courage (civic courage as we call it in times of peace) is the kind of valor to which the monuments of nations should most of all be reared. . . . Robert Shaw had both kinds of virtue. As he then led his regiment against Fort Wagner, so surely would he now be leading us against all lesser powers of darkness, had his sweet young life been spared. You think of many as I speak of one." [21]

It is clear, however, that James did not believe peace in itself to be "the moral equivalent of war." When he composed the essay bearing that title, it was because he believed the admirable martial qualities to be so dependent on war that they could be preserved only by its simulation. The essay was published in 1910 by the Association for International Conciliation, and had a great *succès de réclame*. Over 30,000 copies of the leaflet were distributed, and it was twice republished in popular magazines. Letters of approval poured in from all quarters, not only from confirmed pacifists, but from many, including army officers, who were attracted by James's candid recognition of the psychological and moral claims of war. He made no bones of the natural blood-thirstiness of man, and sympathized with those who apologized for war as the great preserver of the ideals of hardihood and daring: —

"Its 'horrors,'" they argue, "are a cheap price to pay for rescue from the only alternative supposed, of a world of clerks and teachers, of coeducation and zoöphily, of 'consumer's leagues' and 'associated charities,' of industrialism unlimited, and feminism unabashed. No scorn, no hardness, no valor any more! Fie upon such a cattleyard of a planet! So far as the central essence of this feeling goes, no healthy-minded person . . . can help to some degree partaking of it."

The object of the essay was to support the cause of peace by suggesting a way of sublimating this martial spirit: "We must make new energies and hardihoods continue the manliness to which the military mind so faithfully clings. Martial virtues must be the enduring cement; intrepidity, contempt of softness, surrender of private interest, obedience to command, must still remain the rock upon which states are built." By "a conscription of the whole youthful population to form for a certain number of years a part

[21] *M.S.,* 57, 59.

of the army enlisted against *Nature*," James thought that "the military ideals of hardihood and discipline could be wrought into the growing fibre of the people," but without the callousness, cruelty, and degradation that attend war.[22]

[22] *M.S.*, 276, 287–8, 290–2.

LXVII

SOCIAL AND POLITICAL SENTIMENTS

THOUGH there are two well-marked principles in James's moral philosophy, that of militant self-assertion and that of humanity, it is, as we have seen, the second which is the more fundamental both in theory and in practice.

James's sentiment of humanity sprang from several sources. First, he had the sufferer's sensitiveness to the suffering of others. I refer to that extreme sensitiveness which occasions distress to the subject and even sometimes to the object. There were moments when this sensitiveness assumed in James, as in his father, an almost morbid aspect. A study of his relations with his sister Alice through her lifelong illness and lingering death furnishes a most revealing record of this trait. But what might easily have become a weakness was through the compensating and moderating effect of other qualities ultimately a source of strength. The extreme delicacy of his sympathetic response, instead of leading to an evasion of life, was compounded with other elements into loving friendships, an active loyalty to mankind, and even a pluralistic metaphysics.

The presence in James of an irrational compassionateness to which both his ideas and his practice had to accommodate themselves is exemplified by his total inability to drop a case of distress from his mind when once it had been brought to his attention. He would swear off only to yield again to an irresistible impulse. This obsessive compassion led James to the verge of agreeing that "pity is a vice to be exterminated along with its object." "I believe that to be a lie," he said, "but I admit the canalization of pity to be a difficult engineering problem."

The other side of pity is the hatred of cruelty, which was to James most hateful when combined with a profession of high purpose. Even duty forfeits its claims when it hardens the heart. Hence the temper of his judgment on the Inquisition, in which, after alluding to the "curious rat-hole feeling" which it inspires (its "combination of authority with feebleness of intellect — powers of life and death with a mental make-up that is almost idiotic for its meanness, timorousness and unmanliness — a mind not bigger than a pin's head, guiding a will that stuck at nothing in the way of cruelty"), he concludes: "Strange as it may sound, there can be little doubt that a good-natured scepticism and willingness to let the devil have his head a bit, is for the public purposes a better state of mind than too exalted a notion of one's duty towards the world."

The effect of pity was to cause James invariably to side with the "under dog" — with the Boers and the Irish against England, with the Filipinos against the United States, with religion or psychical research against science, with privates or laymen against officers, with the disreputable against the respectable, with heresy against orthodoxy, with youth against age, or with the new against the old.

Another and quite independent sense of James's humane feeling was his sociability. He was a highly socialized individual, not in the sense of being impregnated with tradition, or dominated by the group, but in the sense of his peculiar relish and gift for human intercourse. He was *concretely* humane. He tolerated mankind not in principle merely, but in practice; and he did not merely tolerate them, but enjoyed their presence in the flesh. When he was in the mood he was free, open, and expansive in his relations with others, but this mood, like all of James's moods, was liable to periodic fluctuations. He hated formal or crowded occasions, when pleasant human relations were at one and the same time encouraged and rendered impossible. Knowing the utter desolation of a sensitively social individual in an insensitive social milieu, he sometimes sympathized on this score even with his own guests. It will be remembered that he once hustled hatless through his back door one of his students whom he mistakenly supposed to be yearning for escape from the rigors of hospitality. Another instance of the sort is recorded: —

"During one of my courses with him, James invited me to an afternoon reception or tea at his house. I was a shy youth and dreaded going, but thought I ought to go. When I went in there seemed to be a good many people there and I was decidedly uncomfortable. I met James in the entrance hall. There was something about him which invited entire confidence and I found myself telling him just how I felt. 'Yes, I know,' said he, 'when I see these people who know exactly what to do and say at one of these things, I feel like smashing their heads with a paving stone.' The sympathetic understanding of my feelings and his characteristically forcible language gave me great satisfaction." [1]

There is an aspect of James's humanity that is more difficult to describe. The term "promiscuity" would be too strong, while to describe it negatively as an absence of fastidiousness would be too weak. From certain pages of *Notes of a Son and Brother* we gather that Henry James felt that William James lacked taste in his choice of associates.[2] The fact was that William had something of the clinician's freedom from prejudice — a suffering mortal is a suffering mortal. He had his chosen comrades, and none was quicker than he to perceive the difference between the congenial and the uncongenial. But he went behind and beyond this impression. He was not unoffended by externals, but the offense was negligible if there was something to be found within. It was a part of his genius to find something within when others failed to find it, and a part of his philosophy to believe that there is always something within to find. The generalization of James's tender-heartedness into a humanitarian sentiment and creed was in no small measure due to his lack of squeamishness and the catholicity of his taste. His character was somehow capable of uniting a selective taste which chose his intimate friends and preferred companions with the indiscriminate sympathy which gave sincerity to his humanitarian creed.

All of James's humane qualities appear in his friendships. Strangeness and formality quickly melted in his presence, acquaintance ripening into affection and affection into enduring love. His gift for friendship has been illustrated by his youthful relations with Ward and Holmes, and by his later relations with Hodgson, Robertson, Renouvier, Gurney, Stumpf, and Flournoy. A few further instances may be permitted here. The warmth which fructified the seed of friendship and quickened the growing plant is found in letters to Mrs. Francis J. Child and to Charles Eliot Norton. The first was written in reply to a letter of congratulation on his appointment to a full professorship of philosophy. Mrs. James was at this time ill with scarlet fever.

[1] From a letter to the author by George D. Burrage, Harvard '83.
[2] *Cf.* 323–8.

[Cambridge], March 27 [1885]

Dear Mrs. Child, —

Your letter is the best thing about my promotion — worth more than all its honors, powers and emoluments. It lights up our home with the effulgence of affection and sympathy. I have just read it to Alice through the door with the cracks stuffed with cotton which is the channel of our communion, and all I get from her is a sort of inarticulate cooing and purring, in a voice "choked with tears" of joy. She feels, as I do, that one note of true sympathy is worth all the philosophies and professorships thereof in the world. With love to your blessed family, believe me ever affectionately yours,

WM. JAMES

P.S. As the immortal Schopenhauer says, "Anyone can feel Mit*leid;* aber zur Mit*freude* gehört ein Engel!" [3]

Twelve years later James presented the same friend with his *Will to Believe,* inscribed to "Mrs. Child from her loving W.J.," and accompanied by the note: "This is *not to be read,* — simply *owned,* and smiled at occasionally for love of the author."

The old friendship between the Jameses and the Nortons was continued throughout William James's life in his intimacy with Grace Norton and Charles Eliot Norton: —

Cambridge, Nov. 16, 1907

Dear Charles, —

I cannot let your eightieth birthday pass without the meed of some melodious tear. You will probably be having *Glückwünsche* innumerably showered upon you today, but none will be heartier or more sincere than Alice's or mine, — or our children's either, for they "were nursed upon the self-same hill," and to their minds you have been the tutelary genius of the neighborhood — a sort of benignant half-uncle, always with a word or a present for them, and ever to be remembered among the friendly powers that overarch the universe of childhood. It seemed to me a great achievement to have lived down eighty solid years, each panting to devour one,

---

[3] "Anyone can sympathize with another's sorrow, but to sympathize with another's joy is the attribute of an angel."

"trampling their strata with æonian tread" and storing up all that experience.   Even with the experience passive, the achievement is great; but when it has been as active as yours, with a part played energetically in every better effort and enterprise that was going, and when one has given help and countenance to so many others who were struggling, retrospect of the whole career ought to yield contentment.   You are among those who in the best sense have made of their life a success. . . .   That your future years will be many, and increase the tide of general good-will that sets in towards you, is the prayer of your affectionate friends,

WILLIAM AND ALICE JAMES

Cambridge, Dec. 14, 1907

Dear William, —

The delightful letter which you sent to me on my birthday has since then lain open before me on my much-used writing-pad, giving me fresh pleasure every day.   And yet it, like the other cordial expressions of regard and affection which came to me a month ago, seems to me addressed not so much to me as to some image of me which exists in the hearts of friends, and which is a likeness that I hardly recognize.   Truly Norton's Woods must produce some "little Western flower" with which their eyes have been touched so that they see me not in my natural garb but invested with "trailing clouds of glory"!   But however it be, I am glad and grateful for your affection.   It is a good blessing. . . .   Your affectionate and proud old friend,

C. E. NORTON [4]

What James's friendship meant to others is illustrated by letters from European friends who waited for the warmth and light of his periodic passages. The first of these letters is from Delbœuf, whose instant captivation by James in 1882 has already been recorded.[5] He was absorbed by the care of his wife, who was suffering from an illness that proved fatal three years later: —

---

[4] For Norton's opinion of James, cf. Letters of C. E. Norton, edited by S. Norton and M. A. De W. Howe, 1913, Index. For James's final judgment of Norton as one having a "power of appreciating merit," and an "eagerness to help other and younger men who had it, to get it into play," cf. W.J. to Barrett Wendell, Dec. 30, 1908, Scribner's, Dec. 1928.
[5] Cf. above, I, 687–8.

Ramet [Belgium], Nov. 2, 1886[6]

Dear Friend, —

I no longer leave the house, I no longer go anywhere; I live surrounded by my books, close to my poor wife, receiving, at rare intervals, a visit, — and nevertheless beginning already to calculate the time when you will be able to return to Europe: four years, is it not? It will be a great day, one to mark with a tablet when we see you again. . . . Oh! how often have I in my thoughts crossed the sea to sit by your fireside and chat with you! My most cordial greetings to you and all of yours, — and from all of us,

J. DELBŒUF

The next is from the friend of his youth, Charles Ritter, who was four years James's senior, and who died in 1908 after some years of broken health: —

Geneva, June 15, 1902[7]

Dear and illustrious Friend, —

Your magnificent volume (*The Varieties of Religious Experience*) reached me last Monday, June 9, and filled me with joy, as a sign of life from an old friend, as proof that you have been able to carry out a project in which I was so much interested, and, finally, for its own sake. . . . And now, dear Friend, crown your kindness to an old invalid of the rue St. Léger by sending him the photograph of your dear self, of Madame William James, and of your dear children. If you (or Madame) could add a short account of your present life that would be perfect. . . . Give to an old friendship, after forty two years, a St. Martin's summer, a glorious late autumn sun. All this week, while running through your beautiful volume, I have paused to recall the stages of that friendship:

First the fine days of 1860, "quand sur ton beau front riait l'adolescence," days all too short, alas! and in particular the spring-time fête at Moudon, when you made fun of my youthful enthusiasm for Renan, and when you cited his words: "pour moi je pense qu'il n'est pas dans l'univers d'intelligence supérieure à celle de l'homme" — certainly not a very orthodox formula!

[6] The original French text will be found below, Appendix IV.
[7] Translated by the author.

Then your visit to Geneva in 1868, and our interview in a hotel bedroom.

Then the charming reunion at the Berne railway station in June, 1892, ten years ago.

Then the delicious day at Meggen on the shores of Lake Lucerne in May, 1893.

Finally the good times of April, 1900, at M. Flournoy's, and the brief meeting in the autumn.

And now in fifteen days I shall be reaching my sixty-fourth year, having been born on June 29, 1838. . . . I cannot complain too much, — on the contrary, I ought to regard myself as privileged in this adventure of human life, so difficult and so subject to chance. In any case, one of the happiest chances which have fallen to my lot was that of meeting in my twenty-second year the charming friend who was destined to become an illustrious man, and whose hand I press with all tenderness and the most loyal affection. . . .

CHARLES RITTER

The last of these evidences of friendship is from Charles Peirce, written shortly after James's death to the latter's son Henry: —

Milford, Sept. 21, 1910

My dear Mr. James, —

Your father was the very last of those few men who pulled much upon my heart-strings; and no man ever did so much as he, not even his father. Few days passed without my longing to be with him, and when I was in Prescott Street, and would look out the window and would see him at length pass by, how I used to wish he would come in! But I did n't wish to have him come as a matter of conscience; and he was the most conscientious person I ever knew. — I see that I am only talking about myself! I knew it would be so. His *Varieties of Religious Experience* I think the best of his books. His penetration into the hearts of people was most wonderful; and he was not one of those who chiefly see the evil things in hearts. No doubt many things escaped even his penetration. I think his summings up of cases like the supposed communications from Hodgson very judicious, — though for my part I don't believe them genuine and do not want to. If they *are*, we must suppose that they come while the soul is still half-stunned by the novelty of its situation or by the shock. I think we have a *full logical right* to entertain high *hopes* of a future life, a life of work, long or perhaps endless. But it is clear to me that it has not been intended (so to speak) that we should *count upon* it too implicitly. . . .

I know that my letter must sound to you very egotistical; but he was such an exquisitely lovable fellow, that it is in vain that I tell myself how much more those must suffer who saw him every day; I cannot help being overwhelmed with my own grief. . . . It seems as if La Fontaine must have known him when he wrote:

> Qu'un ami véritable est une douce chose.
> Il cherche vos besoins au fond de votre cœur;
> Il vous épargne la pudeur
> De les lui découvrir vous-même.

His last three books may be criticized; but all the sound heads and sound hearts will forever honour and love the MAN.

C. S. P.

The softness of James's heart did not spread to his head. It involved him in acts of kindness which often cost him much trouble, but he was not more fallible than others in his personal judgments. The difference was that while he saw men's weakness as well as their strength, he admired them for their strength instead of despising them for their weakness. He refers to T. H. Green as "this apostolic human being but strenuously feeble writer": had he known Green personally, he would have addressed the apostolic being and ignored the feeble writer.[8]

James is supposed to have been *blinded* by compassion, especially his compassion for "cranks." The fact is that long experience gave him a shrewd knowledge of the species, and when he was kind to a crank he was perfectly aware that it was a crank to whom he was being kind. But even in cranks of the lower orders he found *something* that touched his heart. The following was to Henry Holt: —

Cambridge, June 19, 1896

Dear Holt, —

A poor crank of a Russian Jew, a regular Spinosa . . . has been melting the heart out of me by his desire to get his *magnum opus*

---

[8] *Principles,* II, 11, note.

(which is only 300 typewritten pages, boiled down from an original 1400) published. He is literally dying of grief because he can't. The stuff might have made some stir in 1650, but of course it is hopeless now. Nevertheless as a fellow crank I am moved by human sympathy to subscribe with the aid of friends $50 towards its publication, and I have written him that I would consult a publisher of my acquaintance, meaning you. About how much ought a publisher to require as a guarantee in such a case — say a 300 page book, 500 copies, got out cheaply and of course not stereotyped? Should you be willing to let it bear your name? The old fellow has quite a grand style in his way. Always truly yours,

WILLIAM JAMES

This habit of addressing his regard to the admirable part of a man had a profound influence on James's professional relations. The rays of his affection fertilized the soil they shone on — often a hitherto barren soil hidden away unsuspected in some obscure and timid soul. Students and colleagues tried to live up to the good that James thought of them. He once wrote to Münsterberg: "I am reading Ostwald's *Vorlesungen über Naturphilosophie,* and find it a most delectable book. I don't think I ever envied a man's mind as much as I have envied Ostwald's, — unless it were Mach's." This reservation in favor of Mach gives James away entirely. He envied nearly everybody's mind; for he saw *some* good quality there which he did n't have himself, and acknowledged its value by expressing the wish that he had it.

James believed and practised the maxim that people flourish most in the sunshine of approval. When his friend Flournoy congratulated him warmly on the *Varieties,* James replied: "Imagine how delighted I am at receiving your post-card this morning, the first real *praise* that I have yet had for this work, and from such a quarter — you, who, having worked at the subject yourself, *know* 'what's what' in it! What my friend Howison said is true: 'What your genuine philosopher most craves is *praise,* rank, coarse praise. Harris . . . calls it *recognition,* but it's *praise* which we all need and work for. Since your praise I feel that my book is *certain* to be a success."

The result of James's presence was usually to raise the general temperature of cordiality. Men said pleasant things to one another, and being in turn recipients of good-will they instinctively sought to earn it — which illustrated his philosophical maxim that if you *will* believe well of your fellow men you may create the good you believe in.

"The great use of a life," James said in 1900, "is to spend it for something that outlasts it." This outlasting cause was then, as in earlier days, the happiness of mankind. But he was not a utopian. "I devoutly believe," he said, "in the reign of peace and in the gradual advent of some sort of socialistic equilibrium." [9] This was written in 1910. A dozen years before he had said: "Society has, with all this, undoubtedly got to pass toward some newer and better equilibrium, and the distribution of wealth has doubtless slowly got to change: such changes have always happened, and will happen to the end of time. But if, after all that I have said, any of you expect that they will make any *genuine vital difference,* on a large scale, to the lives of our descendants, you will have missed the significance of my entire lecture. The solid meaning of life is always the same eternal thing, — the marriage, namely, of some unhabitual ideal, however special, with some fidelity, courage, and endurance; with some man's or woman's pains. — And, whatever or whenever life may be, there will always be the chance for that marriage to take place." [10]

Between these dates there was, I believe, a change of emphasis, induced in part by the Fabian socialism of H. G. Wells.[11] But the change was not radical enough to remove a fundamental ambiguity. Was the good life to be found in that state of things that would begin *after* the victorious conquest of evil, or was it to be found in the conquest itself? On the one hand, James loathed evil, and loathed the condoning of evil. On the other hand, he felt that the redeeming quality of life was that heroism which can exist only when there is a live evil to be resisted and overcome; and thus to recognize in evil an indispensable condition of good is to condone it, and to lapse into that "subjectivism" whose insidious philosophical charms he had so well understood and so sternly repulsed in the still earlier '80s.[12] There is a way, a Jamesian way, by which this seeming

---

[9] *M.S.,* 286.
[10] *T.T.,* 298–9.
[11] Especially this author's *First and Last Things,* which James read with high approval.
[12] *W.B.,* 169 ff.

contradiction can be avoided. What is needed to make life significant is a "real fight," actual risks and genuine obstacles. If one thought that the risks and obstacles were merely put there for their moral effect, one's adventurous spirit would be undermined. The best of all possible worlds from a moral point of view is, therefore, a world which is not designed for that purpose — a world in which the conditions of the significant life are accidental and not intended. Since as a matter of fact these conditions do occur, and occur equally in every age, there is no progress as regards the qualitative significance of life. But the significant life may be more or less humane; and it is here that one should look for progress — in rendering the highest quality of one individual's life less costly to others. "We are all ready to be savage in *some* cause. The difference between a good man and a bad one is the choice of the cause." [13]

The root of James's politics is to be found not in his ethics and philosophy, but in the fact that he belonged to the educated class, and accepted on that account a peculiar rôle and a peculiar responsibility. He was a mugwump, an anti-imperialist, a civil-service reformer, a pacifist, a Dreyfusite, an internationalist and a liberal. What physiognomy do these features compose? Clearly, the advocate of light as opposed to force and emotion. Neither his democracy nor his gospel of action implied a leveling of differences. He did not believe either that one man was as good as another, or that all causes were equally worthy. His politics was governed by the principle of discrimination. The educated man was the man who knew how to criticize, and it was his rôle in politics to offset to the best of his power both the self-seeking of the ambitious and the blind passion of the crowd.

Undoubtedly the greatest single influence upon James's political thinking was that exerted by E. L. Godkin. During Godkin's residence in Cambridge in the late '70s he had been an intimate of the James household. William and Henry James and the circle of their Cambridge friends read the *Nation* and the *Evening Post,* and wrote for them. Godkin's papers were the most important medium of the day by which the emancipated and disinterested mind found effective political expression. There were periodic lapses and revivals of attachment on James's part, the lapses being due to a dislike of

[13] *L.W.J.,* II, 28.

Godkin's negations and polemics, the revivals to a feeling that on important issues Godkin was always fighting valiantly on the right side. The following was written by James to Godkin in 1889 : —

"In the earlier years I may say that my whole political education was due to the *Nation;* later came a time when I thought you looked on the doings of Terence Powderly and Co. too much from without and too little from within; now I turn to you again as my only solace in a world where nothing stands straight. You have the most curious way of always being *right,* so I never dare to trust myself now when you 're agin me." [14]

And writing six years later, at the time of the Venezuela incident, James pledged his loyalty and warmly congratulated Godkin on his courage, but urged him in the interest of effectiveness to be as "non-expletive" and patiently explanatory as possible: "Don't curse God and die, dear old fellow. Live and be patient and fight for us a long time yet in this new war." [15]

Godkin withdrew from his journalistic activities early in 1900, and a year later retired to England, living first at Lyndhurst in the New Forest, afterwards at Castle Malwood, near Stony Cross, Torquay, and finally at Greenway on the River Dart. Before his death in 1902 he suffered much from a malady which he bore with conspicuous fortitude. This being the time of James's protracted visits to Europe both on account of his health and for the purpose of delivering his Gifford Lectures, the James and Godkin families renewed their old intimacy. The Venezuela incident and the Spanish War being succeeded by the controversy over imperialism, Godkin, once a fighter in the foremost ranks, was compelled to play the rôle of spectator : —

Rye, June 25, 1901

My dear Godkin, —

Passing through London on Saturday, I saw Theodora,[16] who told me of your arrival and condition, in a way that inspires me to write an affectionate word of greeting. . . . I wrote you a letter of sympathy two years ago when you were taken ill; but I fancy you never got the letter, and I only hope you did n't think my heart

[14] *L.W.J.,* I, 284. The *Nation* had expressed itself freely (*e.g.,* in 1886) on the "Knights of Labor Convention," and T. V. Powderly, their "Master Workman."
[15] *L.W.J.,* II, 30.
[16] Theodora Sedgwick.

had "grown cold." It is hard to change from the attitude of a fighter to that of a spectator, and you must have passed many a morose hour. Curious that what men so long for and idealize when they are in the "heat and burden" should seem so dolefully insipid when adopted as a profession late in life. One must have been brought up to it from childhood not to find it pall. Nevertheless as a spectacle, it seems to me that the world was never more interesting than now, nor the turn which the warfare of light against darkness will have to take, the tactics it will have to adopt, less certain and more full of possibly good forms of surprise. The enemy at any rate is lively — but neither are we at our last gasp. . . . With warmest regards, dear old Godkin, — to both of you, my wife joining, I am always affectionately yours,

WM. JAMES

Lyndhurst, July 9 [1901]

My dear James, —

You have little idea how much pleasure the receipt of your letter gave me. . . . At the period of the beginning of the war your letters had been the great source of my comfort and my consolation. You seemed to be the one man left worthy to wear Sidney's cask of steel. . . . Like other people I mourn the loss of my aggressive years of youth, but confess that I enjoy my leisure, my peace, and the English landscape, on which I gaze with delight. My years of combat have been so unsatisfactory that I do not care to protract them, and I have long felt the need of friends' society, and am now bent on enjoying it.

I am greatly gratified on finding that you are again in the field, — would I could think that old McKinley would again feel your rod. I am looking forward to your stopping here on your way back through England, if it is only for a night. . . . Affectionately yours,

E. L. GODKIN

Silver Lake, N. H., Sept. 15, 1901

Dear Mrs. Godkin, —

. . . We had a good voyage and our "home" looked pathetically sweet, but we have been too long away, and the veil of strangeness intervenes again between one and one's native land. The awful

catarrhal nasality on the steamer was a bath of alienation! and
the sweet little New Hampshire landscape, which I once embraced
with no reserve, seems now so pathetically poverty-stricken and
over-simple! One must n't mix one's hemispheres! Don't *you*
ever come back — and I will try never to go away! Poor McKinley! the news of whose death comes last night. Verily the foolish
things confound the mighty. But in the general carnival of fool-
ishness I can't get up as acute a set of emotions over this poor ass
of a Czogolsz as I suppose I ought to. It makes McKinley safe
of his place beside Washington and Lincoln; which from the point
of view of ethical truth is to be regretted. Roosevelt will probably
prove weaker in action than he *sounds* to be. A good deal of
rhetorical and emotional manifestation in that Character's strength.

I devoutly hope that E. L. G. holds his own and advances. . . .
Good-bye! Warmest affection to you both, especially to the Martyr,
whose good spirits and saintly resignation are an unforgettable example. Ever affectionately yours,

WM. JAMES

Cambridge, March 14, 1902

Dear Mrs. Godkin, —

An envelope has been lying addressed to you for a month as a
daily reminder of what I wished to do. . . . Meanwhile Godkin's
photograph has come — a very pleasant memento and acquisition,
and ten days ago, your two letters. I hail it as a very good sign that
he should have felt like writing himself, though I 'm sorry to find
him indulging "the old animosities," — which reminds me of the
following anecdote. A man named Gignoux settled near us at
Chocorua, and after driving madly about the country all summer
with four quarrelsome dogs, and getting into a row with almost
all his neighbors, went home in the fall and died in the winter.
When I went back the following spring, the stage-driver told me
that Mrs. G. had opened the house and was going to stay on. I
asked if she was going to keep up "the old animosities." The reply
was: "Well, she 's brought back the setter and the two span*nils* —
the Saint Bernard, I believe, is dead." Which I thought was a
good explication of the word "animosity." Advise E. L. G. to
get rid of all his! Tell him — or rather this letter is to him *and*
to you — that I went yesterday to a "lunch" of the so-called Anti-

imperialist League, and found myself at one of the small tables along with Edward Atkinson, Gamaliel Bradford and F. B. Sanborn. There were a couple of hours of five minute speeches. I came away saddened by the sight of what I knew already, that when you get a lot of pure idealists together they don't show up as strong as an equal lot of practical men. In fact *this* crowd rather justified the "low grade" of the veneration with which the usual voter regards it. Moorfield Storey and Gamaliel Bradford, however, made speeches, each with a good practical outcome. It is evident that public opinion is changing on the subject. "Attention" is being aroused: Storey told me that he understood that Schurman was ready to put up a good fight for promising withdrawal. If the Democrats had sense, they could do a great deal just now. McKinley's star seems to have set. He stood for nothing but certain interests and his own adroitness, and leaves no idea to rally on in his wake. . . .

Prince Henry of Prussia has swept through the country, receiving from us an L.L.D. degree, at a specially convoked meeting in Sanders Theatre. President Eliot's speech to him would have been a fine one, save that he enlarged upon his royal grandmother and made no mention of his imperial brother — a most extraordinary thing, which set all the Germans wondering what the studied insult could have meant. It meant nothing but Eliot's naïveté in matters diplomatic; and the best that can happen is that it should go to swell the general account among the crowned heads of Europe of American boorishness and lack of tact. It's a pity, though, that Harvard University should have to contribute to *that* fund. The Prince seems to be a very good fellow indeed. . . .

I am so glad that the English winter has proved so much of a success and so glad that you, dear old Godkin, can keep up such a splendid fight against inactivity and depressing influences. With spring a new life ought to begin. With most affectionate regards and thanks, in which Alice joins, I am yours ever,

WM. JAMES

Godkin's death occurred two months after the above letter was written. In his letter of condolence James said of him that "to my generation his was certainly the towering influence in all thought concerning public affairs, and indirectly his influence has certainly been more pervasive than that of any other writer of the generation, for he influenced other writers who never quoted him, and determined the whole current of discussion." In 1903 steps were being taken to establish a memorial "Godkin Lecture-ship" at Harvard. The following exchange of letters with Major Henry L. Higginson grew out of a conversation held, apparently, at a dining club, concerning Godkin's influence on the men who were there present. The first is from Higginson to James: —

Boston, Feb. 7, 1903

My dear Mentor, —

Conversation of yesterday remains with me. If Godkin's name is to be honored by a lectureship and needs my help, it shall be given, — and the call remains with you. . . .

So long as Godkin . . . was not admired, his words were valu-able; but later they were so twisted and stained by great conceit, arrogance, evil temper, that they lost their fairness, their perspicac-ity, their virtue and therefore their value. . . . He never doubted himself or questioned fate, or — so to speak — never spat in the river and contemplated the universe and his God. . . . I was shocked at his carping at — indeed slandering — the motives and conduct of Brimmer and Eliot. I was disgusted with his nasty language about Charles S. Fairchild, once Cleveland's Secretary, — a real gentleman who knew and did the high-minded, intelligent thing. You said that he taught me and us all more than anyone, — more than we know. It seems to me that he came into my vision and ken at a time when I was clearer and more open than I 've ever been, and he helped in my education; but I 've learned ten times as much from many a man and woman — notably Mr. Emerson, Mr. Mill, my wife and yours, Ellen Gurney and her husband, some of my young friends, who absolutely formed my life and dyed it in fast colors, and far more from you, friend and mentor. I mean every word I 've said, — absurd or not. Last Saturday I went to the Palmer service, [17] because I knew very little of her and did not fancy her — and tried to cure my fault. I should help in this other case on the same ground. But here I see his value, — in the past. Don't answer me, for writing is wearisome, and you are needed for better things. Yours.

HENRY

[17] The funeral service of Alice Freeman Palmer.

Cambridge, Feb. 8, 1903 [18]

Dear Henry, —

I am sorry to have given you a wrong impression, and made you take the trouble of writing — nutritious though your letters be to receive. My motive in mentioning the Godkin testimonial was pure curiosity, and not desire to promote it. We were ten "liberals" together, and I wanted to learn how many of us had been alienated from Godkin by his temper in spite of having been influenced by his writing. I found that it was just about half and half. I never said — Heaven bear me witness — that I had learned more from G. than from anyone. I said I had got more *political* education from him. You see the *Nation* took me at the age of 22 — you were already older and wickeder. . . . Godkin's "home life" was very different from his life against the world. When a man differed in type from him, and consequently reacted differently on public matters, he thought him a preposterous monster, pure and simple, and so treated him. He couldn't imagine a different kind of creature from himself in politics. But in private relations he was simplicity and sociability and affectionateness incarnate and playful as a young opossum. [19] . . . Don't subscribe, dear Henry. I am not trying to raise subscriptions. . . . Ever affectionately yours,

W. J.

James was a "mugwump" both in the historical and in the generalized sense. The following letter touches on the Blaine campaign during which this label first came into vogue. F. G. Bromberg had been a classmate at the Lawrence Scientific School and a member of Congress from Alabama: —

Springfield Centre, N. Y., June 30, 1884 [20]

My dear Bromberg, —

. . . What you say of Blaine is . . . moving. I had hoped to find you in the "young" Republican party. It is quite true Blaine has never been confounded with the grosser pecuniary corruptionists. The slips with which he is charged are relatively venial in

[18] Reprinted from *L.W.J.*, II, 182.
[19] "Unique mixture that he was of humor and gloom, affectionateness and antipathies, delight in observing and energy in reacting. We shall never know the like of him again." (W.J. to Mr. Lawrence Godkin, Nov. 13, 1907.)
[20] A sentence from this letter is used above, 92.

that line, but I hold it right to make the very most we can of them — for what does Blaine stand for in any other line? Nothing but his own personality, that of a brilliant and unscrupulous partisan debater, and master of machine intrigue. His waving of the bloody shirt and hounding of the Confederate "brigadiers" eight years ago was in my eyes a simple piece of diabolism, — without the excuses of a Logan, for it was perfectly cold-blooded.[21] His proposal to distribute the surplus revenue among the states lately is a sample of him. But it's less for what he *is* than for what he *is n't* that we are ready to bring the Democrats in to defeat him. He is blind, and the whole section of Republicans whom he represents are blind, to the real life of the country today. Old dead shibboleths are all they can think of. They live on hatred and prejudice against the Democratic name, as the Democrats live on hatred of the Republican name. If any recent Democrat be nominated, I shall be too happy to vote him in, in order to get the present fossil Republican party permanently killed, and to be able four years later to drive out the Democrats in the same way in the name of a new national party with something of an intellectual character in purposes, which will devote itself to civil service and economical reform, and perhaps ultimately to certain constitutional changes of which we are in pressing need. Look at the Barnum advertisement called the Republican platform! Can you possibly wish to see a party like *that* cumber the earth any longer? I hope not.

But I can't write politics, and I dare say from your point of view you will rejoin things to which I may not feel ready to reply. . . . Always your friend,

WM. JAMES

James was also, quite consciously and avowedly, a mugwump in the more generalized sense. He allied himself with that minority whose function it was to apply critical reflection to public affairs, and whose destiny it was — to remain a minority. In economic matters the mugwump would look beyond the immediate motive of gain to underlying ethical principles or the broad humane purpose of social institutions. Emancipated from a purely national out-

---

[21] James G. Blaine in the campaign of 1876 had goaded Southern Congressmen into indiscreet statements which revived violent sectional animosities.

look or a chauvinistic patriotism, he would esteem superior human qualities regardless of their place or power. In domestic politics he would be bound by no party allegiance, but would use his vote to tip the scales in favor of rationality and righteousness.

As regards the mugwump's duty James had no doubt, and as regards his effectiveness no illusions. He questioned whether education really made any difference for the good, since educated men seemed to be on both sides of all questions, and to lend or sell the fruits of their education for the support of any passion however base. His qualified appraisal of higher education caused some misunderstanding, and in 1905 he was compelled to write to Eliot from Chicago and explain that he had not meant to say that the colleges "were training schools of crime!" "I only saw one newspaper report, a single paragraph — but that was diabolical. It was sent me by an unknown correspondent who said he thanked God for raising 'one man courageous enough to tell the truth about the colleges,' — adding, 'I never had a college education, the blood of Jesus is enough for me.'"

James realized the superiority of the professional politician: "the strongest force in politics is human scheming, and the schemers will capture every machinery that you can set up against them." He understood propaganda, that "curious auto-intoxication which society practises upon itself with the journalistic secretion." But he refused to despair, believing that the party of critical intelligence might offset their lack of heat by their greater steadiness. On January 9, 1902, he delivered an address before the Graduate School at Harvard, in which he dwelt upon the critical function that the educated classes might exercise in public affairs: —

"So far, then, as the mission of the educated intellect in society is not to find or invent reasons for the demands of passion, it reduces itself to this small but incessant criticizing, or equalizing function. It reëstablishes, because it never forgets, the normal perspective of interests, and keeps things in their proper places in the scale of values. For this it has to blow cold upon the hot excitement, and hot upon the cold motive; and this judicial and neutral attitude sometimes wears, it must be confessed, a priggish expression and is generally unpopular and distasteful. The intellectual critic as such knows of so many interests, that to the ardent partisan he seems to have none — to be a sort of bloodless bore and mugwump. Those who anticipate the verdict of history, the abolitionists, *les intellectuels,* as the university professors were called who stood out for Dreyfus, the present anti-imperialists etc., excite an almost corporeal antipathy. Living mugwumps have indeed a harder row to hoe than members of the regular organizations. Often their only audience is posterity. Their names are first honored when the breath has left their bodies, and, like the holders of insurance policies, they must die to win their wager. . . .

"Speaking broadly, there are never more than two fundamental parties in a nation: the party of red blood, as it calls itself, and that of pale reflection; the party of animal instinct, jingoism, fun, excitement, bigness; and that of reason, forecast, order gained by growth, and spiritual methods — briefly put, the party of force and that of education. . . . The Tories in any country and the mob will always pull together in the red-blood party, when the catchwords are properly manipulated, as a while ago they were by Disraeli; and liberalism will be between the upper and the nether millstone if it have no magnetic leader. . . . The chronic fault of liberalism is its lack of speed and passion. Over and over again generalizations get into such a deadlock that a hole in the dam must be made somewhere, — then the flowing water will enlarge it. A rifle bullet makes a hole by its mere speed, where the dead pressure of a weightier mass does nothing. But occasionally a leader with liberal ambitions has the *vis viva* of the rifle bullet. He may be a fanatic, a Cromwell, a Garibaldi, or he may be a Bismarck, or he may be an adventurer like Napoleon. Happy the country that proves able to use such men for what they are worth, and to cast them off before they victimize it. That country indeed is educated!"

The mature definition of James's political rôle is to be found in an address entitled "The Social Value of the College-Bred." [22] It is the function of the college-bred to guard the "tone" of society, to promote the "critical sensibilities" or "admiration of the really admirable," and to "divine the worthier and better leaders": "We ought to have our own class-consciousness. *'Les Intellectuels!'* What prouder club-name could there be than this one, used ironically by the party of 'redblood,' the party of every stupid prejudice and passion, during the anti-Dreyfus craze, to satirize the men in France who still retained some critical sense and judgment!" [23]

[22] Delivered Nov. 7, 1907. First published in *McClure's Magazine* in Feb. 1908, and reprinted in *M.S.*
[23] *M.S.*, 314, 319–20, 323.

LXVIII

JAMES AS A REFORMER

IN the light of James's general ethical creed and conception of his rôle in social and political reform, it is now in order briefly to review his activities.

As early as 1881 James addressed the students of Harvard College on the subject of temperance, and twice thereafter he spoke before the Total Abstinence League. In his early address he dealt mainly with the injurious effect of alcohol as demonstrated by experimental physiology.[1] In his later addresses, while continuing and developing this theme, he devoted attention to the moral and social aspects of the question. It is evident that he had a fundamental antipathy to the use of stimulants — the more remarkable because of his curious and open-minded interest in all exceptional experiences (among which intoxication might naturally have been included), and his sympathy with that deliverance from inhibitions which is thought to be one of the merits of alcohol. His fundamental maxim of purity and wholesomeness was no doubt at the root of the matter, but there was at the same time a counter-attraction: he found abstinence more intoxicating than indulgence. The following notes were made in preparation for an address of 1894 or 1895: —

"The great *excuse* is conviviality. . . . Even here you *pay*. But here if anywhere is what you pay for worth the price. . . . The whole bill against alcohol is its *treachery*. Its happiness is an illusion and seven other devils return. . . . From every point of view we see one conclusion. It is *safer* to drink cold water, or hot water, or any kind of water. In this over-burdened [age], especially here in America, every ounce of handicap that is added should be avoided, and the daily use of even the smallest amount of alcohol is probably a real handicap, increasing the fatigue and wear and tear of life, diminishing reserve force and elasticity, and

---

[1] "William James on Temperance," *Independent,* June 23, 1881.

tending to shorten existence. Say what you will about quality of existence . . . the gas-lit spurious hilarity with sickness afterwards is not the real quality. . . . It seems . . . a mean way of deciding a question like this, by fear. . . . The best way to wean people from intemperance is to fill them with a love of temperance for its own sake. In other words, replace the drink idol and ideal by another ideal. What is the other ideal? It is the ideal of having a constitution in perfect health that is as elastic as cork, and never cracks or runs rusty or finds any situation that it can't meet by its own buoyancy.

"'Intoxication is not the pleasantest and most desirable state of mind. . . . I know, for I never felt even from Veuve Cliquot, — no, nor after the opening of those stupendous yellow seals which reveal apocalypses of Johannisberg, such exhilaration as one feels from simple, sober, perfect *health* on a fine Indian-summer morning. I have tried both — the one in Schloss Johannisberg itself, and the other everywhere — and of the two, the best excitement was that of my own bounding life-blood.'"[2]

But while James's personal feelings, judgments, and habits were on the whole favorable to abstinence, his repugnance to social machinery alienated him from every organization devoted to the cause. The following letter to Professor Francis G. Peabody was written at about the same time as the address, and was in reply to an invitation to join a Committee of Fifty for the Study of the Liquor Problem: —

Cambridge, Oct. 18 [1894]

Dear Peabody, —

I hate to say no to anything, especially to anything proposed by you, but pray don't propose me for this committee of fifty, council of ten, or Garibaldi thousand, whatever it may be. Do you fellows think you can scare alcohol by the portentousness of your names? Never! It seems to me we *know* quite enough for all practical purposes already, and that this is a kind of swell-front to a house about three feet deep. I confess that the sight of the report of the physiological committee with its proposal to have more dogs sacrificed, and an expert in the library to look up the

[2] These notes state that he had addressed the Total Abstinence League when it was founded, which was in 1882. The last paragraph is a quotation from C. G. Leland's *Sunshine in Thought*, 1862, 83.

literature of the subject for several weeks, made me quite sick inside.

What is *effective,* it seems to me, is the example of abstinence, and the gradually progressive weaning of the people from the habit of expecting to drink on all occasions. Your aqueous dinners to the Club, *e.g.,* do more than your name on this circular will ever do. As in all things, the real cure is the substitution of the better ideal — one need n't then be at pains to drive out the worser one. For our students, *e.g.,* the admiration of, and belief in that pure early-morning health, that is better than all drunkenness and no man that has drunk anything the day before can ever feel, will do more for temperance than anything. I admit that it is something to *live up to!* Excuse the appearance of churlishness that this letter wears I am no man for committees, anyhow. Yours fondly,

W. J.

During the '90s James was also occupied with such educational problems as confronted a member of the Harvard faculty. His individualistic and libertarian creed brought him, as a rule, to the support of Eliot's policies. His scientific training and general modernism inclined him to favor the liberalization of the curriculum at the expense of the privileged position of the ancient languages. "We must," he said, "shake the old double reefs out of the canvas into the wind and sunshine, and let in every modern subject, sure that any subject will prove humanistic, if its setting be kept only wide enough." [3]

Between 1890 and 1909 there was a prolonged attempt to reduce the normal period required for the A.B. degree from four to three years. James was a member of the various committees of the faculty which deliberated upon the proposal,[4] and in 1891 he defended the new plan in an article on "The Proposed Shortening of the College Course," contributed to the *Harvard Monthly*. The following passages are characteristic: "Every teacher soon has forced upon his attention a certain anthropological fact. That fact is that there is a deeply rooted distinction between two sorts

---

[3] *M.S.,* 321.

[4] The result of the agitation was to make the three-year degree *possible* by an increase of the number of courses taken each year. This possibility having proved more and more unrealizable, the number of men who thus obtained the degree soon became negligible.

of student. . . . The one sort of man is born for the theoretic life, and is capable of pressing forward indefinitely into its subtleties and specialties. . . . The other class of men may be intelligent, but they are not *theoretical,* and their interest in most subjects reaches its saturation-point when the broader results and most general laws have been reached. . . . And their teacher also realizes heavily enough the weight of those eternal laws which render it impossible to make an herbivorous animal out of a carnivorous one by offering the latter a continuous diet of hay. . . . These excellent fellows need contact of some sort with the fighting side of life, with the world in which men and women earn their bread and butter and live and die; there must be the scent of blood, so to speak, upon what you offer them, or else their interest does not wake up; the blood that is shed in our electives, fails to satisfy them very long." The A.B. degree should be accommodated to the needs of students of this second category, and for them the three-year course is long enough.[5]

In 1894 and 1898, James used his influence against bills before the Massachusetts Legislature designed to require the examination and licensing of medical practitioners. James was moved by his interest in the new mental therapy, as well as by his chronic distrust of orthodoxy. It seemed to him highly important that hopeful experiences and experiments, therapeutic as well as others, should not be cut off by the spirit of professionalism or the assumption of infallibility. It may well be that "the relation of person to person," or "the free play of personal force and affinity will prove fruitful of beneficent results."

In 1898 James appeared before a committee of the Legislature and pleaded the same cause. Medical knowledge, he said, is highly imperfect and rapidly changing, and experience should be welcomed from any source. He preferred education to legislation, tolerance to prohibition, and experiment to prejudgment.[6] His appearance at the legislative hearing caused much scandal to his colleagues of the Medical School; but he could "face their disapproval much more easily" than that of his own conscience. He wrote to John Jay Chapman: "Says I to myself, Shall civic virtue be confined

---

[5] *Harvard Mo.,* 11–2 (1890–1), 132–5.
[6] *Boston Evening Transcript,* March 24, 1894; March 2, 1898. "I assuredly hold no brief for any of these healers." (*L.W.J.,* II, 69.)

entirely to Zola, J. J. C., and Col. Piquart? Never, says I, so in I goes."

President Cleveland's Venezuela message was dispatched December 17, 1895. The crisis which followed seems to have impressed James for the first time with the danger which lurked in "the fighting instinct" — "three days of fighting mob-hysteria at Washington can at any time undo peace habits of a hundred years." [7] It was a political crime, James felt, to take any steps which would arouse these passions. He wrote to his Congressman, Samuel W. McCall, a letter of protest against what he described as "a wanton and blustering provocation to war." [8] He contributed a letter to the *Harvard Crimson*. Roosevelt, who was at this time President of the Board of Police Commissioners of New York City, had previously written in the same columns to protest against the pressure exerted on Congress by opponents of the administration's policy: "The stock-jobbing timidity," he had said, "the Baboo kind of statesmanship, which is clamored for at this moment by the men who put a monetary gain before national honor, or who are still intellectually in a state of colonial dependence on England, would in the end most assuredly invite war."

To which James replied: "We are evidently guilty of *lèse-majesté* in Mr. Roosevelt's eyes; and though a mad President may any day commit the country without warning to an utterly new career and history, no citizen, no matter how he feels, must then speak, not even to the representative constitutionally appointed to check the President in time of need. May I express a hope that in this University, if no where else on the continent, we shall be patriotic enough *not* to remain passive whilst the destinies of our country are being settled by surprise. Let us be for or against; and if against, then against by every means in our power, when a policy is taking shape that is bound to alter all the national ideals that we have cultivated hitherto. Let us refuse to be bound over night by proclamation, or hypnotized by sacramental phrases through the day. Let us consult our reason as to what is best, and then exert ourselves as citizens with all our might." [9]

[7] *L.W.J.*, II, 28–9.
[8] Dated Dec. 21, 1895, and published in the *Congressional Record*, XXVIII, Part I, 399.
[9] *Harvard Crimson*, Jan. 7, 9, 1896.

The following letter to Frederic Myers was written during these same stirring days: —

Cambridge, Jan. 1, 1896

My dear Myers, —

Here is a Happy New Year to you with my presidential address [10] for a gift. *Valeat quantum.* . . . Well, our countries will soon be soaked in each other's gore. You will be disemboweling me, and Hodgson cleaving Lodge's skull. It will be a war of extermination when it comes, for neither side can tell when it is beaten, and the last man will bury the penultimate one, and then die himself. The French will then occupy England and the Spaniards America. Both will unite against the Germans, and no one can foretell the end. But seriously, all true patriots here have had a hell of a time. It has been a most instructive thing for the dispassionate student of history to see how near the surface in all of us the old fighting instinct lies, and how slight an appeal will wake it up. Once *really* waked, there is no retreat, so the whole wisdom of governors should be to avoid the direct appeals. This your European governments know; but we in our bottomless innocence and ignorance over here know nothing, and Cleveland, in my opinion, by his explicit allusion to war has committed the biggest political crime I have ever seen here. The secession of the southern states had more excuse. There was absolutely no need of it. A commission solemnly appointed to pronounce justice in the Venezuela case would, if its decision were adverse to your country, have doubtless aroused the liberal party in England to espouse the policy of arbitrating, and would have covered us with dignity, if no threat of war had been uttered. But as it is, who can see the way out? Everyone goes about now saying war is not to be. But with these volcanic forces, who can tell? I suppose that the offices of Germany or Italy might in any case, however, save us from what would be the worst disaster to civilization that our time could bring forth. The astounding thing is the latent anglophobia now revealed. It is most of it directly traceable to the diabolic machinations of the party of protection for the past twenty years. They have lived by every sort of infamous sophistication, and hatred of Eng-

[10] Reprinted from *L.W.J.*, II, 30–2. *Cf.* above, 164.

land has been one of their most continuous notes. . . . Ever thine,
— I hate to think of "embruing" my hands in (or with?) your
blood.

W. J.

On the merits of the Monroe Doctrine as affirmed by Cleveland
and Olney, James wrote at length, in 1896, to his wife's brother-in-
law, W. M. Salter: —

"In the abstract it is very pretty, no doubt, though rather comical
in its limitations, but in the concrete it seems to me to need cold
water pumped on it more than any living thing. . . . Can any
serious man pretend that the 'doctrine' has in the mind of one
American out of a thousand an ethical significance? . . . It claims
as an ideal what Mr. Olney says is already a fact, the position of
having our *fiat* recognized as law on this continent. We are pleased
at challenging the big powers of Europe by this attitude, and apart
from that exciting sensation there is n't one of us in ten thousand
who has any use for such a doctrine. . . .

"Such affirmations of 'our will shall be law' form an integral
part of nation's lives, and this 'doctrine' may in *some shape* be considered a part of ours. They are primarily expressions of ambition, but naturally they seek [by] precedent and argument to justify
themselves. Cleveland had not only a right but a duty (considering all things) to worry England into willingness to arbitrate,
and of course he could have done so. . . . *That* policy would
have made us real apostles of civilization, and it need n't in the
least have gone out of the limits of the particular case, or flourished
any hardened theory like Olney's unspeakable rot . . . about the
moral interests of America being irreconcilably diverse from those
of Europe, about permanent political union between European and
American states being unnatural and inexpedient, about South
American republics being our natural congeners and allies, about
our invariable wisdom and justice and equity, and the rest. Things
were in a state where a nascent dogma could harden or not harden,
and in my eyes the whole wisdom of disinterested critics at such
a time consists in resisting the hardening process."

The political issue which stirred James most deeply and exacted
from him the greatest expenditure of time and effort was that
of imperialism. He published eight or more articles and letters,

including an address before the Anti-Imperialist League of which he was at one time vice president. The Spanish War, like the Venezuela incident, first impressed James with the irresistible power of the war fever. The following account was written to his friend Flournoy when the war was two months old.[11]

Cambridge, June 17, 1898

My dear Flournoy, —

Your delightful letter reached me many weeks ago, and now that the College work is over, and a little detachment of mind and feeling of vague new possibility is stealing over me, one of the first acts of my developing freedom is to write you — for you after all, are the point in the old world where I feel most *at home*.

All sorts of things have been happening. You wrote that your household had been so excited over Armenian, Grecian and Parisian atrocities as to have preserved no capacity for taking an interest in Cuban affairs, which are so far away. May I venture to hope that that sluggish state of mind has passed away, and that the young ladies and Henri now leap at the news of the American victories? Seriously speaking, this whole business has thrown a most instructive light on the way in which history is made, and has illustrated to perfection the *psychologie des foules!* The basis of it all is, or rather was, perfectly honest humanitarianism, and an absolutely disinterested desire on the part of our people to set the Cubans free. . . . On this, various interests worked for their purposes in favor of war. The explosion of the *Maine* and the diplomatic negotiations ensued, together with the preparations for possible defense and attack; and by that time Congress was entirely mad, supposing that the people was in the same condition, as it probably was, in less degree. Congress, unfortunately, by our constitution has the right to declare war, and in the psychological condition in which it was, that was the only possible direction of discharge. We were winning the most extraordinary diplomatic victories, but they were of no use. We were ready (as we supposed) for war and nothing but war must come.

It is the worst blow at the *prestige* of popular government [12] that

[11] *Cf.* also the letter to Pillon of nearly the same date, *L.W.J.*, II, 73.
[12] "The worst of it is the complete destruction of the old belief in the *vox populi*. There is no doubt of collective attacks of genuine madness sweeping over peoples and

I have *erlebt*. . . . Our Congress was *absolutely* sincere in disclaiming any desire of conquest or annexation. But see how in the twinkling of an eye a nation's ideals will change! With Dewey's sudden victory, an "imperialist" party has arisen here, which, as it will command all the crude and barbaric patriotism of the country, will be a hard thing to resist. After all, it is on that pure instinctive masterfulness and ambition, that sense of a great destiny, that the greatness of every great nation is based; and we have it in a great measure. But one must "live up" to a great destiny, and alas! our education as a nation, so far, little fits us for success in administering islands with inferior populations. Spain deserves to lose them, but do we deserve to gain them? Whatever happens, in any event, will happen not as the result of any particular reason, but as the result of passion, and of certain watchwords that nations have learned habitually to obey. We have some pretty good ones of the latter sort, which will make for reason. But the *great* passion undeniably now is the passion for *adventure*. We are in so little danger from Spain, that our interest in the war can only be called that in a peculiarly exciting kind of *sport*. And, after all, has n't the spirit of the life of all the great generals and rulers and aristocracies always been the spirit of sport carried to its supreme expression? Civilization, properly so-called, might well be termed the organization of all those functions that resist the mere excitement of sport. But *excitement!* Shall we not worship excitement? And after all, what is life for, except for opportunities of excitement?! It makes all humdrum moralizing seem terribly dead and tame! And it beautifully corroborates the "chance" theory of history, to find that the critical turning-points in these great movements are purely accidental. A victory often depends on the weather. Without the *Maine* explosion we should still very likely be at peace, — that was the last item in the summation of stimuli, and that explosion was possibly due to the free-will of one of the molecules in the dynamite magazine! . . .

Your letters are always a rare delight, so be liberal with them. Much love from both of us to Mrs. Flournoy and all the younger Flournoys. *Idem* from me to yourself.

W. J.

---

stampeding them. And liberalism must slowly and sadly go to work against the possibility of them." (W.J. to H.J.², April 10, 1898.)

Thus at first James saw some good even in the Spanish War. There was not only the opportunity for adventure, but "our isolation from Europe, absurd abstraction that it was, is pretty well broken into. Europe has got to be taken account of, and that will help to educate us." This detached and psychologizing spirit did not last long. As soon as the war against Spain was superseded by the benevolent coercion of the Filipinos his own belligerent passions were aroused. To Salter, who had advocated such a policy on ethical grounds, he wrote as follows: —

Cambridge, Nov. 18, 1898

Dear Mack, —

. . . I read your lecture on the Philippines,[13] etc. with admiration of the *manner,* but with no conviction of the wisdom of the matter of it. . . . Philanthropic empire, educative for freedom, is *in concreto* and now, just *empire.* It means the killing of Aguinaldo and all who may resist us. It means the presumption to force our ideals on people to whom they are not native. It means definitive entrance with army and navy into the old system of international hates and jealousies, from which providence and our situation have spared us hitherto, and from which, if we would *stay* out, we might be, through arbitrations and influences, able to help the other countries in their efforts to emerge. . . . Against all this there is nothing to urge, it seems to me, but the vague hope that where motion and action are, success is always among the *possibilities.* Of course that feeling is sacred, but in the concrete fact of us now, what does it consist in? In absolutely nothing but the uplift of mere *excitement,* — empire and war being the great excitements of peoples, in the face of which all ordinary prudential talk (such as individuals would carry on their affairs with) is deemed base, if not treasonable. These excitements and ambitions are of course the forces that make nations great (when they do not ruin them), and it may be that war is to be the only force that can hammer us into decency, as it is the great force that has hammered the European states. Only it seems to me that men . . . who stand . . . for reflection are in a rather

[13] The lecture referred to was "A New Nation and a New Duty," delivered before the Society for Ethical Culture of Chicago on Oct. 2, 1898. Salter later changed his attitude on the Philippine policy from one of commendation to one of condemnation.

odd rôle when they fan the flames of such excitements by lending
. . . high sounding words to decorate the business withal. . . .

It shows that there is no danger of mankind, however civilized,
ever growing emasculated with senility. We have seen Bentham-
ism succeeded by the glittering nationality-principles of the Second
Empire; and they by those old-fashioned animal ambitions for
mastery and mere success which seem now to be sweeping away the
world, and us at the wake. This is the real and concrete spring of
action, it seems to me, that is exciting us; and raising and educat-
ing inferior races, is mere hollow pretext and unreality. . . .
I write this with great haste, and an appearance of vehemence
which in me is inseparable from the writing act. I mean no
offense . . . only thinking you take a rather abstract view of an
exceedingly concrete situation, and being unable to distinguish in
practice, as you seem to do so beautifully, between the lofty and
elevating appropriation of the Philippines for their future freedom
and the appropriation of them *sans phrase*. Our outward acts
must be the same in either case. . . . Affectionately,

W. J.

James saw imperialism as an outlet for blind passion masked by
a profession of benevolence: "We gave the fighting instinct and
the passion of mastery their outing . . . because we thought that
. . . we could resume our permanent ideals and character when
the fighting fit was done. We now see how we reckoned without
our host. We see . . . what an absolute savage . . . the passion
of military conquest always is, and how the only safeguard against
the crimes to which it will infallibly drag the nation that gives
way to it is to keep it chained forever. . . . We are now openly
engaged in crushing out the sacredest thing in this great human
world — the attempt of a people long enslaved to attain to the
possession of itself, to organize its laws and government, to be
free to follow its internal destinies according to its own ideals. . . .
Why, then, do we go on? First, the war fever; and then the
pride which always refuses to back down when under fire. But
these are passions that interfere with the reasonable settlement
of any affair; and in this affair we have to deal with a factor altogether peculiar with our belief, namely, in a national destiny
which must be 'big' at any cost. . . . We are to be missionaries

of civilization, and to bear the white man's burden, painful as it
often is! . . . The individual lives are nothing. Our duty and
our destiny call, and civilization must go on! Could there be a
more damning indictment of that whole bloated idol termed 'modern civilization' than this amounts to? Civilization is, then, the
big, hollow, resounding, corrupting, sophisticating, confusing tor-
rent of mere brutal momentum and irrationality that brings forth
fruits like this!" [14]

"As if anything could be of value anywhere," James wrote to a
friend, "that had no native historic roots. We have destroyed in
Luzon the one sacred thing in the world, the spontaneous budding
of a national life. We are destroying their souls even more than
their bodies." It was a case of that "blindness in human beings"
to which James had already called attention: "It is obvious that
for our rulers at Washington the Filipinos have not existed as
psychological quantities at all. . . . We have treated [them] as
if they were a painted picture, an amount of mere matter in our
way. They are too remote from us ever to be realized as they exist
in their inwardness." [15]

On April 11, 1899, Roosevelt made his famous speech on "The
Strenuous Life," which evoked a long reply from James in which
he accuses Roosevelt and the whole imperialistic group of "ab-
stractness." They mouth formulas such as "unfit to govern themselves," without seeing the population of the Philippines "face to
face as a concrete reality." The "strenuous life" is another abstraction, which solves no problem, since strenuousness is a quality
which is shared by the advocates of both sides of any issue: —

"Shall Governor Roosevelt be allowed to crow all over our national barnyard and hear no equally shrill voice lifted in reply?
Even the 'prattlers who sit at home in peace with their silly mock-
humanitarianism' must feel their 'ignoble' and 'cowardly' blood
stirred by such a challenge; and I for one feel that it would be
ignominious to leave him in uncontradicted possession of the
field. . . . Of all the naked abstractions that were ever applied
to human affairs, the outpourings of Governor Roosevelt's soul
in this speech would seem the very nakedest. Although in middle
life . . . and in a situation of responsibility concrete enough, he is

[14] Letter to *Boston Evening Transcript,* March 1, 1899.
[15] *Ibid.,* March 4, 1899.

still mentally in the *Sturm und Drang* period of early adolescence, treats human affairs, when he makes speeches about them, from the sole point of view of the organic excitement and difficulty they may bring, gushes over war as the ideal condition of human society, for the manly strenuousness which it involves, and treats peace as a condition of blubberlike and swollen ignobility, fit only for huckster- ing weaklings, dwelling in gray twilight and heedless of the higher life. Not a word of the cause, — one foe is as good as another, for aught he tells us; not a word of the conditions of success. . . . He swamps everything together in one flood of abstract bellicose emotion. . . . To enslave a weak but heroic people, or to brazen out a blunder, is a good enough cause, it appears, for Colonel Roosevelt. To us Massachusetts anti-imperialists, who have fought in better causes, it is not quite good enough." [16]

In May 1900, James, who was supposed to be ill, sent from Geneva to the *Springfield Republican* a six-column translation of the diary of a French naval officer who was an eyewitness of the scenes in Manila in the spring and summer of 1898.[17] A month later he wrote (again from Switzerland) calling attention to a work on the Philippines by Ferdinand Blumentritt and enclosing a trans- lation of the closing pages in which the American conquest was severely condemned.[18] James was still in Europe during the Presi- dential campaign of 1900, but wrote to his friends urging them to vote for Bryan, whom he had at first distrusted, but of whom he later wrote to Francis Boott: "I have fallen in love with him so for his character, that I am willing to forget his following. . . . The worst thing said is . . . that in public affairs he is an ama- teur. So are you and I!"

James's active participation in the anti-imperialist movement came to a close with his address before the Anti-Imperialist League in Boston in the fall of 1903. The movement had failed of its immediate object and could now hope only that the Filipinos might be granted their independence in the more or less remote future. There is a distinct spirit of disillusionment, — Americanism in the old sense is dead, — but there is still a cause uniting the intel- lectual liberals of all countries: —

"I think we have candidly to admit that in the matter of our

[16] Letter to the *Boston Evening Transcript,* April 15, 1899.
[17] *Springfield Republican,* June 4, 1900.
[18] *Ibid.,* July 2, 1900.

Philippine conquest we . . . have failed to produce much immediate effect. 'Duty and Destiny' have rolled over us like a Jug-
gernaut car. . . .

"Angelic impulses and predatory lusts divide our heart exactly
as they divide the hearts of other countries. . . . Political virtue
does not follow geographical divisions. It follows the eternal division inside of each country between the more animal and the
more intellectual kind of men, between the tory and the liberal
tendencies, the jingoism and animal instinct that would run things
by main force and brute possession, and the critical conscience that
believes in educational methods and in rational rules of right. . . .
The great international and cosmopolitan liberal party, the party of
conscience and intelligence the world over, has, in short, absorbed
us; and we are only its American section, carrying on the war
against the powers of darkness here, playing our part in the long,
long campaign for truth and fair dealing which must go on in all
the countries of the world until the end of time. Let us cheerfully settle into our interminable task. Everywhere it is the same
struggle under various names, — light against darkness, right against
might, love against hate. The Lord of life is with us, and we
cannot permanently fail." [19]

Interesting and instructive are James's alterations of attitude
to Theodore Roosevelt. In the year 1877–1878 the latter was a
member of James's course on the "Comparative Anatomy and
Physiology of Vertebrates." He could already boast of some attainment as a field naturalist, having frequently made excursions
to the country for birds and to the Boston wharves for specimens
of lobsters and fish. I quote from the recollections of another
member of the class: "Many were the *rencontres* between him and
Dr. James. T. R. *always* had the last word. . . . Those little
sparring matches I think threw considerable light on his characteristics. He was a great lime-lighter! My impression of his material, in these instances, was that it was largely irrelevant and
far-fetched. At all events, Dr. James would never continue the argument, and I can see him now in his double-breasted blue coat and
flowing tie, settling back in his chair, in a broad grin . . . and
waiting for T. R. to finish." [20]

[19] *Report* of Fifth Annual Meeting of the New England Anti-Imperialist League,
Nov. 28, 1903.
[20] From a letter to the author by Dr. Samuel Delano, Harvard '79.

As a fighter for ideals Roosevelt was a man after James's own heart; while the roughness of his methods — his lack of taste, sympathy, and discrimination — was profoundly offensive. On August 21, 1902, Charles Norton delivered a speech at his annual dinner at Ashfield, and bitterly arraigned the "designing politicians" who rushed the country into the "criminal" war with Spain. Roosevelt had recently spoken in Hartford in support of legislation affecting Cuba and the Philippines. James congratulated Norton promptly and emphatically : —

" 'I wish to say right here' that I thank you from the bottom of my heart for organizing that rebellious dinner at Ashfield, which, I hear indirectly, has caused local bad blood and tribulation. The more the better! May the wound never heal till decent acknowledgment of sin is made. On the whole I have rejoiced in Roosevelt so far, but I 've done with the man who can utter such brazen and impudent lies as he knew he was uttering at Hartford when he spoke of the Philippine business. His moral fibre is too irredeemably coarse. . . . If only one had the pen of a Voltaire !"

Three years later, however, James was advocating the election of Roosevelt to the presidency of Harvard: "Think of the mighty good-will of him, of his enjoyment of his post, of his power as a preacher, of the number of things to which he gives his attention, of the safety of his second thoughts, of the increased courage he is showing, and above all of the fact that he is an open, instead of an underground leader, whom the voters can control once in four years, when he runs away, whose heart is in the right place, who is an enemy of red tape and quibbling and everything that in general the word 'politician' stands for. That significance of him in the popular mind is a great national asset, and it would be a shame to let it run to waste until it has done a lot more work for us." [21]

Two years later the pendulum had swung again. On February 23, 1907, Roosevelt had made a speech at the Harvard Union in which he had humorously derided scholarship to the delight of the students and at the expense of the members of the faculty who sat in the gallery. This was too much for James. Though he preached the gospel of robustness, he cared very deeply what one

[21] *L.W.J.*, II, 232, and note.

was robust about. There was always a prior condition of legitimate belligerency — namely, the purity of one's cause.

James's anti-imperialism is an application of his individualistic
internationalism. Dickinson S. Miller once wrote of James: "Not
detachment, but attachment, was his quality." [22] This is a profound
observation. James's wide and almost promiscuous sociability did
not detach him from his family, but simply multiplied his attachments. Similarly his cosmopolitanism did not detach him from
America, but enriched and diversified his attachments by presenting
new human objects to his apparently insatiable appetite. Though
he was by no means blind to their faults, he found something to
respect and like in every nation that he knew. Once after praising
Italy and England, he added: "Yet I believe (or suspect) that ours
is eventually the bigger destiny, if we can only succeed in living up
to it. . . . Meanwhile, as my brother Henry once wrote, thank
God for a world that holds so rich an England, so rare an Italy!" [23]
He would have said the same of so vigorous a Germany, so polite a
France, or so honest a Switzerland. Thank God for a world that
is generous enough to hold them all!

James's standard of international politics was an application of
his individualism: tolerate differences, and enjoy them. To this
he added the usual corollary, that intolerance is intolerable. He
was fond of saying that he "went in for small nations and small
things generally." "Damn great Empires! including that of the
Absolute. . . . Give me individuals and their spheres of activity."
Here is a completer statement of the matter: "I am against bigness
and greatness in all their forms, and with the invisible molecular
moral forces that work from individual to individual, stealing in
through the crannies of the world like so many soft rootlets, or
like the capillary oozing of water, and yet rending the hardest
monuments of man's pride, if you give them time. The bigger the
unit you deal with, the hollower, the more brutal, the more menda-
cious is the life displayed. So I am against all big organizations
as such, national ones first and foremost; against all big successes
and big results; and in favor of the eternal forces of truth which
always work in the individual and immediately unsuccessful way,

[22] "Mr. Santayana and William James," *Harvard Graduates' Magazine*, XXIX
(1920–1), 351.
[23] *L.W.J.*, II, 305.

under-dogs always, till history comes, after they are long dead, and puts them on the top." [24]

The evil of the "great empire" lay in its fictitious values, its insincerity and its brutality. James sensed the inwardness of the great nations with as much relish as that of the small. But he believed that the great empire was blind to the essence of nationality in others, and at the same time in danger of losing its own soul through attention to mere quantity.

James's Americanism was never seriously shaken. He was instinctively loyal to his own, whether family, friend, institution, or country. A momentary weakening of his national attachment only served to reveal the infrangible strength of the tie. In 1901, when his illness, together with the Gifford Lectures, had kept him abroad for the better part of two years, he said: "I long to steep myself in America again and let the broken rootlets make new adhesions to the native soil. A man coquetting with too many countries is as bad as a bigamist, and loses his soul altogether." [25] This was a characteristic and invariable reaction to any prolonged absence from home. His national pride was wounded by the new imperialistic policy — a nation which wantonly disgorges its historic soul, he wrote in 1899, "tends to loosen the hold of her children." "But," he continued, "I don't despair yet. The many-headed monster has good points, and is today far less corrupt than any European country. One's duty and one's business is there with one's own people."

James's patriotism ran with two of his fundamental moral attitudes. Elaborating the charge that Europe was relatively corrupt, he said: "[American] millionaires and syndicates have their immediate cash to pay, but they have no intrenched prestige to work with, like the church sentiment, the army sentiment, the aristocracy and royalty sentiment, which [in Europe] can be brought to bear in favor of every kind of individual and collective crime — appealing not only to the immediate pocket of the persons to be corrupted, but to the ideals of their imagination as well. . . . We 'intellectuals' in America must all work to keep our precious birthright of individualism, and freedom from these institutions." [26] America.

24 *L.W.J.*, II, 90.
25 *L.W.J.*, II, 152.
26 *L.W.J.*, II, 100–1.

in short, was less highly institutionalized, less subject to control by impersonal, corporate entities, than Europe. As an individualist James had an antipathy to organization, mechanization, and officialdom. He was willing to endure disorder if it was the necessary price for spontaneity. The other attitude which strongly reënforced James's Americanism was his repugnance to the decadent and effete — his preference of the simple, the natural, the vigorous, the forward-looking. He found these qualities in America, and in the end they outweighed the counterattractions of European countries, powerful as these were: "Still, one loves America above all things, for her youth, her greenness, her plasticity, innocence, good intentions, friends, everything." [27]

On July 23, 1903, James contributed a long letter to the *Springfield Republican* on the subject of lynching. This letter was widely reprinted and received so much comment that on July 29 James gave an interview to the *Boston Journal* on the same subject. These published utterances brought him many letters of commendation from the North and of protest from the South.

To James lynching and mob rule were psychological as well as moral phenomena, illustrating the powers of emotional forces, when socially stimulated, to sweep away all ordinary restraints. There was unmistakable evidence of the survival (however much overlaid with decent appearances) of the primal instincts of the brute: "The average church-going civilizee realizes, one may say, absolutely nothing of the deeper currents of human nature, or of the aboriginal capacity for murderous excitement which lies sleeping even in his own bosom. . . . The water-tight compartment in which the carnivore within us is confined is artificial and not organic. It never will be organic. The slightest diminution of external pressure, the slightest loophole of licensed exception, will make the whole system leaky, and murder will again grow rampant. It is where the impulse is collective, and the murder is regarded as a punitive or protective duty, that the peril to civilization is greatest. Then, as in the hereditary vendetta, in dueling, in religious massacre, history shows how difficult it is to exterminate a homicidal custom which is once established."

In the case of the "lynching epidemic," as in the case of mili-

[27] *L.W.J.*, II, 105.

tarism and chauvinism, James was profoundly disturbed by the new rôle of the popular newspaper : —

"Our American people used to be supposed to have a certain hardheaded shrewdness. Nowadays they seem smitten with utter silliness. Their professed principles mean nothing to them, and any phrase or sensational excitement captivates them. The sensational press is the organ and the promulgator of this state of mind, which means . . . a new 'dark ages' that may last more centuries than the first one. Then illiteracy was brutal and dumb, and power was rapacious without disguise. Now illiteracy has an enormous literary organization, and power is sophistical; and the result is necessarily a new phenomenon in history — involving every kind of diseased sensationalism and insincerity in the collective mind." [28]

The last of the causes that enlisted James's support was Mental Hygiene. In 1906, Clifford W. Beers sent him the manuscript of his now famous book, *A Mind That Found Itself*. James read it with enthusiasm, helped him to find a publisher, and was from this date a warm advocate of Beers's programme for developing a more enlightened public opinion on the treatment of mental diseases.[29] Despite his limited strength, his burden of work, and his loathing for organizations of any sort, James participated actively in the new project throughout the remaining years of his life. He wrote Beers over forty letters, assisted him in the organization of the National Committee for Mental Hygiene, finally founded in 1909, helped him to raise money, and gave him warm personal encouragement. Writing to Beers in 1917, President Eliot said: "Among your friends and supporters, the most interesting and remarkable personage, to my thinking, was William James. His letters to you about your work, and his gift of a thousand dollars to your cause — for him a very large gift — must have been very delightful to you, and helpful also. They moved me very much as I read them last evening." [30]

The reasons which actuated James are best set forth in the long letter which he addressed in 1909 to Mr. John D. Rockefeller, Sr.,

[28] July 27, 1903, to Dr. Samuel Delano, who in a letter on lynching, *Evening Post*, July 24, 1903, had emphasized the importance of public opinion.
[29] The story of Beers's enterprise, including his relations with James, will be found in the Fourth Edition of *A Mind That Found Itself*, 1920, vii, viii, 319 ff.
[30] Jan. 17, 1917; reprinted in part from C. W. Beers, *The Mental Hygiene Movement*, 1921, 310.

in the hope of obtaining financial support for the cause: "During my life as a 'psychologist' I have had much to do with our asylums, and I have had so painfully borne in upon me the massiveness of human evil which the term 'insanity' covers, and the inadequacy of our arrangements for coping with it, that I long ago registered a vow that if I myself, by Heaven's grace, should ever be able to leave any money for public use it should be for 'insanity' exclusively. . . . Our usual arrangements take no heed either of prophylaxis or of after-care; what should be regarded as a common functional disease is handled as a social stigma. . . . Everywhere routine and safety are the first consideration, and prevention and cure take the second place. . . . There must from now onward be a tremendous campaign waged for prevention and cure. . . . The occasion of bringing my own dissatisfaction . . . to a practical head, has been the recent publication of a very remarkable book, *A Mind That Found Itself*, by Clifford W. Beers of New Haven. . . . It is he who has convinced the rest of us that the hour for doing something — and not merely feeling and wishing — has struck."

James's active support of "causes" reveals the precise nature of his practical idealism. The good is not something to be contemplated, but something to be brought to pass. It is to be felt, yes — but as the agent and not as the spectator feels it. Ideals are objects of will, rather than of taste. It is this view that underlies his vigorous reaction to Santayana. In 1900, having read Santayana's *Poetry of Religion,* James wrote to Palmer as follows: —

"The great event in my life recently has been the reading of Santayana's book. Although I absolutely reject the Platonism of it, I have literally squealed with delight at the imperturbable perfection with which the position is laid down on page after page. . . . It is refreshing to see a representative of moribund Latinity rise up and administer such reproof to us barbarians in the hour of our triumph. . . . Nevertheless, how fantastic a philosophy! — as if the 'world of values' *were* independent of existence. It is only as *being,* that one thing is better than another. The idea of darkness is as good as that of light, as ideas. There is more value in light's *being*. And the exquisite consolation, when you have ascertained the badness of all fact, in knowing that badness is inferior to goodness, to the end — it only rubs the pessimism in. A man whose egg at breakfast turns out always bad says to himself, 'Well, bad and good are not the same, anyhow.' That is just the trouble! Moreover, when you come down to the facts, what do your harmonious and integral ideal systems prove to be? in the concrete? Always things burst by the growing content of experience. Dramatic unities; laws of versification; ecclesiastical systems; scholastic doctrines. Bah! Give me Walt Whitman and Browning ten times over, much as the perverse ugliness of the latter at times irritates me, and intensely as I have enjoyed Santayana's attack. The barbarians are in the line of mental growth, and those who do insist that the ideal and the real are dynamically continuous are those by whom the world is to be saved. But I 'm nevertheless delighted that the other view, always existing in the world, should at last have found so splendidly impertinent an expression among ourselves." [31]

The letter containing these paragraphs was sent by Palmer to Santayana, who replied as follows: —

Cambridge, Easter, 1900

Dear James, —

Palmer has just sent me your delightful letter, by which I see with joy that you are full of life again in this season of resurrection. May the revival be perennial for you and full of fruits! You must have thought me very unfeeling not to write and make personal inquiries during all these months; it has not been for lack of concern but merely from perplexity in finding the right moment and the right words, as well as from the knowledge of how little my platonic sympathies would count in the midst of the affection of your many friends. But I am as glad as any of them can be at the change for the better, and full of confidence that you underestimate the amount of energy that you will find again in yourself ere long.

I see that you have discovered me in the *Poetry and Religion* more than in my verses or the *Sense of Beauty,* although I fancy there is no less of me in those other books. But there is more to come, and although I daresay you won't like the *Life of Reason* much better than you like my attitude hitherto, I think you will find that, apart from temperament, I am nearer to you than you now believe. What you say, for instance, about the value of the good lying in its *existence,* and about the continuity of the world of values with that of fact, is not different from what I should admit.

[31] *L.W.J.*, II, 122-3.

Ideals would be irrelevant if they were not natural entelechies, if they were not called for by something that exists and if, consequently, their realization would not be a present and actual good. And the point in insisting that all the eggs at breakfast are rotten is nothing at all except the consequent possibility and endeavour to find good eggs for the morrow. The only thing I object to and absolutely abhor is the assertion that all the eggs indiscriminately are good because the hen has laid them.

You tax me several times with impertinence and superior airs. I wonder if you realize the years of suppressed irritation which I have passed in the midst of an unintelligible, sanctimonious and often disingenuous Protestantism, which is thoroughly alien and repulsive to me, and the need I have of joining hands with something far away from it and far above it. My Catholic sympathies did n't justify me in speaking out because I felt them to be merely sympathies, and not to have a rational and human backing; but the study of Plato and Aristotle has given me confidence and, backed by such an authority as they and all who have accepted them represent, I have a right to be sincere, to be absolutely objective and unapologetic, because it is not I that speak but human reason that speaks in me. Truly the Babel in which we live has nothing in it so respectable as to put on the defensive the highest traditions of the human mind. No doubt, as you say, Latinity is moribund, as Greece itself was when it transmitted to the rest of the world the seeds of its own rationalism; and for that reason there is the more need of transplanting and propagating straight thinking among the peoples who hope to be masters of the world in the immediate future. Otherwise they will be its physical masters only, and the Muses will fly over them to alight among some future race that may understand the gods better.

If I get to Europe this summer I shall hope to see you, but it is doubtful: I may stay here or go to Japan — a wholly new sphere for me, where a friend who has gone before is tempting me to follow him. I should n't like Japan very much, but I should like to have seen it. . . . May . . . all things physical and metaphysical go on well and rapidly. Always sincerely yours,

G. SANTAYANA

While James vigorously opposed a Platonic divorce of the good from the realm of existence, and insisted that the "ideal and the real are dynamically continuous," he was not less opposed than Santayana to any *reduction* of the ideal to the real.   The ideal is a preferred form of life — something *to be made real* through the energy of the will.   Thus James consistently refused to identify meanings with origins, differences of value with physical differences, importance with magnitude, or moral progress with natural history.[32]

[32] *W.B.*, 100; *L.W.J.*, II, 345–6.

LXIX

VARIETIES OF RELIGIOUS EXPERIENCE

THE period of James's preoccupation with practical philosophy culminated in the Gifford Lectures of 1901 and 1902, and their publication in the latter year under the title of *The Varieties of Religious Experience*. This was, in the first place, an act of filial piety. Writing to his wife immediately after his father's death in 1882, he said: "You have one new function hereafter, or rather not so much a new function as a new intellectualization of an old one: you must not leave me till I understand a little more of the value and meaning of religion in Father's sense, in the mental life and destiny of man. It is not the *one* thing needful, as he said. But it is needful with the rest. My friends leave it altogether out. I as his son (if for no other reason) must help it to its rights in their eyes. And for that reason I must learn to interpret it aright as I have never done, and you must help me."

The *Varieties* is the fulfillment of this pledge, after the lapse of almost twenty years. It is perhaps surprising that there should be in these lectures so few specific indications of his father's influence.[1] But that influence did not extend to details, nor did it embrace the theological doctrines which filled his father's works. James once said: "I myself believe that the evidence for God lies primarily in inner personal experiences." The father's influence appears in James's general inclination to credit these "personal experiences," of which the chief was the sustaining sense of support from a higher power.[2]

As regards James himself the ideas which are developed in the

---

[1] He refers to his father's conversion at Windsor in 1844 as an instance of "panic fear," but did not introduce it because there was "too much context required." (*V.R.E.*, 161; W.J. to F. Abauzit, June 12, 1904.) There is something reminiscent of his father in the vivid thrust at Calvinism in a footnote: "The very notion that this glorious universe, with planets and winds, and laughing sky and ocean, should have been conceived and had its beams and rafters laid in technicalities of criminality, is incredible to our modern imagination." (*V.R.E.*, 448.)

[2] *Pragm.*, 109; cf. *L.R.H.J.*, 13–4, 72.

Varieties represent one of two threads which can be traced back continuously to his youth. There were always two kinds of faith, the fighting faith and the comforting faith; or, as they might be called, the faith upstream and the faith downstream. The former is the faith that springs from strength. Preferring the good to the evil, the moral person fights for it with the sort of confidence that the brave man feels in himself and his allies, exulting in the danger and in the uncertainty of the issue. This is the faith of James's tough-mindedness,[3] the bracing air which he prefers to breathe when his hygienic tone is good; and it is also the faith of last resort, when skepticism has deprived him of every other support. It is the kind of religion that is characteristic of *The Will to Believe*. The second is the faith that springs from human weakness, and asks for refuge and security.[4] In the fighting faith religion is a stimulant to the will; the comforting faith, on the other hand, is at the bottom of one's heart, relaxing. Though one may row with great earnestness, one is aware of being carried to port — safely, inexorably — by the very current in which one floats. The need for this sort of faith James understood both from his own periodic weariness and from his sympathy with that extremity and tragic plight which is the common lot of man. To this second faith, the comforting faith, James devotes special attention in the Gifford Lectures.

There is also a close relation between James's view of religious conversion and his own "crisis" in 1870–1872. His sense of black despair and morbid fear is used in the *Varieties* to illustrate the state of "the sick soul." He tells us that the experience made him "sympathetic with the morbid feelings of others"; and that both his melancholy and his emergence from it had "a religious bearing." His own "salvation" came through self-reliance and the idea of moral freedom, rather than through a sense of supporting grace — but he experienced a marked alteration of mood, and a feeling of renewed life similar to that of "the twice-born."[5]

At the same time that the Gifford Lectures sprang from James's filial piety and from his personal experiences, they also expressed the psychological interest which had governed him during the '90s. Religion afforded the greatest single group — greatest both in vol-

---

[3] Opposed to "tender-mindedness," *cf. Pragm.*, Lect. I; not to be confused with "healthy-mindedness," as James discusses it in the *Varieties*.
[4] This alternative appears clearly as early as 1861; *cf. L.W.J.*, I, 128 ff.
[5] *V.R.E.*, 160–1; *L.W.J.*, I, 145–8.

ume and in dignity — of those "exceptional mental states" with which he was also concerned in his "psychical research," in his observation of war and mob violence, and in his studies of psychopathology. "I regard the *Varieties of Religious Experience*," he wrote in 1902, "as in a sense a study of morbid psychology, mediating and interpreting to the philistine much that he would otherwise despise and reject utterly." [6]

Nor must it be forgotten, though the exigencies of orderly arrangement permit only a passing reference to it here, that the first public announcement of pragmatism took place in 1898, shortly after James had embarked on the preparation of the Gifford Lectures. In the California lecture on "Philosophical Conceptions and Practical Results" he made a special application of pragmatism in a passage which clearly defines the field of religious investigation: "What keeps religion going is something else than abstract definitions and systems of logically concatenated adjectives, and something different from faculties of theology and their professors. All these things are after-effects, secondary accretions upon a mass of concrete religious experiences, connecting themselves with feeling and conduct that renew themselves in *sæcula sæculorum* in the lives of humble private men. If you ask what these experiences are, they are conversations with the unseen, voices and visions, responses to prayer, changes of heart, deliverances from fear, inflowings of help, assurances of support, whenever certain persons set their own internal attitude in certain appropriate ways." [7]

Although James's appointment to a Gifford Lectureship was not formally made until 1898, it was proposed as early as 1896, and he began in his characteristic way to collect bibliographies, books, clippings, citations, descriptions, letters — material which he did not begin to put into finished written form until 1900. The period of composition coincided with the severe illness which followed his overexertion in the summer of 1899. He was depressed in spirits, and physically disabled. Much of the actual writing was done in bed, at times when two or three hours a day was the maximum of work which his strength would support. [8] It was necessary to postpone the lectures from 1900 to 1901, and there was always the haunt-

---

[6] For the close relation between the Gifford Lectures and the Lowell Lectures on "Exceptional Mental States," *cf. L.W.J.*, II, 56 ff.
[7] *C.E.R.*, 427–8.
[8] *L.W.J.*, II, 126–7.

ing fear that he might not be able to deliver them even if he could complete their preparation. The first series of lectures began at Edinburgh, on May 16, 1901. Only two weeks before he had written: "As for my sad self, I feel reasonably sure now of reading my lectures myself (they begin May 16, — on which date please offer up silent prayer). If I can stand the sociability it will be a great thing, — I have grown so pusillanimous in the past two years about everything, that I dread that like a nightmare. I have become a vegetable, a suffering vegetable if there be such a thing; and, as like seeks like, I shan't get seriously better until I can get my back onto some American vegetation with an American tree over my head and an American squirrel chittering at me."

The lectures were a success, both in the number and in the interest of the auditors, and success restored the lecturer's confidence in himself. After a winter at home he returned to Edinburgh again in the spring of 1902. On June 9 he wrote to Flournoy: "The last lecture went off today, — about 400 auditors, very silent and attentive, and tremendous enthusiasm at the end. But *how* glad I am it is all over! Hereafter I will make no such contract again. I am *deadly* tired and going home to my own normal conditions, to get well."

The lectures had been prepared for the press before James left America for Edinburgh, and appeared in June under the title, *The Varieties of Religious Experience, a Study in Human Nature.* The book, like the lectures, was signally successful. Writing the following January, again to Flournoy, he said: "The book has sold extraordinarily well in English, for a book that costs over three dollars. The tenth thousand is already being printed; I get enthusiastic letters from strangers; and the reviewers, although, *without a* single *exception,* they all use the word 'unsatisfactory,' having eased their conscience by that term, they proceed to handle me with sympathy and praise." This success was not unexpected; indeed, James had anticipated it with some misgivings when he said, it "will doubtless be a popular book, — too biological for the religious, too religious for the biologists." [9]

The thesis of the *Varieties* is best stated in a letter to Miss Frances R. Morse: "The problem I have set myself is a hard one: *first,* to defend . . . 'experience' against 'philosophy' as being the

[9] *Cf.* above, 199.

WILLIAM JAMES AND THEODORE FLOURNOY, MAY 18, 1905

real backbone of the world's religious life . . . and *second,* to make the hearer or reader believe, what I myself invincibly do believe, that, although all the special manifestations of religion may have been absurd (I mean its creeds and theories), yet the life of it as a whole is mankind's most important function." [10]

In other words, religion is not a secondary product, a mode of feeling or action evoked by a secular view of the world, but has its own direct and independent evidence. There are religious *data,* or *facts,* and not merely religious ideas or sentiments. As early as 1884 James had written to Davidson that he rather despaired of any "popular religion of a philosophic character," and found himself wondering "whether there can be any popular religion raised on the ruins of the old Christianity without the presence of . . . a belief in new *physical* facts and possibilities. Abstract considerations about the soul and the reality of a moral order will not do in a year what the glimpse into a world of new phenomenal possibilities enveloping those of the present life, afforded by an extension of our insight into the order of nature, would do in an instant." [11] It was with such "phenomenal possibilities" that the *Varieties* was concerned. But while James identified religion with certain specific experiences, and with specific facts, events, forces, and entities which these experiences revealed, he did not identify religion with any particular creed. By religion he meant historic religions, but in respect of their common content and not their particular claims.

Religion is something more primordial than reason and of equal authority. "Faith branches off from the high-road before reason begins," said James to a skeptical student. In notes made during the preparation of the Gifford Lectures, he wrote, under the heading of "Faith": "The struggle seems to be that of a less articulate and more profound part of our nature to hold out, and keep itself standing, against the attempts of a more superficial and explicit or loquacious part, to suppress it. The profounder part believes; but it can *say* so little. Ought it to be cowed? to submit? or ought it to stand by its own lights? . . . One *can't* convert a genuine disbeliever in religion any more than one can convert a Protestant to Catholicism. . . . My exhibition of extravagant and irrational in-

[10] *L.W.J.,* II, 127.
[11] *L.W.J.,* I, 236–7.

stances will probably confirm such disbelievers entirely.   Just see,
they will say, *how* absurd!   Yet I must shape things and argue to
the conclusion that a man's religion is the deepest and wisest thing
in his life.   I must frankly establish the breach between the life of
articulate reason, and the push of the subconscious, the irrational
instinctive part, which is more vital. . . .   In religion the vital needs,
the mystical overbeliefs . . . proceed from an ultra-rational region.
They are *gifts*.   It is a question of *life,* of living in these gifts or
not living. . . .   There is a chance to do something strong here, but
it is extremely difficult."

The original paragraph which James wrote for the opening of
the Gifford Lectures stressed the uniqueness of the religious experience and the breach with "articulate reason": "There is something
in life, as one feels its presence, that seems to defy all the possible
resources of phraseology. . . .   Life defies our phrases, not only
because it is infinitely continuous and subtle and shaded, whilst our
verbal terms are discrete, rude and few; but because of a deeper discrepancy still.   Our words come together leaning on each other
laterally for support, in chains and propositions, and there is never
a proposition that does not require other propositions after it, to
amplify it, restrict it, or in some way save it from the falsity by
defect or excess which it contains. . . .   Life, too, in one sense,
stumbles over its own fact in a similar way; for its earlier moments
plunge ceaselessly into later ones which reinterpret and correct them.
Yet there is something else than this in life, something entirely unparalleled by anything in verbal thought.   The living moments —
some living moments, at any rate — have somewhat of absolute
that needs no lateral support.   Their meaning seems to well up
from out of their very centre, in a way impossible verbally to describe.   If you take a disk painted with a concentric spiral pattern,
and make it revolve, it will seem to be growing continuously and
indefinitely, and yet to take in nothing from without; and to remain, if you pay attention to its actual size, always of the *same*
size.   Something as paradoxical as this lies in every present moment of life.   Here or nowhere, as Emerson says, is the whole
fact.   The moment stands and contains and sums up all things;
and all change is within it, much as the developing landscape with
all its growth falls forever within the rear windowpane of the last
car of a train that is speeding on its headlong way.   This self-

sustaining in the midst of self-removal, which characterizes all
reality and fact, is something absolutely foreign to the nature of
language, and even to the nature of logic, commonly so-called.
Something forever exceeds, escapes from statement, withdraws from
definition, must be glimpsed and felt, not told. No one knows this
like your genuine professor of philosophy. For what glimmers and
twinkles like a bird's wing in the sunshine it is his business to
snatch and fix. And every time he fires his volley of new vocables
out of his philosophic shot-gun, whatever surface-flush of success
he may feel, he secretly kens at the same time the finer hollowness
and irrelevancy. . . .

"Especially is this the case when the topic is named as the philosophy of religion. Religion is the very inner citadel of human life,
and the pretension to translate adequately into spread-out conceptual
terms a kind of experience in which intellect, feeling and will, all
our consciousness and all our subconsciousness together melt in a
kind of chemical fusion, would be particularly abhorrent. Let me
say then with frankness at the outset, that I believe that no so-
called philosophy of religion can possibly begin to be an adequate
translation of what goes on in the single private man, as he livingly
expresses himself in religious faith and act."

Religion is irrational, and it is also individual. It has to do
with "what goes on in the single private man." The social or institutional side of religion did not interest James or seem to him important. Religion concerns "the way an individual's life comes
home to *him,* his intimate needs, ideals, desolations, consolations,
failures, successes." This, at any rate, was what counted — the rest
was merely the instrument.

From James's emphasis upon the uniqueness of the religious experience, and its specific factual implications, arose his paradoxical
relation to contemporary Christianity. Religion of the sort in which
he was interested was closer to the simple piety of the evangelical
sects than to that of modern religious liberalism. To James, as
to Methodism, religion was a clearly recognizable and memorable
event in the history of the individual. He was fond of more or less
playfully mentioning his evangelical orthodoxy to his friends among
the liberal clergy. Borden P. Bowne, professor of philosophy at
Boston University, was a Methodist of so modern and philosophical
a type that he was tried for heresy. In 1899 he published an essay

on "The Christian Life," in which he contended that salvation must be "ethically understood," dismissed the experience of conversion as unimportant, alluded pointedly to "those non-ethical conversions which are the product of neuropathology and social contagion," and condemned those who "confuse honest inquirers by sending them to grope in the labyrinths of obscure emotional psychology which has been mistaken for religion." [12]   The following is James's acknowledgment : —

Geneva, March 31, 1901

Dear Brother Bowne, —

I thank you sincerely both for your most friendly letter and for *The Christian Life,* which came duly several weeks ago.   [It] seems to me an admirable piece of clearness, compactness and good practical sense. . . .   From the theological point of view, it makes an outsider like myself wonder at the relaxing of ancient doctrines, to see such a document emanating from the Methodist body — the body that used to speak of the Universalists as they did!   It seems to me that all our sects are doctrinally coming together on the basis of theism much like that of earlier Unitarianism.   I am sure that, as you intimate, there have been cries enough of protest against you; and I mysélf have enough of old Lutheran sentiment in my bones to believe that you are too unsympathetic with the mystical needs of man, in making as light as you do of the theological symbols in which they have clothed themselves.   It seems to me that extravagance of some sort is essential to the *direct* religious life.   For the mass, who live at second-hand anyhow, I have no doubt that such sobriety as you defend is a better model to imitate than the morbidness of the more original theologians.   Yet is it as readily *imitable?* I have found this book so very useful to my own thought that since you write of having published "two others of the same sort" (happy fecundity!) I am going to ask you to send them to me also!   This is shameless; but necessity knows no law.   So secluded have I been as not to have heard of their existence.   Pray be good to yours always truly,

WILLIAM JAMES

[12] B. P. Bowne, "The Christian Life," reprinted in *Studies in Christianity,* 1909. With the moralistic, individualistic, fideistic, and Lotzean strains in Bowne's thought James was in sympathy.   His teachings have been perpetuated in the school of "Personalism," of which the organ is *The Personalist.*   His *Metaphysics* (1882) and *Theism* (1902) were carefully read and approvingly annotated by James.

In the *Varieties* James made an untimely allusion to *The Christian Life* as a "rationalistic booklet," [13] when Bowne was hard-pressed by his ecclesiastical opponents. Bowne evidently wrote a letter of expostulation, to which James replied: —

Dec. 29, 1903

My dear Bowne, —

Your letter finds me in my nineteenth day of immersement, with grippe, still weak as a "cat," both cerebrally and muscularly, but a better Methodist than you, I still believe, in spite of your efforts to persuade me to the contrary. If the ass and the blatherskite succeed in their attempt to weed you out of the Body, I hope that they will have the wisdom to get me voted in to fill the vacuum. Seriously speaking, I regret that my use of the word "rationalistic" should in any way have added to your annoyances. . . . Truly yours,

WILLIAM JAMES

In sending a copy of the *Varieties* to his colleague Professor Francis G. Peabody, James wrote: "You will class me as a Methodist, *minus* a Saviour!" To Flournoy he reported: "An enthusiastic clergyman wrote me yesterday that I am of the company of Isaiah and St. Paul. I have just replied (after Whistler): 'Why drag in St. Paul and Isaiah?'" Masked by this pleasantry there lay the serious meaning of James's whole endeavor. He believed that liberalism had saved the intellect at the cost of repudiating the great historic phenomenon of religion. In notes for his lectures he said: "Remember that the whole point lies in really *believing* that through a certain point or part in you you coalesce and are identical with the Eternal. This seems to be the *saving* belief both in Christianity and in Vedantism. . . . It *comes home* to one only at particular times. . . . Bowne's attitude is sensible and prosaic. The more original religious life is always lyric — 'the monk owns nothing but his lyre' — and its essence is to dip into another kingdom, to feel an invisible order . . . *au prix duquel* the common sense values really vanish. Hence, indeed, the genuine antagonism between common sense religion like Bowne's, and that of the more extrava-

[13] 502, note.

gant prophets of whatever kind.   Each is foolish to the other, for each lives in the light of a different world."

In the summer of 1902 James gave two lectures before the Harvard Summer School of Theology.   Writing to Münsterberg from Chocorua on July 11, he said: "I lecture in Cambr. on Monday and Tuesday.   If I go on at this rate, they 'll make me a bishop.   As for my book, don't read it till you 're on your deathbed, when it will save your soul.   I fancy you 're destined to abhor it if you look at it now." [14]   In these lectures and the series of five lectures which he gave in the summer of 1906, he continued to stress the antithesis between the modern rationalizing tendency and the essence of historic religion: "Between the ordinary church-goer and the passionate saint, there is the inveterate feud of those who instinctively tend to keep religion 'reasonable' and those who would obey it in ways that are uncompromising and inconvenient.   At bottom it is the feud between a naturalism with a softened outline, and a positive supernaturalism with its centre of emphasis outside the margin of this world altogether.   My own solution seems to favor this latter view. . . .   The moderate and reasonable men will always be in the majority, and though we may consequently say that reasonable religion is the best for the race 'on the whole,' or abstracting from the more specialized members, yet the vitally *important work* will always be done by these latter, for it is about their contributions that all the warfare revolves."

Even within the party of supernaturalism James identifies himself with the left wing.   There is a "natural supernaturalism" (after Carlyle) — an "immanent or universal supernaturalism."   It distinguishes value from fact, is indifferent to the scientific description of particular existences, and construes the totality as supernatural. James does not absolutely reject this tendency — in discussing religion he rejects *no* tendency, since it is an essential part of his view to accept and to respect as religious any form of piety whatsoever that carries with it a sense of salvation.   But he proceeds, for his part, to defend the cause of the old "dualistic," "particular," or "piecemeal supernaturalism," which admits the supernatural into the same realm of fact with the natural.   He revives this "as a possibility," adducing abnormal psychology and the religious experiences of mankind as evidences in its support.   To most people such con-

[14] Reprinted also in M. Münsterberg, *op. cit.,* 89.

creteness is shocking, but with James himself it is just the reverse. *He* is shocked at "abstract and remote ways of considering individual facts." [15]

It will have been noted that the *Varieties* bore the subtitle, "A Study in Human Nature." It was originally intended that the first series should be "descriptive" and the second "metaphysical," but the descriptive task expanded so greatly that the metaphysical task had to be postponed to another occasion. Such, at least, is the statement of the author. He professed to present the facts and leave the reader to draw his own conclusions. "There is lots of human nature in it," he wrote to a friend, "and I think it must be written rather 'objectively,' for both God's friends and his enemies appear to find in it ample justification for their differing views." [16] The impression left on the reader, however, is that God's friends get much the best of it. James's description was not of the sterilized variety which is commonly called scientific. It is true that he introduced distinctions such as "once-born" and "twice-born," for purposes of classification. But he attached little importance to them, and he made no systematic use of the explanatory hypotheses of general psychology, — either those which he had himself introduced in the *Principles*, or those in vogue at the time when he published the *Varieties*, — with the exception of the unorthodox notion of the "subliminal consciousness." He let his religious documents speak for themselves; or, rather, he *helped* them to speak for themselves. Thus while he regarded the *Varieties* as "in a sense a study of morbid psychology," he took great pains in the opening lecture to rid his auditors of any prejudice they might feel against a state of mind merely because it was pathological. "Mere sanity," he said on another occasion, "is the most philistine and (at bottom) unessential of a man's attributes." [17] The reader receives the impression that James regarded religious experiences, even though they be judged pathological by strict psychiatric standards, as in some sense and in some degree inspired. Their "exceptional" character commended them to him.

Unquestionably James was justifying, and not merely describing, the religious experience. He stationed himself at the centre of the

[15] The same theme, of "crass" *vs.* "refined" supernaturalism, is briefly presented in *V.R.E.*, 520 ff.

[16] *Cf. V.R.E.*, v.

[17] *Letters of Charles Eliot Norton*, Houghton Mifflin Co., 1913, II, 348.

believer's consciousness and tried to convey its warmth and appeal as they were originally felt. He was concerned with religious values, with the hope or exaltation of concrete individuals, which must be rendered sympathetically if they are to be conveyed at all. And then, especially in the latter part of the book, the author *defended the claims* of religious experience. Philosophy, in the person of William James, confirmed its truth.

There are three tests which are applicable to religious truth: "immediate luminousness," "philosophical reasonableness," and "moral helpfulness." These are new names for criteria of knowledge which appear repeatedly in James's philosophy. There is the direct evidence of fact, as in perception; there is the consistency of alleged fact with beliefs already accepted — in short, the indirect evidence of fact; and there is the congruence of belief with the passional nature, especially with the resolute will. The universal claim of religious faith, "that the conscious person is continuous with a wider self through which saving experiences come," satisfies all of these criteria. "Mystical experiences are . . . direct perceptions of fact for those who have them." They are consistent with science, thanks to the new psychological hypothesis of a subliminal self.[18] Their consistency with philosophy is obtained through the hypothesis of pluralism. Mysticism is commonly monistic, and supernaturalism is commonly dogmatic; but James proposes a radical departure: a pluralistic mysticism, and an experimental supernaturalism. This was not a special pleading on James's part, but the proper culmination of one of the lines of his philosophical development. As early as 1874 he had read Benjamin Paul Blood's *Anæsthetic Revelation,* one of the "stepping-stones" of all his thinking thereafter. The last work to be written and published during his own lifetime was in praise of this writer, and bore the title "A Pluralistic Mystic." In 1888 he had been attracted by Edmund Gurney's "hypothetical supernaturalism" — with its idea of an "invisible order continuous with the present order of nature"; and from this there is a natural transition to the "piecemeal" or "crass" supernaturalism of 1902.[19]

Finally, the "moral helpfulness," or passional congruence, of such a pluralistic religious faith lies in its imparting a sense of open oppor-

[18] *V.R.E.,* 18, 515, 423–4, 242; cf. *P.U.,* 299, 309.
[19] James's review of Gurney's *Tertium Quid,* in *Nation,* XLVI (1888). The *Varieties* ends with a reference to this writer.

tunity and of serious responsibility to the individual agent. With it goes that "ordinary moralistic state of mind" which makes the salvation of the world dependent upon "the success with which each unit does its part." [20]

[20] *V.R.E.*, 526.

LXX

RECEPTION OF THE "VARIETIES"

THE *Varieties* had been circulated in Cambridge before James's return from Edinburgh. One of the first to receive a copy was Royce, who passed it on to Eliot: —

Chicago, June 20, 1902

Dear James, —

. . . As to your book: I had it for *a day,* or perhaps two or three days. Harry gave me a copy. I looked at it a very little, as I had time. Thereupon, just before Faculty meeting, Eliot eagerly inquired whether a copy was accessible yet, anywhere. I said that I had one, and as he seemed very eager, I went home, got my copy, brought it to him, laid it beside him as he sat in the Faculty, — and have never seen it since. I told him at the time that it was my own advance copy. But he must have forgotten. So much for Eliot's variety of religious experience. But to lose the book thus gave me still another "variety," from which I have n't recovered yet. The few hours spent over your book gave me great delight. It is a wonderful thing. . . . Yours always,

JOSIAH ROYCE

Asticou, Maine, Aug. 9, 1902

Dear Doctor James, —

I have been reading carefully your Gifford Lectures, finding them very interesting and instructive. The lectures I like best are the first two, Lectures XIV and XV on "The Value of Saintliness"; Lecture XVIII on "Philosophy," and Lecture XX. The very best chapter, to my thinking, is that on "The Value of Saintliness." The only criticism which I should make upon the book bears upon some of the narrations which you assume to be statements of fact, or accounts of actual religious experience. I often found myself doubting whether these narrations answered to any facts whatever. You seem to me to have not made allowance enough for the irresistible tendency of some imaginative human beings to "spin yarns."

Did you ever hear Clarence King [1] telling his personal adventures? If so, you will remember that it was quite impossible to tell whether any of the events that he described had ever happened. I have known three men of science — teachers and writers — concerning whose narratives of personal experience it was impossible to say whether any facts lay at their foundations. As an example, I should cite Mr. S. H. Hadley's narrative, page 201. I happen to have had some dealings with Mr. Hadley about a pal of his, named Samuel F. Jones, who printed a mass of elaborate lies about his experience at Harvard University, in a tract called "Saved by a Sandwich." [2] This material he was also in the habit of reciting frequently at mission meetings. Jones confessed that his tract was all a lie; and as to Hadley, I formed, from conversation with him, the definite judgment that I should be unable to believe a single word that he said on any subject, unless confirmed by others. I think a good many of your readers will probably feel as I did, — quite unable to accept as records of actual experience some of the narratives which you print. It may be said, however, concerning these baseless fictions, that they constitute in themselves a remarkable group of phenomena.

To have written those lectures, when you were not feeling nervously vigorous, seems to me a considerable feat; for the subject is an exciting or nervous one. . . . Very truly yours,

CHARLES W. ELIOT

Chocorua, Aug. 13, 1902

Dear President, —

I am much gratified at your caring enough for my book to have read it so carefully — and in particular that Chapter XX passed muster with you. I think my account has been fairly objective, for persons of all sorts of dispositions towards religion seem to find material for corroboration of the prepossessions they may start with.

As regards the narratives of conversion, it may fairly be said that *no man's* account can be accepted as literally true, of that sort of thing. Everyone aims at reproducing an ideal type which he

[1] An American geologist.
[2] Hadley had just published *Down in Water Street;* a story of sixteen years' life and work in the Water Street Mission. Jones was an undergraduate at Harvard for the year 1873-4.

thinks most significant and edifying. But in a general account of religious experience I think these inaccuracies of detail of no great moment; for ideals all are *pointed to* by experience (*and reached in some cases*), and of the general fact of automatic seizures there can be no doubt whatever. I am quite prepared for what you say of Hadley. I don't understand you to cast doubt on his really being a reformed drunkard, however. . . . Ever truly yours,

WM. JAMES

The following letters were written in reply to friendly comment from Mrs. Glendower Evans and Miss Grace Norton: —

Chocorua, Aug. 25, 1902 [3]

My dear Bessie, —

. . . You are sweet to take my book so seriously. I thought, when writing it, that it could have no originality, but the reception it gets makes me feel that it is original in temper at least. No previous book of mine has got anything like the prompt and *thankful* recognition that has come to me in letters about this — many of them from strangers. But I can't myself say on reflection that I do anything [except] leave the subject just where I find it, and everybody knows that the real life of religion springs from what may be called the mystical stratum of human nature. Exploration of the subliminal may not show that in other respects it pans out as rich as Myers thought it would, and in that case (but it will be a hundred years hence) my suggestion (if remembered by anyone) will appear to have had small value. Still the volume is selling well and will no doubt help to sell my other books. I want now if possible to write something serious, systematic, and syllogistic; I 've had enough of the squashy popular-lecture style. . . . Yours as ever,

WM. JAMES

Chocorua, Sept. 12, 1902

My dear Grace, —

. . . Your letter about my book arrived duly and filled me with mixed feelings of interest and sorrow. . . . I don't wonder that the mouldiness and measliness of so many of my saints gave you

---

[3] Reprinted, with additions, from "William James and His Wife," *Atlantic,* CXLIV (1929), 377–8.

a revulsion away from other-worldliness to naturalism and humanism. Yours is much the best letter I have received from that point of view, because it is the most gravely expressed and the most profoundly felt. The two points of view, I believe, must work upon each other until they acquire a common content and way of living together, the *material* of the blessed life being thought of in terms of humanity, exclusively, the *inspiration* being felt as a relation to a higher portion of the universe now out of sight. But it will be long ere different persons' formulas will not produce misunderstandings in each other's minds. A real practical difference, so far, is between the healthy-minded (among whom I count you as writer of your letter) and those who seriously despair of straightforward healthy-mindedness as a radical solution. I myself don't see how it can be a *universal* solution, when the world is the seat of so much unhappiness really incurable in ordinary ways, but *cured* (in many individuals) by their religious experience. One can neither ignore the unhappy individuals nor the peculiar form of their relief, as facts of human history; and I, surveying human history objectively, could n't help seeing *there* its possibly most characteristic manifestation. But I am intensely an individualist, and believe that as a practical problem for the individual, the religion he stands by must be the one which he finds best for *him,* even though there were better individuals, and their religion better for them. Such Stoicism as you stand up for is one of the noblest all-round attitudes yet found out, and as against the insanities of theistic devotion, certainly has an immense part yet to play.

The summer wanes, and I wane too. Possibly 't is only "need of change," but it is discouraging, in conditions that seem quite paradisiac, to find that the progress of so many weeks gives way to retrogression. I have no doubt that things will move upward again when the term recommences. Thank you again, dear Grace, a thousand times for your good letter, and all the good advice contained in it, and believe me, with loving regards from Alice, your ever affectionate
WM. JAMES

There was a lively interchange of impressions between James and his colleague and former pupil, Professor Barrett Wendell,[4] who

[4] From "A Packet of Wendell-James Letters," by M. A. De W. Howe in *Scribner's,* LXXXIV (1928), 675–87.

had just been appointed Clark Lecturer at Trinity College, Cambridge : —

New Castle [N. H.], Aug. 22, 1902

Dear James, —

When your book came, I did not know you had come home; and so was at a loss where to address you.   Then, when I had read it, I wanted to write so much about it that I have been waiting for the moment — which never comes — when I could send you a letter worth having.

The book is divinely shameless.   God himself could n't discuss his manifestations with more glorious freedom from self-consciousness, or more serene disregard of what trivialities present themselves to mere humanity as values.   There are lots of things I argue with; and lots I don't; not a chapter I should n't like to talk about. But, in fact, I am too utterly tired out, with some unutterably dull lectures I am making for Cambridge, to talk or to write about anything.   So, after all this delay, I just send this word of thanks for the friendly thought which has brought me such sincere pleasure. . . .   On the 17th we sail for England.   Where we shall pass the winter, God knows.   As his closest intimate with whom I can pretend intimacy perhaps you can tell me.   If so, I shall be grateful for the word. . . .   Sincerely yours,

BARRETT WENDELL

Chocorua, Aug. 24, 1902

Dear Wendell, —

Thank you for your letter and for having read my book, which seems to add fuel to the fire which burns in the hearts of God's enemies as well as to that which burns in those of his friends. Your epithets I confess to be slightly obscure, — is it that the "divine shamelessness" which you say I exhibit refers to the two "cases" at the end of the chapter on healthy-mindedness, the which possibly you may have taken (as others have) to be confessions of my *own?*   Heaven forfend!   I am having the possibility of such an interpretation removed in a second edition![5]   I meant to, but did n't, write to congratulate you on your appointment at Cambridge — just the man to form the entering wedge of our all-

---

[5] This change seems never to have been made.

conquering culture (!) — and I [am] right glad to hear it. But it must be a heavy strain to plump right into that complication. I went to pieces on the sociability in England, and am resuscitating here on the bare ground. Cambridge is very nice, what I 've seen of it, but Frederic Myers, the only man there whom I knew well, and who would have immensely got along well with you, is gone. Good luck to you, and best regards from both to each. Always yours truly,

WM. JAMES

Boston, Sept. 22, 1902

Dear James, —

Except for a physical collapse, which has delayed my sailing till Wednesday, I should have answered you long ago. I had no idea that you were in any sense a confessor. What I meant was that God, so far as I am aware, finds himself in a position which permits him any utterances imaginable without the shameful and inhibitory consciousness of self characteristic of fallen man. And to one so deeply fallen as I — the last of the Calvinists who would n't expect a maker that did n't damn us — your glorious freedom from any inhibitory impulse seems admirably illustrative of what that same God had in mind when he started to make man in his image and had n't made a botch of it. Your intellect works like what I dream of Eden. As for me, my carriage, mental and physical, sorrowfully reminds me of Adam's. And so, I spitefully call God — and you — shameless. In which blessed company I leave you, on Wednesday, for a year. . . . Sincerely yours,

BARRETT WENDELL

Passing on to James's philosophical and psychological colleagues, we have first to note the following comment from Ernst Mach: "Your fine and remarkable book, *The Varieties of Religious Experience,* has gripped me powerfully. Religious inspiration is certainly very similar to the scientific inspiration which one feels when new problems first present themselves in a form which is as yet not wholly clear. There is an as yet unmeasured depth into which one is gazing." [6]

James sent a copy of the *Varieties* to his friend Stumpf, and on

[6] Translated from a letter to W.J. of Dec. 16, 1902.

January 1, 1904, wrote in the spirit of their earlier intimacy to ask whether the book had been received.[7] Stumpf replied with an account of his own "religious experience":—

Baden-Baden, March 26, 1904[8]

My dear friend James,—

Now at last, far from Berlin, I am getting around to answering your good letter of January 1, and first of all must tell you how much pleased and touched I am that you think of me with the old-time attachment. In my own behalf I may say that bonds such as those which exist between us endure in my heart indissolubly. It is really just the Hydra of daily work that has made me so dilatory in correspondence — new heads appear to grow every year without the old ones being cut off. My longings look in the same direction as yours, — some remotest valley would be my dearest abode. I, too, should like and ought sometime to bind my sheaves, but at present I see no possibility of escape except in the holidays, and shall probably be obliged to stick to my post in Berlin as long as my bodily powers permit.

I had first accepted Münsterberg's proposal[9] because the adventure attracted me, but as early as last summer I wrote him again declining; my nerves would not have stood it. The whole undertaking is really not gratifying, and nothing will come of it. It is intended that everyone shall speak on the relation of his science to other sciences, — think of something like twenty volumes filled with such purely methodological considerations!

But now as to your fine book. It is indeed very wrong of me to have written nothing about it beyond the card, which you must have failed to get. Forgive a man so beset! There was certainly no want of interest on my part. Indeed in my early youth I cherished for years the idea of becoming a Catholic priest, and actually buried myself in theology, until the inner contradictions of dogma drove me, with many qualms, to abandon it. What you report about religious experiences I have for the most part experienced in my own person. I have, however, subsequently become the more insistent on the control and critique of all these emotions, and am obliged to say now that everything sentimental, ecstatic, fulsome and unc-

---

[7] *Cf.* above, 200.
[8] The German original of this letter is to be found below, Appendix VIII.
[9] To attend the St. Louis Congress.

tuous in these things on the part of grown men, is in the highest degree repugnant to me; and that nothing seems to me to be of value that does not translate itself into active, neighborly love.

Nor can I, in spite of my knowledge of my defects and faults, produce that tortured consciousness of sin on which, according to the pious, religion rests. "Something wrong about us" — I agree, but there is still more evil outside of us than in us; and we need salvation not merely from our sins, but from all the infinite horror of the world which is supposed to have been created by the very God at whose hands man hopes for salvation. In all this the religion of the religious seems to me to be perverse and unnatural.

But I agree completely with what you say (page 485) about religion in the broader and genuine sense, and in every moment of my life I feel the connection with the invisible spiritual realm that surrounds us, and the power that flows from it. Shall I now tell you something, too, about my "over-belief"? I do not know whether I shall ever make up my mind to publish such thoughts as these during my life, though they occupy me daily. To you, however, in confidence, I impart them willingly.

Personal immortality stands for me in the foreground. Your sentence: "If our ideals are only cared for in 'eternity,' I do not see why we might not be willing to resign their care to other hands than ours," [10] seems to me to contain a sort of inner contradiction. The realization of ideals *is* only possible on the presupposition of individual immortality. Psychical values cannot be added together. If new individuals continually succeed one another the later may be better than the earlier, but even so they fade away into nothing, and a summation of values that have no existence except in an individual person is absurd. Let the earth become frozen, let no new individuals arise, then where is the realization of ideals to be found, if the spiritual does not endure? This is for me the first condition, if life is not to be absolutely without consolation and meaning. It is not egoism, — the spiritual must endure not because it is I, but because it is the carrier of values; and I would certainly be ready to renounce further existence if this were a condition of spiritual value outside of me.

[10] P. 524.

That part of us which endures, however, will be only the morally valuable part, which a good will has drawn into its sphere and established there. In a certain sense, therefore, individuality will vanish — not only physical but spiritual as well — provided one takes the essence of individuality to consist in those trifling accidents which our "individual psychology" employs as its criterion. The best analogy for a future life seems to me to be afforded by the state of exaltation induced by the enjoyment of art, or when a great ethical idea completely possesses us: even then the "I" is present, but freed from accidental trifles, raised into a higher sphere, and accompanied by a most blissful sense of unity of being with all the good and exalted spirits of all time. Such moments and hours are to me just like the living presence of my loved ones — of all who have gone before me; these seem to surround me and to speak to me, in the same way as do they who in the empirical present sit near me, silently possessed by the same feelings.

These are my two articles of faith, both of which are at the close of the Athanasian Creed — "communion of saints" and "life everlasting" — whereas all the other articles have dropped out, even the existence of the Christian God. The frightful evils of the course of nature, and the human wickedness which goes with it, exclude this last assumption. But if we are willing to have a pantheistic God, then we can easily introduce for that purpose precisely such a communion of the blessed, which grows from day to day, and at the same time forms an inner unity. I will not explain to you in further detail how I harmonize these ideas with my psychological and cosmological views, but even without this you will easily discover many lines of connection with my short articles on body and mind and on the evolutionary theory. Our views here agree in many respects. Even your pluralism is not so alien to me as to most of our colleagues (though I think that you underestimate the value for feeling of the oneness of the supreme being). Only I would not like to connect the conception of God with the subconscious. What I know about that does not appear to me to point in this direction; I am more inclined to believe that these states belong to the bodily and perishable, and not to the eternal part of us. . . . Hearty greetings to your family, and to you yourself the sincerest good wishes, from your old friend

C. STUMPF

Chocorua, July 17, 1904

My dear Stumpf, —

I got your delightfully cordial and deeply interesting letter last March, and acknowledged it by a post-card. Now that the fatigues of the Cambridge year are over, and that we are all together on our little country place in the mountains, I have repose enough of body and mind to write to you at greater length. First, I congratulate you at not being at St. Louis. The heat in September there will be exterminating, and to my mind the empty immensity of the whole affair is repugnant. Like yourself, I can only see in these twenty-four volumes of methodological considerations in three languages (for such, I believe, is the hoped-for outcome of the whole scheme) one of those enormities which our present-day civilization abounds in and which add to the burdens of humanity. Surely there is enough thought in the world that spontaneously publishes itself, without getting all this mass of it published to order! Nevertheless Münsterberg's organizing genius is very great. His *philosophy* seems to me thoroughly artificial.

Your own confidences as to your religious state of mind interest me deeply. I agree that a God *of the totality* must be an unacceptable religious object. But I do not see why there may not be superhuman consciousness of *ideals* of ours, and *that* would be *our* God. It is all very dark. I never felt the *rational* need of immortality as you seem to feel it; but as I grow older I confess that I feel the practical need of it much more than I ever did before; and that combines with reasons, not exactly the same as your own, to give me a growing faith in its reality. I wish that you, some day, anonymously or over your name, would expand and publish these reflections. I think that these states of mind, which are what people live by, are thoroughly normal; but the artificial rationalistic conscience of professional *Gelehrten,* makes them so often ashamed of the public expression of these inner faiths, that the literature of the world is getting too much weighted the other way; and, lacking examples of faith in minds whose intellects they respect, common people grow ashamed to have any faith of their own. You will probably have seen already Stanley Hall's new *American Journal of Religious Psychology and Education.* I wish that there might be many such documents as yours published therein. I do not suppose that it will continue for many years, but I imagine that for five or six years there will be abundant good material to publish. . . .

I ought to be writing a book; but at Cambridge last year I succeeded in writing just *thirty-two* pages! Pity me! I have become much interested of late in the philosophy of John Dewey of Chicago. Have you seen his *Logical Studies?* I have just written an article for the October number of *Mind* (Bradley having attacked the point of view in this July number), in which you may possibly be interested.[11] Bradley is a man of great subtlety, but *perverse,* in my opinion, so that the importance of his writings is not at all commensurate with their originality. Your ever affectionate

WM. JAMES

Among James's friends and colleagues were many who had given special attention to the topic of religion.[12] Professor Edwin D. Starbuck, from whose *Psychology of Religion* James made frequent citations, also placed at the latter's disposal a collection of manuscript material. His review of the *Varieties* published in the *Biblical World*[13] presented three objections: that the examples which James selected were too extreme; that he overemphasized feeling, neglecting the instincts or modes of organic response that must underlie both the emotional and the intellectual manifestations of the religious life; and that he exaggerated the rôle of a "Higher Power" in religion. James replied at length. "Extreme" cases, he contended, throw more light on what is distinctly characteristic of any given experience than do the "tamer" ones. As to the more fundamental principles of behavior that underlie religion, James asked for more light. The question of the rôle of the "Higher Power" was crucial, and elicited from James a flat affirmation of the veridical character of the mystical experience: —

"I think that the fixed point with me is the conviction that our 'rational' consciousness touches but a portion of the real universe and that our life is fed by the 'mystical' region as well. I have no mystical experience of my own, but just enough of the germ of mysticism in me to recognize the region from which their voice comes when I hear it. I was much disappointed in Leuba's review of my book in the *International Journal of Ethics*. . . . I confess

---

[11] "Humanism and Truth."
[12] The criticism by Émile Boutroux and James's reply are reserved for a later context, below, 562.
[13] XXIV (1904).

that the way in which he stamps out all mysticism whatever, using the common pathological arguments, seemed to me unduly crude. I wrote him an expostulatory letter, which evidently made no impression at all, and which he possibly might send you if you had the curiosity to apply." [14]

The reviewer referred to at the close of this letter was Professor James H. Leuba. James's attention had been attracted by an article from his pen which appeared in 1901. [15]

Florence, March 25 [1901]

The *Monist* with your article has only just been received, having been detained at home. I am *delighted* with two points: (1) the priority of individual over institutional religion; and (2) the asininity of a "definition." On the latter point you are particularly charming. In my Gifford Lectures, of which one course is written but not yet delivered, I have made the same two points, but less emphatically and effectively. The invariable way in which religions are always treated as something tribal, collective, superpersonal, and mysterious has ever been (to a rabid individualist like myself) a source of amusement and astonishment. I hope the rest of your book is all ready. It will be a good one.

WM. JAMES

In July of the same year Leuba published a second article, "The Contents of Religious Consciousness," in which he denied that there was any *specific* religious impulse, since that impulse is identical with "the love of life at any and every level of development." Religion is concerned not with God's existence or attributes, but with the *use* to which he may be put: "Not God but life, more life, a larger, richer, more satisfying life, is in last analysis the end of religion." [16] Of this passage and its context, James wrote to the author: "I consider it as scattering more clouds and confusion than anything I know in the literature of the subject."

But while James welcomed the emphasis which Leuba put on the vital, personal, and pragmatic bearings of religion, he was by no

---

[14] *L.W.J.*, II, 210.

[15] "Introduction to a Psychological Study of Religion," *Monist*, XI (1900–1). This writer has developed his position more fully in *A Psychological Study of Religion*, 1912 (*cf.* especially Ch. XI on "Theology and Psychology"); and *The Belief in God and Immortality*, 1916.

[16] *Monist*, XI (1900–1), 571–2.

means prepared to abandon the objectivity of God. Religion affirms such an object as the ground of its emotional attitude, and James was concerned to show that this affirmation was justified by the same criteria as those applied to any other object. Unless the cognitive claims of religion are credited, it is left in the precarious situation of an as-yet-undetected superstition. The view advanced by Leuba in his article on "Professor William James' Interpretation of Religious Experience," [17] was that of a "scientist" who would describe the religious experiences and explain them without residue by "psychological" causes. He did not object to James's use of the hypothesis of the subliminal consciousness, but argued that such a hypothesis had no metaphysical implications, and robbed the religious experiences of all cognitive import.

It is clear that the real issue between James and his critic concerned the grounds of knowledge. James took the position that in the last analysis all knowledge, including so-called "scientific knowledge," depends on accepting the deliverances of original experience at their face value. The religious experiences, like perceptions, are experiences *of* something; and they are entitled to acceptance until they are disproved by appeal to other original experiences. In other words, James justified religious experience by the application of a radical and well-considered theory of knowledge which he was prepared to apply to all other cognitive claims, including those of his "scientific" critics.

James's reply to Leuba's article was as follows: —

Cambridge, April 17, 1904 [18]

Dear Leuba, —

I have read your article with great interest, admiring its clearness of statement, and rejoicing in the way in which you go to the heart of my contentions, straight and without floundering. Only of your characterization of my thesis as that of "spirit-intervention" do I complain.[19] No reader . . . could possibly guess that the

---

[17] *Inter. Jour. of Ethics*, XIV (1903–4).

[18] The original of this "expostulatory" letter is missing, and the following is made up of several fragmentary versions which have been found among the James papers.

[19] The passage to which James objects contains the statements that there are "spread throughout the book, with marvelous skill, the mysterious, imaginary shadows of spirit agents"; "the reader is almost unavoidably thrown into the temper of the materializing seance"; "ghosts pop out of the very places he has just shown you to be empty," etc. (*op. cit.*, 337).

only spirit that I contend for is "God." Unless he knows my book he will suppose that I am a "spiritist" out and out, which I am not. This is unfair.

I also find the same fault with this article that I have found with its predecessors. You hide your own religious cards, so that one does [not] know exactly how to reply to you. You may think there is no God, nothing but Nature, and that all these vague experiences are "poppy-cock" and nerves. Or you may think there is a God, but that the evidence for him must always be indirect — induction from sensations, or "philosophic" reasoning. Most readers, from your evident anti-"pathological" bias, would infer the former; and if that be your state of mind, reply to you is harder. If, however, you do concede the possibility of a God, and your final sentence is not merely diplomatic,[20] argument grows easier. For then, just as the foundation of "natural" knowledge is sensation, due to immediate non-rational influence of either body on body (or, if you are an idealist, of mental fact on mental fact), so there might be a similar direct influence from God, and our knowledge might be partly at least founded thereon. So far as the feelings of influence harmonized with the rational evidence, the hypothesis that God was the source of influence would be corroborated. Otherwise not. They are bound to harmonize in part, because the mystical and the rational spheres of life are not absolutely discontinuous. It is evident that our intellectual stock in trade plays a suggestive part in our mystical life, and that this suggestive part changes with the progress of our thoughts, so that Vedantic and Christian mysticism have slightly different forms.

If mystical states with all their differences have a common nucleus, then this nucleus should be reckoned a coördinate factor with reason in the building of religious belief. The intellect is interpretative, and critical of its own interpretation, but there must have been a thesis to interpret, and that thesis seems to me to be the non-rational sense of a "higher" power. Religious men largely agree that this sense has been that of their "best" moments — best not only in passing, but when looked back upon. The notion of it has leaked into mankind from their authority, the rest of us being imi-

---

[20] The concluding sentences are: "It may not be useless to add that the rejection of spirit-interference does in nowise commit one to Materialism. It leaves a clear field to Absolute, as well as to many forms of Pluralistic, Idealism."

tative, just as we are of scientific men's opinions. Now may not this mystical testimony that there is a God be true, even though his precise determinations, being so largely "suggestive" contributions of our rational factor, should widely differ? It seems to me that to throw out, as you do, the whole mystical life from a hearing, because of the facility with which it combines with discrepant interpretations, would be like throwing out the senses, for a similar reason, from recognition as factors of our "rational" knowledge. . . . It is evident that our data are complex, however we confine them, and that *sifting* is necessary, be the mystical door left open or kept closed. The truth is what will survive the sifting — sifting by successive generations, and "on the whole." Your critical method sifts out everything, lets nothing survive of mystical authority in God's favor, even though (let me suppose) you admit the possibility of a God.

I find it preposterous to suppose that if there be a feeling of unseen reality shared by large numbers of best men in their best moments, responded to by other men in their "deep" moments, good to live by, strength-giving, — I find it preposterous, I say, to suppose that the goodness of that feeling for living purposes should be held to carry no objective significance, and especially preposterous if it combines harmoniously with our otherwise grounded philosophy of objective truth. *You* say we must consider it a purely subjective affection. But this opens the whole subject of what the word "truth" means, and I cannot enter that except to say that if inferences from "good for life" to "true" were on principle forbidden, not religion but the whole notion of truth would probably have to be the thing overhauled and revised.

My personal position is simple. I have no living sense of commerce with a God. I envy those who have, for I know that the addition of such a sense would help me greatly. The Divine, for my active life, is limited to impersonal and abstract concepts which, as ideals, interest and determine me, but do so but faintly in comparison with what a feeling of God might effect, if I had one. This, to be sure, is largely a matter of intensity, but a shade of intensity may make one's whole centre of moral energy shift. Now, although I am so devoid of *Gottesbewusstsein* in the directer and stronger sense, yet there is *something in me* which *makes response* when I hear utterances from that quarter made by others. I recognize the deeper voice. Something tells me: — "thither lies truth" — and I am sure it is not old theistic prejudices of infancy. Those in my case were Christian, but I have grown so out of Christianity that entanglement therewith on the part of a mystical utterance has to be abstracted from and overcome, before I can listen. Call this, if you like, my mystical *germ*. It is a very common germ. It creates the rank and file of believers. As it withstands in my case, so it will withstand in most cases, all purely atheistic criticism, but *interpretative* criticism (not of the mere "hysteria" and "nerves" order) it can energetically combine with.

Your criticism seems to amount to a pure *non possumus:* "Mystical deliverances must be infallible revelations in every particular, or nothing. Therefore they are *nothing,* for anyone else than their owner." Why may they not be *something,* although not everything? Your only consistent position, it strikes me, would be a dogmatic atheistic naturalism; and, without any mystical germ in us, that, I believe, is where we all should unhesitatingly be today. Once allow the mystical germ to influence our beliefs, and I believe that we are in my position. Of course the "subliminal" theory is an inessential hypothesis, and the question of pluralism or monism is equally inessential.

I am letting loose a deluge on you! Don't reply at length, or at all. *I* hate to reply to anybody, and will sympathize with your silence. But I had to restate my position more clearly.[21] Yours truly,

WM. JAMES

[21] The last two paragraphs are reprinted from *L.W.J.*, II, 211-2.

LXXI

JAMES'S PERSONAL FAITH

It is difficult to distinguish between James's own personal faith and those faiths of others which he not only tolerated and respected, but understood with so much sympathy that he felt their echo in his own breast. Furthermore, it was a part of his creed that there should be many gospels, and it is not easy to tell when he was illustrating this general principle and when he was expounding that particular gospel by which *he* was saved. In a sense his whole genius lay in multiplying differences and alternatives, and in justifying each idiosyncrasy in its own terms. Finally, he was a man of fluctuating moods. The sort of faith which he relished depended on the state of his spiritual palate, and this, in turn, reflected his general bodily and mental tone.

In James's youth he was wont to preach the gospel of Stoicism, especially to his friend Tom Ward, whom he exhorted, in the midst of "December darkness," to remember that the world is "really" as full of life and joy as ever.[1] This motive persisted. Having a tendency to hypochondria himself, James was touched and stirred to admiration by the uncomplaining fortitude of others. Being himself peculiarly subject to moods, he sought to dispel them and to purge his view of their distorting effect: "Our consolation has to be found in falling back upon the general. It is mean to complain, in one's own case, of that which all flesh — even the most decorative members of the species — have to suffer; and after all, the world is as full of youth and maidenhood as it ever was, if we would but realize the fact when our own beards are grizzling."

There is, then, a last reserve of manliness and objectivity by which a philosopher is reconciled to his world however little it may suit him. This was a persistent part of James's gospel, but the least characteristic part. The following confession, written in 1876, reveals both his dissatisfaction with a gospel of sheer fortitude, and

[1] *Cf.* above, I, 258–60, 287, 293.

the supplementary motives that actuated him with increasing strength as the years passed — acceptance of religion as a historic fact, the justification of belief by subjective need, the reservation of religious belief for the moments when this need is most extreme: "The hardness of my Stoicism oppresses me sometimes. My attitude towards religion is one of deference rather than adoption. I see its place; I feel that there are times when everything else was to fail and that, or nothing, remain; and yet I behave as if I must leave it untouched until such times come, and I am drawn to it by sheer stress of weather. I am sure I am partly right, and that religion is not an every day comfort and convenience. And yet I know I am partly wrong."

The most characteristic element in James's gospel is his insistence that where human subjectivity is sufficiently deep and universal it may properly impose its demands on the environment. What was the subjective demand which James felt most profoundly and deemed most valid? It was, as we have seen, the demand of the moral will for a world in which the cause of righteousness, being freed from complicity with evil, is dependent for its realization on the daring and zeal of its devotees. But there was another motive which James understood, both vicariously through sympathy, and directly through his own suffering. This was the longing for safety and security. This longing never ceased to move James even though it was clearly subordinated to his keener relish for novelty and danger. Thus, although in 1885, in "The Dilemma of Determinism," he declared for a war of extermination against evil, he hesitated to close every door to peace. In the same year in *The Literary Remains of Henry James,* he expounded pluralism and healthy-mindedness in his own behalf, and the monism of the sick soul in behalf of his father. But then he went on to say: "We are all *potentially* such sick men. The sanest and best of us are of one clay with lunatics and prison-inmates. And whenever we feel this, such a sense of the vanity of our voluntary career comes over us, that all our morality appears but as a plaster hiding a sore it can never cure, and all our well-doing as the hollowest substitute for that well-*being* that our lives ought to be grounded in, but, alas! are not." [2]

"Pluralism is a view to which we all practically incline when in the full and successful exercise of our moral energy"; and this was

[2] P. 118.

James's gospel when he was at his best.[3] But a man is not always at his best, and the failure of pluralism *in extremis* is an argument against it. In 1907, comparing his moralistic pluralism with the monistic philosophy of the Absolute, he said: "Both beliefs confirm our strenuous moods. . . . [Monism] suits sick souls and strenuous ones equally well. One cannot say thus of pluralism. Its world is always vulnerable, for some part may go astray; and . . . its partisans must always feel to some degree insecure. . . . The needs of sick souls are surely the most urgent; and believers in the absolute should rather hold it to be great merit in their philosophy that it can meet them so well. The pragmatism or pluralism which I defend has to fall back on a certain ultimate hardihood, a certain willingness to live without assurances or guarantees."[4]

Since man is not always hardy, the gospel of pluralism does not always meet his needs. But James was, on the whole and in the long run, spiritually hardy, hence *his* gospel was pluralism. Furthermore, since he uses the term "healthy" for pluralism and "sick" for monism, it is impossible to avoid the inference that a proper spiritual hygiene would bring man to that better state in which pluralism is palatable — that the strong man eager for battle and enjoying the risk is the more ideal type.

James's essential religion, then, is of the moralistic-pluralistic type. The value of God is as "a more powerful ally of my own ideals." It is this felt *need* of God and of religion as a reënforcement of the moral will that is the chief cause of his personal belief. James was not a man to shun the rigors of the intellect. He kept his intellectual muscles fit. "After taking a bath in religion," he once said to his students, "come out and take another bout with philosophy." But as to religious truth itself, he attached comparatively little importance to philosophical arguments, even his own. The *convincing* evidence, he thought, was practical and immediate.

James did not himself have an experience of the presence of God, but his own experience did justify the acceptance of such testimony on the part of others. He was impressed by "the extraordinary vivacity of man's psychological converse with something ideal that *feels as if* it were also actual." He was persuaded to accept this feeling of actuality as authentic because, though he did not experi-

---

[3] *Ibid.*, 116; *cf.* the important self-analysis in *L.W.J.*, I, 199, and below, 699–701.
[4] *M.T.*, 226–9.

ence it himself, he did have *analogous* experiences: not merely the normal experiences which formed the central feature of his philosophical and psychological empiricism, but also "exceptional" experiences of the mystical type. There was, for example, that night in the Adirondack forest, when he received the "boulder of impression" of which he left so vivid a description. He did not claim that he felt God, but only that he was thereafter enabled to understand how people might feel if they did feel God. "Doubtless," he said, "things in the Edinburgh lectures will be traceable to it." This is but one of many instances of that "mystical germ" [5] which led James to credit the full-flowered mysticism of others; or of that acquaintance with the genus of mysticism which led him to accept its religious species.

Did James believe in the immortality of the soul? It is evident that here, as in the case of the belief in God, he first defended the *legitimacy* of the belief, not on his own private account, but for mankind generally. In his lecture on *Human Immortality* he argued that immortality was "not incompatible with the brain-function theory of our present mundane consciousness."

He was there concerned to defend the theoretical possibility of immortality. But what of his own personal attitude? He tells us that the belief was never "keen." He was not one of those who find the thought of their own death intolerable. It is true that when he felt the rush of the creative impulse he disliked the thought of being interrupted: "But, lord! how I do want to read as well as write; and with so much left undone, I am getting really anxious lest I be cut off in the bud." [6] There was always, however, an underlying resignation. Writing of his illness in 1899, he said: "What the outcome will be, Heaven only knows. It is rather discouraging, for I should like to get out these two volumes of Gifford Lectures before turning my back on this world's vanities. But 'man appoints, God disappoints,' to use a little Cambridge Negro's version of the French proverb, and I shan't fret over the event whatever it turns out to be. Of all the vanities, when you come to look penetratingly at them, lectures on the philosophy of religion by mortal men may take the first prize."

[5] *L.W.J.,* II, 77, 211–5, 269; above, 323; below, 676.
[6] Other parts of this letter used below, 376.

It was thus a part of James's code that a man should meet death bravely, or even casually. In his youth, when the Stoical teachings made a strong appeal to him, he wrote the following entry in his diary upon learning of the death of his cousin, Minnie Temple: "By that big part of me that's in the tomb with you, may I realize and believe in the immediacy of death! May I feel that every torment suffered here passes and is as a breath of wind, — every pleasure too. Acts and examples stay. Time is long. One human life is an instant. Is our patience so short-winded, our curiosity so dead or our grit so loose, that that one instant snatched out of the endless age should not be cheerfully sat out. Minny, your death makes me feel the nothingness of all our egotistic fury. The inevitable release is sure; wherefore take our turn kindly whatever it contain. Ascend to some sort of partnership with fate, and since tragedy is at the heart of us, go to meet it, work it in to our ends, instead of dodging it all our days, and being run down by it at last. *Use* your death (or your life, it's all one meaning), 'tut twam asi.'" [7]

Although he came to view the matter less solemnly, this motive never ceased to govern him. In 1900 he proposed that the attitude to death should be a blend of "gentlemanly levity," "high-minded Stoicism," and "religious enthusiasm." [8] As regards the moral significance of immortality, he took the negative view from which Stumpf dissented. He did not see why we might not be willing to resign the care of our ideals "to other hands."

But as James grew older he came to *believe* in immortality. In 1904 he had acquired a feeling of its "probability." Although he did not feel a "rational need" of it, he felt a growing "practical need." What was this practical motive? In explaining why he was now, late in life, acquiring the belief for the first time, he said, "Because I am just getting fit to live." Five years later he wrote: "I had often said that the best argument I knew for an immortal life was the existence of a man who deserved one as well as Child did." [9] With his temperamental love of the living, his affectionate sympathies, and his glowing moral admirations, he had come more and more to feel that death was a wanton and unintelligible nega-

---

[7] "Thou art that." Entry for March 22, 1870.
[8] Above, I, 759.
[9] *L.W.J.*, II, 214; *Proc. of the Amer. Soc. for Psychical Research*, III (1909), Pt. I, 580.

tion of goodness.   This motive or mixture of motives appears in comments on the death of two of his friends.   The first two were written in 1904, and the third in 1906: —

"I came down to Sarah Whitman's funeral, and being here, have stayed till Commencement, but return today.   I can't go without an overflow to you, Sarah Whitman's death was so abrupt and bewildering.   Pathetic, inscrutable, lover of life, outreacher to the good, spreader of friendliness, — where is she now?   And what does it all mean?   I never had the pathos or the mystery brought so sharply home, and one's thought of her now is all one tenderness. How much more real are people's lives than all our criticisms of them!   It is a lesson to cultivate each other, all of us, while we yet have each other." . . .

"Everything in this beautiful world is good except old age and death if one supposes no 'behind the veil' of any kind.   Mrs. Whitman's funeral was wonderful for beauty.   The crowd of friends at the grave were all swayed by the one pathetic emotion.   And now she seems in retrospect like a little slender, lonely, trustful, blind creature, passionately curving and twisting her naïf little life to that black coffin as its terminus.   It's queer!" . . .

"Poor [Richard] Hodgson's death was the event, before I left. Absolutely sudden, dropt dead while playing violent handball.   Had said to a friend, a week before, that he thought he could count reasonably on twenty-five more years of life.   All his work unfinished. No one can ever learn those records as he knew them — he would have written certainly two or three solid books.   Too bad, too bad! And the manliest, unworldliest, kindliest of human beings.   May he still be *energizing* somewhere — it's not a case for *requiescat.*"

Very early in his life James expressed his dissatisfaction with funerals, and his resolution to have "nothing more to do with them" until they improved.   He did not find the institutional forms of Christian worship either natural or agreeable.   He could not pray because he felt "foolish and artificial." [10]   Writing to Schiller from Edinburgh in 1902, he said: "Just been to Church! — automatisms throughout!   Let us beware of the day when pragmatism becomes automatism in *our* mouths."   He attended daily prayers in the Harvard Chapel, but he was no doubt attracted by the simplicity of the worship and the paucity of the congregation.   And as a neg-

[10] Above, I, 212; *L.W.J.,* II, 214.

lected and somewhat forlorn cause, Chapel may have appealed to his chivalry! He endeavored to acquaint his children with the scriptural teachings, as has been recorded by his sister. Writing on October 10, 1890, she said: —

"William has, for several years past, read the Bible to his boys, and expounded (!) as he went. The other day Billy exclaimed: 'But, Father, who is Jehovah, anyhow?' This must have been a blow, after three years of complacently supposed lucidity. Some years ago, when Harry was five or thereabouts, William undertook to explain to him the nature of God, and hearing that He was everywhere, asked whether He was the chair, or the table. 'Oh, no! God is n't a thing; He is everywhere about us; He pervades.' 'Oh, then, He is a skunk.' How could the word 'pervade' suggest anything else to an American child?" [11]

When James was asked whether the Bible was authoritative, he said, "No. No. No. It is so human a book that I don't see how belief in its divine authorship can survive the reading of it." He felt the antithesis between nature and the church: "The spirit of the two systems is so utterly diverse that to an imagination nurtured on the one it is hardly conceivable that the other should yield sustenance. . . . I must personally confess that my own training in natural science has completely disqualified me for sympathetic treatment of the ecclesiastic universe. . . . It is impossible to believe that the same God who established nature should also feel a special pride at being more immediately represented by clergymen than by laymen, or find a sweet sound in church-phraseology and intonation, or a sweet savor in the distinction between deacons, archdeacons and bishops. He is not of that prim temper." [12]

James's religion took the form neither of dogma nor of institutional allegiance. He was essentially a man of faith, though not a man for any one church or creed against the rest. Unlike his father, he was not interested in the elaboration and specific formulation even of his own personal beliefs. He confined himself to the intellectual acceptance of what he regarded as the substance of all religions, and to highly generalized emotional attitudes. He insisted upon retaining not only the ideality but also the *actuality* of God — as a conscious power beyond, with which one may come into benefi-

[11] A.J., *Journal.*
[12] *L.W.J.*, II, 214; and notes for lectures at Harvard Summer School of Theology, 1902, 1906.

cent contact; he believed in the triumph, through this same power, of the cause of righteousness to which his moral will was pledged; and he entertained a hopeful half-belief in personal immortality. These specific doctrinal affirmations, together with his belief in believing, his sympathy with every personal belief which brought to an individual the consolation or the incentive that he needed, and the quality of tenderness and ardent good-will which pervaded all of his relations with his fellow men, make up the substance of his personal religion.

The following letter, added to what has gone before, conveys the peculiar flavor of his attitude. It was addressed to Charles Eliot Norton when the latter was afflicted with the illness of which he died four days later: —

Cambridge, Oct. 17, 1908 [13]

Dear Charles, —

. . . I was . . . grieved at the account . . . of all your sufferings and frustration. What a wrong-way-foremost thing senescence seems to be, and how strange the inharmonious share our different organs take in it! Your brain appears to have no appreciable share, and one hardly knows whether to congratulate or to condole with you, for its functions being so little blunted. I am as convinced as I can be of anything that this experience of ours is only a part of the experience that is, and with which it has something to do; but *what* or *where* the other parts are, I cannot guess. It only enables one to say "behind the veil, behind the veil!" more hopefully, however interrogatively and vaguely, than would otherwise be the case.

I thank you, dear Charles . . . for the superb chrysanthemums, which show that however bedridden a man may be, he can still play a part in the graciousnesses of the world. "Toujours le soleil poudroie par quelque trou." . . . I'm going to Chocorua in a couple of hours. . . . I hope and trust that when I come back I shall be able to come and "hold your hand." Believe, dear Charles, in your present straits, in the deep and warm reverence and affection in which you are held — by no one more profoundly than by yours ever lovingly,

WM. JAMES

[13] This letter has not been compared with the original.

PART VI

THE ULTIMATE PHILOSOPHICAL SYSTEM

LXXII

DEEPENING OF THE METAPHYSICAL INTEREST

THERE is a common opinion that philosophers spend their declining years in reclaiming the beliefs which in the full vigor of their faculties they have doubted or rejected. Being arterially sclerotic and preoccupied with the salvation of their souls, they are supposed to lapse from criticism into edification and dogmatic piety. If there be any such rule, James is the exception. Although the stream of his interests was never confined to any narrow channel, the last decades can be clearly distinguished by their emphasis: in the '80s on general psychology, in the '90s on ethics and religion, and between 1900 and 1910 on systematic philosophy. Instead of devoting his last years to faith, practice, and sermonizing, he gave them to the technicalities of theoretical inquiry.

That his attempt was largely frustrated was due to a series of accidents of a sort to which he was peculiarly susceptible. He was perpetually being invited to lecture, and he usually, with much groaning and dread, accepted. The agencies primarily responsible for James's failure to produce his systematic metaphysics were the trustees of the Gifford and Hibbert Foundations, and of the Lowell Institute, to which should perhaps be added the authorities of Harvard and Stanford Universities. Lectures drained off the flow of ideas which might otherwise have gone into the production of a systematic work. It was his fame that brought him these invitations, and their acceptance brought him greater fame. To have declined them would have required an inhuman and un-Jamesian degree of asceticism. But it is tempting to speculate on the contents of that "Principles of Philosophy" which might have resulted from a decade of rigorous and consecutive philosophizing, similar to that psychologizing of the '80s which resulted in the *Principles of Psychology*.

None of the five books which James wrote in the first decade of the century *was* the systematic metaphysics which he projected and to which he made such frequent allusions. This work was to be technical — designed for his colleagues or for advanced students, rather than for the layman. But when James wrote lectures he wrote them for hearers, and not for readers; and he was not a man to overestimate the capacity either of public audiences or of immature students. The result was that while he attained a vogue and influence almost unique among philosophical writers, he persisted in his "squashy popular-lecture style," and failed to produce that "something serious, systematic and syllogistic" [1] which he intended. To this judgment certain exceptions should be made. The articles which were published after his death under the title of *Essays in Radical Empiricism* were written for philosophical periodicals, to be read by scholars. The same is true of some of the replies to his critics, published in *The Meaning of Truth*. It should also be said that portions of *Some Problems of Philosophy,* such as those dealing with the topic of infinity, are probably as "serious" and "syllogistic" as anything that James was likely to write under any conditions. But the fact remains that no systematic treatise, in which his doctrines were assembled and set forth both rigorously and consecutively, was ever completed. Happily his unpublished remains throw some light on what it might have been.

James's philosophical ideas were, of course, maturing steadily during the '90s; and there were already grumblings from his intellectual conscience. To Baldwin he wrote in 1894: "I am at present trying to dig some rational truth out of myself . . . but it comes hard and has to be blasted, and I fear will result in shapeless débris." In December of this year he delivered before the American Psychological Association his presidential address on "The Knowing of Things Together," in which he specifically anticipated some of the central ideas of his radical empiricism. He still professed idealism of the Berkeleyan type, but it was clear that his thought was already disloyal to that creed. In the *Principles* he had allowed himself the conveniences of dualism. But the whole trend of his philosophical thought both before and after the publication of the *Principles* had been *against* that provisional makeshift. He now saw with increasing clearness that he could not hold one view as a psychologist and another as a philosopher; and as his rejection of dualism became a more and more dominant motive in his thought, he saw that he would have to correct his psychology.

[1] Above, 338; below, 583.

In the year 1895–1896 James devoted the second half of his Psychological Seminary to the "Discussion of Theoretic Problems, as Consciousness, Knowledge, the Self, the Relation of Mind and Body etc." His notes indicate that he was resolved to adopt the hypothesis of *phenomenism* and to carry it through. The "phenomenon" was also called the "datum" or "the pure experience." The central idea was to substitute "fields" of such "stuff," — homogeneous and in some sense continuous, but standing in peculiar functional relations, — both for the dualistic antithesis of mind and matter, and for the monistic reductions of mind to matter or matter to mind: —

"If, therefore, one wants to describe the process of experience in its simplest terms with the fewest assumptions, one must suppose:

"(1) 'Fields' that 'develop,' under the categories of continuity with each other — [categories such as]: sameness and otherness [of] things [or of] thought-streams, fulfilment of one field's meaning in another field's content, 'postulation' of one field by another, cognition of one field by another, etc.

"(2) But nothing postulated whose whatness is not of some *nature* given in fields — that is, not of field-stuff, datum-stuff, experience-stuff, content. No pure ego, for example, and no material substance. This is the hypothesis that we are trying to work out.

"(3) All the fields commonly supposed are incomplete, and point to a complement beyond their own content. The final content . . . is that of a plurality of fields, more or less ejective to each other, but still continuous in various ways. . . .

"What have we gained . . . by substituting various contents continuing in certain respects (which 'respects' are also contents) into each other, for stable things and changing 'thoughts,' the latter of which know the former? What by substituting 'fields' or 'points of view' for egos? We certainly have gained no *stability*. The result is an almost maddening restlessness. . . . But we have gained concreteness. That is, when asked what we *mean* by knowing, ego, physical thing, memory, etc., we can point to a definite portion of content with a nature definitely realized, and nothing is postulated whose nature is not fully given in experience-terms. Whereas the common sense terms with all their stability are 'mysteries' so-confessed. . . .

"The datum in itself and intrinsically considered is no more inner than outer. . . . It can be strung (in its intrinsic entirety) either on a vertical thread, so to speak, which unites it to associates that together with it make the inner world, and also on a horizontal thread with associates that together with it make an outer world. . . .

"There *is* no stuff anywhere but data. The entire world (objective and subjective) at any actual time is a datum. Only, within that datum there are two parts, the objective and the subjective parts, seen retrospectively; and as, within the datum, the one part is to the other, so will the datum itself in its entirety appear as the subjective part in the next datum which will contrast it with the objective part of its own content."

In other words, there is a constant shifting of status, by which a first immediate presentation, being superseded by a second, passes from objectivity to subjectivity — what was "this" has become "that" : —

"As the field alters and the older content shrivels, it forms connection in its new subjective value with the new objective content that marginally comes in. *That* was an appearance of *this,* from the earlier point of view; *this* is a predicate, then unknown, of *that.* . . . In the changed content the central parts . . . are now superseded and corrected; and, so corrected, they are inner, but *significant of* that larger outer. . . .

"We thus reach the abstract notion of an inner part of the field *meaning* and *knowing* another . . . part. We can explain what signifying and knowing mean; and, generalizing the notion, we can say by anticipation that all fields, even the present and the future one, are vehicles of knowledge. . . . Around every field a wider field that supersedes it . . . the truth of every moment lying thus beyond itself. . . .

"Once the notion of a not-actually-given is formed, of a merely possible experience, it seems quite in order that it should be indeterminate as to who should have it. . . . It is so far only an abstract notion, which may later be determined as excluding mine, or as excluding yours, or as including both. The important point is that the abstract notion itself should be an inevitable generalization from the content of every field. The solipsistic character of the present field seems then by *implication* removed. . . . The eject, the more, the reality, *qua* physical, tends to assume a certain form whenever we represent it — the invincible form of a stable permanent world of matter in space. *It there* is the fountain of all our data-fields; our experiences are its aspects from shifting points of view. But what is this but a more-than-*any* experience, a solid supposed as the source of all these points: they never exhaust it, it always exceeds, therefore it falls under the general category of a more or eject. . . . What is the difference between a field in which a memory . . . figures, and a field that contains your thought among its objects? Only a species of the great generic difference that must first be explained, between the *presented überhaupt* and the merely *meant*. Your thought is never presented, always meant, but I know the kind of thing it is. My past thought is now meant, but was once presented. 'Matter' is never presented, always meant." [2]

In the Preface of *The Will to Believe,* written in December 1896, James says (somewhat apologetically) that his radical empiricism "admits of being argued in as technical a shape as any one can desire," and that possibly he "may be spared to do later a share of that work." [3] It is evident that he was already doing it. In 1897–1898 this work was resumed in his seminary under the heading of "Philosophical Problems of Psychology." Some of his notes are recognizable as an anticipation of the views later worked out in his presidential address (1904) before the American Psychological Association on "The Experience of Activity." In the main, however, he was preoccupied with "the pure experience hypothesis" — in a determined effort to resolve certain *entitative* differences of traditional thought into *relational* or *functional* differences. According to this hypothesis, the same, taken over again in different contexts, can be subsumed under different categories, but without involving the discontinuities that are the most prolific source of philosophical difficulties. These notes both reveal the extent to which James anticipated his *Essays in Radical Empiricism,* and at the same time illustrate his persistence and self-criticism.

[2] James's reading for the seminary of 1895–6 included Avenarius, Mach, Bradley, Stumpf, H. Cornelius, Meinong, G. K. Uphues, Baldwin, H. Rickert, as well as his earlier sources. Selections such as the above convey no adequate impression of the many pages covered by the doubts, tentative proposals, amendments, etc., with which James struggled to clear his mind on these and kindred subjects.

[3] *W.B.,* ix–x.

PHILOSOPHICAL PROBLEMS OF PSYCHOLOGY

1897–1898

Various original contents, preserving their "logical" identity, can figure in various combinations with each other, forming parts of diverse systems. . . .

(1) The field of Plato's classificatory conception of "ideas," where the originals meant are the various abstract qualities or types-of-nature that may appear in any field. The relations here are those of comparison.

(2) The system of ideal values, æsthetically or ethically arranged. The relations are those of worth, and the field is one of appreciation.

(3) The system of physical nature, where the terms are sensations or hypothetic objects sensationally defined, and the relations those of sequence and coexistence or quantitative equivalence. . . .

(4) The psychologic system of individual streams of consciousness, if such a collection can be called a system. . . .

What places the same content now in one system, now in another system, is the fact that there are so many relations in which it can stand. . . . Thus, as compared by mere difference of quality, things connect themselves into system 1; by mutual *fitness* or desirability into system 2; when referred as effects to a set of entities conceived with quantitatively measurable properties as having a permanent existence in space, with definite position there, and movement, they enter into system 3; but when conceived in their immediacy, as limiting each other merely in time, without reference to space and without reference to epistemologic function, they enter into system 4. . . . Since, within each system, the relations that govern the content in other systems are abstracted from, we have so many mutually exclusive points of view of the content; and what is true of it from one point of view is either false from another or is so irrelevant that it cannot be treated as positively true. . . .

Sunday, April 3, 1898. The whole *use* of the "change of base" to pure experience is to see whether one may thereby solve certain problems which are *stickers* on the usual dualistic categories, *e.g.:*

(1) The paradox that though sensations and sensible attributes are one, the former are deemed inextensive, the latter extensive.

(2) Psycho-physical causality.

(3) The idealistic paradox, — brain being a condition of consciousness, whose creature brain nevertheless is.

(4) The discrepant cycles of activity, — cerebral and psychological.

(5) The perceptual and conceptual worlds.

(6) The composition of mental states.

Could the facts that enter into these problems be smoothly formulated without paradox or contradiction on the basis of the pure-experience or pure-phenomenon hypothesis, then the latter would certainly score a great triumph. . . .

The primal *facts* which the pure-experience hypothesis must recognize are, first, the *continuity* of experience *in concreto* (giving systems 4); second, its *decomposability* into objects; third, the *identifiability* of these objects in different fields — or, in other words, the noetic function of fields relatively to each other; and fourth, the *discontinuity* of the various sorts of . . . relation on which the different systems are based. . . . Is it owing to the existence of all these discontinuous kinds of relations that pure experience does fall into so many independent systems? . . . Might a synthetic account be found by following out the analogy of a line getting into an angular direction by curving gradually? . . . If *not,* then one could express the facts that experience develops into so many diverse systems by saying that experience offers diverse ultimate *points of view,* mutually exclusive, or insuspectible of combination into one point of view. In other words, it forms an irreducibly plural collection of systems of fact. . . .

Sunday, April 10. It seems to be a case of "many-dimensional continuum." . . . *Selection* . . . of certain interesting lines of relation would . . . appear to be the actual subjective condition which permits experience to fall into so many different systems; whilst the objective condition would be the fact that a plurality of relations are there in the content, and may logically and possibly be found and followed out. And the *occurrence,* in the stream, of objects which, *when they occur, occur with specific noetic fringes developable into termini,* is the initial peculiarity of experience to which all I write about may be traced. . . . Provisionally . . . this may be considered a sufficient *psychological analysis* of the matters which concern us. But such an analysis does not yet throw a ray of light on the questions asked [above]. . . . Let us revert to them. The trouble with them seems rather to be of a *logical* order.

Take question 3, the idealistic paradox. . . . It obviously contradicts logic to say that a portion of a field is the cause (in the ordinary sense of that word) of the entire field itself, or rather such words seem quite devoid of any intelligible meaning. By what discriminations, then, might the matter be cleared up? Will the distinction between object in its sensational immediacy, and object *qua* remote terminus, help? . . . The brain thought-*of* is not entitatively the brain thought-*with.* But if diverse entitatively, in what sense *are* they the same? The one thought-*of* potentially *terminates* in the one thought-*with.* It is as *terminus* that it *causes* the thought field of which entitatively it forms a portion. . . .

Friday, April 15. Does n't it seem like the wrigglings of a worm on the hook, this attempt to escape the dualism of common sense?

And is not the contrast I have been forcibly led to between the brain terminatively or entitatively considered and the brain "in the field" (= the brain *representatively* considered) indistinguishable from the common sense contrast between the objective brain and the brain-thought of? It looks so. Let me, then, try some one of the other problems for better luck! . . .

Friday, April 29. The great difference between the phenomenist and the common sense view is that the latter gives *stable* elements whilst the former is afflicted by a restlessness which is painful to the mind. In it one never gets out of the conception of flux, or process; although it might well seem that all the *actual* found its place in the flux. . . .

Sunday, May 1. . . . My point must be to show that *the beyond is part of the same continuum,* whereas for common sense dualism it is discontinuous, and separated by the epistemological chasm. . . .

If asked, we reply that . . . contemporaneous things do exist in the part of the room from which our faces are turned. . . . What does it mean now to say that he answers "truly" who answers "yes" to the question . . . *"do* they now exist?" . . . Isn't the difficulty this? — *to get out of a solipsism without jumping a chasm?* . . . Suppose there *were* conterminousness . . . what would result? how should my description run? Why, thus, — that my field with the question "more?" and the answer "yes!" terminates where yours begins, — say in this table or that human body, and yours terminates where someone else's begins, and so *de proche en proche* until the whole world gets covered. It *is* covered, *now,* just as common sense thinks it is, and independently of my verification; but it is not *one field* now, as monistic absolutism declares it to be. Arrived at the table in my field, I say "more" — *viz.,* that it is your table too, or that molecules are in it . . . and so far as *my* verification goes, I end there, getting no farther. But the "truth" of my "more" consists in the fact that my "table plus more," which is my terminus, is *conterminous* with you and with the molecules, — there is no "chasm." *So the notion of conterminousness has to be defended.* Not only percepts seem conterminous; concepts seem so too, — minds meet in truths as well as in facts. . . .

Sunday, May 15. . . . Yon bed . . . as I turn my head becomes first a marginal present object, then in immediate memory a conceptual object, then grows (as I turn back or still farther round), into a sensibly present object again, all the while with no "chasm" of otherness to break the continuity of its objective self-identity as meant or known by me through all these changes. . . . It is always *that* bed which is in question for me, and if I bring you in as a second participant, it is *that* bed which I understand *your* deliverances . . . to concern themselves with. . . .

Monday, May 22 and 29. . . . Take me solipsistically if you

will. My talk is merely a description of my present field of experience. That field is an experience of physical things immediately present, of "more" physical things "always there beyond" the margin, of my personal self "there," and of thoughts and feelings belonging to that self, together with "other" thoughts and feelings connected with what I call "your" personal selves. Of these various items some, as fully realized, are "sufficients"; others, the physical things "beyond" and "your" thoughts, come as insufficients — they connect themselves with the marginal "more." But . . . that marginal "more" is part of the experience under description. No one can use it mystically and say that self-transcendency or epistemological dualism is already involved in the description — that the "more" is a reference beyond the *experience*. The "more" is more than the vividly presented or felt; the "beyond" is beyond the centre of the field. . . . My actual field as I speak is full of *thises* and *thats*, *thens, theres, thuses, sames,* and *soons,* all as portions of its content, in the first instance, and in so far forth without the transcendent reference which dualism ascribes to cognition.

On August 26, 1898, James gave his address on "Philosophical Conceptions and Practical Results" at the University of California. This was the lecture in which he launched the philosophical movement to which he gave the name of "practicalism" or "pragmatism"; for which he gave the credit to Charles Peirce; and which he identified with "the great English way of investigating a conception." [4] The movement did not gather headway at once. In fact the lecture did not excite much comment until after 1904, when it was reprinted with slight changes, under the title of "The Pragmatic Method." [5] Even then, as this revised title indicates, the address revealed only that part of "pragmatism" which touches the *method* of philosophy. It did not embrace the pragmatic doctrine of truth, which later became the great polemical issue. "Pragmatism" occupied the centre of the philosophical stage in England and America only after the appearance in 1907 of James's book bearing that title. But although the public controversy over pragmatism must therefore be reserved for discussion in a later context, this postponement must not be allowed to obscure the fact that the pragmatic motive was one of the original roots of James's thought, asserting itself strongly from 1898, and playing an important part in the formation of his "system of metaphysics" after 1902.

[4] *C.E.R.,* 410, 434, 437.
[5] *Jour. of Philos.,* I (1904).

In 1898–1899 James gave a course on metaphysics, in which he announced that he would discuss "The Fundamental Problems of Theoretical Philosophy; The Unity or Plurality of the World-Ground, and Its Knowability or Unknowability; Realism and Idealism; Freedom, Teleology and Theism." The texts were B. P. Bowne's *Philosophy of Theism*, Bradley's *Appearance and Reality*, and Royce's *Conception of God*. From the scanty notes which survive it does not appear that this course marked any significant forward movement in James's thought. His central theme was the defense of "a restless, moralistic world," against the timeless Absolute of Royce and Bradley, and the monism of Lotze. The years 1899–1902 were years of broken health during which his working hours were, as we know, devoted to the composition, delivery, and publication of the Gifford Lectures on religion. In these lectures he "suggested rather than stated" his philosophical conclusions, and expressed the hope of developing them further "at some later day." "All facts and no philosophy," he wrote to Schiller.[6] The present volume was to be "followed by another . . . in which not only Professor Royce's arguments, but others for monistic absolutism shall be considered with all the technical fulness which their great importance calls for."

In the autumn of 1902 circumstances seemed to favor this undertaking. There was loss of time from illness, fatigue, and the usual interruptions (including the rereading of Emerson for the purpose of a "fifteen-minute address!").[7] But it is evident that he believed his metaphysics to be ripe for delivery. "I am going, if I live, to write a general system of metaphysics" — so he wrote to Bergson in December.[8] Ten years before, he had written in reply to Howison, who had alluded expectantly to a "book on metaphysics": "I have never attained to the dream of the possibility of such a thing, much less to the execution, and I now foresee that I never shall. . . . My intellectual higgledy-piggledyism can never lead to a system of metaphysics."[9] This change of attitude reflects his steady development during the '90s, both in the comprehensiveness of his view and in the firmness of his grasp. Two fertile principles now offered a way of rounding up his diverse doctrines, at the same time that they

[6] Cf. *V.R.E.*, 454 (note); *L.W.J.*, II, 165.
[7] *L.W.J.*, II, 187.
[8] *L.W.J.*, II, 179; cf. *ibid.*, 181.
[9] Above, I, 774.

suited the genius of his mind and strengthened his self-confidence. These were pragmatism and the doctrine of pure experience.[10] James felt, in other words, that he had something to say to philosophers, something to contribute to the stream of philosophic enlightenment. It would be a "demolition of the dualism of object and subject in perception," which "will reconcile many of the old inveterate oppositions of the schools" — a *system of tychistic and pluralistic philosophy of pure experience."* [11]

Meanwhile, during this same college year, 1902–1903, James set his fundamental thought in order for a course on "The Philosophy of Nature" (Philosophy 3). The syllabus which he prepared for this course, although it consists in large part only of headings, is perhaps the most *comprehensive* statement of his philosophy that James ever made. It corresponds closely to the description of his system which James gave a year later to Pillon: "My philosophy is what I call radical empiricism, a pluralism, a 'tychism,' which represents order as being gradually won and always in the making. It is theistic, but not *essentially* so. It rejects all doctrines of the Absolute. It is finitist; but it does not attribute to the question of the infinite the great methodological importance which you and Renouvier attribute to it. I fear that you may find my system too *bottomless* and romantic. I am sure that, be it in the end judged true or false, it is essential to the evolution of clearness in philosophic thought that someone should defend a pluralistic empiricism radically." [12]

In Philosophy 3, after announcing that pragmatism would be his method and "pluralistic panpsychism" his doctrine, he first expounded the instrumental view of scientific laws; and, in order to explain the harmony between nature and the scientific mind, advanced Peirce's hypothesis of the evolution of physical order through the "survival of the coherent." Turning to the problem of the unity of the world, he explained such degrees and varieties of unity as the world possesses, in terms of experienced relations. To avoid subjectivism, he argued for the "conterminousness" of minds, that is, their convergence in or towards the same experiences — defending this view against the skeptic on the one hand and the absolutist on

[10] Phases, respectively, of the "experimentalism" and "experientialism" which we have seen to be the fundamental and constant motives of James's empiricism.
[11] *Cf.* below, 606, 609.
[12] *L.W.J.*, II, 203–4.

the other. Borrowing Peirce's term, he adopted the "tychistic" theory that the ultimate origins of things are both plural and spontaneous. No philosophy, he said, can really avoid the recognition of a sheer datum at some point. But beings of independent and accidental origin can *come into* interaction with one another, through a spreading "consciousness of transition." This notion suggests different "spans" of consciousness, and the possibility of a consciousness such as God with a span far exceeding that of man. Change occurs in "finite increments"; and the "quantity of being" is finite, though *conceptual* space and time be infinite. Such a view of the world is not only the most economical description of the discoverable facts, but commands itself as the best postulate for action. It eliminates the problem of evil, and "goes with empiricism, personalism, democracy and freedom." [18]

James circulated the "Syllabus of Philosophy 3" among his philosophical colleagues. F. C. S. Schiller, who received one, had written to congratulate him on the "progress of his system," while at the same time dissenting on minor points, such as the omission of God! He also suggested "joining forces with the Chicagoans." In the same month Schiller had published an enthusiastic review of the *Varieties*,[14] in which, however, he refused to follow James in crediting the noetic claims of the mystical experience. The following letter from James is in reply both to the letter and to the review: —

Asheville, April 8, 1903

Dear Schiller, —

I believe that I am indebted to you for two good letters, for which this languid scrawl will hardly be a meet reply. Your strictures on my poor syllabus, docked and clipped as it was, were characteristically energetic and definite, but many of them would have proved to have had no application had my hand been more fully shown. That is, I should myself have been on their side. As for the infinite, I don't think we should quarrel about that either. There was something you said about "God" which I thought disclosed a somewhat deeper divergence, but as I have not your letters with me, I had better let that drop.

[18] The whole of this syllabus is reprinted below, Appendix IX. For Peirce's comment, *cf.* below, 425–6.
[14] *Proc. of the Soc. for Psychical Research,* XVII (1903).

Has one A. W. Moore of Chicago sent you a paper of his? It tickled me hugely, and I wrote urging him to send it to you and to Sturt.[15] It seems to me a masterly pragmatic production, and it appears now that, under Dewey's inspiration, they have at Chicago a flourishing school of radical empiricism of which I for one have been entirely ignorant, having been led to neglect its utterances by their lack of "terseness," "crispness," "raciness" and other "newspaporial" virtues, though I could discern that Dewey himself was laboring with a big freight, towards the light. They have started from Hegelianism, and they have that temperament (that is, such men as Mead and Lloyd have it strongly) [16] which makes one still suspect that if they do strike Truth eventually, they will mean some mischief to it after all; but still the fact remains that from such opposite poles minds are moving towards a common centre, that old compartments and divisions are breaking down, and that a very inclusive new school may be formed. Once admit that experience is a river which made the channel that now, in part, but only in part, confines it, and it seems to me that all sorts of realities and completenesses are possible in philosophy, hitherto stiffened and cramped by the silly littlenesses of the upper and lower dogmatisms, alternating their petty rationalistic and naturalistic idols of the shop. . . .

Charles Peirce is now giving six public lectures on "pragmatism" at Harvard, which I managed to get up for his benefit, pecuniary and professional. He is a hopeless crank and failure in many ways, but a really extraordinary intellect. I never knew a mind of so many different kinds of spotty intensity or vigor. Miller's health is keeping good, and, although there is a strong basis of old-fashioned rationalism in his mind, which won't give way, I think it is dissolving in spots, and that he will erelong be a full-fledged child of the light.

I am forgetting in all this to notice your review of my "Vagaries" in the *Proceedings,* and that (I now perceive) is what I meant by this second "letter" of yours which I had not acknowledged. It was as usual ultra-generous, and I thank you for it. The energy

[15] "Existence, Meaning, and Reality in Locke's Essay and in Present Epistemology," reprinted from *The Decennial Publications, First Series,* III (1903). For H. Sturt, *cf.* below, 496.
[16] Profs. George H. Mead of the University of Chicago, and Alfred H. Lloyd of the University of Michigan.

and literary ease you show fills me more and more with admiration. You ought to get less teaching work, and do more writing. As regards the matter of mysticism, I should like to talk it over with you. I doubt whether you do full justice to its strength. . . . I shall go up to Chocorua on May 1st, and doubt not that I shall recuperate and *on the whole* be as much better next year than this, as I have been this year than last. But lord! how I do want to read as well as write, and with so much left undone, I am getting really anxious lest I be cut off in the bud. Another pathetic Keats case!

I have just composed the first sentence of my forthcoming book — the only one yet written: "Philosophy is a queer thing — at once the most sublime and the most contemptible of human occupations." There is nothing like having made your start! I should n't be surprised if the rest were like rolling down hill. I am sure that a book of the systematic sort *can* be written — a philosophy of pure experience, which will immediately prove a centre of crystallization and a new rallying-point of opinion in philosophy. The times are fairly crying aloud for it. I have been extraordinarily pleased at the easy way in which my students this year assimilated the attitude, and reproduced the living pulse of it in their examination and other written work. It is the first time I ever tried to set it forth *ex cathedra*. My success makes me feel very sanguine.

We are about to have a philosophy building, "Emerson Hall," so-called. I learn here by the papers that the subscription is secure, and work will probably commence speedily. I don't care a great deal for it myself, but it will please Palmer egregiously, as well as Münsterberg, whose laboratory is now in very bad quarters. I wrote a review of Myers's book for the *Proceedings* just before leaving home.[17] I was dog tired and it went with difficulty. I wish you had done it. I could n't go into criticism of detail, so I simply skeletonized the argument, which was very likely a useful service. My opinion of the man is raised by reading the volumes, but not of the solidity of the system. The piles driven into the quicksand are too few for such a structure. But it is essential as a preliminary attempt at methodizing, and will doubtless keep a very honorable place in history. . . . Yours ever fondly,

WM. JAMES

[17] *Proc. of the Soc. for Psychical Research*, XVIII (1903).

Although "the first sentence of the forthcoming book" had been written in April, this seems not to have been counted, to judge by the following report to Howison, written July 4, 1903, on the eve of James's departure for Chocorua: "I have been getting one obstruction after another out of the way, and on my return to the country tomorrow shall start my new 'System der Philosophie.' It will be a genooine empiricist pluralism and represent the world in such gothic shape that people will wonder how any philosophy of classic form could ever have been believed in. You, dear H., are a classicist, in spite of your pluralism." [18]

There cannot have been much time for consecutive writing during this summer, since in August James was on his way to the Adirondacks, where, towards the end of the month, he delivered five lectures on "Radical Empiricism As a Philosophy." His mind was "working on the infernal old problem of mind and brain, and how to construct the world out of pure experiences." [19] He began the college year with high hopes of rapid composition, as his teaching schedule was light. But in the spring of 1904 he was complaining to his friends of the frustration of his plans. To Lutoslawski he wrote: "Two years ago, the *Varieties* being published, I decided that everything was cleared and that my duty was immediately to begin writing my metaphysical system. Up to last October, when the academic year began, I had written some 200 pages of *notes, i.e.* disconnected *brouillons.* I hoped this year to write 400 or 500 pages of straight composition, and could have done so without the interruptions. As a matter of fact, with the best will in the world, I have written exactly 32 pages!" [20]

And to Flournoy, in June: "The interruptions to work are so incessant that I have written exactly 32 (!) pages of my immortal new work since last October. It is rather pathetic; and I ought to get out of the University. I resigned this year, but they refused to accept my resignation; and the special difficulties of the University this year made it more honorable for me to continue. But *next* year I shall get out for good, and then I hope to do more writing."

[18] *Cf.* W.J.'s letter to Pillon of the same day; above, I, 710.
[19] *L.W.J.,* II, 198. The lectures were not written out and his notes have disappeared.
[20] *L.W.J.,* II, 171-2.

LXXIII

NOTES, BROUILLONS, AND PROVISIONAL DRAFTS

The personal and external difficulties were not the only hindrances to the completion of James's metaphysical task. There were the inherent difficulties of the problems themselves. The introductory pages, which afforded no such difficulties, were actually written, and the following paragraphs will convey their tenor. The title of the book was to be, "The Many and the One."

THE MANY AND THE ONE

INTRODUCTION II [1]

Philosophy is a queer pursuit, reckoned, as it sometimes is, to be the most sublime, and sometimes to be the most trivial, of human occupations. . . . Be it trivial or sublime, philosophy is as indestructible a human function as art is. Men always have attempted and always will attempt to make their minds dwell in a more reasonable world, just as they always have sought and always will seek to make their cities and their homes more beautiful. The thinker philosophizes as the lover loves. Even were the consequences not only useless, but hurtful, he must obey his impulse. . . .

Frankly recognizing the divided state of opinion about philosophy, I prefer to start upon this work romantically, as it were, and without justification. The justification, if the philosophy is good, will come at the end, in the reader's feelings of relief and satisfaction. For *myself* the results I shall try to set forth will be true, or as conducive to ulterior truth as I can make them. But even were such confidence as this a false persuasion on a philosopher's part, the fear that it might be so ought not to check his venture. General scepticism, based on induction, has no authority in individual cases. The lovers marry in spite of the fact that all previous lovers have been under some illusion, and the human race continues because of their imprudence. . . .

It makes no difference what pretensions the philosopher may pa-

[1] James left two drafts of the Introduction to his book, which are marked in his hand "Introduction I" and "Introduction II." I have drawn first from Introduction II, though they may have been designed as *alternatives*.

rade as to the coercive nature of his arguments.   Whatever principles he may reason from, and whatever logic he may follow, he is at bottom an advocate pleading to a brief handed over to his intellect by his peculiarities of his nature and the influences in his history that have moulded his imagination.   The reasons that have seemed so coercive to a man with one hypothesis have in point of fact usually seemed fallacies or irrelevancies to men with different hypotheses. . . .   The pattern of construction of the universe is, after all, a question of fact, and it is quite enough for the dignity of a system of philosophy, if, without pretending to invulnerable certainty, it succeeds in giving to the hypothesis for which it argues a supreme, or even a superior, degree of persuasiveness. . . .

It will conduce to clearness if in a general way I indicate immediately the sort of picture of the universe for which I am going to plead.   It has grown up in my mind gradually, as one detail after another seemed so to fall into its most natural place; and the portions of experience which appear to me to have served as the chief patterns in this world-picturing industry of mine are drawn from the mental and social spheres of life.   Both mental and social life are growths, resulting partly from addition, as new experiences are given and new men are born, and partly from subtraction, as when old events are forgotten, and institutions and leaders die and are replaced.   Mental and social life are at all times a strange blending of purpose, accident, and passive drift.   Both in biography and history, designs are modified to suit events which interfere with the original plan, and although when one looks back upon a certain finished cycle in either it is possible to trace lines of fulfilment, these are always general and abstract. . . .   No man, no nation, ever carried out a plan foretold in all its details.   No consciousness ever embraced in a single act of thought the whole of either an individual or a national life. . . .   I am willing . . . to believe that there may be larger souls than my own, whether connected or disconnected with the larger material aggregations.   The existence of such larger souls may be called a theological question, and I believe that such questions should be discussed as any other question is discussed, in all the ways which may make a decision seem probable or not.   But I do not believe, picturing the whole as I do, that even if a supreme soul exists, it embraces all the details of the universe in a single absolute act, either of thought or of will.   In other words, I disbelieve in the omniscience of the deity, and in his omnipotence as well.   The facts of struggle seem too deeply characteristic of the whole frame of things for me not to suspect that hindrance and experiment go all the way through.

This picture of the irremediably pluralistic evolution of things, achieving unity by experimental methods, and getting it in different shapes and degrees, and in general only as a last result, is what has made me give to my volume the title of "The Many and the One." "The Moment of Experience" is what I should have called it, if I had thrust into the foreground the second aspect of my picture, of which I next make mention. How, on the supposition that the manyness of things precedes their unity, does any unity come into being at all? And of all the different kinds of unity which the universe of our experience encloses, which is the essential kind, after the pattern of which we may imagine the other kinds to be constructed? The essential kind, in my view . . . is the continuity, the absolute nextness of one part to another, which we find in the minutest portions of our inner experience.

INTRODUCTION I

At the present day, as always, we find philosophies divided by chronic warring tendencies. Empiricism and rationalism and materialism and spiritualism, are the names for the most important pairs of these, and they intertwine their effects in such a way that, as things stand, it is hard for a man to find an empiricist philosophy which does not also commit him to the materialist tendency, and hard, if he follow the spiritualist tendency to escape a philosophy which will force him to be a rationalist as well. . . .

By empiricism I mean the tendency which lays most stress on the part, the element, the individual, treats the whole as a collection, and calls the universal an abstraction. By rationalism I mean the tendency to emphasize the universal, and to make the whole prior to the part, in the order both of logic and of being. The temper of rationalism is dogmatic: it willingly claims necessity for its conclusions. Empiricism is more modest, and professes to deal in hypotheses only. By materialism I mean the tendency to explain the higher by the lower, and to give to the lower elements the foremost place in being and in power. Spiritualism, on the other hand, regards the lower elements as secondary, makes of the ideal order the enveloping order, and gives the last word to the highest things. . . .

As things actually stand . . . a student . . . can either be a rationalist or an empiricist; but if he join the reigning school of empiricism he must become a materialist into the bargain; and if he follow the prevailing sort of rationalism, he must become a monist as well. Materialism is the only way of escape from monism, monism the only way of escape from materialism, at the present day. "Monism or materialism" is therefore the alternative offered, and he who wishes neither finds himself in a hard plight.

This was precisely James's plight — his book was to be that rare conjunction of ideas, empiricism and spiritualism. He proceeded first to give an account of common sense, with its categories of body, soul, and causality; and having first testified to the practical serviceability of these categories, he then referred to their deliquescence under the attacks of philosophical criticism.   But at this point, where he found himself face to face with special problems, the project was suspended.   Instead of advancing to the summary conquest of the domain of metaphysics, the author divided his forces, and laid siege to fortresses and walled towns which had to be reduced before he could pass them by.   The record of these local engagements, including the "200 pages of disconnected *brouillons*" above referred to, is to be found in a series of notebooks, containing miscellaneous jottings together with memoranda for the Metaphysical Seminary on "A Pluralistic Description of the World," given in 1903–1904; and in a set of manila envelopes, bearing labels such as "Continuity," "Common Object of Two Minds," "Necessity," "World of Pure Experience."

The Metaphysical Seminary followed the order of topics presented in the "Syllabus of Philosophy 3."   "I want to come *out*," he says, "with a collective *pluralism,* purposive impulse, and *nextness* as the principle of unity.   Best to *foreshadow this* rather early, as my intention.   Begin construction by the question of *Realism vs.* Idealism."   Varieties of idealism are then considered — Berkeleyan, Kantian, pluralistic, monistic, and panpsychistic. The value of idealism lies not in its proving its own case, but rather in its disproving the opposite, namely, the materialistic view of physical nature.   The argument is reënforced by the modern interpretations of scientific concepts.   Here, following Stallo, Karl Pearson, Mach, Poincaré, Ostwald, Le Roy, and others, James shows that physical laws as well as concepts are descriptions of experience, chosen for their utility.

Turning to his own characteristic view, he says, "All that is is experiences, possible or actual.   Immediate experience carries a *sense of more. . . .*   The 'more' develops, harmoniously or inharmoniously; and terminates in fulfilment or check. . . .   The problem is to describe the universe in these terms."   There are "certain difficulties" : —

"(1) 'Develop' implies either 'change' of one being, or 'continuity' in succession of many.

"(2) We imply many experients, yet one world.   The experients are ejective to each other, — how can they know one another or the same objects?

"(3) 'Possible' — so much remains only possible for each experient, that the question comes: *what is* being that is only *possible?*

"(4) How can the diverse come into relation at all? Bradley, Royce, Lotze's monism.

"(5) What do we mean by 'one'?

"(6) What do we mean by 'same'?"

His "program," James continues, is to solve these puzzles "by the principle of nextness, conterminousness," which is defined as "outer relation with nothing between." There follows a long argument for community of objects between two or more minds; and for an externality or adventitiousness of relations that shall permit of the *growth* of unity, without the need of assuming a preëxisting and "absolute" unity of the monistic sort. In short, things may arise plurally by chance ("tychism") and then "form a universe after they have arisen": "The essence of my contention is that in a world where connections are not logically necessary, they may nevertheless adventitiously 'come.' Series of independent origin and purpose may inosculate by 'chance-encounter,' and thereafter mingle their causalities, and combine their effects."

It is true that much relatedness preëxists as a "possibility," but we must avoid thinking this as "a way of being, even now, of the future or doubtful thing." Possibility is of two sorts: the "bare possible," which is "anything of which you can frame an idea which is neither self-contradictory, nor contradicted by something known as real; and the "grounded possible," which is "anything of which part of the conditions exist" — "absence of known hindrance" being supposed here also.

The following represent "various degrees of unity" or relatedness: "(1) Coexistence, withness, togetherness in space and time. (2) Noetic unity. (3) Likeness and difference. (4) Change. (5) Interaction. (6) Unity of substance. (7) Unity of origin. (8) Absolute noetic union." Of these degrees of unity James accepts the first five, but refuses to accept the remaining three as more than doubtful hypotheses. They *may,* but *need* not, be true. They do not do anything to remove the mystery of existence. In the last analysis "empiricism is the only method." How a *what* becomes a *that,* or a *possibility* a *fact,* cannot be explained in any case, and whether we take our ultimate spontaneity piecemeal or all at once makes no logical difference.

The probability, as distinguished from the admissibility, of the pluralistic hypothesis is supported by an appeal to the statistical character of scientific laws and the merely approximative character of scientific concepts. The growth of a universe out of a plurality of chance happenings would depend on things coming to "affect" one another at their boundaries; or on the appearance of "associability." The original of this idea is to be found in the "moment of experience" — which, with its sense of activity, memory, expectation, desire, fulfillment, and development, is like the "line of fire in burning grass." There alone the universe lives *qua* universe — there "the common life is realized" : —

"In these experienced cases, since what comes is continuous with something else and is preceded by an ideal, it may be likened to a *graft*. A graft is an *additive* to a tree. Nobody can contend that it is essential. Yet it combines harmoniously, replaces another branch that would have come, or another scion that might equally well have been grafted, and re-defines the 'whole tree.' It is strictly among the tree's possibilities. . . .

"The merits of the *graft*-theory are as follows: It means anarchy in the good sense. It means *individualism, personalism:* that the prototype of reality is the *here and now;* that there is a genuine novelty; that order is being *won,* — incidentally reaped; that the more universal is the more abstract; that the smaller and more intimate is the truer, — the man more than the home, the home more than the state or the church. . . . It means tolerance and respect. It means democracy as against systems which crush the individual. . . . It means hero-worship and leadership. It means the vital and the growing as against the fossilized and fixed, in science, art, religion, custom, government. It means faith and help; in morals, obligation respondent to demand."

The emphasis on evolution is a notable feature of this outline of James's system, and it leaves him with doubts as to its satisfying religious demands. "Does the pure experience philosophy," he asks, "offer any guarantee beyond possibility?" This question he does not answer with entire confidence : —

"Man is too helpless against the cosmic forces, unless there be a wider Ally. Religion, the belief in this Ally, has thus the simplest of *motives*. Its *arguments* for me lie in the conviction that our normal experience is only a fraction, and in the mystical phenomena. But by this extension of experience only *possibilities* are opened, and what most men want are certainties. They are not *bare* possibilities, however. To make a live possibility, more than an existent stock for a graft is required. The stock must, by idealizing the graft, exert tractive force upon it. . . . How to formulate it? I don't know. . . . If we cling to pure experience, it is in part experience of *activity* . . . a kind of experienced transition, a part of the content. . . . It involves sense of *direction*. . . . If present experiences cannot only welcome, but introduce, then there are *live* possibilities. Leave as problem!

"Meanwhile I ask whether a world of hypothetical perfection conditional on each part doing its duty be not as much as can fairly be demanded." [2]

To the same period belong jottings of a more random nature, which, though their thought is familiar, are so Jamesian in spirit and style as to deserve preservation: —

"The essence of my system is that there is really growth. . . . The world exists only once, in one edition, and then just as it seems. For the usual philosophies it exists in two editions, an eternal edition, complete from the start, in which there is no growth or novelty; and an inferior, side-show, temporal edition, in which things seem illusorily to be achieving and growing into that perfection which really preëxists. This reduplication of the same is absolutely irrational, in whatever way it be considered; and incompleteness and pluralism, in spite of their æsthetic scurviness, are intellectually to be preferred. . . . Transcendentalism has two editions of the universe — the Absolute being the edition *de luxe*. . . .

"Somewhere Being breasts immediately nonentity — cuts against the black inane, as the luminous orb of the moon cuts the cerulean abyss. . . .

"I wonder if my notion of pure experiences with all the other categories formed by additive relations among them may not be as fertile a principle in ontology as association has been in psychology! *Quien sabe?* . . .

"Ostwald, telling of his difficulties with consciousness in his energy-scheme, says that after a week of walking in his garden

[2] Notes for Metaphysical Seminary, 1903-4.

mulling over the matter, he felt a 'knock' in his mind, as when an umbrella turns inside out, — and after that all was clear to him." [3]

The manila envelopes, to which allusion has been made, contain manuscripts which are evidently rejected drafts of metaphysical chapters. There is a manuscript on "Pragmatism," in which the philosophy of pure experience is introduced as providing an example of the pragmatic method applied to the problem of mind and matter. There is a manuscript on "A World of Pure Experience," and headed "Chapter I," which may have been designed to follow the "Introduction" from which extracts have been made above, and may contain the "thirty-two" pages which were all that James had completed on June 14, 1904. In any case the book of which this was to form the first chapter was to be called "Radical Empiricism" — signifying the "refusal to go beyond concrete experience," and the "insistence that conjunctive and disjunctive relations are, when experienced, equally real." There is a definitive break with idealism : —

"By the adjective 'pure' prefixed to the word 'experience,' I mean to denote a form of being which is as yet neutral or ambiguous, and prior to the object and the subject distinction. I mean to show that the attribution either of mental or physical being to an experience is due to nothing in the immediate stuff of which the experience is composed — for the same stuff will serve for either attribution — but rather to two contrasted groups of associates with either of which . . . our reflection . . . tends to connect it. . . . Functioning in the whole context of other experiences in one way, an experience figures as a mental fact. Functioning in another way, it figures as a physical object. In itself it is actually neither, but virtually both."

In other notes of the same period the philosophy of pure experience is applied to the topics of "possibility," "continuity," "common object of two minds," and "activity." "Necessity" is reduced to the three alternatives of "logical identity," "inner fitness," and "coercive sequence"; of which the last is interpreted in terms of felt effort and resistance, and can have no place in physical nature except on the hypothesis of panpsychism.

This winter of 1903–1904, during which James felt himself to be perpetually foiled, was a period of gestation which soon bore

[3] Notes, 1903–6.

fruit — though not of the sort for which he had hoped. His spear-head had not been stopped, but it had been splintered. Between July 1904 and February 1905, he prepared and delivered a new set of lectures and wrote "eight new philosophical articles."

The lectures were given in a course on metaphysics (Philosophy 9, 1904–1905), in which he retraced the outlines of his system, shifting the emphasis to points that required special attention. "Experience" is to be "the primal term," chosen for its "neutrality, concreteness, convenience and inclusiveness." The universe is taken as "concatenated" rather than "consolidated"; and there is much discussion, therefore, of the question of relations, with a view to arguing their reality and their relative externality against the dialectical monism of Bradley. There is a continuation of the lifelong argument with Royce, the always formidable advocate of an Absolute that unifies the world by an all-at-once knowing of it. An attractive hypothesis, says James, but not in the least necessary. When the Absolute is invoked as the knower of facts that fall outside the sphere of finite experience, there is always a more simple alternative, which is to deny such facts. The ultimate has to be begged, whatever be the name by which it is called: whether chance — no outside grounds; freedom — no outside constraint; necessity — no outside possibilities; law — no outside disturbances; truth — no outside hypotheses; or fact — no outside reason. A discussion of causality leads to a statement of James's doctrine of activity; and the question of the relation of mind and body to a comparison of the views of Bergson and Strong. No solution of this last question is presented — "The only surely false theory would be a perfectly clear and final one." The course ended with a restatement of the subliminal doctrine of God, and with the following résumé: —

"Pragmatic Method. Principles of Pure Experience. Conjunctive Relations. Concatenated World. Theory of Knowledge, — Realistic. Mind and Matter Functional Terms. 'Absolute' rejected because (a) Useless; (b) Enigmatical. Additive Universe, — Graft. Tychism and Indeterminism. 'Truth' newly interpreted. Causality is Real Activity. Theology."

LXXIV

RADICAL EMPIRICISM

THE "eight articles" written between July 1904 and February 1905 were those published after James's death under the title (already chosen by James) of *Essays in Radical Empiricism*.[1] What was the relation of these essays to his metaphysical system? The following letter, written at this time to the Italian translator of his *Principles of Psychology,* reveals their central importance.

Cambridge, Feb. 22, 1905

My dear Ferrari, —

. . . Your letter of the 26th of December has been long lying in my pile of letters unanswered. . . . It was extremely interesting and *réjouissante* (how I wish I could write French like you!) by its contents — the sale of 2000 copies of my psychology, which must encourage the publisher as well as yourself . . . and second, all you say of my influence (!!) in the pages of *Leonardo,* and of your own hopes in the new journal which you are founding.[2] I have the first number which you sent me, and it looks promising. . . . I don't think that I am likely to contribute anything to your journal, for I have got to working altogether outside of psychological lines, as some articles which I have recently sent you will show. I am interested in a metaphysical system ("Radical Empiricism") which has been forming itself within me, more interested, in fact, than I have ever been in anything else; but it is very difficult to get it into shape for any connected exposition: and, though it contains very practical elements, I find it almost impossible to put it into popular form. *Technical* writing on *philosophical* subjects, meanwhile, is certainly a crime against the human race! . . . Yours faithfully,

WM. JAMES

[1] Presumably the first eight essays of that volume, most of which appeared during the academic year 1904-5 in the *Jour. of Philos.*
[2] Ferrari's "new journal" was *Rivista di Psicologia.*

It is clear from this statement that radical empiricism was so dear to his heart and so central to his thought that James did not hesitate to give its name to his entire system; also, that it forced him into contact with those technical aspects of philosophy from which he felt a periodic revulsion of feeling. He could never be as clear, in this context, as *he* liked to be. But the notion of pure experience was his deepest insight, his most constructive idea, and his favorite solvent of the traditional philosophical difficulties. Pragmatism provided his method or technique, and pluralism the architecture of the finished product; but radical empiricism gave him his building material.

The *purity* of "pure experience" means its original or pristine character — its priority to distinctions; and in particular to the distinction between subject and object. It was difficult for James's readers to realize that he had abandoned idealism, and construed experience as a larger area *within* which the boundaries of consciousness and self can be defined. For this misunderstanding he himself was largely to blame.[3] He was a recent convert from idealism, and lapsed readily into its habits of speech. Nor did he ever become perfectly clear in his own mind on the crucial issue between idealism and realism — the status, namely, of those parts of nature that lie beyond the mental reach of man. They consisted of further experiences, no doubt — but *whose?* It would have been more consistent if James had rejected this as a false question. For if pure experience is prior to consciousness and self, then the personal pronoun is not applicable to it. But he hesitated between imputing these further reaches of experience to lower forms of mind (after the manner of panpsychism), and treating them as the "possible" experiences of man. It is not surprising that he was obliged constantly to reiterate his adherence to realism; and that he was misunderstood, even by his most sympathetic readers, such as Flournoy: —

Geneva, Oct. 9, 1904[4]

My dear James, —

Thank you kindly for sending your "Does Consciousness Exist?" — it is very difficult to transpose into French, in view of the fact that "conscience" is indispensable, for lack of another word, as a

[3] *E.R.E.*, 76.
[4] Translated by the author.

means of expressing knowing, knower, etc. How fortunate are the English and the Germans to be able to manufacture terms without any prohibitive rules! Is there a real and essential difference between your "pure experience" and the *Empfindung* of Mach, the *phénomène* of Renouvier, etc.? It seems to me not, and I believe that the consciousness, *Bewusstheit,* menstruum, etc., that you combat with good reason, have for some time ceased to exist in French thought. It was at bottom the ancient idol of Cousin and the classic manuals — now quite out of fashion with us, but still in vogue, it is true, with many Germans. . . . Yours always,

TH. FLOURNOY

To Flournoy, then, it seemed that James's view was essentially the same as that of Renouvier and Mach. The phenomena or representations of Renouvier were intrinsically bipolar, being *both* subjective (as represent*ative*) and objective (as represent*ed*). With this view James had been in agreement in his phenomenism of earlier days. But pure experience was intrinsically *neither* objective nor subjective, these being differences of external relation or function. It could be said to be potentially dual, or to possess this distinction as a sort of destiny; but in itself it was "neutral."

As to Mach, it is true that his "sensations" (*Empfindungen*), despite their name, were elements *common* to both minds and bodies, and therefore belonging to neither exclusively. But they were far from composing in themselves that field of reality which James found in pure experience. Mach did, to be sure, suggest that a direct study of these elements themselves might lead to a science which would embrace both the physical and the psychical; and to this passage James attached the query, "Can this mean 'pure experience'?" So far, then, James felt a kinship with Mach, and regarded his view as a step in the right direction. But Mach was fundamentally a positivist, for whom the neutral elements were data, requiring some sort of scientific construction before they yielded knowledge. And the type of construction to which his training and temper of mind disposed him was that of physics. Thus we find him defining the domain of psychology as the dependence of the sensations or elements on the central nervous system. "Decidedly *not,*" remarked James [5]

[5] *Cf.* James's copy of Mach's *Analyse der Empfindungen,* 1903, 42, 83. This work contains numerous references by Mach to James, especially a note indicating his admiration of "The Sentiment of Rationality"; *cf.* 241, note.

— for this could only mean the reduction of psychology, through psychophysics, to physics; while for James psychology had its *own* categories, scientifically as authoritative as those of physics and metaphysically more fundamental.

Richard Avenarius, Karl Pearson, Henri Poincaré, and Joseph Petzoldt [6] also appealed to James through their identifying the content of the physical and mental realms. Avenarius, with his philosophy of "immanence" and "pure experience," explained the traditional dualism of outer object and inner representation as an illusory effect of "introjection." But, like Mach, he was essentially a positivist; and positivism is either skeptical of all metaphysics, or is under suspicion of begging the metaphysical question in favor of naturalism. To James, proponent of a spiritualistic metaphysics, either alternative would be objectionable. He read Avenarius's *Der Menschliche Weltbegriff* with admiration and close attention. But he found it obscure and inconclusive. "Avenarius's effort is very sincere, beautifully written, and must be taken account of by all who are trying their hands at similar problems; but I can't make out what becomes of the universe." While James had much in common with contemporary positivism, — namely, the appeal to experience and the recognition of a standard of utility or convenience in the framing of hypotheses, — he was profoundly unsympathetic to its negations.

James's view of experience, then, was not derived from contemporary positivism any more than from Renouvier. It was in agreement with a *general* tendency of the times; [7] and it was the culmination of a tendency which had governed his own thought from early years. The same desire to escape the dualism of subject and object which had led to his "phenomenism" drove him to look beyond the intrinsic duality of phenomena. In 1884, in the earliest working out of his theory of knowledge, [8] he substituted a relation *within* consciousness for the supposed relation *of* consciousness to an outside object; and described "knowledge by acquaintance" as the case in which the mind actually crosses the path of nature, through a point of intersection common to both. In the *Principles* he per-

[6] A follower of Avenarius. His *Philosophie der reinen Erfahrung* was well known to James.

[7] *E.R.E.*, 1–2.

[8] "On the Function of Cognition," *Mind*, X (1885). For an important summary of the agreement and difference between James's views in 1884 and 1909, cf. *M.T.*, 41, note.

petually converted the *subject* of consciousness into *content* of consciousness. With such doctrines germinating in his mind for twenty-five years there is no need of attributing his radical empiricism to any source outside of James himself.

The first of the *Essays in Radical Empiricism* bore the arresting title, "Does Consciousness Exist?" and set forth the fundamental thesis of "pure" or "neutral" experience. The essays that followed dealt with the applications of this thesis: the relation of cognition to its object; the rôle of concepts and percepts; the general problem of relations; the sense in which two minds can be said to have the same object; the place of feeling in experience; the relation of mind and body; the question of causal activity and efficacy; the nature of truth. There is a new tone of intellectual self-confidence in these essays. He had achieved a sufficient nucleus of doctrine and a sufficient degree of clearness to warrant his promulgating a system of his own.

But his difficulties were by no means over. In the first place, had he really succeeded in distinguishing between pure experience and *subjective* or conscious experience? Did he not betray a partiality for spiritualism as indefensible as the naturalistic partiality of the positivists? Did he not, by construing causal efficacy in terms of "the sense of activity," virtually conceive the physical world as inwardly mental? Finally, accepting his repeated avowal of natural realism, how did he dispose of the fact which is not consciously experienced by any human mind? Must it not either lie outside experience altogether or be experienced by itself — if not by an idealistic absolute?

Professor Warner Fite, discussing "The Experience-Philosophy," said that "experience," despite the claim that it was prior to the distinction between subjective and objective, invariably turned out to be subjective; and at the same time he entered a general protest against the notion that "experience," or anything else, could be an "absolute datum." [9] To which James replied as follows: —

Riverside, Cal., April 3, 1906

Dear Fite, —

I have but just "got round" to your "Experience-Philosophy" article. . . . You seem to think that "experience" means necessarily

[9] *Philos. Rev.*, XV (1906).

subjective experience. "Pure" experience for me antedates the distinction. It is my name for your ambiguous reality from which, wherever conceptually developed, the two sets of data come. It is not an "ultimate" in the sense which you condemn. Its determinations are all retrospective, drawn from what it develops into; and, in so far as the present developments are as perplexingly dualistic as you represent (I confess I had never thought of them as so conflicting, but you may be quite right), it also is a dualism *in posse*. As for your account of our present stage of development, it (the account) seems to me identical with Deweyism and Schillerism. At any rate, *I* read you all alike. If you take the world as "experience" in the "subjective" sense, what is that experience *of?* What is its "content"? Nothing but real things, "objective" both in the epistemological and in the physical sense. On the other hand, what is the content of the "things"? Nothing but sensation-stuff, etc. "Pragmatism," for you, seems to mean confining oneself to the latter truth. For me it means carrying the two truths abreast. The pragmatist in my eyes *must* be a natural realist, and believe in extra-mental facts. He has n't the resources of (say) Rickert, whose second edition of the *Gegenstand der Erkenntnis* I have just been reading, for he can't believe in a *Bewusstsein überhaupt,*[10] to engulf all individual experiences, with their natural-realistic mutual relations, in a higher monistic idealism. That would be one of your ultimates, but the pragmatist can't look out of the finite stream. The two ways of handling this which you so vividly end by describing, are determinants of each other, from step to step, and each determinant has to stay as true until replaced. The past was no less there because the condition of its being experienced *as* past is present. The bank can't say, "I made the river," any more than the river can say, "I made the bank." The right leg can't say, "I do the walking" any more than the left leg can. Taking "experience" concretely, as Schiller and Dewey do, seems to me the only way in which to leave all its determinations real so far as they are attained, and at the same time to leave always a *determinable* (which is never an ultimate in your sense) that provides for what is fertile and developable in the process.

[10] Consciousness in general. Heinrich Rickert's *Gegenstand der Erkenntnis* provoked James to most lively criticism, some of which appeared in his "Abstractionism and 'Relativismus,'" *M.T.*; the rest being recorded on the margins of the book.

Why you, who are now in my eyes one of the best protagonists of pragmatism, should join the crowd in insisting on subjectivism or solipsism as the only admissible synonyms of that word, I can't see. But I do admit [the] difficulty of thinking and expressing one's thought here, and know how lamely I, for one, must have expressed myself to be taken so *à rebours.* . . . Truly yours,

WM. JAMES

P.S. Fact is determined noetically only by assuming the subjective form of "truth"; but its transubjective status is constantly shown by its forcing the truth to redetermine itself. Two variables, of which concrete experience consists, each independent, yet dependent mutually from step to step, — there must be some mathematical analogue that I don't know.

Over a period of two and a half years, beginning in the autumn of 1905, James kept a sort of intellectual journal of his thinking on what he called the "Miller-Bode" objections — advanced by B. H. Bode in a series of articles, and by Dickinson S. Miller in letters and in an unpublished manuscript. James respected these objections because they coincided with his own doubts. His struggle to overcome them is recorded in more than three hundred closely written pages.[11] On the flyleaf of the second of the notebooks devoted to this purpose, he wrote: "The writhing serpent of philosophy, to use a phrase of Blood's, is one gigantic string of mares' nests." Underlying this prolonged and doubly figurative self-torture there lay a conflict of doctrine so fundamental as to require a reconsideration of almost all of James's philosophical ideas. In the *Principles* he had done everything to accentuate the uniqueness and indivisibility of the individual stream of consciousness. Every state of mind was deemed so impregnated with its context as to be incapable of repetition. James could then take this view without prejudice to the existence of a common and permanent world because of his distinction between thoughts and their *objects,* the latter possessing the

[11] Presumably a part of the "hundreds of sheets" to which James refers in *P.U.*, 206–7. Selections from these pages are printed below as Appendix X. For Bode's objections, cf. *Jour. of Philos.*, II (1905); and *Philos. Rev.*, XIV (1905). For James's published reply to the former, cf. *E.R.E.* Miller's objections are published in part in *Essays in Honor of William James*, 1908; and in his controversies with E. A. Singer, Jr., and E. B. McGilvary, *Jour. of Philos.*, VIII, IX (1911–2), and *Philos. Rev.*, XXI (1912).

commonness and permanence which the former lacked. But now he had definitely renounced dualism, and in place of thoughts *and* things there were only "experiences." If these possessed the uniqueness and indivisibility of thoughts, they must lose the commonness and permanence of things; and there would remain only the desperate alternative of solipsism. If, on the other hand, they possessed the commonness and permanence of things, then they could never enter directly into a uniquely individual conscious experience. How to conceive experience so that it could retain both sets of properties, composing both the immediate and the transient life of the subject *and* the stable world of common objects — that was James's problem.

The problem had ramifications. How can the same object be both with ("co") another object in my mind, and at the same time without ("ex") that other object in your mind? How can a personal experience be both isolated ("ex"), as it is in me, and also joined with the experiences of other persons ("co") as it is in God? How can an experience point beyond itself to another which does not yet exist? If all facts are facts of experience, then where (or whose experience) are the relations *between* personal streams of experience? No wonder that James felt "boggled and muddled," as he confessed to Miller; and that he distrusted any "summary executions!" [12]

At the same time that James was endeavoring to meet the criticisms of Miller and Bode, he was engaged in deciding whether or not to accept the panpsychism pressed upon him by his friend Strong, and impressively set forth in a book by G. Heymans, entitled *Einführung in die Metaphysik*.[13] He had always been attracted to panpsychism, and had for brief periods succumbed to its charms. It provided an interpretation of physical nature that was realistic without being materialistic. It was also a convenient auxiliary to radical empiricism: imputing to every entity an inner experience of its own, and thus providing in experiential terms for regions of value falling outside the experience of man. But on the other hand,

[12] *L.W.J.*, II, 236. For the outcome of this intense and protracted effort, *cf. P.U.*, Ch. V–VII; below, 586 ff.
[13] Published in 1905. "Heymans' book is a wonder." (*L.W.J.*, II, 237.) James regarded Dr. Morton Prince (*The Nature of Mind and Human Automatism*, 1885) as belonging to the same school, which he alluded to as "Heymans, Strong & Co." *Cf.* also *P.U.*, 313; W. T. Bush, "William James and Panpsychism," in Columbia University *Studies in the History of Ideas*, 1925, Vol. II.

panpsychism was a variety of substantialism, — it gave things a core, — whereas James had been reared on the empiricist doctrine that a thing is the sum of its appearances. James was disinclined to accept any unbridgeable chasms; and panpsychism, despite its name, introduced a profound dualism — that, namely, between the psychical inwardness of things and their physical outwardness. What the tree, for example, *really* is man can never know, for lack of the tree's experience. And why what feels to itself like a tree, however that may be, should look like a tree to man remains an unsolved problem. James felt, too, that although panpsychism was subject to the "Miller-Bode" difficulties in an aggravated form, it left that battle to others. It was a seductive friend, but not a vigorous ally.

In 1903 Strong published his book entitled *Why the Mind Has a Body*. James found it "charming" and "surely destined to renown"; but, he added, "he has not convinced me yet." [14] James read the book with care and wrote down certain observations of which the last is worthy of preservation: —

"My difficulty with Strong's theory is partly this: that although he distinguishes realities from appearances, he leaves no stable difference of nature between them, but allows the same kind of thing to be at one time real, at another only apparent. This pencil, *e.g.* . . . is, so far as it is my percept, a reality, but so far as it symbolizes so much alien mind-stuff, an appearance. . . . *My* 'pencil' (*i.e.,* my percept so-named) is a reality, of which my 'brain' is the appearance to an anatomist . . . while that very same brain-appearance is reality so far as it is a fact of perception. In short, every appearance is a reality *somewhere,* but not in the place in which it appears. . . . There is a chase, a puss-in-the-corner business. Each when it leaves its own place is represented by a different reality, — its effect. My 'pencil' percept is a 'brain' percept by the time it gets to you. It seems odd to substitute two such homogeneous things for each other, and yet to say they belong to different 'worlds.' "

Santayana, though he was more directly exposed to Strong's persuasiveness, and though some years later he enlisted with Strong under the same banner of "Critical Realism," rejected panpsychism unhesitatingly. He wrote to James from Rome after receiving the

[14] *L.W.J.,* II, 198.

articles "Does Consciousness Exist?" and "A World of Pure Experience":—

Rome, Nov. 29, 1904

Dear Mr. James,—

Thank you very much for your two articles which have reached me here and filled an evening with very refreshing home thoughts, after the merciless biograph of mere phenomena which one gets in travelling. I am here with my old class-mate Loeser, whom you will remember, and who wishes me to send you his love. He has an eighteenth century statuette of Locke which he wishes to present to you. . . . Since I left America I have had glimpses of England, Belgium, Holland, Germany and France, besides six weeks . . . in Avila, and almost a month in Florence with the advantage of being near Loeser and Berenson.[15] I am profoundly out of humour with "æsthetics," yet I have been feeling the new *douche* of it which these friends of mine have drenched me with as a rather invigorating change; one gets so dry in America with no food for the senses, especially if one is obliged to pump up theory every day. From here I mean to go on to Naples and Sicily, Egypt and Greece — all new ground for me; and I hope to return in the autumn a new man, with a fresh supply of "pure experience" and a budding crop of new ideas.

Your articles, apart from their intrinsic importance, have interested me particularly on account of a certain harmony which there is between what you make for and what I have fallen into myself. Doubtless you have from of old let seeds fall into my mind which have sprouted there into what I feel to be quite native convictions; and it comes to me now as a rather surprising happiness that I can invoke your authority in support of a great deal that I feared might seem rash in my opinions. It is the general attitude which Bergson also encourages, although of course it may be turned in various ways and expressed in various vocabularies. What I don't quite understand in your way of stating the matter is whether the conceptual world has *only* its immediate status. Of course, every conception, taken existentially, is a part of the flux, which as you say is largely chaotic in its immediacy; but things and truths have also

[15] *Cf.* above, 256.

a systematic, and more or less static, dimension. For instance, if a candle which was nine inches long when left burning in an empty room is found to be six inches long on the observer's return, was it ever really eight inches in length? Of course the eight-inch candle will draw a potential sort of being from the philosopher's views, themselves immediate experiences of his; the *conception* that the candle passed through that phase will be an absolute item in the universal inventory. But the question seems to me to be whether the eight-inch candle has *only* that imputed being; or, rather, whether imputed being is not what we mean by reality, and the immediate flux itself by appearance. The forthright intellect seems to be the life of the mind, and what it rests in seems to be alone important, true, or efficacious. The eight-inch candle is something to be believed in, because in the material world which the intellect has discovered it is a needful element, that counts and rewards our confidence in its reality. The materials which experience is composed of must therefore be credited with an existence which makes them material elements and gives them a mechanical order, since they exist *also* permanently, potentially, and beyond our range.

If this is what is implied in your views, and I conceive that it is, the result seems to be quite different from panpsychism, and far more rationalistic. According to panpsychism the eight-inch candle exists only by virtue of its inconceivable psychic substance, that mass of irrelevant experience of which a candle at best is but a remote symbol or effect. The *real* eight-inch candle is not eight inches long and is no candle at all. It is perhaps a conclave of political worms electing an infallible pope to maintain that the universe is nothing but a musical composition. According to your view — if I understand it — and to mine, on the contrary, the material qualities of the candle themselves subsist, and it is a cylindrical white body that is really eight inches long at an assignable instant. The world of science, for us, then, would not be a mere fiction, but a real efficacious order discovered in the chaos of immediate experience; a system consisting bodily of the given elements, but of course involving many more, and the longer subsistence of them. Am I right? . . . Very sincerely yours,

G. SANTAYANA

Cambridge, Feb. 8, 1905

Dear Santayana, —

Your letter from Rome of November 29th came duly, and startles me now by the remoteness of its date. If left to my own mere impression I should have sworn to having received it not more than two weeks ago. It is pleasant to hear of the excellent Loeser again, for whom I have a warm affection. As for the statuette of Locke, why did n't he donate it to *you* on the spot instead of merely wishing to donate it to me? Emerson Hall should be its shrine anyhow — possibly the statue of Emerson might hold it in its hand, or dandle it on its knee. But when will either you or I, to whom Locke's mind was that of a street *polisson* in point of subtlety and "truth," have statuettes? A statuette is much more honor than a statue.

I am very glad you find some of my ideas so congruent with yours. Yours are still one of the secrets of the universe which it is one of my chief motives to live for the unveiling of (I swear that 's a good sentence in spite of Hill's rhetoric). I seem to see on all sides (except Bradley's & Co.) symptoms of a greater *Einverständigung* than ever being in the air, and I should be glad, for my own part, to become flexible and make compromises and adopt any new vocabulary in reason, to compass the result. Your letter is too short and pregnant for me to be sure of exactly what you mean by your candle realism, so I don't know how far to subscribe to it and how far not. So I won't enter into the discussion at present, but hang your letter up. In [George S.] Fullerton's new book (wonderful for clearness, though narrow) he professes a realism that sounds like yours. As for the reality of concepts *überhaupt* I believe them to be as real (or to be susceptible of as great reality) as percepts. We have to take account of them and mind them, even more; — but that opens a chapter with many discriminations.

We in the department have been concerned about the fact . . . of your being invited to lecture in France next year. . . . I can't conceive a better man for our university to put forward among the first. The plan . . . is to make *me* the lecturer the next year, 1906–7, and I am feeling so hearty again that I don't say nay. You the Baptist! I the Messiah! (That 's the way it looks to my wife!) Pray write to me again and tell me how the whole thing is looking at your end.

I have got through my half of Philosophy 9 finely and with no fatigue. Also shall have published nine articles since September 1. In consequence of which I am going to "let myself out" and have taken passage on the *Romanic* for Gibraltar, March 11th. . . . I should like much to meet you somewhere. . . . Ever truly yours,

WM. JAMES

In the autumn of 1905 James wrote Santayana a letter in which he commented on the latter's *Life of Reason,* just out, and made inquiries concerning the exchange professorship at the Sorbonne. This letter is unfortunately lost, but something of its tenor can be gathered from a letter written to Miller on November 10: —

"Santayana's book is a great one, if the inclusion of opposites is a measure of greatness. I think it will probably be reckoned great by posterity. It has no *rational* foundation, being merely one man's way of viewing things: so much of experience admitted and no more, so much criticism and questioning admitted and no more. He is a paragon of Emersonianism — declare your intuitions, though no other man share them; and the integrity with which he does it is as fine as it is rare. And his naturalism, materialism, Platonism, and atheism form a combination of which the centre of gravity is, I think, very deep. But there is something profoundly alienating in his unsympathetic tone, his 'preciousness' and superciliousness. The book is Emerson's first rival and successor, but how different the reader's feeling! The same things in Emerson's mouth would sound entirely different. E. receptive, expansive, as if handling life through a wide funnel with a great indraught; S. as if through a pin-point orifice that emits his cooling spray outward over the universe like a nose-disinfectant from an 'atomizer.' . . . But it is a great feather in our cap to harbor such an absolutely free expresser of individual convictions." [16]

Santayana's replies to the missing letter wander far from the subject of panpsychism and even from "pure experience," but they throw an interesting light on the fundamental philosophical differences between the two men: —

Paris, Dec. 5, 1905

Dear Mr. James, —

I am very grateful for your letter: I feel how *generous* it is, and how like you. I may say something about my book — in reply —

[16] *L.W.J.,* II, 234-5.

if there is room at the end, but first let me answer your questions
about the Sorbonne lectures. As you may imagine my experience
has been, so far, wholly unlike Wendell's.[17] He seems to have
grasped with avidity every opportunity to see things and to know
people, and seems to have lectured as if he was borne on a bubbling
wave of international enthusiasm. I have come, thinking only of
my subject, seeing only my personal friends, having only official
relations with officials, and keeping away as much as possible from
the American colony. . . . Of course, even if you wished to
take things as I am taking them, it would be impossible. You
are too famous; everyone here speaks of no one in America but
you; you would have enormous audiences and a host of invitations,
all of which you would find it impracticable to refuse. Nevertheless I don't see why you should n't refuse the American (the
most persistent) set of them; and the French people, if I may trust
my impression and experience so far, are perfectly willing to let
one alone. . . . The Hyde foundation has been a success; audiences have been found; the idea of lectures in England is fashionable and politically opportune. But it is an incident lost amid a
thousand others, a thing of importance to half a dozen persons.
Paris could live without it, and if a man likes the undertaking, as
I do, from the purely personal, academic, scholarly point of view,
he ought to attempt it. It is a delightful and a moderate task.
The freedom of speaking in a foreign language among foreigners —
I mean the intellectual *room* — is exhilarating. You can say what
is *really true*. You need n't remember that you are in Cambridge,
or are addressing the youth entrusted to your paternal charge.
I have never felt so grown up as I do at the Sorbonne; after our
atmosphere, this is liberty. . . .

I have spent, as you may have head, some weeks with Strong at
Compiègne. We had many rather unsatisfactory discussions about
idealism and mind-stuff. He tells me you are a convert to his
theory: is this serious? I should think the same empirical reserve
or abstention which makes you rebel against my materialistic
Platonism would make you rebel against his reversible universe,
perfectly concave and perfectly convex, matter-lined throughout

---

[17] The French exchange professorship was inaugurated in 1898, through the
initiative and generosity of James Hazen Hyde. The first Harvard lecturer at the
Sorbonne was Barrett Wendell, who gave the lectures afterwards published as *Liberty, Union and Democracy*, 1906.

with mind. It is a scholastic artifice, *n'est-ce pas?* It is not science, nor nature, nor moral truth. Strong himself, let me add, seemed to me more heroic and admirable than ever, and I enjoyed renewing our old friendship. . . . Yours sincerely,

G. S.

Paris, Dec. 6, 1905

Dear Mr. James, —

I forgot yesterday to answer one of your questions, which I remember may be of importance to you. The lectures are at five o'clock in the afternoon on Tuesdays and Saturdays. I have no doubt they would change the hour for you if you wished. To everything they say, *"comme vous voudrez"*; and things here, as in England, seem to go by prerogative. You could also give as many or as few lectures as you chose — the great Hyde consenting.

Another omission. Blood's poem,[18] after about six readings, has become intelligible to me, and I like the thought very much, also the diction, but the *composition* is deplorable. Why can't people begin and end, and give one some indication of what they are talking about? As to the tychism of it, it seems to me a good surface philosophy, a good expression of consciousness and the look of the flux. Of course what must be, if it must be, would never be *known* beforehand; and the machinery that may actually support our feelings does n't deprive them of their dramatic novelty and interest, any more than the printed *dénouement* of a novel, extant in the last chapter, takes away from the dreamful excitement of perusing it and of wondering what will come next.

Now that I am launched I will say a word about some of the criticisms in your letter. You are very generous; I feel that you want to give me credit for everything good that can possibly be found in my book. But you don't yet see my philosophy, nor my temper from the inside; your praise, like your blame, touches only the periphery, accidental aspects presented to this or that preconceived and disparate interest. The style is good, the tone is supercilious, here is a shrewd passage, etc., etc. And you say I am less hospitable than Emerson. Of course. Emerson might pipe his wood-notes and chirp at the universe most blandly; his genius might be tender and profound and Hamlet-like, and that is

---

[18] Probably "Reveries of One," reprinted in part in *M.S.*, 402–3.

402 ULTIMATE PHILOSOPHICAL SYSTEM

all beyond my range and contrary to my purpose. I am a Latin, and nothing seems serious to me except politics, except the sort of men that your ideas will involve and the sort of happiness they will be capable of. The rest is exquisite moonshine. Religion in particular was *found out* more than two hundred years ago, and it seems to me intolerable that we should still be condemned to ignore the fact and to give the parson and the "idealists" a monopoly of indignation and of contemptuous dogmatism. It is they, not we, that are the pest; and while I wish to be just and to understand people's feelings, wherever they are at all significant, I am deliberately minded to be contemptuous toward what seems to me contemptible, and not to have any share in the conspiracy of mock respect by which intellectual ignominy and moral stagnation are kept up in our society. What did Emerson know or care about the passionate insanities and political disasters which religion, for instance, has so often been another name for? He could give that name to his last personal intuition, and ignore what it stands for and what it expresses in the world. It is the latter that absorbs me; and I care too much about mortal happiness to be interested in the charming vegetation of cancer-microbes in the system — except with the idea of suppressing it.

A more technical point. You say "activity" can be spiritual only. Is your activity, or sense of activity, not rather an ἐνέργεια than a δύνμισα? Of course I should be the first to agree that activity, in the sense of actuality and conscious stress, belongs only to consciousness or even to the rational and reflective energy of thought. But *efficiency,* in the sense of regular predictable contiguity with other specific events, belongs only to δύναμις, to the potential (= the potent). In a dream there is the sense of activity, there is commotion and actualization, ἐνέργεια: but there is no δύναμις, no material efficacy, save through the underlying metabolism in the brain; the story in the dream stops short; its purposes evaporate. This may be contrary to common-sense, meaning ordinary ways of expressing oneself; but it seems to me quite of a piece with common-sense of a progressive sort, with science. It might be contrary to common-sense to say that the sun is larger than the earth, but not to common-sense applied to the full situation. So this doctrine seems to me reasonable in its method and result, though as yet paradoxical in its language.

I have read practically no reviews of my book so that I don't know if anyone has felt in it something which, I am sure, is there. I mean the *tears*. "Sunt lachrimae rerum, ac mentem mortalia tangunt." Not that I care to moan over the gods of Greece, turned into the law of gravity, or over the stained glass of cathedrals, broken to let in the sunlight and the air. It is not the past that seems to me affecting, entrancing, or pitiful to lose. It is the ideal. It is that vision of perfection that we just catch, or for a moment embody in some work of art, or in some idealized reality; it is the concomitant inspiration of life, always various, always beautiful, hardly ever expressible in its fulness. And it is my adoration of this real and familiar good, this love often embraced but always elusive, that makes me detest the Absolutes and the dragooned myths by which people try to cancel the passing ideal, or to denaturalize it. That is an inhumanity, an impiety, that I can't bear. And much of the irritation which I may betray and which, I assure you, is much greater than I let it seem, comes of affection. It comes of exasperation at seeing the only things that are beautiful or worth having, treated as if they were of no account.

I seldom write to anyone so frankly as I have here. But I know *you* are human, and tolerant to anything, however alien, that smells of blood. Always sincerely yours,

G. SANTAYANA

How the news of James's "conversion" to panpsychism had reached Santayana is set forth in a letter from Strong written during the preceding summer: —

Compiègne, Aug. 23, 1905

Dear James, —

Your card from Hurricane came several days ago and your letter from Ridgefield last night. Heymans's book was indeed a very great satisfaction to me, but your announcement that you are now inclined to accept the theory is if anything a greater. I feel, as I wrote Santayana three days ago, much as the early Christians must have felt when they heard of the conversion of the Emperor Constantine. I don't wonder that Heymans's book has been the means of your conversion, it is so superbly clear and well argued. He has worked out the theory in much greater detail than I did, and this is an important thing, for I realize now that my account of it was far too brief.

You must have been struck, in reading the book, with the similarity of some of his positions to your own: the doctrine that the heterogeneity of mental and physical is not a heterogeneity of elements, but of the laws connecting them; the notion of interpolation and extrapolation; and your doctrine of the will, or rather right, to believe.   I was interested to see that he bears Bergson out in his contention that, while to every psychic state a definite brain-event must correspond, it is not true conversely that to every brain-event must correspond a definite psychic state: this by way of *deduction from the panpsychistic theory.*   I have written Bergson calling his attention to this; you know it was the point of his paper at Geneva.[19] . . . Yours ever,

C. A. S.

That "Heymans's book," though it made panpsychism more than ever seductive, did not in fact overcome James's doubt appears from notes which he made in 1905 just after reading it.   That Strong himself soon recognized the incompleteness and transitoriness of the conversion appears from the following paragraph which he wrote to James in the autumn of 1906: —

"(1) Santayana means by 'consciousness' the transitive cognitive function, not the existent that exercises it; (2) he thinks the psychic element of things lies wholly in this function, and is essentially a sort of nodding towards or throwing kisses at reality, or off into vacancy.   Hence he calls the existent that exercises the cognitive function, without regard to the special equipment it may have for exercising it, 'matter.'   Whereas, in my opinion, we must distinguish, in what is commonly called consciousness, between cognition and luminosity.   Cognition is essentially representation and can take place in the way it actually does only because the existent that represents is intrinsically luminous.   The psychic character in things lies in the existent and not in the function.   Here is the boundary line between panpsychism and materialism.

"My doctrine is of course the same as yours except that I emphasize the fact that in all elementary knowledge, the perception

[19] "Le Paralogisme psycho-physiologique," read at the Second International Congress of Philosophy in Geneva.

no less than memory, there is an experience represented. Current pragmatism is correct as far as it goes, but errs by overlooking this ulterior experience. If the latter be admitted, truth, however subjective and humanistic, is not without relation to it. Sometimes it consists in copying it, as in memory, but always it enables us to adjust our relations to it."

On both of the issues raised in this letter James's view was opposed to the panpsychism of Strong. For the latter the primal experience was in some sense inherently psychic, while for James it was inherently neither psychical nor physical, but consisted of "neutrals, indifferents, undecideds, posits, data, facts." Since for the panpsychist the psychical must be a primitive and not a derivative character of being, he has, James thought, a peculiar obligation to clarify this concept: "He needs to define what he means by 'psychic' as an immediate determination or 'primal quality' of existence. Radical empiricism tries a pragmatic definition. Strong tries none." [20] In the second place, while in James's radical empiricism the physical object was directly presented to human perceptions, or was what it was perceived to be, in Strong's panpsychism the real physical object could be directly presented only to itself, or was as it felt itself to be. These were far-reaching differences.

[20] Marginal annotations and synopsis of an unpublished MS. by Strong, 1907; *cf.* below, 535–7.

LXXV

INFLUENCE OF CHARLES PEIRCE

CHARLES PEIRCE, lifelong intellectual friend and irritant, again enters upon the scene. We have considered the early relations of the two men, and have introduced Peirce's comments on James's earlier works; we have also discussed their reciprocal influence, so far as this depended on personal traits and on their intellectual idiosyncrasies; but now that James's system is reaching its mature form we must compare them as philosophers. Their similarity is more obvious than profound or certain. Many of the terms which James was most fond of employing and to which he has given vogue — terms such as "pragmatism," "tychism," and "synechism" — were derived by him from Peirce. It does not follow, however, that he meant the same things by them.

Peirce's earliest group of writings, 1868–1871, "interested" [1] James "strangely," but can scarcely be held responsible for any of his philosophical ideas. In fact they were largely devoted to the exposition of ideas which James explicity rejected. Peirce argued against immediate or intuitive knowledge, which always occupied a central place in James's thought. Peirce defined truth in terms of agreement, and reality in terms of truth — " the immediate object of thought in a true judgment *is* the reality." In other words, both truth and reality are defined in terms of the ideal consummation of the thinking process. When all the thinking is done, and when all are brought to agreement in a final and conclusive judgment — then *that* is true, and what is there judged is real. Nothing could be more foreign to James's empiricism, according to which both truth and reality are mundane things, given or achieved in the daily experiences of men. [2]

In one respect, however, Peirce's earliest writings (or conversations) seem to have left an unmistakable imprint on James. The

---

[1] Including three articles in the *Jour. of Specul. Philos.*, 1868; and the review of Berkeley, *North Amer. Rev.*, CXIII (1871).

[2] James recognized the *ideal* of agreement, but did not reserve truth for this ideal; *cf. M.T.*, 263–6.

latter was disposed to nominalism, both by the philosophical literature on which his mind was mainly nourished and by his taste for
the particular and concrete.   But he never became a nominalist.   In
one way or another he always found a way to provide for universals,
generals and concepts, however much he might disparage them.
This persistent retention of a modicum of Platonic realism, despite
the general tendency of his thought to the contrary, was largely due
to Peirce's insistence on the rights of thought as opposed to sensation.

It will be convenient to group the further consideration of
Peirce's influence under the heads of pragmatism and pluralism.
In the lecture "Philosophical Conceptions and Practical Results,"
delivered in 1898, James writes that he heard Peirce enunciate "the
principle of practicalism, — or pragmatism, as he called it," in Cambridge in the early '70s.[3]   This statement agrees with the conclusion which we have already reached, that the philosophical club
in which James was associated with Peirce and Chauncey Wright
was most active in the years 1870–1872.[4]   In his account of this
club Peirce emphasizes the influence of Nicholas St. John Green:
"His extraordinary power of disrobing warm and breathing truth
of the draperies of long worn formulas, was what attracted attention to him everywhere.   In particular, he often urged the importance of applying Bain's definition of belief, as 'that upon which
a man is prepared to act.'   From this definition, pragmatism is
scarce more than a corollary; so that I am disposed to think of him
as the grandfather of pragmatism." [5]   But if Bain was the grandfather of pragmatism and Green its father, then James was born
a pragmatist as truly as Peirce,[6] though Peirce may well have been

[3] *C.E.R.*, 410.   In the review of Berkeley written in 1871, Peirce said: "A better
rule for avoiding the deceits of language is this: Do things fulfil the same function
practically?   Then let them be signified by the same word.   Do they not?   Then
let them be distinguished" (p. 469).

[4] *Cf.* above, I, 536.

[5] From a paper (*circ.* 1906) entitled "Pragmatism," published for the first time
in the Preface of Vol. V of the *Collected Papers of Charles Peirce*.   The remainder
of this document is used above, I, 535.   Some years earlier Peirce's recollections
seem to have been less clear.   On Nov. 10, 1900, he wrote to James: "Who originated the term 'pragmatism,' I or you?   Where did it first appear in print?   What
do you understand by it?"

[6] As a matter of fact Peirce states explicitly, in his contribution to the article
on "Pragmatist and Pragmatism" in the *Dictionary of Philos. and Psychol.*, 1902,
that he derived his view from Kant.   But it would be equally correct to attribute
his view to Duns Scotus, or to the influence of scientific technique.   Though the
origin of pragmatism be obscure, it is clear that the idea that pragmatism originated
with Peirce was originated by James.

the first to christen it and to seize on its wide implications. James and Peirce were no doubt both of them confirmed in this tendency by the positivism of Chauncey Wright. For positivism, springing from the experimental method in science, insists on construing concepts in terms of the verifying experiences or "operations" to which they lead.

As to Peirce's influence on James, it is well to compare the latter's various acknowledgments. The first was published in 1884. After arguing that it should be our aim to find "sensational *termini*" for our thought, he said, "If two men act alike on a percept, they believe themselves to feel alike about it." Whereupon he quoted the following from Peirce: — "There is no distinction of meaning so fine as to consist in anything but a possible difference of practice. . . . It appears, then, that the rule for attaining the [highest] grade of clearness of apprehension is as follows: Consider what effects, which might conceivably have practical bearings, we conceive the object of our conception to have. Then, our conception of these effects is the whole of our conception of the object." [7]

In the address of 1898, James credits Peirce with giving his thought "the most likely direction in which to start up the trail of truth," and defines this "direction" as the idea that "the effective meaning of any philosophic proposition can always be brought down to some particular consequence, in our future practical experience, whether active or passive; the point lying rather in the fact that the experience must be particular, than in the fact that it must be active." [8] In this address and in an allusion of 1902 James identifies pragmatism with "the great English way of investigating a conception," namely, to look for its "cash-value in terms of particular experience"; and credits Peirce with singling out and naming the principle by which English and Scotch philosophers "were instinctively guided." [9] In 1904 he credits Peirce with the word "pragmatism," and says that he (James) uses it to indicate "a method of carrying on abstract discussion," according to which "the serious meaning of a concept lies . . . in the concrete difference to someone which its being true will make." [10]

It appears from these passages that Peirce made James acutely

[7] *M.T.*, 40.
[8] *C.E.R.*, 412.
[9] *C.E.R.*, 434; *V.R.E.*, 444.
[10] *C.E.R.*, 448; *M.T.*, 51.

conscious of an idea which he had already imbibed, and continued to imbibe, from many sources; and that this idea was to the effect that the meaning of a concept lay in its putting a particular face on a situation and thereby provoking a particular action.   James assumes that when perceived facts are altered, something is done about it, and that the meaning of a concept consists in perceptual (and therefore practical) expectations.   If these expectations are the same, two concepts mean the same; if there are none, a concept is meaningless.

But while it is clear that this is the idea which Peirce helped to lodge firmly and centrally in James's mind, it is by no means clear that this was Peirce's idea.   It is quite possible, in fact probable, that Peirce's idea underwent clarification and that when he first discussed it in the early '70s it was sufficiently flexible to justify James's interpretation of it.   It is probable even that James's interpretation stimulated Peirce to sharpen his own interpretation. In any case, Peirce's pragmatism became so different a thing from the pragmatism which James attributed to him that he felt obliged to change its name, although he did not decline the honor. Writing to Mrs. Ladd-Franklin in 1905, he said: "Although James calls himself a pragmatist, and no doubt he derived his ideas on the subject from me, yet there is a most essential difference between his pragmatism and mine." [11]   In the same year, speaking of the current misuses of the term, he said: "So then, the writer, finding his bantling 'pragmatism' so promoted, feels that it is time to kiss his child good-by and relinquish it to its higher destiny; while to serve the precise purpose of expressing the original definition, he begs to announce the birth of the word "pragmaticism,' which is ugly enough to be safe from kidnappers." [12]   Now it is a nice question whether it is possible to "derive" from a philosopher ideas which he has never had; or whether one may not reasonably doubt the paternity of a bantling which, as it grows older, becomes increasingly dissimilar to its father.   Perhaps it would be correct, and just to all parties, to say that the modern movement known as pragmatism is largely the result of James's misunderstanding of Peirce.

According to his own definition, Peirce's pragmatism (or pragmaticism) differs from that of James in two respects.   In the

[11] *Jour. of Philos.*, XIII (1916), 718.
[12] *Monist*, XV (1905), 165–6.

first place, the meaning of a concept is construed in terms of conduct, and not in terms of sensation; and, in the second place, it is construed in terms of generality and not in terms of particularity. Peirce urges us to "consider what effects, which might conceivably have practical bearings, we conceive the object of our conception to have." [13] James, on the other hand, in what Peirce called "an exegesis not very deep," identifies the meaning of a conception with the practical consequences of its being true, but then goes on to specify "consequences either in the shape of conduct to be recommended, or in that of experiences to be expected."

So far, then, Peirce puts the emphasis on conduct, while James speaks of future details of experience *or* conduct — "future practical experience, whether active *or* passive." [14] Construed in the light of James's empiricism, the explicit provision for passive experience is significant. With James, thought points to sensory acquaintance. Peirce, on the other hand, interprets thought not in terms of immediacies to which it leads, but in terms of operation and control. At the same time, he had little or no interest in the *"will* to believe" — he supposed the "effects which might conceivably have practical bearings" to be prescribed by the object. Peirce was as constitutionally averse to credulity as was James to skepticism. [15]

The second difference reflects Peirce's emphasis on generalization. "Practical bearings" mean bearings on the *purpose* of action — which turns out to be "concrete reasonableness," or becoming "governed by law," or "instinct with general ideas." Pragmatism thus obtains a new statement: "The entire intellectual purport of any symbol consists in the total of all general modes of rational conduct which, conditionally upon all the possible different circumstances and desires, would ensue upon the acceptance of the symbol." [16]

In short, for Peirce a conception has meaning only in so far as it expresses and promotes the idea of a well-ordered life. It is

---

[13] "How to Make Our Ideas Clear," *Pop. Science Mo.,* XII (1878), 293. This is from the authentic definition, cited above; repeated by Peirce in the article "Pragmatic and Pragmatism," *Dict. of Philos. and Psychol.,* 1902; and in his "Issues of Pragmatism," *Monist,* XV (1905), 481.

[14] *C.E.R.,* 412, 417.

[15] *Cf.* Peirce's early article on "Fixation of Belief," *Pop. Science Mo.,* XII (1877) ; and his remarks on James's *Will to Believe,* above, 222–3.

[16] *Dict. of Philos. and Psychol., loc. cit.; Monist,* XV (1905), 481 ; above, 222.

a habit reflecting the stability and uniformity of things; and its formation is at once an adaptation to this stability and uniformity, and a participation in its growth.   With James, on the other hand, the significance of a conception lies in its leading into the field of particulars and adapting the agent to the exigencies that arise therein.   It is not merely that Peirce is more explicit in linking pragmatism to an ethical ideal, but also that there is an important difference *in* that ideal.   For Peirce the good lies in coherence, order, coalescence, unity; for James in the individuality, variety, and satisfaction of concrete interests.

Another group of Peirce's ideas influenced James's metaphysical pluralism.   These ideas saw the light in a series of articles published in the *Monist* in the years 1891–1893, and which James predicted would "prove a gold-mine of ideas for thinkers of the coming generation." [17]   "Tychism," "synechism," and "agapism" were Peirce's terms for his doctrines of chance, continuity, and love, respectively.   Their relation to James's corresponding doctrines is parallel to the case of pragmatism: James found labels, as well as stimulation and confirmation, in Peirce, but the two sets of ideas were profoundly different.   James, who liked to dwell on doctrinal similarities and philosophical coöperation, emphasized the likeness; while Peirce, who cared more for the precision of his views than for their general physiognomy, emphasized the unlikeness.

With James, tychism, or the doctrine of chance, first commended itself as providing for moral freedom.   It was also agreeable to his fundamental empiricism — to his view that in the last analysis existence is inexplicable.   But Peirce was not interested in either of these ideas, and the second was repugnant to him.   He always refused to accept pure data, whether as limiting explanation or as providing intuition in its place.   To him tychism was acceptable primarily because it reflected the logic of probability, or the statistical and approximative method of science.   And he generalized it to mean that order is a derived and growing aspect of the world: nature acquires laws as a man acquires habits, and in this consist both its evolution and its progress.

As time went on James's view of chance as the sheer impact of the inexplicable, a happening out of the blue, gave way to the idea

[17] *P.U.*, 398.   In this passage James goes on to identify Peirce's ideas with Bergson's.

of "novelty." The novel is in a sense inexplicable, but it need not be abrupt; it may *grow out* of what precedes it, and in that way *belong* to the context in which it arises.[18] "Synechism" meant for James that reality, in being thus continuous and flowing, escapes the logic of identity. For Peirce, on the other hand, synechism was a way of reconciling chance with logic. The continuity of things means that there is always room for further analysis. The pressure of logic forces us to regard every terminus as further explicable. For James there is an unexplained which is inexplicable, and which *needs* no explanation because experience conveys it adequately. For Peirce this same residuum of the unexplained means that the universe is forever explicable.[19]

Peirce gave the name of "agapism" to his doctrine of "evolutionary love." There is a kinship between this doctrine and the fundamental place which James gives to the experience of activity in his later writings. But the disagreement in detail is very striking. For Peirce embraces hate within love as one of its necessary aspects, thus solving the problem of evil in that monistic fashion which James so emphatically repudiates; and Peirce lays stress on the social or corporate personality in a manner quite incompatible with James's uncompromising individualism.[20]

The correspondence between James and Peirce was one-sided, Peirce's letters being literally *voluminous*. It was not that James had less to say, but that he had other channels of distribution. To James, Peirce was one among dozens of correspondents, hundreds of friends, and thousands of readers; while to Peirce, James served both as confidant and as public. And when James wrote to Peirce he was usually so preoccupied with Peirce's personal problems that his mood was unsuited to philosophizing. This correspondence has already been followed intermittently down to the publication of *The Will to Believe,* in 1897. In order to trace the influence of Peirce on James's ultimate metaphysics, however, it is necessary to return to the spring of 1892. James was about to depart for Europe, where he was to remain for fifteen months; and Peirce was in Cambridge, apparently lecturing.[21]

[18] Cf. *P.U.*, 391-2, note; *S.P.P.*, Ch. XII, XIII.
[19] Cf. Peirce's article on "Synechism" in the *Dict. of Philos. and Psychol.*
[20] *Monist,* III (1892-3).
[21] Peirce did not begin his Lowell Institute course (twelve lectures) on "The History of Science" until Nov. 28, 1892, and at that time James was in Europe.

[Cambridge, May 1892]

Dear Charles, —

It has been a great chagrin to me to have you here all this time without meeting or hearing you. I especially wanted to hear you on "Continuity," and I hear of a godlike talk at Royce's. But "Continuity" will appear in the *Monist*. *Talks* can never come again!! "Was man von der Minute ausgeschlagen, gibt keine Ewigkeit zurück." [22] . . . I meant to write you long ago to say how I enjoyed your last paper in the *Monist*.[23] I believe in that sort of thing myself, but even if I did n't it would be a blessed piece of radicalism. Pray send it to Charles Renouvier . . . and to J. Delbœuf. . . . It will strengthen their hands. . . . Ever fondly thine,

W. J.

In 1893 Peirce drew up the prospectus of a work on "The Principles of Philosophy," in twelve volumes: —

Milford, Jan. 1, 1894

My dear James, —

A happy New Year to you, and unless your situation has been exceptional, may it be as unlike the dead year now in hell as possible! I wrote to you enclosing a copy of a prospectus of my treatise on philosophy. I directed it to Columbia College, where I assumed you would be, and asked you to write me a letter·expressive of your interest with leave to print the same. No answer has yet come. Perhaps you were not there. I now enclose *another* prospectus. A third and fourth are to come. I do not feel at all sure of getting subscribers enough to begin. If I do begin, I feel pretty sure there will be interest enough in the thing before I get through.

There is nothing in your psychology which serves my purposes better than your distinction between "substantive" and "transitive" parts of the train of thought. I had been forced to emphasize a precisely corresponding distinction in logic, where one of the most important and difficult operations is to catch the transitive on the wing and nail it down in substantive form. But the word "transitive" has been used for other purposes. For one thing, in the

---

[22] "That which is excluded from the moment no eternity will restore."
[23] "Continuity" appeared under the title of "The Law of Mind," *Monist*, II (1891–2); and the "last paper" was "The Doctrine of Necessity Examined," *ibid.*

logic of relatives (by De Morgan and me) ; by another in the closely related theory of substitutions ; and now you propose to add to the confusion and render your own thought hard to get at, by using this same word.   Why is this word better than "transient" for your purpose?   If I were you, having called the other "substantive," a word well chosen and derived from the terminology of grammar, I would call these others "adjective."   I would either go to grammar for both terms or for neither.   You might term them "volatile" and "sessile"; or, after Homer . . . "winged" and "unwinged"; or, if you want Greek, "planetic" and "aplanetic."   Perhaps you mean "transitive" to be taken from grammar.   If so, the analogy is not clear.   Besides, that would spoil your "substantive," which surely has nothing to do with the substantive verb.   I wish to make use of the distinction, and hence would like to know what improved terminology you would accept.   Very faithfully,

C. S. PEIRCE

In reply to the request for a letter expressive of interest in Peirce's "treatise," James sent the following, which Peirce printed and circulated : "I am heartily glad to learn that you are preparing to publish the results of your philosophizing in a complete and connected form.   Pray consider me a subscriber to the whole series. There is no more original thinker than yourself in our generation. You have personally suggested more important things to me than perhaps anyone whom I have known; and I have never given you sufficient public credit for all that you have taught me.   I am sure that this systematic work will increase my debt."

Cambridge, Jan. 24, 1894

My dear Charles, —

My interminable "grip" has thrown me into such arrears that I am lucky to write to you at all.   You have very likely forgotten by this time your question about "substantive" and "transitive" states.   To my mind it is well not to strain language already in use any more than one can help in creating technical terms. "Volatile" and "sessile" seem decidedly too metaphorical; and in thinking over the matter I don't see why plain "relational" is not after all the most practical epithet to adopt.

I hope that subscribers to your *magnum opus* come in.   It may be that if the more distant thunder had been held in reserve, and the first three volumes alone announced at present, the circular would have met with a better response; but it ought to be responded to as it is. . . . People are afraid of schemes too vast and ambitious — and also threatening to be too expensive. *I* hope for the whole set, but all men are not as I! Yours heartily,

WM. JAMES

P.S. Do you, by the way, know of any other author than Delbœuf and in a manner yourself, who has treated the inorganic as a sort of product of the living? I know I have come across such a speculation but I can no longer think where.[24]

Milford, Jan. *27*, 1894

My dear William, —

The objection to my book that it is so long is a real one, but it seems to me intrinsic. The peculiarity of my philosophy is that it leads to positive predictions comparable with observation. Without that, it would be a nonentity. Now that cannot be shown except at great length. . . . To compress the work into twelve volumes requires the severest kind of selection of materials. But the volumes will be small and of small specific gravity. Nothing so light has been written in philosophy since Voltaire. . . . Very faithfully,

C. S. PEIRCE

Milford, Jan. 28, 1894

Dear William, —

. . . You ask whether I know of anybody but Delbœuf and myself "who has treated the inorganic as a sort of product of the living"? This is good. An instance, no doubt, of that wonderful originality for which I am so justly admired. Your papa, for one, believed in creation, and so did the authors of all the religions. But my views were probably influenced by Schelling, — by all stages of Schelling, but especially by the *Philosophie der Natur*.[25] I consider Schelling as enormous; and one thing I admire about him is his freedom from the trammels of system, and his holding

---

[24] *Cf*. above, I, 472, note 9.
[25] For the doctrine that physical laws are habits of nature, *cf*. also F. Ravaisson's *De l'Habitude,* 1838, influenced by Schelling.

himself uncommitted to any previous utterance. In that, he is like a scientific man. If you were to call my philosophy Schellingism transformed in the light of modern physics, I should not take it hard. . . .

I consider "relational" as the most perversely bad designation it would be easy to give for your "transitive" states. If you find "volatile" and "sessile" too metaphorical it probably indicates that you conceive the states a little differently from what I do. . . . Homer speaks of winged and unwinged words to denote two different kinds or grades of attention. That is, that is what seems to be meant, if anything is meant. Words are always winged in the *Iliad,* I believe, and unwinged in the *Odyssey.* Shall we say "pteroent" and "apteroent"? Yours faithfully,

C. S. PEIRCE

James was indefatigable in his efforts to improve Peirce's situation. He succeeded in finding him temporary lectureships, but the effort made in 1895 to secure a regular appointment at Harvard was fruitless. President Eliot was courteous, but unmoved: —

Cambridge, March 3, 1895

Dear President, —

I hate to hunt you down with disagreeable college problems, but how is a Supreme Being to hide from his creatures? The problem is this. The Philosophic Department has met to arrange the courses for next year, and my taking charge of psychology means, as I told you, that I ought not to do anything else and that the important course in "Cosmology" or "Philosophy of Nature" . . . must either be dropped for next year or given to some outsider. Now I want to propose to you no less a person than Charles S. Peirce, whose name I don't suppose will make you bound with eagerness at first, but you may think better of it after a short reflection. . . . He is the best man by far in America for such a course, and one of the best men living. The better graduates would flock to hear him — his name is one of mysterious greatness for them now — and he would leave a wave of influence, tradition, gossip, etc. that would n't die away for many years. *I* should learn a lot from his course. Everyone knows of Peirce's personal uncomfortableness; and if I were President I should n't hope for a harmonious wind-up to his connection with the University.   But I should take that as part of the disagreeableness of the day's work, and shut my eyes and go ahead, knowing that from the highest intellectual point of view it would be the best thing that could happen for the graduates of the Philosophical Department.   It would also advertise us as doing all we could, and making the best of every emergency; and it would be a recognition of C. S. P.'s strength, which I am sure is but justice to the poor fellow.   I truly believe that the path of (possibly) least comfort is here the *true* path, so I have no hesitation in urging my opinion.   A telegraphic answer to *me* will be understood: "yes," for "invite him"; "no," for "let the matter drop." . . .   Always truly yours,

WM. JAMES

P.S. There is no one beside Peirce who could be thought of to do cosmology.   We have been able to think of no other name. . . .

Eliot's cable reply to this read: "Neither Peirce nor Ladd. Consider Fiske and Russell"; and in a letter he added, "All that you say of C. S. Peirce's remarkable capacities and acquisitions is true, and I heartily wish that it seemed to me possible for the University to make use of them."

Provided a sufficient number of subscribers were obtained, Peirce's *magnum opus* was to be published by the Pike County Press.   James sent the following note in the autumn of 1895: "Here goes my subscription to the Pike County Press, a most extraordinary sounding vehicle for your lucubrations, but such seems to be *la comédie humaine*.   I don't know whether you know a most exquisite literary metaphysic genius named B. P. Blood who lives in Amsterdam, N. Y., and publishes his flights in the *Albany Times*.   Your case transcends his both in the loftiness of the matter and the lowliness of the channel."

The intellectual relations between James and Peirce were most intimate in the decade of 1897–1907.   Peirce was much touched by James's dedication of *The Will to Believe,* and as James began to put together his system of metaphysics he felt that Peirce was on his side, as a partisan not only of practicalism, but of "cosmic variableness."   As the years passed, however, the surface of agreement was rubbed away, exposing the hard ribs of difference, both

in method and in detail.   A subordinate, but persistent and illuminating theme is provided by the problem of Peirce's public lectures — when, where, what, how?

Writing to James on May 30, 1897, Peirce said: "I heard some
months ago through Dr. [Paul] Carus that you were endeavoring to
get me some opportunity to teach logic in Cambridge. . . .   In the
main — that is, in holding that belief is fundamentally a practical
matter — you and I seem to be in full accord; and if we were together there, we would make an impression upon the philosophical
world, and thus upon scientific men, upon teachers, and ultimately
upon the current of the world's thought."   In December, Peirce sent
James an outline of the proposed eight lectures.   The headings were
as follows: 1. Logical Graphs.   2. Lessons of the Logic of Relatives.
3. Induction and Hypothesis.   4. The Categories.   5. the Attraction of Ideas.   6. Objective Deduction.   7. Objective Induction
and Hypothesis.   8. Creation.   The following is James's acknowledgment: —

Cambridge, Dec. 22 [1897]
Dear Charles, —

. . . I am sorry you are sticking so to formal logic.   I know
our graduate school here, and so does Royce, and we both agree
that there are only three men who could possibly follow your graphs
and relatives.   Are not such highly abstract and mathematically
conceived things to be read rather than heard; and ought you not, at
the cost of originality, remembering that a *lecture* must succeed
as such, to give a very minimum of formal logic and get on to
metaphysic, psychology and cosmogony almost immediately?

There is stuff enough in the first two volumes of the prospectus
of your system,[26] to give a short course without infringing on any
mathematical symbolism, I am sure — to say nothing of the other
volumes.   Now be a good boy and think a more popular plan out.
I don't want the audience to dwindle to three or four, and I don't
see how one can help that on the program you propose.   I don't
insist on an audience of more than fifteen or sixteen, but you ought
certainly to aim at that, and that does n't condemn you to be wishy-
washy.   *You* can hardly conceive how little interest exists in the

[26] According to the prospectus, the title of Vol. I was "Review of the Leading
Ideas of the Nineteenth Century," and of Vol. II, "Theory of Demonstrative Reasoning."

purely formal aspects of logic.   Things on that subject ought to be *printed* for the scattered few.   You are teeming with ideas, and the lectures need not by any means form a continuous whole.   Separate topics of a vitally important character would do perfectly well. There would be sure — you lecturing — to be enough unity involuntarily there.   What *I* should like is anti-nominalism, categories, attraction of ideas, hypothesis, tychism and synechism. . . .   Write, now, that you accept all these conditions, and pray keep the lectures as unmathematical as in you lies.   With the best of hopes, I am yours ever,

WM. JAMES

New York, Dec. 26, 1897

My dear William, —

I accept all your conditions.   I have no doubt you gauge the capacity of your students rightly.   It agrees with all I hear and the little I have seen of Cambridge, though the method of graphs has proved quite easy to New Yorkers, whose minds are stimulated by New York life, — people as remote from the mathematical world as anybody in New York.   My philosophy, however, is not an "idea" with which I "brim over"; it is a serious research to which there is no royal road; and the part of it which is most closely connected with formal logic is by far the easiest and least intricate. People who cannot reason exactly (which alone *is* reasoning), simply cannot understand my philosophy, — neither the process, methods, nor results.   The neglect of logic in Cambridge is plainly absolute. My philosophy, and all philosophy worth attention, reposes entirely upon the theory of logic.   It will, therefore, be impossible for me to give any idea of the nature either of my philosophy or of any other of any account.

In consequence of your saying you wanted to hear something about *synechism* and the tychism which is a corollary of it, I have already written my Lecture VIII — the most difficult, supposing that all the rest had been given as I planned them.   But as long as you think that lectures to fifteen or sixteen of your students will be more valuable, I will begin again, and will endeavor to write out some of the "ideas" with which I am supposed to be "teeming" on "separate topics of vital importance."   I feel I shall not do it well, because in spite of myself I shall betray my sentiments about such "ideas"; but being paid to do it, I will do it as well as I possibly can.   After all, I have no reason to distress myself that my philosophy does not get expounded.   Your Harvard students of philosophy find it too arduous a matter to reason exactly.   Soon your engineers will find it better to leave great works unbuilt rather than go through the necessary calculations. And Harvard is only a little in advance of the rest of the country on this road, and this country a little in advance of Europe.   The Japanese will come and kick us out, and in the fulness of time *he* will come to the questions which my philosophy answers, and with patience will find the Key, as I have done. . . .

I am perfectly indifferent about times and hours.   I shall be clay in the hands of the potter.   I wish I had to sing comic songs and dance, though I should do *it* badly.   But I am not puritan enough to understand the pleasure of these chins on "topics of vitally important character."   The audience had better go home and say their prayers, I am thinking.

C. S. P.

It is unfortunate that James's reply to this letter is not extant. Presumably he was still trying to persuade Peirce to be "a good boy," though with only partial success, as the following will indicate: —

Milford, Jan. 4, 1898

Dear William, —

Neither of your interpretations of my letter were right.   (It is so cold in this room, 34°, that I can hardly write.)   I saw the force of what you said, but was deeply disappointed.   I have, however, commenced all over again and have written one lecture, and rewritten it, to condense it, and still it is twice too long, — and not very much in it either.   But I drop that for the time being and am half way through another.   I have my eye on the Corporation, but as you know that my style of "brilliancy" consists in a mixture of irony and seriousness —the same things said ironically and also seriously, I mean — I doubt if said Corporation will see the point.   I fear they will think they had better steer clear of me. . . .

I propose to entitle the course "Detached Ideas on Vitally Important Topics." The first lecture is about "vitally important topics," showing that where they are "vital" there is little chance for philosophy in them . . . vitally important topics are, as I say, "the outline of huge mountains above which we descry a silvery peak far higher yet." The second lecture is about "detached thoughts," and is intended to show that however little time people may have for connected thought outside their business, yet it is better to make it as connected as possible, not shunning detached ideas, but seeking to assimilate them. This enables me to say something about "Nominalism and Realism," and apropos of that of my own philosophical labors. My third lecture is to be upon the highest maxim of logic, — which is that the only strictly indispensable requisite is that the inquirer shall want to learn the truth.

In another lecture I have determined to say something about "Time and Causation." . . . What I shall say in the other lectures I have as yet no idea whatever. I dare say something may occur to me. Very faithfully and gratefully,

C. S. PEIRCE

The eight lectures were eventually delivered (beginning February 12, 1898) at the residence of Mrs. Ole Bull on Brattle Street, Cambridge. The title announced for the whole course was, "Reasoning and the Logic of Things." [27] It was of these lectures that Royce wrote to James in 1901: "As for thoughts, of late I seem to myself to be on the track of a great number of interesting topics in logic. Those lectures of poor C. S. Peirce that you devised will always remain quite epoch-making for me. They started me on such new tracks."

[27] For the first lecture, cf. Collected Papers, Vol. I, Bk. IV, Ch. 5. The topics of the several lectures were as follows: 1. Philosophy and the Conduct of Life. 2. Types of Reasoning. 3. The Logic of Relatives. 4. The First Rule of Logic. 5. Training in Reasoning. 6. Causation and Force. 7. Habit. 8. The Logic of Continuity.

LXXVI

JAMES AND PEIRCE: RELATIONS PHILOSOPHICAL AND PERSONAL

IN 1903 Peirce interested himself in James's election to the National Academy of Sciences. In supporting this nomination Peirce was in part influenced by the fact that in the previous year he had criticized James (and Royce) in a manuscript which was circulated in Cambridge — the original draft of the opening part of his "Minute Logic." In this manuscript James was recognizable as a "man of strength" who "proceeds slap-dash," and "has but the vaguest notion of how he has come by his principles." As to Royce, he was linked with Descartes as representing that library of modern metaphysics which contains hardly "a single argument which does not leave room to drive a coach and four through it, commodiously." [1] A letter of explanation was written to James's wife: —

Milford, April 12 [1902]

My dear Mrs. James, —

. . . I am starting for Washington tomorrow in order to become a member of the Committee on Anthropology, and have the matter righted; since as it stands, it is hardly to the credit of the Academy, much less to its advantage. I write to you about it, simply because there are always people in the world who are placed here apparently for the sake of putting the conduct of others into the worst light; and I do not want any friends of William to think that I have not asserted his just claim to be called the first psychologist living or that ever lived. I wish if you hear any such whispers that you would say vaguely that you are assured that I have the highest admiration for William.

Of course there are some points on which I disagree with him and in manuscript I have said so in exaggerated terms which result

---

[1] These disparaging remarks were deleted by Peirce himself from the typewritten copy reproduced in *Collected Papers*, Vol. II, Bk. I, Ch. 2, § 9.

from my hermit life. But before going to press, I shall take measures to correct that. I have spoken of Royce in the same manuscript in language still further from my real opinion. You see it is like this. I came back from ten days' absence in the last week of November. Yesterday I met the village clergyman and had a talk with him of twenty minutes. During the interval, I had had not over half a dozen chats with my wife, chiefly sustained by her in French, and otherwise had n't spoken two consecutive sentences to anybody. There were four or five months' silence. It is not an exceptional period. I live always so. In this life I find I lose all discernment of grades of expression; and, in particular, in endeavoring to express mild divergence of views use language that is adapted only to convey the idea of utter hostility. . . . I felt I must explain myself, or run the risk of being horribly misinterpreted by William James's friends, to all of whom, as friends of his, I entertain deep feelings of respect and regard.

C. S. PEIRCE

At the same time that Peirce was pressing James's election to the National Academy, James was engaged with a number of other influential persons in an unsuccessful effort to persuade the Carnegie Corporation to subsidize Peirce during his preparation of a *magnum opus* on logic. In his "emphatic letter to Gilman" James stated that he had learned more from Peirce than from any philosopher except Royce.

Ryc, May 2, 1902

Dear Charles, ——

Your letter to my wife was a touching mark of your considerateness to me, but an overestimate of my possible feelings about the National Academy of Science. When Cattell was elected, I thought it absolutely correct, —— he for every reason should be a member. Agassiz asked me a year ago if I should accept membership if offered (and I replied that I would) so I supposed that some movement might be going on. But it would be in my case, I suppose, little more than a formal honor, and I shan't lose appetite for a single meal at being passed by. I thank you most heartily for the interest you show and (as I now learn) have shown in the matter, and beg you to take no more trouble on my account. That *you* should elect me is morally better than election by the Academy!

I wrote shortly before leaving home a most emphatic letter to Gilman in favor of your receiving a Carnegie Grant. I was finishing my own book [*Varieties*] under pressure of time, and could read but little of the logic manuscript which J. M. Peirce gave me. Royce read more of it. It was, of course, *great*. The personal abuse which you now accuse yourself of lavishing upon my undeserving head escaped, I am sorry to say, my attention. It would no doubt have enhanced my admiration, for I delight in abuse if it be only racy enough, and in this case it needs no explanation by the effects of social isolation upon your powers of expression. Royce enjoyed the passage in which you coupled his name with Descartes. . . . My wife and I both thank you for your so kind-hearted letter, and I am always your friend,

WILLIAM JAMES

Milford, June 12, 1902

My dear William, —

I owe you the expression of my gratitude for what you have done to induce the Carnegie Institution to aid me to produce my Logic. Try to think of something further to do; for things look blue. . . .

There is a point of psychology which has been interesting me. . . . The question is what passes in consciousness . . . in the course of forming a new belief. . . . I had got to that point when the expressman came in bringing me the copy of your new book. I have spent five minutes turning over the leaves. I can see what the general feature of your position is, sufficiently to say that I am heartily in accord with you. I say to people — imaginary interlocutors, for I have nobody to talk to — you think that the proposition that truth and justice are the greatest powers in this world is metaphorical. Well, I, for my part, hold it to be *true*. No doubt truth has to have defenders to uphold it. But truth creates its defenders and gives them strength. The mode in which the idea of truth influences the world is essentially the same as that in which my desire to have the fire poked causes me to get up and poke it. There is efficient causation, and there is final, or ideal, causation. If either of them is to be set down as a metaphor, it is rather the former. Pragmatism is correct doctrine only in so far as it is recognized that material action is the mere husk of ideas. The brute element exists, and must not be explained away, as Hegel seeks to do. But the end of thought is action only in so far as the end of action is another thought. Far better abandon the word "thought," and talk of "representation," and then *define* what kind of a representation it is that constitutes consciousness.

But I want to tell you that you should study the new ideas about multitude and continuity (I alone as yet understand continuity, and have published nothing since I mastered it). Ah, my logic will give a tremendous boost to spiritual views! I hope it will get finished, although *personally* it makes mighty little odds to me. . . . With your notions of spiritual influence, why don't you join the Church? Surely you won't allow metaphysical formulæ, dead as the dust of the catacombs, to deprive you of your RIGHT to the influences of the Church. I have been studying Royce's [*World and the Individual*]. The ideas are very beautiful. The logic is most execrable. I don't think it very good taste to stuff it so full of the name of God. The Absolute is, strictly speaking, only God in a Pickwickian sense, that is, in a sense that has no effect. Forgive the garrulity that comes of my eremitical life and God bless you!

C. S. PEIRCE

Milford, Jan. 23, 1903

Dear William, —

I this morning received your "Syllabus of Philosophy 3," [2] which you have neglected to *date*. It is a work demanding long study and will be extremely valuable to me. Its brief form is a great assistance and it is marvellously clear. I will now make such remarks as occur to me on a first perusal of it.

Berkeley on the whole has more right to be considered the introducer of pragmatism into philosophy than any other one man, though I was more explicit in enunciating it.

To the question "How explain this harmony?" [3] you give a number of answers. None of these *are* explanations, but they are *proposals* of *how* to try to explain the harmony. They do not conflict with one another. They simply have different purposes in view. The theistic idea is the only one that satisfies practical needs. But a "design" is a thought. A thought by its nature

[2] *Cf.* Appendix IX.
[3] Between nature and our rational demands.

cannot be present, — it only exists in the sense that it is destined to work itself out. So, at least, says pragmatism. Hence . . . it is needful to introduce the idea of the co-evolution of mind and reality . . . some hypothesis of the nature of tychism, the value of which can only be estimated when sufficient time has elapsed to enable us to see what hopes there may be of predicting future knowledge on that basis. That which for scientific purposes can only be regarded as chance must undoubtedly be regarded by the pragmatist as designed, if it always tends to rationalization. . . .

I can't admit at all your metaphysical tychism, which seems to me untenable. The true solution of the problem of evil is precisely that of *Substance and Shadow*.[4] There may be a something over us not infinite, but *that* it is a misnomer to call *divine*. The continuous is the potential. But the real is composed of the potential and actual *together*. As for Zeno's "argument" — *what* argument, I should be glad to know? State it definitely to a mathematician. I can't admit your statement of the pragmatical conception of infinity. I don't think you have sufficiently studied infinity. Very faithfully, but stopping abruptly to catch mail.

C. S. PEIRCE

In the spring of 1903 (March 26–May 14) Peirce again lectured in Cambridge, this time under the auspices of the University, and on the subject of "Pragmatism"; and in the autumn of the same year (November 23–December 17) he gave a course of Lowell Lectures in Boston on "Logic and Other Philosophical Subjects." There were the usual preliminaries between him and James. Thus "William" to "Charles" on March 13: "At last, 'under Providence,' I have been able to give a slight boost to your affairs. The Corporation of Harvard University have voted to authorize six university lectures by you. . . . You can *name* them as you like. The fifty students whom I have had in Philosophy 3 (of which I sent the syllabus) are well primed with 'pragmatism' and 'tychism,' and would be glad to hear of them from you direct. For 'synechism' you have virgin soil."

To which Peirce replied on March 16: "I just received your letter this afternoon. Nothing could be so gratifying to me. . . . I . . . think that the six lectures had better be confined to the single subject

[4] Referring to the book by H.J.'

of pragmatism, which, as I understand it, is one of the propositions of logic. Its foundation, definition and limitation, and applications to philosophy, to the sciences, and to the conduct of life will make quite enough for six lectures. . . . My dear William, I do not yet thank you. . . . You are of all my friends the one who illustrates *pragmatism* in its most needful forms. You are a jewel of pragmatism."

None of these lectures were published during Peirce's lifetime, but they were written out and preserved. The manuscript of two of them was left in James's possession.[5]

Chocorua, June 5, 1903

Dear Charles, —

I return your two lectures under a separate envelope to Milford, but send this to Cambridge, thinking you may possibly still be there. They are wonderful things — I have read the second one twice — but so original, and your categories are so unusual to other minds, that, although I recognize the region of thought and the profundity and reality of the level on which you move, I do not yet assimilate the various theses in the sense of being able to make a use of them for my own purposes. I may get to it later; but at present even first-, second-, and third-ness[6] are outside of my own sphere of practically applying things, and I am not sure even whether I apprehend them as you mean them to be apprehended. I get, throughout your whole business, only the sense of something dazzling and imminent in the way of truth. This is very likely partly due to my mind being so non-mathematical, and to my slight interest in logic; but I am probably typical of a great many of your auditors — of the majority — so my complaint will be theirs.[7] You spoke of publishing these lectures, but not, I hope, *tel quels*. They need too much mediation, by more illustrations, at which you are excellent (non-mathematical ones if possible), and by a good deal of interstitial expansion and comparison with other modes of thought. What I wish myself is that you might *revise these lectures* for your Lowell

[5] The Cambridge lectures on "Pragmatism" appear in *Collected Papers*, Vol. V, with short extracts in other volumes.

[6] "Firstness," "secondness," and "thirdness" are the names given by Peirce to the three fundamental categories of "quality, reaction and mediation" (*Collected Papers*, Vol. I, 280). "Abduction" is the method of hypothesis (*cf. ibid.*, Vol. I, II, Index).

[7] "Your mind inhabits a technical logical thicket of its own into which no other mind has as yet penetrated." (W.J. to Peirce, July 10, 1903.)

course, possibly confining yourself to fewer points (such as the uses of the first-, second-, and third-ness distinction, the generality involved in perception, the nature of abduction — this last to me tremendously important); make each of them tremendously emphatic, avoid collateral matter, except what is illustrative and comparative, avoid polemic as such (you have very successfully done so), keep the ignoramus in view as your auditor, and I have no doubt you'll be a great success. As things stand, it is only highly skilled technicians and professionals who will sniff the rare perfume of your thought, and *after you are dead,* trace things back to your genius. You ought to gain a bigger audience *when living;* and, if next year you can only score a popular success, it will do much to help your later prospects. I fear that if you make a new course of lectures altogether, they will prove too technical and wonder-arousing and not flagrantly illuminating enough. Whereas, by revising these, you will not only give yourself less trouble, but also do the best possible thing for your audience. You cannot start with too low an idea of their intelligence. Look at me, as one!

Your visit to Cambridge was a refreshing interlude to all of us, I only wish that I had not been in such abominable condition. It was a great pleasure to both myself and my wife to know Mrs. Peirce, to whom pray give our warm regards. Have a good summer, and believe me ever truly yours,

WM. JAMES

Milford, June 8, 1903

My dear William, —

I got your letter and the two lectures this morning. As for my Lowell Institute lectures, I intend to have just as little pure theory in them as possible. I don't think even my Harvard audience was quite fit for that. What they need is logical training — lessons, not lectures; and I mean to have my Lowell Lectures approach as near to practical lessons in reasoning as *lectures* can.

It rather annoys me to be told that there is anything novel in my three categories; for if they have not, however confusedly, been recognized by men since men began to think, that condemns them at once. To make them as distinct as it is in their nature to be is, however, no small task. I do not suppose they are so in my own mind; and evidently, it is not in their nature to be as sharp as ordinary concepts. But I am going to try to make here a brief statement that, I think, will do something for them.

By the phenomenon I mean whatever is before our minds in any sense. The three categories are supposed to be the three kinds of elements that attentive perception can make out in the phenomenon. The practical exigencies of life render "secondness" the most prominent of the three. This is not a conception, nor is it a peculiar quality. It is an experience. It comes out most fully in the shock of reaction between ego and non-ego. It is there the double consciousness of effort and resistance. That is something which cannot properly be conceived. For to conceive it is to generalize it; and to generalize it is to miss altogether the *hereness* and *nowness* which is its essence. . . . All the *actual* character of consciousness is merely the sense of the shock of the non-ego upon us. Just as a calm sea sleeps except where its rollers dash upon the land.

If we imagine that feeling retains its positive character but absolutely loses all relation (and thereby all *vividness,* which is only the sense of shock), it no longer is exactly what we call feeling. It is a mere sense of quality. It is the sort of element that makes *red* to be such as it is, whatever anything else may be. I do not see how that can be described except as being such as it is, positively, of itself [firstness], while secondness is such as it is relatively to something else. . . .

The third element of the phenomenon is that we perceive it to be intelligible, that is, to be subject to law, or capable of being represented by a general sign or symbol. . . . The essential thing is that it is capable of being represented. Whatever is capable of being represented is itself of a representative nature. The idea of representation involves infinity, since a representation is not really such unless it be interpreted in another representation. . . .

That is a very bald statement. An immense number of items might be added. But I endeavor so to draw it up that these ideas may appear less of the nature of will-o'-the-wisps to you, — as steady lights. The more you reflect upon them the steadier they will become; at least, such is my experience. . . . Rest and jollity to you and recuperation. With warm regards to Mrs. James and to all of you. As ever,

C. S. PEIRCE

The spectacle of two philosophers complaining that they do not understand one another is not uncommon, nor is it always edifying. The interest of the present case lies in the association of misunderstanding with so much agreement, sympathy, and good-will. After 1903, James's letters (and he appears to have written only briefly and intermittently) are almost entirely missing. Peirce, on the other hand, kept up a running fire of comment on James's writings, attempting to clarify his own views to James and lamenting the latter's reckless inaccuracies.

Milford, March 7, 1904

Dear William, —

. . . I want to thank you for your kind reference to me in your piece about Schiller's *Humanism*.[8] . . . You and Schiller carry pragmatism too far for me. I don't want to exaggerate it, but keep it within the bounds to which the evidences of it are limited. The most important consequence of it, by far, on which I have always insisted — as, for example, in my notice of Frazer's *Berkeley* in the *North American Review* of October, 1871 — is that under that conception of reality we must abandon nominalism. That in my opinion is the great need of philosophy. . . . I also want to say that after all pragmatism solves no real problem. It only shows that supposed problems are not real problems. But when one comes to such questions as immortality, the nature of the connection of mind and matter . . . we are left completely in the dark. The effect of pragmatism here is simply to open our minds to receiving any evidence, not to furnish evidence. . . . Come up and see our waterfalls, therein is peace.

C. S. PEIRCE

The letters immediately following deal mainly with the articles on pure experience or radical empiricism, beginning with "Does Consciousness Exist?" In September 1904, Peirce wrote a letter in which, having complained of the obscurity of James's notion that "consciousness is often regarded as an 'entity,'" he advanced the view that "the conception of the *real* is derived by a *mellonization* (Greek μέλλων, the being about to do, to be, or to suffer) of the constraint-side of double-sided consciousness." James replied that

[8] James's review appeared in the *Nation*, LXXVIII (1904).

he did n't "understand a word," and the following is Peirce's rejoinder : —

Milford, Oct. 3, 1904

Dear William, —

. . . It is very vexatious to be told at every turn that I am utterly incomprehensible, notwithstanding my careful study of language. When I say it is vexatious, I don't mean that I don't wish to be told so.   On the contrary, I am aware that my modes of thought and of expression are peculiar and gauche, and that twenty years of a recluse life have made them more so, and am grateful to people who help me by correcting me.   But when, as in the present case, I am able to show that the accusation is a mere auto-suggestion due to your having told yourself that everything that Peirce says is unintelligible, and really having commanded yourself not to understand, it gives me a certain glee to feel authorized to yield to my natural vexation.   You will be gratified, with your truly kind nature, to have afforded me so much innocent pleasure. . . .   Your mind and mine are as little adapted to understanding one another as two minds could be, and therefore I always feel that I have more to learn from you than from anybody.   At the same time, it gives great weight in my mind to our numerous agreements of opinion.

Perhaps the most important aspect of the series of papers of which the one you send me is the first, will prove to be that it shows so clearly that phenomenology is one science and psychology a very different one.   I know that you are not inclined to see much value in distinguishing between one science and another.   But my opinion is that it is absolutely necessary to any progress.   The standards of certainty must be different in different sciences, the principles to which one science appeals altogether different from those of the other. . . .   Phenomenology has no right to appeal to logic, except to deductive logic.   On the contrary, logic must be founded on phenomenology.   Psychology, you may say, observes the same facts as phenomenology does.   No.   It does not *observe* the same facts.   It looks upon the same world, — the same world that the astronomer looks at.   But what it *observes* in that world is different. . . .

You speak of various worlds.   But the number is not so great. F. E. Abbot, one of the strongest thinkers I ever encountered, first showed me that there were just three; the outer, the inner, and the logical world. The others are not distinct worlds. . . . What you call "pure experience" is not experience at all, and certainly ought to have a name. It is downright bad morals so to misuse words, for it prevents philosophy from becoming a science. One of the things I urge in my forthcoming *Monist* paper [9] is that it is an indispensable requisite of science that it should have a recognized technical vocabulary, composed of words so unattractive that loose thinkers are not tempted to use them; and a recognized and legitimated way of making up new words freely when a new conception is introduced; and that it is vital for science that he who introduces a new conception should be held to have a *duty* imposed upon him to invent a sufficiently disagreeable series of words to express it. I wish you would reflect seriously upon the moral aspect of terminology. . . . Ever faithfully,

C. S. PEIRCE

On James's suggestion [10] that the Kantian "I think" (supposed to attend all objects of consciousness) could be reduced to the experience of breathing, Peirce commented as follows: "As for your theory that the 'I breathe' must accompany all thoughts, I call your attention to the circumstance that many people, of whom I am one, involuntarily hold their breath while thinking. . . . People sitting by me have occasionally remarked how I keep holding my breath, which suggests that it is a mere personal peculiarity. . . . If I have got to believe that I think with my lungs I will take as my equation: *Ich denke* $=$ I don't breathe."

Milford, Dec. 6, 1904

My dear William, —

Thank you very much for your paper "Humanism and Truth." You have a quotation from me which greatly astonishes me. I cannot imagine when or where I can have used that language: "The serious meaning of a concept lies in the concrete difference to some one which its being true will make." [11] Do tell me at once where I so slipped, that I may at once declare it to be a slip. I do not think I have often spoken of the "meaning of a concept" whether "seri-

[9] "What Pragmatism Is," *Monist,* XV (1905).
[10] *E.R.E.*, 37, and elsewhere.
[11] *Mind, N.S.*, XIII (1904), 457. In James's text this passage is *not* quoted.

ous" or not. I have said that the concept itself "is" *nothing more* than the concept, not of any concrete difference that *will* be made to someone, but is nothing more than the concept of the *conceivable* practical applications of it.

As for people who say that pragmatism means believing anything one pleases, my answer to that will be found in the *Popular Science Monthly* for November, 1877; and is, in brief, that if one could believe what one pleased that would be true. But the fact is that one cannot. I wish I had Royce's text where he asks how the mere pragmatist can feel it a duty to think truly,[12] for he was present at my lecture where I showed that pragmatism (*my* pragmatism) makes logic a mere special case of ethics. . . . Please let me know where that singular quotation from me came from. Very faithfully,

C. S. PEIRCE

Milford, July 23, 1905

My dear William, —

. . . To begin with I want to emphasize my particular gratitude for your papers. . . . I read the French paper[13] first. . . . I found it entirely clear as well as beautifully written. When you write English (it is better to say the disagreeable thing) I can seldom at all satisfy myself that I know what you are driving at. Your writing would, I can see, be immensely forcible if one knew what you meant; but one (No. 1) don't. Now, for example, when you talk about doubting whether "consciousness" exists, you drive me at once to consulting a lot of books (in that particular case just twenty-three, without counting the dictionaries of Baldwin, Eisler, etc.) to see what you could mean; and they left me as much in the dark as ever. But now that you are tied down to the rules of French rhetoric, you are perfectly perspicuous; and I wish, and I am sure lots of others do, that you would consider yourself so tied down habitually. Because one sees that it only aids your force of style. Of course, you can smile at my undertaking to advise you about anything whatever. The fact that you can do so, if you like, emboldens me to say what I say.

I also agree to every word you say in this French article to the

---

[12] "The Eternal and the Practical," *Philos. Rev.,* XIII (1904), 129.
[13] "La Notion de conscience"; *cf. E.R.E.*

full, with one exception, that is that I am quite sure the doctrine is not at all so novel as you say. Of course it is all the better for not being novel. . . . I have myself preached immediate perception, as you know; and you can't find a place where I distinguish the objective and subjective sides of things. I think I will mail you a paper of mine that was printed January, 1901, in the *Popular Science Monthly,* where you will see this; not developed in the beautiful way you do, but plainly enough stated, I think.[14] . . .

I hope the word "pragmatism" may be accepted . . . as the term expressive of those things (perhaps we cannot be sure just what they are) in which the group of us are in agreement, as to the interpretation of thought. As for humanism, it appears to me to be an allied doctrine, in perfect harmony with pragmatism, but not relating exactly to the same question. . . . I prefer the word "anthropomorphism," as expressive of *the scientific opinion.* . . . To . . . anthropomorphism I subscribe in the main. . . . Pluralism, on the other hand, does not satisfy either my head or my heart. I am as sure as I am of anything that the logical doctrines connected with it, Achilles and the tortoise, etc., are utterly false.

As for the "problem of evil," and the like, I see in them only blasphemous attempts to define the purposes of the Most High . . . but that particular problem has received the most beautiful and satisfactory solution in *Substance and Shadow.* We had a tramp working for us for a few days not long ago. One day he started the problem of evil. In twenty words I put before him the *Substance and Shadow* solution. He saw it at once, did my tramp; and after a few moments of reflection he looked up and said to me, "Yes, I guess that is just it." There is, however, nothing more wholesome for us than to find problems that quite transcend our powers, and I must say, too, that it imparts a delicious sense of being cradled in the waters of the deep, — a feeling I always have at sea. It is, for example, entirely inscrutable to me why my three categories have been made so luminous to me without my being given the power to make them understood by those who alone are in a condition to see their meaning — *i.e.* my fellow-pragmatists . . . and the blackest depression under which I suffer . . . comes from that very thing. Yet when I lay the wail before my God, I see that as long as I can say that I have exhausted all my endeavours, it is a

[14] "Pearson's Grammar of Science." Peirce referred James especially to 301 ff.

happy thing that my responsibility ends, and that the matter is in the hands of the Author of all thought. When I began this letter I was suffering agonies at the non-realization of the hope of that week in the summer school, as well as with some lesser but great woes. . . . But simply setting down and running over these few points concerning the true theism has brought a joy that already begins to reduce the pain. I perceive that I am not to hope for a class. How inscrutable! . . .

C. S. P.

Hurricane, Aug. 1, 1905

Dear Charles, —

I wrote to you in a great hurry as I was leaving Cambridge, and now, having re-read your letter, feel like writing again. Your encouragement to me to become a French classic both gratifies and amuses. *I* will if *you* will, — we shall both be clearer, no doubt. Try putting your firsts, seconds, thirds into the Gallic tongue and see if you don't make more converts! The queer thing about that effort of mine was that I wrote it twice as fast as I ever wrote anything in English. At first this seemed quite paradoxical, but on reflection I saw that it was natural. When I write English I have a choice of possible ways of expressing myself, and forever seek to improve. In French the first sentence was my only possible shot, and had to stay; and I was so tickled at having been able to write it at all that it seemed perfect at once, so I rushed on to another of the same kind, — all of them stored-up reminiscences of sentences that I had read, automatically reproduced.

My starting point is, of course, the doctrine of immediate perception; but the farther elaboration I have n't met elsewhere, except recently in two Germans, Petzoldt and Heymans, where the non-dualistic view explaining "mental state" and "physical thing" by different relations to context is made much as I make it. . . . I am much obliged for the little paragraph referring to my French paper in the *Evening Post* of last night. I read your long notice of Wundt a fortnight ago [15] with admiration of its cleverness. You have the journalistic touch very well now, and in addition to that your articles always contain some original thought or bit of learn-

[15] These reviews of James and Wundt appeared in *N.Y. Evening Post*, July 21 and July 31, 1905. In the former Peirce speaks of James's article as "a fine stone to be added to the edifice the humanists are building up."

ing. I've given up reading Wundt, — he gets up philosophy as Winston Churchill *et al* get up historical novels.

When you wrote of the "summer school" I thought you meant either Harvard or Chicago. It appears you meant this place. Have no regrets. I have given two lectures to about a dozen auditresses . . . and two men who can understand philosophy. It's lamentable; and the cash would doubtfully cover your journey. Shed no tears for that! I come here because I love the place, and bought long ago a building lot here that I like to come and gloat upon.

I'm awfully sorry, dear Charley, for your hard plight. . . . Believe me, ever faithfully yours,

WM. JAMES

When James's volume on *Pragmatism* appeared Peirce was in Cambridge lecturing before the Philosophy Club at Harvard.

Cambridge, June 13, 1907

My dearest William, —

. . . I have just this minute received your book, *Pragmatism*. I just turned to the index and looked out Peirce, C. Santiago [16] S. I found a statement of my own thoughts, which I can appreciate, having been laboring and crowding my way for months and months — crowding through throngs of technicalities, objections, and stupidities — to try to express. There you have put it on your page with the utmost lucidity and apparent facility. Nothing could be more satisfactory.

I am not in a position to teach young men anything, and in this worm-eaten university I am happy to think that I should be even more out of place than you; but if I had some young philosophers to aid I should certainly hold myself up as a warning against withholding publication until one can be quite satisfied with his expression. The result is that I am so hemmed in with analyses upon which I labored until they are brought to a presentable finish, that I am completely cut off by them from the mass, even of the philosophical world. . . . With best regards to Mrs. James and your family, I am, the same old sixpence,

C. S. PEIRCE

[16] A name adopted by Peirce, presumably in honor of James.

P.S. . . . Believe me, my dearest William, that I would not give you pain for the world, and the day is past when I wanted *anything* for my personal satisfaction. That is more true than you think; but never mind, think what you like. I just have one lingering wish, for your sake and that of the countless minds that, directly or indirectly, you influence. It is that you, if you are not too old, would try to learn to think with more exactitude. If you had a fortnight to spare I believe I could do something for you, and through you to the world; but perhaps I do not sufficiently take account of other psychical conditions than purely rational ones. . . . I have often, both in my lectures and in my printed papers, pointed out how far higher is the faculty of reasoning from rather inexact ideas than of reasoning from formal definitions; and though I am so bound up in my narrow methods as often to lament that you could not furnish me with the exact forms that I am skilled in dealing with, yet I see myself, with admiration and wonder, how you, nevertheless, come to the right conclusions in most cases, and still more wonderfully how you contrive to impart to audiences as near to the exact truth as they are capable of apprehending. That faculty makes one useful, while I am like a miser who picks up things that *might be* useful to the right person at the right time, but which, in fact, are utterly useless to anybody else, and almost so to himself. What is utility, if it is confined to a single accidental person? Truth is public.

The following complaint was occasioned by the receipt in proof of Appendix C to the *Pluralistic Universe,* in which James says that the "axiom of skipped intermediaries and transferred relations . . . cannot be applied offhand to concrete objects," because novelty is perpetually entering into any actual train of events. James proceeds in the same context to liken Peirce to Bergson, as believing that real novelty occurs, and that its external abruptness is mitigated by its internal continuity.[17]

Milford, March 9, 1909

My dear William, —
The instant I got the proof sheets you sent me I sat down and studied them, and as soon as I had mastered Appendix C I sat down

[17] According to which if a is more than b and b is more than c, then a is more than c, etc. P.U., 395 ff.

to write to you about it.   But I write slowly on account of the need of weighing every word when I discuss points of logic, and when I had filled forty sheets and was going on to the forty-first, I concluded that the matter would not interest you.   I hold to my "tychism" more than ever; but on that account to liken me to a person who talks about *devenir réel* strikes me much like a doctor who should pronounce that a patient had something like *locomotor ataxia* because he had a soft corn under his heel.

It makes me genuinely and heartily unhappy to find you saying, or seeming to say, that one fact is the cause of a second which is the cause of a third and yet that the first is not the cause of the third. . . .   This is obviously to attack every chain of reasoning whatsoever, and is, therefore, to confess that your assertion has no reason to support it.   For my part, I think philosophy is, or should be, an exact *science,* and not a kaleidoscopic dream.   Why did you put your "principle of skipped intermediaries" in your psychology if it can only be talked of *in abstracto?*

I thought your *Will to Believe* was a very exaggerated utterance, such as injures a serious man very much, but to say what you now do is far more suicidal.   I have lain awake several nights in succession in grief that you should be so careless of what you say. . . . The only thing I have ever striven to do in philosophy has been to analyze sundry concepts with exactitude; and to do this it is necessary to use terms with strict scientific precision. . . .   But that being my only claim to consideration, and it being a deeper conviction with me that philosophy is either a science or is balderdash, and that a man who seeks to further science can hardly commit a greater sin than to use the terms of his science without anxious care to use them with strict accuracy, it is not very grateful to my feelings to be classed along with a Bergson who seems to be doing his prettiest to muddle all distinctions. . . .   Very faithfully, lovingly, and gratefully,

C. S. Peirce

Cambridge, March 10, 1909

Dear Charles, —

Before whom have I cast that pearl of an Appendix?   I imagined it to be in the purest spirit of your synechistic tychism; and I think still that my only mistake was in sending it to you without the whole text that introduced and justified it. Of course you are right in the logical world, where every term is changeless to eternity, but the real world is incongruent, as I always thought you held (it being indeterminate, except partly), and the logical terms only mark static *positions* in a flux which nowhere is static. But wait till you see the book, of which I enclose a circular! I hope to send it to you in four weeks, and repent now of having stirred you to such a troublesome premature reaction. Forty sheets! Lord help us! . . . Affectionately yours. . . .

Wm. James

Milford, March 14, 1909

My dear William, —

I must have been in a hazy condition of mind when I wrote to you, if I did not make it clear, as I intended to do, that you had skilfully stated my position so far as the universe of existence goes. But I wish you would consider — as a vitally important, and quite indispensable condition of making yourself clear — that you must have some invariable or exactly certain yardstick. . . . 'T was that acute but shallow fellow, Chauncey Wright, whom I only availed myself of as a whetstone of wits, but whom you looked up to far too much, who probably entrapped you in his notion that in some part of the universe one and one perhaps do not make two. . . .

My dear William, there is *something* about your mode of expressing yourself that makes plain folk like me unable to comprehend what you mean; and I think that *this* is what it is. You want to make the universe of the possible (because it indubitably is a real universe) as inexact as I hold the existential universe to be. But that can't be, because the possible is our only *standard* of expression. . . . I could make the whole matter clear to you as the noonday sun, if it were not that you are *wedded* to the theory that you can't understand mathematics! If you would only allow that *perhaps* you are mistaken about that, I guarantee I would make a mathematician of you. But when a person lays it down, as Axiom I, that he can't understand mathematics, that is to say, can't understand the *evident,* that blocks the road, don't you see? . . .

Now I have a particular petition to lay before you, as usual. One winter, about forty years ago or less,[18] I used almost every

[18] *Cf.* above, I, 536.

day to dine with your brother Harry and we used to talk a great deal (so it is reported by my rather reporter-like memory) about the novels he meant to write. I dare say his impression might now be that he had been discreetly reserved, and as near silent on the subject, as he could without offence be. But I was greatly interested in our discussions at the time, and I have very, very often desired to read some of his books. . . . If you will only pick me out one at a time, and will send them to me, I want to try a specimen of each kind that he writes. . . .

C. S. P.

Cambridge, March 21, 1909

Dear Charles, —

I don't deserve as elaborate and instructive a letter as you have written, nor do I fully deserve all your censure, even though I was conceived and born in philosophic sin, for I expressly *do* believe with you that in the universe of possibles, of merely mental truth, as Locke calls it, relations *are* exact. Time that *equabiliter fluit* is a conceptual entity, against which your time felt as tedious and mine felt as flashing by, can be artificially plotted out and equated, to the great convenience of human practice; and all their exact relations form a splendid artificial scheme of tabulation, on which to catch whatever elements of the existential flux can be made to stick there. My tychism, like yours, relates only to the flux. But wait till you see my forthcoming book! . . .

I will send you a copy of my brother's *Golden Bowl,* which is the most elaborate thing in his "third manner." I hope you'll be able to finish it! I will also send you *Tono-Bungay,* a splendid new thing by H. G. Wells. Yours as ever . . .

Wm. James

LXXVII

PRAGMATISM: ITS PLACE IN JAMES'S DEVELOPMENT

In the autumn of 1906 James wrote to his brother: "This is definitely my last year of lecturing, but I wish it were my first of non-lecturing. Simplification of the field of duties I find more and more to be the *summum bonum* for me; and I live in apprehension lest the Avenger should cut me off before I get my message out. Not that the message is particularly needed by the human race, which can live along perfectly well without any one philosopher; but objectively I hate to leave the volumes I have already published without their logical complement. It is an esthetic tragedy to have a bridge begun and stopped in the middle of an arch." [1]

During James's late years his desire to round out his system and his weakness for public lecturing were perpetually at war. In the spring and summer of 1905 he delivered a series of five lectures: first, March 3–10 at Wellesley; then, June 30–July 7, at Chicago; and finally, July 22–August 3, at Glenmore. They were successful, especially at Chicago, where he attracted an audience of five hundred. "I felt them," he wrote to Eliot, "pulling on my line like one fish." During the same spring he journeyed to Rome, where on April 30 he delivered his "Notion de la conscience" before "a really splendid audience for quality . . . even though they did n't understand." [2] He lectured during this period as one having a message to deliver. He was evidently moved by a characteristic impulse to communicate his latest ideas to others without waiting to give them technical or systematic form; and he was at the same time eager to put his private thoughts to the social test. In spite of his intermittent resolves to be technical, he could never be *satisfied* with any product of his pen which was not readable. In letters to Papini he speaks of writing a "popular synthetic book,"

[1] *L.W.J.*, II, 259.
[2] *L.W.J.*, II, 227.

of "sketching the universe of radical empiricism *à grands traits*," and reserving the "indigestibilities" of his system for "a volume of appendices."

The lectures given at Wellesley, Chicago, and Glenmore were substantially the same, setting forth what he called "the individualistic philosophy." He began with praise of philosophy in general, as consisting in the exercise of "the critical function" by the individual, and defended it against the charge of being unprogressive. Recent philosophy would, he said, be much more astonishing to the Ionians than would modern science. He repudiated the prevailing opposition between philosophy and science — "both are just man thinking, by every means in his power." The best philosophy will avoid "smugness," and endeavor always to keep in touch with "the character of vulgar reality." The lecturer then reviewed pragmatism — naming Locke, Berkeley, and Hume as "the first pragmatists," and citing Kant's conception of God as an illustration of the pragmatist method in contrast with that of mediæval theology. Pluralism he developed by applying the pragmatic method to the problem of "the one and the many." Certain types of unity, such as "unity of substance" and "abstract noetic unity," are set aside as meaningless or trivial. "Mechanical" and "generic" unity are excluded as plainly contrary to fact. There remain "concrete noetic unity," "unity of origin," and "unity of purpose." These are meaningful hypotheses, and they are not capable of disproof — but both appearance and practice are against them if they are construed absolutely. The world seems to be *partially* unified in these respects, or to be *achieving* such unity; this being the belief of common sense, and the assumption of the moral will. All views of the universe as a whole are based on the analogy of one of its parts. Some have chosen "the lower necessities," others "the higher ideals": thus the world has been conceived as a thought, a sentence, a piece of music, a dream, a work of art, a grab-bag. Radical empiricism, says James, proposes "the social analogy: plurality of individuals, with relations partly external, partly intimate, like and un-like, different in origin, in aim, yet keeping house together, interfering, coalescing, compromising, finding new purposes to arise, getting gradually into more stable habits, winning order, weeding out." This is the tychistic world, which is in agreement with the new "individualistic" ideas of science (uniformity being only statistical);

and which provides for novelty, freedom, real efficacy of the will, and the uncompromising rejection of evil. The only drawback is the sense of "insecurity." This must be "minimized." Optimism being rejected on theoretical grounds, and pessimism being practically and emotionally impossible, there remains the alternative of "meliorism." The best is "possible" — not merely in the negative sense of non-contradiction, but in the positive sense that its conditions are partially present and that it has champions who are pledged to its promotion. Such a melioristic faith is consistent with theism, and is supported by the evidence for a supernormal mind. God is not the whole — but only "the ideal part. He helps us and we can help him." In its moral implications this individualistic philosophy is libertarian, tolerant, democratic, militant, humane.

In 1905–1906 the course on metaphysics (Philosophy 9) was repeated with changes reflecting the shifting emphasis of James's thinking. He was now looking beyond the essays in radical empiricism to the ideas which were elaborated in *Pragmatism* and *A Pluralistic Universe*. There were introductory lectures discussing types of philosophy and suggesting a middle course between materialistic empiricism on the one hand, and a rationalistic spiritualism on the other; the aim of the course was "to unite empiricism with spiritualism." Then follows an examination of the problem of knowledge with a view to escaping solipsism. A solution is sought in the pragmatic identity of your object and mine. Our activities lead to a common terminus, through which we influence one another, and which, though it may transcend experience, lies in an experienced direction and is a "more" of the same experiential kind. Whether this "beyond," this thing-in-itself, shall be interpreted panpsychistically, is questioned and again left unsettled. "Explain, and confess difficulty of explanation" is James's note on the subject.

Then follows a vigorous attack on the Roycean noetic Absolute — "bloated and puffy with superfluous consciousness and information. . . . All the hairs in our head are numbered. Omniscience of this silly sort, so far from being sublime, is idiotic or dropsical." There is the further difficulty that the Absolute, knowing all, cannot possibly embrace those human experiences which depend on privation. The "Absolute has the victory as well as the defeat, but even for him it is both. For the defeated party it is nothing *but* defeat." It is as if, by the fact of being written in a novel, each character should have a life of his own in addition to his life for the author or the reader. The "congenial" features of the pluralistic hypotheses are summarized as follows: "It redeems us from abstraction, from carrying on our book-keeping in two accounts, like Sunday Christianity. It restores to philosophy the temper of science and of practical life, brings the ideal *into things.* It allows order to be increasing, — therefore is a philosophy of *progress.* It makes *us* factors of the order. It frankly interprets the universe after a *social* analogy. It admits different systems of causation relatively independent, — *chance,* therefore, in so far forth."

We are to "take evolution *au grand sérieux,*" providing for real change, real novelty, and real advance. "If evolution, Gods may be one of the results." Religion is essentially a reliance on "reserve" or "vital resource," "a life in us finding an answering life." But the divine so conceived "may be impersonal," like the Emersonian "over-soul." "For myself, not getting beyond the Emersonian stage, I should be happy to be at the Fechnerian. I would accept the assurances of others, were parts of them not inconsistent with what I believe, *e.g.:* (1) Fact, — specifications of visions at variance with facts elsewhere known; (2) Logic, — compounding of selves; (3) Metaphysics, — 'souls' *vs.* pure experience. In any case religion is indestructible because private life is indestructible."

Finally, there is a discussion of the nature of the humanistic doctrine of truth. *"Pragmatic method* asserts that what a concept *means* is its consequences. Humanism says that when these are satisfactory, the concept is *true."* [3]

During the first half of the academic year 1905–1906, James also gave, as Philosophy 1a, a systematic outline of his philosophy in a form adapted to beginners. This course was repeated during the second half-year at Leland Stanford University.[4] While there (on January 8, 1906), he wrote in his diary, "Feel lonely and scared"; but on January 10, "Funk is over! It went all right."

---

[3] These lectures were never published, but full notes have been preserved.
[4] Also at Harvard in 1906–7 as Philos. D, James's last regular course of instruction.

It continued to go "all right," and led to a varied and exhausting life, full of social engagements, and of miscellaneous lectures in San Francisco and Berkeley as well as at Stanford. His letters express his enthusiasm over Stanford University and the "freshness and eagerness" of his auditors. "The human vacuum is curious . . . the historic silence rings in your ears. . . . But this generation is only the first coat of paint, the fallow clover-crop ploughed into the soil. . . . Such simplification! Such freedom from distraction, and such pure, severe and noble surroundings!" [5]

For Philosophy 1a, James prepared a printed syllabus, and he revised it for use at Leland Stanford. The content of the course was determined first of all by its introductory character. It was not only simplified in exposition, but contained restatements of stock philosophical ideas and detailed comments on Paulsen's *Introduction to Philosophy,* which was used as a text. Nevertheless the course played an important part in James's philosophical development. It led to the writing of the unfinished volume, published after James's death but in accordance with his instructions, on *Some Problems of Philosophy,* considerably over one half of which follows the printed syllabus verbally as well as in the order of topics. This course also forced James to think of his philosophy as a whole, and was more comprehensive than any one of his published works. It can be looked upon as an essay in systematization.

Only one feature of this elementary presentation of his views calls for further comment. The syllabus for the Harvard course contains a long discussion of idealism, which did not afterwards appear either in the Stanford revision or in *Some Problems of Philosophy.* He defended Berkeley against the charges of nihilism and solopsism, credited him with introducing "the whole phenomenalist way of thinking," summarized, sympathetically, the case against naïve realism, and finally left his own position in doubt: —

"Phenomenalism or idealism is usually accused . . . of denying the 'objective' import of experience. It is important in discussion to disentangle certain ambiguities in the word 'objective' as used here. That an idea represents an 'object' may mean that it represents something either: — 1. Trans-*personal* — as when my object is also *your* object; or, 2. Trans-*corporeal* — as when my

[5] *Cf.* also *L.W.J.,* II, 239–41.

object is outside of my body; or, 3. Trans-*cerebral* — as possibly in my body, but out of my brain; or, 4. Trans-*visible* or trans-*palpable* — as when it is defined either as a 'scientific' entity (like the atom or ether-wave) or as a panpsychic entity; or, finally, 5. Trans-*mental* altogether, as when it is said to be altogether 'unknowable.' . . .

"Our only intelligible notion of an object *in itself* is that it should be an object *for* itself, and this lands us in panpsychism and a belief that our physical perceptions are effects on us of 'psychical' realities. . . . Even if we don't become panpsychists, we can still describe the entire course of our experience as a system of possible sensations connected by definite laws with actual sensations (Mill), and keep a place in our description for every verifiable fact, without invoking any entity of which sensation does not constitute the nature. *That* something exists when we as individuals are not thinking it, is an inexpugnable conviction of common sense. The various stages of idealist reflection are only as many successive attempts to define *what* the something is that thus exists. The upshot tends pretty strongly towards something like panpsychism. But there are various shades of opinion here."

During the year 1905–1906, when James was so busily occupied with popular lectures, "The Book" still occupied his thoughts. There are two sketches of it as it appeared to its author at this time. The first is in the form of directions: "Best begin the Book by the order of Philos. 1a, Chicago, Glenmore, etc. Apply pragmatic method to 'knowledge,' and establish common sense point of view. Apply it to 'oneness' and establish empiricist point of view. Revert to common sense identification of subject and object in perception, and expound idealism. Discuss noetic absolutism; demolish it. Set up pluralism as alternative. From this slide into trans-subjective realism, scientificism. Then radical empiricism, panpsychism, etc."

The other sketch is in the form of chapter headings: "1, 2. Philosophy. Paint pictures. Empiricism *vs.* rationalism. 3, 4, 5. Portrait of absolutism (historic) (good with bad). Psychological explanation. Postpone mystical aspect. 6. Empiricism. 7. Pragmatic method. 8, 9. Question of unity. 10. Question of Knowledge. 11. Common sense. 12. Realism *vs.* idealism. 13. Social analogy. 14. Laws of nature, — stable state, statistics. Spencer, Petzoldt. 15. Social forces, Tarde. 16. Dynamic connection. 17, 18. Activity, free-will, — creation. 19. Possibility. 20. Infinite. Finite constitution. 21. Theism. 22. Theism. Mysticism. 23. Truth. Conceptual short-hand. Conservation of energy. Reality of concepts. 24. Will to believe. Fideism. Probability. 25. Brain. 26. Bergson and Strong. Fechner. 27. Lecture V, Chicago." [6]

Instead of executing the plans here formulated, James allowed himself to be again drawn into popular lecturing. During the summer of 1906, he gave a brief course before the Harvard Summer School of Theology; and in the autumn, November 14 to December 8, he gave the Lowell Lectures on "Pragmatism," which he repeated at Columbia University, January 29 to February 8, 1907. In the interval he had begun (January 7) the composition of the book on *Pragmatism*, and had given (January 22) his last college lecture [7] with its "oration, inkstand and loving cup." The Columbia lectures were delivered before an audience of over one thousand, and he spoke of those few days in New York — the lectures and his reception — as "certainly the high tide of my existence, so far as *energizing* and being 'recognized' were concerned." [8] Nevertheless both the lectures and the ensuing volume were dictated by personal and by strategic reasons rather than by the logic of his philosophical development. And the public attention which they received involved the author in so great a volume of acknowledgment, interpretation, and controversy that the technical treatise had again to be postponed. Such was the penalty of success!

To the title of his *Pragmatism* James appended the subtitle: "A New Name for Some Old Ways of Thinking." James meant, no doubt, that he had not himself invented these ways of thinking; not only could their roots be traced far into the past, but they represented a broad contemporary tendency which James shared with others. This tendency embraced: the newer logic of Mill, Lotze, and Sigwart, with its emphasis on the instrumental as distinguished from the representative function of ideas; the doctrines of evolution and historical relativism, stressing change, plasticity, and adaptation in human knowledge; the vogue of probability and hypothesis

---

[6] The fifth lecture at Chicago was devoted to a summary of James's moral, social, political, and religious beliefs.
[7] To Philos. D.
[8] *L.W.J.*, II, 265.

in scientific method. James also meant that he had himself been familiar with these "ways of thinking" and had espoused them from the beginning of his own philosophical career.[9]   There are two of them which transcend the rest in importance, and may fairly be called the cardinal principles of pragmatism.   The first, the pragmatic method, proposes to interpret concepts in terms of their consequences for experience or practice.   The second is the pragmatic theory of truth: to the effect, namely, that truth is an attribute of ideas rather than of reality; and that it attaches to ideas in proportion as these prove useful for the purpose for which they are invoked.   But when these two cardinal principles are stated, it is at once evident that they coincide broadly with the two doctrines which constitute James's "empiricism," and which constituted it from the beginning of his philosophical maturity: namely, experientialism and experimentalism.

The following note was written by James in 1873: "Religion in its most abstract expression may be defined as the affirmation that all is *not* vanity.   The empiricist can easily sneer at such a formula as being empty through its universality, and ask you to cash it by its concrete filling, — which you may not be able to do, for nothing can well be harder.   Yet as a practical fact its meaning is so distinct, that when used as a premise in a life a whole character may be imparted to the life by it.   It, like so many other universal concepts, is a truth of orientation, serving not to *define* an end, but to determine a direction."

This cannot be said to be a pronouncement in favor of pragmatism, but it indicates clearly that James was already disposed to recognize that if a concept cannot be translated into terms of experience or practice, it is meaningless.   James's preoccupation with the British empiricists followed soon after, and the public announcement of the pragmatic doctrine in 1898, in the address on

---

[9] *Cf.* M. Baum, "The Development of James's Pragmatism Prior to 1879," *Jour. of Philos.*, XXX (1933).   It is no part of the present study to trace the earlier anticipations or contemporary parallels of James's pragmatism except so far as James was influenced by them.   A reader who would like to pursue the history of pragmatism further might begin with: D. S. Miller, "Prof. James on Philosophical Method," *Philos. Rev.*, VIII (1899); A. Lalande, "Pragmatisme et pragmaticisme," *Revue philos.*, LXI (1906); W. M. Horton, *Philosophy of Abbé Bautain*, 1926, 199–203, 289–96; R. Berthelot, *Un Romantisme utilitaire*, 1911; and É. Leroux, *Le Pragmatisme américain et anglais*, 1922.   Useful information regarding the history of the word "pragmatism," and suggestions regarding historical anticipations and analogies, will be found in "A German Critic of Pragmatism," *Monist*, XIX (1909).

"Philosophical Conceptions and Practical Results," identified that doctrine with "the great English way of investigating a conception," exemplified by Locke, Berkeley, Hume, and their lesser followers.   Although this address had something of the character of a *pronunciamento,* it is clear that James was not aware of having reached any new stage in his philosophical development.   The topic which he selected resulted from his desire to select something "sufficiently popular and practical" from his existing arsenal of ideas.[10] It served as a review of his philosophical beginnings, and as an acknowledgment of indebtedness to Charles Peirce, who in "the early '70s" had enunciated explicitly the method which the English empiricists had followed "instinctively." [11]

With James himself the method ceased to be merely "instinctive" at a very early date.   Upon his first thorough reading of Locke's *Essay,* perhaps as early as 1876, he wrote the term "practicalism" in the margin opposite the passage in which that author argues that it does not matter of what substance the self is made, provided its functions remain the same — the term "practicalism" which he later employed as a synonym for "pragmatism."   Replying in 1878 to the positivistic contention that the question of materialism was insoluble or meaningless, he said: "Every question has sense and imposes itself unmistakably, when it produces a clear practical alternative, in such wise that according as one answers the question one way or the other, one is obliged to adopt one or the other of two lines of conduct." [12]   Pragmatism in the first or methodological sense, as a canon of meaning, thus dates from the time when James first began to have a philosophical mind of his own.   It reappears more or less explicitly in all of his later writings.

The second or experimentalist principle is not less deeply rooted in James's philosophical past.   As soon as he had any doctrine of his own concerning the human mind he insisted on its activity, initiative, and congenital bias.   Man thinks because he is prompted to do so by the interests and the purposes which govern him.   Here again James found the way prepared by the great empiricists.   Reading Locke's *Essay,* he applauded that writer's view of "nominal essences" as "teleological" instruments.   He was quick to note Locke's recog-

---

[10] *L.W J.,* II, 79.
[11] *C.E.R.,* 410, 434.
[12] *C.E.R.,* 76; translated by the author.

nition of the practical motives in knowledge; and selected the following passage as a suitable "motto for practicalism": "He that will not eat till he has demonstration that it will nourish him, he that will not stir till he infallibly knows the business he goes about will succeed, will have little else to do but sit still and perish." [13]

At approximately the same time (soon after 1875) James set down the following note, indicating his disposition to regard truth as *pro*spective rather than *retro*spective: "The truth of a thing or idea is its meaning, or its destiny, that which grows out of it. This would be a doctrine reversing the opinion of the empiricists that the meaning of an idea is that which it has grown from. . . . Unless we find a way of conciliating the notions of truth and change, we must admit that there is no truth anywhere. But the conciliation is necessarily made by everyone who reads history and admits that an [earlier] set of ideas . . . were in the line of development of the ideas in the light of which we now reject [them]. . . . In so far as they tended to induce these they were true; just as these will induce others and themselves be shelved. Their truth lay in their function of continuing thought in a certain *direction*. Had they tended out of that direction they would have been false."

Taken as *prospective,* truth is to be interpreted in terms of the *purposes* or *ends* which govern thinking. This was the theme of the first systematic work which James planned to write, and of which "The Sentiment of Rationality," published in 1879, is the most important fragment. How far it is *legitimate* that these ends should govern the acceptance of an idea, especially when the ends are practical and emotional rather than theoretic, is the central question of the essay on "The Will to Believe." Meanwhile in the *Principles* James not only had elaborated his general teleological view of mind, but in the last chapter, on "Necessary Truths and the Effects of Experience," had developed *in extenso* his view that the mind is governed by innate predispositions which, like Darwinian variations, owe their survival to their function of adaptation.

Among the earlier statements of the pragmatic theory of truth, however, James attached unique importance to the essay "On the Function of Cognition," published in 1885. It is "the *fons et origo* of all *my* pragmatism," he wrote in 1907; he gave it the leading place in the volume on *The Meaning of Truth;* and cited Charles

[13] Locke's *Essay,* 1853, 499.

Peirce as an exponent of the same doctrine.[14]   The historic significance of this essay is due to several facts.   It marks the definitive
and final identification of "truth" with the success of ideas.[15]   It
applies this notion not to the palpably practical situation, but to the
so-called *theoretical* situation, showing that this, in a more subtle
sense, is also practical.   It shows just how in such a situation the
idea points to a suitable terminus or practical *dénouement;* how it
leads to its object through intermediaries, all of which lie within
the same field of experience; and how its success may be interpreted
in terms of safe arrival at its destination.   In short, this essay
surpassed previous utterances on the subject in the degree to which
it subsumed theoretical and practical processes under a common
formula, and in the effectiveness with which the formula was applied to the concrete details of cognition.

[14] *M.T.*, I, 136; *Mind.* X (1885), 43, note.
[15] Up to this time James was still using the term "truth" for the objective aspect
of experience.

LXXVIII

THE RECEPTION OF PRAGMATISM

Pragmatism appeared in May 1907. It is abundantly evident that James was drawing upon his own past; giving a name, an emphasis, and a new formulation to doctrines which he had held for over thirty years. It does not follow that he experienced no sense of innovation and leadership. Quite the contrary was true. He felt that he might now make these ideas *effective* by his mode of presenting them and in conjunction with the trend of the times. There is a note of exhilaration in his comments and predictions, as appears from the following letter to Theodore Flournoy: —

Cambridge, Jan. 2, 1907 [1]

Dear Flournoy, —

This is a rather belated New Year's epistle, but no matter, if it only find you able to receive our greeting and assurance of continued affection, even though communication in these days gets more rare. . . . All is well with the James family — all but an increase of my arterio sclerotic symptoms in the last six months. But after nine more lectures at Harvard and eight, a month hence, at Columbia University in the City of New York, I am free from that particular *corvée* for eternity, and mean to lead a life without excitement or strain. It makes me almost tremble to look forward to such freedom! . . . I want to make you all enthusiastic converts to "pragmatism" (something not necessarily connected at all with "radical empiricism") on which I gave eight Lowell lectures to a fine audience in Boston this winter (these are the lectures which I shall repeat in New York). I did n't know, until I came to prepare them, how full of power to found a "school" and to become a "cause," the pragmatistic idea was. But now I am all aflame with it, as displacing all rationalistic systems — all systems, in fact, with rationalistic elements in them; and I mean to turn the lectures into a solid

[1] For Flournoy's reply to this letter, *cf.* below, 456.

little cube of a book which I hope to send you by next October, and which will, I am confident, make the pragmatic method appear, to you also, as the philosophy of the future. Every sane and sound tendency in life can be brought in under it. . . .

My reading is more philosophical than psychological in these days, but I have to confess that I meet no books that come upon me with the force of revelations; and I have, as we all have, to read so many — the immense majority — unopened. The world is getting too big. You are fortunate in living in Switzerland — you ought once to see New York! an earthquake *en performance*. I wish never to go there again. . . . How tremendously interesting is the condition of France. *Vive* Briand! *Vive* Clemenceau! To think of court-martials abolished and Picquart Minister of War! Pure poetic justice *does* then sometimes prevail here below! Compare this French republic with that of 1793, and one sees that the pragmatic method has made progress. . . . Your ever affectionate

WM. JAMES

James attributed the success of *Pragmatism* in part to its historic timeliness — with humanism, its *alter ego,* it was "like one of those secular changes that come upon public opinion overnight, as it were, borne upon tides 'too deep for sound or foam.' " [2] But at the same time he felt that his own style would ensure the book's receiving public attention. Thus he wrote to his brother: —

"I have just finished the proofs of a little book called 'Pragmatism' which even you *may* enjoy reading. It is a very 'sincere' and, from the point of view of ordinary philosophy-professorial manners, a very unconventional utterance, not particularly original at any one point, yet, in the midst of the literature of the way of thinking which it represents, with just that amount of squeak or shrillness in the voice that enables one book to *tell,* when others don't, to supersede its brethren, and be treated later as 'representative.' I shouldn't be surprised if ten years hence it should be rated as 'epoch-making,' for of the definitive triumph of that general way of thinking I can entertain no doubt whatever — I believe it to be something quite like the protestant reformation." [3]

Evidence of the success of *Pragmatism* is to be found not only

[2] *M.T.,* 54.
[3] *L.W.J.,* II, 279.

in the number of its followers and the volume of their applause, but also in the passionate opposition which it evoked. As a critique of certain authoritative and traditional tendencies in philosophy, it clearly reached its mark. Others, who read the book without resentment, complained of its ambiguity. James and his allies were thus called upon both to defend and to restate their doctrine. Many of James's own replies to the critics of pragmatism were published in *The Meaning of Truth* (1909) and need not, with one exception, be included here. This exception is the exceedingly interesting footnote appended to "The Function of Cognition." Here James summarizes the difference between his earlier pragmatism as represented by the article of 1885, and his later pragmatism as represented by the volume bearing that name.

The earlier pragmatism, he says, recognized the cognitive situation as consisting in the knower's idea together with an external reality. The reality, though independently given, is accessible to the knower through intermediate experiences; and in order that it may be said to be known it must be "pointed" to through these intermediaries. The pointing consists in resemblance and in a projected train of action ultimately impinging upon the reality pointed to. There is no action at a distance, no "epistemological gulf," whether left as an agnostic chasm or bridged by an Absolute. The whole process of knowledge, not only the idea, but its aim, — the flight of the arrow and the mark which it hits, — falls within the cycle of the knower's experience. James's pragmatism here draws upon his peculiar radical-empiricist view of the continuity and objectivity of experience, just as in his radical-empiricism, on the other hand, he makes use of the pragmatic method. The two doctrines coalesce as they are deepened, and the independence which James occasionally attributes to them can only mean that they proceed from independent premises and *might* be held independently.

The advance of the later over the earlier pragmatism is summarized by James as follows: to a large extent cognitive reference is indirect, leading to the object's associates rather than to the object itself; the object's resemblance to its object is not so important as was formerly supposed; the essential relation of an idea to its object is one of "satisfactory adaptation." The last two of these alterations were crucial.

In reducing the importance of "resemblance" James moved a step further away from the orthodox theory of correspondence — away from a structural and towards a functional conception of knowledge and truth.   He continued to find confirmation of this in the current tendency of science to treat its concepts as instruments wherewith to "handle" nature, rather than as "duplicates" of reality;[4] and in the important rôle which is played by verbal imagery.   The experience of Helen Keller furnished a case in point: —

Cambridge, Dec. 17, 1908

Dear Helen Keller, —
. . . I have no explanation of the lack of emotional memory you speak of, and in general I am quite disconcerted, professionally speaking, by your account of yourself before your "consciousness" was awakened by instruction.   But whatever you were or are, you're a blessing!   It is no paradox that you live in a world so indistinguishable from ours.   The great world, *the background*, in all of us, is the world of our *beliefs*.   That is the world of the permanencies and the immensities, and our relations with it are mostly verbal.   We think of its history and structure in verbal terms exclusively — the sensations we have of the remote and the hidden, being the merest incipiencies and hints which, as you so well show, we extend by imagination or add to by analogy.   But it makes no difference in what shape the content of our verbal material may come.   In some it is more optical, in others more acoustical, in others more motor in nature.   In you it is motor and tactile, but its functions are the same as ours, the relations meant by the words symbolizing the relations existing between the things. . . .   Believe me, faithfully yours,

WM. JAMES

In the conception of "satisfactory adaptation" James found an aid to generalization.   The various motives, whether theoretical or practical, to which he had traced the activity of thought, could all be brought under this formula.   It afforded a means of uniting the two basic relations between the thinker and the object, namely, action and sensation — for to deal with an object successfully, and to receive from it the impression which one expects, are in some sense both modes of adaptation.   And it also united the ranks of

[4] *S.P.P.*, 90-1, note.

the pragmatists, enabling James to find common ground with Dewey and Schiller.

Among the friendly and approving salutations of pragmatism the first came from Flournoy. He wrote before the book appeared, but he was already familiar with the doctrine from James's articles and letters: —

Geneva, March 16, 1907 [5]

My dear James, —

. . . I quite understand your being enthusiastic over the power and fecundity of the pragmatic method, which you handle as its genuine creator; for the brave Peirce does not appear to me to have been more than the slight push, the occasional cause, which would have had no result without the real motive force, the power to convert potentiality into reality, which you have yourself supplied entirely. And what would have remained of the fragmentary pragmatist tendencies hatched spontaneously by Bergson, Boutroux, Mach, etc., if you, together with Dewey and Schiller, had not provided them with *une sorte de centre de ralliement et de coordination!* So far as my obtuse brain and my insufficiently philosophical faculties permit me to understand pragmatism, radical empiricism, tychism, and "pure experience," — *je m'y sens tout gagné.*

In our country our general cultivated public is becoming every day better acquainted with your thought; and the translation of your *Talks to Teachers* by Pidoux, following so soon after the *Expérience religieuse* by Abauzit, is having a most favorable effect upon this diffusion of your ideas in French-speaking Switzerland. There is, moreover, an evident and curious affinity between our temperament and the general allure of your mentality: our public finds in you something that it needs and which it finds neither in French nor in German philosophers of the present day. . . . Believe me, devotedly yours,

TH. FLOURNOY

Cambridge, March 26, 1907 [6]

Dear Flournoy, —

. . . I have grown more and more deeply into pragmatism, and I rejoice immensely to hear you say, "je m'y sens tout gagné." It

[5] Translated from the French by the author.
[6] *L.W.J.,* II, 267–8.

is absolutely the only philosophy with *no* humbug in it, and I am certain that it is *your* philosophy.   Have you read Papini's article in the February *Leonardo?*   That seems to me really splendid. You say that my ideas have formed the real *centre de ralliement* of the pragmatist tendencies.   To me it is the youthful and *empanaché* Papini who has best put himself at the centre of equilibrium whence all the motor tendencies start.   He (and Schiller) has given me great confidence and courage.   I shall dedicate my book, however, to the memory of J. S. Mill.

I hope that you are careful to distinguish in my own work between the pragmatism and the "radical empiricism" . . . which to my own mind have no necessary connection with each other.   My first proofs came in this morning, along with your letter, and the little book ought to be out by the first of June.   You shall have a very early copy.   It is exceedingly untechnical, and I can't help suspecting that it will make a real impression. . . .   A good *coup de collier* all round, and I verily believe that a new philosophic movement will begin. . . .   Love to you all from

W. J.

Among James's personal friends there were two who found the negations of pragmatism congenial without adopting its metaphysical and religious applications.   Thus to Barrett Wendell pragmatism meant that "we live and die in terms of surmise," and that "finality is nowhere within human ken." [7]   Similarly, it was the irony and not the enthusiasm of the pragmatist cult which appealed to Judge Holmes.   Reference has already been made to the divergence of vocation and philosophy which separated these lifelong friends.   But James sent his published works to Holmes, and Holmes had rarely failed to respond with his half-appreciative, half-dissenting comment.   Upon receiving a copy of the *Principles,* he wrote: "I have read the book — and every word of it — with delight and admiration.   I think it a noble work, and don't doubt it will give you a reputation of the kind our generation most values, here and in Europe.   Some of the chapters are schemes of all possible *belles lettres* in scientific form, yet preserving the *esprit* and richness of empirical writing." [8]   But he had refused to accept James's

[7] *Scribner's Magazine,* LXXXIV (1928), 686.
[8] Nov. 10, 1890.

theory of the freedom of the will. In acknowledging *The Will to Believe,* he wrote: —

Boston, May 24, 1896

Dear William, —

Thank you very much for the little book which I have read with much pleasure. With its general aim or end I sympathize deeply — I mean the justification of the idealizing impulse; in detail, I somewhat diverge. I think the demands made of the universe are too nearly the Christian demands without the scheme of salvation. I long ago made up my mind that all that one needed was a belief in the significance of the universe. And more lately it has come to seem to me that even that might be ambiguous. For all I know "significance" is an expression of finiteness and incompleteness, and the total, if there is one, is too great a swell to condescend to have a meaning. The basis of my content is precisely the denial of the possibility of that attitude of rejection and scorn for which you quote Carlyle and the *City of Dreadful Night.* Of course a man may say, "I hate it," as a mere fact of temperament, and may talk big against God while the lightning is quiet. But what warrant a sceptic can have for assuming that he is a god outside the show, with a ποῦ στῶ for criticizing it, I don't understand. This you will recognize as my ever recurring view ever since we have known each other. I won't write a lecture, but just hint my reserves and repeat my thanks. Affectionately yours,

O. W. Holmes

As to the *Varieties,* which he read with Royce's *World and the Individual* ("very able — but thimblerigging, I thought it, on the first rapid perusal"), Holmes had rejected the conclusions, and at the same time applauded the style and the "delicate appreciation of all aspects of the human." He added, writing in 1902: "Some day, here, in Heaven, or in the world outside of time and space where Royce is God, we shall talk together again with that intimacy of understanding and mutual stimulus which we have known and which I never forget."

Pragmatism interested Holmes above James's other writings, and presented issues on which Holmes held definitive views of his own. His remark that "the best test of truth is the power of the thought to get itself accepted in the competition of the market"[9] was plainly pragmatistic; the general philosophical conclusions which he drew were peculiarly his own.   Of what was relativistic and skeptical in James's view, Holmes felt confident; but of James's confidence, metaphysical and religious, Holmes was — skeptical.   James sent him copies of the articles which appeared early in 1907, in advance of the book: —

Washington, March 24, 1907

Dear Bill, —

I have read your two pieces about pragmatism[10] (pedantic name) and am curious to hear the rest.   Meantime I will fire off a reflection or two.   For a good many years I have had a formula for truth which seems humbler than those you give . . . but I don't know whether it is pragmatic or not.   I have been in the habit of saying that all I mean by truth is what I can't help thinking.   The assumption of the validity of the thinking process seems to mean no more than that: I am up against it — I have gone as far as I can go — just as when I like a glass of beer.   But I have learned to surmise that my *can't helps* are not necessarily cosmic can't helps — that the universe may not be subject to my limitations; and philosophy generally seems to me to sin through arrogance.   It is like the old knight-errants who proposed to knock your head off if you did n't admit that their girl was not only a nice girl but the most beautiful and best of all possible girls.   I can't help preferring champagne to ditch water, — I doubt if the universe does.

But a reference to the universe seems to let in the Absolute that in form I was expelling.   To that I answer that I admit it to be but a guess.   I think the despised *ding an sich* is all right.   It stands on faith or a bet.   The great act of faith is when a man decides that he is not God.   But when I admit that you are not my dream, I seem to myself to have admitted the universe and the *ding an sich*, — unpredicable and only guessed at, as somewhat out of which I come rather than coming out of me.   But if I did come out of it, or rather, if I am in it, I see no wonder that I can't swallow it.   If it fixed my bounds, as it gives me my powers, I have

[9] Dissenting in 1919 in *Abrams* v. *United States,* 250 U. S. 616, 624 (*Dissenting Opinions,* 1929, 50) ; *cf. Collected Legal Papers,* 1920, 310–6.
[10] "Pragmatism's Conception of Truth," *Jour. of Philos.,* IV (1907) ; and "A Defense of Pragmatism," *Pop. Sci. Mo.,* LXX (1907).

nothing to say about its possibilities or characteristics except that it is a kind of thing (using this phraseology sceptically and under protest) that has me in its belly and so is bigger than I. It seems to me that the only promising activity is to make *my* universe coherent and livable, not to babble about *the* universe. Truth then, as one, I agree with you, is only an ideal — an assumption that if everyone was as educated and clever as I he would feel the same compulsions that I do. To a limited extent only do men feel so in fact, so that in fact there are as many truths as there are men. But if we all agreed, we should only have formulated our limitations. . . . I think the attempt to make these limitations compulsory on anything outside our dream — to demand significance, etc., of *the* universe — absurd. I simply say it contains them, and bow my head. To defy it would be equally absurd, as it would furnish me the energy with which to shake my fist. Most of us retain enough of the theological attitude to think that we are little gods. It is the regular position of sceptical French heroes, — like the scientific man in Maeterlinck's "Bees."

I have written more of a letter than I have time to write, but I add that I don't think fundamental doubt at all inconsistent with practical idealizing. As long as man's food produces extra energy he will have to let it off, *i.e.,* to act. To act affirms, for the moment at least, the worth of an end; idealizing seems to be simply the generalized and permanent affirmation of the worth of ends. One may make that affirmation for purposes of conduct, and leave to the universe the care of deciding how much it cares about them. Again I bow my head and try to fulfil what seems to me my manifest destiny. . . . As to pain, suicide, etc., I think you make too much row about them, and have had thoughts on the need of a society for the promotion of hard-heartedness. It is as absurd for me to be spearing my old commonplaces at you as it would be for an outsider to instruct me in the theory of legal responsibility, but you see, *mon vieux,* although it is years since we have had any real talk together, I am rather obstinate in my adherence to ancient sympathies and enjoy letting out a little slack to you.

I think your "Defense of Pragmatism" an admirable piece of writing. Also it commands my full sympathy so far as I see. Its classification reminded me (in the freedom merely) of Patten's

Development of English Thought — a most amusing and suggestive book — one of those that like your piece makes me say, "Give me the literature of the last twenty-five years and you may destroy the rest" (when I want to horrify the cultured). In general nowadays I would rather read sociology than philosophy; though I was interested by Santayana's four volumes, spite of their slight tendency to improvise; and though I devoted a certain time, the summer before last, to enough study of Hegel's *Logic* to enable me for the moment to say specifically what I thought the fallacies, and then dismissed it from my mind. Adieu. Yours ever,

O. W. Holmes

P.S. I have just read your other paper,[11] also good. Your general line of thought has been used by protectionists — that protection unlocks energies and gets more out of men. . . .

Washington, April 1, 1907

Dear Bill, —

Thanks for the additional article[12] which I have read. We start from surprisingly similar premises, and our conclusions fit as opposites sometimes do. Your world is convex and mine is concave, but I don't see but you come out on the arbitrary as I do. That is, unless your *better for us* means what feels better, you still are defining truth by truth, which is like seeking the limit of space in terms of space. Starting with a feeling, and starting with a can't help, seem to me a good deal alike except in their implications. I am reminded by some things you say of an observation of mine to which I attach some value in the legal aspect. I say that truth, friendship, and the statute of limitations have a common root in time. The true explanation of title by prescription seems to me to be that man, like a tree in the cleft of a rock, gradually shapes his roots to his surroundings, and when the roots have grown to a certain size, can't be displaced without cutting at his life. The law used to look with disfavor on the statute of limitations, but I have been in the habit of saying it is one of the most sacred and indubitable principles that we have; which used to lead my predecessor

---

[11] "The Energies of Men," *Philos. Rev.*, XVI (1907).
[12] Second installment of "A Defense of Pragmatism," *Popular Sci. Mo.*, LXX (1907).

Field to say that Holmes did n't value any title that was not based on fraud or force.   Yours ever,

O. W. HOLMES

Upon receiving a copy of *Pragmatism,* Holmes summed up his verdict: "I heartily agree with much, but I am more sceptical than you are.   You would say that I am too hard or tough-minded, — I think none of the philosophers sufficiently humble."

Professor John E. Russell was one of the earliest critics of pragmatism.   In an article of 1906,[13] he argued that knowledge involves relations which transcend the knower's experiences — logical relations which no introspective account can ever embrace.   On the flyleaf of his copy of this article James wrote his comment: "You think . . . that likeness, cause, beyondness and what not find no lodgement in my system.   But I lodge them along with every other form of relation, in the content.   They are overtones that tinge the everlasting undertone of nextness. . . .   All content as such terminates in its own immediate self, you think; whereas the plain fact is that all content . . . is immediately *of* other content — is *so given.*   It *is* not; it *passes.* . . .   Satisfaction 'transcends' backwards, as the 'more' transcended forwards. . . .   'Truth' *is* not, concretely. . . .   It is not an *esse,* but a *fieri,* a function.   It lives only in passage; in short, it is 'what passes.' "

Early in 1907, James wrote to Russell: "The New Yorkers were bad enough; I lectured to them on pragmatism at Columbia eight times; they compassed me about, they wagged their tongues at me on four several evenings; I replied to them *straight* each time; they found nought to say in return, but not one confessed himself convicted of error."   Russell was destined to be James's one exception to the rule that philosophers never confess their errors.   In the correspondence which followed, and a part of which was afterwards published, Russell insisted upon distinguishing the *truth* of an idea from the experience of its *proving* true; while James challenged him to give any meaning to the first except in terms of the second. In the end Russell conceded the point and went over from intellectualism to the camp of James, Dewey, and Schiller.[14]

James reckoned among his allies the experimental scientists who

[13] "Some Difficulties with the Epistemology of Pragmatism and Radical Empiricism," *Philos. Rev.,* XV.

[14] *C.E.R.,* 470–83; cf. *Jour. of Philos.,* VII (1910), 23.

offered a pragmatic interpretation of their own technique.   Among
these he frequently named Ernst Mach, Karl Pearson, W. Ostwald,
and H. Poincaré.[15]   From Mach James had learned something of
what he knew about the history of science, and he had readily accepted his view of the biological and economic function of scientific
concepts.   That was in the earlier days.   In his insistence on the
practical motives of knowledge, James had now gone so far that
he could obtain from Mach only the sense of a somewhat lagging
support: "W. J., but not emphatic enough," he wrote in the margin
of his copy of Mach's *Erkenntnis und Irrtum*.   The latter's acknowledgment of *Pragmatism* was brief and somewhat perfunctory:
"I have read the book through hurriedly from beginning to end with
great interest, in order to study it again later.   Although I am by
my entire training a scientist and not at all a philosopher, nevertheless I stand very close to pragmatism in my ways of thinking, without ever having used that name.   By following out this line the
unprofitable differences between philosopher and scientist could be
resolved."

Other approving comments on *Pragmatism,* coming from Dewey,
Bergson, Strong, and Schiller, are reserved for special consideration below.   The majority of his contemporaries and colleagues
received the book with profound misgivings.   It confirmed Stumpf's
"growing divergence."   Royce not only disagreed but disapproved.
C. C. Everett voiced an objection whose force James quickly acknowledged.   In "Philosophical Conceptions and Practical Results,"
James had argued that matter and God were pragmatically the same
if their results were the same; and that if there were no future life
awaiting us it would make no difference whether we had sprung
from one or the other.   This passage was reprinted in *Pragmatism,*
but in the *Meaning of Truth* the author tells us that he had "perceived a flaw" at once.[16]   Origins make an *emotional* difference regardless of ulterior consequences.   James spoke of the "automatic

[15] *Pragm.*, 48, 57. James read all of these writers. Poincaré's *Science et
l'hypothèse, Valeur de la science,* and *Science et méthode* were all read and annotated between 1902 and 1908, and Karl Pearson's *Grammar of Science* ten years
earlier.   Reading Ostwald's *Vorlesungen über Naturphilosophie* in 1902, James
wrote the term "pragmatism" in the margin opposite the author's interpretations of
scientific concepts in terms of their experimental consequences (114, 366).   During this same year he received letters from Ostwald recognizing the similarity of
their views and urging James to formulate the pragmatic theory of scientific concepts.
[16] *C.E.R.*, 414 ff.; *Pragm.,* 92–100; *M.T.,* 189, note.

sweetheart" — Everett, who may have originally drawn James's attention to the "flaw," spoke of the incubator-chicken: —

Cambridge, Oct. 29, 1898

My dear James, —

I thank you for your pamphlet, which I read with much interest, as I do whatever you write that comes my way. If I may venture a suggestion in regard to this, it seemed to me as I read it, that perhaps too little regard was had for *sentiment per se*. We speak of chicken-hearted men. Suppose we think of a human-hearted chicken. It seems to me it would make considerable difference to one approximating this type, whether it had a mother-hen brooding over it or was kept warm in an incubator — even though it got everything out of the incubator that it could out of the hen. Is not at least one difficulty with materialism that it changes the world into an incubator? — There are enough more. Excuse this hasty suggestion and believe me, with love and admiration, yours very truly,

C. C. EVERETT

James Ward was one of many who regretted pragmatism the more poignantly because of their sympathy with other motives in James's thought: —

Diablerets (Switzerland), July 18, 1907

My dear James, —

I owe you many thanks for sending me a copy of your lectures on *Pragmatism*. I have, I believe, read the whole of it, but I must candidly confess that I cannot get excited about pragmatism. It is not that I think . . . it of no importance. On the contrary, it has emphasized a side of experience too much ignored by certain influential thinkers. But the main point, the primacy of the practical, has been fully made out and I am content to leave the dead to bury their dead. What interests me in your work is what you have to say about pluralism. I was very much struck years ago by the remark of a clever young Frenchman, [Émile] Boirac, that the problem of the one and the many would be *the* philosophical problem of the twentieth century, and I am taking it up myself in my new Gifford Lectures. But I find the difficulties appalling; at the same time, I am satisfied that the first step towards a solution of the main problem is to have the pluralist position fully worked out. Knowing your pluralistic tendencies I have been anxiously awaiting a systematic exposition from your pen. Meanwhile I have been attempting to work out one of my own, and it is now about half done. I have gone to work a different way from you, but I incline more and more to admit your result that "absolute monism is shattered." . . .

Your last lecture disappointed me and I fancy will disappoint many of your readers. Just when one is expecting at least some hint of the sort of theism you conceive to be compatible with pluralism, you say: "I cannot start upon a whole theology at the end of this last lecture"; and then refer to your *Varieties of Religious Experience,* as if the problem had not been shelved there too. Well, at least we shall look out for a complete work on "Radical Empiricism," and hope you will leave such secondary matters as pragmatism to your juniors, Dewey and Schiller. By the way, I found the lady with whom we are staying, who is a great admirer of yours, was busy reading *Pragmatism* when we came. She is greatly shocked at your "want of academic dignity," and she thinks you are getting worse! I tell her I know of no writer except Huxley who has such appositeness and vigor. . . . With kindest regards, yours sincerely,

JAMES WARD

Frederick Pollock provided a perfect illustration of James's observation that a disquieting novelty is often attacked as an accepted commonplace: —

London, Oct. 5, 1907

My dear James, —

It was bad luck that I could not be within reach of you during my visit to New England. Since I came back I have read *Pragmatism.* If the pragmatic method teaches anything it would seem to be that agreement and disagreement to philosophical propositions in the lump are of very little value, so I shall not say whether I agree with you or not. Moreover, I understand your pragmatism, at any rate, to consist not in affirmation or denial of specific propositions about the universe but in a way of regarding the whole spirit of philosophical inquiry. Taking it so, my difficulty is not to conceive pragmatism as a working method, but to think of any notable philosopher who was not a pragmatist. Socrates was assuredly one, the first and greatest; his objection to the Sophists was that they treated serious questions merely as themes for rhetoric and dialectic. The Schoolmen were such bold pragmatists that they adopted the heathen Aristotle as the main pillar of Catholic philosophy. Descartes was a pragmatist — what he wanted was *marcher assurément dans cette vie* — and so following down to William James & Co. Materialism can be pragmatical, too, as witness the great Virgilian panegyric on Lucretius, — three lines only, but what lines! [17] And Thomas Hobbes of Malmesbury, who contrived to combine a thoroughly materialist psychology with an eschatology worked out in some detail.

For my own part, I have thought for many years that even competent people's opinions in both philosophy and politics are a function of temperament as much as of dialectic, or more. No logic would ever reason a Carlyle into optimism or an Emerson into pessimism. . . . Yours very truly,

F. POLLOCK

Shadworth Hodgson was too much of a rationalist at heart to have any sympathy with pragmatism. By this time he and James were gazing affectionately but sadly across an ever-widening gulf of philosophical dissent.[18]

London, June 18, 1907

My dear James, —

Many thanks for so kindly sending me your book on *Pragmatism*, through the London publishers. I shall read it with the greatest pleasure and the greatest attention; though I must confess that I am strongly pre-possessed against what I know are its tenets, and can hardly imagine it possible that I should be convinced by it. You describe the name "Pragmatism" as a new name for some old ways of thinking; — I go no farther than your title-page for this. Of course, — *old* and *ever-recurring*. The names "Pragmatism" and "Humanism" alike announce its partial character, and therefore its

---

[17] "Happy the man who has gained a knowledge of the causes of things," etc., *Georgics*, Bk. II, lines 490–2.

[18] *Cf.* above, 1375 ff. In 1911 Hodgson attacked pragmatism in an essay, "Some Cardinal Points in Knowledge," *Proc. of the British Academy*, V.

total unfitness to be a *philosophy*. How can you dream of elevating the needs, the desires, the purposes, of Man into a "measure" of the Universe? You have surely first to ask, what experience *compels him to think of* Man, and the Universe, and the relation between them, as *really being,* before you can even ask the question of how much those needs, desires, or purposes, reveal of the nature of the Universe.

But enough of this *old* criticism of an *old* way of thinking. Let me congratulate you on your election as a corresponding member of the British Academy. I am greatly rejoiced thereat, as a humble member of that body. I am, as ever, sincerely yours,

SHADWORTH H. HODGSON

James felt that most of the objections to pragmatism were due to misunderstandings, sometimes on his part and sometimes on the reader's, but in either case quite capable of being removed. He set himself the task of removing them because of a firm conviction that his was the true gospel, which would ultimately prevail and which it was his duty to propagate. A letter to his friend Thomas Sargeant Perry illustrates this attitude: —

South Lincoln, Aug. 1, 1907

Dear Thomas, —

I was "unfeignedly" delighted by your appreciative words lately about "pragmatism," not only that *you* should have been so cordial and shown yourself the genuine philosopher I have always accused you of being, but because I took your letter to be "representative" of a certain body of non-professional opinion, and your heartily favorable reaction seemed to me an example of what I may expect elsewhere. My colleagues absolutely refuse to understand my doctrine of "truth," perverting it in the most shamelessly stupid way. It convinces me that I am original. I think I entirely disconcert them by my non-technicality of statement. They are so brought up on technical ways of handling things that when a man handles them *bare,* they are non-plussed, can neither understand, agree, or reply. . . . Have you read B. Shaw's last volume, *John Bull's Other Island,* etc.? — the *most* utterly delightful body of truths I've ever had in my hands. Love to you all!

W. J.

During the years 1907 and 1908, Jean Bourdeau published a series of articles on Papini and on pragmatism — articles with a strongly irreverent and journalistic flavor, and containing a delicately ironic allusion to *le genre de philosophie que l'on peut attendre des Yankees,* but on the whole sympathetic with the new movement as an expression of the youthful and experimental mind.[19]   Perry sent James these articles and evoked the following response: —

"Thanks for . . . the last Bourdeau.   Poor man! he seems not to be able to get rid of the subject; but the pragmatism that lives inside of me is so different from that of which I succeed in wakening the idea inside of other people, that theirs makes me feel like cursing God and dying.   When *I say* that, *other things being equal,* the view of things that seems more satisfactory morally will legitimately be treated by men as truer than the view that seems less so, *they quote me as saying* that anything morally satisfactory can be treated as true, no matter how unsatisfactory it may be from the point of view of its consistency with what we already know or believe to be true about physical or natural facts.   Which is rot!! . . . I am sending you an *American Magazine* with Mr. Dooley on pragmatism.   Its fortune 's made!"

James's sensitiveness to the charge of subordinating theoretical to crudely practical considerations appears in the following protest written to his brother on September 8, 1907: "I want to write and publish, if I can do it, another immortal work, less popular but more original than *Pragmatism,* which latter no one seems rightly to understand, — representing it as a philosophy got up for the use of engineers, electricians and doctors, whereas it really grew up from a more subtle and delicate theoretic analysis of the function of knowing than previous philosophers had been willing to make.   I know that it will end by winning its way and triumphing!"

[19] Bourdeau was a writer on historical and philosophical subjects and a regular contributor to the *Journal des débats.*   The articles appeared in this paper, but are most readily accessible in the *Revue hebdomidaire,* Jan. 25, March 1, Aug. 30, Sept. 27, Nov. 8, 1907, Jan. 24, Feb. 28, 1908.   Bourdeau based his articles largely on A. Lalande's "Pragmatisme et pragmaticisme," *Revue philos.,* LXI (1906).

LXXIX

THE DEFENSE OF PRAGMATISM

IT was important for the orientation of pragmatism that there should be a clear understanding of its relations to the neo-Fichtean movement represented in contemporary German philosophy by Windelband and Rickert. This school, like pragmatism, affirmed "the primacy of the practical reason," which point of agreement, however, only served to accentuate a fundamental divergence. Neo-Fichteanism was *a priori* in its theory of knowledge and absolutistic in its metaphysics, while pragmatism was empirical and naturalistic. One of the leading proponents of neo-Fichtean doctrine was James's friend and colleague, Münsterberg, who followed James's development closely, and was quick to call attention to his departure from the more orthodox Kantian path.

Cambridge, March 16, 1905

Dear Münsterberg, —

It is a great compliment to my stuff that you should read it so hot from the press.[1] Too precipitately, possibly, for you to have grasped its full "inwardness." Of course I have long been familiar with the essay in Windelband's *Präludien* on Kant; and with Rickert in both editions.[2] As Schiller, Dewey and I mean pragmatism, it is *toto coelo* opposed to either the original or the revived Kantism. What similarity can there possibly be between human laws imposed *a priori* on all experience as "legislative," and human ways of thinking that grow up piecemeal among the details of experience because on the whole they work best? It is this rationalistic part of Kant that pragmatism is expressly meant to overthrow. Both its theory of knowledge and its metaphysics go with an empiricist mode of thought. When the other lectures of my course get published you will certainly see this, as you cannot see it now. I have n't read

[1] Apparently "The Essence of Humanism," which had just appeared in the *Jour. of Philos.*, II (1905).
[2] *Gegenstand der Erkenntnis*, 1892 and 1904.

Simmel's longer works — only his original pragmatistic article
(which seemed to me rather crude, though essentially correct)[3] and
his work on the science of history, so I can't compare him with
Dewey and Schiller. But as for Rickert, in spite of his exquisite
literary talent, and clearness of statement, it seems to me that he
just buries his doctrine alive. It is the cleanest case I know of an
abstraction (the transcendental *Ich,* namely) first shown to be
equivalent to absolute zero, then opposed in glory and dignity to
all the particulars from which it is abstracted, as their real source
and ground. Rickert's chapter on "Relativismus" (*Relativismus*
being exactly identical with pragmatism in the discussion in question) seems to me *erbärmlich,*[4] really *infantile.* But these are hasty
and dogmatic words of mine. You can't fully understand my position till you read this lecture on truth in its setting among the
others. There, it is irreconcilable with anything in Kant, — only
the most superficial resemblance obtaining. Yours as ever,

W. J.

In his *Science and Idealism,* given as an address at Yale in 1905–
1906, Münsterberg set forth the antithesis between the realm of
describable existence and the deeper reality of the indescribable will,
whose four "postulates" of "identity," "harmony," "fulfilment,"
and "unity" define the realms of science, æsthetics, ethics, and religion.

Cambridge, June 28, 1906

Dear Münsterberg, —
I thank you both for the *Psychological Studies* and for *Science
and Idealism.* Also for your remarks on my Papini article. I confess I am sorry that you consider my criticism of our American
articles uncalled for. Such uncouthness and obscurity I have never
met before so systematically characteristic of a movement, — though
I suppose that Fichte's and Hegel's time paralleled it. The only
clear writers are Schiller on one side and Taylor on the other.[5] . . .

---

[3] Über eine Beziehung der Selektionslehre zur Erkenntnistheorie," *Archiv für
systematische Philos.,* I (1895).
[4] Pitiful. For James's defense against "relativismus" and his counter-charge
of "abstractionism" against Rickert and Münsterberg, *cf. M.T.,* 246 ff. For his
recognition of his agreement with Rickert, *cf. Pragm.,* 228, 236.
[5] *C.E.R.,* 460; A. E. Taylor, *Philos. Rev.,* XIV (1905); *McGill Univ. Magazine,* III (1904).

I have read *Science and Idealism* with great care, and with every effort to assimilate your attitude. *That* book, at least, is superiorly well written! But were it not for my fixed belief that the world is wide enough to sustain and nourish without harm many different types of thinking, I believe that the wide difference between your whole *Drang* in philosophizing and mine would give me a despairing feeling. I am satisfied with a free, wild nature; you seem to me to cherish and pursue an Italian garden, where all things are kept in separate compartments, and one must follow straight-ruled walks. Of course nature gives material for those four hard distinctions which you make, but they are only centres of emphasis in a flux, for me; and as you treat them, reality seems to me all *stiffened*. The will-attitude which you describe . . . and its postulations, are also really there, but resultantly and tentatively, along with rival tendencies; and the sort of decree-fulminating prior authorities you make of them strike me as monstrously artificial. My "will to believe" shrinks back from such dogmatic behavior as that! But emphases and tempers are only the colors the world is painted in. If the same content is there in every color it would seem all right to let us choose our colors as we please. But when you substantify the "over-individual" timeless self as you do, and make it (an absolutely empty abstraction according to me) the law-giving supporter *a priori* of all the contents of reality, you seem to me to introduce a mythological content. Its "will" as described by you means . . . absolutely *nothing* real for me. It is *pure* fiction. . . .

But, dear Münsterberg, I don't wish to inflict polemic upon you. The world is wide enough! Do your best; and I'll do my best; and the next generation will do better than either of us, and keep whatever either of us may have contributed to the good. Don't answer; but if you do, be sure that I will not strike back. Sincerely yours,

WM. JAMES

Clifton, July 1, 1906

Dear James, —

I am sincerely grateful to you for your philosophical letter. Believe me that no one can agree with you more than I do in your chief thesis that each one ought to do his best in expressing himself, and that in this way by the dissensus of opinions the truth will be developed. Certainly self-expression is the central dogma of my whole system. Also our differences: yes, the world of immediate experience is to me also a wild nature without ways and flower-beds, and [with] plenty of weed. But I think our life's duty makes us gardeners, makes us to unweed the weeds of sin and error and ugliness; and when we finally come to think over what kind of flowers were left as valuable, and we bring together those which are similar — then we have finally indeed such an Italian garden as the world which we are seeking, as the world which has to be acknowledged as ultimate.

You say, you do not find such wills in you. Neither do I. If I found them as experience, my investigation would be a psychological one; I discover that will in the effects. I find realities in me which I cannot understand if I do not consider them as the fulfilment of such will behind the scene, as transcendental power. Just, therefore, my way is that of critical philosophy, as against a dogmatism which conceives the reality always as something experience-able and substantive. You want that reality is an existing object — that is in my eyes an untenable dogmatism. To me reality is an activity, a subject, whose effects alone I perceive; *otherwise I should not understand why something is to me valuable without having any value for me personally.* And that is really *my fundamental problem: why do I care for a moral deed or a true astronomical calculation if they do not bring any advantage to me?* In short the problem of absolute values is in the centre of my philosophy, not the question of knowledge which absorbs you pragmatists. Of course that short address for Yale was quite unsatisfactory; but I am writing at present a full book, "Kritik der Werte"; [6] I hope to complete it in October, and that I hope will answer some of your doubts. . . . Yours sincerely,

H. Münsterberg

The following letter to Mrs. Glendower Evans was written in reply to her complaint that James had caricatured absolutism. The correspondence occurred immediately after the conclusion of the Lowell Lectures on pragmatism, and related specifically to the lecture, "What Pragmatism Means," in which James had insisted that if absolutism was to mean anything it must be interpreted in terms

[6] The title of the published work was *Philosophie der Werte* (1908); in English, *The Eternal Values*, 1909.

of the specific emotional difference which it makes to the person who accepts it. This difference consists in the trust which the absolutist can feel, and which permits him to enjoy an occasional "moral holiday," knowing that the cause of righteousness is in safe hands.[7]

Cambridge, Dec. 11, 1906 [8]

Dear Bessie, —

I shall continue to love every word *you* say, however wicked — thus should pragmatists and absolutists take each other! Your wickedest word is to accuse me of caricaturing the Absolute. As pragmatism is little more than an attempt to think clearly, that charge would kill me dead, if true; so in spite of you, I *must* reply to it on paper. *Vaguely,* everyone is both monist and pragmatist. One lives in the detail of one's experiences; and one supplements those in sight by a *more,* which most of us imagine consolingly. 'T is when you try to be not vague but definite about the more, that the trouble arises. You can take it as quantitative addition, indefinite in amount, and merely prolonging the finite; or you can take it as totalizing and surrounding the finite, altering the form of experience, therefore (or rather presenting it in another form than that in which we get it) : eternal or absolute form.

If you take it as *prolongation,* your consolations are probable at best, and your world a meliorism. If you take it as totalizing, your consolations are certain or necessary and your world a dogmatic optimism. It flows from the very form of totality that it should lack nothing, for it does n't refer beyond itself. You surely don't mean *this* when you accuse me of caricaturing! *As realized "eternally,"* then, everything is good. Evil is seen along with what over-rules it, monistically. Is it a caricature to say that we ourselves are advised to seek peace by ascending as far as possible to the eternal point of view? What can such peace come from in that case but from the abstract reflexion that in the whole every part is needed and symphonic? No perception of the particular atonements is needed for this, by us; the Absolute Experient has the perception, but for us the monistic form *per se* is a guarantee of the total excellence. How is it a caricature to say that this permits of quietism?

[7] *Pragm.,* 71–9.
[8] Published in *Atlantic,* CXLIV (1929), 376–7. James retained a copy of this letter, indicating that he attached importance to it. *Cf. M.T.,* viii–ix.

You yourself write of issues being "guaranteed" by the larger order. Guaranteed *anyhow,* without specification of remedy. It permits equally of strenuosity, of course. It *dictates* nothing, but *justifies* all *fact* qua element of absolute experience. It thus helps sick souls more than pragmatism does; and as their needs are the sorest it has always seemed to me that this is a towering merit, to be weighed against absolutism's demerits.

But after all, *how* does an Absolute make so for optimism, blindfold on our part, clear-sighted on that of the Eternal? Surely by the "overruling" content which it postulates as complementing the bad parts of experience. . . . The pragmatic value of the Absolute consists in nothing but these *atoning facts.* The pragmatist postulates them by faith, *sans phrase,* the absolutist by his extra machinery, which is supposed to certify them. In any case *our* only way of realizing them is as a prolongation. The only thing *we* gain by assuming the eternal point of view is the *permission of blindfold optimism.* To those who don't care for it, the invariable reply is: "Go back to the finite point of view! Hate and deplore things to your heart's content; for the 'now,' the evil part *as such,* exists in the Absolute to be deplored exactly as we deplore it. Only as overruled, is it justified, only as He sees it." And that is what I meant by the "shuffle." The Absolute has become only an abstract name, like "Nature," for the indefinitely prolonged content of experience, and we are all pragmatists again together. There may *be* an Absolute, of course; and its pragmatic use to us is to make us more optimistic. But it is n't forced on us by logic, as Royce and Bradley think, and its cash equivalent is the *atoning experiences believed in.* Pardon so long a rigmarole. Yours affectionately,

W. J.

In the summer of 1907, R. B. Perry published two articles, in the second of which [9] he argued that the meaning and truth of ideas should be identified with their *cognitive* use, that is, their reference to experienced reality, rather than with the ulterior practical uses which they also serve; and called attention to the difficulty of supposing, especially in the case of the past, that the world is modified by the knowing of it. James's reply is illuminating: —

[9] "Review of Pragmatism As a Philosophical Generalization," *Jour. of Philos.,* IV (1907).

South Lincoln, Aug. 4, 1907

Dear Perry, —

Your second article has just reached me. . . . The two . . . help to clear up many things. They make me, for instance, realize how unlucky a word pragmatism has been to attach to our theory of truth. It seems to most people to *exclude* intellectual relations and interests, but all it *means* is to say that these are subjective interests like all the others, and not the sole ones concerned in determining the beliefs that count as true. I think that . . . you have fallen into this trap yourself. You have failed to grasp the exceedingly wide bearings of Schiller's contentions. You . . . use [the word "practical"] as *excluding* intellectual practice. The pragmatic test of a concept's meaning is a difference in possible *experience* somewhere, but the experience may be a pure observation with no "practical" use whatever. It may have the tremendous theoretical use of telling which concept is true, however; and that may remotely be connected with practical uses over and above the mere verification, or it may not. The "cognitive intention" . . . is an intensely peculiar part, when developed, of our human emotional endowment; involving, as it does, curiosity for new fact, insistence on non-contradiction, and on simplification of form, and love of tracing applications. You treat it as if it lay apart from all other human urgencies, whereas psychologically it is only one species of the genus human urgency, and in this case simple formulas are reached only by treating the whole genus together. . . .

You speak, again, as if the "degree of satisfaction" was *exclusive* of theoretic satisfactions. Who ever said or implied this? Surely neither Dewey, Schiller nor I have ever denied that sensation, relation, and funded truth "dispose," in their measure, of what we "propose." Nothing that we propose can violate them; but, *they satisfied,* what in addition gratifies our æsthetic or utilitarian demands best will always be counted as *more* true. My position is that, *other things equal,* emotional satisfactions count for truth — among the other things being the intellectual satisfactions. Certainly a doctrine that encouraged immortality would draw belief more than one that did n't, if it were *exactly as satisfactory* in residual respects. Of course it could n't prevail against knock-down evidence to the contrary; but where there is no such evidence, it will incline belief. And how can truth be *known* save as that which inclines belief?

Truth must indeed *fit* "sensation, relation and funded truth," but the term "fit" is ambiguous — there are as many ways in which our ideas can fit an object as there are ways in which animals can fit their environment.   The truest fit is the *richest* fit — it will be held so. You surprise me by talking like those critics who assume that in the truth-relation the object alone is determin*ant,* the idea determin*ed.* They are *co-*determinants, of a result due to two variables reaching a final equilibrium or equation.

You speak of *"the* world."   *The* world is surely the *total* world, including our mental reaction.   The world *minus* that is an abstraction, useful for certain purposes, but always envelopable.   Pure naturalism is surely envelopable in wider teleological or appreciative determinations.   Most men try so to surround it.   You talk as if from the point of view of truth such trials were condemned in advance.   But we pragmatists not only justify them, but say that the constitution of the world of naturalistic truth itself can only be understood by bringing it into line with the appreciative truth. Subjective needs have played a part in both. . . .   In haste, yours as ever, and with much admiration for your essay in spite of my animadversions.

Wм. Jаmеs

The question of knowledge of the past was raised very ingeniously by a pupil of the old days, Alfred C. Lane, professor of geology and mineralogy in Tufts College.   In a letter written to James in October 1907, he formulated three alternatives: (1) the whole time-process, past and future, is rigidly determined, and can conceivably be surveyed by an all-seeing mind; (2) only the past is so determined; (3) nothing is so determined — the universe, past, present, and future, being, even to an all-seeing eye, naught but a writhing worm.   The originality of Professor Lane's formulation lies in his supposition of an instrument analogous to a microscope by which the past and future can be brought into view: —

"Suppose, to return to the likeness of our four-dimensional microscope, we are observing not a dead and rigid rock section but a living worm.   It turns and wriggles, and changes not merely the appearance in the focal plane, but above and below.   We cannot be sure of anything except that which we immediately see.   And in a cosmos constructed on this plan we could be sure neither of the past nor of the future. We could say that which is is, but we could not go on to affirm that that which has been was! In such a universe it might be literally true that sins were 'blotted out,' that the 'Absolute forgot' our transgressions, the future would change the past — the part of the worm above the focal plane move that below — as well as the past influence the future. And yet it would be neither without law nor control.

"Now in this last horn I have no faith. . . . I think the facts are against it; that, as I understand the structure of the universe, a physicist on some fitting fixed star could today see the cohorts crucifying Christ on Calvary, or hear the bellowing of prehistoric beasts, had he instruments of sufficient delicacy, and that to sufficiently refined sensibilities the cosmos would be one echoing whispering-gallery of all past time. . . . Thus so far as the past is concerned I must, must I not, class myself as a 'tender-minded softy'? Verification means to me not making the idea true, it is making me know it to be true. Is the truth less true before it is verified? Or does its difference to me make any difference in it? It would doubtless make a great practical difference to me as a deacon of an orthodox church if Christ did not take that walk to Emmaus. It would, so far as I know or can see, make no difference to anyone if the youngest uncles of Thotmes III had ever swam in the Nile. But I cannot see that my life or anyone else's affects the truth of the propositions. . . .

"I do not know whether you really adopt this third alternative and believe in the modification of the past by present and future, because your outlook seems to be by habit forward, — not like that of the geologists, backward. . . . I would really like to know whether you grasp the second or third horns, or both, as perhaps to some extent I do the first and second."[10]

Cambridge, Oct. 28, 1907

Dear Lane, —

I am very glad to get signs of life from you again, and I send back your tip-top letter as requested. I have had such a mass of correspondence about "Prag" lately that I am rather tired of writing on the subject, so you will excuse my brevity. The three alternatives

[10] This letter, dated Oct. 20, 1907, together with James's reply as printed below, appeared in an article by A. C. Lane, "The Trilemma of Determinism," *Western Journal of Education*, Ypsilanti, IV (1911).

you analyze so clearly are all familiar to my thought, though I never thought of microscope-focusing as representing the subjective time change in which a static order, or even a writhing "worm," may appear, and I find the image very luminous.

The second horn of the trilemma is mine, — with the future partly indeterminate while the past is given fully. The third horn (with the writhing past) I absolutely repudiate, for I can frame no notion of the past that does n't leave it inalterable. Truths involving the past's *relations* to *later things* can't come into being till the later things exist, so such truths may grow and alter, but the past itself is beyond the reach of modification. What I have done to deserve the preposterous misunderstanding which I am accused of on all sides, but which you only express hesitatingly (for which, thanks!), I can't imagine. I should like to see a single sentence from my book which gives color to it. Probably it comes from confusing the terms "reality" and "truth," — realities are independent variables, but truths about them are functions also of other variables, and must alter. I cannot enter into the general question of what motives we may have for assuming indeterminate futures, but am, with old-time regard, yours very truly,

WM. JAMES

In the autumn of 1907 James was "interviewed" in his study in Cambridge, and after an informal conversation he "went to his desk and wrote down this statement." It is interesting both as an example of extemporization and as an expression of James's earnest desire to make pragmatism both intelligible and acceptable. After complaining that certain of his critics had construed pragmatism as a resort to practise in default of theory, he proceeded as follows: —

INTERVIEW IN N. Y. TIMES, 1907

It is true that pragmatist writers have laid more stress than any previous philosophers on human action. But nothing could be more ludicrous than to call this their primary interest, or to explain it by their belief that purely theoretical knowledge of reality, and truth as such, are unattainable. Pragmatism's primary interest is in its doctrine of truth. All pragmatist writers make this the centre of their speculations; not one of them is sceptical, not one doubts our ultimate ability to penetrate theoretically into the very core of reality. . . .

Instead of being a practical substitute for philosophy, good for engineers, doctors, sewage experts, and vigorous untaught minds in general to feed upon, pragmatism has proved so over-subtle that even academic critics have failed to catch its question, to say nothing of their misunderstanding of its answer.   Whatever propositions or beliefs may, in point of fact, prove true, it says, the truth of them consists in certain definable *relations between them and the reality* of which they make report. . . .   Philosophers have generally been satisfied with the word "agreement" here, but pragmatists have seen that this word covers many different concrete possibilities. . . . There are all sorts of ways of having to do with a thing.   To know it, we must mean *that* thing, and not another thing; we must be able to portray or copy its inherent nature; and we must know innumerable things *about* it and its relations to other things.   To know it rightly, moreover, we must not go astray among all these many ways of knowing it, but select the way that fits in with our momentary interest, be the latter practical or theoretical, and select the way that will work. . . .   Thus the first vague notion of "agreement" with reality becomes specified into that of innumerable ways in which our thoughts may *fit* reality, ways in which the mind's activities coöperate on equal terms with the reality in producing the fit resultant truth. . . .

Mind *engenders* truth *upon* reality. . . .   Our minds are not here simply to copy a reality that is already complete.   They are here to complete it, to add to its importance by their own remodeling of it, to decant its contents over, so to speak, into a more significant shape.   In point of fact, the *use* of most of our thinking is to help us to *change* the world.   We must for this know definitely *what* we have to change, and thus theoretic truth must at all times come before practical application.   But the pragmatist writers have shown that what we here call theoretic truth . . . will be . . . irrelevant unless it fits the . . . purpose in hand. . . .   And, moreover, it turns out that the theoretic truth upon which men base their practice today is itself a resultant of previous human practice, based in turn upon still . . . previous truth . . . so that we may think of all truth whatever as containing so much human practice funded. . . .   Thus we seem set free to use our theoretical as well as our practical faculties — the practical here in the narrower sense — to get the world into a better shape, and all with a good conscience.   The only restriction is that the world resists some lines of attack on our part and opens herself to others, so that we must go on with the grain of her willingness. . . .   Hence the *sursum corda* of pragmatism's message. . . .

There never was such confusion.   The tower of Babel was monotony in comparison.   The fault has lain on both sides.   Dewey is obscure; Schiller bumptious and hasty; James's doctrine of radical empiricism, which has nothing to do with pragmatism and sounds idealistic, has been confounded with his pragmatism; pragmatism itself covers two or three distinct theses; the critics . . . opened fire before the pragmatists had got their words out; everyone has spoken at once, and the upshot has made one despair of men's intelligence. But little by little the mud will settle to the bottom. . . . We shall soon find ourselves at home in the pragmatic view and temper, and will then say that it was not worth so much hubbub.[11]

Professor A. O. Lovejoy, writing to acknowledge the receipt of James's *Pragmatism,* urged the need of sharpening certain distinctions: first, that between the pragmatic theory of meaning and the pragmatic theory of truth; second, that between the consequences following directly from a proposition itself, and those following from *believing* the proposition. A mechanical and a personal cause might have the same consequences, but believing the one or the other would have very different emotional effects. The writer then went on to express his assent to James's pluralism. "I should like very much," he said, "to see your pluralistic metaphysics stand on its proper logical legs, and throw away the weak and treacherous crutch of a pragmatist epistemology."

St. Hubert's, Sept. 13, 1907

Dear Lovejoy, —

Such a letter as yours from Bern is a rare treat. . . . The book was never meant for a treatise, but for a sketch, — to make air and room for an empirical philosophy that might not necessarily be irreligious, to breathe in. Finer and more accurate work was reserved for the future. This was only to *win a platform* for more accurate discussion, and the single-word title of *Pragmatism* was chosen for tactical purposes (since it was already in use) to group my different tendencies together, and rally those who could sympathize, under one banner. It will certainly serve that purpose, as "humanism" (the only alternative) would not have served it; so its ambiguity and lack of precision may be condoned.

This virtually replies to your strictures on my treatment of the "One and the Many." I never meant to refute monism in that lecture, but only to gain a place for fair discussion of pluralism; and I showed how easily the pragmatistic way of entering a question

[11] From W.J.'s mss. The interview, by Edwin Bjorkman, appeared in the *N. Y. Times,* Nov. 3, 1907.

brought the two views *onto the same level as hypotheses.* Absolutists call pluralism absurd and irrational *ab initio,* even as an
hypothesis.   To win an *even place* for it as an hypothesis was a
good illustration of what the pragmatic method could do, and I
used it to that end.   To seriously discuss monism with a view to its
refutation, one would have to explode its *arguments,* not one of
which I considered in that book.   But I'm very glad you like that
lecture! . . .

I have always been aware of what you lay out in so masterly a
way, — the heterogeneity between the pragmatic method of tracing
the meaning of ideas, and the pragmatic theory of truth. . . .
But when it comes to your distinction between two meanings in the
first meaning of pragmatism, I have to frankly cry *peccavi* — you
convict me of real sin.   Consequences of true ideas *per se,* and
consequences of ideas *qua believed by us,* are logically different
consequences, and the whole "will to believe" business has got to
be re-edited with explicit uses made of the distinction.   I have been
careless here, and I hope that you, in your article, will spread out
that matter at the length it deserves.   Failure to do it on my part
has been a misdemeanor. . . .

You ask what I do about propositions asserting past realities,
or other persons, their "meaning" not consisting of future consequences.   As a pragmatist (in the first sense) I reply that if objects
be represented so devoid of any context as to make no connection
whatever (logical or physical) with any item in the world's future,
their existence is not only unverifiable, but really meaningless.
Fellow-minds and past history expressly abound in such connections,
by which we approach their neighborhood or mentally remount time
towards them; but we can imagine, as coexisting with our experience,
myriads of entities absolutely isolated from it.   In that case, however, we can not only not *verify* which of them truly exists, but,
apart from some *possibility* of coming into touch with ourselves,
we cannot even conceive what . . . the real existence of any one
of them would mean. . . .

As for Kant, I do hope that you will treat him as a finite human
being and not as a supernatural oracle.[12]   As a human being he is

---

[12] In the letter cited above Lovejoy had announced his intention of writing an appraisal of Kant — "a sort of *was soll Kant uns sein.*"   Cf. "Kant and the English
Platonists" (*Essays Philos. and Psychol. in Honor of William James*), in which

delectable, as an oracle awful. I am *very* glad you are putting him in his setting, I'm sure he can't be properly understood (his home *influence,* at any rate, can't be understood) without that contrast-effect. As overcomer of Baumgarten, Crusius *et al.,* he was no doubt great. But it is the fashion to treat him as primarily an overcomer of Hume, which he emphatically was not. I have for years wished that someone would edit a *selection from Kant's contemporaries* (the philosophic texts in vogue before he wrote) as an *Apperceptionsmasse* for understanding him better. No one seems to read up them critters. You appear to have been doing it. . . .
Yours always truly,

WILLIAM JAMES

P.S. Have you read Bergson's *Évolution créatrice?* I find it perfectly glorious, though terribly obscure and unfinished.

Early in 1908 Lovejoy published two articles entitled "The Thirteen Pragmatisms," in which he suggested that, ten years having elapsed since the announcement of pragmatism, it was "perhaps not too much to ask that contemporary philosophers should agree to attach some single and stable meaning to the term." [13] The galleys of these articles were sent to James and he returned them to the author with profuse marginal comments. He occasionally referred to Lovejoy's criticisms as "cavils," *Spitzfindigkeiten,* "captious," and so on, but on the whole he contended that the multiplication of different (not incongruous) pragmatisms only amplified the pragmatist thesis and proved its fertility.

Cambridge, Dec. 22, 1907

Dear Lovejoy, —

I began your galleys with high hopes, so jollily and clearly written, but got somewhat disappointed ere the end. . . . I admire your good English and your genius for distinguishing, and think that some of your distinctions, possibly all of them, are useful and help the final clearing up. Many of them are familiar to all of us, but you *emphasize* them most usefully.

As a pragmatist, I welcomed all your distinctions and more.

Lovejoy goes far towards justifying James's view that "the true line of philosophic progress lies . . . not so much *through* Kant as *round* him." (*C.E.R.,* 437.)
[13] *Jour. of Philos.,* V (1908), 5.

They all fit into and build out the general pragmatist scheme for
which you show no sympathy and (it seems to me) little understanding.   Your reader does n't know whether you are condemning
or developing it.   I take you as developing it, though I doubt
whether you take yourself so.   That scheme is to establish a completely concrete account of what men mean by "truth."   They may,
upon occasion, mean each or any of the things you enumerate; and
a complete pragmatistic account would enumerate, subordinate, and
locate them all.   You give an impression (certainly not intended)
of arguing as if, because so many things go into the natural history
of live truth, they must cancel each other, and the learner *must* have
to fall back on "intellectualism," with its unexplicated term "agreement."   I could re-write your article, changing its censorious tone
for an enthusiastic one, and using (I think) every one of your distinctions to make the pragmatist account more solid.   The only
censure the article really *comports* is that we have been too hasty and
rushed into print with an inadequately concrete account.   Yours,
notwithstanding,

WILLIAM JAMES

Montrose, Pa., Jan. 1, 1908
Dear Professor James, —
   I am obliged to you for letting me see your marginal comments
on my "Thirteen Pragmatisms" paper as well as the more general
commentary of your note. . . .   So far as I can see, there is no more
any such thing as "Pragmatism" than there is (to steal an illustration
of your own) such a thing as the weather, over and above the
sequence of temperature and air-pressure states. . . .   Let a man
say which of the thirteen or more propositions he accepts; if he
accepts them all, let him say whether he takes them as independent
items of opinion, resting each on its own grounds, or as common
deductions from a higher general principle; if the latter, let him say
just what this general principle is, and show that his particulars
are really deducible from it.   Let us have pragmatism brought
down from glittering generalities about "concrete descriptions of
truth," "the practical" and what not, and reduced, itself, to its proper
cash-value.   And let us not be fooled, as a large part of the public
now seems to me to be fooled, by labels.   I, for my part, a good
deal question whether on the issues that seem to *me* to "make a differ-

ence" in philosophy, there is much in common between yourself, Dewey and Papini. I detect a similarity of party names, and of some favorite formulas; but I appear also to detect a profound divergence of essential tendencies. . . .

Your most general observation on my paper is that it implies no reflection on pragmatism even though all its distinctions and antitheses be admitted as just; for pragmatism has room for all these and more. . . . I can't think it a merit in a system of thought that it should be able to swallow up all of the disconnected and in part antithetic propositions enumerated in my paper. If it's one kind of "pragmatism" to lose one's respect for the sharp, clean *"entweder-oder* of the stiff-necked Understanding," that certainly is a feature of the movement with which I can't sympathize. . . . On the whole, I'm sure, pragmatism has been a big and useful thing; but it has, I'm equally sure, now reached the point where it's in danger of doing more harm than good if the movement be not purged of certain latent tendencies — if its own "characteristic excess" be not now recognized and corrected. And perhaps the first correction needed is that we should all cease thinking of the movement as a movement, reduce pragmatism to certain cold-blooded and entirely specific propositions, and begin to examine, first, their precise meaning; second, their consistency and relations *inter se;* and third, the reasons for thinking any of them true. . . . With cordial regards, yours,

ARTHUR O. LOVEJOY

It was an essential part of pragmatism to distinguish between beliefs on the one hand and reality on the other, and to attach truth exclusively to the former. Cleaving to this duality, James rejected the notion of an intermediate "proposition" or "supposal." The position is clearly stated in the following letter to Henry N. Gardiner.[14]

[Cambridge], Jan. 9, 1908

Dear Gardiner, —

Thanks for your most lucid letter, which makes clear to me one of the difficulties which I have to meet. I meet it by asking you

[14] *Cf.,* also, *M.T.,* 282 ff. The views of Gardiner to which allusion is here made were published under the title of "The Problem of Truth," *Philos. Rev.,* XVII (1908).

squarely whether the "supposal" of which you make so much be not a purely linguistic entity for which there is no place among the realities involved in the discussion. *"That"* Cæsar existed, *e.g.,* is not an intermediary between the objective fact "Cæsar-existed" and the other objective fact "someone's-belief-that-Cæsar-existed," but a muddle of the two facts, made to appear as a medium of connection between them by granting to it the objectivity of the first fact and the truth of the second. Surely truth can't inhabit a third realm between realities and statements or beliefs. If mythology be a "disease of language," then your "supposal" (excellent term, however) is certainly a mythological being. It is easy to see how it arose, for we say indifferently "the fact *that* Cæsar existed," and "the belief that Cæsar existed"; so that it becomes natural to marry fact and belief together by this *tertium quid* of a *that* which is neither fully objective nor fully subjective, and can mean sometimes what is real and sometimes what is true. It seems to me the great merit of pragmatism to have stepped right over all such mongrel figments and to have put discussion on the solid ground of facts and relations-between-facts, that are also facts. . . . I am very curt, being in a hurry, but I wish you'd search your heart seriously about this mongrel cur of a supposal, begotten upon you by the unspeakable Meinong and his English pals. Yours ever,

W. J.

The most distinguished critic of pragmatism was F. H. Bradley, whose *Logic* James had so greatly admired twenty years before. The correspondence between these champions of opposing schools testifies to their magnanimity. Bradley was a formidable and often supercilious controversialist, an acute dialectician, and an invalid somewhat withdrawn from human intercourse. Philosophically he was one of the foremost champions of absolutism, who greeted every fresh philosophical opinion with the claim that it was to be found in Hegel, and whose *a priori* rejection of the categories of experience and common sense has led to his being parodied as the author of "The Disappearance of Reality." [15] Although these qualities could scarcely have commended him, the strength of James's respect and attachment was unmistakable. Indeed there was more than this — a personal sympathy which led him to say of Bradley

[15] *Mind!* a parody of *Mind*, published in 1901, 51.

(in a manner more gentle than ironical) : "He is, really, an extra humble-minded man, I think, but even more humble-minded about his reader than about himself, which gives him that false air of arrogance." [16]   Bradley, on his part, testified in 1895 that James held "an honored place among those from whom he has learnt and hopes to learn." Of Bradley's *magnum opus* James wrote in 1894: "I have just read a book *Appearance and Reality* . . . published a year ago, which is destined to bring the whole of English philosophical discussion up to a higher plane, dialectically, than it has ever known before. I mistrust it, both premises and conclusions, but it is one of those vigorous and original things that have to be assimilated slowly. . . . It undoubtedly will be epoch-making in our literature." A few years later Bradley read James's *Will to Believe* and wrote a letter of half-approving criticism. Both the *Essays in Radical Empiricism* and *A Pluralistic Universe* afford evidence of James's preoccupation with Bradley's arguments. He felt him to be too dangerous an adversary to leave in his rear.

In July 1904, Bradley published in *Mind* a long and vigorous polemic entitled "On Truth and Practice," directed against the authors of *Personal Idealism*,[17] and particularly against Schiller as their "self-elected leader." He possessed an aptitude for sarcasm and personal castigation, and in this case he chose to exercise it. Citing Schiller's statement (in the Preface of his *Humanism*) that certain older modes of philosophizing are "flung aside with a contemptuous smile by the young, the strong, the virile," he added: "This is certainly young, indeed I doubt if at any time of life most of us have been as young as this." He warned James that "a writer can be discredited by the extravagance and the vulgarity of his disciple." [18]   At the same time he wrote privately to James, stating that he felt an obligation to rebuke Schiller, and regretted that this might seem to reflect on Schiller's allies. He was "far from suggesting that there is nothing in 'pragmatism,' " and assured James of his continued esteem and respect.[19]

[16] *L.W.J.*, II, 142.
[17] *Cf.* below, 495–7.
[18] *Mind, N.S.,* XIII (1904), 310, note, 330. He justified this charge against Schiller by a reference to the latter's "Useless Knowledge," *Mind, N.S.,* XI (1902). These personalities were omitted when this article was reprinted in *Essays on Truth and Reality* (1914), where the author inserts an Introductory Note, restating his general position with reference to pragmatism.
[19] Writing to James five years later, he still refused to see any good in personal idealism, and went on to say : "I believe now that pragmatism has nothing to do with

Both Schiller and James received advance proofs of Bradley's attack, and both replied to it in a temperate and conciliatory manner, the latter in his "Humanism and Truth," and the former in an article entitled "In Defence of Humanism." [20] James also replied privately. The following fragment, written June 16, 1904, is all that remains of his long and numerous letters to Bradley: —

"Have you read Royce on pragmatism in the *Philosophical Review* for April? [21] He acquiesces in all its contentions and simply lets his Absolute absorb it. I don't see how anyone can possibly deny a single one of its *positive* contentions, and your own Absolute is there for you to oppose to its negations. The doctrine of your admirable *Logic* is that reality is the primal 'that' of which all our 'whats' are determinations. That is identically Schiller's doctrine, save that for him the original 'that' may vanish in the infinitely regressive superposition of human '*whats*' — we can't today unpeel them wholly. True 'whats' are those of which the scroll of them, previously rolled up, will at this date suffer the application. That scroll and the novelties of experience, actuating us together, put rather narrow limits on our waywardness of predication. The ultimate 'that,' according to Schiller, is a $\ddot{v}\lambda\eta$ which, as you say, we merely 'encounter,' and which we handle by our predicates — as best we may. This is perfectly compatible in my eyes with your Absolute, since you expressly deny that our predicates copy the latter; and your notion of 'truth' as relative to the final amount of translation into Absoluteness which all our predicates in the end require, can simply add itself to the humanistic notion thereof. I do not believe in your Absolute, neither does Schiller: but nothing debars you from believing in our humanism, bag and baggage — you need only throw your Absolute round it, and give yourself the richer world you require.

"I believe that humanism, whether with or without the Absolute container, is a 'true' account of our finite knowing, and I suspect that, methodically and morally, it will prove full of regenerating

---

personal idealism and is consistent with the flat denial of it." Bradley sought to drive a wedge between James and Schiller, which operation James resisted. It was, in fact, one of the most persistent motives of James's thought to insist on the solidarity of his views with those of Schiller and Dewey. (*Cf., e.g., M.T.,* 242.)

[20] Both appeared in the Oct. number of *Mind.* Cf. also *M.T.,* 51. James was much concerned that Schiller should not reply to Bradley *in kind.* For his letter to Schiller on this matter, *cf.* below, 503.

[21] "The Eternal and the Practical," *Philos. Rev.,* XIII (1904).

power. Moreover, there is nothing definite to oppose to it. You yourself only oppose the vague notion of 'corresponding' with reality. But anything corresponds with reality, so far as given, which we can apply to it so as to fit, and thus enrich both it and our lives; and the fitting process has terribly difficult conditions, notwithstanding its great margin of indeterminateness. Don't you think that philosophy would gain more if philosophers would try conciliation — see how much of each other's views they could adopt rather than reject? You, in your article, seem to me to have sought for whatever interpretation of Schiller would allow you to reject the most of him. *Ditto* Taylor in his really farcical interpretation of my *Will to Believe* [22] — luckless title, which should have been the '*Right* to Believe.'"

Oxford, Oct. 15, 1904

Dear Professor James, —

I ought long ago to have written to thank you for your friendly letter and for the proof of your article. I did not do so because I wished (as you suggested) to read your proof carefully first. . . . Certainly I agree very largely with your view, that is, with a large amount of it. You must remember that I was brought up in that development of Kantianism which ended in humanism, or at least was said to end in it. That there was no reality beyond human experience, and no possibility of copying or following anything from the outside, was a sort of watchword even. "No Transcendence," in short. For myself I have had in some respects to diverge from this "humanism" as I received it. You have diverged still more vitally (as I understand), but for all that we have retained much of a common basis. And I a little object to the common basis being ignored. What would have been "sympathetic" would have been for you to take the doctrine of "No Transcendence" as common ground between you and the main Kantian development; and then to show how you worked it out with regard to various well-known controversial questions. I, however, recognize that this could scarcely be done in an article.

As you mention the fact that you may perhaps write others, I think that if I write something to point out where I do not see

---

[22] "Some Side Lights on Pragmatism," *McGill Univ. Magazine,* III² (1903–04).

what your view is, this may be useful.[23] If you feel inclined to say in return that I ought to have seen, I shall not be hurt at all. Quite seriously, I know that I have not a very sympathetic intelligence; and quite seriously, I think that in some ways I can on this account be more useful — naturally in some ways only. Naturally you do not write merely for the sympathetic. . . . Yours truly,

F. H. BRADLEY

Later letters from Bradley raised the question of the rights of the "theoretical interest" : —

Oxford, April 28, 1905

Dear James, —

. . . With regard to pragmatism, I do not seem to know exactly where we now are. I am beginning to wonder whether I have not always myself been a pragmatist. At least I have never thought that mere theory had more than a subordinate place in life. On the other hand, I do think that theory has a place in the human end, however small that place may be. It is here with truth more or less as it is with beauty. If you tell me that these are subordinate, I ask you "to what?" — and I fail to get any answer that I understand. "To the whole of life and to life as a whole?" Yes — I am with you there. But if you mean that this precludes the independent pursuit of truth and beauty within certain limits, I do not agree. The pragmatic test appears to me to be illusory, and as impossible to apply, in the case of speculation as it would be in the case of art. I venture to think that a great deal more of explanation is wanted here, and that after this explanation the difference between you and myself would be much reduced. I do not know how you take the human end, and in what you think it consists. That is one reason why controversy apart from further explanation would, I think, lead to nothing. I do not think that in the human end you can subordinate its various aspects and elements to anything but the whole. I am here, you see, something of a "pluralist." And it is here that I have no idea where the "pragmatist" stands. What to him is the end and the good?

I have been much interested in reading your papers as to a world of experience etc. . . . Your view strikes one at first sight as

[23] This article appears not to have been written.

being a kind of phenomenalism.   It recalls to some extent — with a difference — the controversies connected with J. S. Mill's view.   I find myself to some extent here asking the same questions, and not seeing the answers. . . .   Actual experience seems to be immediate experience.   But, with us, immediate experience is of limited span. It is a "now" of feeling containing a diversity and a duration and a lapse, but *not* containing in the same sense the past and the future which is outside its span.   If so, what of experience as the universe? . . .

I have been very greatly interested by your apparent adoption of the view that the contents of various selves may be partly identical. This doctrine I thought that *we* (*i.e.,* the absolutists) had been preaching for years.   I remember I felt justified myself years ago when preaching it in the name of Hegel to take the tone of a "voice of one crying in the wilderness."   And now?   Is it conceivable that *you* of all persons have adopted it, and are preaching it against *us?*   If so I rejoice, for I don't care how the doctrine is spread so long as it is spread.   But I think I must be under some misapprehension here. . . .

Have we one great immediate experience containing all things and selves?   If so, how does the one self among others know the whole? . . .   We come back here again to the old question, "Is experience *actual* experience?" and, if not, is it experience at all? . . .   And of course a volume is wanted to reply to this letter, so you see what I do and do not expect in answer.   Yours truly,

F. H. BRADLEY

Oxford, March 25, 1909

Dear Professor James, —

I have returned here . . . to find . . . your article in the *Journal of Philosophy* for December, which you were kind enough to send me.[24]   I have read it and I still do not know whether and how far I am a pragmatist.   I also do not know if Hegel was one.   I am sure that he was not an "anti-pragmatist," and that I am not one. But I am still a long way from understanding you. . . .   The doctrine that truth is the working of an idea is, I understand, Hegel's view.   Subject to certain reservations, I, of course, accept it.   But I understand the working to be *theoretical*. . . .   Pragmatism (I

[24] A review of Marcel Hébert's *Le Pragmatisme.*

and others supposed) flatly denied this, and maintained that *all* such working was merely practical. . . . Now I understand that *you,* at least, both say and have said that this interpretation is wrong. Pragmatism accepts theoretical working as one among other workings, and does *not* subordinate in all cases theory to practice (in the ordinary sense). If so, the difference between you and me would be merely as to the right of these other "non-theoretical" workings to be *also* called truth. That is a difference which is a small one (comparatively). But I do not know if you speak here for other pragmatists as well as yourself. And, if this is the only difference between us, I cannot understand some of the language which has been used by pragmatists, or the attitude which some at least of them have taken towards preëxisting philosophy. . . . Yours truly,

F. H. BRADLEY

The last of Bradley's letters on pragmatism followed the reading of James's article "On a Very Prevalent Use of Abstraction." In this article James defended himself against the charge of "psychologism," and made a plea for "absolute truth" as an "ideal" based upon certain "postulates." [25]

[Oxford], May 30, 1909

Dear James, —

Do not be afraid that I am writing you a long letter, or one that requires an answer. This is only to say that I have read your paper in the *Popular Science Monthly,* for which I send thanks. You were quite right in thinking that this paper might make the position of pragmatism clearer. . . . As against your critics there your case seems to me a good one. They (I also) have criticized you in a way which was at least partly mistaken. But why was this so? It was, I think, mainly because we did not understand what it is that pragmatism postulates. *If* you make certain postulates your doctrine is, I should say (if "practice" is taken widely enough), quite consistent and intelligible. These postulates, are, however, rather large ones.

All experience is becoming a *consensus,* hence all the reality which ideas need take account of is contained in experience. Anything which anticipates the character of the final consensus is so far true,

[25] *M.T.,* 266. The article originally appeared in *Pop. Sci. Mo.,* LXXIV (1909).

and is true *now*. The idea of possible disconnected and ultimately divergent experiences in the universe is excluded *absolutely*. The idea of an "Other" which from the outside can radically alter our ideas is excluded. The idea of our experience and all experience being liable to change and divergence is excluded.

Now what does all this rest on? Observation of *our* experience, that of a few passing parasites on a speck of dust? Apparently so. . . . I suppose "humanism" comes in here, but what does *that* mean, and what does *that* postulate? How *can* your critics know?

Really at a guess I should say (from what is before me) that you are no "empiricist" at all any more than I am. If your critics are to criticize pragmatism intelligently they ought to have whatever is postulated set out plainly, I should say. If that were done I don't suppose you would be troubled with many more criticisms of the kind you answer in this article. Of course others would take their place. Personally I feel that I myself can do [no] good by criticizing what I am sure I do not understand. . . . Yours truly,

F. H. Bradley

Thus for James the nature of truth was exhibited in the working of human ideas, *so far as* these proved satisfactory; whereas for Bradley it lay rather in that *complete* satisfactoriness which is approximated in human knowledge, but must always lie beyond it. The following passage from a letter written to James by Bradley in 1909, indicates a tendency to shift the emphasis in James's direction.[26]

"I am afraid that I have laid too much emphasis on the imperfection of all truth and all reality, forgetting perhaps at times that I believe quite as much in relative degrees of perfection, and of our power and duty to produce these, both in the intellectual world and also outside it. It is possible that I have given an idea that to me all is barren and worthless which stops short of ultimate perfection, — an idea which I do not believe to be true. If I had been and were able to enlarge on these relative degrees of perfection I would have done so or would do so. But I have not the necessary knowledge and power. Certainly I agree that this is a great

[26] Bradley's *Essays on Truth and Reality,* 1903, had already shown this tendency.

defect, the 'thinness' you have spoken of, and I feel it to be so. But the task is for another."

In spite of this rapprochement between James and Bradley their metaphysical conclusions are radically different. For James the absolute truth is a goal: it is definable, and it determines the direction of effort, but its attainment is problematic. The world *may* be such that imperfect, that is, only relatively satisfactory, knowledge speaks the last word. Bradley, on the other hand, would insist that without perfect truth there is no truth; and since truth must be assumed if there is to be any thinking whatsoever, its perfection must be affirmed — hence the Absolute. In other words, to use Kantian terms, that ideal of complete satisfactoriness which for James is "regulative" only is for Bradley "constitutive." This divergence was predetermined by the fact that James was fundamentally an empiricist, accepting the particular perceptual or practical experiences of men as the ultimate disclosure of existence; while Bradley was fundamentally a rationalist, reserving the rationalist's privilege of deducing existence from the necessities of thought.

LXXX

JAMES AND SCHILLER

THE difference between James and F. C. S. Schiller is inescapable, but not easy to formulate because their philosophical doctrines are so inextricably interwoven with temperamental traits. The difficulty is aggravated by the fact that James and Schiller, if not Dewey, made every effort to consolidate their forces against the common enemy. "As I . . . understand Dewey and Schiller," said James, "our views absolutely agree." He did, however, recognize a difference. He spoke of Schiller's "butt-end-foremost statement of the humanist position." He said of Schiller that "he starts from the subjective pole of the chain, the individual with his beliefs, as the more concrete and immediately given phenomena"; whereas he, James, starts with two things, "the objective facts and the claims." He implied that in the end the two views would coincide, since Schiller must come out with an objective view of reality and he with a subjective view of truth.[1] But this difference of emphasis does in fact involve a difference of metaphysics, which might be expressed by saying that while James had a metaphysics over and above his theory of knowledge, Schiller (like Dewey) took the cognitive process itself as a sample of reality. His world was a pragmatic world — a world in the making, after the manner of truth-making.[2]

But there is another difference. James was, as we have seen, reared in the tradition of British empiricism, and he was never emancipated, — while none of his pragmatic colleagues or disciples acknowledged the same allegiance.[3] As a good empiricist of the

---

[1] *Pragm.*, 243; *M.T.*, xix, 169, 242.

[2] *Cf., e.g.*, Schiller, *Humanism*, "The Ethical Basis of Metaphysics"; and *Studies in Humanism*, "The Making of Reality"; *cf. C.E.R.*, 444. This is truer of Schiller's later writings than of his *Riddles of the Sphinx*. It might be said that Schiller and James develop in reverse directions, the former becoming less and the latter more metaphysical.

[3] Ernst Mach and Dickinson S. Miller should, perhaps, be excepted; but the former disavowed metaphysics altogether, while the latter was too good a British empiricist to follow James in his radical fideism and pragmatism.

British school, James attached a peculiar importance to sense perception and to the immediacies of experience generally. Thus, while he was prepared to admit that our categories are man-made, and must therefore introduce a human factor into all thinking about reality, his humanism was always qualified by his affirmation that in certain situations reality speaks for itself, with its own voice and in its own accent. James tells us that whereas both the scholastics and the panpsychists believe in a real "core" within the man-made wrappings of knowledge, Schiller and Dewey recognize only a "limit" to the process of mediation, or a plastic material which has no characters save such as thought confers upon it.[4] Although James was too tolerant to exclude other alternatives, it is clear that he is on the side of the "core," and that he identifies that core with sensible experience.

Schiller's *Riddles of the Sphinx,* published in 1891, was described by James as "A pluralistic theistic book, of great vigor and constructive originality . . . that of a young man, and crude and disproportioned, but very suggestive, and quite in the lines which I incline to tread." In 1897 Schiller wrote a laudatory review of the *Will to Believe,* and congratulated its author on having "thrown his bomb shells into the stifling *aura* which surrounds many a hoary prejudice of the philosophic world."[5] This review encouraged James to believe that he already had a philosophy, and that (with the collaboration of others such as Schiller) he might found a school. How Schiller came to the defense of James when his *Will to Believe* was under attack in 1899 has already been described. His essay on "Axioms As Postulates," published in 1902, was conceived by its author as a development of "the *Weltanschauung* which Professor James has called *pragmatism* and *radical empiricism." Personal Idealism,* of which this essay forms a part, was reviewed by James in *Mind.*[6]

Chocorua, Aug. 6, 1902

Dear Schiller, —

I have . . . written and posted the notice of *Personal Idealism* which I promised. It is a terrible summary and superficial affair,

---

[4] *Pragm.,* 249–51.
[5] *Mind, N.S.,* VI (1897), 554. For James's humorously modest acknowledgment, *cf. L.W.J.,* II, 65–6.
[6] *Personal Idealism,* 1902, 63; *Mind, N.S.,* XII (1903). Schiller describes him-

but the book was too intricate either to report on or to criticize in detail, and I don't myself believe in minute reviews. I never read them; so I just hinted at the import of each essay and said a favoring word as to the import of the whole attempt. I think the essays all vulnerable in spots, but have enjoyed them immensely, especially Marett's, Bussell's and Gibson's. But they make me feel the sore need of a *systematic* and radical metaphysics affirming that whole point of view with as classical rotundity as the object — the Universe, which is no rounded or finished whole as yet — admits of. Pray spend the flower of your young life in composing such a thing, while I will similarly spend the dregs of mine.

What I meant by quoting your "unmoved mover" as a mystical document was that it tried to rationalize the essentially mystical intuition of a completed oneness and stillness in which nevertheless life's fulness is enjoyed.[7] The "antinomy" of fruition-disappointment, is both by your reasons and the mystic's experience put to naught. I regard this as an all-important step, and a novel one, so far as your share goes. It fills one of the big gaps in our reasonable view of things. . . . Yours ever,

W. J.

Oxford, Sept. 26, 1902

Dear James, —

. . . I was delighted with your review, and thought it admirably calculated to draw professional attention to our enterprise. . . . I note that you have estimated the whole thing as a contribution to metaphysics rather than to the special sciences; and though that no doubt is right, it does n't tell me . . . how far the general method . . . can be applied to the elucidation of the special problems of logic, and how far my attempts to do this may be said to have succeeded. . . . Personally, I cherish pragmatism chiefly as a method for the extraction of concrete results from refractory material: merely as a general point of view for judging the universe at large, it would seem to me as futile as other sorts of meta-

---

self as having been a pragmatist as early as 1892 (*Humanism*, 1903, ix). *Personal Idealism* was edited by Henry Sturt with the collaboration of G. F. Stout, F. C. S. Schiller, W. R. B. Gibson, G. E. Underhill, R. R. Marett, F. W. Bussell, and H. Rashdall.

[7] In 1900 Schiller wrote for *Mind* an article entitled "On the Conception of Ενέργεια 'Ακινησίας," in which he represented unchanging activity as an ideal experience. In his *Varieties of Religious Experience*, which had appeared shortly before this letter was written, James had referred to this article as a serious attempt to "mediate between the mystical region and the discursive life." (*V.R.E.*, 422, note.)

physics. And I believe that methods are the really great things, that in the end a good working method is what really tells even with the professional philosophers. And I cannot help thinking that you rather overestimate the importance of the system and scholastic formality which your soul abhors, and that it is a case of "optat ephippia bos, equus impiger optat arare," [8] when you demand it so urgently; just as when Ward with his thoroughly academic mind wants to write a "psychology for the British people." I don't believe that when you or I make a system of it, it will be any more acceptable. . . . Ever thine,

CANNING SCHILLER

Cambridge, Nov. 27, 1902

Dear Schiller, —

It gars me greet, that I have left your splendid letter of Sept. 26 with no response for all this time. I accomplish but little, yet my strength is so neatly adjusted to the things that are required, that works of supererogation like letters have to be shirked as long as they safely can. But this is a sour northeasterly Thanksgiving Day when no laws of sobriety hold. You are too easily pleased with my dry little review of *Personal Idealism* in *Mind*. I hope the book sells well, — it ought to. I recommend it on every hand. . . . As I tried to say when at Oxford, I don't think that you have quite succeeded with the example of identity which you have taken. I wish you had n't tackled that example, or else treated it a little differently, for the enemies will make the most of it and ignore the rest of the article.[9] I agree with what you say in your letter, about pragmatism being more important as a method than as a *philosophy,* and methods are for handling concrete cases.

I am for the first time in my teaching life trying to construct a universe before the eyes of my students in systematic lectures, with no text.[10] *Es geht schlecht;* but I get some instruction out of it myself. I have to refute Royce (as well as Bradley) to his own pupils; and sooth to say his *reasonings* are almost inconceivably bad, so the task is so easy that I am afraid to bear on lest I should tumble through altogether. But he is the same perfect-tempered ball of equanimity throughout all. You make some pointed objection to

[8] "The ox longs for the saddle, the spirited horse for the plough."
[9] Schiller develops the "postulate of identity" from "the felt self-identity of consciousness." (*Personal Idealism,* 1902, 94–104.)
[10] "The Philosophy of Nature" (Philos. 3).

him which needs a definite reply, and his invariable reply is simply
to restate his whole system, so it does n't pay to object. . . .

I have just been reading up a lot of articles by some pupils of
Bergson, Le Roy and Wilbois, in the last volumes of the *Revue de
métaphysique et de morale.*[11] They work your notion of nature
per se being a kind of ὕλη beautifully and extensively, but they are
bavards, and although filled with sacred enthusiasm and physical
learning, they are *slack,* philosophically. Still it is an important
movement, and one must re-read Bergson to see just what the dickens
he does mean. . . . Have you read Ostwald's *Naturphilosophie?*
I supped last night with a club of young instructors here, physicists,
chemists, biologists, and philosophers, who meet for discussion of
each other's deepest problems,[12] and they discussed that book. It
is an awfully *burly* thing, it seems to me. But which of us will
ever state the *blinding* truth? Farewell! Yours affectionately,

WM. JAMES

In 1903 Schiller received a copy of the famous "Syllabus in Philosophy 3," and wrote a letter of detailed criticism, in the course
of which he suggested that he and James "join forces with the
Chicagoans," meaning John Dewey and his school. How James
replied, expressing his enthusiastic interest in Dewey and Moore,
and playfully alluding to the beginning of his own "forthcoming
book," has already been described. The following letters throw
light on the origin of the name "humanism," which Schiller proposed and which James recognized, although he refused to accept
it as the best name of the movement *as a whole.* Schiller admitted
pragmatism as a species of humanism, while James admitted humanism as a species of pragmatism![13]

Oxford, April 24, 1903

Dear James, —

. . . I have been inspired this morning, *à propos de rien,* with
THE *name* for the only true philosophy! You know I never cared
for "pragmatism"[14] . . . it is much too obscure and technical, and

[11] Vols. IX, X (1901–2); *cf. C.E.R.,* 450; *M.T.,* 65.
[12] The "Wicht Club," whose members were G. W. Peirce, W. H. Sheldon,
E. E. Southard, G. N. Lewis, W. B. Cannon, E. B. Holt, R. M. Yerkes, A. O.
Norton, R. P. Angier, and R. B. Perry.
[13] For James's articles on "humanism" and his many references to it, *cf. Bg.* and
Pragm., and *M.T.* For Schiller's statement of the matter, *cf.* "William James and
the Making of Pragmatism," *Personalist,* VIII (1927); *Personal Idealism,* 63, note.
[14] *Cf. Personal Idealism,* 1902, 63, note.

not a thing one can ever stampede mankind to. Besides the word has misleading associations and we want something bigger and more extensive (inclusive). It does not express the whole meaning of what we are saying, and I feel that I'm constantly stretching the term. But why should we not call it HUMANISM? "Humanism" as opposed to scholasticism; "humane" as opposed to barbarous (in style and temper); human, living and concrete as opposed to inhuman, fossil, and abstract; in short, not "anthropomorphism" (horrid word!) but "humanism." Consider, *e.g.,* how much better your remark about *"rehumanizing* the universe" sounds![15] I propose, therefore, to call myself henceforth a humanist, and my volume of essays "Humanism: Philosophical Essays by F. C. S. S.," or something of the sort, and shall devote the preface to expounding what I mean. Not that we need drop "pragmatism" on that account as a technical term in epistemology. Only pragmatism will be a species of a greater genus, — humanism in theory of knowledge. . . . As ever thine,

CANNING SCHILLER

Oxford, June 9, 1903

Dear James, —

. . . I have lived in hopes of receiving from you an answer to what is just now the most important question in the philosophic universe, *viz.* — ARE YOU A HUMANIST? I am — more than ever, having meanwhile worked out some of the implications of the term in the Preface to *Humanism.* They are beautiful, and I should like, if it does n't worry you too much, to send you the said Preface in manuscript. Meanwhile I append a new Pythagorean "table of contraries" under the head of

1.	*The Good and Finite* vs.	*The Evil and Infinite*
2.	Humanism	Scholasticism
3.	Pragmatism	Verbalism
4.	Personal Idealism	Naturalism
5.	Pluralism	Absolutism
6.	Radical Empiricism	Apriorism
7.	Voluntarism	Intellectualism
8.	Anthropomorphism	Amorphism
9.	Britticism	Germanism
10.	Witticism	Barbarism

[15] James had spoken of "a re-anthropomorphized Universe," as the outcome of personal idealism (*C.E.R.,* 443).

That is comprehensive enough, don't you think? . . . It appears to me . . . that the thick of the fight (once we get to close quarters) is going to be about the indetermination of truth and reality prior to experiment. The other side all hold to a rigid preëxistent system which is not made, but only found, and try to fasten upon us a belief in chaotic indetermination. I reply that a *plastic* universe cannot be either, and try to make them see how the nature of the question goes to determine the answer, and how our behaviour therefore helps to shape reality. . . . Ever thine,

CANNING SCHILLER

To which James replied: "I owe you for three letters, but from my graphophobic personality this post-card must suffice. Don't *you* be discouraged, however, but keep up the correspondence. . . . 'Humanism' does n't make a very electrical connection with my nature, but in appellations the individual proposes and the herd adopts or drops. I rejoice *exceedingly* that your book is so far forward, and am glad you 'll call it 'Humanism' — we shall see if the name sticks. All *other* names are bad, most certainly — especially 'pragmatism.' "

Chocorua, Sept. 10, 1903

Dear Schiller, —

Your proof came last night,[16] and it is needless to say that I admire both the spirit and the form of it. I believe the harvest is ripe, or almost ripe, for cutting, though I confess I did get an impression from my audience at Glenmore, mostly of intelligent world's people, of the lack of any acute need of philosophic clearness on the part of the educated public; and of the pragmatic adequacy of common sense, with a covering of absolutistic theism for emotional and speculative purposes, to most of their requirements. I am struck by your tribute to common sense. More than ever have I this summer been impressed by the perfect magnificence as a philosophical achievement of the *Denkmittel* by which common sense has straightened out the chaos of individual experiences, — the categories of "thing" and "property," the dualism of mind and matter, and the notion of causal efficacy. They are so adequate to ease of

---

[16] Proof of *Humanism,* dedicated "To my dear friend the humanest of philosophers, WILLIAM JAMES, without whose example and unfailing encouragement this book would never have been written."

living, that when any more fine-spun philosophy returns to them again, we warm towards it as to something sound and sane, and redeemed from artificiality. From the pragmatistic point of view an ode has yet to be written to common sense.[17] . . . I am *sure* these essays will strike deep. Yours ever,

W. J.

Salisbury, Nov. 15, 1903

My dear Schiller, —

I don't know what you will have thought of my silence about your book, but the explanation of it is *on ne peut plus simple.* The day it came I started to write to "accuse" the reception, and express both my enthusiasm at the promise of racy reading which the volume expressed, and my *attendrissement* at the dedication, but I was prostrated on that day, and from day to day was prevented by pressure of other things from even looking at the volume, until the habit of not writing to you on that subject became easy; and here I now am with the volume in my bag . . . but probably with no liberty to sit down and read it all through again for several weeks. So here goes, with the belated bald acknowledgment. I have had all sorts of outside things shoved upon me since my return a month ago to Cambridge. . . . The best of the lot was reading up the output of the "Chicago School of Thought," and reporting it at a "conference" which Royce has organized. It is splendid stuff, and Dewey is a hero. A real school and real thought. At Harvard we have plenty of thought, but not school. At Yale and Cornell, the other way about. It is particularly fine to have Chicago and Oxford, in total independence of each other, enter the same path, and I am sure that the theses now thrown down by the pair of you will be the topic of philosophical discussion for twenty-five years to come. Dewey needs a great deal of building out and following of his principles into all sorts of questions of detail. But it's a noble work. Pity that their style should be so dry and abstract; and lucky for the cause that you should be such a jolly splendid writer. You catch all sorts of things on the wing which escape them, but you're a splendid team. . . .

I am greatly tougher than last year, and with good husbandry shall have a good winter. I have written almost nothing of my own

[17] *Cf. Pragm.*, Lect. V.

stuff, but my seminary is helping me to get it into shape, and it will doubtless prove a good ally to your efforts. You and Chicago have built out beyond my sight on the "truth" question — all the more welcome to me is your work. I must say that Royce, whose system is terribly cut under by Dewey, etc., demeaned himself in an admirably amiable and candid way on the night of my report. . . . Good success to you, and heartiest thanks for the undeserved honor of the dedication. Yours ever,

WM. JAMES

Tallahassee, Feb. 1, 1904

Dear Schiller, —

By a curious coincidence, your letter of Jan. 15 with the *Times* review, reaches me this A.M. at breakfast just nine hours after I mailed my own review of *Humanism* to the *Nation*.[18] The *Times* review seems to me almightily cleverly done. . . . Evidently it is the pouring out of a long smothered volcano of irritation at your general tone of belligerency and flippancy, and of dislike of a philosophy which seems to the reviewer partial and shallow because he has never taken in the profounder vistas which it opens up. *What do we mean* by "truth"? What is it known-as? Those are questions which if once opened up for discussion, will make each side respect the other a little more. I am amused at the way *my* name has been dragged in as that of the father of all this way of thinking. I recognize it as a continuation of partial thoughts which I have expressed; but "pragmatism" never meant for me more than a method of conducting discussions (a sovereign method, it is true), and the tremendous scope which you and Dewey have given to the conception has exceeded my more timid philosophizing. I welcome it, and admire it, but I can't yet think out certain parts of it; although something inside of me feels sure that they can be successfully thought out, and that it will then be a great day for Philosophic Man. "Humanism" (the term) which did not at first much "speak" to me, I now see to be just right. *Vivat et floreat!* [incomplete]

In his review of *Humanism* James remarked that Schiller had not solved the problem of the external world. It is necessary to ac-

[18] The *Times* review appeared in the [London] *Times Literary Supplement*, Jan. 8, 1904. For James's *Nation* review, *cf. C.E.R.*, 448.

count for the fact that the existing world fits our conceptions, and for the fact that these have a "retroactive significance." In his review of *Personal Idealism* James suggested that Schiller "tone down a little the exuberance of his polemic wit." [19] In the summer of 1904, as we have seen, Bradley had written a provocative article against Schiller. The latter's reply was sent to James in proof.

Chocorua, Aug. 9, 1904

Dear Schiller, —

. . . Personally I relish greatly your irony and flights of metaphor, but from the point of view of party politics I am sure that they ought not to be allowed full headway, *und zwar* for the following reasons.

I rejoiced when you wrote me that your rejoinder to Bradley was to be scrupulously polite (or words to that effect), because (as I believe I once wrote you) it is astonishing how many persons resent in your past writings what seems to them "bad taste" in the way of polemical jeers and general horse-play. Solemn as an owl and tender as a dove, should be your watchword from now on if you are to outlive these arrears of debt to the proprieties. Now I believe that this October *Mind* will be the first artillery fire of an important general engagement, in which it behooves us to risk no disadvantage of *any* sort. . . . Bradley has put himself flagrantly in the wrong by his personalities and sarcasms; and the important point tactically is that he should be left there high and dry; and should not be able to point at anything in your reply and say: "There! did n't I tell you of his self-advertising, and swaggering over his 'new philosophy,' and general juvenility and crudity?" . . . I think your whole mental tone against our critics is overstrained. They don't try to misrepresent, — they simply have "absoluteness" so ingrained in them that they can't conceive of what any alternative can mean. There has been no conspiracy of silence, — there has simply been *failure to hear* what was worthy of an answer of some sort. The older ones will never be converted; but by arguing patiently and avoiding personal bitterness, we shall much sooner win the sympathy of the younger fry. After all, our side is only half developed. I am sure that not one of us has any clear idea of what the ultimate *pre-human fact,* which we encounter and which

---

[19] *C.E.R.*, 443.

works, through all our stratified predicates, upon us — the ὕλη as you call it — really is or signifies; and the relations of truth to *time* (truth being so often retroactive legislation, and existing even now before it is discovered) have never been explicitly thrashed out. Anyone is excusable for being recalcitrant. . . .

I am going immediately to write an article entitled "A World of Pure Experience," which Woodbridge promises to print in his new *Journal of Philosophy*, etc., before October, and which will, I hope, somewhat clear up the jungle. Have you read Hobhouse on us twain (although he names us not) in the *Aristotelian Proceedings?* [20] A lovely-written article, ending with my will to believe doctrine, beautifully expressed, and offered as an *alternative* to the incredible travesty of you and me which he begins by laboriously substituting for it. What is the virus, the insane root, the screw loose (or what), that condemns these fellows to judicial blindness in their reading? It's a queer experience for us. But Taylor [21] goes far beyond Hobhouse, whose article as to all its positive contentions I find very *simpatico*. Who and what is he? Gentleman? Professor? What? I know that you'll forgive my animadversions, wrung from me by the need of the "cause" only, and believe me, ever fondly yours,

WM. JAMES

Schiller wrote regretting his inability to comply fully with James's suggestion — because it was too late, and because he did not agree. [22]

Chocorua, Sept. 2, 1904

Dearest Schiller, —

Your long and *köstlich* letter of the 21st . . . came yesterday. Yours is a superabounding nature . . . superabounding in truth, acuteness, humor, gall, wrath — and *I* think, *delusions* about the state of the enemy's mind. Their faults are less moral and more intellectual than you suppose. Bradley, I am sure, can't see outside of his own categories, and the humanistic view has been so scantily developed as yet, that we must have patience — a *quantity* of food

---

[20] For the letters exchanged with Hobhouse apropos of this article, *cf.* above, 245-7.

[21] The reference is to A. E. Taylor, "Truth and Practice," *Philos. Rev.*, XIV (1905).

[22] Schiller's reply to Bradley was, nevertheless, restrained; *cf,* above, 487.

must go down for assimilation to occur. Even Taylor and Hob-house may have been more innocent than they seem, although that is a thesis that requires some Will to Believe. . . .

Wheeler has invited me to go next summer and join you and Dewey at Berkeley. I want to awfully, and I suspect that certain obstacles now in the way can be removed. What a triumvirate we shall be, and how humanism will hum — drowning the roar of Russo-Japanese artillery across the Pacific. . . . I am curious to see what you will think of my articles in the *Journal*.[23] They are not directly on the pragmatic line, but close to it. . . . Yours ever,

W. J.

P.S. In a letter from C. H. Hinton [24] yesterday, he says: "The academic mind secretes thought and contempt together, in about equal proportions." Good!

The following paragraph, written to Schiller from California in 1906, indicates James's growing sense of the constructive possibilities of the new movement as represented by his allies: —

"What I really want to write about is Papini, the concluding chapter of his *Crepuscolo dei Filosofi,* and the February number of the *Leonardo*. Likewise Dewey's 'Beliefs and Realities,' in the *Philosophical Review* for March. I must be very damp powder, slow to burn, and I must be terribly respectful of other people, for I confess that it is only after reading these things (in spite of all you have written to the same effect, and in spite of your tone of announcing judgment to a sinful world), that I seem to have grasped the full import for life and regeneration, the *great* perspective of the program, and the renovating character for *all things,* of Humanism; and the outwornness as of a scarecrow's garments, simulating life by flapping in the wind of nightfall, of all intellectualism, and the blindness and deadness of all who worship intellectualist idols. . . . It is queer to be assisting at the *éclosion* of a great new mental epoch, life, religion, and philosophy in one."[25] . . .

Schiller read the manuscript of *Pragmatism* and urged James to

[23] The *Essays on Radical Empiricism.*
[24] Charles Howard Hinton, English writer on philosophical subjects.
[25] Reprinted from *L.W.J.,* II, 245–6.

adopt the name of "humanism," but James replied that it was too late. Much as he disliked the term "pragmatism," it seemed "to have *international* right of way at present." Bradley again attacked pragmatism in *Mind,* and Schiller prepared a reply, which he sent in proof to James. The latter was anxious that Schiller, who had been "treated like an impudent school-boy who deserves a spanking," [26] should afford his opponents no excuse for such treatment.

Cambridge, May 18, 1907

Dear Schiller, —

. . . One word about the said proof. It convinces me that you ought to be an academic personage, a "professor." For thirty-five years I have been suffering from the exigencies of being one, the pretension and the duty, namely, of meeting the mental needs and difficulties of other persons, needs that I could n't possibly imagine and difficulties that I could n't possibly understand; and now that I have shuffled off the professional coil, the sense of freedom that comes to me is as surprising as it is exquisite. I wake up every morning with it: "What! not to have to accommodate myself to this mass of alien and recalcitrant humanity, not to think under resistance, not to have to square myself with others at every step I make — hurrah! it is too good to be true. To be alone with truth and God! *es ist nicht zuglauben!* What a future! What a vision of ease!" But here you are loving it and courting it unnecessarily. You 're fit to continue a professor in all your successive reincarnations with never a release. It was so easy to let Bradley with his approximations and grumblings alone. So few people would find these last statements of his seductive enough to build them into their own thought. But you, for the pure pleasure of the operation, chase him up and down his windings, flog him into and out of his corners, stop him and cross-reference him and counter on him, as if required to do so by your office. It makes very difficult reading, it obliges one to re-read Bradley, and I don't believe there are three persons living who will take it in with the pains required to estimate its value. Bradley himself will very likely not read it with any care. It is subtle and clear, like everything you write, but it is

[26] *L.W.J.,* II, 270–1; *Pragm.,* 66–7. Bradley's article was "On Truth and Copying," *Mind, N.S.,* XVI (1907); and Schiller replied under the title of "Mr. Bradley's Theory of Truth" in the same volume.

too minute. And where a few broad comments would have sufficed, it is too complex, and too much like a criminal conviction in tone and temper. Leave him in his *dunklem Drange* — he is drifting in the right direction evidently, and when a certain amount of positive construction on our side has been added, he will say that that was what he had meant all along — and the world will be the better for containing so much difficult polemic reading the less.

I admit that your remarks are penetrating, and let air into the joints of the subject; but I respectfully submit that they are not *called for* in the interests of the final triumph of truth. That will come by the way of displacement of error, quite effortlessly. I can't help suspecting that you unduly magnify the influence of Bradleyan absolutism on the undergraduate mind. Taylor is the only fruit so far, — at least within *my* purview. One practical point: I don't quite like your first paragraph, and wonder if it be too late to have the references to me at least expunged. I can't recognize the truth of the ten years' change of opinion about my *Will to Believe*. I don't find anyone — not even my dearest friends, as Miller and Strong — one whit persuaded. Taylor's and Hobhouse's attacks are of recent date, etc. Moreover, the reference to Bradley's relation to me in this article is too ironical not to seem a little "nasty" to some readers, therefore out with it, if it be not too late. . . . All that humanism needs now is to make *applications* of itself to special problems. Get a school of youngsters at work. Refutations of error should be left to the rationalist alone. They are a stock function of that school. . . . I hope that you'll like the chapter on "Humanism" in my lectures. The whole book is a loose popular *cadre* which invites to a tremendous task of filling in. . . . Affectionately thine,

W. J.

Oxford, May 27, 1907

Dearest James, —

Your letter and your book arrived together this morning. . . . Endless thanks for both. Both are superb, and enough to go down immortally to posterity withal! I think you are quite right in every word you say in both. It is absolutely the right way, — for you. It is the way of arguing which fits your personality and brings out

what is best and strongest in you. And its appeal is world-wide,
— to all whose hearts are in the right place to be reached by reasoning like that. Unfortunately there are others, who must be dealt
with differently. And fortunately we too are capable of other
methods. In virtue of this I may be right — too, and Dewey as
well. Dewey's primary appeal is to those who like their philosophy
difficult and technical, and will respect nothing that is not obscure.
Mine is to the dialecticians, and logic-choppers and controversialists,
the men that wield the microscope and microtome. My duty is to
show them that we can beat them at their own despicable game, that
we can reason quite as closely and distinguish quite as finely: nay,
my aim is to show that *judged by their own standards,* their thinking is loose and their doctrines are inadequate. . . .

It is possible that I sometimes get subdued to the material I have
to work in, and am in danger of becoming too intellectualist in refuting intellectualism. It often happens in controversy that one becomes contaminated with the spirit of one's opponents. It may
also be that I develop too much gusto in controversy, from a feeling
that it is a game which best evokes *my* powers and one at which I
fear no antagonist. But I believe myself to be fundamentally a man
of peace, nevertheless, who has risen in revolt against a brutal, degrading and irrational tyranny, and who would lay aside the sword
as soon as a real freedom of thought and independence of spirit
is secured to all. At any rate, at present *solche Käuze wie Knox* [27]
und ich are indispensable. We guard your most vulnerable flank,
and by repelling counter attacks secure your advance. Remember
that just as you hear the criticism on me I hear that on you — low,
petty and dishonest as it generally is. It makes me angry. But
I can foresee and foretell the sort of thing that two-thirds of the
dons here will say: "Shockingly popular! Why even a pass man
could understand it! . . . Why does n't he write that systematic
metaphysic we could break our jaws upon? We don't believe he
can. There is only *one* system, and that is absolute. It was pro-
mulgated by Plato, continued by Aristotle, and perfected by Hegel.
All else is vanity and vexation of spirit!" . . . I hope you will
now take a good rest in the shade of your laurels (one of the slow-
est growers of trees!), and remain ever thine,

CANNING SCHILLER

[27] H. V. Knox, author of *The Philosophy of William James,* 1914.

In the following letters the issue of realism comes to the fore and divides the relatively objective James from the relatively subjective Schiller: —

Cambridge, Jan. 4, 1908

Dear Schiller, —

. . . I got back a week ago from the meeting at Cornell University of the Philosophical Association. *Very* nice: almost all the papers read were epistemological, but the "symposium" on "truth" was abortive, not being a discussion at all, but a delivery of five unconcerted general essays on the subject, of which I gave the first.[28] . . . Your name was in many mouths, no one persuadable that you could possibly admit an "objective" reality. I, being radically realistic, claimed you to be the same, but no one believed me as to either of us. Would n't you subscribe to the paper I enclose? Is n't the ὕλη which you speak of as the primal bearer of all our humanized predicates, conceived by you epistemologically as an independent *that* which the *whats* qualify, and which (in the ultimate) may be decided to be of any nature whatsoever? I hope so; for that position seems to me invulnerable, and in the end must win against all the muddlers and misunderstanders. Don't answer me too minutely; if tempted to do so, refrain; I only want to be able to quote you as agreeing. If you *don't* agree, the bare fact suffices, the reasons can come later. . . . *Addio!* "Yours for the truth" —

W. J.

Schiller's reply accused James of too great a deference towards the realists. The following is James's rejoinder: —

Cambridge, Dec. 4, 1909

Dear Schiller, —

. . . As regards your animadversions, both public and private, on my tactics, they don't trouble me much, though I see well what you drive at, and admit your superior formal or "economic" elegance. We both assume a situation to discuss, don't we? in the shape of someone claiming truth and getting there or not. Your procedure lets him get there all alone, mine [lets him] get there to someone else's satisfaction; that someone being supposed as a sort

[28] Published in *M.T.*, under the title of "The Meaning of the Word Truth."

of outside custodian of the object aimed at, who can recognize the success of the first man's aiming and talking. It seems to me really fantastically formal to ignore *that* much of the truth that is already established, namely, that men do think in social situations. The externality and independence of our "objects" means primarily that even if *we* be annihilated they are identifiable with objects that are still there for other people. I *simply assume the social situation,* and I am sorry that Marett [29] and you balk at it so much. It is not assumed merely tactically, for those are the terms in which I genuinely think the matter. The *essential* thing, of course, is the expulsion of the static saltatory, by the working ambulatory, definition; and that is done by both of us with equal success, notwithstanding that we discuss slightly different "situations."

Your "situation" allows a more comprehensive and elegant treatment of man's general theoretic life, though even human life at large may have a superhuman *socius* who can ratify or reject man's theories. It may be better adapted to make converts in England, but I find mine better here. My mental field is small and simple, and it always fills me with amazement to see how many *points* you can articulate and handle at once. If I think of one, I have to drop all others. . . . Thine ever,

W. J.

In the last year of his life James was largely engaged on the work which appeared posthumously under the title of *Some Problems of Philosophy,* while Schiller was writing his *Formal Logic.*[30] The two friends exchanged manuscripts and comments. Their difference of opinion turns again on Schiller's relatively subjectivistic and voluntaristic emphasis as opposed to James's realism. According to Schiller *all* knowledge is pragmatic and provisional, including the knowledge of so-called facts. The object is always what it is, *for* a subject, and *on the ground* of the satisfaction afforded by so conceiving it. James, on the other hand, stresses the original and ineradicable aspect of objective givenness, without which the pragmatic operation would have no application or meaning; and which is itself known, independently of that operation, in immediate experience. And James accepts, furthermore, the com-

[29] R. R. Marett, tutor in philosophy at Exeter College, Oxford.
[30] Published in 1912, and dedicated to James.

mon-sense categories which, having been pragmatically justified, may now be generally assumed in describing the cognitive operation itself. Thus James's world, for all his romantic temper, assumes a familiar form. There is a something *there* over against the subject and independent of it; and *what* it is that is there has long since been established by cumulative pragmatic evidence. Schiller was still harassing Bradley in the pages of *Mind,* and returning blow for blow.

                                        Rye, April *27*, 1910

Dear Schiller, —

I have had your long and interesting letter for two days. The thing for you now is to . . . get . . . out your logic at the earliest possible date. *Stop all occasional and polemical writing* for that purpose! . . . What you write of my manuscript makes me see again how much more radically and deeply you and Dewey place yourselves than I do. . . . The problems I started with were more superficial and I have kept closer to their neighborhood. Of course I see the splendid sweep of your program and what your letter says makes me red-hot for the publication of your logic. *No* other thing you can possibly do will be as important. I was struck by what you said of "designation" in *Mind* . . . when it appeared, but the much briefer formulation in the forthcoming article took hold of me much more.[31] . . .

There may be an advantage, from the point of view of converting the public, in our working at different levels. For example, in a book for college use like mine (I want it to *sell*) the "eternal" view of concepts can do no particular harm, for they are *relatively* eternal (and some of them actually so, so far as we yet know), and the distinguishing of them as such is a rather definite stage in thought, practically attained by opinion concerning them, on which the student can start easily and keep step with you. (I think you are unjust to "copying," for surely one of the most voluminous purposes of our thinking is to know what things are "like.") I send you herewith the introductory pages of my chapter, which I spared you before on account of their relative triteness. You can see how easy it would be for me to put myself quite on your ground by de-

---

[31] *Mind, N.S.,* XIX (1910), 40–3, 537 ff. The writer insists on the importance of the concrete act of pointing, as giving meaning and truth to judgments.

veloping here at greater length the notion of "meaning," and thereafter making all boundaries more fluid, as you do.[32] But I question whether, for didactic purposes (as well as for your priority rights!) I hadn't better keep my level, and leave yours to you. I shall make use of some of your marginal scribblings, and altogether I have found this last letter of yours a very eye-opening communication. Yours ever,

W. J.

Rye, May 4, 1910

Dear Schiller, —

I return your logic chapter which I find intensely interesting and am very glad to have read. I shall also profit by the annotations on the pages of my manuscript . . . and by your accompanying letter. I understand entirely what you are driving at, and the last Appendix of my *Pluralistic Universe* will show you that I have caught the meaning of the fluidity of concepts long since.[33] Also have I always known that percepts (in the plural) are just as much artifacts as any "concept" is. . . . You have aimed at describing the whole process of knowledge, from an initial zero. I start (especially in this book for students) from the common-sense level at which, as you admirably say, "many discriminations of proved pragmatic value have already been effected." It is important to show the public that the function of concepts is practical, but it disconcerts the beginner to be told that the very concepts you use in doing so are themselves deliquescent; and after all, our experience ought to have by this time established *some* of them in pragmatic solidity. . . . I thus pedagogically insert the thin end of the wedge with which you and Dewey are engaged in splitting up the whole thickness of the cake of epistemology. There is room for both of our methods; but the result of your notes and criticisms will be to make me confess more explicitly to the provisionality of my forms of statement. . . . I can see cavils which will be made right off to your Chapter I, — it is a program to which the following chapters will give concreteness! Receive my blessing!

W. J.

---

[32] *Cf.* "The Import of Concepts," in *S.P.P.*

[33] "On the Notion of Reality As Changing." James does not withdraw his older position (*Principles*, Ch. XII) that concepts themselves are unchanging, but asserts that the existent world has to be constantly reconceptualized.

On the eve of his departure for America, less than three weeks before his death, James wrote a last letter to Schiller, in which he said: "I leave the 'Cause' in your hands. . . . Good-bye, and God bless you. You shall hear of our safe arrival. Keep your health, your splendid health! It's better than all the 'truths' under the firmament. Ever thy W. J."

LXXXI

JAMES AND DEWEY

JAMES refused to admit that the differences between himself, Dewey, and Schiller were more than differences of emphasis or approach. He credited Dewey with a wider pragmatic "panorama" than his own or Schiller's; with introducing the generalized conceptions of "adaptation" and "satisfaction," in such wise as to assimilate theory to practice; and with seeing the ethical implications of pragmatism. To Dewey himself the differences were more fundamental and more explicit.[1]

Dewey's pragmatism or "instrumentalism" is more single-minded than that of James. He is primarily concerned with the analysis of the cognitive process. He is not satisfied with general statements of its essentially practical character, but undertakes a meticulous examination of its structure. He is interested in the technique of truth-making. Having analyzed the cognitive process in pragmatic terms, he takes the process so analyzed as his philosophical *fundamentum*. His ethics stresses the central place of thought in conduct — as with Socrates, virtue is knowledge.[2] His metaphysics, if he can be said to have a metaphysics, is not so much an application of his pragmatism as it is a projection of it. He says that "knowledge *is* reality making a particular and specified sort of change in itself,"[3] and this sort of change is taken as typical of reality as well as of knowledge. In addition to pragmatic "knowledge about," James provides an alternative, namely, knowledge by acquaintance; and this, however rare or impure it may be, does at any rate afford a cognitive footing outside of the processes of thought. We can know what the world is "like" without thinking about it, and, knowing what the world is like, we can see that thinking is only one corner of it. Dewey, on the other hand, al-

---

[1] James's fullest statements of his philosophical relations to Dewey and Schiller are found in *M.T.*, xvi–xix, 42, 56, 169. For Dewey's views of the matter, *cf.* the several articles cited immediately below.

[2] "The Development of American Pragmatism," Columbia *Studies in the History of Ideas*, II (1925).

[3] *Essays Philosophical and Psychological in Honor of W.J.*, 1908, 59.

though he affirms that things *are* what they are immediately experienced as, limits this cognitive rôle of experience to the case in which
experience functions as the meaning or evidence of thought.[4]

James regards pragmatism as a method to be freely used, and
applies it to the standard doctrines of metaphysics, as though any
of these might be considered available. It is true that the metaphysics which he adopted — the metaphysics of change, freedom,
and manyness — does to some extent reflect the exigencies of a
pragmatic theory of knowledge; but pragmatism is much less exigent
with James than with Dewey. James's philosophical thinking,
both his ethics and his metaphysics, abounds in ideas which are
irrelevant, if not alien, to his pragmatism. He felt misgivings on
this score, and was disposed to regard Dewey as more radical and
more self-consistent; while Dewey, though he admitted the richness and tolerance of James's thought, did in effect charge him with
a lack of rigor.[5]

These differences are no doubt related to the general philosophical
temper of the two men, as well as to their early influences. James is
more conciliatory and hospitable to ideas, Dewey more systematic.
The interest of James is strongly metaphysical and religious, that
of Dewey social and logical. Both men feel the influence of Darwin
and of modern experimental science, but while James springs from
British empiricism crossed with the voluntarism and fideism of Renouvier, Dewey has his roots in Hegel and in neo-Kantism. James
is interested in content, while Dewey's preoccupation with method
amounts in effect to a naturalistic panlogism, in which content *is*
method. To James the ultimate vision is intuitive, while to Dewey
it is discursive. Or, while James *is* percipient, artistic, and religious,
Dewey elaborates ideas *about* perception, art, and religion. With
James the essence of life and experience can be grasped only in the
living and in the experiencing, and this conviction springs from
the abundance and vividness of personal living and experience;
whereas with Dewey the essence of things emerges only upon reflection, and this conviction springs from his characteristic and perpetual thoughtfulness. This must not be taken to imply that Dewey
would abandon life for thought but that his ideal of life is *thoughtful* living.

4 "The Postulate of Immediate Empiricism," *Jour. of Philos.*, II (1905).
5 "What Does Pragmatism Mean by Practical?" *Jour. of Philos.*, V (1908).

The correspondence between James and Dewey extends over a period of eighteen years. In 1886 James read Dewey's *Psychology* and wrote to Croom Robertson: "Dewey is out with a psychology which I have just received and but one-half read. I felt quite 'enthused' at the first glance, hoping for something really fresh; but am sorely disappointed when I come to read. It 's no use trying to mediate between the bare miraculous self and the concrete particulars of individual mental lives; and all that Dewey effects by so doing is to take all the edge and definiteness away from the particulars when it falls to their turn to be treated." Dewey's reaction to James's *Principles* was very different. He relished its lively style, and acknowledged it to be the "spiritual progenitor" of the whole philosophical movement of which he was the leader.[6]

In 1888 Dewey published a "Critical Exposition" of Leibnitz's *New Essays Concerning the Human Understanding,* and James evidently wrote a belated letter of comment, to which the following is a reply: —

Ann Arbor, May 6, 1891

Dear Professor James, —

I wish to thank you for the kindness and frankness with which you wrote me about my *Leibnitz.* I assure you that your words have anything but "forwardness" to me, and that coming from you they have given me great encouragement. I know that in a good deal of my work I have shown more zeal than discretion, but I have always believed that for a man to give himself away is one of the best methods for him to get rid of himself. The public can always protect itself effectually enough. I must protest against the imputation of considering you a barbarian; or if I do consider you one then I believe that the chief function of civilization is to produce barbarians — unless civilization means sophistication. On my side, I presume to think that I am more of a Yankee and less of a "philosopher" than sometimes may appear. . . . Sincerely yours,

JOHN DEWEY

The following letters on ethics resulted from the publication in 1891 of Dewey's *Outlines of a Critical Theory of Ethics,* and James's article on "The Moral Philosopher and the Moral Life." Each read the other's work and they exchanged comments: —

[6] Below, 521.

Ann Arbor, May 10, 1891

My dear Professor James, —

Your hearty note regarding the *Ethics* was very welcome to me. The book has received a little of what is called "favorable comment" as well as more or less of the reverse, but so far as reported you are the first man to see the point, — and that I suppose is the dearest thing to a writer. The present preceptual structure is so great, and such a weighty thing, both in theory and in practice, that I don't anticipate any success for the book, but when one man like yourself expresses what you wrote me, the book has already succeeded.

But unless a man is already living in the gospel and not under the law, as you express it, words thrown at him are idle wind. He does n't understand what you mean, and he would n't believe you meant it, if he did understand. The hope seems to be with the rising generation. . . . Many of my students, I find, are fairly hungering. They almost jump at any opportunity to get out from under the load and to believe in their own lives. Pardon the somewhat confessional character of this note, but the man who has seen the point arouses the confessional attitude. . . . Sincerely yours,

JOHN DEWEY

P.S. I don't know that I told you that I have had a class of four graduates going through your psychology this year, and how much we have all enjoyed it. I 'm sure you would be greatly gratified if you could see what a stimulus to mental freedom, as well as what a purveyor of methods and materials, your book has been to us.

Ann Arbor, June 3, 1891

My dear James, —

I have been putting off writing you day by day as theses etc., piled up about me. Besides, although I had read your ethical article once and recommended it to my class to read, I wanted to read it again. The article rejoiced me greatly . . . two things more than others . . . your statement that any desire, as such, constitutes a claim and any claim an obligation, and your discussion of rules. I was only sorry that the discussion of obligation, in particular, had not appeared before I wrote my *Ethics*. I think it is the best and simplest statement I have ever seen.

I should say that there is something back (and something ahead) of whatever freedom of sight and treatment there is in my ethics. I got it from Franklin Ford to whom I refer in the Preface.[7]   By some sort of instinct, and by the impossibility of my doing anything in particular, I was led into philosophy and into "idealism" — i.e., the conception of some organism comprehending both man's thought and the external world.   Ford, who was a newspaper man (formerly Editor of Bradstreet's in New York) with no previous philosophical training, had been led by his newspaper experience to study as a practical question the social bearings of intelligence and its distribution.   That is to say, he was on a paper and wanted to inquire.   The paper would not let him: the more he was stopped, the more his desire to inquire was aroused, until finally he was drawn into a study of the whole matter — especially as he found that it was not any one newspaper, but rather the social structure, which prevented freedom of inquiry.   Well, he identified the question of inquiry with, in philosophical terms, the question of the relation of intelligence to the objective world, — is the former free to move in relation to the latter or not?   So he studied out the following questions: (1) The conditions and effects of the distribution of intelligence especially with reference to inquiry, or the selling of truth as a business; (2) the present (or past) hindrances to its free play, in the way of class interests; or (3) the present conditions, in the railway, telegraph, etc., for effectively securing the freedom of intelligence, that is, its movement in the world of social fact; and (4) the resulting social organization.   That is, with inquiry as a business, the selling of truth for money, the whole would have a representative as well as the various classes, — a representative whose belly interest, moreover, is identical with its truth interest. Now I am simply reducing what was a wonderful personal experience to a crude bit of cataloging, but I hope it may arouse your interest in the man and his work.

What I have got out of it is, first, the perception of the true or

[7] The Preface to Dewey's *Outlines of a Critical Theory of Ethics* contains the following: "I may call attention to the idea of desire as the ideal activity in contrast with actual possession; to the analysis of individuality into function including capacity and environment; to the treatment of the social bearings of science and art (a point concerning which I am indebted to my friend, Mr. Franklin Ford); to the statement of an ethical postulate; to the accounts of obligation, of moral rules, and of moral badness" (vii–viii).   Franklin Ford later published *Municipal Reform, a Scientific Question,* 1903.

practical bearing of idealism — that philosophy has been the assertion of the unity of intelligence and the external world *in idea*
or subjectively, while if true in idea it must finally secure the conditions of its objective expression. And secondly, I believe that a
tremendous movement is impending, when the intellectual forces
which have been gathering since the Renascence and Reformation,
shall demand complete free movement, and, by getting their physical
leverage in the telegraph and printing press, shall, through free
inquiry in a centralized way, demand the authority of all other so-
called authorities. It is impossible to convey what I mean in a
page or two, but, as I am all the more anxious to see you and talk
with you on this very account, I hope I may not have made you suspicious of me. I shall have with me in the summer a number of
Ford's own writings which will convey it in an orderly and rational
way. I do not think that anyone who, like yourself, has the intellectual interest developed, the thirst for inquiry with no special
interest or precept or church or philosophy to "save," can fail of
being interested both in his theoretical discovery and in his practical
project. . . . Sincerely yours,

JOHN DEWEY

The group which formed around Dewey at the University of
Michigan and afterwards at the University of Chicago, forming
the nucleus of the so-called "Chicago School," and of the general
movement known as "instrumentalism," began to attract James's
attention and excite his enthusiasm at the beginning of the century.[8]
The correspondence which follows reflects James's eager interest
and sympathy. In the summer of 1903 the annual meeting of the
National Educational Association was held in Boston, and in the
preceding March James wrote to Dewey in behalf of his friend
Mrs. Pauline Agassiz Shaw, who had been selected to preside over
the sessions devoted to the kindergarten. To this letter he added
a postscript: "I have just read, with almost absurd pleasure,
A. W. Moore's *Existence, Meaning and Reality*. I am years behindhand in my reading, and don't know how close *you* may have
come to anything like that since 1898. I see an entirely new 'school
of thought' forming, and, as I believe, a true one. Who and what
is Moore, and how old?" Dewey replied as follows: —

[8] *Cf.* above, 375; and *L.W.J.*, II, 201–2.

[Chicago, March 1903]

[My dear James, —]

. . . [I walked] on air for a long time after getting such a letter from you. Moore . . . has taught here since about '95. . . . The flexibility and freedom of his mental operations I need n't speak of, — his articles do that. He has n't had fair play, he has been so loaded with "sections" . . . but probably has gained maturity from his enforced inhibitions. . . . I am tremendously glad that you liked his article, and very appreciative of the fact that, liking it, you expressed your satisfaction so generously. As for the standpoint, — we have all been at work at it for about twelve years. Lloyd and Mead were both at it in Ann Arbor ten years ago. Did you ever read Lloyd's *Dynamic Idealism?* I can't see much difference between his monism and your pluralism, — barring a little exaggeration of the plural on its own account, if I may venture. Mead has difficulty of articulation in written discourse, as you know; but I suppose he is more effective than any man in our Department in giving capable advanced students independent method. He works himself (and *it*) out mainly in biological terms. "Life-process" is his terminology for the developing reality. We have turned out some doctors who are beginning to do more or less. . . . They are all young, all busy with teaching; and I think on the whole it speaks well for them (and for their standpoint) that they have been fairly conservative in publishing. . . .

As for myself, — I don't know whether you ever read my psychological articles on "Emotion" and the "Reflex Arc Concept," — the one on "Effort" I know you read because you were good enough to write me. The "Savage Mind" article (thank you for your good word which I did n't acknowledge but appreciated) does n't appear very near (even less perhaps than the others referred to), but I have evolved them all from the same standpoint. The articles on "Evolution Applied to Morality" ought to bore you, and are not sent for you to read, except . . . the criticism of both empiricism and rationalism as non-genetic and hence absolutistic.[9] (I think you

---

[9] These articles appeared in *Psychol. Rev.*, I (1894), II (1895), IX (1902); *Univ. of Chicago Contributions to Philos.*, I (1896); *Philos. Rev.*, VI (1897), XI (1902). Of the "Savage Mind" article James had already written to Dewey: "I cannot refrain from thanking you for a thing so 'concrete' and full of veracious psychological imagination. Also humane, and calculated to dampen the conceit of our all-destroying 'Civilization.' Pray keep up that line of study" (Sept. 28, 1902).

must state your plurality as a matter of historic significance, and hence of relativity). . . .

I am sending you, herewith, some proof from a forthcoming Decennial volume, *Studies in Logical Theory*, written by [A. W.] Moore, [S. F.] McLennan, [H. B.] Thompson, [H. W.] Stuart, one or two others and myself as Editor. You may not have time nor inclination to read, but I wish you would glance the pages over enough to see whether you could stand for a dedication to yourself. Unfortunately my own things come first and are the only ones in page proof yet. (Overlook the disrespectful allusion to your pluralism in a foot-note, — I can but feel that your plurality as it now stands is æsthetic rather than logical.) But so far as I am concerned your *Psychology* is the spiritual *progenitor* of the whole industry; and while we won't attempt to father you with all the weak kidlets which are crying in the volume to be born, it would afford us all (and me in particular, if that does n't reflect on the pleasure of others) very much satisfaction if you will permit us to dedicate the volume to you.

We hope to get to East Hill [10] soon after the middle of June; — we have been congratulating ourselves much ever since we learned that you were coming up. . . . Faithfully yours,

JOHN DEWEY

Cambridge, March 23, 1903

Dear Dewey, —

Thanks for your amazingly obliging and interesting letter. . . . What you write of the *new school of truth* both pleases and humiliates me. It humiliates me that I had to wait till I read Moore's article before finding how much on my own lines you were working. Of course I had welcomed you as one coming nearer and nearer, but I had missed the central root of the whole business, and shall now re-read you (I had read *all* the articles you quote with great pleasure, but with this semi-blindness still), and try again a hack at Mead and Lloyd of whom I have always recognized the originality, but whom I have found so far unassimilably obscure. I fancy that much depends on the place one starts from. You have all come from Hegel and your terminology *s'en ressent,* I from empiricism, and though we reach much the same goal it superficially looks dif-

[10] At Hurricane, N. Y., the place of Thomas Davidson's "Summer School for Cultural Sciences."

ferent from the opposite sides.   I enclose a syllabus [11] to show you where I'm working. . . .   Yours faithfully,

WM. JAMES

Chicago, March 27, 1903

My dear James, —

. . . I feel rather ashamed to have given you the impression that I was writing about a new school of thought.   I do not think you will find it worth while rereading the articles I mentioned; or, if you do, that you will find anything in them that is in any way indicative of new developments.   It is simply that upon the psychological side the articles all go back to certain ideas of life activity, of growth, and of adjustment, which involve teleological and dynamic conceptions rather than ontological and static ones.   None of them attempts any metaphysical applications, with the possible exception of some of the implications of the one on the evolutionary method as applied to morality.   I have been at work with my classes more or less on the metaphysical — or logical side, as I prefer to call it — for some years, but I never felt until this year that I had anything in shape to publish. . . .

Thank you very much for your syllabus, which I have read with very great interest.   I hope that you are going to put the thing out in such objective shape that we can all get the benefit of a completed exposition.   Your reference to monism's doubling up of the world into two editions emboldens me to refer to my review of Royce . . . where I have made some remarks on the same reduplication.[12]

It may be the continued working of the Hegelian bacillus of reconciliation of contradictories in me, that makes me feel as if the conception of process gives a basis for uniting the truths of pluralism and monism, and also of necessity and spontaneity.   Pearson leaves his co-evolution of the perceptual world and the conceptual a blank unmediated thing, which accordingly suffers from the defects of any theory of parallelism and of preëstablished harmony.[13] Yet I cannot help feeling that an adequate analysis of activity would exhibit the world of fact and the world of ideas as two correspondent objective statements of the active process itself, — cor-

[11] The "Syllabus in Philos. 3."
[12] *Philos. Rev.*, IX (1900), XI (1902).
[13] Karl Pearson's *Grammar of Science* (2nd edition, 1900).

respondent because each has a work to do, in the doing of which it
needs to be helped out by the other. The active process itself
transcends any possible objective statement (whether in terms of fact
or of ideas) simply for the reason that these objective statements
are ultimately incidental to its own ongoing — are for the sake of it.
It is this transcendence of any objectified form, whether perceptual
or conceptual, that seems to me to give the clue to freedom, spontaneity, etc.; and to make it unnecessary to have recourse to such a
hypostatizing of chance as Peirce seems to me to indulge in. I
always feel as if he were engaging (as respects his "chance") in
just the same sort of conceptual construction he is protesting against.
I must say, however, that I can see how far I have moved along
when I find how much I get out of Peirce this year, and how easily
I understand him, when a few years ago he was mostly a sealed
book to me, aside from occasional inspirations. . . . Yours sincerely,

JOHN DEWEY

The spring of 1903 saw the appearance of *Studies in Logical
Theory,* by John Dewey, "with the coöperation of Members and
Fellows of the Department of Philosophy" of the University of
Chicago. The Preface contained the following words: "For both
inspiration and the forging of the tools with which the writers have
worked there is a preëminent obligation on the part of all of us to
William James, of Harvard University, who, we hope, will accept
this acknowledgment and this book as unworthy tokens of a regard
and an admiration that are coequal."

Cambridge, Oct. 17, 1903

Dear Dewey, —
I was about to write to you in any case this afternoon when your
ultra friendly letter came. On returning from the country yesterday, one of the first things that greeted my eyes was your *Logical
Studies,* and the to me surprising words that close its Preface.
What have I done to merit such a tribute? The Lord, who know-
eth all things, knows doubtless about this too, but I accept it rather
blindly, and most delightedly, as one of the good things that life
sometimes strews in one's way. I feel so the inchoateness of all
my publications that it surprises me to hear of anything definite

accruing to others from them. I must do better, now that I am "looked up to" so. I thank you from the bottom of my heart! As for the foot-note, I fear I gave an exaggerated impression to Mrs. Dewey. You are certainly taking it too hard. I would n't have it expunged for anything now.[14]

It rejoices me greatly that your School (I mean your philosophic school) at the University of Chicago is, after this long gestation, bringing its fruits to birth in a way that will demonstrate its great unity and vitality, and be a revelation to many people, of American scholarship. I wish now that you would make a collection of your scattered articles, especially on "ethical" subjects. It is only books that tell. They seem to have a penetrating power which the same content in the shape of scattered articles wholly lacks. But the articles prepare buyers for the books. My own book, rather absurdly cackled about before it is hatched, is hardly begun, and with my slow rate of work will take long to finish. A little thing by Harald Höffding, called *Philosophische Probleme,* which I have just read . . . is quite a *multum in parvo* and puts many things exactly as I should put them. I am sure of a great affinity between your own "monism," since so you call it, and my "pluralism." Ever gratefully and faithfully yours,

WM. JAMES

James felt that two of his labels, "the will to believe" and "pragmatism," were unfortunate. The following letter suggests that the label of "instrumentalism" was not less so. "Instrumentalism" seems to imply submission to external circumstance, or the variable means to a fixed end. But the "intelligence" which Dewey praises is a principle of freedom and innovation; not a mere condition of life, but an enrichment of experience and expansion of powers which, in the ideal sense, *constitute* life.

Chicago, Dec. 19, 1903

Dear James, —

This is the third letter I have got into since receiving yours, — but the others were written in sections at intervals and became too disjointed, so I 'll start on a briefer one in the hope of finishing.

---

[14] In a footnote Dewey speaks of James's "satisfaction in the contemplation of bare pluralism, of disconnection, of radical having-nothing-to-do-with-one-another." (*Studies in Logical Theory,* 81.)

But it must be long enough to tell you how much philosophic encouragement, to say nothing of purely personal pleasure, your letters give. . . .   For a number of years I have funded for my own intellectual capital more of the ideas of other people — students and colleagues — than I can tell, and Moore has given at least as much as he has received.   As for the whole point of view, it needs working out in all kinds of directions, of course.   But one thing that makes me believe in it is that students, graduates and some of the undergraduates, get hold of it and make it a working method.   The people who have written for the *Logical Studies* — and there are four or five others who might have written — have n't repeated, I know, a lesson that had been taught them.   They have made a personal tool of discussion, and inquiry out of a "point of view." And that is a good criterion, — for a pragmatist anyway.   But when you say it needs psychological development I wonder sometimes if you fully appreciate how much of all of this is in your two volumes of psychology.   I have a good mind sometime to make an inventory of all the points in which your psychology "already" furnishes the instrumentalities for a pragmatic logic, ethics and metaphysics. . . .

I am going to do Schiller for the *Psychological Review*.[15]   His temper and style, and some of his positions, trouble me, but I shall endeavor to put my hyperæsthesias one side.   It does seem to me, however, that the concept of a "changeless activity" is absolutism all over again.[16]   What does "will" mean?   What becomes of the instrumental interpretation of cognitional activity?   And where is emotion without the disturbance and excitation of change?   And what is "feeling" if all emotional coloring is excluded?   Either we have an Absolute beyond experience, in our sense of experience, or else a Bradleyan Experience in which will, feeling and cognition are all eternally one.   If our final philosophic conception is a Completed Activity, and we try to describe this in terms of psychical experience, — what is this anyway but Bradley's Reality in his *Appearance and Reality?*

I thank you very much for writing the notice of the *Logical Studies*. . . .   I have something brewing in my head on what I call to myself "Truth As Stimulation and As Control," a com-

[15] *Psychol. Bulletin*, I (1904).
[16] *Cf.* above, 496, note 7; and *Humanism*, Essay XII.

mentary in effect upon your "Sentiment of Rationality"; to point out that in certain situations truth is that which liberates and sets agoing more experience, in others, that which limits and defines, which adjusts to definite ends.   It seems to me this will straighten out some objections to pragmatism, its seeming over-utilitarianism (the "control" side), and provide a place for the æsthetic function *in* knowledge — "truth for its own sake," harmony, etc. (the liberation side).   And I believe this has a bearing on the indeterminate character of experience, and hence upon freedom, etc. Schiller from this point of view overdoes relatively the control side of truth, its utility for *specific* purposes, not making enough of the tremendous freedom, possibilities of new growth, etc., that come from developing an "intelligence" that works along for a time according to its *own* technique, *in abstracto* from preconceived and preëxperienced ends and results. . . .   I 'm getting to another documentary letter, but "truth for its own sake" has upon complete pragmatic principles, it seems to me, not only a justification, but an absolutely indispensable function; without which the last word would be with an "environment" which finally determines what is and what is n't useful; and it makes little difference whether this environment is called "matter" or a complete system of thought-relations, or Experience *per* Bradley or *per* Royce. . . .   Yours as always,

JOHN DEWEY

James's enthusiastic review of the *Logical Studies* appeared early in 1904 under the title of "The Chicago School" — enthusiastic save for the remark that the book contained no "cosmology" or explanation of the "common world." [17]   In his prompt acknowledgment, Dewey wrote: "I need hardly say what I have said before, such approval as you feel drawn to give means more to us than that of anybody else.   None the less as far as I am concerned I have simply been rendering back in logical vocabulary what was already your own."

In February of the same year James presented the "New Thought" before a group of Dewey's colleagues and students in Chicago; and in the following September Dewey read the first of the articles on "radical empiricism" — "Does Consciousness Exist?"

[17] *Psychol. Bulletin,* I (1904) ; *cf. C.E.R.,* 445–7.

Grenoble, Nov. 21, 1904

My dear James, —

. . . I read the article on "consciousness" with profound assent. I think the idea of consciousness which you contend against is at the root of many of the arguments against pragmatism . . . which charge it with subjectivism. Holding the conception themselves, the critics confer the idea upon others, and then charge up against them the consequences to which they have rendered themselves liable. As for the last few pages, they seem to leave the subjective consciousness in an unnecessarily otiose state. That the mental fire does n't burn appears to be the first prerequisite of our managing the fire that does burn, — of having it burn when, how and where we wish. In logical phrase, without the psychical no abstraction, and without abstraction no prescient control. This is the point of view which, if I understand him — and unfortunately he is n't easy reading — Mead has set forth in his "Definition of the Psychical." [18]

Of course, we come back everywhere, to the difficulty of stating the nature and reasons of the fact that the objective, the fire which burns, is pliable, and submits to the exactions which we, in our subjective or psychical capacity, make upon it. . . . This is just the fundamental question of morals, — the interaction of persons and things, or the relation of personal freedom and the stable order. And one of the many advantages of the pragmatic approach is that it identifies this ethical problem with the general problem of the relations of the objective and subjective in experience, instead of leaving the ethical in a small corner by itself. And there is much to be said concerning an order which is . . . fixed within limits, and which yet gives to the impulsion of prescient action, and the whole conception of evolution as . . . reality which changes through centres of behavior which are intrinsic and not merely incident. All of this is very vague, but I trust to you to fill it up enough to give it some meaning. I am glad also to have your paper as a souvenir of the evening you spent with us in Chicago, as I recognize the continuity of what you said to us then and your article . . . .

Mrs. Dewey joins me in regard and in affection for both yourself and Mrs. James. Very sincerely yours,

JOHN DEWEY

[18] *Decennial Publications* of the University of Chicago, First Series, III, 1903. James had distinguished the mental from the physical series by the fact that in the

When in 1906 he turned to the composition of the lectures and volume on "Pragmatism," James was acutely and enthusiastically aware of the support which he was receiving from different quarters. He was eager to consolidate the movement, if not by agreement, then by a frank recognition of differences. Dewey contributed to this clarification and mutual understanding.

New York, Nov. 28, 1907

Dear James, —

I have just finished, for Woodbridge, an account of the pragmatic movement, based on your book.[19] This reminds me that I have not even acknowledged the book, at least I can't remember doing so. I am culpable, flagrantly so, in the matter of acknowledgments and correspondence generally, but this is one of my worst sins of omission. If I had been less interested and absorbed in the book I should probably have written of its receipt long ago! As it is, I shall have to count on your antecedent knowledge of my appreciation of and indebtedness to all you do.

I have not attempted a review of the book, but rather of the pragmatic movement with reference to what present controversy seems to me to indicate as the points which require more explicit statement and development. Among other things I have become conscious of some points of possible divergence between Schiller, yourself and myself, taken two by two all the way around; and I am not sure that some misunderstandings among our critics might not be cleared away, if our points of respective agreement and possible disagreement were brought out. For example, the antecedents of humanism, via personal idealism, were distinctly an idealistic metaphysics. My own views are much more naturalistic, and a reaction against not merely intellectualistic and monistic idealism but against all idealisms, except, of course, in the sense of ethical ideals. Now, I seem to myself to be nearer you than I am to Schiller on this point, yet I am not sure. On the other hand, Schiller in his later writings seems to emphasize that the good consequence which is the test of an idea, is *good* not so much in its own nature as in meeting the claims of the idea, whatever the idea is. And here I

---

former the terms do not *act*. "Mental fire is what won't burn real sticks." (*E.R.E.*, 33.)

[19] "What Does Pragmatism Mean by Practical?" *Jour. of Philos.*, V (1908).

seem to be nearer to him than to you; and yet again I am not sure.
If there are real differences, and our critics are inclined to make
combinations of our respective doctrines which no one of us alone
would stand for, this may account for some of the unsatisfactory
misunderstandings in the present state of controversy. Yours
sincerely,

JOHN DEWEY

It will be recalled that in 1907 James had delivered his lectures
on pragmatism at Columbia University. In 1908, James was presented with a volume of *Essays Philosophical and Psychological,*
written in his honor by "his colleagues at Columbia University,"
and "intended to mark in some degree its authors' sense of Professor James's memorable services in philosophy and psychology, the
vitality he has added to those studies, and the encouragement that
has flowed from him to colleagues without number." [20] To this
volume Dewey contributed the essay entitled, "Does Reality Possess
Practical Character?" and which to James seemed the most
"weighty." [21] It served, together with the previous article "What
Does Pragmatism Mean by Practical?" to define the author's interpretation of James and of the doctrine which they held in
common.

In 1908 and 1909 James was busily engaged in the double
task of refuting critics and smoothing the way to agreement. In
the former year he published an article entitled " 'Truth' *versus*
'Truthfulness,' " at the conclusion of which he proposed to surrender
the word "truth" to those who wished to emphasize "the preliminary
and objective conditions of the cognitive relation," reserving the
term "truthful" for that functional value of ideas which pragmatism
emphasized. Dewey disapproved of the proposal, and it was withdrawn by James when he reprinted the article in *The Meaning of
Truth.*[22]

New York, Feb. 24, 1909

Dear James, —

In view of what you told me about reprinting your essays on
truth, I am going to be impertinent enough to ask about one essay,

[20] Title-page and prefatory note.
[21] *L.W.J.*, II, 310.
[22] *Jour. of Philos.*, V (1908), 181; *M.T.*, 225.

viz., that on "Truth versus Truthfulness"; provided, that is, you are thinking of reprinting that as it stands. My remarks have to do with the two closing paragraphs. For a pragmatist to say that the question is "almost purely academic" gives the unbeliever too much chance to blaspheme, does n't it? Or, on the other hand, if this is an almost purely academic question, how can it be admitted that "truthfulness" is so much the more important idea, as the last paragraph indicates? I should not venture to write you about this if I did not know positively that these two paragraphs have been both a stumbling-block to those who had not made up their minds, and a cause of congratulation to the anti-pragmatists. . . .

While my main purpose in writing is merely to raise this question of advisability, it seems to me that Strong's article [23] . . . brings out very clearly the confusion of your critics which you are endeavoring to meet by your distinction between "truth" and "truthfulness." "Is it true that Napoleon landed in Provence on the last day of March, 1814?" If this means anything, it means either (*a*) Is the *statement, idea or belief* that Napoleon landed etc., true? or, (*b*) Is the landing (the bare existential fact) of Napoleon a truth? Now the thoroughgoing rationalist (*e.g.,* Royce) holds, as I understand him, that the bare existential fact *qua* fact *is* itself of the *nature* of truth, *i.e.* is already, externally at least, an absorbed element in a truth (and therefore intellectual) system. Now Strong (and many of your other critics) do *not* hold this any more than you do. Strong's "true that Napoleon landed" can only be an elliptic statement for, "the idea or belief is true." Now it seems to me that we need only hold the critics (of the non-absolute-idealism type) up to the distinction between brute existences or occurrences (which certainly are not "truths") and the intellectual . . . statements *about* those existences (to which alone the character of truth-falsity does appertain), to make them see that the confusion lies with them, and that truth (and not merely truthfulness) may well be a relation between the *effects* of the existence in question and the *effects* of the intellectual position or assertion in question. And the case of the truth of a historic statement, a statement about an event in the past (and this not by the nature of the case open to direct inspection), seems to be a particularly strong case on your

[23] "Pragmatism and Its Definition of Truth," *Jour. of Philos.,* V (1908).

side. "Cæsar's existence" is, then, in no sense a *"truth* 2000 years old"; the question is whether a belief or statement that Cæsar did certain things 2000 years ago is true.

You will pardon this suggestion, I hope, but it seems to me that to concede, for the sake of better understanding, to the critic that a happening is the same as a truth, is to admit the very point in which his own confusion resides, and, by encouraging him in that confusion to prevent exactly the better understanding which you have aimed at?   Sincerely yours,

JOHN DEWEY

In the Preface to *The Meaning of Truth* James undertook to represent the views of Dewey, Schiller, and himself as complementary rather than conflicting.   Schiller's universe was "psychological," his own "epistemological," and as for Dewey's — it was "the widest of the three," but he "refrained from giving his own account of its complexity."   James had originally written Dewey down as "ontological" to complete the trilogy, but having submitted the passage to Dewey he had "refrained," at the latter's earnest request.   "Even the humblest and most obscure writer," wrote Dewey, "has perhaps a natural reluctance, while he is still vocal, to be authoritatively explained by others, even though he recognize that he is fair game for criticism."   James's request for further explanation evoked the following: "Of course I had no intention of passing upon your references to Schiller.   No, I don't think your statement about me is false; but, pragmatically, falsity and inadequacy run into each other.   The 'ontological' reference is, I think, misleading, considering the historic and conventional associations of that term.   My most serious objection is that I do not think such summary resolutions of complicated matters really clarify the discussion.   They create as many new questions as they resolve and often produce a new crop of misunderstandings."

In the same Preface, James insisted that Schiller, Dewey, and he absolutely agreed "in admitting the transcendency of the object (provided it be an experienceable object) to the subject, in the truth-relation."   Then follows a passage on "Dewey in particular," which conforms to, and in some cases verbally reproduces, the following letter.[24]

[24] *M.T.,* xvii.

New York, March 21, 1909

Dear James, —

. . . It is perhaps inconsistent of me to make a positive suggestion, but . . . it occurred to me that the sentence "as firmly as I do to independent objects" might be finished up as follows, "since his instrumental theory of knowledge is clearly self-contradictory unless there are independent existences of which ideas take account and for the transformation of which they function."

Of course I am not trying to supply *you* with language; but I have never been able to see why a critic . . . if he really believed (except for controversial purposes) that I do not believe in anything beyond mental states, should not point out the self-contradiction that that involves me in. Of course I have repeated *ad nauseam* that there are existences prior to and subsequent to cognitive states and purposes, and that *the whole meaning of the latter* is the way they intervene in the control and revaluation of the independent existences. And I am quite sure that if you will read over carefully the passages quoted from me in the accusations of my critics, or turn to what in your Preface . . . you refer to as "certain sentences," you will find them to be sentences which refer to the empirical character of the extra-cognitional existences; — sentences which can be paralleled, of course, over and over again from your own writings. In fact, I find (in conversation) that many critics regard your doctrine as much more subjectivistic than mine, because I, following the lead of your *Psychology,* "Reflex-Action and Theism" etc., emphasize (more than do your later writings) the biological *origin* of ideas and intellectual operations.

In short, you will find (unless I am mistaken badly) that the critics who make this charge . . . *always* shift the ground from the analysis of *truth* to the meaning of *experience,* and having themselves a thoroughly subjective (and hence dualistic) notion of experience, they read it into us. And to point out this shift of ground on their part seems to me more important than reiterations on our part of our belief in independent existences, which they can always go on ignoring by claiming that even if we hold these things, we *ought* not to logically. Sincerely yours,

JOHN DEWEY

It is clear that this discussion led to no breach between James and Dewey, but tended rather to confirm their agreement. James continued to follow the development of Dewey's thought with interest and admiration.[25] The temper of their correspondence was worthy of their common vocation. They were wholly unlike in the genius of their minds; and if it be true that the style reveals the man, then they were certainly different men. James had great difficulty in understanding Dewey's ideas with their "unchained formlessness of expression"— Dewey must have found James precipitate and over-exuberant. But to both these were trivial considerations, and they sought by sympathy and understanding to emphasize the truth which they held in common, rather than by disputation to aggravate their differences.

[25] Thus he read and annotated Dewey's *How We Think,* published early in 1910.

LXXXII

JAMES AND STRONG

THE commonest charge against pragmatism was the charge of subjectivism. In replying to his critics, therefore, James was primarily concerned to reaffirm the existence of independent objects — independent, not of experience, since they *are* experience (or are *as* experienced), but of ideas about them, being a prior condition of the meaning and truth of these ideas. In taking this position he believed that he enjoyed the support of Dewey, Schiller, and other fellow pragmatists. He looked also for agreement from other avowed realists, such as Charles A. Strong.

Up to 1907 the principal topic of discussion between James and Strong had been panpsychism, which Strong advocated and which James *almost,* but never *quite,* accepted. In 1904 Strong published an article on "The Naturalistic Theory of the Reference of Thought to Reality" [1] which led James to regard him as an ally. The important article, "A Word More about Truth," which James published in the summer of 1907, identified pragmatism with "the notion of satisfactory working or leading," and in expounding this notion James cited Strong in his support, and borrowed his terminology.[2] In the later correspondence James was increasingly insistent that this "satisfactory working or leading" of an idea, its *referring* to an object and *proving* true, must fall completely within the knower's experience. He evidently felt that Strong took the matter too lightly — speaking, as he did, of "similarity," "vision," and so forth, as though there were no problem at all.

Early in 1907 Strong heard the lecture which James delivered at Columbia on Pragmatism, and read in proof one or more articles

[1] *Jour. of Philos.,* I (1904). In this article Strong speaks of "cognition" as "nothing but a way of entering into relations with a reality"; and hails James's and Miller's formulation of this view as "destined to form one of the foundation-stones of the evolutionary psychology of the future" (253). But Strong evidently accepted it with metaphysical (panpsychistic) and logical reservations.

[2] *Jour. of Philos.,* IV (1907), 397 ff.

which James had prepared on the same subject. He was especially interested in the religious applications of pragmatism, and in March wrote to urge the distinction between "the God of things as they should be, and the God of things as they are. The latter exists . . . but he does not deserve to be worshipped, — is, indeed, a false God; the former is worshipful, but he does not exist." He concluded with the exhortation: "If you cannot come out squarely for an ideal God . . . at least give him . . . an even chance with the other, *indicate the alternative;* and the hearts of those who have suffered through inability to believe will bless you." This was the "tightly woven little letter," the "warning" against his "superstitious tendencies," to which James replied on April 9, stating that his God, being only a "part of a pluralistic system," could be *both* existent and ideal: "What harm does the little residuum or germ of actuality that I leave in God do? If ideal, why . . . may he not have got himself at least partly real by this time? I do not believe it to be healthy-minded to nurse the notion that ideals are self-sufficient and require no actualization to make us content. It is a quite unnecessarily heroic form of resignation and sour grapes. Ideals ought to aim at the *transformation of reality* — no less!"[3]

In the same month in which the above letter was written Strong sent an unpublished manuscript on "Theory of Knowledge" and "Evolutionary Psychology," which James annotated and summarized.[4] Strong here describes his theory of knowledge as "substitutional," borrowing the term from James,[5] and meaning that an immediate subjective experience is substituted for an external object. This function of external reference, or "projection," constitutes "consciousness"; and is distinguished from the psychical reality, or "feeling," which constitutes the universal character of existence. The same manuscript contains two references to the pragmatists: first, as "holding that [knowledge] has no reference beyond experience, and that questions of truth and falsity relate to future experience and the actions to be recommended in view of them"; second, as ignoring the reference of experience to an ulterior external object.

[3] *L.W.J.,* II, 269–70.
[4] *Cf.* above, 405. Apparently this was an early draft of the article entitled "Substitutionism" which Strong contributed to *Essays Philosophical and Psychological in Honor of William James.*
[5] *E.R.E.,* 62 ff.

Cambridge, June 1, 1907

Dear Strong, —

Your manuscript has been in my hands for ten days at least, and has been read twice over with minute care.   But don't expect a "minute" reaction from *me* just now!   I have been busy with Ph.D. work, and other manuscripts, and have just been constrained to write "a last word about Truth" for the *Journal* myself.[6] . . .   All I can say now is that the whole thing represents an extremely successful *systematization,* with wonderful clearness of discrimination, and happiness of statement in many parts, but so concise and often so elliptic as not to be *criticizable* until published in fuller form. Your great and fundamental point, the distinction between feelings as primary and consciousness of them as secondary, I am sure I don't yet rethink just as you think it.   I don't positively object to it, and I can see what an alleviation it would be to almost everything, but I can't think it *out,* so I will say nothing about it now.   Your epistemology seems absolutely at one with my own, and I think the term "substitutional theory" is very likely to help it down.   I don't know whom you have in mind by your "pragmatists," — possibly Mach.   But Mach's pure phenomenism is expressly denied by him to be a *philosophy,* it is only a point of view which he calls sufficient for scientific purposes.   Schiller, Dewey and I are all (I, at *any* rate!) epistemological realists, — the reality known exists independently of the knower's idea, and *as* conceived, if the conception be a true one.   I can see that some bad parturient phrases of my radical empiricism might lead to an opposite interpretation, but if so they must be expunged.   As a pragmatist I have not given a word of excuse for such an interpretation.

I leave on Tuesday next for Keene Valley, where I shall stay, more or less alone, as many weeks as I can stand it. . . .   I shall as promptly as possible buckle down to my own puzzling over the fundamentals, where I grapple on my own account with the maxim a feeling is as it is felt, and where the whole conception of "consciousness" must be overhauled.   If I find myself drawn straight into your own paths, delightful will be the experience of agreement.

---

[6] "A Word More about Truth," *Jour. of Philos.,* IV (1907).   In "ambulatory" relations the terms are continuous or adjacent, as in real existence or immediate experience; while "saltatory" relations, like similarity and other logical relations, leap over intervening terms and act at a distance.

I hope it will turn out so, — you are evidently *very* near to a solution of everything. . . . Affectionate regards!

W. J.

P.S. I have borrowed your terms "saltatory" and "ambulatory" in my just-finished article on truth, — giving you full "credit"!![7]

Glion, June 20, 1907

Dear James, —

Thank you for your generous words about my typewritten notes, as well as for *the book,* on the completion of which I congratulate you. I am grieved that you should think me unjust to pragmatism. I'm afraid my carping references to it, in the notes, even seemed to you unmannerly, written as they were after hearing but half your lectures and before I had read your book. In the first passage where I refer to the doctrine I had Dewey's account of perception in mind, and the view criticized might better perhaps have been called "immediate empiricism." The later references, however, were aimed at your account of truth. Granting that you admit a thing-in-itself beyond the perceptive experience — do you (1) regard it as the *object* of the latter? (2) admit it to be really, though perhaps inadequately, *known?* This is the position to which I have come round, largely under the influence of Santayana. It can hardly be your view, for then you would recognize truth to be a relation between the perceptive experience and the thing-in-itself. . . .

I am reading Bergson's extraordinary book.[8] In form it is a rare work of art. I feel inclined to draw a line between the panpsychism and the vitalism of it, accepting the former but cherishing doubts about the latter. Yours ever,

C. A. STRONG

Cambridge, July 1, 1907

Dear Strong, —

Yours from Glion of June 20th comes this morning. That I should not yet have made clear my notion of knowledge to *you* shows how desperately hard is *Einverständigung*[9] in these regions. I send you a duplicate proof of an article written *at* the Columbians,

[7] *M.T.,* 138.
[8] *L'Évolution créatrice.*
[9] Reaching agreement.

at Miller especially, which will perhaps make me clearer to you, though I should like you also to read it in its revised and augmented form when it appears.   I have just mailed to Woodbridge the manuscript of another shorter article in reply to a recent clever one of J. B. Pratt's.[10]   Bit by bit I hope that light will break through the apparent impenetrable opacity of my words.

In reply to the questions in this letter of yours — "Granting a thing in itself beyond the perceptive experience, do you (1) regard it as the *object* of the latter? (2) admit it to be really though perhaps inadequately *known?*" — I say "yes," with a stentorian voice, provided you allow the word "object" to cover a scale of objects, from the first representative that we have in sensation to the ultimate thing-in-itself, and the word "known" to cover a possibly absolute telepathic confluence, as well as every grade of imperfect symbolic copying or approach.   A scheme will perhaps help : —

KNOWLEDGE
^

adequate   SYMBOLIC
^   ^

Confluence	nextness	concept	concept	concept	percept	sensation	our idea

Reality in itself

The vertically written words mean the scale of *approaches* to *adequate* knowledge of the object as critically ratified by an omniscient onlooker (I can only conceive of it as conflux or identification, such as common sense assumes in sense perception where the sensation *is* the object).   All the other stages of the scale are inadequate, and more or less symbolic and representative, but they are all projections towards *that* reality in itself, and in any one of them our finite fallible mind may rest as if we had adequate knowledge. — Good-bye!   I leave in a week for Keene Valley.   Bergson's book is *divine* — though I can understand it but partially.   Yours as ever,

W. J.

[10] "A Word More about Truth," and "Prof. Pratt on Truth," *Jour. of Philos.*, IV (1907).

St. Moritz, July 20, 1907 [11]

Dear James, —

. . . It seems to me that the new article on truth attacks the issue in the most fruitful way, since it goes at the underlying presuppositions, which are certain conceptions as to the relation between subject and object. You say that cognition is essentially a process of leading, and that it would find its perfect fulfilment in confluence with the objects. I cannot admit either of these propositions. . . . Not all the objects of knowledge are or involve possible future experiences of mind; thus, a physical event happening *now,* yet not under my eyes, or one that happened years ago, or a thought past or present in another mind. No process of leading could conduct me anywhere but away from such objects as these. . . . Suppose what I think of is a tiger, accidentally escaped from a cage. I don't want to be led towards him, much less to become confluent with him. I want to *adjust my relations* to him. . . . Suppose what I am thinking of is another person's toothache. Again I want no confluence, but rather to take the proper measures for affording my fellow-being relief. This is again adjustment of relations. *But the adjustment is not now to future experiences of mine, but to present experiences of another person, unshareable by me because essentially other and beyond.* And two-thirds of all our objects of thought are in this case. . . .

Now to the final point about truth. Each possible object of cognition, located at some definite point of space and of past, present, or future time, *has a determinate nature* . . . and this nature constitutes an absolute standard, to which the fact that knowing is largely mere adjustment, rather than copying, does not exempt it from conforming. . . . You see, dear James, where I at present find myself. It seems to me that in your thinking you conceive objects transcendentally as possible future experiences of mine, rather than realistically as actual experiences now existing, or that once existed or will exist, of somebody or something else; and that this is why you can say that truth is merely a matter of consequences, and a thing in our own hands, rather than a revelation . . . of (for the most part) inexorable fact. . . . Ever truly yours,

C. A. STRONG

[11] For comment on this letter and its subject matter, *cf.* James's letter to Miller of Aug. 5, 1907, in which he proclaims himself a "natural realist," and asserts that the function of knowledge is to *select* from experience. (*L.W.J.,* II, 295–6.)

South Lincoln, Aug. 4, 1907

Dear Strong, —

Yours from St. Moritz of July 20th finds me temporarily here and with no writing paper, so excuse! How I wish I could have thrashed the matter out orally with you and Santayana! I won't send your letter to the *Journal of Philosophy,* — it would be obscure to the uninitiate, and I think that my own *Auseinandersetzungen* had better stop for a while in print. Your objections to my statement seem largely based on not giving due weight to my insistence that the leading may be *towards* as well as *into* the independent reality known. Evidently my statement has been very faulty, for "towards" means "into the neighborhood of" (or, to put it most widely, "into the universe of"), and that includes generic similarity and similarity of associates, as well as time and space propinquity.[12] . . . The essential point in my theory is that both idea and reality form mutually separated parts of a common world of experiences, and that the *fundamentum relationis* of the fact that the idea may mean and point to that reality, and know it truly, is to be found in the enveloping experiences and nowhere else. Take them out and the meaning and the knowing lose their foothold.

Of course the simplest case is *perception,* and one must use that as one's first paradigm in expounding. Complete knowledge of me by you is actual perception (complete, at any rate, in one way) and the percept *is* the reality, for common sense. If you extrapolate my mind, you at first know it only conceptually, and my supposition of a later confluence was only hypothetical. If ever you should get an acquaintance with my mental present as close as your optical acquaintance with your own hand is to your kinesthetic acquaintance with the same hand, or with my mental past as close as is your acquaintance with your own past, then, from the height of that telepathic knowledge, you would call your present conceptual knowledge of me inadequate and lacking in truth. I see no obstacle to supposing that such telepathic fusion might some time be realized, but if you consider it eternally impossible or self-contradictory, drop it. I only used it *ad hominem* as a type of what my adversaries *might* mean by absolutely final truth.[13]

[12] *Cf. M.T.,* 42, note, where W.J. says that he came in his later writings to emphasize the relation of the idea to the independent reality not directly, but *indirectly,* through other realities.

[13] This is a different conception of ideal truth, — more closely allied to mysticism and intuitionism than the conception of agreement. The latter view is closer to Peirce and Dewey, the former to Bergson.

Now the experiential environment, which both separates the idea and the reality and mediates between them, affords many types of adjustment of the one to the other. We take cognizance of a tiger as much by shunning as by seeking him. It is *that* tiger whom we must shun, so proved by our haunts not being *his* haunts, and the total map of haunts is partly verified negatively by ourselves, and partly positively by other men who are themselves parts of the environment common to us both. If no one verifies the whole, then who knows whether we thought a real tiger at all, and what *constitutes* our meaning any particular tiger out of the possible universe of tigers? The toothache-case is exactly similar, save that I can't possibly (at present) have direct perception of it. But by means of our common environment I can get so "near" it as to cure it, or so far from it as to avoid seeing the man suffer, in both cases proving by my action that *it* is the reality my mind points to, and means, and knows. It is through the "adjustment of my relations" to these independent realities that my *taking cognizance of them* is established. The way *my own future* (on which you lay such stress) comes in is that it is a term to which both the reality and my present idea converge by appropriate lines of context leading from each.

How should I not agree with you that the *determinate nature* of the reality is a fixed stake in the relation, that controls? But controls what? Controls the *denotation,* so to speak of the idea, the rest of which depends on our subjective interest also. To *take account of* is an essentially ambiguous phrase. Thought "adapts" itself in as infinitely numerous ways as animal organisms do, but it is tethered. You take account of tigers by loving as well as by hating, and your ideas may be "true" in either case, apart from *other* ideas which might be violated by them. The common notion of truth as conformity (into which you seem about to drop near the end of your letter) is passive conformity. "True" architecture must conform to gravity, just as true belief must conform to reality; but to represent true belief as meaning absolute conformity (as intellectualists do) is like saying that architecture is a pure effect of gravity. You can't work any real meaning into either phrase. In fine, I conceive realities as existent, as having existed, or about to exist, in absolute independence of my thought of them. But I deny that you can express the varied facts of knowledge by the empty term "conformity." It is not like a coat that has to be made to "fit" a fixed figure. Rather is the fit an equilibrium between two mutually independent variables.   There's where the humanism comes in! . . .   The word "pragmatism" is evidently a very unlucky one.   It suggests sordid practical interests, and all the critics take it to *exclude* logical ones.   But the interest in "truth" *per se* is an intensely *peculiar* human one, which most men are without.   It resolves itself into curiosity about new facts, love of consistency, and love of simplification — immense practical urgencies.   In haste, yours,

W. J.

St. Moritz, Aug. 6, 1907

Dear James, —

The number of the *Journal of Philosophy* containing your article came yesterday, and I have spent the morning on it, taking notes.[14] . . .   In the present account you leave out of consideration the whole element of *agreement* and *correspondence* between idea and object, and so the fact that the idea may have a *vision* of the object before actually getting to it. . . .   My criticisms still hold good.   For you, the only proof that the idea has to do with the object at all is an eventual or possible confluence.   But I have shown that in cases where confluence is not only undesirable, but even inconceivable, we still cognize the object. . . .   No, not "total conflux," but *exact duplication:* complete agreement between our idea and the thing itself. . . .   If what I am thinking of is somebody else's toothache, my thought is truest if I conceive the toothache exactly as it is. . . .   Then I shall be surest to run for a remedy, or to give him the address of a dentist, since I realize completely what his having the toothache means.   A less preposterous case would be that of sympathy for colored people (I have been reading Wells's book on America), due to realizing entirely what it means to be personally worthy yet be treated with contempt as an inferior. . . .

In short, (1) an adequately representative image, that may assist us (2) to assume the right practical relations to a reality — these two things are the essence of cognition: not being led towards, with the ultimate prospect of merging into, the reality.   But the difference between these conceptions is, that the latter gives an account of cognition in terms of *actual or possible experiences for me,*

[14] *Jour. of Philos.,* IV (1907), 404–5.

and therefore defines truth as merely a matter of "consequences," while the former gives one in terms of experiences *existing beyond me,* and therefore defines truth as a relation of thought to realities beyond it. If all realities could be switched around so as to be brought into the track of my future experiences, the doctrine of "consequences" would cover all cases: but they cannot. . . .

"Their whole notion of a standing reality grows up in the form of an ideal limit to the series of successive termini to which our thoughts have led us and are still leading us." Not at all! The limit is a perfect *idea* of the object. . . . The notion of the object as merely a limit involves a confusion of the logical with the metaphysical; such realism is not true realism at all, and James would do well to moderate his "stentorian voice" . . . until he has something more truly realistic to say. . . .

"*Telepathic* confluence": that word introduces a new complication. It indicates that you hold a kind of empiricism according to which experience is, as I say, "afloat," and not properly in space and time at all: so that, if my experience exactly reproduces another, *they are the same experience.* . . . To which my reply is, that experiences are really in space and time . . . and that experiences which are the same in quality but in a different place and time are *not* the same experience, but only alike. In other words, telepathy could only give me the perfect idea of an object. Ever yours sincerely,

C. A. STRONG

South Lincoln, Aug. 21, 1907

Dear Strong, —

Yours of the 6th from St. Moritz is just in and makes me despair of ever making myself intelligible, in spite of every effort to be clear in my writing. It seems as if the whole world had conspired to insist that I *shall* not be a realist, in spite of anything I may say I am to the contrary. Dewey and Schiller are in the same boat; but my own troubles are enough for me, so I leave them to take care of themselves. My own brother-in-law, Salter, having just read my *Pragmatism,* writes to remind me that facts are facts, and we have to take account of them whether we want them or find them satisfactory or helpful, or not — and we *must* take account of them. It ought all to help me to a less foggy statement of the position, so I will try again with *you,* without farther loss of time, though I think that my last letter . . . may partly have dispelled the darkness. You and I are so very much closer together in the tracks we make over the field of thought than anyone else, that we ought, ere we get through with each other, to coalesce in the same formulas. I think the word "pragmatism" has been very unlucky. Everyone takes it as *exclusive* of purely intellectual interests, or purely mental adaptions to reality, making us signify that all our agreements with reality must be of an externally and immediately utilitarian sort. You don't do this, so I bless you. Miller can apparently digest my book so little that he writes me that he can say nothing articulate about it at present. In general, Boutroux, Gardiner, and Bergson are the only persons who accept heartily the general attitude of the book. Everyone else is noncommittal or critical, and no one seems to notice what in my . . . mind I had been a little conceited about, namely the well-kept-up "popular" style throughout. Perhaps, after all, that is a demerit in philosophy! Let me now re-state my view, for your consumption.

First of all, I absolutely agree with you (and thought I had said so) that knowledge of a reality is a state of mind that puts us into relation with a reality — any relation, almost, provided it be with *that* reality. "Confluence" was only a hypothetical case, assumed to be represented by my critics, and "escape" from tigers is as real a relation as approach to them, on my system. When I spoke of "leading towards," I was evidently too fond of a brief formula, supposing that the reader's imagination would interpret the words properly as meaning "leading into the general environment of." I suppose that you yourself agree that without some common mediating environment, there can be no basis for the reference to *this* reality, rather than to any other which resembles it, on the part of the idea. The toothache you speak of, or the "souls of black folk" which we may copy so intimately, must be proved the toothache of *that* sufferer, or the feelings of *those* darkies, by some *traceable process,* connecting my mind, through my body, with their bodies, and thence with their feelings. Otherwise the "reference" has no foundation in experience.

So much agreed, I say (and have always meant to say or imply) that a case of knowledge implies several factors, with relations between them. These are:

(1) Our thoughts and our acts, with the relations between them;

(2) Our acts and our "objects," with the relation between *them* (environmental). These are direct relations. Another direct relation that obtains only in cases of maximum knowledge of the object is

(3) that our thoughts shall *resemble* it, the more completely the better, so to be "true" *portraits* of it.

(4) The fourth relation is the indirect one, between the thought and *that* object, established by means of (1) and (2).

Relations (3) and (4) are the only ones that common "epistemology" recognizes. Most of our critics accuse us of *denying* (3) and (4), consequently of denying genuine knowledge to exist. What I contend for is that you can't know *that* object (in distinction from any other object like it) unless you reinstate (1) and (2). Our opponents regard (1) and (2) as inessential complications. In reality they are essential to found the very minimum of knowledge upon. Almost no resemblance will suffice, so long as our thought carries us adaptively into the environment of which the reality forms part; while, on the other hand, the extreme of similarity will not carry reference to any particular reality with it, or make of our thought a "portrait," unless there be some real path to the individual thing portrayed. Thus the bare function of knowledge ("reference," or "taking account" of *überhaupt*) demands (1) and (2), and gives (4) when taken abstractly and saltatorily; while the *perfection* of knowledge, or of "truth," requires (3) as well.

Please observe that this whole statement starts by assuming a reality independent of our thought and numerically additional thereto. In other words, it is a realistic account of knowing. The object is assumed all along by me, the describing epistemologist, to be "outside" of the thought. You seem to have been very much perplexed by my doubtlessly poor tactics in taking a very simple type of cognition, imagination of a sensible "thing," namely, as my paradigm to expound by, and leaving the reader to supply the additions and restrictions necessary for other types and cases. In this case we *do* verify by being led up to, and apparently . . . becoming "confluent" with the reality. If on deeper reflection it proves impossible that we should ever be confluent, let confluence go! My general epistemological scheme remains, on any metaphysical assumption. We can at any rate *approach* reality in various degrees;

and the nearer we approach, the "truer" we become. You either say or imply that I can only mean *spatial* approach, and am debarred . . . from meaning approach in *likeness*. I have none of my writings here, so I can't give references, but the point was always in my mind, and I have a strong impression of having carefully said (and in several places) that approach meant "generic" approach, and nextness meant "logical" nextness, as well as neighborhood in space. These are essential to the acquaintance with, or "portrayal" by, thought of the *that* to which it "refers." Yet portrayal is so intermittently required for thought's uses, that likeness can be dispensed with more than half the time.

So far, I seem to be identically on your ground. But you quote my phrase that reality grows up in the form of an ideal "limit" to successive termini to which our thought leads, and attack me on the word "limit," as being incompatible with the object's independent existence. The limit must fall within the thought-series, you say. I never meant to use the word technically, but in point of fact no mathematical series includes its own limit, so I'm technically all right. In actual practice we never reach the limit in our pursuit of "fact" — so in that line of pursuit, for me as well as for you, reality lies always beyond the subjective series.

Keeping close together so far, there comes a point where we might begin to diverge. I have assumed realities outside of thought, and assumed that, in crucial instances of verification, thought might be led close to them, even "next" to them (or even *into* them, if one require it). Also that thoughts may be exactly *like* them. But who can verify these verifications, prove the thought to *be* like, and to really touch (by the acts they inspire) the very realities they are "of"? The thoughts trust their own verifications; I, the describer, now assume both the realities and the thoughts and the truth of the latter, and thus corroborate the said verifications, but who warrants that there *is* such a world apart from my description? In other words, how do we anywhere escape solipsism in the end? . . You claim that there *shall* be a reality beyond the thought. The thought itself *assumes* one. No one *proves* it, — it simply proves itself by the process of continuing without refuting itself.

But these ulterior considerations lie wholly outside of the pragmatistic truth-debate. That starts and ends with realistic postulates;

and the soundness of my contention stands or falls with the analysis of knowing into its four elementary relations, as above laid down. I say that (1) and (2) are needed to establish "reference," — that is my main point. I also talk much of "leading." If you once construe that word to mean any sort of "taking account" of a reality, that *could* prove itself (if challenged) by touching some object of sense somewhere, *I don't see how you can possibly object to anything that I say.* Of course the knowledge of universal truths remains over, but there, too, the formulation need be little changed. The paradigms to which all cases reduce are direct percepts of relation, ethical, mathematical, or what not; and these are not "true" so much as "real." They correspond to sense percepts in the realm of outer fact.

I have written very rapidly, and I beg you to keep this, for I may wish to see it again. I can't help hoping that some of your reluctancy may be overcome. It seems hard to be accused of thinking what one never thought, even though one may have seemed in one's clumsiness to say it. Good-bye, affectionately yours,

W. J.

Paris, Sept. 4, 1907

Dear James, —

. . . Santayana and I (he has just left for London this morning) have been greatly interested by your article on Pratt.[15] We did not know you would acknowledge so roundly that truth is a relation between an idea and a reality beyond it, often quite separate from human experience, and it almost seems to us a complete change of face. We thought the pragmatist doctrine was that truth is a relation between the idea and *subsequent human experiences,* — that it "consists in the consequences" in this sense. Dewey certainly seems to teach that ideas are merely instrumental in resolving tangles in experienced situations, and that it is a fallacy to give them any other validity than that which they have as fulfilling this function. And as to the thoroughness of Schiller's idealism I have no further doubt after the discussions I have just had with him in the Engadine. He said he was n't able to understand your article "A Word More about Truth"; which I think very likely. So I venture to predict that your developing realism will at once alarm your pragmatist col-

[15] "Professor Pratt on Truth," *Jour. of Philos.,* IV (1907).

leagues and astonish those who have hitherto been your critics, who will think you are at last coming to your senses.

While your declarations in the article on Pratt are completely satisfactory on the score of realism, I think you must make one further admission, namely, that, *in so far* as "correspondence" exists between the idea and the reality . . . knowing involves an anticipatory vision of the thing known, and truth therefore consists in the correctness of this vision though not in this solely; instead of knowing's being, as you seem to say, wholly a matter of ambulatory relations.   You seem at moments to argue almost as if there were no such thing as saltatory relations (*e.g.,* similarity) — as if they were an intellectualist absurdity.   Of course neither these nor the ambulatory relations alone are the relation of knowing, which is rather a name for the whole complex situation. . . .   Yours ever,

C. A. STRONG

St. Hubert's, N. Y., Sept. 17, 1907

Dear Strong, —

Yours from Hotel Metropolitan, Sept. 4th, is at hand.   I 'm beginning to get angry!   That you, after my laborious explanations, in and out of print, should still insist that I *shall* not be a realist, *dépasse la mésure.*   You speak as if I were only now "acknowledging" and "coming to my senses," whereas in that article "The Function of Cognition," which is the *fons et origo* of all *my* pragmatism (in its second sense as "theory of truth"),[16] you will see that I had to create a reality by miracle in order to provide my idea with something to "know."   If that is n't independent reality, what is?   The "subsequent human experiences" that you and Santayana think are meant by me to *supersede* antecedent reality, are precisely the experiences that lead towards it or to it and connect our ideas with it, so that reference *to it* and truth *of it* may be predicable *of* them. How anyone can establish the cognitive relation without such intermediaries I cannot, nor could ever, see.   The one further "admission" that you now ask of me, is what I have always emphasized, in that article and ever since, in articles, books, letters, and talk. Our idea must not only lead into the physical and mental neighborhood of the reality, but (in ideally complete knowledge) *resemble* it.   Where did I ever give color to your reproach that I have argued

[16] *Cf.* above, 450-1.

almost as if the saltatory relation of similarity were a non-existent intellectualist absurdity? I should like to see chapter and verse. I have indeed argued that copying is not *per se* identical with knowing, and that much in knowing is not copying, but these are not what you accuse me of.

I should n't write this at all, dear Strong, feeling rather hopeless of ever getting understood, save that I fear that if I don't make a strong protest just now you may some day feel it right to get into print with your interpretation of me, and make confusion worse confounded. You are the man who has least right to misrepresent me, for to no one have I ever talked so fully; and with epistemological realism at the very permanent *heart and centre* of *all* my thinking, it gives me a queer "turn" to hear you keep insisting that I shall and must be treated as an idealist.

You say that Dewey and Schiller are at any rate idealists; but after the way you interpret *me,* how can I accept your interpretation of your conversation with Schiller as decisive? Schiller I conceive to stand identically where I do, and I should be surprised to learn that he did n't. Dewey's system of thought overlaps mine on all sides, and he is, I confess, hard to interpret. On the reflective level in which knower and known are talked *about,* I conceive him to be a perfect realist, though on the plane of the immediate *talking* one may accuse him of *Identitätsphilosophie.*

Well! Enough! I hope you won't take the acerbity of this brief scrawl as arguing that I 'm "mad" with you. But my persistent failure to get myself understood of late is breeding in me a sort of despair as to whether there 's any use in discussion, or whether any philosopher will ever get himself understood by anybody. . . . Affectionately yours,

WM. JAMES

Chocorua, Oct. 2, 1907

Dear Strong, —

. . . I rejoice at your taking my last letter in such good part. Please remember that what you were writing to me about was *Pragmatism,* and I defied you to find in the definition of truth therein contained anything incompatible with realism. That in my essays on "Radical Empiricism" (which in the preface to *Pragmatism* I expressly said was not to be confounded) you can find sentences that squint towards idealism, I have no doubt, — so be at no pains to look them up for my conviction! But the problem there was metaphysical, not epistemological; it was an analysis of the *nature* of what is experienced, not of the meaning of knowing, and whatever epistemology I may have brought in was by the way, and illustrative, not fundamental. In those articles I was groping and fumbling anyhow, and doubtless guilty of much confusion. But when *expressly* writing about "knowledge" and "truth" as in *Pragmatism,* I have always *intended* (though I have probably made verbal slips) to be realistic, and to be called an idealist (as by Montague,[17] and others) makes me feel queer. I send you a "snopsis" of your typewritten manuscript, which pray return at your leisure. Have I made any big mistakes? Good luck. Yours,

W. J.

Pocantico Hills, Oct. 5, 1907

Dear James, —

. . . You will find many passages in your recent articles where you assume that physical things are identical with the experience of them, that they "consist of sensation." . . . For instance, where you speak of the two stages.[18] The notion of "conterminousness" again is founded, is it not, on the conception that an object is identical with the experience of it?

Well, in your latest articles on truth, "A Word More etc.," and "Professor Pratt on Truth," you seemed to me to be rapidly veering in the right direction, and particularly in your letters to me to be making your object more and more genuinely realistic (by saying that the ambulation was not into its *neighborhood* but into its *universe,* the confluence not an existential but a *logical* one), and so — this is the great, great point — *making your empiricism not an empiricism of* APPEARANCES *but of* SENTIENT EXISTENCES *or* MIND-STUFF.

For here is the great difference between empirical philosophies, as I believe will be found in the end: that one class means by "experience" *the presentation of an object,* and the other class means

---

[17] W. P. Montague: "The Relational Theory of Consciousness and Its Realistic Implications," *Jour. of Philos.,* II (1905); cf. 316 *passim.*
[18] The common-sense stage in which the real object is identified with the perception, and the stage of philosophical criticism in which the real object is identical with *ulterior* perceptions or with the *limit* of perceptual completeness; cf. *M.T.,* 127–33.

a feeling. Dewey and Bergson are objectivists: their universe consists of nothing but appearances (although they endow them with a reality or existence which appearances properly have not) ; you, in your "World of Pure Experience," are rather on their side than on mine. . . . Ever yours sincerely,

C. A. STRONG

New York, Jan. 5, 1908

Dear James, —

I read your manuscript twice through on the train, and posted it to Creighton soon after arriving.[19] It is true that we now agree as to the facts, but I fear some serious disagreement still remains as to the proper naming of them, and particularly as to the locus of the thing named "truth." I am forced to say that truth is a matter, and exclusively a matter, of resemblance or copying, and that what is additional to this is mere utility, and misnamed either truth or truthfulness. You seem to take truth in a large sense in which it ceases to mean something true about the object, and means mere adaptation to it; any view is true that helps us to act rightly, whether it conveys anything about the object or not. . . .

It is important, as I have said before, to distinguish between pragmatism as a theory of objective reference and pragmatism as a theory of truth. I agree with you that the reference of the idea to the object cannot be established without taking account of the totality of concrete connections, including the workings; but I should say that truth lay neither in the causal relations by which the idea is called forth nor in those by which it works, but solely in that relation of correspondence which makes it possible for the idea to work, — or rather (this is an important addition) in the relation of correspondence plus the spatial or quasi-spatial relations that hold idea and object in relation to each other.

Truth, as you admitted (when asked whether, if the world should cease at this moment, my idea of Cæsar's assassination would not still be true, though it would have no consequences), — *truth consists rather in the potentiality of the right kind of consequences than in their actual occurrence. Now this potentiality is exactly equivalent to the relations of space and of correspondence which predeter-*

[19] Apparently "The Pragmatist Account of Truth and Its Misunderstanders," published in Jan. 1908, in the *Philos. Rev.,* of which Professor J. E. Creighton was the editor.

mine what the consequences shall be. Truth, then, is anterior to the consequences. . . . Yours ever,

C. A. STRONG

Cambridge, Jan. 6, 1908

Dear Strong, —

Yours received — pardon haste in reply! Truth is a quality of knowledge. If resemblance were the essential thing, all specimens of a genus would be "true" of each other. If space relations were the essential thing, *all* things in space would be "true" of each other. *Ditto* of all other relations. Evidently something else is essential, *viz.,* cognitive reference and adaptation. You can't get either constituted without the workings. *That* the object is, *what* it is, and *which* it is of all the objects with that *what,* are things determinable only by the pragmatic method. The *which* means our pointing to a locus; the *what* means some selection on our part of an essential "aspect" to apperceive the object by (and this is wholly relative to our "situation," as Dewey calls it); the *that* means the attitude aroused in us of recognizing reality, our *acknowledgment.* Surely all these things are *indispensable* to the truth of anyone's cognition. Surely anything less is insufficient to constitute the notion! In haste,

W. J.

LXXXIII

BLOOD AND BOUTROUX

AT the same time that James was striving so eagerly to explain pragmatism, writing voluminously both letters and articles in behalf of its saving gospel, he was looking beyond pragmatism to the metaphysics which he believed to be its complement. With some of his friends such as Blood and Boutroux, though they might discuss pragmatism, metaphysics was the chief bond. His relations with these friends may serve, therefore, to lead us over from *Pragmatism* to *A Pluralistic Universe*.

In the ten years that elapsed between *The Will to Believe* and *Pragmatism*, James had not lost sight of Blood, though their correspondence seems to have languished. It will be remembered that in 1897 James had looked upon Blood as a literary mentor. Later it was James who was advising Blood and helping him to some kind of adequate utterance of his thought. In 1905 Blood wrote frequently, enclosing poems, "sermons," and drafts of more ambitious literary ventures. In 1907 he returned to his old theme of the "anæsthetic revelation," which he could find a way of introducing into any context. It was this which had brought him recognition and letters from famous men, such as Stevenson, Stirling, Story, Emerson, Bryant, Holmes, and Wendell Phillips. It was this which had first commended him to James, and this was his message to the world. But he realized that such esoteric truths must be reserved for the few, and that for the wider appeal in which James was interested he must confine himself to plainer and more sober doctrines.

Amsterdam, March 6, 1907

My dear Sir, —

I am hot after the opportunity to make a wider audience for your memorable words at Edinburgh in 1902: "Those who have ears to hear, let them hear: to me the living sense of its reality comes only in the artificial mystic state of mind."[1] Ere long this will be regarded as the most significant and memorable utterance of the nineteenth century.   Behind it was Sir Humphrey Davy, Sir William Ramsay, my own forty years' experience, Tennyson's normal insight, various experimenters collated and discussed by the society at 20 Hanover Square, London, and the psychological and metaphysical unrest of all the world.[2] I therefore got into type the printed matter herewith, omitting what I most desired to say, lest it should handicap any endeavor you could persuade yourself to make to have it well published — that is, the connexion of pluralism, etc., with the anæsthetic revelation. . . .   Now I beg you will kindly go through this article rough shod, regardless of all but the most advisable conclusions — an unnecessary admonition I confess.   Perhaps I could give it some literary charm, — I have not thought of that.   Most respectfully yours,

BENJ. PAUL BLOOD

P.S. Another thing I would impress: the conceit and big-headedness that gives the universe a primary reference to man, saying that it *must* be rational, and to him; he cannot be content to be a visitor and spectator . . . but he must be of the blood royal. The genius of the anæsthetic revelation does not make him such a referee.   He is but a witness in the case: his reason and all about him is but incidental and inconsequent.   One born under a monarchy, a pauper amidst the wealth and splendor of the Church, should take more readily to the truth.

To assist Blood's researches James sent him the volume of the *Proceedings of the Society for Psychical Research* which contained Sir William Ramsay's study of "Partial Anæsthesia," and Blood returned it some months later with the explanation: "If you wonder why I have not long since returned your book, let me tell you

---

[1] *V.R.E.*, 388–9.

[2] In 1800 Sir Humphrey Davy experimented with "laughing gas" (nitrous oxide) and described the effects in *Researches, Chemical and Philosophical*, etc. In 1882 Prof. William Ramsay undertook similar experiments; *Proc. of Soc. for Psychical Research*, IX (1893–4). "20 Hanover Sq." refers to this Society. Tennyson wrote to Blood on May 7, 1874. His own "revelation" came without anæsthetics; cf. *Memoir*, by his son, II, 158, 473; and "Tennyson's Trances and the Anæsthetic Revelation," by J. I. Lexow, perhaps written and privately printed by Blood under this pseudonym.

of the fellow who stayed late, and expected his wife to lecture him, and then stayed later so that she would get anxious and be glad to see him, and so forget the lecture. . . . Eternal spring to you!"

The "printed matter" referred to above was published in the *Amsterdam Recorder* for March 5, 1907, under the title "After This, What? — An Advancing Revolt from Monism to Pluralism." The author paid his respects to James in the concluding paragraph, in which he says that pluralism is "the aroma, or the caviare, of occasional utterances of certain living men of genius, — James, of Harvard; Howison, of California; Jastrow, of Wisconsin and other subtle spirits, whose searching lights reveal the foreground of a new régime, a cosmical readjustment." The clipping contained several of the purple passages which so delighted James and which he culled for his later article on "A Pluralistic Mystic." [3] Blood was gifted, after the manner of James, in *depicting* a pluralistic universe, but James's power of sustained and coherent thought he wholly lacked. "For single far-flung and far-flashing words and sentences," writes James in acknowledgment, "you're the biggest genius I know; but when it comes to constructing a whole argument or article it seems to be another kettle of fish." [4]

The discussion of pragmatism begins with Blood's reading of James's "Defense of Pragmatism," [5] published in this same month.

Amsterdam, March 13, 1907 [6]

My dear Sir, —

. . . I received gratefully your article in *Popular Science,* which I read last night and again this morning, with wonder that you should say so much and so well before you assume to have said anything to the purpose proposed. That is where the professor comes in, I suppose, and the long training in the art of refinement, which still renews the vocation of the German doctors. But what you are going to do, or have done, is to me a live and lively question. You speak of philosophies in the plural, as of so many novels; there are good and bad novels, but each is able to hold itself together — is legitimate as a story; so good and bad philosophies, but all *philosophy* — all having a consistency that must be respected, and for-

[3] *M.S.,* 401.
[4] W.J. to Blood, March 8, 1907.
[5] March 1907. Reprinted as "The Present Dilemma in Philosophy," in *Pragm.*
[6] Quoted in part in *M.S.,* 392–3.

given for its "temperament" — as if philosophy in general were honest dough, and each man flings out a batch of it fashioned his way. I don't see what kind of "empt'ins" they are using to assure this common consistency, — it must be the school logic; and you are proposing something eclectic, of the *modus vivendi,* pot-boiling order, that shall get away with all good fellows. What else, if your prescription is "philosophical" instead of "mystical"? Do you not foresee that I am coming from Edinburgh [7] with the claim that not only has philosophy failed and passed, but something has come to replace it — something that *I know,* if I cannot articulate it, which must make philosophies seem the toys they are? The systems you treat so respectfully (by implication) don't go, have no propulsion. Reason is an equation: nature is excess, — she is ever-more. Go back into reason with a sufficient intelligence, and you come at last to fact, nothing more: a given, a something to wonder at and yet admit, like your own will. And all these tricks for logicising originality, — self-relation, absolute process, subjective contradiction, making something out of nothing by "driving the business," will wither in the breath of the mystical fact — they will swirl down the corridors before the besom of the everlasting Yea! You hear me? And so, "to use a vulgar phrase," God bless you! and yours!

B. P. BLOOD

To which James replied: "Bravo Blood! You are splendid! You must put this last letter of yours into the article or book or whatever you make of it."

In the following summer Blood sent James his impressions of pragmatism as a whole. It is evident that he is willing, with James, to reduce rational truth to practicality only provided that a higher irrational truth is put in its place. He is forever appealing beyond James the pragmatist to James the mystic: —

Amsterdam, Aug. 28, 1907

My dear Sir, —

I received from Longmans a copy of *Pragmatism.* . . . I have read it over and over, and laid it down and taken it up again and again, to see just what and where was the matter with it. It will be

---

[7] Referring to James's acknowledgment at Edinburgh of the claims of mysticism, repeatedly cited by Blood.

assailed, and not understood as it might be, on account of an over-sight in the weak *emphasis* allowed throughout the book to the asser-tion . . . that "there can *be* no difference anywhere that does not *make* a difference elsewhere — no difference in abstract truth that does not express itself in a difference in concrete fact, *and in conduct consequent upon that fact,*" [8] etc. . . . If the abstract surely ap-pears in the concrete, and the concrete is the more feasible and con-venient, the case of the practical is won, and the pragmatic method is approved and must be endorsed. To generalize and popularize the method is good industry. But as you advance into your store-house of truths . . . and then and there proclaim the pragmatic method as a relief from the worry and frustration of the unsuccess-ful student (neglecting the emphasis I first quoted), he resents your ideals as worldly and undignified: he wants to "know" though the heavens fall. . . . The student of your *Pragmatism* will think that you propose to treat . . . topics as idle unless he can show some ethical good which their discussion promises. I happen to know that you don't mean any such thing. You perceive that philosophy is vain, because mysticism and not reason is the final word. He does not see this; he makes you hold the available in practice as *the true, per se,* — and so soil the robes of Truth, and insult in-telligence.

Of course, no less on account of the Revelation, thinking will have to go on: that does not explain the mystery, but only settles and em-phasizes the fact that the final word *is* mystery. . . . The book is highly entertaining, — rich with *ingenuities.* Ever truly yours,

BENJ. PAUL BLOOD

Amsterdam, Sept. 29, 1907

My dear Sir, —

. . . And still I am taking up and laying down your *Pragmatism,* — the most provoking thing, in a way, that I have encountered. Usually I do not get mystified. I can give you, mentally, the cube root of six figures in as many seconds, if the root is a whole number; and I can make a pretty good show of multiplying by three big fig-ures, and even by four small ones, at once. This book of yours is the fastest, the brainiest head-on collision with experience that I have been into; yet I have to stir the dish with my own spoon before

[8] *Pragm.,* 49–50.

I can swallow it. It is this way: when you say to your audience "pragmatism is the truth concerning truth," the first "truth" is different from the second. About the first you and they are not at odds; in the first your vocation and honor are at stake, and you speak from ground common to both you and them. As to this truth, you are not giving them liberty to take or leave it, encourage or suppress it, according to its practicality for them, — its satisfactory or working quality for their private uses. . . . You concur on the higher ground, *or you would not be talking their language.* On that higher ground there *is* an absolute, or absolutistic definition of truth, which would be something like this; truth is the proper relation between subject and object; or, *the* truth is the conformity, or harmony, of the sufficient intelligence with objective totality. From the rationalist viewpoint, and from every viewpoint which has not *expressly denied* reason and intelligence as the ultimate and primal ground of being, there must be such a truth; and short of this denial on your part, the opposition may claim that you dethrone a sacred conception. It is in trying to see that without this express declaration you have still said enough, .and still feeling so confident that you must have said enough, that I keep clubbing myself at not finding the declaration, or "something just as good."

I think you will agree that there is no objective totality, nor any unified sufficient intelligence. If there is anything I am sure of, it is that wonder and not smirking reason is the final word for all creatures and creators alike. And pragmatism is the only method of philosophizing (if we must go on thinking) after that insight is attained. We can only go for the practical, in the largest and longest sense, whether right or wrong, as they sang of the Union. Pardon this throwing my botheration up to you, and of all things do not tax your tired nerves to set me right. I shall swim out. . . . Heaven keep you well and strong, — and happy.

BENJ. PAUL BLOOD

Cambridge, Oct. 11, 1907

Dear Blood, —

I got your letter of the 29th when in the country, and deferred my answer till I should have your former letter about *Pragmatism* under my eye, thinking that they ran into one. It pleases me greatly that the book should interest you so much. It sticks in the crop of almost everyone of any technical learning, and those who applaud it do so from a very shallow notion of what it means. I will only say one word, about the difficulty in your second letter, because it is one that almost everyone feels, and yet is easily replied to.[9] Your words are: — "When you say to your audience 'pragmatism is the truth concerning truth,' the first truth is different from the second." . . . The objector seems to think that if a man places truth in satisfactions he is debarred from believing his own satisfactions to be sufficient guarantees of the truth of what he says. It is quite the reverse. A man's "reasons" satisfy him, his satisfaction produces the reaction called belief, which varies in intensity according to the psychology of the individual. The belief is n't a part of the *logic,* if logic there be in the reasons; it is a result of the logic and of many other things, and carries with it the "truth" of what he believes, for the believer. This is the "first truth" you write of. Such truth when we feel it, we feel impelled to spread and propagate, to infect others and set an example. Let my satisfactions as a pragmatist become a model for yours, etc. What I say about truths in general (my "second truth") is thus in no wise inconsistent with what I do about my first truth. . . .

I do (in your words) expressly deny reason ("smirking reason" — thanks for that noble word!) as the ultimate and primal ground of being, and all my tilting against "rationalism" has that meaning. But I have evidently not made it explicit enough. Reason deals with consistencies only, truth with consistencies *plus* facts; belief is itself a part of fact and a part-maker of fact, life includes all these elements and rolls reason along in its flood, — enveloping it, not enveloped by it. The live pragmatist, who stands for a concrete cross-section of the whole flood, is the only person who is all right. . . . Yours as ever,

W. J.

Amsterdam, Jan. 20, 1908

My dear Sir, —

. . . Now then, as to pragmatism. . . . What I understand by [it] is plain American sense, as applied to mental industries and exploitations among topics which have been run into ruts of prejudice and superstition. I understand you to look askance at the old

[9] *M.T.,* 70 ff.

canon and criterion of "truth" which philosophers have exalted into contradiction and contempt. I think of pragmatism as poetry in overalls and blouse, — as the brother of Plato was found mending a bridle, while yet capable of repeating from memory the whole argument of *Parmenides*. It follows that you must have your own criteria of truth, *your own working definition*. I understand that you, like Bacon, prefer fruit and physic to froth and metaphysic. You want theories that will work, and you profess gall enough to insist that the work shall confirm the theories, rather than that the theories shall determine the work.

I see nothing in this to carp at, nor anything else at all in the discussion on your part, except a certain tantalizing reserve. You say to your critics: "This is my notion of truth; if you don't like it, give me a better one of your own!" — while you know very well that you could drive them to contradiction if they attempted it. Why not say to them as you said to your audience in Edinburgh, that the living sense of reality comes only in the artificial mystic state of mind? — But have it your own way. Everything goes. . . .

> Doubt that the stars are fire
> Doubt that the sun do move,
> Doubt "truth" to be a liar —
> But never doubt my love!

PAUL

Émile Boutroux [10] had published as early as 1874 a work *On the Contingency of the Laws of Nature*. This work had brought him almost instant recognition, and he was already ripe in years and in fame when his intimacy with James began. For though there had already been a letter or two exchanged, James did not "make his acquaintance" until the autumn of 1908.[11] He at once found him *"simpatico."* Boutroux, like James, was a champion of freedom against the claims of science; and like James he held that truth expresses the moral and æsthetic, as well as the more narrowly intellectual, part of man. As holding these congenial doctrines, and as being the simple and upright man that he was, he made a strong appeal to James. As though to make up for the wasted opportunity

[10] Professor at the Sorbonne, 1888–1902; from 1902 until his death in 1921, Director of the Fondation Thiers.

[11] *L.W.J.*, II, 314.

of past years, their friendship ripened quickly into love, and formed one of the most significant episodes of the last two years of James's life. There were reasons, however, why they could not be close philosophical allies. James was naturalistic and evolutionary in the premises of his thought, while Boutroux belonged in the tradition of French spiritualism with its roots in Schelling. Their philosophical relations reveal one of the routes of thought leading from James's pragmatic "corridor," but one which James himself did not follow.

In November 1905, James wrote to Boutroux to thank him for his long and highly sympathetic Preface to the French translation of the *Varieties of Religious Experience*.[12] In this Preface Boutroux's peculiar spiritualistic emphasis is evident. Thus he tells us that to a pragmatic empiricist like James personal activity is "the sole reality that we immediately apprehend." It is also the *fundamental* reality in which the conflicting claims of science, morality, and other interests are reconciled. Religion in concerning itself with the life of the soul thus takes precedence of other forms of knowledge as being the most concrete, the most unified, and the most deeply satisfying.[13] Now if James does hint at this, — imply it, consider it, *almost* say it, — he never *does say* it. He says that "private and personal phenomena," or moments of conscious life, are more complete of their kind than are physical objects as conceived by science. Religious experience makes up in concreteness something of what it lacks in clearness and cogency. Qua concrete it is to be credited with conveying a sense of what reality is like. All this James says in a few pages, with his accustomed willingness to speculate freely in the full view of his public.[14] But there is in Boutroux's interpretation an accent of monism, of rationalism, and of finality that is wholly foreign to the conjectural and experimental genius of James.

Boutroux received a complimentary copy of *Pragmatism,* and his comments show how consistently he emphasized what he took to be its underlying metaphysical activism, rather than its biological description of cognition and its naturalistic-utilitarian standard of truth: —

[12] *L'Expérience religieuse,* translation by F. Abauzit, 1906. The Preface is dated Oct. 18, 1905.
[13] *Op. cit.,* xiv–xv, translated by the author.
[14] *V.R.E.,* 498 ff.

Paris, June 27, 1907 [15]

Dear and honored colleague, —

Cordial thanks for sending me your volume on *Pragmatism*. I have just read it at a sitting with pleasure as well as profit. I believe with you that the great difference is between those who believe that things are, purely and simply, and those who think that they happen, and that we are among the artificers which contribute to their happening. In the first case, there is no serious occupation but science; all the rest is vanity and illusion. One does not even see very clearly what idea, in this case, we should form of scientific work — its motives, vicissitudes and progress. In the second case, our entire life, the scientific life included, has a meaning that is both clear and interesting. Every moment of practical activity pleads for this second way of looking at the matter, while the reasons urged against it in the name of science do not appear to be convincing. Let us proceed, therefore, as if we lived our life effectively, and as if it deserved, by its effectiveness, to be lived.

I find many a passage in your work of unusual clarity and force; and I think it will contribute, among us also, to spread ideas which undoubtedly have glorious antecedents, but which a persisting scholasticism still has the power to thwart. Accept, dear and honored colleague, my respectful and deep regard,

ÉM. BOUTROUX

In January 1908, Boutroux wrote an article on "William James et l'expérience religieuse," which formed a chapter of his book, published a few months later, entitled *Science et religion dans la philosophie contemporaine.*[16] He concluded this review of James with some pages of mildly critical comment, beginning with the statement that as a radical empiricist James regarded "objects outside of us" as "fictions of the imagination or artificial constructions of the understanding." [17] In other words, like so many of James's friendly critics, Boutroux found a stumblingblock in the apparent subjectivism of a philosophy which limited itself to "experience."

[15] This and the following letters from Boutroux to James are translated from the French originals, which are reprinted below, Appendix XI.
[16] The article appeared in *Revue de métaphysique et de morale*, XVI (1908). The book was carefully read by James, and annotated with special reference to its allusions to pragmatism.
[17] *Op. cit.*, 331–5.

Rye, July 20, 1908

Dear Professor Boutroux, —

I must begin by a *peccavi, peccavi!* The envelope which includes these lines was addressed to you at Cambridge, Massachusetts, about four months ago, if I remember rightly, after I had read your chapter on my *Varieties* in the *Revue de métaphysique et de morale;* and was to contain my immediate "reaction." But I postponed reacting from day to day, because I was trying desperately to finish some lectures which I had been asked to give at Oxford, and because an abominable attack of influenza came, which made it impossible for me to write more than a very short time each day. Your book arrived before I got to writing, so I said, "I will read the whole book first" — and now on this blessed 20th of July I have but just attained to reading it! The truth is that my head has been in a very bad condition, and I have been so fatigued with social obligations since coming to the British Isles that I have hardly been able to read anything at all. I know that to my *peccavi* you will reply *"absolvo te."* I have now come to a quiet harbor in my brother's house, and hope ere long to be able to rest away the effects of the long nervous strain.

I am naturally both elated and touched by the extremely serious way in which you treat my own work, in writing which I had so little of an ambitious aim that the success it has achieved (your chapter being the apogee thereof) has surprised me not a little. The only merit I should claim for my *Varieties* is that it is a *sincere* piece of composition, in which the facts cited do the work themselves. The delicacy with which you reproduce my thought, whilst improving and amplifying it in many points, seems to me admirable. I don't know whether your remarks from page 331 onwards are meant altogether to be a restrictive criticism, on your own part, of my doctrine. I am *not,* epistemologically, a subjectivist, in spite of what I call my radical empiricism; and I hold with you that faith in the existence of an object is inseparable from the consciousness of it, so far as that consciousness is effective in our life. It seems to be extremely difficult to formulate all these relations in a universally intelligible and satisfactory way; to do so, will be a fine task for the philosophers of the next generation to perform. I feel sure that whatever they will succeed in *tirer*-ing *au clair,* the whole of it will probably fall within the lines which you have drawn in this masterly book, which seems to have taken every possible point of view into consideration, and which reads like the summing up, on the part of an absolutely wise and impartial mind, of all the elements of the situation.   What will remain for others is the emphasizing of particular elements, and the introduction of the note of passion into the exposition, which will make it bite into common people, as your severe and passionless *Auseinandersetzung* bites only into philosophers.   In detail, as in the ensemble, it is a tremendously *true* book, and an extraordinary pleasure to me to read anything [with] which I find myself so *voluminously* in agreement.   I should think that Professor Bergson would feel very similarly about it.   I am still too tired and lazy to go into any of the details with you; I simply give you the dominant impression with which the whole fills my mind.   I think the book will have a lasting influence on all really serious thinkers.

I have been corresponding with Professor Bergson with regard to a possible meeting soon.   If I go to France, I should extremely like to see your face also, to thank you for your literary kindness to my poor person. . . .   Believe me, dear Professor Boutroux, yours faithfully and gratefully,

WM. JAMES

The next letter was written after a meeting in October — in London, not Paris.

Paris, Dec. 18, 1908

Dear Professor James, —

I am very grateful for your kind thought of me, and I have read with eager interest the very clear and precise article in which you successively distinguish pragmatism from subjectivism.[18]   It is not there that the difficulty lies for me.   It lies in the word "satisfactorily."   If this word means, "in a manner corresponding to the expectation of the subject," how does your definition of truth differ from the idea which scientists, common sense and the intellectualists themselves form of it in so far as they take the practical point of view?   I sometimes fear, when I read certain definitions, that everybody is a pragmatist.   The side of the doctrine that seems to me to be the most important and distinctive

[18] The review of Hébert (*M.T.*, 230) had just appeared.

is the actual indetermination of the future, and in consequence the conception of the laws of nature as simple contingent facts. As for myself I adhere whole-heartedly to this doctrine, which you support with so much force and clarity. The intelligence is not sacrificed by it, but is emancipated from ἀνάγκη,[19] and united with life, with love, and with individuality.

My wife and I always remember with happiness the moments spent with you in London. Like you I find that the abstract is as nothing compared with the concrete. I see you, I hear the sound of your words, I taste the flavor of your courtesy: what description of your person could replace this sensation. I am always hoping that we shall sometime have the pleasure of having you here as our own. Meanwhile I beg you to think of us from time to time, as we love to revive our memory of you. To you and to Mrs. James we send our best wishes for the year which is just beginning. To you yourself the assurance of my deep sympathy. Yours ever,

ÉM. BOUTROUX

Paris, May 2, 1909

Dear Professor James, —

Thank you heartily for sending me your new book.[20] I read it like all your writings with particular pleasure because I seem to hear you, and to be in communication with you personally, as well as with your philosophy. The latter, furthermore, is profoundly acceptable to me. It seems to me that I present the philosophical problem precisely as you present it: "Either absolute independence or absolute mutual dependence — this, then, is the only alternative allowed by these thinkers. . . . Possibly you will yourselves think, after hearing my remaining lectures, that the alternative of a universe absolutely rational or absolutely irrational is forced and strained, and that a *via media* exists." And I would solve the problem as you yourself do: "In the each-form . . . a thing may be connected by intermediary things with a thing with which it has no immediate or essential connexion." [21] It is precisely that which I call contingent relation or connexion, intending

[19] Necessity.
[20] *A Pluralistic Universe.*
[21] W.J. was refuting the monists and absolutists, such as Lotze, Bradley, Royce, and McTaggart. *P.U.*, 76, 81, 324.

by this term to exclude pure chance as well as mechanical or logical necessity.   I believe that the search for the best connexions between things really distinct and logically irreducible, is properly what common, living speech means by reason; and that is why I think that an activity can be said to be reasonable when it is not chained, fixed and brought to a stop by the iron law of an intellectualistic monism.

I do not know whether you have heard that I have received and accepted the invitation to come and give the Hyde Lectures at Harvard next spring.   I propose to deal with this very subject, which lies especially near to my heart: How can things have relations with one another without losing their reality, their individuality, their spontaneity, their liberty?   The real and living connexion, — that is what I am trying to find.   I would be happy if my plan had some chance of interesting you.   I need not tell that what attracts me most in the prospect of going to Boston is the pleasure of finding you there, and of meeting Mrs. James.

Meanwhile we send you our remembrances and best wishes.   Very cordially yours,

ÉM. BOUTROUX

In the autumn of 1909 Boutroux read James's *Meaning of Truth* "with profound interest."   "I attach myself above all," he said, "to this idea: that properly speaking there is no being, but only 'doing' (*faire*), and that consequently experience is above science and life above formulas." [22]   In January 1910, as president of the French Academy of Moral and Political Sciences, Boutroux had the pleasure of announcing the election of James as a foreign associate for America, and in March he gave at Harvard a series of lectures which James heartily applauded.   Writing in April to Flournoy of the incident connected with the American visit of Eusapia Palladino, the Italian medium, he said: —

"Much more pleasant is the subject of Boutroux's visit, — the gentlest and most modest of philosophers, without an enemy in the world.   They stayed with us for two and a half weeks and we were able to protect him from too much fatigue.   *She* needed no protec-

---

[22] In a letter written two months later Boutroux again expresses the belief that the thesis of *The Meaning of Truth* is "unattackable"; affirms his adherence to the doctrine that "the world is still in process of making"; and says that he has been oriented in this direction from the beginning of his philosophical thinking.

tion, excellent wife that she is. His lectures, of which he gave twelve, were exquisite for clearness, breadth and sincerity, and I think that the book which will follow, *Contingence et liberté,* will inevitably have success, the times being now fully ready for that way of thinking, as they were not when he published his first book. I found him very easy to talk with, our ideas being so fundamentally alike." [23]

In an article entitled "A Great French Philosopher at Harvard," which he wrote for the *Nation,* James gave Boutroux credit for being "the leader *de jure* of the reaction against the abstract, and in favor of the concrete point of view in philosophy," explaining that Boutroux was the historic precursor of the movement which was represented in its more "strident" and "revolutionary" phases by Bergson and himself. "The most important features of 'pragmatism' and 'Bergsonism,' " he said, "find clear expression" in *La Contingence des lois de la nature,* published by Boutroux over forty years before. In expounding Boutroux's philosophy it is evident that he is at the same time expounding his own: —

"Whereas the classic and scholastic tradition is that reality is above all the abstracted, simplified, and reduced, the inalterable and self-identical, the fatal and eternal, Boutroux took the diametrically opposite view. It is the element we wholly live in, it is what Plutarch's and Shakespeare's pages give us, it is the superabounding, growing, ever-varying and novelty-producing. Its real shape is biography and history. . . . Not chance . . . but 'contingency,' is the idea which Professor Boutroux prefers to work with; and by contingency he means the element of spontaneity which characterizes concrete human life — where the consciousness of the present is ever of *many* future possibilities, and contains always enough causality for either of them, when realized, to be regarded as its natural effect. . . .

"The great originality of M. Boutroux throughout all these years has been his firm grasp of the principle of interpreting the whole of nature in the light of that part of it with which we are most fully acquainted, namely, our own personal experience. . . . Those readers who know something of present-day philosophy will recognize in my account the same call to return to the fulness of concrete experience, with which the names of Peirce, Dewey, Schiller,

[23] Another selection from this letter is printed above, 170.

Höffding, Bergson, and of many minor lights are associated.   It is the real empiricism, the real evolutionism, the real pluralism; and Boutroux (after Renouvier) was its earliest, as he is now its latest, prophet." [24]

On April 23, 1910, soon after his return to Paris, Boutroux delivered an address before the Academy of Moral and Political Sciences, and took as his theme "observations on his voyage to America."   The address was delivered in the presence of ex-President Theodore Roosevelt as well as other notables.   It was, he said, with the university world that he had come into contact in America: —

"The more so since I had the good fortune to stay with Professor William James, whom we have recently elected an associate member of this group.   How charming was the house of the illustrious philosopher!   Standing by itself amidst lawns and trees, built of wood in the colonial style like most of the houses of the university part of Cambridge; large, filled with books from top to bottom, a dwelling-place marvelously suited to study and meditation.   Reflection, furthermore, is here in no danger of degenerating into egotism.   For there reigns a most amiable sociability.   The 'library,' which serves as Professor James's place of work, contains not only a desk, tables and books, but couches, window-seats, morris-chairs, welcoming visitors at all hours of the day, so that it is in the midst of merry conversations, among ladies taking tea, that the profound philosopher meditates and writes."

Boutroux then went on to hail James, with his "marvelous sense for the concrete and for life," and with his "metaphysics of action, pluralism and universal creation," as a symbol of American life. And in this the speaker associated the absent James with the present and newly elected member, Roosevelt.[25]

James followed Boutroux to Europe only a few weeks later. During the tragic months of his last illness the Boutroux were much in his thoughts.   He visited them at the Fondation Thiers, was introduced at the Academy, and exchanged a number of brief notes for the making and unmaking of appointments.   On the eve of his return to America, and six weeks before his death, James wrote from London: —

[24] *Nation,* XC (1910), 312–4.   Only one of these lectures seems to have been published, "Hasard ou liberté," *Revue de métaphysique et de morale,* XVIII (1910).
[25] *Compte rendu,* de l'Académie des Sciences morales et politiques, 1910, premier semestre, Paris, 1910.

"Ever since leaving Nauheim I had been getting worse and worse. . . . Under the circumstances a visit under your hospitable roof was out of the question, to our great regret. . . . Spasmodic attacks, in the early morning hours . . . leave me ill all day. I say this not by way of complaint, but of excuse, rather! Don't waste 'sympathy' on me, for I deserve on the whole more misery than I am having! To have known you is one of the pleasantest episodes of my life, and the memory of it will always be a satisfaction; especially does seeing you and Madame Boutroux and those intelligent young laureates at the Fondation, leave a characteristic picture. I regret now to have left to you the trouble of having the Pascal mask packed safely to come to me by postal package. If not impossible, will you have it sent to 'Lamb House, Rye (Sussex),' my brother's place, where we shall stay until our date of sailing, August 12th? . . . I must now stop. Pray give my best regards to Madame Boutroux . . . and receive my fraternal and affectionate adieux." [26]

Within a year after James's death Boutroux wrote a little book on his friend's life and philosophy. At the end of this book, after an admirably sympathetic rendering of James, the author undertook to bring him into line with the great classic tradition. It would not be contrary, he suggested, to the deeper tendencies of James's thought to recognize a "living and concrete reason" which, while it would be distinct from the purely logical understanding, would nevertheless be one with the νοῦς of Plato and Aristotle, and play much the same metaphysical rôle. And then, like all good Frenchmen, Boutroux concluded by attributing this highest insight to Descartes.[27] All of which betrayed in Boutroux a philosophical inheritance quite foreign to that of James; so that the more he honored James by assigning him to the company of the elect, the less was it James that he honored.

[26] July 16, 1910. The mask is in the Library of Philosophy in Emerson Hall, Harvard University.
[27] *William James*, 1911, 129–42.

LXXXIV

PRAGMATISM IN ITALY AND GERMANY

In the spring of 1905, being in Rome for the purpose of attending the Fifth International Congress of Psychology, James wrote as follows: "I have been having this afternoon a very good and rather intimate talk with the little band of 'pragmatists,' Papini, Vailati, Calderoni, Amendola, etc., most of whom inhabit Florence, publish the monthly journal *Leonardo,* at their own expense, and carry on a very serious philosophic movement, apparently *really* inspired by Schiller and myself (I never could believe it before, although Ferrari had assured me), and show an enthusiasm, and also a literary swing and activity that I know nothing of in our own land. . . . It has given me a certain new idea of the way in which truth ought to find its way into the world. The most interesting, and in fact genuinely edifying, part of my trip has been meeting this little *cénacle,* who have taken my own writings, *entre autres, au grand sérieux.*" [1]

These men, together with Prezzolini and others, formed a group which met informally for philosophical discussion, and which was sometimes referred to as "The Pragmatic Club." Thus did James stumble, quite unawares, upon a band of devotees already engaged in the practice and propagation of the new gospel. The period of their collective enthusiasm coincides with the life of *Leonardo,* from 1903 to 1907. In its pages they published numerous articles on pragmatism, — its history and its leaders, — reviewed James's works as they appeared, and acclaimed the sale of 2000 copies of the translation of his *Psychology.* Giovanni Vailati died in 1909, Mario Calderoni in 1914. Their articles, representing a relatively sober and moderate version of pragmatism, were published after their death with a Preface by Papini.[2] Of the others, Giovanni Amendola became a liberal statesman, opposed Fascism, and died

[1] *L.W.J.,* II, 227, 228.
[2] Lanciano, 1920. Largely reprinted from *Leonardo* and *Rivista di psicologia.*

in 1926 of the effects of "lessons" supposed to have been administered by unofficial agents of the government. Giuseppe Prezzolini veered away from pragmatism in the direction of the idealism of Croce, and Giovanni Papini himself passed through a succession of phases culminating in Christian piety. The latter's book *Sul Pragmatismo*, "the doctrine which had from Peirce its name, from James its fame," [3] was designed to appear in 1906, simultaneously in Italian, French, and English — there was talk of a preface by James for the English edition. But it did not see the light until 1913, and was then a record of the past rather than a declaration of faith.

So long as the movement lived it was very much alive. It was this liveliness, especially as embodied in Papini, that stirred James to one of his characteristic enthusiasms. He liked the spirit of the group, their "frolicsomeness," and even their "literary swagger and conscious impertinence." He liked their "tone of feeling, well fitted to rally devotees and to make of pragmatism a new militant form of religious or quasi-religious philosophy." [4] He liked their style, and that of Papini in particular: "What a writer! and what fecundity! and what courage! . . . and what humor and what truth!" This feeling seems to have been reciprocated. Papini speaks of James's "simplicity," "charm," and "profundity." It was he who "conquered" at the Psychological Congress of 1905, of which his paper on "La Notion de conscience" was the "high light." [5]

The following exchange of letters reveals the spirit of this relationship, so characteristic of James in its unhesitating ardor and in its disregard of the disparity of ages: —

Del Monte, April 27, 1906

My dear friend and master, Papini, —

I have just been reading your *Crepuscolo dei filosofi* and the February number of *Leonardo*, and great is the resultant fortification of my soul. What a thing is genius! and you are a real genius! Here have I, with my intellectual timidity and conscientiousness, been painfully trying to clear a few steps of the pathway that leads

[3] "Quella dottrina ch'ebbe dal Peirce il nome e dal James la fama" (*Sul Pragmatismo*, 1913, viii).

[4] "G. Papini and the Pragmatist Movement in Italy," originally published by James in 1906; *C.E.R.*, 460, 465. The writings of Papini which chiefly interested James were *Il Crepuscolo dei filosofi* (1906) and the *Leonardo* articles afterwards republished in *Sul Pragmatismo*.

[5] *L.W.J.*, II, 246; "Gli Psicologi a Roma," *Leonardo*, III (1905), 123–4.

to the systematized new *Weltanschauung* and you with a pair of bold strides get out in a moment beyond the pathway altogether into the freedom of the whole system, — into the open country.   It is your *temper of carelessness,* quite as much as your particular formulas, that has had such an emancipating effect on my intelligence.   You will be accused of extravagance, and *correctly* accused; you will be called the Cyrano de Bergerac of Pragmatism, etc., but the . . . program . . . *must* be sketched extravagantly.   "Correctness" is one of the standards of the older way of philosophizing, that looks in the particular fact for the ghost of some "principle" that legitimates its being, and takes *creation* out of reality.   If creation takes place in particulars, as I have always "seen reasons for believing" but now "believe," "correctness" is not a category for judging anything real. . . .   I shall soon write a notice of the *Crepuscolo* and *Leonardo* for Woodbridge's *Journal* and call you the master of the movement now.   You 're such a brilliant, humorous and witty writer!   It is splendid to see old Italy renovating us all in this way.   I have just written to John Dewey of Columbia University in New York, calling his attention to these writings of yours.   You must immediately read his article "Beliefs and Realities" in the *Philosophical Review* for March.   It is a little obscure in style, but very powerful, and the weightiest pragmatist pronouncement yet made in America!   Continue to think and write!   Yours faithfully,

WM. JAMES

Florence, May 3, 1906 [6]

Dear Master, —

I have received your letter from Del Monte, and assure you that it has almost overwhelmed me.   To hear the master whom I have studied and whom I admire say to me things that seem too flattering even for my pride (which, I might say, is not inconsiderable) has been for me one of the most intense joys of my intellectual life.   I know well that your sympathy for what I am trying to do predisposes you to enthusiasm, but I would not hope to be able to give my dearest master in return a fraction, however small, of the intellectual excitement which he had given me.   I am still quite young, dear mas-

[6] This letter was written in French and is translated by the author.   Papini's "little book" was *Il tragico quotidiano.*

GEORGE SANTAYANA, ABOUT 1887

GIOVANNI PAPINI, 1903

ter — only twenty-five years old — and I am eager to go on working in *your* path. I hope that you will continue to support me — your confidence in me will be one of my sustaining forces.

Only a few days ago I published a little book of philosophical fables: I am sending it to you. I am working on the new Italian edition of your *Psychology*. In June this will be finished. I am working also on my book on pragmatism — I shall send you the proofs. Write me again. Will your metaphysics soon appear? Cordially yours,

G. Papini

P.S. I have received and read Dewey's article. I shall speak of it later. I await your notice of *Leonardo*.

Then, two months later, when Papini had received and read James's promised article in "Woodbridge's *Journal*," he wrote: "You can well imagine the emotion I have felt in reading it, not only for what you say of my ideas but above [all] for the heartfelt sympathy that animates your words. Theories may die and you and I may very well, in two days or two years, have opposite opinions, but the inclination you show for my way of thinking and writing gives me a pleasure of a special kind that men of mere knowledge perhaps never feel."

In a chapter of his *L'altra metà*, Papini says that pragmatism, affirming the utility of knowledge, may be taken in two quite opposite ways according as one does or does not cleave to utilitarianism. To a utilitarian, the utility of knowledge will commend it, and confirm its authority; but to a non-utilitarian the utility of knowledge will disparage it and bring deliverance from its yoke. Papini is of the latter persuasion. "The true greatness of man," he says, "lies in his doing the useless precisely because it is useless." [7] In proportion as science is useful it becomes a positive duty to despise it, and to turn one's activity into more disinterested channels! There is a similar distinction between the "puritanic" and "conciliatory" pragmatisms, the former manifesting itself in restraint and economy of thought, and thus continuing the tradition of positivism; the latter being exuberantly speculative, as a result of hav-

[7] "La vera grandezza dell'uomo deve consistere nel fare l'inutile, appunto perchè inutile," *L'altra metà*, 1922, 203. The first edition appeared in 1910.

ing discovered and escaped the limits of science.   Another of Papini's distinctions is that which he draws between "pragmatisti
sociali" and "pragmatisti magica."   The former are sober men and
find in pragmatism an instrument of organization and policy; while
the latter are intoxicated with the creative spirit.[8]

Papini himself represented in each of these antitheses the freer
and bolder alternative.   His appeal to James lay both in his recognition of the many doors which open out from the pragmatist corridor,[9] and also in his choosing for himself the door of heroic imprudence, free speculation, and aggressive faith.   He was the
"dithyrambic" voice that aroused men's "divinely-creative functions."[10]   He was the "youthful and *empanaché* Papini, who has
. . . put himself at the centre of equilibrium whence all the motor
tendencies start."[11]   This was the pragmatism which adopted "action" as the standard by which to judge all human instruments,
truths among the rest;[12] and the James to whom this gospel appealed was the James who found "life worth living" because of its
heroic moments.[13]

Papini's distinctions suggest two connections of pragmatism with
modern social and political developments.   Communism, so far as
its motives are technological, will readily accept a philosophy in
which all knowledge is judged by its applications, in which these
applications are construed in terms of a control of environment, and
in which both knowledge and its applications are socialized.[14]   This
is *one* of the strains in pragmatism, albeit more characteristic of
Peirce and of Dewey than of James.   But the more powerful impulse communicated by pragmatism to social and political thought
seems to spring from another source, namely, from its exaltation of
direct action, and hence both of revolution and of dictatorship.

[8] *Leonardo*, IV (Feb. 1906), 58–61.
[9] *C.E.R.*, 462.
[10] *Pragm.*, 257.
[11] *L.W.J.*, II, 267.
[12] "Energies of Men," *Philos. Rev.*, XVI (1907); published in *Leonardo*, V
(Feb. 1907).   Here pragmatism offers no *Weltanschauung* of its own, but permits
man to choose any that suits his moral and æsthetic demands, and arouses an
"eccitamento mentale" by making man conscious of his creative power and superiority to science.   (*Op. cit.*, 34.)   For the affinity of Schiller's humanism to this
gospel of defiance, *cf. e.g.*, *Humanism*, 1903, xvi.
[13] E. Palmieri in his *G. Papini*, 1927, states that the doctrine of *The Will to Believe* is central in Papini.
[14] For a hint of this communism of science, a common knowledge for common
ends, *cf.* A. Lalande, "Pragmatisme et pragmaticisme," *Revue philos.*, LXI (1906),
144.

While a Papinian pragmatist would have had only contempt for a purely economic state, he would have found himself much in sympathy with a cult of violence and danger.

In April 1926, Mussolini gave an interview to the press in which he named James, along with Nietzsche and Sorel, among his philosophical masters. Being asked which influence was the greatest, he replied: "That of Sorel. Nietzsche enchanted me when I was twenty, and reinforced the anti-democratic elements in my nature. The pragmatism of William James was of great use to me in my political career. James taught me that an action should be judged rather by its results than by its doctrinary basis. I learnt of James that faith in action, that ardent will to live and fight, to which Fascism owes a great part of its success. . . . For me the essential was to act. But, I repeat, it is to Georges Sorel that I owe the greatest debt. It was that master of Syndicalism who by his rugged theories on revolutionary tactics contributed most decisively to the forming of the discipline, the energy and the power of the Fascist cohorts." [15]

It would be unwise to take this statement too literally. The list of Mussolini's acknowledged masters is already long and is growing longer.[16] That which he found in James he could easily have found elsewhere, as it was widely disseminated and had many parallels. And James was a prophet on the other side as well. The fate of Amendola has already been alluded to. In his account of life among the political prisons on the island of Lipari, Emilio Lussu describes the time spent in discussing James, and the suspicions excited in the breast of the police agent who "intervened one day and inquired, in the name of the law, who Signor James was." [17] But there is no good reason for doubting that the young Mussolini knew at least fragments of Jamesian doctrine and found them to his liking. He remembers also to have made James's personal acquaintance.

The time and the means of Mussolini's contact with pragmatism are obscure. There is a current story that towards the end of the

[15] *Sunday Times,* London, April 11, 1926. The interview was obtained by the Spanish journalist, Dr. André Révesz.

[16] Machiavelli, Schopenhauer, Strindberg, etc.; *cf.* H. W. Schneider, *Making the Fascist State,* 1928, 230–1.

[17] The agent referred the matter to his superiors, who apparently thought James to be, if not a teacher of the true gospel, at any rate innocuous. "The Flight from Lipari," *Atlantic,* CXLVI (1930), 31.

first decade of the present century (1908 or 1909) Mussolini spent some six months in Paris and went frequently to Péguy's shop on the Rue de la Sorbonne to hear Sorel expound Bergson. According to the story, Lenin was meeting Sorel at the same time, so that both of these great revolutionists were imbibing anti-intellectualistic doctrine from the same source.[18]   Lenin read and wrote philosophy voluminously.   He was attracted by Sorel's syndicalism, in which class war was defended as a heroic myth — *una interpretazione will-to-believ-istica* of Marxism, as Papini expressed it.[19]   But any reference to Lenin's pragmatistic affiliations has to be qualified by the fact that in the name of materialism he roundly denounced and elaborately refuted the "empirio-criticism" of Ernst Mach espoused by his rival, A. A. Bogdanov.   He was suspicious of this philosophy because it seemed to open a fideistic way to "the God-makers," and because of its general spirit of "conciliatory quackery."   The followers of Mach were a "wretchedly pulpy . . . contemptible party of middle-roaders," who concealed the irreconcilable conflict between idealism and realism.   Lenin was instinctively, and perhaps strategically, opposed to modernist interpretations of Marx; preferring the premise of materialistic determinism to more flexible philosophical doctrines having no fixed economic and political implications.[20]

Mussolini, whether he did or did not meet Sorel in 1908, was in any case familiar with his writings, and through them he undoubtedly heard of Bergson.   But that he should have heard of James from the same source is altogether improbable.   Sorel's most famous work, *Réflexions sur la violence,* contains many allusions to Bergson, but none to James, despite the striking similarity of the doctrine of the soul-sustaining myth to that of *The Will to Believe.* To the second edition of *Les Illusions du progrès* Sorel added an appendix on "Grandeur et décadence" in which he drew upon James's *Varieties of Religious Experience,* but this was not until 1911. His attention does not appear to have been attracted to James's *Pragmatism* until after the French translation of that book appeared — also in 1911.   Then, in 1921, having read the French transla-

---

[18] I owe this story to Prof. M. Mauss of the Collège de France, who does not vouch for its accuracy.   I have been unable to verify it.

[19] *Leonardo,* IV (1906), 60.

[20] Nikolai Lenin, *Materialism and Empirio-Criticism* (Vol. XIII of *Collected Works*), 1927, 294 and *passim.*

tions of *The Meaning of Truth* and *A Pluralistic Universe,* Sorel published a book entitled *De l'Utilité du pragmatisme.* The *Avant-propos* was written in 1917, and announces the author's acceptance of the doctrine with reservations. He thinks that James has been ill-served by disciples like Papini, "mystifiers whose special function it is to make a smoke-house of any paradoxical novelty," and who find their proper haven in futurism. He thinks that James's pragmatism is provincial, impregnated with the atmosphere of an American, Protestant, and academic environment, and that it needs to be rethought by a European brain. This being done, however (and Sorel proceeds to do it), he concludes that pragmatism may take its place among the classics of philosophy and render an important service to modern thought.[21]

Everything points to 1908 as the year of Mussolini's affair with philosophy. It was in 1908 that he published in *Il Pensiero romagnolo* an article on Nietzsche, entitled "La Filosofia della forza," and wrote a "Storia della filosofia" which was never published.[22] This was the year of his doubtful visit to Paris, and of the undoubted publication of Sorel's *Réflexions sur la violence* (followed a year later by its translation into Italian). And it was in this year that Mussolini came into contact with the *Leonardo* group of Florence, from whom he can scarcely have failed to hear the name, if not the doctrines, of William James. *Leonardo* itself came to an end in 1907; but it was succeeded the following year by *La Voce,* and while this was primarily political and literary rather than philosophical in its interest, it blossomed from the same stem. Prezzolini was its editor; Papini was a frequent, and Mussolini an occasional, contributor. Here Fascismo seems to have associated for a time with Pragmatismo, under the somewhat questionable auspices of Vocismo and Futurismo.[23]

Whatever be the channels of transmission through which individual leaders have been influenced, there can be no doubt of the broad fact that pragmatism and Fascism (as well as Bolshe-

---

[21] Sorel, *De l'Utilité du pragmatisme,* 1921, III, 21–2.

[22] The manuscript being destroyed, so the story goes, by a jealous young woman who mistook the jargon of philosophy for the names of her rivals. (*Life of B. Mussolini,* by M. G. Sarfatti, Eng. trans., 1925, 149.)

[23] *Cf.* H. W. Schneider, *Making the Fascist State,* 1928, VII, 121, 232, 244; W. Y. Elliott, *The Pragmatic Revolt in Politics,* 1928, X, 316. It should be noted that articles from Sorel's pen, anticipating the *Réflexions,* had begun to appear in Italy in 1903.

vism) hold some ground in common; and that Mussolini has a right to cite James, even if it be an afterthought. The contemporary political revolution, construed broadly, is a rejection of liberalism. It is the gospel of force consciously opposed to the gospel of humanitarianism and political democracy. It explicitly rejects the widely accepted dogma that the several individuals who compose society, since it is *their* interests which are at stake, shall be the final judges both as to what is good and as to what means shall be adopted for its realization. William James *was* a liberal in precisely this sense. That he would have had the least sympathy with either Bolshevism or Fascism is unthinkable. We have to do, then, not with a coherent revolutionary philosophy of which James was a forerunner, but with a group of ideas and sentiments, shifting and often unrelated, which here and there overlap the ideas and sentiments of pragmatism.[24]

Fascism sprang from an emergency and expressed the need of prompt and decisive action, ideologies being disparaged because they promote discussion, delay, and irresolution: pragmatism was, therefore, a welcome ally, for having boldly challenged the prestige and authority of the intellect. Fascism was opportunistic, arising as a measure of safety, and continuing to be preoccupied with urgent questions of public and partisan necessity: pragmatism had taught that ideas which do not have an application to the practical situation in which they arise are meaningless and unprofitable. Fascism employed force, both against opposing force and against constitutional rights, was merciless and lawless, excited martial ardor among its own members and threatened its neighbors: pragmatism had taught that ideas and policies may rightly be adopted for their tonic effect upon the will, and that the justification of action may lie, not in its happy consequences, but in the fervor or exaltation of the action itself. For all these ideas with which pragmatistic philosophy supports the exigencies of Fascist policy, it would be possible to cite innumerable texts from James.

There remains the central idea of Fascism, namely, its subordination of the individual to the organic solidarity of the state. This idea was anathema to James, and belongs in the opposite tradition of Hegelianism. It was to a Gentile, rather than to a James, that

[24] Summaries of the philosophy of Fascism will be found in W. Y. Elliott, *op. cit.*, Pt. III; G. Gentile, "The Philosophic Basis of Fascism," *Foreign Affairs,* VI (1928), 290. The most authoritative statement is by Mussolini himself in the article "Fascismo," in Vol. XIV of the *Enciclopedia italiana.*

Fascism must look for the philosophical elaboration of this idea, and as it assumed increasing importance the rationalization of Fascism shifted more and more to idealistic grounds.[25] There is a reason why a political movement which found pragmatism congenial in its early and revolutionary stages should look to idealism in its maturity. Pragmatism of the type represented by the youthful Papini encourages the individual or casual group to become heroes and martyrs in behalf of *any* cause. Its tendency is disruptive and anarchical. But when a revolutionary movement has seized upon the agencies of the state it becomes automatically the champion of the state. For the subjective principle of freedom it is now necessary to substitute the objective principle of common action. For a plurality of militant loyalties which ennoble life diversely, it is necessary to substitute one loyalty, and to give that an exclusive title to nobility. When revolutionists become rulers they can no longer pride themselves on their private force, — for that would encourage a like pride in dissidents, — but must claim that *their* force possesses a peculiar sanction, as springing from something greater than themselves. Their wills can no longer be merely theirs, but must be channels of a higher will; the blood of a greater organism must flood their veins, and a mightier voice speak out of their mouths. Fascism was a party, held together by discipline and sectarian enthusiasm; when the party became the state, these mental characteristics, already developed, were carried over to the state. As a revolution, Fascism created a breach with the past; the doctrine of statism restored and satisfied the sentiment of historic self-identity. This is not pragmatism, — on the contrary, it derives its philosophical sanction from pragmatism's dearest foe, — but it is an authoritarian form of the gospel of action, by which the conquests of violence can be preserved, consolidated, and moralized.[26]

Although Ernst Mach was an important forerunner of pragma-

[25] This nation-worship, submission of the individual to the state, idealization of patriotism, etc., was, of course, a vigorous cult in France with Charles Maurras and *L'Action française*. But although this influence was considerable, it was not philosophical. For Maurras's nationalistic creed, *cf.* his *Au Signe de flore,* 1931, 256–7, 291–3. Maurras goes back to Renan for his creed of nationality.

[26] I may add that, so far as I can see, these pragmatistic and idealistic ideas have nothing to do with the cult of Mazzini, who believed that action should follow swiftly upon thought, because it is of the very nature of thought that it should illuminate action and of action that it should realize thought. This is in no sense opposed to the liberal tradition. It finds the justification of action in the ends which thought forecasts, and not in the action itself or in its subjective authority. (But *cf.* Gentile, *op. cit.*)

tism, while Simmel and Ostwald were greeted by James as allies, pragmatism gained only a slight foothold in Germany, and that mainly in Austria! Even the three philosophers just mentioned accepted it as an interpretation of method in the physical or social sciences rather than as a philosophy.[27] Mach, it is true, has recently been canonized and made the father of a new school of philosophy in Vienna.[28] But this Mach *redivivus* is the positivistic and not the pragmatistic Mach. The substitution of logistics for ethics and metaphysics, as proposed by Mach's latest disciples, is profoundly alien to James in temperament as well as in doctrine.

A German translation of *Pragmatism* appeared in 1908, by Wilhelm Jerusalem,[29] whose motive was to make it known to a hitherto unsuspecting philosophical public. The translator had arrived independently at a similar view, and had carried on a sympathetic correspondence with James since 1900.[30] In the *Vorwort* of his translation he now proclaimed his adherence to the pragmatic school, while expressing his preference for a greater emphasis on the *social* conditions of knowledge.

Professor Julius Goldstein,[31] who afterwards published articles expounding and defending pragmatism, wrote James several enthusiastic letters, to which the latter replied: —

"Schiller had already written to me about you as the only pragmatist now living in Germany. I hope that this will not long be true, but that you may succeed in inoculating your fellow-countrymen with a taste for more empirical philosophy, or rather with a *dis*taste for the elements of absolutism which so many Germans still leave to flourish in the midst of an otherwise very empirical way of thinking." "I am getting numerous acknowledgments of my book, but only one so far has been as enthusiastically sympathetic as yours. It is evident that your mind and mine are cut on the same pat-

[27] Of James's works, the *Principles of Psychology* and *The Varieties of Religious Experience* appear to have been most hospitably received. The translation of the latter in 1907 by G. Wobbermin was a stimulus to the development of the psychology of religion.
[28] The leading spirits of this school are L. Wittgenstein, M. Schlick, and R. Carnap.
[29] W. Jerusalem (1854–1923) was at this time teaching philosophy at the University of Vienna, where he was later made full professor.
[30] In this year Jerusalem sent James his *Urtheilsfunktion,* and James acknowledged its importance and his measure of agreement with it.
[31] Professor of philosophy at the University of Darmstadt. Among the articles which interested James was "Moderne Religionspsychologie," *Internationale Wochenschrift,* III (1909).

tern. . . . The Germans, as you say, are given over to monism — monism in the depths, however empiricist they may appear on the surface. *My* empiricism and pluralism are in the depths also."

Any summary of the influence and later development of pragmatism must take account not only of the several things which it may itself mean, but of the several philosophical destinations to which it may indirectly lead. The unique importance of James lay not only in the initial impulse which he gave to the movement, but in the fact that he foresaw and countenanced so many of the directions which the movement might take. In its narrowest and strictest sense his pragmatism was a description of discursive knowledge, including the rôle of ideas, how they refer to their objects, and what makes them true. All three of these questions are answered in practical terms: an idea is an instrumentality; it refers to its object by inaugurating a train of activities leading thereto, or there-towards; and it is true in so far as it enables the knower to cope with its object successfully. Assuming some such description of discursive knowledge to be correct, what is the metaphysical sequel? One may regard the practical character of discursive knowledge as equivalent to its disparagement. If discursive knowledge is *merely* practical, then it behooves the metaphysician to look for a deeper or purer theoretic insight elsewhere. This is the way of intuition-ism and mysticism, exemplified by Bergson. Or, having discovered that discursive knowledge is *practical,* one may pass on to the under-lying will and assert the general priority of practice to theory. This is the way of activism, exemplified by Papini, Schiller, Sorel, and Catholic Modernism.[32] Or, having accepted a practical inter-pretation of the discursive process, one may take this process itself as the prototype of all activity, not only scientific, but moral and æsthetic as well. This is the positivistic instrumentalism of the school of Dewey. This list of alternatives is not complete, nor are they mutually exclusive. In James himself all three alternatives are retained. Indeed it was the indeterminate richness of its possibili-ties that commended pragmatism to him. Nevertheless, while he joined hands with Papini and Dewey and greeted them as allies in

---

[32] Catholic Modernism owes little or nothing directly to James, so that it falls outside the scope of the present study. A brief account of its relations to the gen-eral pragmatic tendency will be found in the author's *Present Conflict of Ideals,* 1918, 310, *passim.*

the same cause, it is quite clear that he felt a deeper allegiance to the army of the mystics and intuitionists. It was a metaphysics of vision and insight, rather than either activism or positivism, that sprang from the ancient roots of his thought.

LXXXV

A PLURALISTIC UNIVERSE

THE Hibbert Lectures, which were published under the title of *A Pluralistic Universe,* were given at Manchester College, Oxford, May 4–26, 1908. "The audiences were surprisingly large, several hundreds," and "very attentive." The invitation had been received in the autumn of the previous year, and accepted after much hesitation. The writing of the lectures was begun on December 7, and not yet completed when he sailed for Europe on April 21. His hesitation had been due largely to the uncertain condition of his health, and after he had engaged himself he feared that he could not go through with it. He was also reluctant to "relapse into the popular style," just when he thought he had "done with it forever." The strength of this reluctance appears in a letter to Schiller, written in January : —

"I accepted because I was ashamed to refuse a professional challenge of that importance, but I would it had n't come to me. I actually *hate* lecturing; and this job condemns me to publish another book written in picturesque and popular style when I was settling down to something whose manner would be more *strengwissenschaftlich, i.e.,* concise, dry, and impersonal. My free and easy style in *Pragmatism* has made me so many enemies in academic and pedantic circles that I hate to go on increasing their number, and want to become tighter instead of looser. These new lectures will have to be even looser; for lectures *must* be prepared for audiences; and once prepared, I have neither the strength to rewrite them, nor the self-abnegation to suppress them."

"The Present Situation in Philosophy," used as the subtitle of the book, was the original title of the lectures. His major purpose was to present an alternative to monistic idealism, and thus to consolidate the opposition. This he delighted to do at Oxford — in the very stronghold of monistic idealism. But though James threatened "the scalp of the Absolute," and uttered dire threats against that august being's clerical defenders," [1] his belligerency was largely playful — signifying exuberance of spirits rather than homicidal intent.

The exponents of monistic idealism whom he honors as his chief adversaries are all of them old philosophical protagonists with whom he had often done battle before, and from whom he had learned much: Lotze, Royce, and Bradley. He brings the same general charge against them all, namely, that they present philosophy with a false dilemma between utter unity and utter irrelevance. Lotze argues that if two things are distinct, they cannot influence one another; Royce that if two things are independent, they can never become interdependent; and Bradley that if things are two they cannot be related. The conclusion is that since there *is* influence and relationship, implied even in bare plurality, then distinctness and independence must be abandoned: oneness must be the reality, and plurality the mere appearance. All of which argument, says James, is vitiated by abstraction. It proceeds by first singling out some aspect of the concrete thing to the exclusion of the rest, then identifying the thing with this aspect exclusively, and finally showing that the thing so regarded does not provide for the aspects excluded! The argument is not only vicious but unprofitable. The way to find out about influence and relatedness is to look to experience to see how concrete things *do* influence one another, and how they are *in fact* related. The discovery of what *is* renders it quite superfluous to argue whether it *can* be.

Though James was uncompromisingly opposed to a monism of identity, and especially opposed to the dialectical proofs advanced in its support, he was not less opposed to a doctrine of bare manyness and irrelevance. He believed that the world was full of intimacies — indeed, that the most characteristic feature of experience is the interpenetration of one thing with another. This accounts for his friendly overtures to Hegel, the very fountainhead of the doctrine which in Royce, Bradley, and Lotze he repudiates. He had always had a sneaking fondness for Hegel, but insisted on taking liberties with him. He liked him in undress, stripped of his logical regalia. There was, he thought, a homely Hegelian insight: the fact that things contaminate one another, thus becoming something other than themselves.[2] The Hegelian Absolute was to be credited with

---

[1] *L.W.J.*, 303.
[2] *P.U.*, 89–90, 109.

another merit, namely, the sense which it gives its believers that "at bottom all is well with the cosmos," and which permits them to enjoy "moral holidays." But this merit was, he thought, more than offset by the problem of evil — which confronted Hegelianism in a most aggravated form.[3]

There are two connections between the metaphysics of *A Pluralistic Universe* and the *Pragmatism* which preceded it. First, the former is an application of the latter: the pragmatic method and standard of truth are repeatedly applied to the proof of pluralism and the disproof of monism.[4] Second, the latter is applied to the former: that is, the pragmatic account of knowledge affords a special case of the pluralistic metaphysics. The Preface to the *Meaning of Truth* was written in August 1909, over a year after the delivery of the Hibbert Lectures. In that Preface James justified the assembling of his polemical articles on pragmatism by saying that he regarded the acceptance of the pragmatic account of the truth as removing an obstacle to that "radical empiricism" in which he was primarily interested. Pragmatism does not merely provide a method which can be employed in metaphysics — it provides a metaphysics of truth which is consistent with that general metaphysics which James advocates, through bringing the entire process of cognition within the field of possible experience.

It will be recalled that in 1904, when James was summarizing his metaphysics, he spoke of it as composed of four doctrines: pluralism, radical empiricism, tychism, and theism.[5] *A Pluralistic Universe* is primarily concerned with the first and second of these doctrines, though the fourth is reaffirmed. The third constitutes the most distinctive feature of the later work, *Some Problems of Philosophy,* on which James was engaged at the time of his death.

Pluralism is, as we know, almost coeval with James's philosophical maturity. Its personal roots lay in his love of variety and change; its moral roots in his unwillingness to compromise good with evil, or the individual with the universal; and his philosophical roots in his empiricism — especially his experientialism. Motives of the first sort led to his picturesque representations of a world which was unfenced, uncultivated, untidy, and unpredictable — a world which

---

[3] *P.U.,* 114, 116. *Cf.* the Preface to *M.T.,* viii–x, where James withdraws this last concession to monism.

[4] *Cf., e.g., P.U.,* 111 ff.

[5] *L.W.J.,* II, 203–4. For a very much earlier summary, covering much the same points, *cf. W.B.,* 291–5 (written in 1882).

slipped through every ideal container, and resisted the impression of every logical mould. Motives of the second sort, combined with the voluntaristic aspect of his empiricism, led in the direction of an ethical pluralism or monadism — a "republic of semi-detached consciousnesses," with a finite God whose limitations and external relations acquitted him of responsibility for evil. It was the third motive which dominated the *Pluralistic Universe*. In the world as it is given in experience, the connections among things are *de facto,* rather than necessary or constitutional. There is a "free play" of the parts of the world on one another; they "lean on" one another; exist *together,* but without loss of their identity. Things are real *severally,* in their *"each*-form," rather than as taken together, in their *"all*-form." Everything in the world has a real environment, that is, a relation to something which is genuinely other than itself, and which it is compelled to meet and take account of without any sort of antecedent complicity.[6]

Pluralism in this sense is indistinguishable from "radical empiricism," which thus forms the main theme of the book. Radical empiricism consists essentially in converting to the uses of metaphysics that "stream of consciousness" which was designed originally for psychology. Some alterations were necessary, and it was for a long time doubtful whether these were possible. The *Pluralistic Universe* announces that the doubt is dispelled. The result is to silence those qualms of his intellectual conscience which had hitherto prevented a step to which his speculative passion had impelled him — the adoption, namely, of the Fechnerian hierarchy of souls.

There were for James, as there were in fact, two Fechners. When James was writing the *Principles,* Fechner's *Psychophysik* was already a recognized classic in modern experimental psychology. From it James derived many suggestions bearing on imagination, attention, discrimination, and perception. But with the fundamental doctrine of the book he was in profound disagreement. Fechner was "a man of great learning and subtlety of mind," but as regards the great "psychophysical law" on which his fame as a psychologist mainly depended, it was a "patient whimsey" of "the dear old man," which had inspired a literature so dreadful that James refused even to admit it to a footnote. This peculiarly

[6] *P.U.,* 34, 321–3, 358–9.

slighting opinion of psychophysics reflected the little importance which James attached to methods of measurement and to a precise technique in the existing state of the science of psychology, and it is on this ground that his judgment of Fechner has been challenged by experimentalists.[7] But the deeper ground of Jameş's dissent lay in the fact that he regarded Fechner as a peculiarly offending example of atomism and associationism — of that, to James, profoundly erroneous doctrine which teaches that states of mind can be decomposed into elements, constituted by a summation of increments, and measured by the number of their parts. Though its *objects* may be so considered, the state or act of mind itself, thought James, is an organic whole in which the parts are inextricably embedded.[8]

The second Fechner was the metaphysical Fechner, who conceived the universe as a series of overlapping souls from God down through the earth-soul to man, and from man to the unobservable psychic states that lie below the threshold of his consciousness. This daring speculation excited James's imagination, and at the same time satisfied two motives in his thought: he had always been tempted by the panpsychistic view of physical nature, and his religious thought had steadily moved towards the hypothesis of superhuman consciousness. In 1905 he read with great relish Fechner's *Die Tagesansicht* and *Über die Seelenfrage*. Then, in 1907, he wrote to his friends in praise of *Zend-Avesta*, "a wonderful book, by a wonderful genius"; and devoted a whole chapter of *A Pluralistic Universe* to the sympathetic exposition of its doctrine.[9]

There were many reasons why Fechner should attract James — his heroic life, his "intense concreteness," his "fertility of detail," his "thickness," exceeding that of all Hegelians save Hegel himself, his use of analogy and poetic imagery, and above all his confirmation of James's own speculative leanings. But the old difficulty which led James to reject associationism had its application here also. Fechner's metaphysics, like his psychology, was based throughout on a pyramiding of consciousness, a series of levels in

---

[7] *Principles,* I, 534–49. *Cf.* E. G. Boring, *History of Experimental Psychology,* 1929, 285–6.
[8] *Principles,* I, 546, and Ch. VI, *passim.*
[9] *L.W.J.,* II, 300, 309. *P.U.,* Lecture IV. *Zend-Avesta* was originally published in 1851. James read the second edition of 1901. It is to be noted that K. Lasswitz, who had in the '90s influenced James in the direction of a panpsychistic cosmology, was a follower of Fechner.

which the unity of the higher was composed of the plurality of the lower.   James had already transferred this difficulty from the psychological to the metaphysical field in his argument against the Absolute as the container of finite minds.   His wavering between what he took to be the requirements of logic and the alluring speculations of Fechner appears in the following paragraph written to Schiller in 1905: —

"I am more and more impressed by your article on Taylor.   It carries me past a critical point in my attitude towards absolutism — from indulgent tolerance to intolerance, namely.   It must be crushed!   I've just been reading Fechner's *Tagesansicht,* and his *Seelenfrage.*   I can't yet get over the dialectic difficulty of seeing how a wide-span consciousness can be entitatively *constituted* of smaller consciousnesses, but the dear old man's thoroughness and intimacy with his theory, and the inimitable use he makes of the methods of induction and analogy makes all these absolutists with their short-cuts to beatitude shrivel, humanly speaking, to pellicles. Taylor undoubtedly has n't any philosophic *entrails,* — he's all epidermis.   And the extraordinary quality of his surface makes the contrast all the sharper." [10]

In *A Pluralistic Universe* James describes his earlier rejection of "the compounding of consciousness," and the gradual changing of his mind.   He might, had he chosen to pursue this autobiography far enough, have gone back to 1870, when he was looking vainly for some way in which "molecules of feeling could coalesce."   He might have recalled 1876, when he had complained that Renouvier's extreme adherence to the logic of identity led him to neglect the factor of synthesis in mental and moral states.   The view of the *Principles* had been anticipated in 1884, but did not obtain definitive expression until 1890.   According to this view mental states can be unified only through their common relation to something other than themselves.   Not wishing to introduce a soul *ad hoc,* he argued that two states may be unified through knowing the same object, or through being known together as the object of a third state. Higher states emerge from lower, or could be resolved into them, but could never be said to *contain* them.   In 1895 he relaxed this view on the ground that it required a strained interpretation of

---

[10] Schiller's article was "Empiricism and the Absolute," *Mind, N.S.,* XIV (1905), and referred to A. E. Taylor's work, *The Elements of Metaphysics,* 1903.

non-cognitive states. So he proposed to admit that mental states may, wherever convenient, be considered as having parts — distinct, though fugitive. He still felt that neither he nor anyone else had succeeded in laying bare "the nature of that altogether unique kind of complexity in unity which mental states involve." [11]

Ten years later the doctrine of "pure experience" had brought the issue to a crisis. James was now definitely committed to the view that reality and the field of consciousness were one and the same. This implied that portions of the field could be common to two or more minds; that they could, in other words, be identical parts of different conscious wholes. It was clear that something had to break — either the new metaphysics of experience, or the old psychological and logical scruples. This was the crisis which gave rise to the remarkable document to which reference has already been made, and which in the form of an intermittent diary extends from 1905 to 1908 — from the moment of his definitive adoption of the position of radical empiricism, down to the writing of the Hibbert Lectures. [12] It is to this difficulty, and apparently to this document, that James refers in *A Pluralistic Universe* when he says, "I struggled with the problem for years, covering hundreds of sheets of paper with notes and memoranda and discussions with myself over the difficulty." He goes on to say that the "struggle was vain," and that finally, encouraged by Bergson, he resolved to renounce his scruples, and to accept what experience teaches even if it be at variance with what logic proves. [13]

This outcome meant to James a descent into the "bog of logical liquefaction." He felt that he was scarcely called upon to be more faithful to logic than the absolutists who professed to be its friends. But had he *been* a logician he would, perhaps, have spoken not of forswearing logic altogether, but of changing his logical creed. He does refer to "intellectualistic logic" and "the logic of identity," as though there were perhaps "some higher (or lower) form of rationality." [14] He might have welcomed logical developments since his day, and in particular the emancipation from grammatical habits that is made possible by the use of symbols. He would, no doubt,

[11] Above, I, 489–90; *L.W.J.*, I, 187; *Bg.*, 1884–1; *Principles,* I, Ch. VI, especially 162–3 and note; *C.E.R.*, 399–400.
[12] "The Miller-Bode Objections." *Cf.* above, 393–4; and Appendix X.
[13] *P.U.*, 207–8.
[14] *Principles,* I, 163; *P.U.*, 208. Royce had found no difficulty in the inclusion of one consciousness by another: *e.g.*, *World and the Individual*, 1901, II, 238.

have objected to the symbols, but the modern logic of relatives, in providing that the copula of a proposition may signify *any relation,* and not merely the relation of identity, would have put into his hands a tool more suited to his work.

Even so, the outcome of James's thought is not so much to reject logic as to define its limits. What is needed to solve the problem of "compounding" is to be able to say of a certain conscious state that it both is and is not the same as another: that, for example, your experience is the same as mine objectively, but not subjectively. Now "conceived-as-mine" cannot be identical with "conceived-as-yours"; and if the experience *were* only as *conceived,* that would be the end of the matter. But there is no contradiction in saying that the experience, if distinguished from the conception of it, may be conceived in both ways. Whether it lends itself to such duality of conception is a question of fact, and not of logic. And James believes that it is in fact characteristic of existence that its members are both identical with, and different from, their neighbors.[15]

This "endosmosis of adjacent parts of living experience" is, as has been noted, a development and transposition to metaphysics of that "stream of consciousness" which had been so vividly described in the *Principles,* and which had first been introduced to the public in the famous essay of 1884 on "Some Omissions of Introspective Psychology."[16] He had found a powerful support in the "synechism" of Charles Peirce, and received a final confirmation from Bergson. The world as James now depicts it is a scene of perpetual transition, in which the parts, instead of merely succeeding, inherit one another and usher one another in. No event expires until after another has already begun, so that there is always a zone of commingled dawn and twilight through which the one leads over into another. But while each object is thus woven into the fabric of reality, its threads extend only for a limited distance, so that it is only indirectly connected with remoter regions.

Despite its title, *A Pluralistic Universe* is designed to emphasize *both* plurality and unity. If James wished to escape the practical implications of monism, he was not less anxious to escape the theoretic difficulties of atomism, monadism, dualism, or any view in which unity was excluded in advance. He sought a view which

---

[15] *P.U.*, 286; Ch. VI, VII, *passim.*
[16] *Mind,* IX (1884); *P.U.,* 214; *C.E.R.,* 491–2.

permitted unity — as much as theoretic demands might require, or as the facts might yield, or as the religious consciousness might crave. Hence while there is no "universal co-implication, or integration of all things *durcheinander*," there is unity of "the strung-along type, the type of continuity, contiguity, or concatenation." [17] The universe is not a block or an organism, but an all-navigable sea — a great neighborhood embracing lesser neighborhoods, in which accessibility is universal and intimacy proportional to propinquity.

This is the picture of concrete existence. There is another picture which James also knew well how to paint — the picture, namely, of a *selected* world, "dipped out from the stream of time." [18] This motive of selection is one of the aboriginal motives in James's thought. It dominated his conception of mind, his interpretation of concepts, and his pragmatic theory of discursive knowledge. Its subordination in this last of James's inspired works provides conclusive evidence both that metaphysics was his central philosophical interest, and that empiricism was his central philosophical conviction — a new empiricism in which philosophy shall depict or suggest reality in terms as close as possible to the sensible flux of unreconstructed experience.

Another element of James's philosophy which is largely ignored in this work is his realism. There is no reason to suppose that he abandoned a creed so frequently reaffirmed, and so vigorously defended against the critics of pragmatism at the very time when he was writing *A Pluralistic Universe*. But in the absence of any reëxamination of the question, James's position remains uncertain on a metaphysical point of first importance. Must reality be perceived, sensed, or felt in order to be? Rejecting a solipsistic or even humanistic limitation of existence, James represents it as stretching off beyond the horizon of human consciousness — accessible, but out of range. In what, then, consists this ulterior existence? In rejecting the Absolute, James may be assumed to have eliminated one alternative — the alternative, namely, that all existence is housed within the experience of a universal mind expressly provided for the purpose. There remain three alternatives. Residual existence may consist in the *possibility* of experience,

[17] *P.U.*, 325.
[18] *P.U.*, 235.

a view which is hard to reconcile with James's frequent admission that a possibility must always involve the actuality of some of the conditions of its realization. Or, residual existence may consist in experience of infra-human minds, everything which is not for man or some higher subject being conceived as "for itself." This is panpsychism, which James was repeatedly on the verge of accepting, which he constantly praised, but to which he seems never to have given his explicit and unreserved assent. There remains only one last possibility, which is to distinguish *experience* from the *experienced*. Existence would then coincide with the content of experience, but would be independent of any *act* of experiencing on the part of mind. This alternative would be the most consistent with James's theory that mind is a peculiar type of relationship among terms which in themselves are neither physical nor mental.[19] *A Pluralistic Universe* does not clearly affirm this alternative, and even compromises it through identifying the continuum of experience with consciousnesses great and small.

It is in *A Pluralistic Universe* that James speaks most explicitly of the union between empiricism and religion as inaugurating a new era both for religion and for philosophy.[20] The virtue for religion of this union lies in its providing for an intimacy between man and God that does not prejudice either the freedom of man or the innocence of God. It may be described as a pluralistic pantheism: pluralistic because, as James had already expressed it in an earlier work, "God . . . is no absolute all-experiencer, but simply the experiencer of widest actual conscious span," having like other finite beings an external environment for which he is not responsible;[21] pantheism because God is, so far as his limits extend, "the intimate soul and reason of the universe," in whose life man participates directly through the mystical state. When that state occurs, a certain character of isolation ("*ex*-ness") which formerly distinguished man's consciousness disappears, leaving that *co*-consciousness which was formerly only God's, but is now shared by man.[22]

---

[19] This is the view, sometimes referred to as "neutralism," which has been explicitly developed by those later realists who have taken James's "Does Consciousness Exist?" as their point of departure.
[20] *P.U.*, 314.
[21] *M.T.*, 125; *P.U.*, 310–11. *Cf.* also *L.W.J.*, II, 154–5, where James speaks of his view as "polytheistic."
[22] *Cf. P.U.*, 28–31, 299, 309, etc.; *V.R.E.*, 388, and *Mind*, VII (1882), 206; *M.S.*, 201–6; *C.E.R.*, 489–90; above, 133, 334.

In the concluding pages of *A Pluralistic Universe,* James relates his final metaphysics to the earlier chapters of his philosophy. It is the hypothesis of "radical empiricism," defended against "intellectualistic" objections, and verified by experience. But its verification is not conclusive enough to exclude the rival hypothesis of monism. It is to James himself "the most probable hypothesis," but he does not expect that his opponents will recognize this probability as coercive. What he really hopes to obtain, especially on the part of younger thinkers, is a receptivity to the pluralistic alternative, and, in the inevitable exercise of their "will to believe," a more favorable attention to concrete experiences and the *"particulars of life."*

James felt confident of the success of his latest book, and his expectations were promptly verified. Soon after its appearance he wrote to Flournoy: "It is already evident from the letters I am getting about the *Pluralistic Universe* that the book will 1st, be *read;* 2nd, be *rejected* almost unanimously at first, and for very diverse reasons; but, 3rd, will continue to be bought and referred to, and will end by strongly influencing English philosophy." [23]

It is interesting that there should have come from Germany, through the pen of Ernst Mach, praise of James's interpretation of German philosophers: —

Vienna, May 6, 1909 [24]

Most honored Professor, —

Some days ago I received *A Pluralistic Universe* from you. Being quite ill in bed I could read only a little of the book. So far I have read the fourth lecture, on Fechner, which has interested me greatly, inasmuch as I knew Fechner, who was a fatherly friend to me personally as well as in his work. Your setting forth of his stand-point and way of thinking seems to me to be excellent; there is no German, so far as I know, who has achieved it. I came into closer contact with Fechner after the appearance of his *Psychophysik* in the year 1860, and was associated with him at intervals until near the time of his death. His ideas gain ground steadily in Germany, even his ideas concerning the soul-life of plants, with which the scientific botanists would have nothing to do in the years

[23] *L.W.J.,* II, 324. Among the letters which James doubtless had in mind was that communicating Hodgson's "profound dissent"; *cf.* above, I, 651–2.

[24] Translated by the author.

1880–1885. People called Fechner a fool and a fanatic.[25] He was himself in part responsible for this on account of his leaning towards spiritism, manifested in his association with Zöllner and Slade. And one must acknowledge that a little sobriety would have greatly furthered his always scientific thinking. The "Earth-Protecting Angel" [*Erd-Schutzengel*] makes a peculiar impression when one thinks, for example, of San Francisco or Messina.

I have also read the third lecture, on Hegel. I have constantly tried to read Hegel, supposing that I would find profound ideas in him, but I have never succeeded in arriving at a good understanding of him, perhaps because I approached him from the scientific side. Through your third lecture a first understanding of Hegel seems to dawn upon me. For this illumination I am very grateful to you.

To your books, of which I now possess a considerable series, I owe many new points of view, and I hope and most eagerly desire that these writings may have their good effects in Germany. With renewed and hearty thanks, and with best wishes, most respectfully yours,

Dr. Ernst Mach

The "almost unanimous rejection" which James expected was expected, no doubt, on the score of the book's repudiation of logic. And on this score he received much admonition. His colleague Palmer, who thought that this work would put James back "in the high position from which that horrid volume on *Pragmatism*" had tended to pull him down, objected that it was absurd to attack logic by what were after all logical processes (arguing against argument), and resumed his old rôle of Hegel's advocate. If one was dissatisfied with the older logic, why not adopt the Hegelian dialectic, which was expressly designed for a philosophy of change, such as James's? To which James replied that he would appropriate the honey of Palmer's praise, and excuse the gall of his criticism as the "watering of a pair of aged rationalist eyes at the effulgent sunrise of a new philosophic day!"[26]

W. P. Montague, speaking as a realist, said that James's problem of "compounding" could be met (with no offense to logic) if

[25] *Cf.* Stanley Hall's impression, above, 18.
[26] *L.W.J.*, II, 322.

pains were taken to distinguish the .object from the consciousness of it. To which James replied that his discussion of "compounding" had placed itself very explicitly on idealistic grounds." [27] To introduce objects transcending consciousness would be to return to the position of the *Principles* and undo a lifetime of philosophizing. His problem now was to provide for compounds in a world in which objective reality and the stream of conscious experience *coincided,* and this coincidence he evidently identified with idealism; thus again revealing his wavering adherence to his own doctrine of "pure" experience as a "neutral realm" — capable of assuming the rôle of consciousness, but not necessarily or inherently conscious.

Montague's criticism was also directed against James's Bergsonian anti-intellectualism. A. E. Taylor, whom James had frequently cited as an example of intellectualistic excesses, urged James to "recall his recantation" of logic; and urged that the new logic, if not the old, was quite equal to the task of reconciling the many to the one.[28] A. O. Lovejoy, like Montague, accepted the pluralism but refused to sacrifice logic : —

Estes Park, Aug. 27, 1909

Dear Professor James, —

I am unexcusably late in thanking you for the copy of *A Pluralistic Universe* which, through your kindness, came to me from the publishers some three months or more ago. . . . For myself I go along with most of the argument with conviction and even enthusiasm. I balk seriously only at one point, but that one is perhaps to your thinking the most important of all, — the dark Jordan that must be swum through before your Celestial City can be entered. I mean the extreme of anti-rationalism to which the book gives expression. The first lecture, for example, I can't but think, damagingly overstates the degree of dependence of philosophical opinions upon personal temperament and alogical impulses. . . . There is, obviously, always an interworking of personal and logical factors in shaping a philosophical doctrine, especially in causing its oversights and limitations, but to your prefatory denial of the importance of the logical factor, surely one could n't have a better refutation than the book itself, which is an honest and tenacious

[27] Montague, *"A Pluralistic Universe* and the Logic of Irrationalism," "An Explanation," *Jour. of Philos.,* VII (1910) ; W.J., "A Correction," *ibid.*
[28] *Mind, N.S.,* XVIII (1909), 576–88.

and "objective" working out of a conceptual problem by logical methods — under the incitement, doubtless, of personal prepossession — and is *not* merely an exploitation of private idiosyncrasies of taste and sentiment. . . .   In some places it seems to me that, after fetching a long compass, you have come out, via Bergson, at just those enormities which you began by most tellingly castigating in Hegel. As I always admired that castigation, and have always thought you our most resolute apostle of loyalty to the plain old Eighteenth Century Understanding — of the manful acceptance of its *entweder-oder* and its unresolved oppositions, I am now and then a good deal shocked and disappointed at this part of the new book. . . .

If the recognition, with Bergson, of the reality of our temporal experience and of its *durée réelle* implied this throwing overboard of reason, I don't know that I could refuse to accept the consequence. But it is n't clear to me that so great a sacrifice is demanded. . . .   It does not seem likely that any philosophy can long thrive that is generally understood to begin by simply denying the intellectual processes that begot it. And as the philosophy of *A Pluralistic Universe* is one which, in most points, I should very much like to see thrive, I hope that it can be so amended as to give no ground for so injurious an impression concerning it.   Faithfully yours,

ARTHUR O. LOVEJOY

Cambridge, Sept. 4, 1909

Dear Lovejoy, —

I have your letter, which gives me great pleasure by its praise, although when you blame me, it seems to me that you take an extravagantly exaggerated view of my anti-logicality. I am too weary to try to straighten things out in a letter, and I imagine that much war will be waged by many combatants in print before Bergson's thesis gets settled to general satisfaction. All that I contend for is that things *are* as continuous as they seem to be, and that the intellectualist arraignment of experience as self-contradictory and impossible won't pass. If continuity and flow mean logical self-contradiction, then logic must go. B. Russell's disciples pretend that he has saved logic by the "new" infinite.[29] Perhaps he

[29] *Cf.* B. Russell, *The Principles of Mathematics,* Vol. I, 1903; which James read carefully and annotated through Part V.

has, and if so the better, but I wait to be convinced. I wish that you would spread yourself more articulately on the matter, and in print. Thanks again. Yours very truly,

WILLIAM JAMES

In Germany the most ardent admirer of *A Pluralistic Universe* was the Julius Goldstein of Darmstadt whom Schiller had cited to James as the only living German pragmatist. He at once offered to translate the book, and during the spring and early summer of 1910, only a few months before the end, he held a number of conferences with James at Bad-Nauheim. They talked about both the translation and the doctrine itself, of which Goldstein wrote a résumé.[30]

Cambridge, May 21, 1909

Dear Mr. Goldstein, —

I am immensely pleased at your cordial letter about my new book . . . and I think I see what its destiny is going to be. It will stir the puddle, be a ferment and give rise to controversy promptly. But its fruits in the way of conversion to Bergsonism will be small, until much time has elapsed and much more writing occurred. In particular the school of the "new infinite" will resist it tooth and nail, thinking that *their* logic is free from any of the objections which I urge.[31] I greatly admire your article on Bergson, which I thank you for sending me.[32] He is a great genius and I doubt whether you overrate him, but *qui vivra verra!* I am overjoyed that a man of your great literary power should be willing to translate me. . . . Believe me, with best regards and wishes for the success of your enterprise, yours very truly,

WILLIAM JAMES

P.S. From the German point of view much of the polemic against the Absolute will have no relevancy, yet I believe that the English absolutists are taking the intellectualist position in a more *radical*

---

[30] The translation appeared in 1914, under the title of *Das pluralistische Universum*. The *Einführung* of this volume contains an admirable summary and interpretation of James's contributions to philosophy.

[31] Precisely what was done by A. E. Taylor, *op. cit.,* 580.

[32] Published in the *Frankfurter Zeitung*, May 2, 1909; and reprinted in the author's *Wandlungen in der Philosophie der Gegenwart*, 1911, Ch. IV.

way than contemporary Germans, and that their logic is worth killing, even in a country where it is n't very vivacious.

Bad-Nauheim, June 19, 1910

My dear Goldstein, —

You probably had more pages of your manuscript to read me when the dinner interrupted us. I forgot them afterwards, and must now go without! I hope that you will feel free to handle me "without gloves" and in any way you see fit. You understand me better than anyone, apparently, and I feel entirely safe in your hands. If you *criticize*, all the better for the cause of truth.

Apropos of "pantheism," the opposition I had in mind in that first lecture was that between the divine as an *immanent* principle and as an *external* creator. In contrasting "theism" with "pantheism" the words suggest the numerical opposition of dualism and monism, which confuses the reader. Possibly you may find a way, in translating, to mitigate the confusion. . . . Always truly yours,

WILLIAM JAMES

LXXXVI

JAMES AND BERGSON: RELATIONS AND INFLUENCES [1]

WITHOUT doubt the most important philosophical and personal attachment of James's later years was that which he formed with Bergson. A French report of the Fifth International Congress of Psychology, held at Rome in 1905, and at which James had read his paper on "La Notion de conscience," contains the following statement: "No one is unaware — he has himself continually proclaimed it — of what our eminent philosopher, our master-analyst, M. Bergson, owed at the beginning of his career to the works of Americans. It was first and chiefly under the inspiration of Ward, then to a small extent under the influence of William James, that the author of the *Essai sur les données immédiates de la conscience* was led to his famous conception of the internal stream, the *durée réelle* of the deeper and ineffable self, to that psychological mysticism whose precise expression has been his glory. . . . If we have borrowed a psychology from America, we have given them back a philosophy, — for it was impossible to see in the paper of William James anything other than the Bergsonian doctrine of the primacy of action." [2]

This statement evoked from Bergson the following prompt and conclusive reply: "The theory of the inner stream, or rather of the '*durée réelle*' . . . could not have been due to the influence of Ward, for I knew nothing of this philosopher, not even his name, when I wrote the *Essai sur les données immédiates de la conscience*. . . . I come to the reference to William James, a philosopher my love and admiration for whom I can never adequately express. His *Principles of Psychology* appeared in 1891. My essay . . . was worked out and written between 1883 and 1887, and published in 1889. At that time I knew nothing of James except his fine studies of

---

[1] A French translation of this and the following chapter has appeared in the *Revue des deux mondes*, XVII (1933).

[2] Translated from *Revue philos.*, LX (1905). 84.

effort and emotion. (I was not acquainted with the article which appeared in *Mind* in January, 1884, which already contained a part of the chapter on the 'stream of thought.')[3] In other words the theories of the *Essai* could not have been drawn from James's psychology. I hasten to add that the conception of the *durée réelle* developed in my *Essai,* coincides on many points with James's description of the 'stream of thought.' . . . But if one examines the texts one will easily see that the description of the 'stream of thought' and the theory of the *'durée réelle'* have not the same significance and cannot spring from the same source. The first is clearly psychological in source and signification. The second consists essentially in a critique of the idea of *homogeneous time,* as one finds it among philosophers and mathematicians. Now, although I am not qualified to speak for William James, I believe I can say that the 'Bergsonian' influence counts for nothing in the development of his philosophy. . . . I believe that I ought to insist on these two points because the article . . . presents as an accidental and local fact . . . a movement of ideas which has for some years been in evidence everywhere and which arises from causes that are general and profound. In every country, and with many thinkers, the need has been felt for a philosophy more genuinely empirical, closer to the immediately given, than the traditional philosophy, worked out, as the latter has been, by thinkers who were primarily mathematicians." [4]

This statement should be accepted as disposing permanently of the question of priority. Neither philosopher ever made any claims of priority; each rejoiced to find the other in possession of the truth, and was almost extravagantly appreciative of the other's merit. The similarity of their doctrine is not complete or extraordinary — and does not disparage the originality of either.

There is every reason why James and Bergson should have been attracted to one another. They were both men of profound humanity. They both possessed a degree of artistic sensibility unusual among philosophers, and were distinguished masters of prose style. Their styles are very different, it is true. James uses broader

[3] "Some Omissions of Introspective Psychology," *Mind,* IX (1884). The "studies of effort and emotion" were "The Feeling of Effort," 1880, and "What Is an Emotion?" 1884. The former had appeared also in French in the *Critique philos.*
[4] *Op. cit.,* 220–30. *Cf.* also A. Ménard, *Analyse et critique des principes de la psychologie de W. James,* 1911, Ch. VII.

ÉMILE BOUTROUX, ABOUT 1908

HENRI BERGSON, ABOUT 1910

strokes, is more colloquial, humorous, and emphatic; while Bergson's style is chaste, impersonal, restrained. James has something of the quality of a pamphleteer. After the *Principles,* all of his works were either lectures or special articles, written with a view to their immediate effect upon an audience or a philosophical opponent. He was eager to be understood immediately, and was always willing to speak the language of his auditor in order to obtain a hearing. Bergson, on the other hand, composed systematic works, perfected according to their own inner requirements, and expecting like monuments to be approached and studied in their own terms. Even so, both writers are rich in metaphors and imagery, and in their power of intuitive suggestion. According to their common creed reality cannot be analyzed or described, but only *conveyed,* and they both possessed a very unusual capacity to convey it.

In their philosophical doctrines, also, there are many differences. Their systems, being developed quite independently, met, exchanged salutations and gifts, and then proceeded on their way. In no sense did they *coincide,* either as systems or in their particular theorems. It is true that James professed his conversion to Bergsonism, but this was James's way of expressing his moods of personal discovery and agreement. He had in the same sense been converted by Renouvier, Hodgson, Fechner, and almost converted by half a dozen others, but it is clear that the formula of discipleship would scarcely apply to any of these relations. His profound sociability led him to look for a personal embodiment of his ideas, whom he could love and admire; and he liked to expound his ideas by quoting with enthusiastic approval the words of others.

Furthermore, James's Bergsonism was of the spirit and not the letter, so that to enumerate their differences of detail would be to traverse their entire philosophies. Suffice it to mention certain major topics. Bergson, as he himself pointed out, took as his point of departure the logico-mathematical way of thinking, which, in neglecting *real time,* missed, he believed, the very essence of things. James did not, as is commonly said, begin with experimental psychology, but rather with British empiricism, which, in neglecting *felt relations,* also missed the essence of things. In other words, while for Bergson the crucial truth was temporal passage, for James time was only one of many cases of that transitiveness or continuity which was *his* crucial truth. Both thinkers found the key to metaphysics in a certain aspect of conscious experience, namely, its continuity. James saw in this continuity a way of coping with the hereditary difficulties of empiricism — such as dualism, and the problem of the one and the many. Bergson, on the other hand, used it first as a means of correcting the abstract timelessness of the intellectualistic view, whether in physics or in metaphysics.

Both philosophers attached importance to biological evolution, but with differences. Bergson was more biological than James, and there would be a certain point in saying that James developed a biological psychology while Bergson developed a psychological biology. Furthermore, James's biology was profoundly Darwinian — stressing accidental origins, variations, adaptation, and survival; while Bergson's biology had more affinities with Lamarck, and emphasized the dynamic and creative character of the vital impulse. Finally, the general pattern of the evolutionary process tends to be for Bergson divergent and for James convergent. James's unity is in the making — lies ahead as a goal of achievement; while for Bergson there is always a sense of the *aboriginal* unity, as well as of the qualitative sameness, of the stream of life.[5]

James and Bergson agree, as against Peirce and Dewey, in assigning a cognitive rôle both to concepts and to immediate experience. They are unwilling to deny immediacy the title of knowledge, because, although it can reveal only the flowing and qualitative aspect of things, this *is* an aspect of things, to which there is no mode of access save by immediacy. They do not deny conception the title of knowledge because, although it can grasp only the external, static, schematic aspect of things, this, also, *is* an aspect of things, which conception is to be credited with grasping. Both philosophers recognize the problem of accounting for the fact that concepts somehow *work* — for even though concepts do, unless properly supplemented, misrepresent reality, it is nevertheless inherent in the nature of reality that it should be misrepresentable in precisely this manner. So James thinks of concepts as cuts or excerpts from the continuum, while Bergson thinks of them as instantaneous fixations of the flux.[6]

[5] How slight this difference becomes when each philosopher takes account of the other appears in an interesting letter written by Bergson to H. M. Kallen, printed in *Jour. of Philos.*, XII (1915). *Cf.* also the latter's *William James and Henri Bergson*, 1914.

[6] *Jour. of Philos.*, XII (1915), 616. James's final discussion of this question will be found in *P.U.*, 339–43.

For both philosophers reality is immediately given in experience — *is* experience, when that term is properly construed. Their philosophies of experience abound in differences, of which one is important enough to receive special mention. The outstanding problem for James is the interpretation of such experience as lies beyond the periphery of human consciousness. Here Bergson introduces the hypothesis of *unconscious mental states,* thus adding to the alternatives which rendered James's outcome so ambiguous and inconclusive. But here, despite this and other like differences, we touch the region of their profoundest agreement. Both philosophers find that thinking, since it distinguishes, specifies, and arrests, is alien to the genius of existence, which is interpenetrative and flowing. Both men have the same sense of the *copiousness* of reality, and of the pathetic thinness of the concepts with which the human mind endeavors to represent it. They measure the inadequacy of thought by the standard of intuition. They find a way of avoiding the dualisms of subject and object, and of body and mind, by appealing to a concrete reality that embraces both pairs of opposing terms. The reality which is felt or intuited is a temporal, changing continuum from which the mind, governed by its practical interests, selects what is relevant. By a change of attitude from thought to feeling, from action to insight, from periphery to centre, — or whenever one *yields* oneself to things instead of making demands upon them, — then one becomes aware of the plenum of being in which the part is immersed. Whenever either Bergson or James adopts this mode of philosophizing he becomes the perfect exponent of the other. Bergson found himself in James's *Pluralistic Universe;* James, if he had lived to read them, would have rejoiced at the clarity and understanding with which his likeness was portrayed in Bergson's introductions to the French translations of *Pragmatism* and the *Letters.*[7]

A reference in the *Principles* indicates that James read Bergson's *Données immédiates de la conscience* immediately after its publication in 1889.[8] It appears, however, to have made little or no impression on him. When Bergson's *Matière et mémoire* appeared in 1896 he sent an inscribed copy to James, and although it was

[7] *Le Pragmatisme,* 1911, 1–16; *William James: extraits de sa correspondance,* 1924, 7–12.
[8] *Principles,* II, 609.

promptly read it struck no sparks. Then, in 1902, James reread both books with kindling admiration. "Nothing that I have read in years," he wrote early in 1903 to Flournoy, "has so excited and stimulated my thought. Four years ago I could n't understand him at all, though I felt his power. I am sure that that philosophy has a great future. It breaks through old *cadres* and brings things into a solution from which new crystals can be got."

Though he now realized the similarity of Bergson's views to his own, he still found great difficulty in following their detailed presentation. The notes which he made at this time show him to have been both attracted and baffled by Bergson's view of the relation between the inner and the outer worlds. He had himself for many years looked for an escape from dualism in the direction of that theory of "pure experience" which he worked out in 1904, and he was not prepared to substitute Bergson's way for his way.

During the years 1905–1908, when James was engaged in working out his metaphysics of "radical empiricism," and when he was struggling with the crucial problem of "the compounding of consciousness," he recurred frequently to Bergson, trying out the latter's ideas, and increasingly convinced that they were engaged upon the same task with much the same fundamental assumptions. In the spring of 1907 he received and read Bergson's *L'Évolution créatrice.* The effect was immediately made known to his friends. Thus to Strong: —

"Have you read Bergson's *Évolution créatrice?* It seems to me the absolutely *divinest* book on philosophy ever written up to this date. I can assimilate it as yet only in part; but he has killed the beast Intellectualism dead! And he has put the opposition to its categories in the right *place* to be defended — in the *intervals,* namely, the 'conjunctive' places, in which life actually goes on. I am here at Chocorua for a fortnight, and shall spend the summer trying to digest Bergson and you."

There was much of this new book which he could not yet "assimilate." [9] But he was now finding a way of bringing Bergson's views and his own into agreement on the problem of dualism: "For a pure experience philosophy the great distinction is that between inner and outer experiences. The latter are present and wear their qualities adversely — because the present is the time of action. The

[9] *L.W.J.,* II, 290.

former have the same qualities but have dropped their adverseness, — in this dropping lies the passage from what is actual to what is ideal." [10]   At the same time he noted "agreements between B. and W. J.," and wrote down certain questions to "ask him" — for the two men were not yet in direct contact.

They met for the first time in 1905, when James was sixty-three and Bergson forty-six.   This difference of age seems to have made little difference, either in their enjoyment of one another or in the mingled affection and respect which both of them felt.   The date of this first meeting was only five years before James's death, and during the latter's subsequent visits to Europe he was constantly hampered by declining health.   Had he been spared there is every reason to believe that there would have been a growing intimacy, both personal and philosophical.   In the manuscript which James left unpublished Bergson's name appears frequently. Towards the end of this manuscript he refers to the view (of causality) which most resembles his own as "Bergson's, *of which more later.*" [11]

The correspondence opens with a letter from James that appears to have been prompted by his rereading of Bergson's first two books : —

Cambridge, Dec. 14, 1902 [12]

My dear Sir, —

I read the copy of your *Matière et mémoire* which you so kindly sent me, immediately on receiving it, four years ago or more.   I saw its great originality, but found your ideas so new and vast that I could not be sure that I fully understood them, although the *style,* Heaven knows, was lucid enough.   So I laid the book aside for a second reading, which I have just accomplished, slowly and carefully, along with that of the *Données immédiates,* etc.   I think I understand the main lines of your system very well at present — though of course I can't yet trace its proper relations to the aspects of experience of which you do not treat.   It needs much building out in the direction of ethics, cosmology and cosmogony, psychogenesis, etc., before one can apprehend it fully.   That I should

[10] Note in James's presentation copy of *L'Évolution créatrice*.   This topic James refers to in his notes to *Matière et mémoire* as "my problem."
[11] *S.P.P.*, 219 (note), italics mine.
[12] Reprinted from *L.W.J.*, II, 178–80.

take it in so much more easily than I did four years ago shows that even at the age of sixty one's mind can grow — a pleasant thought.

It is a work of exquisite genius. It makes a sort of Copernican revolution as much as Berkeley's *Principles* or Kant's *Critique* did, and will probably, as it gets better and better known, open a new era of philosophical discussion. It fills *my* mind with all sorts of new questions and hypotheses and brings the old into a most agreeable liquefaction. I thank you from the bottom of my heart. The *Hauptpunkt* acquired for me is your conclusive demolition of the dualism of object and subject in perception. I believe that the "transcendency" of the object will not recover from your treatment, and as I myself have been working for many years past on the same line, only with other general conceptions than yours, I find myself most agreeably corroborated. My health is so poor now that work goes on very slowly; but I am going, if I live, to write a general system of metaphysics which, in many of its fundamental ideas, agrees closely with what you have set forth, and the agreement inspires and encourages me more than you can well imagine. It would take far too many words to attempt any detail, but some day I hope to send you the book. How good it is sometimes simply to *break away* from all old categories, deny old worn-out beliefs, and restate things *ab initio,* making the lines of division fall into entirely new places!

I send you a little popular lecture of mine on immortality, — no positive theory but merely an *argumentum ad hominem* for the ordinary cerebralistic objection, — in which it may amuse you to see a formulation like your own that the brain is an organ of *filtration* for spiritual life.[13] I also send you my last book, the *Varieties of Religious Experience,* which may sometime beguile an hour. Believe, dear Professor Bergson, the high admiration and regard with which I remain, always sincerely yours,

WM. JAMES

Paris, Jan. 6, 1903

My dear confrère, —

I have just completed the reading of the book which you were kind enough to send me, — *The Varieties of Religious Experience,* and I am anxious to tell you what a profound impression the reading

[13] *Cf.* above, 132–3, 355.

of it has made on me. I began it at least a dozen days ago, and since that moment I have been able to think of nothing else, so captivating and — if you will permit me to say it — so moving, is the book from beginning to end. You have, it seems to me, succeeded in extracting the quintessence of the religious emotion. No doubt we already felt that this emotion is both a joy *sui generis* and the consciousness of a union with a superior power; but it was the nature of this joy and of this union which appeared to be capable neither of analysis nor of expression, and which nevertheless you have been able to analyze and express — thanks to a quite novel procedure, which consists in giving the reader in sequence a series of *impressions d'ensemble* which intersect and at the same time fuse with one another in his mind. There you have opened a way in which you will certainly be followed by many others, but in which you have at once gone so far that it will be difficult to pass or even overtake you.

If you have had occasion during the last ten or twelve years to talk with French students visiting Cambridge, they must have told you that I have been one of your admirers from the beginning, and that I have lost no opportunity of expressing to my hearers my great sympathy for your ideas. When I wrote my essay on *Les Données de la conscience* I was as yet acquainted only with your article on "Effort," but I had been led, by an analysis of the idea of time and by reflection on the rôle of that idea in mechanics, to a certain conception of the psychological life which is entirely consistent with that of your *Psychology* (save, however, that I see in the "resting-places" themselves "places of flight," on which the fixed regard of consciousness confers an apparent immobility). You will therefore understand that no approval could be to me more precious than that which you are kind enough to give to the conclusions of my book *Matière et mémoire*. Here I have sought — without thereby sacrificing the results of cerebral physiology — to show that the relation of consciousness to cerebral activity is quite different from what the physiologists and philosophers suppose: and I see that on this point, also, we follow two very close and probably convergent routes. That, at least, is the impression left upon me by the reading of the very interesting lecture on *Human Immortality* that you were good enough to send me. The more I think about the question, the more I am convinced that life is from one end to the other a phenomenon of attention. The brain is that which directs this attention; it marks, delimits and measures the *psychological contraction* which is necessary for action; in short, it is neither the duplicate nor the instrument of conscious life, but its most advanced point, the part which inserts itself in events, — something like the prow in which the ship is narrowed to cleave the ocean. But, as you so justly say, this conception of the relation of brain to mind requires us to maintain the distinction of soul and body at the same time that we transcend the old dualism, and consequently we must often depart from the lines of our customary thinking. I wish most eagerly that I might have an opportunity of discussing all this with you. May I ask you, in case you come to France, to be good enough to send me word in advance so that we can arrange a *rendez-vous?* I beg you, my dear confrère, etc.,

H. BERGSON

Cambridge, Feb. 6, 1903

Dear Monsieur Bergson, —

Your letter of a month ago has filled me with delight, but I write now, not to answer it, but to ask a practical question. Shall you still be at Paris about the end of March or beginning of April? I find myself (not being completely reëstablished in health) excessively fatigued with my half year's work, and (since it is impossible to get rest at home) impelled to absent myself for six or eight weeks. I waver between California, and a steamer to the Mediterranean with a return home via Paris and England. I confess that the prospect of some philosophic conversation with you is what would most incline me towards the European trip. But if, on arriving, I were to find that you had gone to Russia or come to these United States, I should be much disappointed. Can you therefore answer me? *und zwar,* since the time is probably too short for an exchange of letters — I sail (if I *do* sail) on Feb. 28th — by cable? If you *can* see your way to an interview, whether at Paris or anywhere between the Riviera and England, it will suffice to send the words: "James, Cambridge, Mass. *Oui.*" Four words will not cost much, or I should regret imposing the tax upon you. A post-card hither might also be risked. Believe me, ever sincerely yours,

WM. JAMES

Cambridge, Feb. 25, 1903 [14]

Dear Professor Bergson, —

Your most obliging cablegram (with eight words instead of four!) arrived duly a week ago, and now I am repenting that I ever asked you to send it, for I have been feeling so much less fatigued than I did a month ago, that I have given up my passage to the Mediterranean, and am seriously doubting whether it will be necessary to leave home at all. I *ought* not to, on many grounds, unless my health imperatively requires it. Pardon me for having so frivolously stirred you up, and permit me at least to pay the cost (as far as I can ascertain it) of the despatch which you were so liberal as to send. There is still a bare possibility (for I am so strongly tempted) that I may, after the middle of March, take a cheaper vessel direct to England or to France, and spent ten days or so in Paris and return almost immediately. In that case, we could still have our interview. I think there must be great portions of your philosophy which you have not yet published, and I want to see how well they combine with mine. *Writing* is too long and laborious a process, and I would not inflict on you the task of answering my questions by letter, so I will still wait in the hope of a personal interview sometime.

I am convinced that a philosophy of *pure experience,* such as I conceive yours to be, can be made to work, and will reconcile many of the old inveterate oppositions of the schools. I think that your radical denial (the manner of it at any rate) of the notion that the brain can be in any way the *causa fiendi* of consciousness, has introduced a very sudden clearness, and eliminated a part of the idealistic paradox. But your unconscious or subconscious permanence of memories is in its turn a notion that offers difficulties, seeming in fact to be the equivalent of the "soul" in another shape, and the manner in which these memories "insert" themselves into the brain action, and in fact the whole conception of the difference between the outer and inner worlds in your philosophy, still need to me a great deal of elucidation. But behold me challenging you to answer me *par écrit!*

I have read with great delight your article in the *Revue de métaphysique* for January,[15] agree thoroughly with all its critical part,

[14] Reprinted from *L.W.J.,* II, 183–5.
[15] "Introduction à la métaphysique."

and wish that I might see in your *intuition métaphysique* the full equivalent for a philosophy of concepts. *Neither* seems to be a full equivalent for the other, unless indeed the intuition becomes completely mystical (and that I am willing to believe), but I don't think that that is just what *you* mean. The *Syllabus* [16] which I sent you the other day is (I fear), from its great abbreviation, somewhat unintelligible, but it will show you the sort of lines upon which I have been working. I think that a normal philosophy, like a science, must live by hypotheses — I think that the indispensable hypothesis in a philosophy of pure experience is that of many kinds of other experience than ours, that the question of $\begin{cases} \text{co-consciousness} \\ \text{conscious synthesis} \end{cases}$ (its conditions, etc.) becomes a most urgent question, as does also the question of the relations of what is possible only to what is actual, what is past or future to what is present. These are all urgent matters in your philosophy also, I imagine. How exquisitely you do *write!* Believe me, with renewed thanks for the telegram, yours most sincerely,

Wm. James

Paris, March 25, 1903

My dear confrère, —

I was much disappointed when I learned that you would probably not come to Europe, and my regret would have been even keener had I not learned that it is the improvement of your health which has led you to abandon the trip. I hope that you may be promptly and completely restored from the fatigue of which you speak, a fatigue that is easy to understand when one thinks of the amount of work and thinking that your last work, *The Varieties of Religious Experience,* must have cost you.

The difficulties which you call to my attention in certain parts of *Matière et mémoire* are only too real, and I am far from having succeeded in completely surmounting them. But I believe, nevertheless, that among these difficulties some are the effects of inveterate habits of our mind, habits having a wholly practical origin, and from which we should emancipate ourselves for purposes of speculation. Such, for example, is the difficulty of admitting present un-

---

[16] "Syllabus in Philos. 3"; *cf.* above, 373–4, 425–6, and Appendix IX.

conscious memories. If we reduce memories to the category of things, it is clear that there is no mean for them between presence and absence: either they are unqualifiedly present to our mind, and in this sense conscious; or, if they are unconscious, they are absent from our mind and should no longer be considered as present psychological realities. But in the world of psychological realities I do not believe that there is occasion for presenting the alternative "to be or not to be" so exclusively. The more I try to grasp myself by consciousness the more do I perceive myself as the totalization or *Inbegriff* of my own past, this past being contracted with a view to action. "The unity of the self" of which philosophers speak, appears to me as the unity of an apex of a summit to which I narrow myself by an effort of attention — an effort which is prolonged during the whole of life, and which, as it seems to me, is the very essence of life. But to pass from this apex of consciousness or from this summit, to the base, that is to say, to a state in which all the memories of all the moments of the past would be scattered and distinct, I realize that one would have to pass from the normal state of concentration to a state of dispersion like that of certain dreams; there would, therefore, be nothing positive to be done, but simply something to be undone — nothing to gain, nothing to add, but rather something to lose: it is in this sense that all my memories are there when I do not perceive them, and that nothing really new is produced when they reappear in consciousness.

The résumé which you kindly sent me of the course which you are now conducting interested me profoundly. It contains so many new and original views that I do not yet sufficiently succeed in grasping the ensemble, but one dominant idea stands out so far: the necessity, namely, of transcending concepts, or mere logic, or the procedure, in short, of that over-systematic philosophy which postulates the unity of everything. The path which I am myself following is analogous to this, and I am quite convinced that if a really *positive* philosophy is possible, it can only be found there. Again, how much I regret that I cannot have the talk with you for which I had hoped. But you will not fail to come to France or England one of these days, and in that case I could always arrange to meet you, at any time and place, provided you gave me notice a little in advance. I beg you, etc.,

H. Bergson

Paris, Feb. 15, 1905

My dear confrère, —

Forgive me, I beg you, for so tardily acknowledging your kindness in sending me your last articles.[17]   I need not tell you that I read — and reread — them as soon as I received them, but I have been over-driven during these last weeks and it has been impossible for me to write you earlier.   These five articles contain the outline of an entire philosophy, and I await with impatience the work which will present its complete development.   But you already indicate a certain number of applications, all extremely interesting.   I believe that on many essential points I could join you, but perhaps I would not go quite so far as you do in the way of "radical empiricism."   The principal difference bears probably (again I am not wholly sure) on the rôle of the unconscious.   I cannot avoid making a very large place for the unconscious, not only in the realm of psychology, but also in the universe in general, the existence of unperceived matter seeming to me to be of the same *genre* as a psychological state which is not conscious.   This existence of a reality outside of all actual consciousness is, no doubt, not the existence-in-itself of the older substantialism; and nevertheless it is not the actually-presented to a consciousness.   It is something intermediate between the two, always on the point of becoming or of again becoming conscious, — something intimately mingled with the conscious life, "interwoven with it," and not "underlying it" as substantialism would have it.   But it is possible that even on this point I am nearer to you than I imagine.

I am very grateful for your kind allusions to my works in many of your articles.   They will attract attention to the common direction of the very considerable movement of ideas which you have created in America and which is more and more gaining ground with us.   I wish that these convergent efforts might succeed in inaugurating a new *positive* metaphysics, that is to say, one that is capable of indefinite progress, instead of having to be accepted or rejected as a whole, like the older systems.   I beg you, etc.,

H. BERGSON

In April 1905, James sailed for a "holiday" in Europe.   After visiting Athens, and attending the Congress of Psychology in

[17] The essays in radical empiricism, "Does 'Consciousness' Exist?" "A World of Pure Experience," etc.

Rome, he went north through Switzerland and France and sailed back to America in June: —

Cannes, May 13, 1905

Dear Professor Bergson, —

I am staying at the Hôtel du Parc here with Strong, and expecting to spend a week in Paris, probably from the 25th of May to the 1st of June. . . . I have to confess that, although I am cerebrally in a rather good-for-nothing condition, *one* of the things that makes me choose my way home via Paris rather than straight from the Mediterranean, is the possibility that, once in Paris, I may see you face to face, and perhaps gain a little better understanding of some of the points in your philosophy that are still to me obscure. This is rather a formidable sounding announcement, as you are a modest man. But pray don't take alarm at it, — my intentions are most innocent, and my curiosities will probably seem to you very superficial. The gist of the matter is that I think it must be always good for two philosophers who are *near* each other to come into personal contact. They will understand each other better, even if they should only gossip away their hour. I hope then that you are to be in Paris at the time when I shall be there, and that you will have time and disposition to give me an hour or two. I shall go to the Hôtel des Saints Pères, in the street of the same name, and a note from you proposing a convenient time and place will get me if addressed thither. . . . I have a number of different things to do in Paris, and if my date with you is fixed first, everything else can be regulated with reference to that.

Hoping that this will find you at home and in good health and not *unsociable!* — I am, with highest esteem and regard, yours truly,

WM. JAMES

Geneva, May 18, 1905

Dear Professor Bergson, —

Your very kind letter . . . just reaches me, and I hasten to reply. It looks now as if I should hardly be able to be at Paris before Friday or Saturday the 26th or 27th. Will Sunday the 28th be a good day for our first meeting? A Cambridge friend, now in Paris, has asked me to come to his *appartement*, which is 28, Rue d'Offémont (Dr. Norton is his name).[18] I shall conse-

---

[18] Dr. Rupert Norton, son of Prof. Charles Eliot Norton.

quently not be at the Hôtel des Saints Pères, and can receive you, or go to your house, on Sunday morning, just as is most convenient to yourself, — I don't like to waste your time by asking you to come and see me. How would Wednesday the 31st do for the *déjeuner* which you offer me? On Thursday, or possibly on Wednesday night, I must start for England.

I have learned from Mr. Claparède this morning that M. Brunschvicg [19] has the kind intention of inviting me to the Société Française de Philosophie. At some other time this would give me extreme pleasure, but it happens that I find myself just at this time in a state of acute neurasthenic fatigue (wakefulness, etc.) and am trying to minimize such occasions of effort and excitement. I shall consequently try, while in Paris, to limit my philosophic *Umgang* to yourself, hoping to make up the loss some other year. Will you therefore kindly not mention to the world at large that this particular transatlantic philosopher is expected? It is humiliating to have so bad a nervous system, *mais "à la guerre comme à la guerre,"* and *my guerre* is with that internal enemy. I shall be at Lausanne until the 24th. I am to stop on the way to Dijon to see some friends. Believe me, dear Professor, yours most sincerely,

WM. JAMES

The first conjunction of these two luminaries took place on May 28, 1905. There is no contemporary record of it save the entry in James's diary for that date: "Visit from Beautiful Bergson." Twenty years later Bergson himself recalled the occasion. He was speaking of James's preoccupation with the things of the spirit: "I believe that we did indeed, say *'Bonjour,'* but that was all; there were several instants of silence, and straightway he asked me how I envisaged the problem of religion." [20]

Professor F. Abauzit was at this time preparing his French translation of James's *Varieties of Religious Experience,* and Bergson took a lively interest in the enterprise.

Cambridge, July 10, 1905

Dear Professor Bergson, —

Returning from a week of lecturing at the University of Chicago, I find two letters from Abauzit, wherein he copies letters (or parts

[19] Léon Brunschvicg, professor of philosophy at the Sorbonne.
[20] Translated from Bergson's Preface to the French translation of James's letters, by F. Delattre and M. Le Breton, 1924, 9.

of letters) from you, expressing a good deal of anxiety lest the freedom of his translation should expose him to the criticisms of the captious. The translation is so faithful to my ideas, and yet written in such spirited French, that I count myself extremely lucky, after reading the first 144 pages of proof, and have written him words to that effect which I have told him he might quote in his Preface. One need not drink the sea to call it salt. I shall therefore not read the rest of his proofs. I have more to do than my strength is good for, and a number of translators, in different tongues, and my only safe policy is not to let myself be made responsible for details. On the whole Abauzit seems to me an admirable translator.

He writes that you will furnish him with a short Preface.[21] I am very glad; but please remember that it was not *I that asked you to.* In truth, I am filled with sorrow at the thought of his having bothered you (as he evidently has) so much with the proofs. Your time should be saved from such drudgery. *Please* pay *no* more attention to the proofs! And don't answer this! Sincerely yours,

WM. JAMES

Paris, July 20, 1905

My dear confrère, —

To my great regret I was obliged to write to Abauzit that I could not undertake the preface which he had kindly asked me to do for his translation. For two or three weeks I have suffered from a general nervous fatigue caused by a very tenacious insomnia: I have no doubt aggravated this condition by insisting on remaining in Paris to work despite it. Thus I am now obliged to break off all work and go on a trip, if I am to be able to resume my courses when I return. I much regret not being able to give to Abauzit this token of my interest, and to your book, permit me to say, this evidence of my great admiration. But never was a foreign work less in need than this of being presented to the French public.

I read the articles which you kindly sent me as soon as I received them, and I want to tell you how much they have interested me.[22] They clear up your doctrine, and answer, it seems to me, objections which have been raised against it. The essential point appears to me to be that which you have treated in the second article:

[21] The Preface was, in fact, written by Boutroux.
[22] The later essays on radical empiricism.

"How Two Minds Can Know One Thing." The more I reflect on it, the more I believe that philosophy will be obliged to fix upon a solution of the sort you indicate: there is *pure* experience, which is neither subjective nor objective (I employ the word *image* to designate a reality of this sort); and there is what you call the *appropriation* of this experience by such and such consciousnesses, an appropriation which appears to me to consist in a unique kind of diminution of the image, but which you would make consist, if I have understood you, rather in the affective states which attend the pure image. Yet I do not believe that these two last views are irreconcilable with one another, for the diminution of which I speak is always made for a practical purpose; it interests our body and should, in consequence, translate itself into an attitude of the body which welcomes or rejects the external image. Now this attitude of the body is perceived at the points where it arises, that is to say in the interior of the body-image. And a perception internal to our body is precisely, it seems to me, what one calls an affective state.

I do not know whether you have read an article in the last number of the *Revue philosophique,* apropos of the Congress at Rome. . . . It is said in this article that the conception of *"durée réelle"* which I set forth in my first work (*Essais sur les données immédiates*) drew its inspiration from the idea of Ward and also a little from yours, — and that, reciprocally, the philosophy which you are now setting forth draws its inspiration from my works. In reply to this article I wrote immediately to the *Revue philosophique* a letter which will appear in the next number, and in which I set forth: first, that my *Essai* was written in ignorance of Ward's and your ideas, and that one can see that the theories developed in that *Essai* have a very different significance and origin; second, that no more could you, on the other hand, have drawn your inspiration from "Bergsonism," for the very simple reason that long before *Matière et mémoire* you had already taken the line which you are now pursuing. I thought I ought to cut this incipient legend at the very root, because, to my mind, one of the most striking arguments that one can invoke (from the external point of view) in favor of American "pragmatism" and the "new philosophy" in France, is precisely that these two doctrines have established themselves independently of one another, with different points of departure and different methods. When, under such conditions, two doctrines tend to coincide, there is a good chance that both of them are in the vicinity of the truth.

I hope most earnestly that you will carry out your plan of coming to spend some months in France. And I am not alone, believe me, in hoping it. I assure you, etc.,

H. BERGSON

LXXXVII

BERGSON AND JAMES: ESTIMATES AND INTERPRETATIONS

THE spring of 1907 brought the publication of Bergson's *L'Évolution créatrice,* and James's characteristic postal-card acknowledgment: —

Cambridge, May 19, 1907

Your new book is just arrived — hurrah! hurrah! hurrah! and thanks. You will receive my little book on *Pragmatism* in a couple of weeks.

WM. JAMES

After reading the book James wrote more fully: —

Chocorua, June 13, 1907 [1]

O my Bergson, you are a magician, and your book is a marvel, a real wonder in the history of philosophy, making, if I mistake not, an entirely new era in respect of matter, but unlike the works of genius of the "transcendentalist" movement (which are so obscurely and abominably and inaccessibly written), a pure classic in point of form. You may be amused at the comparison, but in finishing it I found the same after-taste remaining as after finishing *Madame Bovary,* such a flavor of persistent *euphony,* as of a rich river that never foamed or ran thin, but steadily and firmly proceeded with its banks full to the brim. Then the aptness of your illustrations, that never scratch or stand out at right angles, but invariably simplify the thought and help to pour it along! Oh, indeed you are a magician! And if your next book proves to be as great an advance on this one as this is on its two predecessors, your name will surely go down as one of the great creative names in philosophy.

[1] Reprinted from *L.W.J.,* II, 290–4.

There! have I praised you enough? What every genuine philosopher (every genuine man, in fact) craves most is *praise* — although the philosophers generally call it "recognition"! If you want still more praise, let me know, and I will send it, for my features have been on a broad smile from the first page to the last, at the chain of felicities that never stopped. I feel rejuvenated.

As to the content of it, I am not in a mood at present to make any definite reaction. There is so much that is absolutely new that it will take a long time for your contemporaries to assimilate it, and I imagine that much of the development of detail will have to be performed by younger men whom your ideas will stimulate to coruscate in manners unexpected by yourself. To me at present the vital achievement of the book is that it inflicts an irrecoverable death-wound upon Intellectualism. It can never resuscitate! But it will die hard, for all the inertia of the past is in it, and the spirit of professionalism and pedantry as well as the æsthetic-intellectual delight of dealing with categories logically distinct yet logically connected, will rally for a desperate defense. The *élan vital,* all contentless and vague as you are obliged to leave it, will be an easy substitute to make fun of. But the beast *has* its death-wound now, and the manner in which you have inflicted it (internal *versus temps d'arrêt,* etc.) is masterly in the extreme. I don't know why this later *rédaction* of your critique of the mathematics of movement has seemed to me so much more telling than the early statement — I suppose it is because of the wider *use* made of the principle in the book. You will be receiving my own little "pragmatism" book simultaneously with this letter. How jejune and inconsiderable it seems in comparison with your great system! But it is so congruent with parts of your system, fits so well into interstices thereof, that you will easily understand why I am so enthusiastic. I feel that at bottom we are fighting the same fight, you a commander, I in the ranks. The position we are rescuing is "Tychism" and a really growing world. But whereas I have hitherto found no better way of defending Tychism than by affirming the spontaneous addition of *discrete* elements of being (or their subtraction), thereby playing the game with intellectualist weapons, you set things straight at a single stroke by your fundamental conception of the continuously creative nature of reality. I think that one of your happiest strokes is your reduction of "finality," as usually taken, to its status alongside of efficient causality, as the twin-daughters of intellectualism.   But this vaguer and truer finality restored to its rights will be a difficult thing to give content to.   Altogether your reality lurks so in the background, in this book, that I am wondering whether you *could n't* give it any more development *in concreto* here, or whether you perhaps were holding back developments, already in your possession, for a future volume.   They are sure to come to you later anyhow, and to make a new volume; and altogether, the clash of these ideas of yours with the traditional ones will be sure to make sparks fly that will illuminate all sorts of dark places and bring innumerable new considerations into view.   But the process may be slow, for the ideas are so revolutionary.   Were it not for your style, your book might last 100 years unnoticed; but your way of writing is so absolutely commanding that your theories have to be attended to immediately.   I feel very much in the dark still about the relations of the progressive to the regressive movement, and this great precipitate of nature subject to static categories.   With a frank pluralism of *beings* endowed with vital impulses you can get oppositions and compromises easily enough, and a stagnant deposit; but after my one reading I don't exactly "catch on" to the way in which the continuum of reality resists itself so as to have to act, etc., etc.

The only part of the work which I felt like positively criticizing was the discussion of the idea of nonentity, which seemed to me somewhat overelaborated, and yet did n't leave me with a sense that the last word had been said on the subject.   But all these things must be very slowly digested by me.   I can see that, when the tide turns in your favor, many previous tendencies in philosophy will start up, crying "This is nothing but what *we* have contended for all along."   Schopenhauer's blind will, Hartmann's unconscious, Fichte's aboriginal freedom (reëdited at Harvard in the most "unreal" possible way by Münsterberg) will all be claimants for priority.   But no matter — all the better if you are in some ancient lines of tendency.   Mysticism also must make claims and doubtless just ones.   I say nothing more now — this is just my first reaction; but I am so enthusiastic as to have said only two days ago, "I thank heaven that I have lived to this date — that I have witnessed

the Russo-Japanese war, and seen Bergson's new book appear —
the two great modern turning-points of history and of thought!"
Best congratulations and cordialest regards!

WM. JAMES

Paris, June 27, 1907

Dear Professor James, —

Your letter gave me great happiness, and I must thank you for
it at once. You are right in saying that the philosopher likes
praise, and that in this he resembles the general run of mortals;
but allow me to say that the support for which I was especially
eager, was that of the thinker who has so powerfully contributed
to the refashioning of the soul of the new generations, and whose
work has always excited in me such profound admiration. And
the letter in which you declare yourself ready to adopt the essential ideas of my work, in which you defend them in advance against
the attacks which they are sure to provoke, touches me above all.
I keep it by me, as a sufficient recompense for the ten years of effort
which this book has cost me.

I began to read your *Pragmatism* the very moment the post
placed it in my hands, and I could not put it away until I had finished reading it. It is the program, admirably traced, of the philosophy of the future. By very diverse lines of consideration, which
you have always been able to make converge to the same focal
point, by suggestions as well as by explicit reasons, you convey the
idea, above all the feeling, of that supple and flexible philosophy
which is destined to take the place of intellectualism. Never had
I been so aware of the analogy between our two points of view as
when I read your chapter on "Pragmatism and Humanism." When
you say that "for rationalism reality is ready-made and complete
from all eternity, while for pragmatism it is still in the making," [2]
you provide the very formula for the metaphysics to which I am
convinced we shall come, to which we should have come long ago
if we had not remained under the spell of Platonic idealism. Shall
I go so far as to affirm with you that "truth is mutable"? I believe
in the mutability of *reality* rather than of *truth*. If we could
regulate our faculty of intuition by the mobility of the real, would

[2] *Pragm.*, 257.

not this regulating be a stable thing, and would not the truth —
which can only be this very regulating — participate in this stability? But before attaining to that, many tentative efforts will be
necessary. Once more, dear Professor James, my hearty congratulations on this new work, which is destined to exercise a wide influence. Believe me, I beg you, etc.,

H. BERGSON

Oxford, May 8, 1908

Dear Professor Bergson, —

You will be surprised at seeing where I am. I got here last
Monday and am giving a course of seven (or eight?) "Hibbert
Lectures" on "the present situation in philosophy," — it amounts
practically to a critique of intellectualism, and a vindication of the
immediately *vécu* flux — in short, to Bergsonism. One lecture is
exclusively about your ideas, at least about that part of them, just
as another is about G. T. Fechner's. Can you send me a few data
of fact, for completeness' sake, such as:

(1) the year and place of your birth;

(2) the successive schools in which you studied;

(3) the successive offices, academic or other, which you may
have held;

(4) any remarkable adventures, romantic or heroic, as well as
philosophic, in which you have taken part (!) etc., etc. Details
help interest! The audiences are large, about 500 at the first lecture.
Hoping that you are well, I am as always, faithfully yours,

WM. JAMES

P.S. The lecture on "Bergson" comes off on Monday the 18th.
I expect to publish the volume under some such title as "Intellectualism and Reality," within the year.

Paris, May 9, 1908

Dear Professor James, —

I cannot tell you how much pleasure I felt when, last evening, I
recognized your handwriting on an envelope bearing an English
stamp. Here at last, I hope, is an opportunity of talking with
you. . . .

You do me great honor in devoting one of your Oxford lectures to me. How happy I should have been could I have heard you, both in this and in the other lectures. At any rate I hope that you will not delay bringing them together in a volume.

Here is the information for which you wished to ask me. First, my *"curriculum vitæ."* Born in Paris 1859. Pupil at the Lycée Condorcet, from 1868 to 1878. Student at the École Normale Supérieure (the institution where with us the future university professors are trained) from 1878 to 1881. *Agrégé* in philosophy in 1881, doctor in 1889. Professor of philosophy in various *lycées* in the provinces and in Paris from 1881 to 1898. Professor at the École Normale Supérieure, from 1898 to 1900. Professor at the Collège de France since 1900. Membre de l'Institut since 1901.

Now as to events worthy of note, there have been none in the course of my career, — at least nothing *objectively* remarkable. On the subjective side, however, I cannot but attribute great importance to the change which took place in my way of thinking during the two years which followed my leaving the École Normale, from 1881 to 1883. I had remained up to that time wholly imbued with mechanistic theories, to which I had been led at an early date by the reading of Herbert Spencer, a philosopher to whom I adhered almost unreservedly. It was my intention to devote myself to what was then called the philosophy of the sciences, and to that end I had undertaken, after leaving the École Normale, to examine some of the fundamental scientific notions. It was the analysis of the notion of time, as that enters into mechanics and physics, which overturned all my ideas. I saw, to my great astonishment, that scientific time does not *endure,* that it would involve no change in our scientific knowledge if the totality of the real were unfolded all at once, instantaneously, and that positive science consists essentially in the elimination of duration. This was the point of departure of a series of reflections which brought me, by gradual steps, to reject almost all of what I had hitherto accepted and to change my point of view completely. I have summarized in the *Essai sur les données immédiates de la conscience* (pp. 87–90, 146–149, etc.) the considerations regarding time which determined my philosophical orientation and with which all my subsequent reflections are bound up.

Of all this, and much more besides concerning your last work on Pragmatism, I hope soon to be able to talk with you. Meanwhile, dear Professor James, I send you my affectionate and faithful regards,

H. BERGSON

Oxford, May 12, 1908

Dear Professor Bergson, —

I thank you most heartily for your letter, especially for the account of your mental crisis, which puts the whole difference between reality and scientific formulations of it into a nutshell. I hope that when you read what I have said of you, though of course you will find it very inadequate, you will not say I have "totally misunderstood."

May 15th. I have let this letter stand till I should have seen my brother, who came here yesterday from Paris, and with whom I had to settle certain dates of our own itinerary, since we are to pay him a visit of some weeks at Rye where he lives, and no date had been established for that. It is fixed now for the last half of July and part of August, which sets me comparatively free for the next few weeks. I am greatly pleased, naturally, that you should express a desire for a meeting. I find it hard to define either questions or answers in conversation — the pen is more efficient — but something always comes, and I confess that I should be very glad to talk over certain things with you again. I do not, however, think the end of this month to be propitious. I arrived here, with my lectures not completely written, in a state of extreme nervous fatigue, having had a very bad winter, virulent influenza followed by incessant vertigo, insomnia, etc.; and the need of writing these lectures, and the tremendous hospitality of Oxford added to the rest, will leave my brain quite unfit for any serious discussion of a profitable kind until I shall have had some weeks of rest. Where shall you naturally expect to be during the latter half of June? It will be very easy for me to go to Paris . . . some time thereabouts, and could make my dates agree with yours. Pray let me know as soon as you can conveniently. We shall probably leave Oxford before June 1st, but have not yet fully decided where to go. Believe me, dear Prof. Bergson, with cordialest regards, yours very sincerely,

WM. JAMES

James did not carry out his plan of crossing to the Continent in June, but remained in England, dividing his time between sight-seeing and visits to various friends.

Rye, July 19, 1908

Dear Professor Bergson, —

I have left you a long time without communication, but having now reached a temporary position of equilibrium at my brother's house, I can resume the thread of my more habitual and normal existence, and begin to think and write letters instead of looking at scenery and talking exclusively with persons more or less strangers. I have enjoyed myself, but am profoundly fatigued. You wrote of the possibility of coming to England in July. I, on my part, have made a half engagement to spend a couple of weeks in C. A. Strong's company at Glion on Lake Leman, beginning on the first of August. I naturally still wish to see you, and since in my own case nothing is fixed irrevocably, I now write to ask whether your own plans are fixed, and whether you are to be in England before August, or failing that, where *in the natural course of events* you are to be. On the whole *I* should rather avoid Paris just now; but if you yourself were going to the country in France, I might possibly join you, and even more easily if you were going to Switzerland. Pray let me know at the above address.

Meanwhile I am sending you an (uncorrected) proof of my lecture on Henri Bergson since the book will not appear until next April. I add to it the lecture which precedes it, and half of that which follows, in order that you may appreciate the context and connection in which I make use of your authority. You may keep these proofs and read them at your leisure. You see that I suppress almost all of your philosophy for the sake of emphasizing all the more your critique of intellectualism, which was the point my own lectures were chiefly concerned with. I have very likely misinterpreted you somehow — tell me if I have! — and believe me, faithfully and gratefully yours,

WM. JAMES

Chaumont-sur-Neuchâtel, July 23, 1908

Dear Professor James, —

I must tell you at once the great joy which it has given me to read you. Never have I been in this way fathomed, understood, penetrated. Never have I been so aware of the sympathy and of the sort of "preëstablished harmony" which brings your thought and mine into accord. Let me add that you have not confined yourself to analyzing my ideas; you have transfigured them, without ever in any way disfiguring them. I kept thinking, while reading your exposition of my theses, of those superb reproductions which the masters of engraving have derived from pictures which in themselves were sometimes quite ordinary.

Throughout your fifth lecture and the beginning of the seventh, as well as in the last pages of the chapter devoted to me, I believe that I perceive the essential idea of your book, — an idea important above all others, which will dissipate the difficulties which have been accumulated by philosophers around the question of the relation of the parts of experience to experience as a whole. I hope soon to be able to read the whole of this book, which will form the connecting link between the *Principles of Psychology* and the *Varieties of Religious Experience,* and at the same time give definite shape to the philosophy to which pragmatism seems to point, — a philosophy destined, beyond any doubt, to supersede the old metaphysical dogmatism.

We have finally decided to postpone our visit to London to the first fortnight of October. For the moment we are established in Switzerland, at Chaumont, above Neuchâtel, in a chalet far away in the mountains. Here we shall remain until about the 8th or 10th of September; then we shall go and spend three weeks in Italy, from which we shall betake ourselves directly to London. If you decide to come and pass a part of the month of August in Switzerland I hope that I may be able to meet you there. From where I am it is very difficult to go all the way to Glion — the coach, the trains and the *funiculaire* make bad connections — but we could, if it were not too inconvenient for you, arrange a rendezvous at Ouchy-Lausanne on the shore of Lake Geneva. Perhaps Strong would like to come with you. It is true that from Territet-Glion to Ouchy takes an hour and a half by boat, and I dare not ask you to make this comparatively long crossing. But if the weather were fine you would perhaps not find this trip on the lake disagreeable; I could easily reach Ouchy toward the middle of the afternoon, and if you reached there on your part by the four-thirty boat we would have an hour or an hour and a half to talk together in the garden of the Hôtel Beau-Rivage. And I shall refrain from engaging you in a philosophical "interview"; — they must have pestered and fatigued you enough for the last two months. But I shall be truly happy to see you again before you once more leave Europe, and to thank you besides by the spoken word for the admirable study which you have just devoted to me. Believe me, dear Professor James, etc.,

H. BERGSON

Rye, July 28, 1908[3]

Dear Bergson, —

(Can't we cease "Professor"-ing each other? — that title establishes a "disjunctive relation" between man and man, and our relation should be "endosmotic" socially as well as intellectually, I think.) *Jacta est alea,* I am not to go to Switzerland! I find, after a week or more here, that the monotony and simplification is doing my nervous centres so much good, that my wife has decided to go off with our daughter to Geneva, and to leave me alone with my brother here, for repairs. It is a great disappointment in other ways than in not seeing you, but I know that it is best. Perhaps later in the season the *Zusammenkunft* may take place, for nothing is decided beyond the next three weeks.

Meanwhile let me say how rarely delighted your letter made me. There are many points in your philosophy which I don't yet grasp, but I have seemed to myself to understand your anti-intellectualistic campaign very clearly, and that I have really done it so well in your opinion makes me proud. I am sending your letter to Strong, partly out of vanity, partly because of your reference to him. It does seem to me that philosophy is turning towards a new orientation. Are you a reader of Fechner? I wish that you would read his *Zend-Avesta,* which in the second edition (1904, I think) is better printed and much easier to read than it looks at the first glance. He seems to me of the real race of prophets, and I cannot help thinking that *you,* in particular, if not already acquainted with this book, would find it very stimulating and suggestive. His day, I fancy, is yet to come. I will write no more now, but merely express my regret (and hope) and sign myself, yours most warmly and sincerely,

WM. JAMES

[3] Reprinted from *L.W.J.,* II, 308–9.

Instead of going to Switzerland James visited Belgium and Holland, spent three days in Paris, and returned to London. There the long-deferred meeting took place on October 4, two days before James sailed for home. He wrote to Bergson on the evening of the same day: —

London, Oct. 4, 1908 [4]

Dear Bergson, —

My brother was sorry that you could n't come. He wishes me to say that he is returning to Rye the day after tomorrow, and is so engaged tomorrow that he will postpone the pleasure of meeting you to some future opportunity.

I need hardly repeat how much I enjoyed our talk today. You must take care of yourself and economize all your energies for your own creative work. I want very much to see what you will have to say on the *Substanzbegriff!* Why should life be so short? I wish that you and I and Strong and Flournoy and [William] McDougall and Ward could live on some mountain-top for a month, together, and whenever we got tired of philosophizing, calm our minds by taking refuge in the scenery. Always truly yours,

WM. JAMES

A further record of this interview is contained in James's letter to Flournoy of the same date. Speaking of the various philosophers whom he had been seeing in Oxford and London, he said: "The best of all these meetings has been one of three hours this very morning with Bergson, who is here visiting his relatives. So modest and unpretending a man, but such a genius intellectually! We talked very easily together, or rather *he* talked easily, for he talked much more than I did; and although I can't say that I follow the folds of his system much more clearly than I did before, he has made some points much plainer. I have the strongest suspicions that the tendency which he has brought to a focus will end by prevailing, and that the present epoch will be a sort of turning-point in the history of philosophy. So many things converge towards an anti-rationalistic crystallization. *Qui vivra verra!*" [5]

[4] Reprinted from *L.W.J.*, II, 315.
[5] *L.W.J.*, II, 314–5.

Paris, Jan. 21, 1909

Dear William James, —

I have delayed replying to the letter in which you spoke to me of M. Mitchell's translation; I wanted first to come to an understanding with M. Pogson, who is at this moment translating the *Données immédiates de la conscience,* and who was to have proceeded from that to the *Évolution créatrice.* Since M. Mitchell has already translated this last book, and since you are satisfied with the part of his work that you have read, he is the one that should have the preference. M. Pogson tells me that he is of the same opinion. I am writing to M. Mitchell this very day that things will work out in this way very well.[6] Thanks for your kind assistance in the matter. Indeed your Oxford lectures may have given M. Pogson the idea of translating me.

I have been so busy since my return that I have not yet been able to read Fechner's *Zend-Avesta,* of which you spoke to me in London; I shall apply myself to this study as soon as I am a little freer. But I have had a foretaste of it, the last day or so, from reading your fine article in the *Hibbert Journal.* This hypothesis of an Earth-Soul, which will perhaps seem arbitrary to many people, is in reality the hypothesis which hugs the facts most closely, since it imputes nothing to the cause but what is strictly needed in order to produce the ascertained effects. The really arbitrary thing is to pass immediately from these effects to an infinite cause which is neither commensurable nor in contact with them. You have indicated this so well in your article, and enveloped it all in such seductive poetry, that I am now afraid of being disappointed when I read Fechner himself. Your conception of beings intermediate between man and God seems to me one of those which will come to play a more and more dominating rôle in philosophy. Believe me, I beg you, dear Professor James, etc.,

H. BERGSON

Paris, April 9, 1909

Dear William James, —

I am writing you a hasty word (letters for America must be mailed immediately) simply to tell you of the great pleasure it has given me to read your article in the *Hibbert Journal.*[7] It has

---

[6] Arthur Mitchell's translation, *Creative Evolution,* appeared in 1911.
[7] "The Philosophy of Bergson," VII² (1909).

just come. I was already acquainted with it from the proofs which you were good enough to send me; but it rejoiced me intensely to read again this truly magisterial exposition of the governing idea of my work. That is indeed what I thought; but how I would like to have said it in that way! And how much the idea gains from the original thinking with which you have surrounded and supported it! Thank you, once more. Believe me, I beg you, dear William James, etc.,

H. BERGSON

Paris, April 30, 1909

Dear William James, —

I awaited your new book with impatience, and I thank you for sending it to me. It is an admirable book, which I shall reproach only for being far too modest and for putting forward the names of Fechner and Bergson, when it is with William James — with the word, the thought and the very soul of William James — that we have to do. The book says many things, but it suggests still more than it says. It defines and justifies pluralism, it enables us to place the finger on the concrete relation of beings one with another, it definitely lays the foundations of "radical empiricism"; this is what it *says*. But it suggests something beyond that, — a certain consoling emotion drawn from the very heart of reality. You speak, in your conclusion, of those "saving experiences" which some souls have been privileged to enjoy; unless I deceive myself, your book, combined with the *Varieties of Religious Experience,* will generalize experiences of this sort, introducing them among those who had no idea of them, or developing them where they exist only in a nascent state. That is where the religion of to-morrow is to be found, and the philosophy of to-morrow likewise. . . . This is why your work seems to me destined to have "far-reaching" and profound consequences. But these effects will be produced, no doubt, only gradually. It will be necessary to give the prejudices of the religious mind, and those of the philosophical mind, time to wear themselves out, the one being as tenacious as the other.

I could very well reconcile my conception of the *"élan vital"* with the doctrine of the "Earth-Soul," on condition, however, that one consider the solar system as a whole rather than our planet by itself. On the other hand, that the past is conserved wholly, and that it is conserved automatically, is what experience seems to me to show; for the impartial analysis of pathological as well as normal facts appears to me to reveal the impossibility of the brain's storing up memories. It follows that the memories must conserve themselves.

There are many other points on which your book has set me to thinking. I will speak of them another time. At the moment I can speak only of the impression that the work has made on me. I look forward to having some days of leisure when I can reread at one stroke, one after the other, your last three volumes. My impression of them will then, no doubt, become more *formulable*. But it cannot be more profound. Be assured, dear William James, of my feelings of great admiration, etc.,

H. BERGSON

A Pluralistic Universe was followed soon by *The Meaning of Truth,* which Bergson acknowledged as follows: —

Paris, Oct. 28, 1909

My dear James, —

I am eager to thank you at once for this new book, equally as interesting as its predecessors, written with the same charm of style, and destined to clarify definitively those points of your doctrine that have been most persistently misunderstood. I have already read the greater part of these studies as separate articles; not, however, the first, which has such great importance from the point of view of the genesis of pragmatism, and builds a bridge between your psychology and your philosophy.[8] But it seems to me that when combined they lend one another mutual support and go off together like a single shot. What appears to me to stand out in the book as a whole is chiefly the very clear distinction between reality and truth; — and in consequence the possibility, and almost the necessity, that the pragmatist should be at the same time a realist. It is not to be wondered at that people should have so much trouble understanding this; all our habits of mind, and our habits of speech as well, work in the opposite direction, no doubt because they are both formed in the Platonic mould. When once we have

[8] "The Function of Cognition."

represented to ourselves a world of *things,* we cannot help considering truth as constituted by the set of all the love-matches which
cause these things (or these ideas) to be coupled forever; — so as
to make reality and truth terms of the same order. Much time
will be required to dissipate this mirage completely. It will be
required all the more because people picture pragmatism *a priori*
(I do not know why) as something that must necessarily be simple,
something that it should be possible to sum up in a formula. I
ceaselessly repeat, on the contrary, that pragmatism is one of the
most subtle and *nuancées* doctrines that have ever appeared in
philosophy (just because this doctrine reinstates truth in the flux
of experience), and one is sure to go wrong if one speaks of pragmatism before having read you *as a whole.* . . . Once more, in
haste, all my compliments. Believe me, etc.,

H. Bergson

Early in 1910 James published his popular address on "The Moral
Equivalent of War," and an article [9] in which he described four
peculiar experiences of his own "within the last five years,"
which he thought might throw light on mysticism. In all of these
experiences, three developing from reminiscence and the fourth
from dreams, there seemed to be a sudden "uncovering" of hidden
tracts of reality, continuous with, but lying beyond, the subject's
normal world.

Paris, March 31, 1910

My dear James, —

I hope that you have accepted the invitation which Boutroux
brought to you from the University of Paris, and that we shall
soon see you in France. If, as I hope, it is for this spring or
summer, will you kindly let me know, at least approximately, the
date of your arrival? I shall not fail to be in Paris at the time
you designate.

I have not yet told you how much I enjoyed reading your two
articles: "The Moral Equivalent of War" and "A Suggestion about
Mysticism." The former is certainly the finest and most persuasive
thing that has been said concerning the non-necessity of war, and
concerning the conditions under which it would be possible to

[9] "A Suggestion about Mysticism," *Jour. of Philos.,* VII (1910).

abolish it without thereby diminishing human energy. As to your article on mysticism, it will, I am sure, be the point of departure for much fresh observation and research. I am not sure that I have ever experienced an "uncovering" myself, but perhaps there was something of the kind in the following phenomenon which I have sometimes (though rarely) experienced in dreaming. I believed that I was present at a superb spectacle, — generally a vision of an intensely colored landscape through which I was travelling at great speed, and which gave me so profound an impression of reality that I could not believe, for the first few moments of waking, that it had been a mere dream. Indeed, during the very short time that the dream seemed to last (two or three seconds at most) I had each time the very clear feeling that I was about to have a *dangerous* experience, that it depended on me to prolong it and to learn the sequel, but that something was stretching and swelling in me more and more and would burst if I did not relieve the situation by waking up. And upon waking I had at the same time both a feeling of regret to have had such a dream interrupted and a perfectly clear sense that it was I who had willed its interruption. I give you this experience for what it is worth! It has, perhaps, some relation with yours in so far as it suggests the idea of a momentary extension of the field of consciousness, — due, however, to an intense effort. How I wish that you would pursue further this study of "the noetic value of abnormal states." Your article, taken together with what you have said in the *Varieties of Religious Experience,* opens up great perspectives in that direction. *A bientôt,* I hope. Affectionately and devotedly yours,

H. BERGSON

In the spring of 1910 James again turned his face towards Europe, being moved chiefly by concern for his brother's health. When he received the above letter he was already in Europe and wrote the following postal from his brother's house at Rye: —

Rye, April 20, 1910

Many thanks for yours of March 31st, just forwarded hither from Cambridge. We reach Paris between May 1st and May 15th — impossible to fix date now. I shall have largely to abstain from

social activities, so pray don't think of invitations on my account!!
I will write again as soon as our plans are more settled.

W. J.

James arrived in Paris May 5, and lunched with Bergson on two occasions, meeting Strong and Édouard Le Roy. On May 17 he left for Nauheim, and while there received from Bergson the manuscript of an article which he was asked to transmit to the *Journal of Philosophy* in New York. In April this *Journal* had published an article by W. B. Pitkin entitled "James and Bergson: or, Who Is against Intellect?" in which the writer had taken exception to James's exposition of Bergson; citing texts to prove that Bergson was in fact the friend and not the enemy of the intellect, and that James had therefore unlawfully claimed his support. Bergson now wrote that as regards "a certain theory of *concepts,* and of the place occupied by intelligence in the *ensemble* of reality," James and he were in full accord. "On all that, he has said exactly what I think. I would like to have said it as well." [10] The misunderstanding arose from the fact that while both philosophers were anti-intellectualistic, they also understood the necessity of providing a positive as well as a negative interpretation of this doctrine. It is an important feature of the world that it should have given birth to the intellect, and that for those who live in it the intellect should be practically indispensable. It is always possible to find pro-intellectualistic passages in the one writer to contrast with anti-intellectualistic passages in the other. But for both the central problem was to reconcile the partial truth of conceptual knowledge with the fuller truth of immediacy. It might be said that their very integrity and seriousness of purpose as philosophers lay in their acceptance of responsibility for this problem.

In June 1911, ten months after James's death, Bergson wrote to Mrs. William James that he had just reread all of her husband's recent works in order to prepare himself for the writing of the Introduction to the French translation of the *Pragmatism*. He added that while he had attempted to write of James quite impersonally, he could not avoid betraying something of the peculiar feeling which he had for his memory.

[10] *Jour. of Philos.,* VII (1910), 385, 388.

To this Introduction Bergson gave the title of "Truth and Reality," and, as this title suggests, he was primarily concerned to show that pragmatism was — in its implications, if not in its explicit affirmations — a metaphysics. It implies that reality is "redundant and superabundant," differing from the simplified systems of philosophy and common sense, as life in all its fecundity and irrelevance differs from the selected and unified representations of it on the stage. The origin and inspiration of pragmatism is to be found, says Bergson, in this notion of a reality in which man *participates* — a reality whose nature is revealed to him only when he feels it flowing through his veins, or whose deeper currents he detects in the transports of the mystical experience. Pragmatism is the theory of truth suitable to such a metaphysics. Common and traditional theories suppose that truth is "there" to be extracted like a nut from its shell — a sort of logical armature supporting the posture of the universe. On the contrary assumption, — that reality is flowing, — truth is an aid to action, a guiding thread by which man finds his way and keeps his footing in the midst of perceptual novelty. While for other philosophies truth is a "discovery," for pragmatism it is an "invention." Like any technological device, it depends on the properties of nature, but it is none the less a creation of the human mind. Or, to change the figure, truth is a "route" which man takes in traversing nature: the route must conform to nature, but so far as nature is concerned other routes might equally well have been discovered, laid out, and followed. When routes are once established they constitute those general characteristics of the human mind which make up common sense, or which philosophers call "the categories." The routes of truth differ in the *degree* to which they conform to nature. Contrary to the common impression, the truths of exact science are peculiarly arbitrary. Like the steamer, they take short cuts of their own; while the truths of feeling and sense, like the course of the sailing vessel, coincide more nearly with the prevailing winds and tides.

With this doctrine of truth, as well as with its complementary metaphysics, Bergson was broadly in agreement — and he testified to its profundity, originality, and moral elevation. The vulgar disparagement of pragmatism as skeptical or utilitarian, he said, can only *astonish* those who have known James himself; for no one ever loved truth more ardently or sought it more persistently and self-forgetfully.[11]

In the Preface which Bergson wrote a dozen years later for the French translation of James's letters,[12] he revealed the vividness of his recollection and the depth of his personal understanding. He recognized (as he was so eminently qualified to do) the concrete and sympathetic quality of James's metaphysical vision, and the extent to which this was related to his artistic genius. He saw behind all of James's diversity of interest and doctrine a passion for metaphysical truth, and an image of reality which revealed itself steadily and with increasing clearness. He said of the man himself: "Un foyer ardent était là, dont on recevait chaleur et lumière." [13] This "foyer" is still radiant, in France as well as in America.

The affection and esteem which united James and Bergson provide a remarkable example of friendship without submergence of individual differences. Each paid homage to the other, but without loss of independence or of separate fame. They discovered their doctrinal agreement and their deep personal affinity with no suggestion whatsoever of rivalry, but with a grateful sense of confirmation and a strengthened hope that the truth might prevail.

[11] W. James, *Le Pragmatisme*, trans. by E. le Brun, 1911, 1–16.
[12] *W.J., Extraits de sa Correspondance*, 1924.
[13] *Op. cit.,* 7.

LXXXVIII

BRADLEY AND WARD

F. H. BRADLEY, as we have seen, was continuously interested in the development of James's thought. To James, Bradley was a highly respected and greatly admired proponent of the false doctrine of the Absolute. The correspondence (of which only Bradley's part has been preserved) turns from pragmatism to James's later metaphysics with the following letter on radical empiricism: —

Ilfracombe, Nov. 25, 1904

Dear James, —

Many thanks for your article on "Pure Experience." I have just read both it and the one called "Does Consciousness Exist?" with what intelligence I at present have, which is not much. . . .

What I think is a misfortune both here and in the article on "Humanism" is that you say so much about the neo-Kantian Absolute. I should say myself that there are very few persons indeed who believe it and who understand it as you understand it. Most of us understand it in an opposite sense, — at least I should say so. The result of this may be that less weight may be given to what you have to say than ought to be given to it. After all, even if the Absolute is everything you say it is, the real question is whether your view is able to maintain itself. It seems to me a pity that you should run the risk of getting your views ignored, or rejected summarily, by making assertions or assumptions about what many of us hold, which leave us in wonder. . . . Your idea of the Absolute seems to be something external, trans-phenomenal, — something brought in to serve as a bridge, and to conjoin the separate; something, again, not interested in differentiation, but only in unity. Say the opposite and you will say what *most* of us hold, or at least *think* we hold about the Absolute. . . . Yours truly,

F. H. BRADLEY

The following letters deal with *A Pluralistic Universe,* first the "Fechner" article as it appeared in the *Hibbert Journal,* and then the whole book.

St. Raphaël, Feb. 3, 1909

Dear Professor James, —

I have just been reading your paper on Fechner, which I find very interesting. I don't suppose that people are very likely now to read the *Zend-Avesta* much, but I am sure you are right in thinking that it would do them good to do so. You may possibly remember that I told you that Fechner had influenced me to some extent, and that I had referred to him. I find, on looking, that it is on p. 271 of my book.[1] Where I was influenced by him was that he acted in opposition to the too "humanistic" view of the world which I should say prevails in Hegel; — I, to be frank, do not think that Fechner's arguments as to the earth soul are worth anything. But as to the unlimited possibilities of non-human organic life, I found him conclusive; and you will, I think, see that I have used him as well as referred to him. I do not see how we are to show that there are beings higher than men, and I could not urge this positively. But as to the indefinite possibility of such beings I think I was clear. . . . Don't answer this. I hope you do well. Yours truly,

F. H. Bradley

Isle of Wight, May 14, 1909

Dear James, —

I have now read the book you so kindly sent me. I have read it with interest and pleasure, and among other things which please me is the discovery that we are much more in agreement than I imagined. At least so it seems to me. I am going to write down some things which have occurred to me, on the understanding that they are not an invitation to controversy, but simply for you to read and find useless or not as it may be. . . .

I want first to point out that (as I think) you have not been fair to the other side.

(1) You speak often as if for a pantheistic monism the higher was only a witness or spectator of the lower. This is true of *some* monists, but only of some surely. Take Hegel's view of Ob-

---

[1] *Appearance and Reality,* 1893.

jective Mind. Can it for one moment be supposed that with Hegel the state was only a *witness* of its citizens, and not also their substance and will?

(2) This applies to *intermediate* wholes between the individual and the Absolute. Anyone who does *not* accept these is in conflict with Hegelianism. What's wrong with Hegel (as *I* think) is his exclusive *humanism*.

(3) *The continuity of the given*. The denial of this is surely not part of the monist's position. Green's views (whatever they were) are *his* views. Green was in my opinion no Hegelian, and in some respects was anti-Hegelian even. Now as for what is given being continuous, *I* have supposed that to be Hegel's view. I have myself now long ago advocated it, believing it to be his, though I don't say exclusively his. Last winter I read two of Bergson's books. *Données immédiates* and *Évolution créatrice;* and though I found much to admire, I myself was rather *bored* by his insistence on certain points. *"Connu"* is what I kept saying to myself. Generally, then, I think your case would be stronger and not weaker, if, instead of saying "Fechner and Bergson are the friends — *not* Hegel," you said, *"and even Hegel,* up to a certain point." . . .

The doubt is whether you are not a kind of loose monist and also a dualist. I do not see how your readers can decide. They would want information as to God's "other," how this stands to God and in what kind of whole, if a whole at all.[2] . . . You claim certain practical advantages for your view. God is finite. The moral struggle is the last truth, etc. Of course I see what you get, but what I think you *don't* see is the price at which you buy it. . . . It seems to me that you have taken up with something like Manichæanism, and that Christianity is given up. I mention this because you assume that Christian theology only objects to God's finiteness on metaphysical grounds. But the objection is intensely practical. Christianity says that if I trust in God he will in some sense see me through. "Nothing," it says, "can pluck me out of my Father's hand." But if, as you say, my Father's power is limited, and you can't say exactly how far it is limited, that would appear to be bunkum. Of course in any case my moral duty is the same.

[2] For James's view that God is finite and therefore in relation to something "other" than himself, *cf. P.U.*, 24, 111, 312, etc.

I must stand by my Father, sink or swim. Certainly. But this is *not* Christianity. This is good Stoicism. "Victrix causa deis placuit," etc. I am not myself an orthodox Christian, — far from it. But I wonder that you don't see that here you are going back on Christianity. The question whether it is back to something higher or lower you don't discuss. *I* think to something lower. But then *I* am prepared for the higher doctrine in religion being more glaringly inconsistent. *You as a pragmatist* stand out for theoretical consistency!! Not that you really get it, — and if you *did??* But *I* am only a poor intellectualist. (I don't *mind* being called that. Not in the least. It only seems to me very funny. And I know you don't mind an occasional gibe.)

I am (to pass from that) very glad to learn . . . that I have been totally mistaken as to your view on liberty.[3] Of course if I had known you meant *that,* I would, instead of criticizing you, have supported you to the best of my endeavor. But how was I to know that *this* was what you meant by chance? I wish you would read a part of my *Ethical Studies,* in the first chapter and the appendices thereto. It seems to me that we now say much the same thing, and if I said it then (1876), so much the better. Renouvier is only a name to me. I was following Hegel and Erdmann here,[4] but how closely I now cannot remember. . . .

I expect to go to Oxford at Whitsuntide. There are things I want to do, but I cannot get on and time does not wait. However, I have used up a good deal of my old notes now, God be praised. What vexes one is the idea that what one *has* done should be lost. As to what one has *not* done — that seems to matter little. It is one's own individuality one wants to assert, I suppose. Please excuse the length of this letter. It would take an octavo volume to answer the questions it raises. So let it be the volume — in print. My best wishes. Yours truly,

F. H. BRADLEY

The next letter contains Bradley's comment on *The Meaning of Truth,* in which James had taken up the cudgels for "humanism" against Bradley,[5] and stressed the realistic presuppositions of prag-

---

[3] "The only 'free will' I have ever thought of defending is the character of novelty in fresh activity-situations." (*P.U.,* 391, note.)

[4] Bradley refers to Johann E. Erdmann, *Grundriss der Psychologie,* 1873, p. 124, Section 160.

[5] *M.T.,* Ch. III.

James Ward, 1896

F. H. Bradley, about 1910

Portrait by R. Grenville Eves

matism. It was to this explicit affirmation of realism that Bradley the idealist took exception.[6]

St. Raphaël, Jan. 2, 1910

Dear James, —

I have now read your book and I write mainly to thank you for it. I have not understood your position, and, if I were asked to write a review of the book, I should decline, not only because I never do review books, but also because I could not do justice to your work. But I feel that it has been of use to me, and I cannot think that there is anyone to whom it would not be of use. And, though that is not all that you want, I am sure that you will think it is much. What I mean (to speak merely of myself) is this, that, though I think I *can* answer the questions you have raised, I don't think that I ever have answered them explicitly, and that to answer them explicitly is necessary. I hope I may be able to attempt to do this, *not* in the form of a criticism of yourself. But perhaps I shall not be able.

I think that I now understand your position less than ever. . . . I begin to wonder if I am not asked by you to start with assuming as true a sort of common-sense realism, and to swallow without demur all the difficulties which belong to it. Of course I cannot do this. Of course I hold that since Hegel the thing in itself has been exploded, and that for me knowledge or belief beyond experience is impossible. And yet you seem to me now to ask me to agree that the contrary is true. You seem (*e.g.*) to ask me to believe in a real past fact independent of present experience. Of course I reject such a thing. Of course I at once ask you how, even if it existed, you could know that it existed and get it into your mind. . . . You seem to offer me nothing but what I reject as exploded nonsense. And you even seem to think that I must accept it. . . .

I now pass to another point, — that of possibility. It has been pointed out again and again that Mill, Bain, and the whole school of English empiricism (in order to seem plausible) have to identity the possible and the actual, and do this in a wholly uncritical man-

<hr>

[6] Bradley had already criticized James on this score; *cf.* above, 489. At the same time Strong and others were complaining that James was not realistic *enough!*

ner. Now I don't say that you do this also, but I cannot understand you in any other sense. . . .

I *think* that you *do* admit theoretical activity as more than a mere means to something else, but I am not *sure,* because I cannot understand, if so, some of the language which you have used elsewhere. And Dewey seems clearly, if so, to differ in principle. But, however that may be, what I miss is a statement as to the position of the theoretical test. May I, or may I not, accept as true an idea which is inconsistent with itself? May I put general "working" first, and "consistency" second, or not? You may remember that I have asked this question before. It really is a burning and very practical one in daily life. . . .

What I want to say is that I have found your book interesting, and am sure that it will do good, even if it fails to make converts, — which perhaps after all is a far lesser good. You won't think, I hope, for a moment that those who are not converts fail to appreciate in some sense and to value your work. We all hope that you will have sufficient health and strength to go on for many years working out your views and removing our stagnation, — to put it at the very lowest. Yours truly,

F. H. BRADLEY

In October 1909, Bradley had summed up his philosophical position [7] in a form that excited James's admiration and led him to comment on the extraordinary likeness-in-difference between Bradley and Bergson. Both found the real unity of things in that aspect of wholeness which they present to feeling, and both laid bare the inadequacies of conceptual knowledge. But when it came to their final philosophical creed they parted company, Bergson pursuing the way of empiricism and mysticism, with their reliance on immediacy, while Bradley pursued the way of rationalism — affirming by an act of heroic but gratuitous faith that a promised land of intuition lay somewhere beyond the barren wilderness of conceptual thought. If, says James, Bradley would only follow his own lights, and unite forces with Bergson, the two of them could lay the ghost of rationalism forever.[8]

To which Bradley made no public reply except to credit Hegel (!)

[7] "Coherence and Contradiction," *Mind, N.S.,* XVIII (1909).
[8] "Bradley or Bergson?" *Jour. of Philos.,* VII (1910); *C.E.R.,* 491–9.

with the discovery that unity is given in immediate experience.[9] But James had sent him the proof, and received the following comment: —

St. Raphaël, Jan. 4, 1910

Dear James, —

Many thanks for your letter and for the proof just sent on here. As for taking offence, how could I do so — even if I wished to do so? But as for writing a reply, I don't know what to say. I explained to you that I feel very uncertain as to what the issue is, and still feel the same uncertainty. I do not understand sufficiently the character of the alternatives, advocated by yourself and Bergson, to say anything about it. And, secondly, I think there must have been some misapprehension as to what my point of view is, — though here again I don't feel at all clear. What I have urged is that so far is the Absolute from being useless, that it is our criterion of true and false and generally of better and worse. I don't see how I could have committed myself to this more definitely. . . .

As things are, I see little use in my writing a reply to the effect that I am misunderstood, — so far as I see. The more I see of controversy the lower opinion I have of it. And, as to being misunderstood, anyone can write and complain of that. The reader usually, I think, concludes that the person who complains is in the wrong. . . .

However, I will keep the thing in mind, and in any case I send you my best thanks for the offer and for your eulogism of myself, which, believe me, I value. Yours truly,

F. H. Bradley

P.S. I don't think the fastening together of an originally discrete datum is really Hegelian. I think myself that Hegel is far more on your side.

It is a pity that the letter which provoked the following reply has not been preserved, but its contents can be surmised. That a correspondence conducted with so much good will should end on a note of futility is disappointing, but not without its bearing on the nature of philosophical discussion.

[9] "A Disclaimer," *Jour. of Philos.*, VII (1910).

Jan. 28, 1910

Dear James, —

Yours to hand. I assure you that I do *not* think that a writer fails to be clear because I fail to understand him. I, unfortunately for myself, have an unsympathetic mind, and I sometimes remember this. As to the angels, perhaps they see that philosophy gets on quite as well by misunderstandings as by anything else. After all, *anything* is better than agreement without real understanding. "More power to your elbow" is the wish of yours truly,

F. H. B.

The Gifford Lectures at the University of Aberdeen were given from 1896 to 1898 by James Ward, of Cambridge University; and in 1899 these lectures were published under the title of *Naturalism and Agnosticism*. This work formed an important part of the reaction against science — or rather against the philosophical *claims* of science — which marked the close of the nineteenth century. Ward and James had been acquainted since 1880, and had corresponded on psychological questions. In *Naturalism and Agnosticism* James found an anti-Spencerian polemic which he could not fail to approve in its argument if not in its length, and an interpretation of science as *merely descriptive,* which was quite in the line of his own thought. On the other hand, James and Ward differed profoundly both in temperament and in origins, so that although in his later work, *The Realm of Ends* (1911), Ward announced himself as a pluralist, the two men really drew little sustenance from one another.

The philosophical, as distinguished from the psychological, correspondence between James and Ward begins with a reply to Ward's approbation of *The Will to Believe*: —

Cambridge, May 13, 1897

Dear Ward (Let's drop our titles!), —

Yours of the third has given me keen pleasure. I did n't expect such praise from you, having in my heathen blindness imagined you as of the more "hard-headed" class. And being as hard-headed as I know you to be, your praise is the most welcome that I have yet received. We must all go to work to counteract the *Absolute One* which has its way so freely in metaphysics, and I hope you'll play your part actively. I suppose your Gifford Lectures will be published. I shall fall on them with avidity. For determinism, the *elements* of the world are all *repetitious*. Apropos of the view that they vary, and statistical results alone are repetitious, do you know the remarkable articles by C. S. Peirce?[10] . . .

Thank you again a thousand times. I find your summarized statement admirable, and am surprised to find how closely my thoughts about faith have simply followed in the steps of yours. My own teacher and inspirer in this line has been Renouvier. Faithfully yours,

WM. JAMES

In 1899 James had sent Ward his *Talks to Teachers,* which the latter had acknowledged: —

Bad-Nauheim, Aug. 4, 1899

My dear Ward, —

Your letter of July 9th, just received here, was most welcome. I never expected any express acknowledgment of my *Talks* book, and am all the more gratified at what you say. I don't "dash off" that kind of stuff, any more than any other kind, but forge it all with *blut und schweiss,* and groans and lamentations to heaven, and vows that I will never start to write anything again. To turn from small things to great, I have read your Gifford Lectures with "palpitating interest." I find it a very irregularly composed book; and, with my own dread task before me, can well appreciate your difficulties and sympathize with your pains. But it is a great book, and if I mistake not, it will be recognized as marking the termination of one stage, and the beginning of another, in English philosophical literature. "Naturalism" or scientificism will linger in the by-ways, but on the highways I don't see how it can survive your *sonnenklar* reduction of the physical categories to an abstract shorthand for descriptive purposes. I think you have spread yourself a little too much on poor Spencer, whose matchless genius for blundering in mechanics, etc., needed not so much breadth of exposure. But you have given the death blow, I verily believe, to all that kind of popular philosophy. Its fibres are broken, and its flower will

[10] "The Doctrine of Necessity Examined," etc., *Monist,* II, III (1891–3).

hereafter wear a withered look.   Some of your figures of speech are tremendously *triftig,* and your best pages have an extraordinary dignity and weight of style.

I wish I could find your constructive part as successfully executed. Of course your vindication of the concrete as the real is glorious. But to me your knitting together of the individual consciousness and the general consciousness is profoundly obscure, and I suspect it of not being clearly carried out.   To my taste you follow the Kantian catchwords too much.   This note is only a reaction of *feeling* on my part.   So rich a book cannot be assimilated at a single reading, and I shall have to do much reading between those covers hereafter.   The whole thing has been a great help to me about my second Gifford course,[11] which in many respects is planned to cover similar ground; though I am an out and out pluralist, and mean to make my fight not so much against the tribe of Spencer as against the neo-Kantian transcendental monists, to whom it seems to me you give too much countenance and comfort.   Seeing you do the Gifford thing so naturally makes me feel that it is a natural thing to do.   My first course is to be a purely objective psychological study of religious sentiments, based on documentary material.

I thank you for your invitation for December, and shall be delighted to accept it — probably Mrs. Ward will include my wife, who is to be with me all the year.   I must reserve a loop-hole for possible backing out at the last moment, in case my unfortunate heart behaves ill. . . .   This regular *Kur* life is a loathsome thing to a "free spirit," but beggars can't be choosers.   "Bent is the tree that should have grown full straight," and the rest of my life must be spent in shirking and dodging things that erstwhile were a proper challenge.   But the book is a man's book!   Always faithfully yours,

WM. JAMES

Martigny (Suisse), Aug. 20, 1899

My dear James, —

. . . *Ars est celare artem,* and perhaps I ought rather to have inferred pains and effort from the light and colloquial style of your

---

[11] The second course, given in 1902, was originally designed to be metaphysical (the first being psychological), but as it turned out the metaphysics was only briefly outlined and postponed to a later work.

Talks: at any rate the result is charmingly fresh. I must look again, when I get home, at your *Will to Believe* and see more exactly wherein your pluralism differs from mine. I have long felt that there will always remain something hopelessly insoluble about the relation of the one and the many, and all existing attempts sacrifice one or other term. Spinoza, for example, the many, and Leibnitz the one. My sympathy is so far with the many . . . that it seems to me reasonable to let no theology tamper with the reality of human freedom. The God of Augustine or Calvin reduces me to a puppet, and seems to be himself the Absolutely Dreary. It seems to me that were I such a being I would fain forego the monotony and the tameness of omniscience and omnipotence in order to know the freshness and the zest of *living.*

But again it seems absurd to regard God as merely one of ourselves, the Supreme One *among* the many. . . . Nor is pantheism any better: God as the sum of the many. . . . We do not advance a hair's breadth towards a true unity this way. We must find God within as well as without, — only so do we advance from "cosmic emotion" to veritable religion. . . . But this God-consciousness is a matter of character and will, depends on singleness of eye, purity of heart, a certain childlikeness. And those who attain to it can only say: "Our wills are ours we know not how. Our wills are ours to make them Thine." To the "child of God" the experience seems certain, the "why" intelligible, but the "how" inexplicable or perhaps absurd; for what meaning is there in my asking how God creates and sustains? The one mystery that does press for solution and threatens to drive us again to pantheism, is the mystery of evil. But this brings up afresh the questions as to the reality of finite initiatives and the insipidity of blank omnipotence, etc.

Referring to my Gifford Lectures, you say, and I am sure you say truly, the "knitting together of the individual consciousness and the general consciousness is profoundly obscure." One or two reviewers have made a like complaint, and others, though seemingly approving, have certainly misunderstood. . . . But I must not forget to say how greatly all the kind things you have said of the book have pleased and encouraged me. . . . Believe me, ever most sincerely yours,

JAMES WARD

There is no evidence that James paid his expected visit to Ward in December 1899, but he saw him from time to time during the long residence abroad occasioned by his illness and by the Gifford Lectures of 1901 and 1902. When these lectures were published (*Varieties of Religious Experience*), they were promptly sent to Ward.

Cambridge [Eng.], July 16, 1902

My dear James, —

I left England in the beginning of June and only returned a few days ago. I found the copy of your Gifford Lectures awaiting me, which you had been kind enough to send. For this many thanks. It has occupied me for the last two or three days from morning till night, and I have read it eagerly — but with very mixed feelings. I agree with much of it thoroughly and from much I dissent altogether. I am with you in what you call "pragmatism" . . . and in regarding personal religious experience as fundamental; also in what you call — not very happily — the crasser form of supernaturalism. I differ from you in your estimate of "transcendental idealism," and most of all as regards the rôle you assign to subliminal consciousness.

I do not, of course, object to your taking the subconscious for granted, but I feel that you go too far in accepting Myers's views as so much "gospel truth." So far as I can see the entire presentative content of subconsciousness is derivative: it consists, as you seem to admit, of memories or suggestions. It would, I think, be substantially true to say: "There is nothing in subconsciousness — in the way of idea, at least — that was not first in consciousness." Religious ideas, then, cannot have originated there: the most that can be said is that they may be transfigured and quickened by emotions that have emerged thence. Subconsciousness may be the source of an illumination inexplicable enough to the subject experiencing it, but it cannot, I think, be a source of revelation. Paul, Luther, Bunyan and the rest were full of religious conceptions consciously acquired. In conversion, and all things else distinctly human, the social medium, the *Zeitgeist,* are indispensable. If so, thought and reflexion are necessary prerequisites of religion, — the rational element is a *sine qua non.* Hence your exposition seems to me a complete topsy-turvy, one more instance of individualism overdone!

The only people to feel at home with your theory would be the thoroughgoing Calvinists, but you are far too Pelagian to suit them in other respects. On the one hand, all seems to turn on the extent to which the subconscious door is open or shut, and here the individual is helpless; but, on the other, you still talk of the *will* to believe: "we and God," you say, "have business with each other; and *in opening ourselves to his influence* our deepest destiny is fulfilled." [12] . . . No doubt the relation of the human and the divine wills is a hard, perhaps a hopeless problem, but without some genuine "synergism" an admitted fact, I don't see how anything worth the name of religion is possible. Yet you seem to make it a matter of enthusiasm in the bad sense, of "obsession" and the like: in fact you seem to bring religion so much into line with what is fundamentally pathological, that if I did not know you better, I should be tempted to regard your whole discourse as a practical joke!

The pluralism of which you give hints . . . only adds to my perplexity, for on that tack it seems more than ever essential to lay stress on individual will and reason. I shall await your new book with interest, and devoutly hope you will have both the health and the leisure to push on with it at once. I have had no tidings of you for some time: if you are still on this side we should be glad to see you. Ever yours sincerely,

JAMES WARD

Chocorua, July 29, 1902

My dear Ward, —

I wish whilst you were writing, that you had vouchsafed a word about your health. I have been troubled about you ever since I saw you last year. I hope that the illness is over, for the world can't afford to lose your services yet. That you should have read my book through so eagerly and felt like inditing four pages of admonition looks as if your cerebral functions were all right. *I am slowly recovering, but the quantitative result is still small.*

As for what you say of my results, I am moved to make a brief comment. I don't accept all Myers's opinions as "gospel truth," quite the reverse. But I think Myers's *problem*, the "exploration of the subliminal," to be the most important definite investigation opened of late in psychology, and I think Myers's way of going at it on the whole admirable. Who has brought together and simplified

[12] *V.R.E.*, 517.

as much as he? Have you seen an obituary article on his relation to psychology by me in the S. P. R. *Proceedings* of last year?

As for the derivative nature of the subliminal, it *certainly* in my view is not entire. The existence of supernormal memory (*vide* Flournoy's case)[13] and supernormal cognitions (*vide* Piper) proves that there *is* a region for exploration, and that Myers's problem is genuinely important. The relation of it all to religion is through mysticism. I *can't* ignore the vital prominence of that sort of experience in the religious life. I have fully admitted the necessary coöperation of intellect in elaborating results, and think you misapprehend me as saying "all feeling and no reason."

But I feel sure that contemplative reason would produce no religion (even with desire to prompt results) unless there were in addition some of these other non-rational intuitive processes to clinch persuasion. The persuasion gets *form* from the *Zeitgeist,* etc. But form depends on where quickening emphasis falls, this gives the perspective and fixes the centre, and those non-rational feelings of reality, and automatic promptings towards certain kinds of life, play the same part in our spiritual experience which sensations do in ordinary affairs. They determine the distribution of our energies, and our reason coöperates in the resultant. I may maximize unduly the non-derivative character of these forces, which you minimize. But if one is on a hunt, it is better not to assume at the start that there is no game, or, you won't get what little there is. Pardon this hasty scrawl.

WM. JAMES

Ward's qualified approval of James's pragmatism has already been recorded.[14] It was in the metaphysical sequel rather than in pragmatism itself that he was interested, and here James persistently sought to bring him into pluralistic partnership with Bergson and himself. In the summer of 1904 Ward had gone to the United States, to teach for the summer session at the University of California, and to give an address at the Congress of Arts and Sciences held in connection with the World's Fair at St. Louis. The address was published in November, under the title of "The Present Prob-

[13] The case of "Mlle. Hélène Smith," described by Flournoy in *Des Indes à la planète Mars,* 1900, and "Nouvelles observations sur un cas de somnambulisme avec glossolalie," *Archives de psychologie,* I (1902).
[14] *Cf.* above, 464–5.

lems of General Psychology";[15] and defended the activity and continuity of mental processes together with their subconscious persistence, against current atomistic and mechanistic views. James found this address "pithy" and "extraordinarily suggestive." "I think," he wrote, "that [with] my notion of pure experience and of cognition, yours of a continuum and of activity, and Bergson's ideas generally . . . an efficient compound can be made."

Writing to Flournoy in the autumn of 1908, he said: "I spent three days at Cambridge, where again I saw James Ward intimately. I prophesy that if he gets his health . . . he will become also a militant pluralist of some sort. I think he has worked out his original monistic-theistic vein and is steering straight towards a 'critical point' where the umbrella will turn inside out, and not go back."[16]

James's eagerness for Ward's support grew stronger with the publication of his own *Pluralistic Universe:* —

Cambridge, March 20, 1909

My dear Ward, —

. . . I expect in three weeks to send you my Oxford lectures and shall be curious to know whether in your eyes there will seem any promise in my attempt at a synechistic solution of the one *vs.* many problem, or if the Bergsonian separation of the immediate flux as containing all life's dynamisms, from our conceptual treatment of it as only a map for practical purposes, seems to you worthy of serious consideration. To me it has been tremendously relieving. . . .

Last summer in the beauty of rural England has made the United States seem sadly decayed and slovenly, and in many human respects 1000 years in arrears. . . . I hope now, having got certain other tasks out of the way, to get at writing (very slowly) my little "Introduction to Philosophy." . . . Believe me, with delicious memories of my visit, yours ever truly,

Wm. James

Cambridge [Eng.], April 12, 1909

My dear James, —

Your little stay with us last autumn was very quickening and refreshing to me, but I never expected you to remember it; for you

[15] *Philos. Rev.*, XIII.
[16] *L.W.J.*, II, 314.

are well in "the swim" and I have long been wholly out of it. . . . I have read your articles in the *Hibbert* and am looking forward with interest to the book, where I hope you will have more to say about Bergson. The thing of his that has interested me most is the section on liberty in the *Données immédiates*. But I cannot get to the bottom of his view of matter. There are no things, he says, only actions . . . and matter and *l'élan de vie* are inverse movements. The one is necessity, the other introduces into it as much liberty as possible.[17] . . . The start, then, is with matter, and *l'élan* is after all not absolutely creative! I hope you are going to interpret this "vision" for the rest of us. . . .

I am glad you have not dropped the idea of that "little introduction to philosophy," but I expect you will find it grows pretty big before you have done it. . . . Anyhow, *prosit!* With many thanks for your good friendly letter, ever yours,

James Ward

At the close of the following letter, devoted to James's *Pluralistic Universe,* there is a modest allusion to Ward's own Gifford Lectures, given in the years 1907–1910, and published under the title of *The Realm of Ends* in 1911.

Cambridge [Eng.], April 28, 1909

My dear James, —

Many thanks for the copy of your last book, which reached me yesterday. As I told you, I was eager to see it and "tackled" it at once.

I find it, as I ought to have expected, but did not — very different from the pluralism that I have tried sympathetically to expound in the first course of my new Gifford Lectures. . . . You call your pluralism "synechistic," and that looks like a contradiction: what you seem to have is muchness rather than manyness. The key to your whole position I find in the lecture on the "Compounding of Consciousness," and here you take as the last truth of things a doctrine that even as psychological has always seemed to me indefensible, because unworkable. . . . *Credat Judæus:* I cannot — no, I cannot for the life of me see how either your views or Bergson's are to work. You talk glibly of conscious experiences *freely*

---

[17] *L'Évolution créatrice,* 1907, 270, 273.

compounding and separating themselves without ever, as Bradley would say, reflecting on the shock that you administer. What is a conscious experience that can freely act at all? You talk of taking reality sensibly, and dropping categories; and then, it seems, it consists not of bits or selves or of anything definite, — it is so complete a flux and fusion that it is impossible to talk of anybody in solid singleness "swimming in it." Verily, my friend, if ever man did, you have *das Kind mit dem Bade ausgeschüttet.*[18]

It has long been a favorite notion of mine that the term "consciousness" is just exactly the most treacherous weapon in the philosophical armoury, but I have never known it serve anybody so badly as it seems to me to have served you. . . . Your consciousness is, so to say, a symmetrical relation, so far comparable to gravity. *E.g.,* you say ". . . Just as we are co-conscious with our own momentary margin, etc." [19] To me and to many this is utter nonsense. When I am conscious of a sensation the sensation is not conscious of me. But I do not say that what you *mean* is nonsense. [No doubt], as Bradley would say, "you are prepared to show that our positive doctrine is wrong, and our negative criticism mistaken." But at least you ought not to ignore them altogether.

I expect before long to meet with an exclamation about your book of this sort: — "We see then at length to what pragmatism leads: there is no soul, and no God, and the world is not rational; what we have is not a universe, but a multiverse like a Dyak's head,[20] and feathers smothered with dust and netted over with cobweb!" . . . But don't imagine that I sympathize with such declamation. I agree with your empiricism in saying that we can't get beyond the many, and a finite God or Gods; I agree with your criticisms of absolutism, but I find difficulties when you offer a solution. . . . Why you as an empiricist insist on thoroughgoing continuity I cannot think. I admit the difficulties in the notion of substantial souls, in the idea of dominant and central monads, and I see many difficulties which you never even mention, but I prefer stopping at the difficulties to advancing to your solution. I don't expect to solve the riddle of the universe, and I prefer to stop and make the most of difficulties rather than slur them over. Bradley has said some hard things about "cheap and easy monisms": I am afraid before I

[18] Thrown out the baby with the bath.
[19] *P.U.,* 289–90.
[20] *Cf.* below, 684–5.

have done I shall have — if I live — to say some hard things about "cheap and easy pluralisms"; but without, I think, giving offence to a thinker whom I sincerely esteem and a man whom I truly love. . . . The pity of it is, for my part, that the two Cambridges are not one place. What a stimulus it would have been to me to have been during all these years within earshot of you, instead of having to do all my thinking in solitude!

Well, I must not inflict any more upon you. But in reading over what I have written I feel I have been too confident and outspoken, and in my eagerness to say out my dissent I have forgotten even to mention the many good things and fine passages that I have noted down as I went along. . . . I too am going to lay great stress on religious experience and on faith; and I have already had a fling at absolutism. If it would not bother you I might send you a copy of the syllabus of my first course, but of course it is very jejune and scrappy. With kindest regards in which my wife joins, believe me ever yours sincerely,

JAMES WARD

Cambridge, May 16, 1909

Dear Ward, —

I have read your letter about my *Pluralistic Universe* over and over again, and do not feel inclined to call it a "tale of little meaning" though assuredly "the words *are* strong." The trouble is that they are too oracular and like Jove's thunder, to let me understand *exactly* how they are meant to apply; and I tremble, but don't fully take in their message. Send me the syllabus; and when I have read that and the public lectures, I shall understand the precision of the objections you feel to Bergson and myself better. I don't yet understand the whole of Bergson myself; though, ravished with his expressions, I always feel, in reading him, that I am *about* to understand him in the next moment — but the next moment still flees! I am getting, in these days, lots of *non-possumus* letters about my book. I seem to myself to "see round" the objections so far urged, very completely, so they only confirm me in my error. But I don't focus on *your* objections well enough to see just how they lie in your mind — I only know that they are something awful! Oh, for a week of leisurely conversation together on some irresponsible hill-slope in the country somewhere! I am sure that you and I *ought* to agree, having so much in common, and could easily come to a much closer understanding — especially if Mrs. Ward were near us! — than we now are near. Meanwhile *pazienza!* Let us both write as much as we can, and by defining and defining, see just where we are in relation to one another. Pray send the syllabus! Affectionate regards to your whole household, and wishes for your health. Yours always truly,

WM. JAMES

St. Andrews, N. B., June 15, 1909

Dear James, —

I delayed answering your last because I found I had no more complete copies of my lecture syllabus, and waited till I could get them here. I am now sending off all there are. . . . Well, I am sorry I frightened you by my vague outbursts anent your "poor *P. U."* . . . Bergson has ideas, just as you have too, and I think the same *Ahnung* is working in you both: it comes out in your pragmatism, and comes out, more clearly perhaps, in Bergson's criticism of what he calls intellectualism. All the worth I see in pragmatism is to be found — don't kick — in Kant, in his "primacy of the practical reason," and in his showing that there is "room for faith." In his notion of an *élan vital* Bergson strains to reach a point beyond this, but I fear he is mystical, perhaps even approximating to the philosophies of the Unconscious. He ought to have more to say. What disturbs me in your views is the Dyak's head, and the tychism — in all this I think you have got out of bounds, and I see no way back. It is the same complete deadlock at the one extreme, that absolutism is at the other. The problem is to *reconcile* the one and the many, not to repudiate either. . . . Ever yours sincerely,

JAMES WARD

Cambridge, June 27, 1909

Dear Ward, —

Your letter, syllabus, and review-clipping are all received. Your syllabus whets my appetite greatly for the whole book. Nobody seems yet to have gone over the whole subject of pluralism as you have done. I thank you for making both the name and the thing so respectable.

Only one word *zur Einverständigung* about "tychism." I think the centre of my whole *Anschauung*, since years ago I read Renouvier, has been the belief that something is doing in the universe, and that *novelty* is real. But so long as I was held by the intellectualist logic of identity, the only form I could give to novelty was tychistic, *i.e.*, I thought that a world in which discrete elements were annihilated, and others created in their place, was the best descriptive account we could give of things; and that if the elements were but minute enough, "scientific determinism" could be kept, as approximating the appearances sufficiently for practical error to be avoided in our dealings with nature's "laws." This sticks in the human crop — none of my students became good tychists! Nor am I one any longer, since Bergson's *synechism* has shown me another way of saving novelty and keeping all the concrete facts of law-in-change. Giving up the logic of identity as the means of understanding the essences of concrete things, we justify the Hegelian tendency, without Hegel's own abominations; we put the world of concepts in its definite and indispensable place; we allow novelty to be, and join hands again with life. Not tychism then, but synechism (if we must talk Greek) is the solution! Yours ever fondly,

WM. JAMES

The gap between the pluralisms of James and Ward remained unbridged, but their personal relations grew in intimacy. The following was dictated by James only two weeks before his death: —

London, Aug. 11, 1910

We have been in England for two months this summer, and the natural order of things would have made me look you up, but I have fallen so acutely ill with cardiac asthma that human intercourse has been impossible. We sail tomorrow for home . . . and I send you all these regretful greetings. Always,

WM. JAMES

Cambridge [Eng.], Aug. 16, 1910

My dear James, —

We were away this summer on Dartmoor, and while there heard from our old friend Graham Wallas of your illness. His impression was that you had gone to Nauheim, and it occurred to us at once that there was some chance of our seeing you on your way homewards. Then came your sad but friendly post card with its "regretful greetings."

Well, all the same we shall "hope for the best" or what we think the best, and if that is not to be — well still. Yours, my dear friend, has been a successful life and surely it has been a happy one, for I know of no one more universally beloved. I, at least, never heard an ill word of you from anyone. And I firmly believe that great things are to come out of "pragmatism" when the *Gährung* is over. "Ehe es einen guten Wein giebt muss der Most sich erst toll ge- bärden." [21] I seem to see clearly that speculation in our day has turned over a new leaf, wherever you have made your mark. . . . Ever yours,

JAMES WARD

[21] "To get a good wine it is necessary that the must should first go mad."

LXXXIX

THE UNFINISHED TASK

WARD's letter reached its destination, but it could scarcely have been read. After landing in Quebec, James was taken directly to his beloved Chocorua, where he sank rapidly and died on August 26, 1910. During the closing year of his life he had experienced a revival of interest in the mystical experience. The "Suggestion about Mysticism" appeared in February 1910. The last of his writings published during his own lifetime was an essay entitled "A Pluralistic Mystic," devoted to an exposition of the philosophy and genius of his old friend Benjamin Paul Blood.

The extraordinary relations of James and Blood have already been followed through the period of pragmatism. We have noted that whatever the immediate occasion, Blood usually contrived to put in a word for the "anæsthetic revelation." For James in his most serious philosophical moments, the mystical experience was justified by perception — the abnormal by the normal. If logic was rejected it was because such a rejection seemed to be warranted by the observable data of everyday immediacy. The mystical experience itself was a dubious oracle, needing credentials, and obtaining such as it had from a speculative psychology of the subconscious. The "noetic value of abnormal mental states" remained an open problem in James's mind.[1] For Blood, on the other hand, the mystical experience was the one trustworthy insight — leaving no doubts, and superseding both philosophy and normal experience. His pluralistic intuitions, in which James delighted, were an effective solvent to the classic monisms; but he had his monistic moods as well. The reconciliation of monism and pluralism, and the escape from all like antitheses and paradoxes, — the only abiding satisfaction of the question "Why?" — were to be found in an abnormal and artificially induced "revelation."

Since Blood was a professing pluralist, his praise of James's Hibbert Lectures was to be expected: —

[1] *C.E.R.,* 513.

Amsterdam, April 24, 1909

My dear Sir, —

Let me thank you for the compliment and courtesy of a copy of the *Pluralistic Universe*. I have read it all — every word. It is delightful — rich — inevitable. . . . All these essays call for the Anæsthetic Revelation, — the insight, that Mystery, THE MYSTERY as such, is the final, the hymnic word. You are tearing reason to pieces, you name it oftenest in quotation marks; you use it pragmatically, and deny it "absolutely," — you can't be beaten — be assured of that; but the Fact remains, and, of course, the Mystery. Good-bye.

PAUL

In the spring of 1910 James was preparing his article for the *Hibbert Journal,* and was planning it as a surprise. He wrote to Blood discreetly from Rye: "I am staying here for a while with my brother, and wish to tell a friend the years in which your 'Lion' and 'Nemesis' poems respectively appeared in *Scribner's Magazine.* Answer me as above, keep hearty, *produce!* and believe me as ever your Wm. James."

The article, "A Pluralistic Mystic," drew upon Blood's letters, and upon the whole of his published writings, philosophical, poetical, and occasional — James having read and collected them for many years. It praises Blood's literary talent and illustrates it with copious citations. More important is the acknowledgment of James's philosophical indebtness. He had evidently found in Blood a confirmation of his own empirical Hegelianism — the discovery in actual experience of the reality of otherness and opposition. Beyond this he found in Blood a *mystical verification of pluralism:* "I confess that the existence of this novel brand of mysticism has made my cowering mood depart. I feel now as if my own pluralism were not without the kind of support which mystical corroboration may confer. Monism can no longer claim to be the only beneficiary of whatever right mysticism may possess to lend *prestige.*"

Blood's philosophy, said James, was "not dissimilar to my own"; and he was willing that Blood's "last word" as a mystic should be *his* last word as a philosopher: "Let *my* last word, then, speaking in the name of intellectual philosophy, be *his* word: — 'There is no conclusion. What has concluded, that we might conclude in regard to it? There are no fortunes to be told, and there is no advice to be given. — Farewell!' " [2]

Sending the article to Blood, James wrote the following explanatory letter: —

Constance, June 25, 1910 [3]

My dear Blood, —

About the time you will receive this, you will also be surprised by receiving the *Hibbert Journal* for July, with an article signed by me, but written mainly by yourself. Tired of waiting for your final synthetic *pronunciamento,* and fearing I might be cut off ere it came, I took time by the forelock, and at the risk of making ducks and drakes of your thought, I resolved to save at any rate some of your rhetoric, and the result is what you see. Forgive! forgive! forgive! It will at any rate have made you famous, for the circulation of the *H. J.* is choice, as well as large (12,000 or more, I'm told), and the print and paper the best ever yet. I seem to have lost the editor's letter, or I would send it to you. He wrote in accepting the article in May, "I have already forty articles accepted, and some of the writers threaten lawsuits for non-publication, yet such was the exquisite refreshment Blood's writing gave me, under the cataract of sawdust in which editorially I live, that I have this day sent the article to the printer. Actions speak louder than words! Blood is simply *great,* and you are to be thanked for having dug him out. L. P. Jacks." Of course I've used you for my own purposes, and probably misused you; but I'm sure you will feel more pleasure than pain, and perhaps write again in the *Hibbert* to set yourself right. You're sure of being printed, whatever you may send. How I wish that I too could write poetry, for pluralism is in its *Sturm und Drang* period, and verse is the only way to express certain things. I've just been taking the "cure" at Nauheim for my unlucky heart — no results so far! Sail for home again on August 12th. . . . Warm regards, fellow pluralist! Yours ever,

WM. JAMES

[2] *M.S.,* 374–5, 411.
[3] Reprinted from *L.W.J.,* II, 347–8.

The *Amsterdam Evening Recorder*,[4] which had evidently been shown James's letter to Blood, suggested that "Benjamin Paul Blood, Esq., of this city," known to Emerson, Tennyson, Stevenson, Story, and Stirling, scarcely needed any "digging out." As to Blood himself, he wrote shortly after James's death that the latter had been cut off before having adequately testified to that mystical revelation whose broken and occasional rays had contributed his "real secret" and "oriented his philosophic vision." He felt that after James's passing the mantle of prophecy fell upon him. He would seek a definitive expression of the great mystical truth. "If I can express it," he continued, . . . "my work will be more than one of the 'books of the week,' for therein the fact may appear that Sinai, Olympus and Calvary were but sacred stepping-stones to this secular elevation, where free thought may range hereafter, when the old scares of superstition shall have vanished to the limbo whence they came." [5] Only four months later he wrote to Mrs. James: "I have finished to my intense satisfaction that expression of anæsthetic revelation which he was so insistent that I should attempt. I sigh that he might have seen it." [6]

While James took a strong interest in mysticism during the last year of his life, this was only one item among the rest. That his interest in current problems was as strong as ever is attested by the writing, and publication in February, of "The Moral Equivalent of War." The serious enterprise of James's last days, however, was the composition of the most technical and carefully reasoned of all his books. It grew, as we have seen, out of his introductory courses at Harvard and Stanford and, under the title of *Some Problems of Philosophy,* was designed to serve as a college textbook having a wide circulation. But it was written for readers, and not for an audience; differing in this respect from all of his philosophical works except *Essays in Radical Empiricism* and *The Meaning of Truth,* and differing from these in being conceived as a unified treatise rather than as a volume of independent articles.

This "Introduction," as James at first called it, was begun on March 28, 1909, and was continued intermittently up to the time

[4] July 23, 1910.
[5] *Springfield Daily Republican,* Oct. 16, 1910.
[6] Feb. 27, 1911. Blood's posthumous work, *Pluriverse* (1920), evidently suggested by James's influence, was not, however, completed until sometime after 1913. The Introduction to this volume, written by the editor, H. M. Kallen, contains an illuminating account of Blood and his philosophy.

of his death.   Parts of the manuscript were read and criticized by his friends in Europe during the summer of 1910.   It was never completed, but James left written instructions to publish it: "Say it is fragmentary and unrevised. . . .   Say that I hoped by it to round out my system, which now is too much like an arch built only on one side." [7]   It was dedicated to "the great Renouvier's memory."   Thus at the end James was faithful to his beginnings.

This volume represents a definite turning away from polemics, popular and literary appeal, mysticism, and flights of imaginative speculation.   Writing to a friend in Germany shortly after the appearance of his article on Blood, he referred to it as "a wonderful *Sturm und Drang* utterance for pluralism," but added, "this . . . will be the last of my *Sturm und Drang* period."   In the summer of 1909 he had written to his old friend Pillon: "I believe that philosophy stands at present at the beginning of a new sort of activity, not unlike that which began with Locke, and which will end by defining (in ways not dreamed of till quite recently) the limits of what the conceptual or logical method can accomplish, and the parts of reality which escape treatment by fixed logical categories or concepts.   I am quite sure that in establishing the inadequacy of concepts, the door will be opened to much vagueness and extravagance, and that possibly something like the excesses of the German romantic school in philosophy may yet be in the order of the day. That will doubtless be a pity, and must be counted to the disadvantage of the movement.   But it gives me very little anxiety, for I think that the final upshot and result will be a greater distinctness and clearness than philosophy has ever seen. . . .   But, dear old friend, neither you nor I will be there!!"

Though James thus predicted the excesses of romanticism and had himself freely indulged them, he now, at the close of his life, writes from a mood of restraint and sobriety.   It is true that he continues to affirm the insufficiency of the logic of identity; but he meets logic on its own ground, and goes far to repudiate that "anti-logicality" which, though he had first claimed it as a merit, he did not suffer gladly when applied as a reproachful epithet by others. The present volume represents, in other words, an effort to anticipate that "greater distinctness and clearness" which James believed would follow the romantic phase of the new philosophy; while at

[7] *S.P.P.*, vii, viii.

the same time it discusses certain specific and traditional topics of metaphysics which the author had heretofore neglected from a desire to promulgate his general point of view.

The first eight chapters follow the syllabus of the Stanford University course of 1906 — in the order of topics, and often verbally. They deal with questions which James has already treated fully elsewhere, such as the distinction between "percepts and concepts"; which is, however, here restated to embrace the final outcome of his dealings with Bergson and Bradley. There must always be a discrepancy between concepts and reality, because the former are static and discontinuous while the latter is dynamic and flowing. The attempt to substitute concepts for reality leads to a whole nest of Bradleyan and other "intellectualistic" difficulties which stand in the way of any positive metaphysics. The failure of conception is made good by perception. Concepts are "real" in their "eternal way," they enter into close union with perception, and they play an important rôle in experience; but they are "secondary . . . imperfect and ministerial." This affirmation of the priority of perception to conception, both genetically and cognitively, is *the tendency known in philosophy as empiricism"*; to which, in the remainder of the book, the author will "hold fast." [8] Empiricism implies particularism, pluralism, and *novelty* — it is at this point that important additions are made to the author's thought.

Freedom had always been one of the cardinal tenets of James's philosophy, and his metaphysics had in this respect always been adapted to his ethics. Thus in *The Will to Believe* he uses the term "chance" to indicate not capriciousness or perversity, but a margin of *indetermination* which might leave room for a decisive act of will.[9] In the important "Syllabus of Philosophy 3" (1902–1903) this theme is resumed, and "tychism" takes the central place in the author's metaphysics. It agrees with the recent tendencies of science, satisfies the moral nature, eliminates the problem of evil, and avoids psychophysical dualism. Tychism is, in short, a name, like "empiricism" or "pluralism," applicable to James's philosophy as a whole, turning up that side of it which proclaims the spontaneity and unexpectedness of things. And already the point is made

[8] *S.P.P.*, 93 ff., 98–101, 106–7. James reiterates his rejection of nominalism and harks back to the view which he had announced as early as 1879; *cf. C.E.R.*, 109–15.
[9] *W.B.*, 153.

that while chance when viewed from without is sheer caprice, it may be "self-sufficing life from within." [10]   Then, in the essay on "The Experience of Activity," reprinted as an appendix to *A Pluralistic Universe,* James disclaims any intention of introducing free will as an agent intruding itself into natural processes *ab extra.*   It means only "the character of novelty in fresh activity-situations." And in another appendix to the same volume he points out that this character of novelty does not "jump abruptly in" — but leaks or filters in so gradually as to leave the sense of continuity undisturbed. Viewed inwardly as a progressive unfolding of novelty, chance is convertible into Bergson's *creative* evolution. [11]

Thus James came to look upon his earliest tychism, with its emphasis on sheer chance, as only a negative form of intellectualism. According to intellectualism, the units of which reality is composed either are or are not identical: determinism says that they are, tychism that they are not.   The paradox of tychism — its odiousness to the philosophic mind — lies in its leaving even adjacent existences in a state of total irrelevance one to another.   When the whole effort of philosophy is to make transitions smooth, tychism makes them harsh.   But once the logic of identity is abandoned, it is permissible to say that two successive events both are and are not identical: the first develops into the second, the second emerges from the first.   There is novelty, but it is a novelty which, when it comes, seems natural and reasonable, like the fulfillment of a tendency.   This notion of a "really growing world" is the general theme of the latter part of the *Problems of Philosophy,* the theme which bound him closely to Bergson, and the theme with which he was increasingly occupied during the last years and months of his life.

The topic of novelty connected itself in James's mind with two of the classic problems of philosophy: first, the paradoxes of infinity and continuity; and second, the nature of causality.   The first of these problems had cost James much labor and anxiety in his earlier years, especially during the time when the influence of Renouvier was at its height.   He had now reached a definite conclusion which was not shaken by the exponents of "the new infinite," to whom he had given close attention. [12]   There was, he thought, no difficulty in

[10] "Syllabus of Philos. 3," I.
[11] *P.U.,* 391; 398–9.
[12] B. Russell, Cantor, Couturat, etc.; *cf. S.P.P.,* Ch. XI.

"the standing infinite." [13]   It means that no matter how long one goes on counting there is always an ulterior unit there to be counted. The amount of the actual counting is not prescribed, and may always be finite.   The difficulty with "the growing infinite" is that it seems to imply an actual infinity of counting.   Thus a moving body, if motion be continuous, must arrive at and pass infinitely many points on its way to any given point M.   We might assume some sort of automatic recording device by which these intermediate points were checked off as they were passed.   Then before the body could reach M it would be obliged to count up to infinity by the enumeration of the positive integers, which is impossible.   So James concluded that motion and change must occur by "drops, buds, steps" — "finite in number and discrete."   This is "the radically pluralist, empiricist, or perceptualist position," which James here adopts "in principle." But when he asks the rhetorical question, "Does reality grow by abrupt increments of novelty, or not?" the answer is that he will resume this question after he has taken up the problem of causation.[14]

The problem of causation has remained unsolved, James thinks, because philosophers have oscillated between the two impossible views that cause and effect are identical and that they are external and mutually exclusive.   This is intellectualism again, with its sharp alternatives and logical antitheses.   If we turn to the *"experience* of activity," on the other hand, we find a "transitive" efficacy, which neither unites cause and effect nor divides them — but carries the one over into the other.   "Rather," he says, "does a whole subsequent field grow continuously out of a whole antecedent field because it seems to yield new being of the nature called for, while the feeling of causality-at-work flavors the entire concrete sequence as salt flavors the water in which it is dissolved." [15]   If we ask whether all causes are of this experiential sort, the answer must depend on how we conceive the relation of mind and body, and on whether we accept or reject the panpsychistic view of the physical world.

Here James stopped.   He promised a discussion, in later chap-

---

[13] Or, in fact, in the standing finite.   A first or last in space or time is perfectly thinkable: it does not require to be limited by something other than itself, but "may be limited by its own termination."   For James's earlier views on infinity, *cf.* above, I, 491, 659, 670, II, 596.

[14] *S.P.P.*, 172, 185, 187–8.

[15] *Ibid.*, 218.

ters, of idealism, of psychophysics, and of Bergson.[16]   These promises were, unhappily, never fulfilled.   Had he fulfilled them some of
the gravest difficulties and doubts which his philosophy raises would
perhaps have been removed.   Is it a neutral stream of "pure" experience, or is it the mental series, which constitutes the metaphysical reality?   How can the physical series be the dynamic series if
cause is identified with activity, and if activity is identified with "the
sense of activity"?   Does reality exist when no individual sentient
being is consciously aware of it?   And if so, in what sense, if any,
can such existence be said to be "experienced"?   These questions
are not answered.

Since James never returned from his excursion into the problems
of infinity and causation to resume the discussion of novelty, one
can only guess at the way in which he would have rounded off the
account.   That he would not have left his "abrupt increments of
novelty" unrelieved is clear.   One may surmise that he would have
described a sequence of happenings in which events occur like strokes
or pulses, with a thrust of their own; but in which they would at the
same time be continuous — in the sense of conjunction or nextness, rather than in the sense of connection.   Their continuity
would not consist in the link between them, but in the *absence* of
any such intermediary.[17]   Being thus in direct contact, they would
be subject to "osmosis."   Event *a* would look forward to, and in
some measure anticipate, *b; b,* when it came, would in some measure
fulfill this anticipation, and look back upon *a.*   The prospect of *a,*
and the retrospect of *b,* would overlap; *a* would be qualified by *b-*
about-to-come, and *b* by *a*-just-past.   This would not contradict
the discrete order of dynamic beats or initiatives: they would begin
apart, and run together.   Nor would the progressive character of
the change contradict the requirements of freedom.   Each event
would come as an unfolding, as something "called-for" or "looked-
for," but would also have in it an element of surprise.   Freedom
would signify this residual "character of novelty in activity-situations." [18]

The "angel of death" did in fact strike James down before he
had said all that he had to say.   Not only was much left unsaid,
but there were many problems that he had neither thought out nor

[16] *Ibid.,* 166, note; 216–7, note; 219, note.
[17] *Ibid.,* 187.
[18] *P.U.,* 391, note.

worked out. When death brought him down he was in full flight. But the nature of James's latest preoccupations and the direction of his latest efforts bear out his own statement: "I think the centre of my whole *Anschauung,* since years ago I read Renouvier, has been the belief that something is doing in the universe, and that *novelty* is real." [19]

His philosophy being so interpreted, there is even a certain propriety in the fact that James's task was unfinished. Writing in 1908, he said, "I 've grown fearfully old in the past year, except 'philosophically,' where I still keep young." Philosophically he did not merely *keep* young — he seemed to grow younger. Certainly at no period of his life was he so curious, so receptive, so ardently speculative, as in his last years. While his philosophical powers grew, — his fertility and his self-confidence, — his universe also grew more complex and more interesting. It was inevitable, therefore, that his last glance should look beyond the horizon and that his last act should be a question rather than an answer.

Early in this study I ventured the judgment that James's philosophy as a whole could be subsumed under the conception of empiricism — provided, of course, I were allowed to define that idea. I believe that that judgment is now justified, and I can only hope that I have not taken too many liberties with the idea. I shall have failed if I have not at the same time created the impression that there is a kind of incongruity in applying any label to James. To oversimplify him would be to offend against the spirit of a philosopher who never objected to a flavored experience as too rich, a public Heaven as too crowded, or a tolerant mind as too promiscuous. He always felt imprisoned by doctrinal limitations, even when he applied them to himself. He undertook to be a rigorously scientific psychologist, and yet he exceeded all of the psychologists of modern times in the frequency of his metaphysical infidelities. If the quarry that he was pursuing fled out of scientific bounds he went after it, with no feeling whatever that he was trespassing. In fact he crossed the line between psychology and philosophy so many times that it was totally obliterated. He called himself empiricist, pluralist, pragmatist, individualist, but whenever he did so he began at once to hanker after the fleshpots of rationalism, monism, intellectualism, socialism. He liked body in his philosophizing, and he

[19] Above, 656.

hated to leave out anything that had either flavor or nutritive value. He was much more afraid of thinness than he was of inconsistency. To measure such a philosopher by systematic standards is to omit an essential part of him.   He enlivened everything that he touched, fertilized every idea that passed through his mind, carried a blazing torch in all his meanderings, zigzags, and circles.   This was felt even by his nonphilosophical friends, such as Albert Venn Dicey : —

"One must remember a dictum of William James by which I shall always remember him.   'One must learn to be content with everything, even with oneself.'   This he said to me the last night I was at Boston.   So he is gone.   I saw this in yesterday's *Scotsman*.   There is one good and able man the less among the living to help us.   What may be the merit or the truth of his theories I cannot judge.   My suspicion is that he hit some weak points in prevailing moral and philosophical systems, but did not establish any coherent theory in their place.   He had, however, I am pretty sure, one quality which in my judgment belongs to all great thinkers, in whatever line and in whatever school.   He made incidental remarks which have great merit, whatever be the ultimate worth of his general system." [20]

These "incidental remarks" of "great merit," a merit which Dicey certainly did not exaggerate, account for the peculiar vitality of James's influence.   It spread like the branches of a banyan tree and took root in divers places.   His mind was abundantly fruitful and he scattered its riches far and wide.   He lost no chance of exploration from fear of departing too far from the main highway. The result is that while there are very few pure Jamesians, in the sense of direct descent, the world is full of mixed Jamesians, who acknowledge their common relationship to him without feeling any bond with one another.

James's thought has remained green when that of many of his contemporaries is withered.   This is due not only to the sheer quality of his work, but to its pioneering spirit and prophetic insight.   There *are* elements of James's thought that are at present under an eclipse — psychical research, for example, and individualistic-humanitarian liberalism.   But if we compare the year 1935 with the year 1885, in which James may be said to have come of age, and plot the move-

[20] To Mrs. Dicey, Aug. 30, 1910, reprinted from *Memorials of Albert Venn Dicey*, 1925, 209–10.

ment of the human mind and spirit during this half century, it is remarkable how much of James falls on the line. The attention to "experience"; the free intermingling of psychology and philosophy in the study of perception, thought, and other forms of knowledge; the revolt against the dualisms of subject-object and of body-mind; the passing of scientific dogmatism, in both its mechanistic and its evolutionary forms; the empirical study of religion, and the tendency to ascribe noetic value to the mystical consciousness; the rise of the theory of value; the recognition of the emotional and other personal contaminations of thought; the dethroning of the Absolute and the decline of all forms of extreme monism; indeterminism; the stream of consciousness; the clinical approach to psychology, with its emphasis on personality and on the unconscious; the rejection of associationism, together with the emphasis on integral motor response, and on the organic unity of the conscious field; the development of applied and of social psychology; relativity, in all its wide range of meanings — these are some of the ideas whose vogue would make it quite possible for James to breathe the air of the present time, and whose proponents find it natural to quote him.

CHARACTER AND THOUGHT: MORBID TRAITS

THE character of James, like his thought, escapes simple formulation.[1] "What a real person he is!" said Minnie Temple.[2] He had, in fact, the reality of his own pluralistic universe — abounding and unbounded.

I shall attempt no clinical diagnosis, but observe him with a layman's eye, and with no predetermined set of categories. It would be natural to apply his *own* categories, and to ask whether he was a tough-minded accepter of facts (a "Rocky Mountain tough"), or a tender-minded respecter of principles (a "tender-foot Bostonian").[3] The fact is that he was both; or perhaps it might be more accurate to say that he was tough-minded with many tender-minded concessions, as he may be said to have been a pluralist with concessions to monism. He would not have made the distinction had his own experience not embraced both sorts of mindedness, — had he not had his tough moods and his tender, — and his philosophy, as a way of being true to himself, was under an inner compulsion to satisfy them both.

Another of his famous distinctions is that which he made in *The Varieties of Religious Experience,* between the "healthy-minded" and the "sick soul." The former enjoys a sense of easy or certain triumph over evil; he imposes terms on it, regarding it as alien and conquerable. He enjoys, as James expresses it, "a temperament organically weighted on the side of cheer and fatally forbidden to linger, as those of opposite temperament linger, over the darker aspects of the universe."[4] The sick soul, on the other hand, accepts

---

[1] A writer who finds that "the only way to understand a metaphysical system or theory lies in translating it as far as possible into terms of genetic psychology" once made an interesting attempt to explain James's philosophy by his temperament: E. Tausch, "W. James, the Pragmatist — a Psychological Analysis," *Monist,* XIX (1909). Of James's comments on this article (*op. cit.,* 156) I have made occasional use in what follows.

[2] *N.S.B.,* 511.

[3] *Pragm.,* 12-3.

[4] *V.R.E.,* 83.

evil not only as incurable but as *essential,* and has to make his peace
with the world on terms which evil dictates; suffering is itself a part
of the deeper meaning of life, sublimated into resignation, repentance, purification by pain, or the exaltation of self-sacrifice.
Now James had his times of healthy-mindedness and his times of
soul-sickness, and he knew both; but when he was healthy he was
healthy-minded, and when he experienced soul-sickness he was sick.
His *norm,* in other words, and his *salvation* lay in the recovery of
healthy-mindedness. His own favorite tonic, a sort of open-air
exposure to the perilous adventure of combating evil, would not do
for sick souls. He did, however, have a physician's interest in the
soul-sickness of others, and since his own soul sometimes needed
the medicine which he prescribed, he knew its virtue.

As to the distinction between the "once" and the "twice-born,"
James's life was punctuated by abrupt crises, and his recoveries
tended to assume the form of a dramatic regeneration. Especially
notable was the "crisis" of April 29, 1870, when as a young man of
twenty-eight he found not only philosophical insight but a way of
life in the reading of Renouvier's second *Essai.*[5] There is some
reason, surely, to be reminded of that older young man of thirty-
two, Saint Augustine, who, having heard the words *"tolle lege"* in
his garden at Milan, found a way of salvation, philosophical as well
as personal, in the reading of Saint Paul's Epistles. But there was
in James no such sharp disassociation between the unregenerate and
regenerate phases as marks the twice-born type in its authentic
cases. Had there been, he would not have been a detached observer
of his own experience, or a psychologist of religion.

In short, James transcended his own classifications in the act of
creating them. They cannot be used to define his limits, but only to
prove his many-sidedness. His recognition of them, his understanding of them in terms of his own experience, inclined him also
to admit a provisional plurality of truths. That any man should
find a remedy good, whether it be medicine for the body or medicine
for the soul, created a presumption in its favor. And James not
only made an allowance for diverse truths in the final accounting, but
reserved the liberty of tasting them all himself. In 1900, writing
to Thomas Davidson, who like himself was afflicted with an incurable malady, James said: "One can meet mortal (or would-be

[5] *L.W.J.,* I, 147.

mortal) disease either by gentlemanly levity, by high-minded stoicism, or by religious enthusiasm. I advise you, old T. D., to follow my example and try a playful *durcheinander* of all three, taking each in turn *pro re nata.*" [6] Discount whatever of light-mindedness was designed to cheer the heart of his friend, and this statement contains a residual philosophical conviction that the whole truth somehow includes all gospels whose remedial value is proved in the profounder moments of human experience.

James was never robust and there were many times, short or protracted, when he was disabled by illness. During the Civil War, when he was a young man of from nineteen to twenty-three years of age, he was clearly incapacitated for military service. There were two long periods, one in his youth and one towards the end of his life, when he was unable to use his eyes. From 1867 to 1873 (that is, from his twenty-fifth to his thirty-first year), he suffered from insomnia, weakness of the back, and digestive disorders, and for the next five years he was convalescent. He strained his heart in 1898, twelve years before his death, and from this injury he never recovered. In point of physical health, the best years of his life were the twenty from his marriage in 1878 to the injury of his heart in 1898, but even during these years he suffered frequently from nervous fatigue and from recurrent attacks of grippe, insomnia, and eye strain. There was always a ghost or a premonition of disability. "We are all well," he once wrote to Howison, "I suffering much from the sense of my inadequacy, both intellectual and corporeal, to my tasks; but the years elapse, notwithstanding, with no public exposure." And similarly to Davidson: "There is nothing like being regularly ill or regularly well, the *vermischt* condition is the most unsatisfactory."

Despite these facts, invalidism is about the last word with which to describe William James. He was perpetually expending energy, physical as well as mental; he was alert, quick, and elastic in all of his reactions. He was the sort of man that runs upstairs — two steps at a time. His periods of illness were often the effect of the overwork to which his nature constantly tempted him. There was, furthermore, a notable discrepancy between the incapacity of which he complained and the record of his achievement. Somehow long lists of long books got read when he was unable to use his eyes, and

[6] Above, I, 759.

a considerable flow of ideas poured out of him when he was unable to use his mind. The fact is that a working day of twenty-four hours would never have been long enough — however large the area enclosed, he would have been fretting at the barrier.

His neurasthenia conspired with his impatience to exaggerate his illness — not only the illness itself, but his feeling of it and his expression of that feeling to others. He was very highly charged, and his body was in a peculiar measure the instrument of his will. It is little wonder that he was unable to accept the hypothesis of automatism. Spencer's description of life as "adjustment of inner and outer relations" failed utterly to fit James's own case. He was, and must have known himself to be, a radiant, centrifugal person, whose outward life took on the color of its inner source. This meant that he was the creature of his own moods, and while these were normally buoyant, they were subject to frequent alterations. Of his tendency to hypochondria, his mother wrote in 1874 (during his period of deep depression): "The trouble with him is that he *must express* every fluctuation of feeling, and especially every unfavorable symptom, without reference to the effect upon those about him. . . . Wherever he speaks of himself he says he is no better. This I cannot believe to be the true state of the case, but his temperament is a morbidly hopeless one, and with this he has to contend all the time, as well as with his physical disability."

I begin, then, with what would be regarded as the more malignant of James's mental traits, though reserving doubts as to whether, through the alchemy of genius, they were not in reality benign.

"At . . . moments of energetic living," says James, "we feel as if there were something diseased and contemptible, yea vile, in theoretic grubbing and brooding. In the eye of healthy sense the philosopher is at best a learned fool." [7] An essential element in James's practical philosophy is this eulogy of action and external experience. He once wrote to his brother Robertson in playful earnestness, "My dying words are, 'outward acts, not feelings.'" He accepted Carlyle's gospel of work in his answer to the great question, "What Makes Life Worth Living?" With Carlyle he admired heroic action, and felt that in its absence life was flat and unprofitable. He received morality and even religion in terms of risk and combat. He inferred from the principle of "reflex

[7] *W.B.*, 74.

action" that any completed operation of mind culminated in an overt response, and in his theory of truth he was a pragmatist.

When, however, one looks below the surface, -— and it requires no deep psychoanalytic probing, — one finds that James's exhortation to action was addressed primarily to himself.   He entered upon a philosophical career with deep misgivings because he feared that it would develop a tendency to morbid self-preoccupation.   He found teaching to be a "godsend," because it diverted him from "those introspective studies which had bred a sort of philosophical hypo-chondria."   He turned at first to science because he needed "some stable reality to lean upon"; he was "not strong enough . . . to choose the other and nobler lot in life." [8]   In other words, he had a very definite tendency to brooding melancholy.   He knew it, fought it, and triumphed over it, but he never rooted it out of his nature.   It was a permanent, though intermittent and subordinate, phase of his experience and character.   His gospel of heroism was a moral which he drew for himself from his own experience.   His praise of action and scorn of the unventilated chamber of inner thought and feeling was a call to arms, or a shout of triumph, proceeding from the arena of his own moral struggle where his strength was engaged in combat with his weakness.

In the second place, James was interested throughout his life in what he called "exceptional mental states."   His promotion of psy-chical research and of abnormal psychology generally, his studies of the "hidden energies" of men suddenly revealed in times of stress, his collection and description of religious experiences in all their variety, but with special emphasis on their oddity, his disposition to credit mysticism as a source of knowledge — all testify to this pre-occupation.   How far did James *himself* experience "exceptional mental states"?   We know that sometime in the early '80s he was prompted by the writing of his friend Blood to experiment with nitrous-oxide-gas intoxication, and that he caused some scandal among his philosophical friends by likening the effect to the insight of Hegel.   He recorded the following as the most coherent and ar-ticulate truth revealed to him in this state: "There are no differences but differences of degree between different degrees of difference and no difference."   He said that this had "the true Hegelian ring," and described the "ecstasies of cognitive emotion" with which it was

[8] *L.W.J.*, I, 167, 170–1.

bathed.[9]   Now this incident suggests the child playing with matches, or irreverently mocking the devout.   It was, in fact, both of these things.   James was incorrigibly and somewhat recklessly curious, and he derived enjoyment from deflating the solemnity of the pundits.   There is no doubt that this experiment, and his psycho-pathological approach generally, did make him skeptical of the im-port of the mystical experience of others and slow to credit his own. Nevertheless, the very fact that he used his experience under anæsthetics as a key to the interpretation of Hegel indicates his recognition of its noetic claims.   Later, in his *Varieties of Religious Experience,*[10] he took pains to point out that the causes of an ex-perience "have nothing to do with its truth or value, which are determined by its fruits."   And there can, I think, be no doubt that other experiences, which were not artificially induced, left in his mind an increasing precipitate of conviction.   For he had engaged in extraordinary adventures of this sort — adventures having that character which the unbelieving describe as hallucinatory, and the believing as intuitive.   It was probably in 1870, just prior to his conversion to Renouvier, that he suffered the memorable hallucina-tion of fear which he has so vividly described in the *Varieties:* —

"I went one evening into a dressing-room in the twilight to procure some article that was there; when suddenly there fell upon me without any warning, just as if it came out of the darkness, a horrible fear of my own existence.   Simultaneously there arose in my mind the image of an epileptic patient whom I had seen in the asylum, a black-haired youth with greenish skin, entirely idiotic, who used to sit all day on one of the benches, or rather shelves against the wall, with his knees drawn up against his chin, and the coarse gray undershirt, which was his only garment, drawn over them, inclosing his entire figure. . . .   This image and my fear entered into a species of combination with each other.   *That shape am I,* I felt, potentially.   Nothing that I possess can defend me against that fate, if the hour for it should strike for me as it struck for him. . . .   After this the universe was changed for me alto-gether.   I awoke morning after morning with a horrible dread at the pit of my stomach, and with a sense of the insecurity of life that I never knew before, and that I have never felt since.   It was like a

[9] *W.B.,* 297.
[10] 15 ff.

revelation; and although the immediate feelings passed away, the experience has made me sympathetic with the morbid feelings of others ever since." [11]

A less morbid but not less vivid experience is that which befell him in the Adirondack Mountains in 1898. He had at all times a sense of intimate communion with nature, and especially with nature in its natural states. On this particular occasion he spent a sleepless night on the slopes of Mt. Marcy, in what he described as "a state of spiritual alertness of the most vital description." Writing of this night to his wife, he said: —

"I spent a good deal of it in the woods, where the streaming moonlight lit up things in a magical checkered play, and it seemed as if the Gods of all the nature-mythologies were holding an indescribable meeting in my breast with the moral Gods of the inner life. . . . The intense significance of some sort, of the whole scene, if one could only *tell* the significance; the intense inhuman remoteness of its inner life, and yet the intense *appeal* of it; its everlasting freshness and its immemorial antiquity and decay; its utter Americanism, and every sort of patriotic suggestiveness, and you, and my relation to you part and parcel of it all, and beaten up with it, so that memory and sensation all whirled inexplicably together. . . . It was one of the happiest lonesome nights of my existence, and I understand now what a poet is. He is a person who can feel the immense complexity of influences that I felt, and make some partial tracks in them for verbal statement. In point of fact, I can't find a single word for all that significance, and don't know what it was significant of, so there it remains, a mere boulder of *impression*. Doubtless in more ways than one, though, things in the Edinburgh lectures will be traceable to it." [12]

In the last year of his life, as we have seen, James described four "abnormal" experiences of his own, all of which had occurred after 1905, and which he hoped would throw light on the topic of mysticism. He *believed* that "there is a continuum of cosmic consciousness, against which our individuality builds but accidental fences, and into which our several minds plunge as into a mother-sea or reservoir." [13] This belief was to some extent founded on normal observation, on the reports of others, and on the theory of the

[11] *V.R.E.*, 160–1.
[12] *L.W.J.*, II, 76–7.
[13] *M.S.*, 204.

subliminal consciousness which he adopted from Myers. But the impression is irresistible that it was his own unusual experiences that put the seal of conviction on what would otherwise have been an alluring but open hypothesis. It is true that he refused to credit himself with the mystical experience, or at most admitted that he had a "mystical germ." But in view of all the evidence it seems more correct to say that he did in fact have experiences of the type called mystical; adding that these experiences were infrequent, lacked the character of overwhelming authority with which they are commonly invested, and played only a minor rôle in his philosophy as a whole.

The third of James's morbid traits is his extreme *variability* — the frequency of the barometric and thermometric changes in his temperamental weather. The only published statement which he made about the personal sources of his philosophy contains the following, addressed in 1909 to a writer who had undertaken to make a diagnosis: "I think you overdo my personal mysticism. It has always seemed to me rather a matter of fair play to the various kinds of experience to let mystical ecstasy have its voice counted with the rest. As far as I am personally concerned it is the ordinary sense of life that every working moment brings, that makes me contemptuous of rationalistic attempts to substitute thin logical formulas for it. My *flux*-philosophy may well have to do with my extremely impatient temperament. I am a motor, need change, and get very quickly bored. . . ." [14]

The Jamesian universe was not a Great State of Things, or architectural monument of cosmic bulk and infinite complexity — it was a stream, a passage, a becoming, a history in the making. Now it is certain that whether the universe was really so or not, it would necessarily have *looked* so to James because he was perpetually in motion himself. There was an outward projection of an inward restlessness and nostalgia. He was peculiarly subject to the mirage of absent and distant joys.[15] He became tired of whatever he did long before it was finished, and felt a most powerful revulsion toward it after it was finished. A minor but not insignificant symptom of this was a detestation of proofreading, such as found expression in the following outburst to the editor of the *Psychological Review:*

[14] Letter to E. Tausch, *Monist,* XIX (1909), 156.
[15] For his explanation of this nostalgia as due to a lively imagination, *cf. L.W.J.,* I, 128.

"Send me no proofs! I will return them unopened and never speak to you again. As Mrs. R. says, 'Remove the cuticle from your own polecats,' or get your entrapped victims to help you. I am of the eagle's race and free!" After the publication of the *Principles of Psychology* poor Palmer prepared several pages of *errata,* but he could never persuade James to look at them.

His sister Alice, who was an indulgent but acute diagnostician, found James "just like a blob of mercury" — lacking in power or inclination to "stick to a thing for the sake of sticking." [16] De-scribing to this same sister his experiences with a "mind-cure doc-tress" in 1887, James said: "I sit down beside her and presently drop asleep, whilst she disentangles the snarls out of my mind. She says she never saw a mind with so many, so agitated, so restless, etc. She said my *eyes,* mentally speaking, kept revolving like wheels in front of each other and in front of my face, and it was four or five sittings ere she could get them *fixed.* . . . I thought it might please you to hear an opinion of my mind so similar to your own." [17]

That James's mercurial temperament made him at times difficult to live with was no secret, at any rate within the family. There is an inverted allusion to it in the following passage from a letter writ-ten in 1891 by William in Chocorua to Henry and Alice in London: "I am becoming more patriarchal than ever: Last week we had three nurses at once, — nine women in all, — in the house. . . . I think that even (sister) Alice would feel compunction if she could see me, the idol of the group of relatives and dependents, dignified and serene, never worrying or 'wishing,' never depreciating present possessions, never protesting against the injustice of others' opinions, or contradicting or pinning them down, never discussing personal anecdotes from the point of view of abstract reasoning and absolute truth, never seeking a second metaphor, or a third, when the first or second were good enough, breathing, in short, an atmosphere of peace and rest wherever I go. A *noble et forte personnalité* indeed! But enough of this: since you can't *see* it, it is well that you should *hear* of it at least; and my Alice is, I fear, too shy to write such things."

James complained constantly of a multitude of distractions.

16 *L.W.J.,* I, 289–90.
17 *L.W.J.,* I, 261.

"The constitutional disease from which I suffer," he wrote, "is what the Germans call *Zerrissenheit* or *torn-to-pieces-hood*. The days are broken in pure zigzag and interruption. . . . Give me twelve hours of work on *one* occupation for happiness." [18] Although he usually imputed this state to his environment, and sought to escape it *somewhere*, he knew in his heart that it was his own nature, and not outward circumstance, that tormented him.

Over and above these symptoms of volatility — restlessness, impatience, dispersion of attention and perversity — there were deeper alternations of mood. Thus in June 1865, he was sure that his voyage to Brazil was a "mistake," while in September he was in high spirits and thanking God that he had come. In the autumn of 1887, although his courses were large and successful, and he was writing busily on his *Principles of Psychology,* and his "eyes, sleep and working and walking powers" were all restored, his zest for life was strangely dulled. In October he wrote to his sister: "The Eliots have just returned from a year of absence abroad. I have not seen 'em yet. Whether it be his cold figure at the helm, or what not; whether it be perhaps the fact that I myself never graduated here, I know not; one thing is certain, that although I *serve* Harvard College to the best of my ability, I have no *affection* at all for the institution, and would gladly desert it for anything that offered better pay." The following was written to his brother Henry five weeks later, showing the persistence of the mood: "I am glad you write so sanguinely of your work. That's the way to feel. If only one *can* feel so. A strange coldness has come over me with reference to all my deeds and productions, within the past six months. I don't know whether it be the passage under the meridian of forty-five years, or due to a more reparable cause, but everything I've done and shall do seems so *small*." By the autumn of 1888 this mood seems to have vanished: "The Cambridge year begins with much vehemence — I with a big class in ethics, and seven graduates from other colleges in advanced psychology, giving me a good deal of work. But I feel uncommonly hearty, and shall no doubt come out of it all in good shape. . . . I am to have lots of reading and no writing to speak of this year and expect to enjoy it hugely." [19]

Oscillation, then, of the quick and darting variety, or with the

[18] *Atlantic,* CXLIV (1929), 380.
[19] *L.W.J.,* I, 283.

longer rhythm of exaltation and depression, is profoundly characteristic of James's nature.   It is reflected in his world, which is a scene
of abrupt as well as of continuous change; and in his mind, which is
variable, versatile, and itinerant — perpetually crossing over, turning corners, or embarking on new voyages.

Finally, there was in James a pathological repugnance to the
processes of exact thought.   Whether it can be regarded as a
symptom of soul-sickness to be relatively incompetent in logic and
mathematics, I do not presume to say.   There is also doubt as to
whether James was so incompetent in this direction as he felt himself to be.   In any case, incompetent he did *feel* and *profess*
himself to be.   He made belated efforts to advance his mathematical education.   In 1893 he wrote to Flournoy: "Can you name me
any simple book on differential calculus which gives an insight into
the philosophy of the subject? . . .   I have just been through a
short treatise by one of my colleagues, but it is a thicket of particular formulas and calculations without one general idea, and I
want ideas and not formulas."   But on the whole he was easily
consoled.   He was much pleased when one of his students characterized algebra as "a form of low cunning." [20]   To Peirce he wrote
in 1909: "I am *a*-logical, if not illogical, and glad to be so when I
find Bertie Russell trying to excogitate what true knowledge means,
in the absence of any concrete universe surrounding the knower and
the known.   Ass!"   Thus a lack of mathematics and logic did not
exclude James from intimate relations with the universe — at any
rate, with the Jamesian universe.   On the contrary!

With Charles Peirce this more or less self-righteous plea of
incompetence was no laughing matter.   Towards James he felt a
little as the friends of Mr. Skimpole felt when the latter so blandly
remarked that he was a "child" and "could not understand money."
Not only did Peirce belong to a tribe of mathematicians and
logicians, and practise both subjects with eminent skill, but he
thought that they represented the perfection of clarity, and therefore
the supreme height of intelligibility.   Hence his complaint that
when a person "lays it down," as James does, "that he can't understand mathematics, that is to say, can't understand the *evident*,
that blocks the road" to further explanations. [21]

[20] *L.W.J.*, II, 207.
[21] *Cf.* above, 439.

We have seen that in the Hibbert Lectures of 1908 James solemnly and publicly renounced logic. It is true that there is some question as to the precise scope of this renunciation, since he repeatedly referred to the logic which he renounced as the "intellectualistic logic" or the "logic of identity," as though there might be some better logic to which he remained faithful. It is also true that at the very times when he was resolving to renounce logic he was engaged in mental operations of extreme rigor bearing a remarkable resemblance to what other people called logic. His very refutation of the "intellectualistic logic" was, whether right or wrong, certainly not either dogmatic, impressionistic, or empirical, but a notable demonstration of painstaking analysis. Again, despite the reiteration of his incompetence in mathematics, he examined the new mathematical theory of the infinite with much care, and rejected it not because he disliked it, but because it seemed to him to be invalid. But while James was thus perpetually driven to the processes of exact thought by his desire for clearness and cogency, he was at the same time repelled by a temperamental aversion and distrust; and these feelings, combined with a natural impulse to find metaphysical justification for them, led him to sweeping and extravagant assertions of the irrationality of being.

An inventory of James's pathological traits would embrace, then, tendencies to hypochondria and hallucinatory experience, abnormally frequent and intense oscillations of mood, and an almost morbid alogism, or antipathy to the mode of thinking which employs definitions, symbols, and trains of inference. In terming these traits "pathological," I mean only that taken in themselves they would commonly be regarded as defects. In relation to the character and thought of James, they are *ingredients,* essential to the substance as well as to the flavor of the compound.

XCI

CHARACTER AND THOUGHT: BENIGN TRAITS

TURNING to James's benign traits, I find four that are peculiarly pervasive: sensibility, vivacity, humanity, and sociability. When I say that they are benign I mean not only that in themselves they would commonly be regarded as merits rather than as defects, but also that they dominated James when he enjoyed a sense of well-being, or when he felt himself to be most himself.

In speaking, first, of James's sensibility, I do not mean his susceptibility to feeling or emotion, but the acuity of his *senses* — the voluminousness and richness of the experience which he received through them, and the prominence of that experience and of its underlying motive in his life as a whole. He tells us that he was not a visualizer so far as his memory and imagination were concerned. On the other hand, it is the unanimous testimony of all who knew him that he lived much through the eyes. He wanted to *see* people whom he knew. He exchanged photographs with his friends and made a large "anthropological collection" in order to study the human physiognomy.[1] He was ceaselessly and interestedly observant of all that lay about him — of nature and art, as well as of life. Being a painter, the eye was no doubt his major sense: to use his own expression, he "took in things through the eyes." But although he described himself as a "musical barbarian," he was quick also to discriminate nuances of sound, especially in the quality of a human voice. His psychological writings testify to his discrimination of organic sensations.

Having a high sensuous endowment and being avid of sensory experience, it is not surprising that he should have felt such experience to convey the authentic revelation of reality. It is the unsaid but fundamental premise of his whole metaphysics that only he can speak authoritatively of the universe who is most sensitively attuned to it. Metaphysics is an apprehending of reality in its most

[1] *L.W.J.*, I, 51.

immediate and lifelike aspect, or a listening to hear "the pulse of Being beat." When he said that he found "no good warrant for even suspecting the existence of any reality of a higher denomination than that distributed and strung-along and flowing sort of reality which we finite beings swim in," [2] he was placing his ultimate reliance on the human sensorium.

The same motive appears in all of James's pet philosophical aversions. He was constantly attacking verbalism. How much better, he said, a bill of fare "with one real egg instead of the word 'egg.'" He hated abstractions, and would be like Agassiz, one of the "livers in the light of the world's concrete fulness." [3] He seemed to be forever scooping reality up in his hands in the hope of catching it alive. Caring more for actuality than for ancestry, he took relatively little interest in origins and histories. He thought that the question "why?" was sooner or later a futile question, the last answer being a "what" or "that" for which there is no "why." The world has an ultimate physiognomy, rhythm, flavor, or quality, which, having been discerned, must be accepted as it is. His metaphysics was a perpetual striving to sense that ultimate quality.

James's metaphysics, then, reflects the sensuous, pictorial character of his mind. [4] But this interpretation must not be taken too simply. Intuition, according to Bergson, is immediate, but is not on that account easily attained. So in the case of James the authentic experience of reality is uncommon and difficult. The painter tells us that he paints the scene as he sees it — which sounds very simple, until we discover that only the eye of the painter can really see. Something like this is the case with James's metaphysical vision. There are occasional moments when experience is most fully tasted — in the exhilaration of a fresh morning, in moments of suffering, or in times of triumphant effort, when the tang is strong, when every nuance or overtone is present. James would arrest us at such moments, and say, "There, *that* is it. Reality is like *that*." But our worldly minds are filled with ready-made ideas, and when we experience reality it usually has these ideas already stamped upon it. Our minds are accustomed to various

[2] *W.B.*, 141; *P.U.*, 213.
[3] *V.R.E.*, 500; above, I, 205.
[4] For an interesting study of the figurative quality of James's thought and style, cf. M. Cornesse, *Le Rôle des images dans la pensée de William James*, Grenoble, 1933.

short cuts, omissions, and abbreviations dictated by practical convenience, and what these omit we do not commonly apprehend. Hence the metaphysical vision, like the seeing of the painter, involves a recovery of innocence, a capture of the elusive, an unnatural access of sensitiveness.

The quality which is revealed to James when this metaphysical vision is achieved is *transitivity*. It is characteristic of the mind in its routine operations to dwell upon termini, goals, conclusions; and philosophy usually reflects this characteristic by treating reality as a finished product. Or, revolting at such perfectionism, philosophy may swing to the other extreme and declare reality to be the mere negation of completeness. Both of these views, James thought, are abstract and dialectical. Concretely, — when you seize the sense of it, or get the feel of it, — reality is a movement from terminus to terminus, a pursuing of goals, an *arriving* at conclusions. It is on its way to something. Reality is not the destination, nor is it mere movement, but just that concrete character which is so likely to be missed by the analytic mind, namely, directional or meaningful change. It is neither form nor matter, nor a mere combination of the two, but a plasticity in which matter is in the act of assuming form. James did not invent this view to suit his theoretical exigencies — it was what he discerned when he experienced experience. So whenever the intellect makes distinctions we find him endeavoring to restore the primitive concreteness, not by piecing the distinctions together, but by recovering the original as it was before these were selected and detached.

The following passage will illustrate James's pictorial manner of philosophizing, his effort to convey as faithfully as possible the immediately presented aspect of a situation, and also that peculiar quality of synthesis which distinguishes his way of seeing things. He has been arguing that reality is neither absolutely one nor absolutely many, but a stream whose parts coalesce where they touch, and exclude one another as their interval increases. At the same time he is endeavoring to describe the relations of the private experiences of individuals to the common world in which they live: —

"*Prima facie,* if you should liken the universe of absolute idealism to an aquarium, a crystal globe in which goldfish are swimming, you would have to compare the empiricist universe to something more like one of those dried human heads with which the Dyaks of Borneo deck their lodges. The skull forms a solid nucleus; but innumerable feathers, leaves, strings, beads, and loose appendices of every description float and dangle from it, and, save that they terminate in it, seem to have nothing to do with one another. Even so my experiences and yours float and dangle, terminating, it is true, in a nucleus of common perception, but for the most part out of sight and irrelevant and unimaginable to one another. . . . The distant parts of the physical world are at all times absent from us, and form conceptual objects merely, into the perceptual reality of which our life inserts itself at points discrete and relatively rare. Round the several objective nuclei, partly shared and common and partly discrete, of the real physical world, innumerable thinkers, pursuing their several lines of physically true cogitation, trace paths that intersect one another only at discontinuous perceptual points, and the rest of the time are quite incongruent; and around all the nuclei of shared 'reality,' as around the Dyak's head of my late metaphor, floats the vast cloud of experiences that are wholly subjective, that are non-substitutional, that find not even an eventual ending for themselves in the perceptual world — the mere daydreams and joys and sufferings and wishes of the individual minds. These exist *with* one another, indeed, and with the objective nuclei, but out of them it is probable that to all eternity no interrelated system of any kind will ever be made." [5]

Owing to his sensibility, James was extraordinarily receptive to impressions. But he met his impressions more than halfway — acted on them and sought them out. He was naturally *vivacious*. He said of himself, "I 'm a 'motor,' and morally ill-adapted to the game of patience." He meant, first, that he was one of those who "in memory, reasoning, and all their intellectual operations," make use of "images derived from movements" rather than from sight, hearing, or touch. But he meant also that this motor type of imagery was associated with comparative quickness of reaction. It is impossible to read James's description of the "explosive will," as represented by the man who will be "the king of his company, sing all the songs and make all the speeches, lead the parties, carry out the practical jokes, kiss all the girls, fight the men, and, if need be, lead the forlorn hopes and enterprises" — without catching a note

[5] *E.R.E.*, 46–7, 65–6.

of sympathy and understanding on the part of the writer himself.[6]

This *vivacity,* this eagerness and gusto, marked James from an early age — as a "son and brother." His sister Alice once said of him that he seemed "to be born afresh every morning." "He came down from his bedroom *dancing* to greet me," said his father, who had gone out to Cambridge in 1882 to see him. He was an overflowing and inexhaustible fountain — a fountain, be it remarked, and not a channeled stream. For a fountain scatters itself wantonly. That which was so striking about James was not his capacity for work, though this was remarkable, but his capacity for play. Whatever he did he did with good measure, and with no nice calculation of its utility. It was this more than any other trait that gave the impression of genius. There was a fecundity, a prodigality, an upward rush from hidden depths, that suggested a prime source rather than an artifact or instrument.

There were light as well as serious forms of James's vivacity. He wore bright neckties. He had a highly developed sense of fun, and was usually himself its principal fomenter. He had his days of feeling "particularly larky,"[7] but some degree of larkiness might be expected at any time. Thus he wrote to Flournoy as he was completing his second course of Gifford Lectures, "The old spirit of mischief revives in my breast, and I begin to feel a little as I used to." In the family circles to which James belonged laughter was a major activity. Its waves and detonations not only cleared away the vapors of neurasthenia, but were fatal to any "airs" of pretension or pose. There was wit, but it was gayety and elaborate nonsense which was the characteristic domestic product. In the days of James's boyhood, when juvenile theatricals were in order, it was he, according to the testimony of his brother, that supplied "the motive force," imagined "the comprehensive comedies," and served as "the constant comic star."[8]

His way of making fun of people, himself included, his delightful absurdity and peculiar art of loving caricature, appear in one of the letters to his family, written in his nineteenth year. He describes

---

[6] *L.W.J.,* II, 163; *Principles,* II, 61–5, 538. In distinguishing these types of imagery James followed Ribot, Galton, and especially M. A. Binet. There is no *proved* connection between the motor type of imagery and quickness of reaction time, or impulsiveness of will. I am indebted for light on this topic to my colleague Prof. Gordon W. Allport.

[7] *L.W.J.,* I, 305.

[8] *S.B.O.,* 253.

his "vision of those at home just going in to dinner": "My aged, silvered mother leaning on the arm of her stalwart yet flexible Harry, merry and garrulous as ever, my blushing aunt with her old wild beauty still hanging about her, my modest father with his rippling raven locks, the genial auld Rob and the mysterious Alice, all rise before me, a glorified throng." On this passage — its "pleasantry of paradox," and "evocation of each familiar image by its vivid opposite" — we fortunately have the authoritative commentary of his brother Henry: —

"Our mother, *e.g.,* was not at that time, nor for a good while yet, so venerably 'silvered'; our handsome-headed father had lost, occipitally, long before, all pretense to raven locks, certainly to the effect of their 'rippling'; the beauty of our admirable aunt was as happily alien either to wildness or to the 'hanging' air as it could very well be; the 'mystery' of our young sister consisted all in the candour of her natural bloom, even if at the same time of her lively intelligence; and Harry's mirth and garrulity appear to have represented for the writer the veriest ironic translation of something in that youth, I judge, not a little mildly — though oh *so* mildly! — morose or anxiously mute." [9]

James's correspondence abounds in evidence of the gayety of his spirits, and the rich diversity of their quality and tone. Especially characteristic is the delicious mockery of the early letters to his sister Alice, such as those written in an interval between his cure at Teplitz and his studies at Heidelberg, when he was twenty-six and she was twenty; [10] or the following, written five years later from Florence, upon receiving news of the birth of the first child of his brother Robertson: "We got . . . from Father . . . a letter . . . announcing to us that we had given birth to a nephew. So the third generation of the James family is in full swing! We are uncles, grandmothers, aunts, etc., all drawing our subsistence as such from that one worm-like being in Wisconsin. It seems to me the pyramid points the wrong way, and the spreading end ought to be the youngest, instead of the trunk being more numerous than the twiggery."

A more serious form of James's vivacity was his curiosity. His mind darted like a humming bird. From boyhood he was "addicted

[9] *N.S.B.*, 132–5.
[10] *Cf.* above, 525, 547; for other letters of the same period and in the same vein, *cf. L.W.J.*, I.

to experiments," there being, as his brother Henry remarked, "no possible effect whatever that might n't be more or less rejoiced in as such." [11]   It was this same liveliness of mind that enabled him to enjoy novelty.   It is obvious that he was himself an interesting man, but more significant that he found other things interesting. On that fatal day in 1898 when he overexerted himself in the Adirondacks he fell in with a group of young people, including several Bryn Mawr girls, "dressed," as he described them, "in boys' breeches, and cutaneously desecrated in the extreme." [12]   He afterwards apologized for the "impudence" with which he had commented on their clothes: "I remember so vividly," writes one of the party, "the occasion he mentions, and the keen charm and vigor of his presence, — his laugh ringing out at the end of that long, wonderful, mountain-forest day (and night) with such gayety and spontaneity that I think now with a pang of how little I dreamed he was overtaxing his strength.   The 'impudence' to which he refers was, I think, his praise of us . . . in that Victorian — or Edwardian — era for wearing knickerbockers.   I remember especially that he made us all feel in the van of progress . . . by saying of the convenience of our clothes for climbing, — 'I'm glad it's come.   I'm glad I've lived to see it.'"

Innovations require readaptations, and they are resented by sluggish or habituated minds for the effort they cost.   Not so with James.   He enjoyed such expenditures of energy.   If change did not come, he went out and looked for it.   He was perpetually embarking on voyages of discovery.   His travels, which, inaugurated in his childhood, became an essential part of his life, were always voyages of discovery — in new worlds of people, ideas, art, or "life."   If his body remained in one place his mind made voyages. He "tried" things [13] — nitrous-oxide gas, mescal, Yoga, Fletcherism, mental healers.   He imagined and speculated.   He entertained hypotheses and played with ideas.   His mind was of the roving-animal, rather than the rooted-vegetable variety; and he required an element in which such an unplanted mind could navigate, breathe, and find its nourishment.   It is no wonder that the culminating phase of his philosophy, with which he was preoccupied when death overtook

[11] *N.S.B.*, 123.
[12] *L.W.J.*, II, 76.
[13] *L.W.J.*, II, 35, 37.

him, was the vision of "a really growing world," of which continuous novelty was the central figure.

James's vivacity was tempered by his equally fundamental *humanity,* or tenderness of heart. He admired the spirit of adventure and the bold fighting qualities, but only provided no one was hurt. That hardness which is said to be a condition of supermanly eminence was utterly lacking in him. Humanity exercised a final veto upon heroism; or, the only kind of heroism that was ultimately tolerable to him was a heroic battle against inhumanity. Similarly, that liveliness of temper that led him sometimes to assume a tone of mockery was sure to be, if not commingled with, then remorsefully succeeded by, a melting mood. It was his sister again who could best evoke this familiar blend of banter and affection — seasoned, in this case, with a characteristic touch of homesickness : —

Rome, Dec. 24, 1873

Sweet Beautlington, —

I cannot resist, in spite of strong objections to spoiling you with too frequent letters, taking my pen in hand on this pearly-lighted Christmas Eve and inscribing with its point on thy tender and loving heart some words of kindness and sympathy. Thou seemest to me so beautiful from here, so intelligent, so affectionate, so in all respects *the thing* that a brother should most desire, that I don't see how when I get home I can do anything else than sit with my arm round thy waist appealing to thee for confirmation of everything I say, for approbation of everything I do, and admiration for everything I am, and never, never for a moment being disappointed. What I shall do for you in return for this excellence 't is for you rather than me to say, but I hope not to fall short of any of your exactions. I can imagine the darkling light in the library at this hour, with you lonely three sitting watching the embers and wishing for a fuller house to pass the so-called merrie Christmas Eve. . . . Adieu to dear old Father and Mother, the boys and Aunt Kate, and believe, under the form of impertinent self-conceit, in the true love of your brother

WILLIAM

This same note of playful adoration appears in a letter written by James thirty-five years later to his niece Rosamond Gregor, then eight years of age. Mrs. James was visiting her sister in Montreal.

Cambridge, Jan. 14, 1908

Darling Rosymouth (for you know that *Mund* is the German for mouth) you dear lovely extra —
ordinary
  wonderfle
    beautifle
      intellectual
        heavenly
          practical
            affectionate
              obedient
                industrious
              obliging
              gifted
            witty
              maddeningly
charming THING!

How nice it was for you to write such a letter to your 66 year old uncle and make him feel about 6 years old again! I agree with you about Agamemnon being a fool, but I'm sorry that you love Achilles, for he is a regular *hound,* nothing but pride and sulks. I would spank him if I were able. I hope you didn't read about those tedious fights. Perhaps you read an abridgment.

I hope that you enjoy your Aunt Alice. Underneath all her apparent severity there is a real soft spot, on which you can snuggle down. I am sorry that you give her such cold weather. But the dear spring weather is sure to come, birds and buds and grass and sunshine.

I am glad to hear from my wife that you are so gloriously splendid. Try to make everyone happy about you. Kiss your dear and placid mother for your waspish uncle. She has a big soul, no pettiness or paltriness about *her!* That is the best thing you can say of anyone, except all them things I said of you on the front page. . . .

So now, my own darling lovely, etc., etc., Rosymouth, good-bye, with tenderest regards to your father as well as yourself,

WM. JAMES

There was a flavor of buoyant humanity in all of James's writings which, combined with the directness of his style, gave a peculiarly personal quality to his influences. Thus a distant and casual reader of the *Principles* once experienced a sense of conversion similar to that which the elder Henry James felt on reading Swedenborg. As her conviction deepened she shared it with a friend: "I came to know another mind such as my own had been, a mind sick with doubt, dumb with negations, starved on barren philosophies, and, even as I, so this hungry mind fed greedily upon the tonic truths and came to new courage and hope. . . . Thus two souls are facing the East together and living with Pragmatism and William James for the watchword, and where there had been the depths of darkness, there shines the perfect day." [14]

James's life was as notable for its friendships as for the strength of its family ties. Two weeks before his death he wrote to Howells: "One's ancient affections seem the abidingly real part of it all." And to another correspondent: "Wherever you are it is your own friends who make your world." It is this feeling which accounts for the volume of his correspondence. When he was physically isolated from his friends, he must nevertheless live in their companionship. His friendships, with Tom Ward, Wendell Holmes, and Charles Ritter in the early days, and later with Renouvier, Hodgson, Delbœuf, Davidson, Gurney, Robertson, Myers, Stumpf, Royce, Ward, Flournoy, Bergson and others, were distinguished by their quality as well as by their number. They partook both of love and of admiration. There were an intellectual commerce and a moral comradeship, together with a simple, warm-hearted attachment of man to man. James's official or professional relationships — with colleagues, collaborators, students, teachers, executives, editors, publishers — almost immediately changed into friendships; the man being to William James so much more vivid and important than the particular rôle in which he might happen to be acting.

He took the initiative in the making of friendships. He had a warm heart, and it was not insulated. There was a look of affection in his eyes; and no one knew better than he how to woo the affection of others by translating his affection into spoken and written words. He recognized no barrier of creed or race, his strongest prejudice being that which he felt against prejudice itself. In 1899, he wrote to Davidson concerning a favorite hotel: "The circular appears this year with the precious addition: 'Applications from Hebrews cannot

[14] M.T.M. (Mrs. Wade MacMillan), "The Pragmatic Test," *Harper's Weekly*, April 18, 1914.

be considered.' I propose to return the boycott." He found almost everybody interesting and worthy of sympathy if they would admit him into their inner lives. His was a compassionate love, conditioned by his own suffering, and based on fellow feeling, but with a delicate discernment of the unique flavor of each individual, and a respect for the residual inwardness which must transcend even the most intimate understanding. It was an outgoing and a confident love, which often found in its objects more than up to that moment they had found in themselves.

James liked variety in the objects of his affection, and liked each with a separate liking. Thus he delighted in his juniors because of their promise. Writing to Julius Goldstein, a young and unrecognized German philosopher with whom he talked during his last illness at Bad-Nauheim, he said, "It has been an exquisite pleasure to me to meet a 'rising genius' like you, trying his wings like 'an eagle dallying with the wind.'" He delighted in those whom the world called cranks, either because he relished their idiosyncrasies, or from sheer, unconquerable pity. He was a great lover of animals. The history of the dogs who succeed one another as members of the James household would form a chapter in itself. In 1897 he bought a St. Bernard puppy, of whom he wrote to Miss Pauline Goldmark: "He is a violet, a Saint. I have borne him here so far in my arms, and feel like a nursing mother towards him. Tomorrow I take him to Cambridge in the baggage car. If, in the inscrutable leadings of Providence, a perfect sympathy between him and my wife and babes should fail to develop, or, developing, should undergo retrograde metamorphosis, *he is yours next June,* big, intelligent, *salonfähig,* but still (I am sure) the Saint which he is now. He is absolutely incorruptible and unvulgarizable. But if my children develop such a love for him that to lose him would be like losing their mother or me, you can easily see that with them he must remain, — and, alas! I feel that this is the more likely case of the two." [15]

James's sympathy for animals was an almost physical reaction. His pleasure from driving in the mountains was largely destroyed by his feeling for the horses on the long upward grades, and he was perpetually leaping out to reduce the load. Though he believed that the dog in the physiological laboratory would, if he could know what it all meant, "religiously acquiesce" in the experiments, he was haunted by the thought that this meaning of future good to

[15] *Cf.* also *L.W.J.,* I, 278; II, 26.

others was precisely what must remain absolutely beyond the sacrificial victim's ken.[16]

James felt a sympathy for dogs and meditated upon their inner lives. He also felt a sympathy for underdogs and invariably sided with them. It is clearly impossible to be a partisan of the underdog without sharing the underdog's antipathies. This is the chief root of James's antipathies. He hated hardness, cold-heartedness, complacency, airs of easy superiority. Above all things he hated cruelty. When in his "Dilemma of Determinism" he was casting about in his mind for an instance of unmitigated evil, he chose a recent crime in which a man had murdered his loving and trusting wife.[17] The brutality of the deed itself, the prisoner's self-satisfaction and the mild sentence which he received, not only aroused James's personal detestation, but marked his universe with an indelible stain. He could never bring himself to worship the *whole* of such a universe. "There is something wrong with the world"; and the incontrovertible proof of this indictment was the suffering of mankind together with the cruelty or fatality by which it was inflicted. "There is no *full* consolation. Evil is evil and pain is pain; and in bearing them valiantly I think the only thing we can do is to believe that the good power of the world does not appoint them of its own free will, but works under some dark and inscrutable limitations, and that we by our patience and good will, can somehow strengthen his hands." [18]

The philosophical outcropping of James's tenderness of heart thus appears in his pluralism — in his recognition of the inward significance of individual lives in all their incomprehensible diversity, in his finding a glow of preciousness within every forbiddng exterior, and in his absolutely unrelenting condemnation of inhumanity. James's modesty is allied with his tenderness. He frankly enjoyed the honors which were heaped upon him in his later years, but they did not make him self-important. He was fond of quoting John La Farge as saying that fame comes to those who wait, and increases in proportion to their growing imbecility.[19] He was not so much humble as self-forgetful, the reason being that he was preoccupied with other people. This, at least, was his healthy-minded attitude. Now a person who is interested in what he sees and in whom he meets, whose mind *goes out*, may very properly be an em-

[16] *L.W.J.*, I, 25; *W.B.*, 58.
[17] *W.B.*, 160–1.
[18] To Mrs. Glendower Evans, *Atlantic*, CXLIV (1929), 375.
[19] *L.W.J.*, II, 173.

piricist in his philosophy. He does not regard himself or any of his faculties as the source of truth; he is never sure enough of himself to claim finality for his results; he listens respectfully to other judges; and he never loses his sense that there is more to come — both from the wisdom of his fellow men and from the teeming universe.

James's extraordinary *sociability* is no doubt associated with his vivacity and his tenderness, but it would be a mistake to treat it as though it were a secondary trait. It is characteristic of him that he should in later years have referred to his three months' hospital internship in 1866 as valuable not because of any pathology that he had learned, but because the "dramatic human relationship" with certain people had helped him in the way of understanding human nature. For stiff, artificial, or noisy social relations he felt a strong loathing, and he sought to avoid them. But this is as though a musically sensitive person should avoid bad music. He had a great love and a great capacity for social relations where these were spontaneous and sincere.

When the atmosphere was favorable — and he could usually make it so — he was a great talker, with an abundant flow of wit and wisdom directed very personally and with great good-will to those about him. He considered conversation as a kind of joyful recreation, capable of refinement and subtlety like any art, but requiring openheartedness and fellow feeling as its first condition. The following was written to Howells in 1894, apropos of a letter which the latter had received from an enthusiastic admirer of the elder James: —

"Both Bob and I are much pleased to learn of one more reader of poor old H. J. whose readers in these latter days seem so few. . . . Only as for 'one real American not being afraid of any other,' I fear Father would have snorted at the lack of reality in the dictum. If there is anyone *I* am really afraid of it is the dry-hearted American whom you meet in traveling, and to whom the sort of trivial conversation you engage in with everybody you meet in Europe, is an object of nothing but disdain. I dined yesterday at New Bedford, whither I had rushed for a snatch of Sabbatical rest, at a table with four others. Each of us gulped his food in silence, each fearing the other's contemptuous or painful reception of a sudden remark. I was immensely struck in the south two years ago by the uncomfortable state I threw everyone into to whom I spoke at table. They looked away, became uneasy, and hastened to leave. Speech must have an object, for the 'real' American to tolerate it."

The same complaint is made in a letter of 1900 to Francis Boott: "I confess that one of the things at home that most draws me is the remembrance of your laugh and everlasting sociability and good humor. For you, talking is a substantive enjoyment. For my other colleagues and playmates, except perhaps Mrs. Whitman,[20] it is only a useful and often tiresome means to some ulterior end."

The following recollection by a former student indicates James's desire to establish a human in place of an official relationship: "We found that unless his positions were challenged his lectures might become prosy, whereas the challenge was sure to bring the lightning flashes of his wit and make it extremely interesting. Well do I remember how another student and myself framed a friendly conspiracy alternately to take the dangerous rôle of lightning conductor by trying to badger him. He also at that time had a curious habit of going around to his classes under the pretext of some trouble with his eyes and getting them to read his examination papers to him when, of course, if there was any lack of lucidity it could be at once explained. I think, however, his real object was to get in close touch and friendly contact with the men." [21]

It is clear from this description that James preferred to converse with people who had minds of their own, and who could give as well as receive. It was in 1896 from Chautauqua that James wrote his wife this impression, and this characteristically indulgent judgment, of certain serious and docile people whom he respected but did not enjoy: "I 'm put in conceit of college training. It certainly gives glibness and flexibility, if it does n't give earnestness and depth. I 've been meeting minds so earnest and helpless that it takes them half an hour to get from one idea to its immediately adjacent next neighbor, and that with infinite creaking and groaning. And when they 've got to the next idea, they lie down on it with their whole weight and can get no farther, like a cow on a door-mat, so that you can get neither in nor out with them. Still, glibness is not all. Weight is something, even cow-weight." [22]

These, James's natural benign gifts, — his sensibility, his vivacity,

[20] Mrs. Henry Whitman of Boston and Beverly; above, 357.
[21] A. C. Lane, "The Trilemma of Determinism," *Western Journal of Education,* IV (1911), 161–8.
[22] *L.W.J.,* II, 41. *Cf.* also above, 131.

his humanity, and his sociability, — united to compose his personal charm.   They were all engraven on his face and embodied in his appearance and bearing: in the erectness and firmness of his posture, in his "irascible blue eyes," in his "pleasant and manly voice," [23] and above all in the confident friendliness of his expression.   "I still remember vividly," writes one of his students, "how James used to arrive at class with hat and gloves but no overcoat on fairly cold mornings, and how handsome he looked standing on the edge of the platform and saying in a casual conversational tone: 'There is no primal teleological reagibility in a protoplasm.'"

His personality was radioactive, or, as Bergson expressed it, "un foyer ardent était là, dont on recevait chaleur et lumière." [24]   His flame not only warmed and illuminated, but ignited; bringing him both lasting friendships, and also a wide circle of acquaintances and readers whose admiration glowed with affection.   His personal qualities reached his readers, as well as his hearers, not only because these qualities infused his writing, but because his writing was addressed to his readers as though they were acquaintances or hearers.

Hence the same qualities which afford the key to James's character and personal magnetism also explain his style.   He was much concerned with literary form both in others and in himself.   Writing in 1894 of Stevenson's *Wrecker,* he said: "It seemed to me that the matter had decidedly overflowed and slopped round the form.   Too much inchoate frontierism of event, character and language.   Literature has to assimilate her stuff slowly to get it plastic."   James's own most characteristic species of writing was the lecture or public address.   A being as sensitively socialized as he could not utter monologues in the presence of his kind — he must reach out to them, touch them, and feel their response.   So whatever he wrote began as talk.   His letters were more artful than his talk. [25]   When it came to his published writings, they had to satisfy this social requirement and at the same time expound their subject matter with orderly completeness.   To accomplish

---

[23] *L.W.J.,* I, 25; *Letters of C. E. Norton,* 1913, I, 264. Elsewhere Norton says: "James's spirit and temper do good to whoever comes within their range; and it is as much through their affections as through their intellects that his disciples are attracted to him." (*Ibid.,* II, 412.)

[24] Preface to Delattre and le Breton, *William James: extraits de sa correspondance,* 1924, 7.

[25] "My letters, I find, tend to escape into humorisms, abstractions and flights of fancy." (*L.W.J.,* II, 111.)

both of these results at the same time cost James much labor. He wrote, corrected, and rewrote. "Everything comes out wrong with me at first; but when once objectified in a crude shape, I can torture and poke and scrape and pat it till it offends me no more." When his writing was thus finally acceptable to James, its subject matter was clarified and at the same time so humanized that he could enjoy a sense of common understanding and of friendly intercourse with his audience.

Of course he had his moments of dissatisfaction with this style. In 1908, when it was too late to change his habits even had it been temperamentally possible, he wrote: "I find that my free and easy and personal way of writing, especially in *Pragmatism,* has made me an object of loathing to many respectable academic minds, and I am rather tired of awakening that feeling, which more popular lecturing on my part will probably destine me to increase." But as a rule his style represented his own opinion of what philosophical style should be. "I don't care how incorrect language may be," he once said, "if it only has fitness of epithet, energy and clearness." He hailed Papini with joy, as one in whom he found "instead of heaviness, length and obscurity, lightness, clearness and brevity, with no lack of profundity or learning." [26] James's canons of style, in other words, were dictated by a consideration for his reader and a desire to *reach* him. He hated to be bored himself and he dreaded to give such offense to others. He once wrote to his brother Henry of Bryce's *American Commonwealth:* "A perfect bog of reasonableness, as you once said. One fairly longs for a *screech* of some kind."

James's style was also determined by the fact that he wrote both philosophy and psychology in literary or colloquial English. "Technicality seems to me to spell 'failure' in philosophy." He proposed to Santayana that they unite their forces in an assault on "the desiccating and pedantifying" [27] processes of the American Ph.D. This condemnation of technicality no doubt reflected James's distaste for logic and mathematics, but it also reflected his conviction that all inquiries are directed to the same world, which lies open and accessible; and that there is only one way of knowing, namely, by hypothesis and verification. There is, he said, "just

[26] *L.W.J.,* I, 297; II, 300–1; I, 341; *C.E.R.,* 460–1.
[27] *L.W.J.,* II, 79, 229.

man thinking, whether he be greengrocer or metaphysician." There is no mysterious kind of being or truth behind the known world. There is only that sort of thing with which we are familiar, and which we overlook or despise because it is familiar, and there is *more of the same kind*. Reality being of this intimate sort, re- vealing its innermost character in the human experience of every day, the appropriate style of philosophical exposition is that which vivifies the familiar, and extends its horizon without altering its essential character.

James felt a peculiar aversion towards the translations of his writings. "It is no doubt a piece of neurasthenic perversion of sensibility," he wrote to Flournoy in 1900, "but I confess that translations of my own writings always give me a kind of horror, and the best thing for me is in no way to coöperate. I have n't read a single page of the German translation of my *Essays* or of the Italian translation of my *Psychology*." This feeling was in part his characteristic desire to escape to something new from what had long been on his mind, and in part a feeling of humility that anyone should go to so much trouble on his account. But when he did advise his translators it was to urge them to subordinate literal accuracy to sense. He wanted the French translation of the short *Psychology* to read as if it were originally composed in the French language. When Flournoy was intending to translate the *Varieties,* James wrote: "Feel absolutely free to abridge, invent, expand, paraphrase in *any* way, solely from the point of view of making the French reader content." Again it is the social motive which outweighs every consideration of verbal precision.

Among the most technical of James's writings were the articles collected under the title of *Essays in Radical Empiricism.* They were designed as papers to be published in a philosophical journal and read by his professional colleagues. But before he published them he seized the opportunity to present them in his five lectures before Davidson's summer school at Glenmore in 1904, "just to hear how the stuff would sound when packed into that bulk. It sounded *queer,* and I must make it sound less so to the common mind." In short, James did not write for posterity, still less for eternity, but spoke audibly to those who were visibly present.

CONCLUSION

WE have met two William Jameses: the neurasthenic James, with his unstable nervous equilibrium, his sometimes morbidly vivid and lawless imagination, his oscillation of mood and aversion for rigorous intellectual procedure; and the radiant James, vivid, gay, loving, companionable, and sensitive. We have, in fact, met a third James, in whom the second of these is deepened and enriched through being united with the first. To this third James must be assigned two remarkable essays in self-revelation. The first was written about 1878, when James was thirty-six years of age: —

"I have often thought that the best way to define a man's character would be to seek out the particular mental or moral attitude in which, when it came upon him, he felt himself most deeply and intensely active and alive. At such moments there is a voice inside which speaks and says: '*This* is the real me!' . . . Now as well as I can describe it, this characteristic attitude in me always involves an element of active tension, of holding my own, as it were, and trusting outward things to perform their part so as to make it a full harmony, but without any *guaranty* that they will. Make it a guaranty — and the attitude immediately becomes to my consciousness stagnant and stingless. Take away the guaranty, and I feel (provided I am *überhaupt* in vigorous condition) a sort of deep enthusiastic bliss, of bitter willingness to do and suffer anything, which translates itself physically by a kind of stinging pain inside my breast-bone (don't smile at this — it is to me an essential element of the whole thing!), and which, although it is a mere mood or emotion to which I can give no form in words, authenticates itself to me as the deepest principle of all active and theoretic determination which I possess."[1]

The following paragraphs were written in a notebook twenty-five years later: —

"How can I . . . justify the strong antithesis I constantly feel, namely, that certain philosophic constructions . . . are subjective

[1] *L.W.J.*, I, 199–200.

caprices, redolent of individual taste, while other constructions, those which work with concrete elements, with change, with indeterminism, are more objective and cling closer to the temperament of nature itself. . . . What, on pragmatist terms, does 'nature itself' signify? To my mind it signifies the non-artificial; the artificial having certain definite æsthetic characteristics which I dislike, and can only apperceive in others as matters of personal taste, — to me bad taste. All neat schematisms with permanent and absolute distinctions, classifications with absolute pretensions, systems with pigeon-holes, etc., have this character. All 'classic,' clean, cut and dried, 'noble,' fixed, 'eternal,' *Weltanschauungen* seem to me to violate the character with which life concretely comes and the expression which it bears of being, or at least of involving, a muddle and a struggle, with an 'ever not quite' to all our formulas, and novelty and possibility forever leaking in.

"Münsterberg's Congress-program [2] seems to me, *e.g.,* to be sheer humbug in the sense of self-infatuation with an idol of the den, a kind of religious service in honor of the professional-philosophy-shop, with its faculty, its departments and sections, its mutual etiquette, its appointments, its great mill of authorities and exclusions and suppressions which the waters of truth are expected to feed to the great class-glory of all who are concerned. To me 'truth,' if there be any truth, would seem to exist for the express confusion of all this kind of thing, and to reveal itself in whispers to the 'meek lovers of the good' in their solitude — the Darwins, the Lockes, etc., — and to be expressly incompatible with officialism. 'Officials' are products of no deep stratum of experience. Münsterberg's Congress seems to be the perfectly inevitable expression of the system of his *Grundzüge,* an artificial construction for the sake of making the authority of professors inalienable, no matter what asininities they may utter, as if the bureaucratic mind were the full flavor of nature's self-revelation. It is obvious that such a difference as this, between me and Münsterberg, is a splendid expression of pragmatism. I want a world of anarchy, Münsterberg one of bureaucracy, and each appeals to 'nature' to back him up. Nature partly helps and partly resists each of us."

---

[2] "Münsterberg's Congress" was the "Congress of Arts and Sciences" held at the St. Louis Exposition in the summer of 1904. For his *Grundzüge der Psychologie,* 1900, *cf.* above, 147, 150–1.

"Active tension," uncertainty, unpredictability, extemporized adaptation, risk, change, anarchy, unpretentiousness, naturalness — these are the qualities of life which James finds most palatable, and which give him the deepest sense of well-being. These are at the same time the qualities which he deems most authentic, the accents in which the existent world speaks to him most directly. It seems clear that this metaphysical insight, profoundly temperamental as it is, cannot be imputed to any single element of James's nature, morbid or benign. There is something of his restlessness in it, something of his preference of the unusual to the orderly; it is to some extent his way of escape from a tendency to morbid self-preoccupation. On the other hand, it is a direct expression of his creative and richly imaginal fancy; a projection of his vivacity; and the cosmic sympathy by which he rejoiced in strange and varied otherness.

There is still a fourth James, the James of experience and discipline — a transformation of native qualities into dispositions and habits. One is, perhaps, surprised to discover that a man of James's speculative interests was also a man of the world. He was not, like the proverbial Thales, forever falling into wells while gazing at the stars; nor was he one of those childlike innocents, well known in the European academic world, who need a guardian to manage their affairs. He knew his way around. As was once remarked of his father, he knew how to go close to the edge of impropriety without stepping off.[3] Despite his bold indiscretions, his easy manners, and a mischievous delight in shocking the pedants, he never strayed beyond the bounds of good taste. Or if he did, he knew it. His breeding gave him that sense of security which permits occasional liberties. He took liberties with the English language, but they were clearly privileged liberties, which derived a certain authority from the fact that he took them. He associated with strange characters, and frequented the intellectual underworld; but he did not lose caste, or compromise his essential dignity. Here, in short, was a man who seemed to let himself go, or to be *willing* to make a fool of himself, and who, owing to some unconscious inner check, never did make a fool of himself. He was original, spontaneous, but never "queer."

[3] MS. report of G. H. Howison's "St. Louis Reminiscences," Jan. 6, 1916, University of California Library.

We think of James as cosmopolitan, and of course he was. He began his almost ceaseless travels at the age of two, and learned to feel at home in all parts of Western Europe. Yet he was so crudely patriotic as to make his more emancipated friends feel a sense of superior detachment. It was characteristic of him to write to Norton of England's "magnificently fine state of civilization," to say that "everything here seems about twice as good as the corresponding thing with us"; and then to add, "but I suspect we have the bigger eventual destiny after all" — thereby betraying, as Norton said, his "invincible Americanism." [4] In short, though James moved freely and wandered far, he was never uprooted. His "heart" remained at home.

Worldly wisdom, taste, breeding, domesticity, patriotism — these were some of the forces of control, entering into what we may call the conscience of James, as distinguished from his native traits. There remain the two major constituents of that conscience, the moral and the intellectual.

James was a moralist in the good old-fashioned sense of one who believes that right is right and wrong is wrong, and he enrolled himself under the first in order to combat the second. "Tell him to live by yes and no, — yes to everything good, no to everything bad," was the message he once sent to his youngest son. I shall not attempt to trace this moralism to its source. It is natural to attribute it to his Calvinistic ancestry, though such an explanation loses much of its force when it is remembered that his father, the immediate embodiment of that ancestry, was in antinomian revolt against Calvinism. More important than the question of creed is the fact that his father was a good man and a moral partisan; and there was an image of maternal saintliness which, could it be brought into a clearer light, would no doubt explain much. It is plain, also, that a sense of deportment, associated with those checks of taste and breeding already noted, disposed him to accept traditional moral standards. The intensity of his moral feeling was reënforced by his sympathies, since morals for James were always in the end translated into humanity.

The strength of James's moralism is proved by the fact that it outweighed the warm attachment of old friendships; prevented his ever becoming a mere psychologist of morals, as might have been

---

[4] *Letters of C. E. Norton,* 1913, II, 412.

expected from his interest in the history and pathology of the mind; set limits to his love of life, and sometimes even to his tolerance; and definitively triumphed over his æsthetic sensibility and artistic impulse.

Moralism is only one name for James's fundamental seriousness. With all his gayety and playfulness, he exceeded most of his contemporaries in his sense of responsibility. He refused to use any of the methods, so well known among philosophers, by which a man justifies his leaving the arena and taking a seat among the spectators: "I can't bring myself, as so many men seem able to do, to blink the evil out of sight, and gloss it over. It's as real as the good, and if it is denied, good must be denied too. It must be accepted and hated and resisted while there's breath in our bodies." [5] In short, unlike a later and faltering generation, James united liberalism, tolerance, and humanity with a resolve that these principles should, so help him God, prevail.

James had an intellectual as well as a moral conscience. He had a regard, almost a reverence, for facts. In his early days as a student at Harvard, it was Jeffries Wyman with his scrupulous and modest adherence to the results of observation, rather than Louis Agassiz with his bolder and more dogmatic mind, who was his scientific paragon. His philosophical heroes were always men like Renouvier or Mill whom he believed to be honest and disinterested in the sense of reporting faithfully what they found. He did not object to invention and wishful thinking, but he did object to the pretense that they were anything else. He was an empiricist because he believed empiricism to be the only *open-minded* and *candid* philosophy.

His intellectual conscience appears in his vast erudition, his indefatigable industry, and in the patience with which he controlled his own impatience and devoted years to the untying of a philosophic knot. It took him ten years to answer Royce's argument for the Absolute, and another ten years to solve the problem of the compounding of consciousness. When he died he had just forsworn his *Sturm und Drang* propensities forever in order that he might satisfy his intellectual scruples and the "respectable academic minds" of his colleagues.

James took philosophy as he took life — seriously. He felt that,

[5] *L.W.J.*, I, 158.

like tragic poetry, it was distinguished by its noble theme. Philosophy was not a form of play or craftsmanship, though it might add those values to its own. It was the pursuit of truth. And truth is not worth pursuing unless what you apprehend you also believe. It is by belief that one makes truth one's own — absorbs its nutriment. Hence in his philosophizing James was a believer; and was moved by the believer's missionary zeal. Thus he once wrote to his fellow pluralist, James Ward: "We must all go to work to counteract the *Absolute One,* which has its way so freely in metaphysics, and I hope you'll play your part actively."

There is a simple earnestness in this plea that is of the very essence of James. His power in philosophy and over philosophers was due in no small measure to his teaching that in theory as in practice a man must take his part, believing something, fighting for what he believes, and incurring the risk of being wrong. And with all this eagerness of pursuit and strength of conviction there was no suspicion of complacency. He always left the impression that there was more; that he knew there was more; and that the more to come might, for all one knew, throw a very different light on the matters under discussion. He respected his universe too much to believe that he could carry it under his own hat. These saving doubts arose from the same source as his tolerance and respect for his fellow man. The universe, like one's neighbor, is never wholly disclosed to outward view, and the last word must be a consent that the *other* should be *itself.* In metaphysics, as in human relations, the chief source of illumination is sympathy. The conclusion of the matter was unconsciously formulated by James himself: —

"I merely point out to you that, as a matter of fact, certain persons do exist with an enormous capacity for friendship and for taking delight in other people's lives; and that such persons know more of truth than if their hearts were not so big." [6]

[6] *T.T.,* 267.

APPENDICES

I

PHILOSOPHICAL CORRESPONDENCE BETWEEN
WILLIAM JAMES AND HIS FATHER[1]
(1867)

Berlin, Sept. 5, 1867

My beloved old Dad, —

. . . I have read your article[2] which I got in Teplitz several times carefully. I must confess that the darkness which to me has always hung over what you have written on these subjects is hardly at all cleared up. Every sentence seems written from a point of view which I nowhere get within range of, and on the other hand ignores all sorts of questions which are visible from my present view. My questions, I know, belong to the Understanding, and I suppose deal entirely with the "natural constitution" of things, but I find it impossible to step out from them into relation with "spiritual" facts, and the very language you use *ontologically* is also so extensively rooted in the finite and phenomenal that I cannot avoid accepting it as it were in its mechanical sense, when it becomes to me devoid of significance. I feel myself, in fact, more and more drifting towards a sensationalism closed in by scepticism — but the scepticism will keep bursting out in the very midst of it, too, from time to time, so that I cannot help thinking I may one day get a glimpse of things through the ontological window. At present it is walled up. I can understand now no more than ever the world wide gulf you put between "Head" and "Heart"; to me they are inextricably entangled together, and seem to grow from a common stem — and *no* theory of creation seems to me to make things clearer. I cannot logically understand *your* theory. You posit first a phenomenal Nature in which the *alienation* is produced (but phenomenal to *what?* to the already unconsciously existing creature?), and from this effected alienation a *real* movement of return follows. But

---

[1] For a discussion of these letters *cf.* above, I, 155. The first, which is here reprinted only in part, has already appeared in *L.W.J.*, I, 95–8.

[2] The article here referred to dealt with "Swedenborg's Ontology," and was a review of recent books on the subject. It appeared in the *North Amer. Rev.*, CV (1867).

how *can* the real movement have its rise in the phenomenal? And if it does not, it seems to me the creation is the very arbitrary one you inveigh against; and the whole process is a mere circle of the creator described within his own being and returning to the starting-point. I cannot understand what you mean by the descent of the creator into nature; you don't explain it, and it seems to be the kernel of the whole.

You speak sometimes of our natural life as our whole conscious life; sometimes of our consciousness as composed of both elements, finite and infinite. If our *real* life is unconscious, I don't see how you can occupy in the final result a different place from the Stoics, for instance. These are points on which I have never understood your position, and they will doubtless make you smile at my stupidity; but I cannot help it. I ought not to write about them in such a hurry. . . . I arrived here late last night. My back will prevent my studying physiology this winter at Leipsig, which I rather hoped to do. I shall stay here if I can. If unable to live here and cultivate the society of the natives without a greater moral and dorsal effort than my shattered frame will admit, I will retreat to Vienna where, knowing so many Americans, I shall find social relaxation without much expense of strength. . . . Much love from your affectionate,

WM. JAMES

Berlin, Sept. 26, 1867

My dearest Dad, —

. . . Many thanks for writing so often. I wrote you three weeks ago, just after my arrival, more hastily than the seriousness of the subject required perhaps, and so hastily that I cannot now remember what I said with any distinctness. Whatever I did say, however, was meant rather as a description of the natural *sag* of my mind when left to itself, than as its deliberate opinion when active. Then it becomes wholly sceptical. I do not despair, however, of finding bottom somewhere, and it may be where you stand, if I ever fully understand you. I see much better what you are driving at now than I ever did before, however. I wish you would send me to read again that article on "Faith and Science." [3] I had somewhere among my traps the copy you sent me to Pará. Perhaps Harry can find it. I want you to feel how thorough is my personal sympathy with you, and how great is my delight in much that I do understand of what you think, and my admiration of it. You live in such mental isolation that I cannot help often feeling bitterly at the thought that you must see in even your own

[3] *North Amer. Rev.*, CI (1865).

children strangers to what you consider the best part of yourself. But it is a matter in which one's wishes are of little influence, and until something better comes, you can feel sure of the fullest and heartiest *respect* I feel for any living person. . . .

I have sent Harry with this an ineffably flat article for the *Nation*.[4] Having just read it over it seems to me really hardly worth the postage, so don't let Harry hesitate, through fear of wounding my feelings, from sending it, if he thinks it not adapted for publication. Tell Mother I kiss her more like twice a day than once a month. Give lots of love to Bob, Alice, and all. . . . Ever your loving

WM. JAMES

Cambridge, Sept. 27, 1867

My dear Willy, —

I wrote you by Thursday steamer in haste, and now add what I had n't time to say in that letter. I have no great conceit of my expository ability, and my *N. A. R.* article is full, no doubt, of incapacity, but at the same time it is very evident to me that your trouble in understanding it arises *mainly* from the purely scientific cast of your thought just at present, and the temporary blight exerted thence upon your metaphysic wit. Ontological problems seem very idle to the ordinary scientific imagination, because it is stupefied by the giant superstition we call Nature. That is to say, the man of science admits that every thing he observes by any sense is strictly phenomenal or relative to every thing else; but he is not disconcerted by this fact, because he holds instinctively to an *absolute substance* in which all these fleeting things inhere, this substance being Nature. We all *instinctively* do the same thing, but the difference between the philosopher and the man of science, between the man who *reflects* and the man who simply *observes,* is, that the former outgrows his intellectual instincts or disavows the bondage of sense, and attains to the exercise of free thought. And the first postulate of free thought is that Nature — being a mere generalization of the human mind, intended to give a quasi-unity to the divergent objects of sense — is void of absoluteness, or has no being *in se* but only in the exigencies of our carnal understanding. If we believed instinctively in *creation,* we should have no need of this hypothesis of Nature. For then we should see all the various forms of sense acknowledging a unitary human substance, and would regard any brute unintelligible quantity like what we call Nature, a sheer superfluity or superstition. But while we disbelieve in creation, as we

---

[4] This article was a review of Herman Grimm's *Unüberwindliche Mächte,* and was published anonymously in the *Nation,* CV (1867). It is James's first known publication.

do while we are still the sport of our senses or the dupes of our scientific activity, we must believe in Nature as the objective source or explication (instead of the subjective product or implication) of all phenomena; and so long as this belief lasts, the mind remains puerile, and God — though we may continuously admit his existence out of regard to tradition — becomes a rigid superfluity, so far as the conduct of life is concerned.

Now here it seems to me is exactly where you are as yet intellectually: in this scientific or puerile stage of progress. That is, you believe in some universal quantity called Nature, able not merely to *mother* all the specific objects of sense, or give them the subjective identity they crave to our understanding, but also to *father* them or give them the objective individuality or character they claim in themselves. And of course while this state of mind endures, the idea of creation is idle and superfluous to you, for if Nature is there to give absolute being to existence, what need have we to hunt up a creator?

But let me get down to your particular difficulties. I quote: "I cannot, etc. . . . to the starting-point." I don't know what you mean by the *"unconsciously existing* creature," as all existence implies to my mind consciousness of some sort. Certainly when I speak of my existing phenomenally, I mean that I *exist* or *appear to my own consciousness,* and *to the perception of others. Reflectively* I admit that this appearance . . . has no reality out of consciousness, that is, no absolute reality, being altogether relative or subservient to a higher spiritual and as yet unconscious existence . . . but my reflection is utterly impotent to control the data of sense, and I *feel* my own existence or reality to be as absolute — feel the delivery of consciousness to be as unquestionable — if not indeed more absolute and unquestionable than all other knowledge, sensuous and scientific both, put together. I *know* that I am not God, that I am *other* than infinite, and nothing but disease of my brain, or some overpowering sophistry, can ever possibly shake that knowledge or enfeeble it, but everything on the contrary goes forever to confirm and enhance it.

Thus my self-consciousness eternally projects or separates me from God; stamps me essentially finite where he is infinite, imperfect where he is perfect, contingent where he is absolute; created where He is creative; and so of strict necessity, as it were, originates a free movement of return to Him; that is to say, an inward movement, a movement of my inward or *individual* being. The movement is a spontaneous one, and infallibly leads to that objective or spiritual conjunction with God in which my real being lies. For this separation from God which consciousness affirms as inherent in my *self,* is noway agreeable to me as a selfish being, but on the contrary every way disagreeable and painful; so that my very selfishness prompts me to unselfishness — prompts me to separate myself from myself as it were — in paying some regard to my neighbor, or learning to identify myself to some extent with others. This is that birth of my inward or spiritual and immortal life, to which my natural consciousness has been wholly subsidiary. If, as my consciousness avers, I am alienated from God, or the infinite good, *just in so far as I am myself,* then clearly my aroused self-love binds me to the utmost alertness in getting away from myself, or postponing its interests to those of my fellow-man. By this instinctive movement I begin to put on real or objective being, that being which lies in becoming conjoined actively with the Divine perfection. For the creative love is purely objective as having no subjective ends, no taint or draw-back of self-love; so that if I can become objective even for subjective ends, or at the instigation of my selfish cupidity, *there* at all events is a Divine form superinduced upon my natural consciousness, which will one day be admissive of higher or spiritual substance and will gradually divorce me from my phenomenal foothold and plant me upon reality. That is to say, the lower, natural, passive, subjective side of my consciousness — what allies me with the finite — instead of dominating the higher, spiritual or objective and active side — what allies me with the infinite — will be taken up into the latter, just as the mineral is taken up and glorified in the vegetable, this again in the animal, and the animal in man. To argue then, as you do, that this objective tendency in us is unreal because it has only a subjective provocation or base, is like arguing down my spiritual manhood, my practical objective sympathy with all goodness and truth, because you can scientifically relegate me in all material regards back to animal, vegetable and mineral antecedents. I have the inexpugnable testimony of consciousness to my spiritual reality, a testimony which laughs at all adverse reasoning — which thrives in fact by all outward gainsaying, and only dwindles in an atmosphere of outward concession or acknowledgment.

You go on to say — "I cannot understand what you mean by the creative descent into nature" etc. . . . You mean I don't explain it *physically,* for I have done nothing else but explain it *metaphysically.* It doesn't admit of physical explanation; this is a matter of course, for physics are themselves an *im*plication of the truth alleged, and are themselves therefore only legitimately *ex*plicated by it, without the ghost of a legitimate pretension themselves to explicate it. The palpable metaphysic reason for the descent of the creator into nature, is supplied by the very definition of creation as a marriage of creator and creature. Certainly you see this much to be true, that creative if it mean anything means an equation of the creative and created natures. There is just as certainly, however, no essential or absolute equality between them, so that creation if it take place at all must be purely empirical or contingent; that is to say, *must involve an experience on the creature's part which shall bring him up to level of the creator.* But how shall the creature command the necessary resources for this end? He is in himself absolutely without funds, being as yet utterly unconscious or non-existent, so that unless his creator is rich and gracious enough to make him a loan, by making over *his* existence to him as it were, or allowing him to appropriate it as freely as if it were his own, he will never be able to bring himself up to the required level. He can ascend or come into consciousness, only in so far as the creator previously descends or lapses from consciousness. Now this descent of the creator is what we call Nature, or the universe of existence. *There is in reality or spiritually no such thing as universal existence, all life in the exact measure of its perfection being individual.* But to the finite mind Nature or the realm of universality is unquestionable, so that the creature unhesitatingly refers his existence to it, absolutely affiliates himself to it, blindly, irresistibly *identifies* himself with it, and hence falls into the creative trap without a struggle or so much even as the dimmest suspicion of the true state of the case. What the creature believes in utterly and without any misgiving, is the *universality* — the community — the identity of existence as avouched by what we call Nature; and what consequently he never so much as speculates — what he never so much as dreams of — is a possible individuality of existence, which is not only commensurate with this wide weltering universality, but superior to it and capable of coercing it into its perfect vassalage. Hence the Creator has His own perfect and merciful way with him altogether. By playing upon this superstitious belief of his in Nature — by allowing him to appropriate without stint a personality derived from natural appetite and passion, from natural affection and thought — he gives him that requisite projection from Himself, that needful *self*-consciousness which bases his spiritual reaction towards the Creator, and ends in the ultimate marriage between the two which we call creation. Thus Nature is only a creative form, ceremony, or ritual. It is a living symbol or consecration of the spiritual marriage which is forever going on or deepening between creator and creature; and is *utterly devoid of life but in that aspect.*

But it is time that I put my letter in the mail, and my head aches with the fatigue of writing so much on a stretch. I will write again and doubtless more to the purpose if you answer this letter critically. I am sure I have something better to tell you than you will be able to learn from all Germany — at least all scientific Germany. So urge me hard to your own profit. Let it go at present into your memory — if no further — that in the true order of thought individuality is primary, and universality or community altogether derivative: that is, that the only universal existence is individual existence. In other words, there is but one created or universal species — Man; and all the genera or kinds of existence are only so many implications of that unitary Form. Good-bye. Harry also is going up with a letter for you.

[Unsigned]

Berlin, Oct. 28, 1867

My dear Father, —

I acknowledged your metaphysical letter last week. I will now try as well as my feeble power will let me to reply to it. It helped to clear up many of the points on which your position was obscure to me, though I cannot say that I yet fully understand it. I think much of my difficulty has been from uncertainty as to your use of words; and from having been led astray by your *tone* to look for a *necessary* connection between propositions, where I could not find one, although there was a very intelligible empirical one. Thoughts would naturally in your mind, interwoven through and through it as they have been by long brooding, acquire a substantialness and vividness, and consequently a positiveness and absoluteness of expression, which they would needs be deprived of on their first reception into mine. This applies to almost all your ontological matter. You say that such and such *must* be the way in creation, as if there were an *a priori* logical necessity binding on the mind. This I cannot see at all in the way you seem to, although I may be quite ready to accept the contents of your propositions as an *a posteriori* hypothesis; or, if you object to that word, an "unprovable" affirmation of the heart like those you speak of.

But there occurs an objection at the very threshold which seems to me more important. It refers to the whole conception of creation, from which you would exclude all arbitrariness or magic. Now I don't see what the word "creation" can mean if this be totally excluded, or what there is to justify its discrimination from pantheism. Creation, emanation, have at all times been opposed to pantheism, immanence; and it is evident from the scorn with which you always mention pantheism that you, too, place a broad gulf between them. The essence of the pantheistic conception, if I understand it, consists in there being a necessary relation between Creator and creature, so that both are the same fact viewed from opposite sides, and their duality as Creator and creature becomes merged in a higher unity as Being. Consequently a conception really opposed to pantheism must necessarily refuse to admit any such ratio as this, — any such external ratio, — so to speak, between them; must deny that each term exists only by virtue of the equation to which it belongs; the Creator must be the all, and the act by which the creature is set over against him have its motive within the creative circumference. The act must therefore necessarily contain an arbitrary and magical element — that is, if I attach the right meaning to those words — undetermined by anything external to the agent. Of course it is impossible to attempt to imagine the *way* of creation, but wherever from an absolute first a second appears, *there* it must be; — and it must be magical, for if in the second there be anything coequal or coeval with the first, it becomes pantheism.

So much for the way in which I apprehend the terms, and you will see how I fail to understand why on the one hand you have such an aversion to pantheism, and yet on the other to an arbitrary creation. I can see no essential logical reason for preferring one to the other, and am accordingly ready to accompany you in believing in creation as I understand it. But then it seems that you understand it differently, for you find an opprobrium in the idea of the creature being left in the shape of a mere emanation. To me it seems he can be no true creature outside of that condition; inside of it he may be anything. You say in your article: "To create or give being to things is no doubt an inscrutable function of the Divine omnipotence to which our intelligence is incapable of assigning any *a priori* limit or law." And accordingly, so far as we know the final cause of creation, it may be the production of a consciousness pleasant or of a consciousness painful, of one ignorant of its creatureship or otherwise, filled with love for the creator or with aversion, or entirely unconscious. It seems to me that the "reality" of the creature obtains, that he "truly is," when this end, whatever it may be, is fulfilled. You, on the contrary, appear to claim for him something additional, to insist that he attain an "absolute being," which to me, if it mean anything, means transcending the limits of his creatureship.

You will probably now see my position; its difficulties may be verbal, but even if they are, I cannot help thinking they must have been shared by a good many of your readers. Take for instance this passage, to which I remember referring in my first letter: "God can create only what is devoid of being in itself; this is manifest. And yet what is void of being in itself can at best only appear to be. It can be no real but only a phenomenal existence." It seems to me you slip here from the idea of "being in itself" (or being as uncreated) in the first sentence, to that of "real" being in the last, a less definite term. To make sense to my mind the whole should read: "God can create only what is devoid of being, except as created. And what is thus void of uncreated being, can at best only *appear* to be uncreated. Its *uncreatedness* cannot be real but only phenomenal." This is a very different conclusion to yours. *It* can be real. Why can it not be real *and* created? real *as* created? real in the sense I spoke of on the preceding page?

Oct. 29. To descend a little more into details:—You give the creature a natural consciousness, with which he identifies himself and thus becomes alienated, aware of an opposition in him to the Creator. This opposition under the influence of religion becomes hateful to him, a recoil from his natural consciousness takes place, and with it the true creation, to which what has preceded is merely subsidiary, takes place, by a spontaneous movement of return to the Creator being originated. Do not suppose I am opposed to such a theory—as a filling out of the idea of creation, as a history, as an account of the "physics" of the matter, it is most beautiful and acceptable;—but I cannot see how it leads to a result *qualitatively* a bit different from a process in which the natural consciousness should be a superfluity, and the creature cast off equipped with an instinctive belief in the Creator, and an immediate knowledge of his own estate. I cannot see how those germs of his spiritual individuality from which his true life grows, differ *essentially* from his natural consciousness, nor how, multiply the planes of reflection as you will, and chase the process up and down the angles, you ever come out with more than you put in, namely the sole Creator. He, in the last resort, bears the whole expense of the operation.

What you say in your letter does not explain away the difficulty, because no matter how great you make the difference between the subjective side and the objective side in the creature, they remain at most but opposite poles of the same thing. The life of plant and animal has its root in the mineral life, and draws all its force therefrom; yet its form is totally unconscious therein. Sensation, perception, and reason apparently have their roots in the life of the nervous system, yet their form is entirely new and original. And in the same way my spiritual manhood may be a form wholly different from the moral consciousness in which it has its root, but after all is said, there is *one* sense in which they all fall together, one ratio they have in common, their ratio to the Creator. In the long series from the mineral to the highest form of social love that I can imagine, I can neither see it as possible logically or probable empirically, that there should exist an interrupted link, a gap in which some new quality made its appearance so "spontaneous" as to be in this deepest essence different from the rest, or more "real" as opposed to the Creator. This is the "descent of the Creator into nature" which I told you I did not understand — this sudden appearance of him in a different relation to one part of the chain from that in which he had stood towards the other part. You say I seem to be asking of you a *physical* explanation of this. It seems to me on the contrary that the only difficulty is metaphysical. Considered in their physical differences, it is very obvious that the different links of the created chain look towards the Creator differently.

You probably now see the state of my mind, and where the trouble lies. Either I entirely lose sight of some vital element of the question; or I am led by the natural zeal of your mode of expression to think that you draw fundamental distinctions where you do not really do so. In either case it will now be easier than before for you to set me right. I do not think you will accuse me of wanting to "chop logic" on these, of all matters. Really, my tendency is entirely the other way. For myself, I shrink from trying to image too exactly these things; but if we are to talk about them at all, we must try to work as much clearness into our words as possible. I am sure that I understand you now better than before, though probably still imperfectly. You know how much depends in these matters on a natural bent of feeling, and you probably know how sceptical I am and how little ready to *assert* anything about them. I think that spontaneously I am rather inclined to lapse into a pantheistic mode of contemplating the world, but even if my thoughts were worthier and more serious than they are, I doubt if I should ever care to measure very jealously one way of considering it against another, but would rather let each go as symbols. Your analysis or Swedenborg's of creation into its elements seems to me a most full and beautiful one, and I do not now think that my possible joy in going forth to meet the Creator in the sort of marriage or equation you represent ought to be diminished by my believing that the thing was after all a piece of "magic" on his part. Empirically it is different. I cannot attain to any such "inexpugnable testimony of consciousness to my spiritual reality" as that you speak of, and that must be a decisive moment in determining one's attitude towards such problems. *Practically*, it seems to me that *all* tendencies must nowadays unite in philanthropy; perhaps an atheistic tendency more than any, for sympathy is now so much developed in the human breast that misery and undeveloped-ness would all the more powerfully call for correction when coupled with the thought that from nowhere else than from us could correction possibly come, — that we ourselves must be our own providence.

I have now laid bare to you the general complexion of my mind. I cannot help thinking that to you it will appear most pitiful and bald. But I cannot help it and cannot feel responsible for it. Heaven knows I do not love it, and if in a future letter or letters you are able to sow some seed in it which may grow up and help to furnish it I shall be thankful enough. Good night, my dear old Daddy. I will close this letter here, and write gossip to Alice by this steamer. Ever your loving son,

WM. J.

MEMORANDUM [5]

You posit as preliminary to your construction these three premises:
(1) The creature cannot possibly have a real distinctness or separateness from the Creator;
(2) Yet he must somehow have a logical distinctness, to identify him as created;
(3) He must also be "worthy" of his creative source, or reflect in some way its likeness.

The objections I now have to make are purely logical ones — you have as yet no right to bring in any data from feeling (or psychological ones) to aid in rebutting them.

I say, first, that, though to reconcile (1) and (2) your introduction of the concept *"appearing to exist"* seems quite legitimate, yet you are wrong in claiming this to be synonymous with "appearing *to himself* to exist *as non-created"*; since (in the absence of any third spectator) the appearance may logically be an appearance to the Creator as well as to the creature; and an appearance of createdness as well as uncreatedness. Hence the deduction of your first step is not logically cogent.

Your final step, that after which the process of creation is complete, results in the existence of a creature appearing to himself as such. You assume all along that such a consciousness-as-creature is impossible save with the preliminary experience of a consciousness-as-free, to serve as a foil, or ground to rise from. This seems to me an unnecessary assumption, for the moment you admit any qualitative determination at all of the creature's being, consciousness-as-created would seem as admissible as anything else to be its primitive form. . . .

The conclusion I draw from [the above] premises shrinks up very short in comparison [with] yours. . . . I can only explain [the]

---

[5] These notes were found in W.J.'s handwriting, attached to the above letter. The MS. is unfortunately mutilated and incomplete. The words in brackets have been supplied by the author, and the unintelligible fragments omitted altogether.

greater elaborateness of your construction by supposing that it was not originally deduced in your own mind but formed in some other way, and these premises fitted to it afterwards. In other words, your system starts partly from psychological data — from the empirical fact of a selfhood, whose feeling is in opposition to the dictates of reason, etc., etc., etc. And I think that if your [position] would base itself undisguisedly on the [claims] of our active nature, it would be clearer [and more] persuasive than it is.

II

TURGENEV TO HENRY JAMES, JR.[1]

Paris, lundi, 21 janv., 1876

Cher Monsieur James, —

(Je commence par vous demander la permission de vous écrire en français.) Vous devez me trouver très peu poli de ne pas vous avoir remercié jusqu'à présent du cadeau que vous m'avez fait. La raison en est étrange — mais parfaitement véridique: j'ai de nouveau oublié votre adresse — et je n'ai pas pu retrouver où je l'avais inscrité. Aussi me suis-je décidé à écrire aujourd'hui à l'aventure, avec l'espoir que si, malgré tout, ma lettre vous parvient, vous aurez la complaisance de me le faire savoir. Je continue à être souffrant et à ne pas sortir — ce n'est plus la goutte — c'est une bronchite que j'ai attrapée. Nous avons commencé, Mme. Viardot et moi, à lire votre livre — nous avons lu les deux premiers chapitres — et je suis heureux de vous dire tant le plaisir que cela nous a causé. La scène (avant le départ) entre Rowland, la mère de Roderick, Miss Garland et Striker est faite de main de maître. Je ne doute pas que la continuation de la lecture nous faire le même plaisir — et je ne veux pas tarder davantage à vous envoyer mes meilleures félicitations. Si cette lettre vous parvient, vous seriez très aimable de pousser jusqu'à la Rue de Douai. La dernière fois que vous êtes venu je me sentais mal et me mettais au lit. Je ne bougerai pas de chez moi tous ces jours-ci. Mille amitiés, et au revoir.

Iv. TOURGUENEFF

[1] Enclosed in letter of H.J.[2] to W.J., Feb. 8, 1876, printed above, I, 365.

III

NOTES BY CHAUNCEY WRIGHT
(1874–1875?)

THE following notes are written in Wright's hand on James's manuscript entitled "Against Nihilism," 1874–1875(?); (*cf.* above, I, 525–8). The attribution of these notes to Wright is based on chirographic peculiarities which leave little room for doubt.

[p. 1032, ". . . it is meant"] This, by figure, at least, refers the phenomenon to an assumed intelligent will which as contrasted with it, is posited as non-phenomenal, *i.e.,* noumenal. All phenomena *do* refer to existences besides themselves as individual phenomena, but these existences are what they *mean* or are *signs of:* — and are not what means or intends them, except when they are phenomena of an intelligent will. When the phenomena refer to existences at all determined or determinable, these existences are also phenomena, actual or potential, *i.e.,* present in perception or in conception; the concept being the identicus or *ideographic sign* of a perception not present. . . . The *objectivity* of a phenomenon is its significance. Even the subject becomes an object when any phenomenon is consciously referred to it or is felt to be a sign of it. Not "being meant by," neither "meaning" in an active sense, but being simply and neutrally "a sign of," seems to me to be the substantive reference of a phenomenon in general; and that the active and passive relations are particular ones added to this general neutral one. To be sure, even this is a polar relation — not an equality; since a substance is not conceived as a *sign* of its attributes, but the reverse. A sign as determining must be itself more determined than what it determines. But by "substance" is sometimes meant "essence" or essential attributes; and these may be signs of inseparable accidents. Thus inertia felt by us may signify to us weight, ultimate incompressibility, and indestructibility. In this logical sense "the substance" is a sign of its attributes, or "means" them. In metaphysics "substance" is not a select set of attributes, but *all* attributes actual and potential — and the unknown in general as well as the at present unperceived.

The very individuality of a phenomenon is a determination of it by other phenomena. . . . As individual and actual it is *now;* and "now" is a mutual determination of two series, *ante* and *post.* It may have no relation to space, or such determination in space, as well as time, as an individual thing has; it may have no determination in kind, class or quality, or such as would determine a name or even a thought or any sign of it; still as being actual it is placed between the two series which determine it to be now, and therefore its individuality is not in itself. Neither is it in a common substratum of existence, which negatives all difference and individuality. Common sense is right, but not skilful in distinctions and dialectics; and what is called "nihilism" does not differ from it except in the analysis of being. That which without being present, or in any exact sense existent, is simply signified by what is present, does not gain existence because the sign is believed in. Its concept or sign is distinguished from the mere suggestion or imagination which has no respect to reality. Belief in the sign has respect to reality; and reality is threefold: a past, a present, and a future — one remembered, one perceived, one expected. It is only in the present reality or the present object of belief, that the phenomenon stands for itself; has no fallible representative, is actually itself. And even in the present it is not any kind, class or quality; or instance of a kind, etc; but is to be so determined only by being a sign of remembered or preconceived phenomena; which as a sign it calls up more or less vaguely as present concept.

Reality, or that to which logically, or in a process of thought and action, belief has respect, or is relevant, should be distinguished (as it is not by common sense) from the actuality of a phenomenon, as that beyond which ontologically metaphysics searches for substance. In respect to the quest of metaphysics there is nothing in our knowledge but present phenomena — objective and subjective, and mutually related or mutually determining and determined, but ever passing phenomena, ever coming forth and fading out, though not by chance. There is an order in them. This order is partly in the present group and leads continuously on, though more or less unexpected elements continually modify the cognitive order. These are the elements of objective perception. Orderliness is not what needs explanation by a metaphysical cause, but is what affords explanation and prompts to its quest whenever the unexpected occurs. The *"nothing* besides phenomena and their laws" (the laws themselves embodied and exemplified in present specimen phenomena) — this doctrine of phenomenalism and nominalism — attaches to the word "nothing" a sense which must be understood to relate only to this ontological quest of pure being. The realities of belief are not thereby made present actualities, on the pain of being declared illusory. My expectations are of the real if what I now expect comes to pass or becomes actual; though it has no existence, or no other existence than having a sign in my present consciousness; that is, a conceived, putative, potential existence in a representative which so far as the individual existence of this as a present phenomenon is concerned, is not different from that of merely imagined, unexpected phenomena; seeing that an expectation or belief is not dependent on any but a phenomenal difference between what is believed and what is merely imagined — namely, the remembered order of past phenomena.

But after all, nihilism is rather a discipline than a positive doctrine; an exorcism of the vague; a criticism of questions which by habit have passed beyond the real practical grounds or causes of question. Common sense is opposed only so far as common sense is not critical.

[p. 1032, ". . . having this quality"] This quality appears to me to be a merely negative one — simply as *no part* of the phenomena of our activity. Our passivity toward them is not a compulsion by them of our activities, but simply a non-belonging to our activity. Our activity may govern them indirectly, it is true, in all cases where the outward, objective results of our activity affect the conditions of the phenomena. I may cease at will to see, because seeing depends on the positions of my eyes and their openness, and these depend on my wishes or motives.

The contrast here indicated is not that of a substance and phenomena, but of subject and object phenomena; in the special relation, moreover, of perception to the *active* phenomena of the self. But perceptions are often or for the most part, two-sided, immediately involving *our* passivities or feelings, and their outward significance. As feelings they are signs of us, ourselves; they mean the subject "we are." As perceptions they mean something not us, not in our particular memories or imaginations — some other phenomena present only by their concept signs, and only vaguely perhaps in these.

[p. 1033, ". . . conscious existence"] No feeling except perhaps in unreflective consciousness — in an absolutely unremembered consciousness (if any there be) — exists by itself as an instant conscious existence. It passes (by its relations of resemblance, and contiguous association, or by a significance that is grounded on these) to other feelings, — and this is true quite irrespective of its being a feeling *in* us or a feeling of something else. This *passing* character in a phenomenon, which passes even when continuous or constant in degree, is recognized by all thinkers on both sides. Time is always an element in phenomena, both internal and external, and is the abstract of relations in general.

It is the *continuum* of phenomenal existences. It is their "substance" in the logical sense; that is, their universal attribute.

[p. 1033, ". . . that the self"] It is nothing without *its relations* of resemblance, contiguous association, significance, and in time; and these, when uncompounded of simpler relations belonging to these same highest categories, are self-existent in the sense of not being subject to explanation. If derived there is no evidence, nor any conception of their derivation, which does not contradict their nature as the elements of all conceivable explanation.

IV

LETTERS OF J. DELBŒUF TO WILLIAM JAMES [1]
(1882–1890)

Liége, le 5 mai, 1882

Cher monsieur, —

. . . Votre lecture sur le sentiment de l'effort m'avait jeté dans un vrai enthousiasme. À toutes les personnes que je rencontrais, je demandais: "Avez-vous lu l'opuscule de M. James? lisez cela!" Jugez donc! Du neuf sur cette vieille question, et du neuf d'un bout à l'autre. C'était à ne pas le croire. . . .

Vous me demandez, Monsieur, ce que j'enseigne. Je ne sais si je dois vous le dire. Je suis professeur de philologie grecque et latine à l'université de Liége, et professeur de grammaire grecque à l'École normale des Humanités. J'ai une petite réputation comme philologue —mais le monde ne sait pas que le philologue Delbœuf est le même personnage que le philosophe du même nom. Que voulez-vous? C'est le destin. Ma vocation c'était la physique et la philosophie. . . . Agréez, cher monsieur, l'assurance de mes meilleurs sentiments.

J. DELBŒUF

Liége, le 19 décembre, 1882

Cher ami, —

Car c'est le nom que je veux désormais vous donner — votre carte correspondance que j'attendais avec la plus vive impatience, m'a été remise aujourd'hui à mon retour de mission (à Huy cette fois-ci — dans l'entretemps j'ai été aussi à Namur). . . .

Le déterminisme est un système logique, irréfutable — seulement en contradiction avec le sens intime, le sense pratique et le sens commun. Aux déterministes à expliquer d'une manière *satisfaisante* l'illusion de la liberté, et la distinction que je fais en moi-même entre mes actes libres et mes actes non-libres. . . . Vient maintenant la question de fait. Y a t'il de la discontinuité dans le monde? Je soutiens que oui. . . . Le fait de la discontinuité une fois établi, ma théorie sur la volonté libre, l'explique-t-elle? Oui. Il est certain que par le retard ou le ralentissement dans l'action on peut introduire la discontinuité

---

[1] *Cf.* above, I, 687–8; II, 285, 92.

dans les mouvements sans toucher au principe de la conservation de
l'énergie. . . .

Entre autres énigmes (il y en a plus de *sept*) il y a celle du temps et
celle du libre arbitre. J'ai réduit ces deux énigmes à une seule : le libre
arbitre et le temps sont fonctions l'un de l'autre. . . . Qu'est-ce que le
temps ? Je répondrais volontiers, c'est la forme même de l'exercice de
la liberté. Je vous disais à Liége, que c'était chez moi une espèce de
rêve, de l'Empédoclisme. Écoutez néanmoins. Si toutes les affinités
étaient satisfaites, ainsi que toutes les répulsions, si en un mot, l'équilibre était réalisé, y aurait-il encore du temps ? Vous répondrez non
avec moi, je le suppose du moins. Dans ce cas qu'est le temps sinon
la forme abstraite de la satisfaction (en voie de se réaliser) de toutes
les affinités, de tous les *besoins* des êtres. Le temps est donc plus ou
moins rapide suivant la rapidité même de cette satisfaction. Le temps
s'écoule entre deux termes inconcevables, le trouble absolu, l'équilibre
absolu, mais sa marche n'a rien d'uniforme. À ce temps réel nous
avons dans nos conceptions substitué un temps abstrait qui marche d'un
pas uniforme ; aux êtres réels, animés de besoins, nous substituons dans
notre pensée des points matériels inertes, puis par une imagination instan-
tanée, nous les mettons en mouvement dans un milieu homogène. Qu'y
a-t-il d'étonnant que de sein de l'homogénéité et de l'uniformité rêvées
par nous, ne sortent que l'homogénéité et l'uniformité ? Mais plaçons-
nous dans la réalité vivante, et la ligne tracée par la pierre qui se pré-
cipite vers le sol, réflètera les mouvements de tout ce qui vit, de tout
ce qui est sensible, de tout ce qui se meut, car l'aile du cousin qui voltige
au dessus de l'eau, agite l'air et fait vibrer la pierre. Nos lois physiques
ne sont que l'expression des lois qui règlent la *satisfaction* des affinités
dans *des conditions* déterminées librement par nous (le vide, etc.).

Vous le voyez, je ne résous pas l'énigme, je l'agrandis plutôt, mais
à l'origine de tout mouvement nouveau (même pensée) apparait la
liberté.

M. Ribot m'écrit que vous deviez aller à la Salpétrière. Je suis bien
heureux d'apprendre que la santé vous revient avec le sommeil. Mon
sommeil continue à être très inégal. J'ai fort bien dormi cette nuit.
J'ai trop de besogne, et la tranquillité me serait nécessaire. Mal-
heureusement les circonstances semblent se conjurer contre mon repos.
Ribot m'écrit : "Vous seul pouvez faire l'article sur Fechner." Je ne
sais si c'est absolument vrai ; mais cela a l'air d'être vrai, en France du
moins. Mais à chaque instant j'ai des invitations aussi pressantes.
Voilà que les libraires me demandent des livres populaires. Mes con-
férences sont demandées de partout ; c'est mon seul succès, et je l'en-
registre avec plaisir — j'oublie mes puces. Un journal disait à propos

de celles-ci : nous croyons que c'est le même qui a écrit les conferences. J'aime assez ce genre de remarques sur ma personne ; vous avez pu l'observer vous-même. Je m'amuse très objectivement de la surprise des gens. J'ai joui deux bonnes semaines, lorsque, à la suite de votre question : qu'enseignez-vous ? je vous ai répondu ce que vous savez. Je suivais ma réponse par la pensée ; je voyageais sur le vaisseau qui l'emportait. Enfin elle arrivait à Boston. Vous ouvriez la lettre ; puis voilà que aux seuls noms de grec et de latin, vous laissez tomber les bras et restez plongé dans un abîme de réflexions. Je ne sais pas si la chose s'est passée ainsi ; mais je me suis plu à l'imaginer telle. Vous devez me trouver bien bavard pour un homme si occupé. C'est une de mes rares distractions, c'est de laisser dans une lettre, ma plume suivre le courant de ma pensée légèrement vagabonde.

Ma femme et mes enfants sont sensibles à votre souvenir. Nous n'oublierons jamais la figure sympathique de celui qui est parti de si loin pour venir s'asseoir à notre table ; et nous nous plaisons à espérer le revoir un jour avec sa femme, un enfant peut-être. La même hospitalité, plus cordiale encore si possible, les attend. M. Frédericq m'a dit que vous lui aviez écrit. Vous voilà maintenant relié à Liége par des liens multiples. Votre affectioné

J. DELBŒUF

Ramet, 2 nov., 1886

Mon cher ami, —

. . . Je ne sors plus, je ne vais plus nulle part ; je vis au milieu de mes livres, près de ma pauvre femme, recevant de loin en loin une visite — et pourtant, calculant déjà le temps où vous pourrez revenir en Europe : dans quatre ans, n'est-ce-pas ? Ce sera un beau jour, à marquer d'une pierre blanche, celui où nous vous reverrons. . . . Ah ! j'ai si souvent par la pensée, franchi la mer pour aller m'asseoir à votre foyer et causer avec vous !

Mes amitiés les plus cordiales pour vous et tous les vôtres — et de notre part à tous

J. DELBŒUF

Liége, 5 mai, 1887

Mon cher ami, —

. . . À propos dites moi donc si les boules de Robert Houdin, n'avaient pas elles aussi pris l'habitude de sauter d'elles-mêmes en l'air et de retomber dans sa main ? Car telle doit être la conséquence des comparaisons et des analogies qu'au début de votre article, à la suite de Wundt et de Léon Dumont, vous établissez entre la matière brute et la matière vivante. Pour moi, les canaux creusés par l'eau qui coule, les plis de l'habit, les clefs et les serrures ne me disent rien de bien clair, et partant ne m'expliquent pas les habitudes corporelles ou psychiques. Je sais bien, — "Science *populaire*"; — mais n'est-ce pas un peu trop populaire? . . .

Mille choses affectueuses de notre part à tous les vôtres,

J. DELBŒUF

V

DISCUSSION OF THE ABSOLUTE
(JAMES AND ROYCE, 1899)

EARLY in the year 1899 James wrote and transmitted to Royce the following criticism of the latter's doctrine of the Absolute.[1]

ROYCE'S ARGUMENT FOR THE ABSOLUTE

LET us adopt the idealistic criterion that what is unthought of is no fact, and that anything is a fact just so far as it is thought of and no farther. Then assume any finite fact A: first, without thinking of B, C, D, etc.; then, later, assuming them along with it. We thus know A [first] merely by way of acquaintance or in its first intention, and nothing *about* it. We can't say that at this point knowledge *about* it is even *possible;* for such knowledge would be of its relations, and in the absence of other terms, B, C, etc., the basis for relations does not exist. Let us next think B, C, D, etc., along with A. The thought of A's relations, and the knowledge about A now becomes *possible*. It is not necessarily *actual,* for we can think A and B without *tracing* or *noticing* their relation. There are thus three stages of being for A's relations: first, impossibility; second, possibility; third, actuality.

If we do trace A's relations, suppose that we find them as follows: A coexists with B, precedes C, succeeds D, resembles E, changes into F, is a mile away from G, knows H, is ignorant of I, is out of all relation to J, is better than K, etc., etc. These relations all are extraneous to A's inner nature, which would remain unaltered if B, C, D, and the relations with them, should vanish. By the idealistic criterion, nothing unthought of exists, so we must suppose that we ourselves build up this universe as we successively think its facts and relations, and just in so far as we do so think them. If we supposed no other thinker (not even ourselves yet, as reflective critics) our thoughts would be the vehicle of continuity of the universe. And that universe would not be known all together or at once; for finite minds like ours would grasp its parts in succession, letting fall old ones when they turned their attention towards the new. What was thus forgotten would lapse from being until remembered again, for if facts be made by knowing, where there is no knowing, there is no fact. . . .

[1] *Cf.* above, I, 807–10.

To make our ideas more definite, let us consider one portion of this universe when only partially developed to our knowledge. Take *A,* for example, before it has changed into *F,* and while the supposed mind is as yet innocent of the idea of *F* — ignorant of *F*'s very possibility. *F* is not *for us critics* the absolute zero which it would be if not even *A* were there, for when *A* is there we must call *F* at least possible. And this possibility is itself a kind of fact. Yet what kind of a fact can it now be in that universe on our idealistic principles, since by supposition neither *A* nor any other thinker in that universe now thinks it? Again, the very ignorance of it that pervades that universe is a kind of fact. Yet what kind of a fact can *that* be, if no one exists there to whom that ignorance is known? The habits of our speech tend to make the answer sound paradoxical; yet the truth is that on idealistic principles neither the possibility nor the ignorance of *F* can properly be said to *be* facts in that universe until some one there actually realizes them.

Let *A* be an egg and *F* a chicken. In what sense can you call an actual egg a "possible chicken"? Only in the sense that a chicken *will come,* — you may *expect* him. If you don't expect him there is no objective present feature of the universe corresponding to what you call his possibility except the egg itself. "Possible chicken" is only one way of naming "actual egg," by a mind that considers present and future things together. If there be no such mind, then there is no status for the possibility as such. We have no business to say, with Professor Royce, that since for us discussing critics the possibility is objectively there, the Absolute Mind must be there to support it. What is *there* in the universe itself apart from us, is *the egg* — nothing more — and later, the chicken; distinct facts which may perfectly well be realized in successive steps, each one of which may be a fresh surprise to the learner.[2]

Just so of the ignorance of *F,* the chicken. What do we mean by that? We simply mean that from the minds that exist in that universe the thought of chicken is completely absent. But surely we have no right to treat this non-existence of any thought of chicken as if it were a positively constituted fact, and then with Royce to demand the Absolute as its supporter; [treating] this absence as if it were a presence —

[2] [Note by W.J.] Do you mean to say, the Absolutist might insist, that it is not *true* even before the chicken comes *that he will come?* It *is* true; but only in this sense that *if anybody then and there asks if he will come,* the answer must be *yes,* not *no.* But, if the question remains unasked, there is neither truth nor untruth, neither yes nor no, for there is no hypothesis extant, no proposition to *be* true or false. Even this reply is too good-natured to the Absolute. For if there be no Absolute Mind arbitrarily lugged in, the question is neither true nor false at the time of asking, but only at the moment when the chicken comes. His coming *makes* the truth which does n't *exist* now; it is an error to say that any proposition about the chicken is either true or false in advance of his actual presence.

the presence, namely, of just that absence. Such absence indeed, if stated, can be stated only by a positively constituted proposition and this circumstance is what gives rise to the sophistication. As the fact of absence exists in our supposed universe, no one is assumed to state it. No one asks "where is the chicken?" And *to know egg and not to know chicken* — what is that other than barely to know egg? Yet Royce, with chicken in his mind's eye, seeing you barely knowing egg, says it is a fact that you do know it "without chicken," and since every fact must be known, says he must lug in the Absolute as the knower; although all the time *he himself,* as the first introducer cf the thought of chicken, and perceiver that you leave it out, is the only knower required. . . .

All that the idealistic principle demands is that where there is no knowing there is no fact (no knowing of absence, no fact of absence *then* — no knowing of futures, no futures *now* in any shape, etc.) ; and that so far as we find knowing, there we *have* fact — fact present, fact future, fact possible, fact impossible — just as the knowing may befall. But Royce, behind the first knowing actually found, says that you need a second knowing to account for the *fact* that it *is* found. But whose is this second knowing? It is that of us critics who discuss the first. *We* then are the second knowers, not the Absolute; and so long as nobody discusses us and knows us as such knowers, there is no higher knower in the field. If, later, we proceed to talk about the "fact" of our second knowing, then we should be third knowers, and so on *ad infinitum,* but no Absolute Knower would ever logically be required.

Royce starts with facts *assumed* unknown. He ignores his idealistic *principle* by saying that they are facts, even though unknown. He then says, using now his idealistic principle, that if facts, they can't be unknown, and must therefore be known by the Absolute. Such illogicality is curious, since the only logically necessary consequence which the idealistic postulate carries is this : that if a thing can't be shown to be a fact for any finite consciousness, it is no fact at all.

Altogether Royce's procedure leads to odd conclusions regarding the negative and privative aspects of reality. Every fact is susceptible of representation under such aspects. Of the bare fact *A,* for example, it may be said with truth that it is *not B,* that it is there *without B,* that it *does not know B,* that it *contradicts non-A,* etc., etc. All these propositions express also "facts" about *A.* That is, so soon as anyone considers the matter curiously enough to propound them, he can only be answered with a Yes. *Ergo,* says Royce, they *are* facts anyhow; and for bare *A* to be constituted as a fact at all we must postulate an Absolute explicitly cognitive of all this infinite mass of redundant, negative stuff concerning it, as the indispensable condition of its being. Royce's Absolute thus develops affinities with both Hegelism and Spinozism. Hegelism says that a thing completely is, only in so far forth as it has been mediated by the negation of its own negations. Spinozism says: *Omnis determinatio negatio.* The *A* which *is*, is finitely or barely, only in so far forth as it has been cut out from that mass of environing stuff of which it is the negative, and by knowing which along with it, the Absolute establishes its existence. From all which superfætations and redundancies, a consistent use of the idealistic principle relieves us, and from them we are even more simply relieved if we are not idealistic at all.

What would Royce do with the notion of a *zero*-universe, a universe idealistically described by saying there is nothing in it known because there is nothing to know? He would of course say that these last propositions, being true of that universe, drive us to the Absolute. It makes a splendid "full-circle" system, and the shortest cut from zero to everything, that philosophy can show. Yet how intimately absurd, — as soon as you realize the meaning of the zero-hypothesis, as distinguished from the positive zero-*object* which the grammatical proposition suggests! Hegel's logic revives: to posit nothing is to posit being, and so on through the rigmarole.

The following is Royce's reply to James's memorandum, together with James's rebuttal. James's comments were written on Royce's manuscript, and are here printed in small capitals where they occur. The parenthetical comments are by Royce himself.

March 1899

Dear James, —
Your objections begin with a provisional acceptance of the "idealistic criterion" that you state., . . . This being the case, I have no difficulty in pointing out that your hypothetical instances, cited to refute the idealistic theses as to the Absolute, involve far more "facts," and so far more "thought" — or, as I should now prefer to word it, far more "knowledge" or "consciousness of facts" — than you seem to observe as you go. I have at present time to bring out only this aspect of your discussion.

I

"Let us," you say, "assume any finite fact *A,* first without thinking of *B, C, D.* . . . Let us next think *B, C, D,* along with *A.* . . . We must suppose that we ourselves build up this universe as we successively

think its facts and relations. . . . If we supposed no other thinker
. . . our thought would be the vehicle of continuity of the universe.
And that universe would not be known all together or at once."

The "facts" that your hypothesis here assumes include explicitly
more than *A* alone, or than *A* together with *B, C, D.* Explicitly you
assume three other types of facts: —

1. That the *A* which is first thought alone is identical with, or the
same as, the *A* which is later thought along with *B, C, D.* [TO THE
THINKER IT SO COMES — HE FEELS NO DISCONTINUITY OR DIFFERENCE
EXCEPT THE TIME DIFFERENCE.]

2. That "we," who do this thinking, are in some sense or other . . .
the same thinkers, or that we constitute the same thinking process all
through, since we are, by your hypothesis, such that our thoughts constitute "the vehicle of continuity," and it is said by you to be "we" who
"successively think its facts and relations."

3. That the moment when *A* is alone in our thought, and the moment
when *A* is with *B, C, D,* are objectively real events in one time series,
or that the one moment really follows the other. [IN BRIEF: I ASSUME
"MEMORY," AND THE KIND OF CONSCIOUSNESS OF THINGS WHICH IT
INVOLVES, IN THE FINITE THINKER.]

Now I do not force these assumptions upon you. It is you who have
chosen to make them. By hypothesis they are "facts." By the "criterion," also presupposed, they are known facts, or exist only as facts
thought of. I need not say that these facts are not reducible to the content of either one of the two moments (α) when *A* alone is thought
of, or (β) when *A* is merely thought with *B* and *C.* On the contrary,
the three sorts of fact that I have just pointed out are all of them *facts
about the relations of the contents and consciousnesses and events of
your two moments only in so far as these two moments are together
equally real and are to be viewed as parts of one whole fact.* This
whole fact, with its three aspects, you assume, and by the "criterion" it
is fact only in so far as it is known fact, or fact thought of. [AND
THOUGHT OF IT IS, BY THE FINITE CONSCIOUSNESS SUPPOSED.] . . .

There *is,* then, by hypothesis, a "thought," or as I should prefer to
say here a "knowledge," or a "consciousness," which *knows* (not merely
believes), *thinks* (not merely guesses) this whole fact to be what it is
in these three aspects. If you deny this result [WHY SHOULD I BE
TEMPTED TO DENY IT?], you deny the "criterion" that by hypothesis
you were to accept, and refuse to play the game that you have just
agreed to play. If you accept this result, however, your statement:
"that universe would not be known all together or at once" [AN UN-
FORTUNATELY SWEEPING STATEMENT ON MY PART, SINCE WE WOULD

KNOW SUCH PARTS OF IT AT ONCE AS WE REMINISCIENTIALLY THOUGHT OF TOGETHER. OTHER PARTS WHICH WE FORGOT, WOULD THEN NOT BE KNOWN CUM ALIIS, AND THEIR RELATION BEING UNKNOWN WOULD BY THE IDEALISTIC CRITERION BE NO "FACT"], is forthwith abandoned. You have, indeed, assumed that "we" never know that universe "at once" [I AM SORRY FOR MY SLIP OF LANGUAGE. I MEANT "NEED" NOT KNOW IT ALL AT ONCE], but you have assumed that said universe possesses two sorts of sameness, and one character of objectively real succession, all of which have meaning only for the whole fact, or for the fact of your universe in its wholeness, and of its processes in their entirety of succession. [THEY HAVE MEANING ALL ALONG SO FAR AS THE FINITE THINKER FEELS THEM, FEELS NO DISCONTINUITY IN HIS OBJECT, OR IN HIMSELF, AS HE FEELS TIME FLOW, — SONST NICHT.] If all reality is known, then here is an assumed reality that "we" indeed know not, but that is known and exists only as known.

If you hereupon reply by simply denying that you meant A to be the same A in the two events, or "we" to be the same "we," or the succession to constitute one process in one time, I shall only ask you to try again, and to state your case as you mean it. [I CERTAINLY DID MEAN THEM TO BE THE SAME, FOR THE FINITE THINKER SUPPOSED (SO LONG AS HE THINKS THEM AT ALL) SO THINKS THEM. TO HIM THEY APPEAR NOT DIFFERENT; AND THAT IS WHAT THE "SAMENESS" SIGNIFIES OR IS KNOWN AS.] If you reply that you long ago *disposed* of sameness, ego, etc., in your *Psychology* [I DISPOSED OF IT IN NO HOSTILE SENSE. "SAMENESS" IN ANYTHING MEANS THE SAMENESS FELT THERE, AND THIS TIME FELT BY THE FINITE THINKER], I shall answer that you did so there only provisionally, upon an explicitly realistic hypothesis. . . . But here you are for the time playing quite another game [I CAN'T SEE IT!], namely, that determined by the hypothesis of the "criterion," to which we are now to adhere. If you reply by asking me whether I, then, believe in a transcendentally permanent "we," or in a "same thing" in successive moments of time, I respond that . . . the problem here is not what I think, but is merely what you have here chosen to assume. If the "vehicle" is n't any one vehicle at all, but only the one-horse shay as it was after the crash came; if the A *alone* is n't the A later *found* . . . with B and C [IT IS THAT A, SO FAR AS THE FINITE THINKER MAY NOT HAVE FORGOTTEN IT WHEN HE THINKS B AND C. IF HE HAS FORGOTTEN IT THEN NOBODY THINKS THE FIRST WITH THE LATER FACTS, AND ITS "SAMENESS" CAN'T BE SAID TO EXIST], but if the two are different A's; if the succession in one time process wherein the one event really follows the other, is not real at all; — then, indeed, your whole hypothesis is so far a total incoherence. But if in *any* sense the

sameness of the "vehicle," and of the A, and if in any sense the real
succession of your two supposed events in one time is indeed real, and
if by the "criterion" whatever is real is known, then there is, in your
universe a knowledge of these three aspects.   And these three aspects
are knowable as such only if "that universe is known all together or at
once"; whereby, of course, I do not mean that it is known "all together"
in either one of your temporally successive moments, or at any other
temporal moment, or that "we" as you have defined us, ever know it
at all.   [YOU OUGHT TO PROVE THE IMPOSSIBILITY OF MEMORY, THEN.
WHY SHOULD THE FINITE CONSCIOUSNESS SLIDE ALONG, ACQUIRING
NEW OBJECTS, KEEPING THESE AWHILE WITH NO SENSE THAT THEY
ARE OTHER, THEN LETTING THEM FADE OUT?]

II

Let A change into F, as you desire, and "let A be an egg and F a
chicken."   The "realization in successive stages," the "surprise to the
learner," the former finite "ignorance of chicken," the later "knowledge
of chicken," the real relation of later chicken to that same egg whereof
before there was knowledge when there was no knowledge in the
"learner's" mind of the coming chicken, the sameness of the surprised
learner to whom the new light comes (his sameness, I mean, all through
the process) — these are now the elements of your more specifically
defined universe, as you later assume it to be constituted.

Well, these assumptions are yours, not mine.   You tell the story.
You give to its parts supposed real relations, some of which by your
hypothesis, the "learner" himself never faces.   [ALAS FOR MY LAPSUS
PENNAE WHICH HAS GIVEN YOU ALL THIS TROUBLE.] . . . The case is
just as before. . . .   The whole universe defined is assumed in its real
succession, samenesses, progress, and stages as real.   This reality either
is real as whole, or is not.   If it is not real as whole, then the chicken
comes not from the same egg that before existed.   [THE "LEARNER"
NEVER APPREHENDS IT AS A DIFFERENT EGG, DOES HE?]   The learner
who is surprised is not the learner who was ignorant [HE IS CONSCIOUS
OF NO DUALITY]; the one event does not really succeed the other in any
one time at all; the "vehicle" crumbles, like the one-horse shay, again,
into the dust of mere separate facts, and your whole story remains a
tale signifying nothing.

But if the whole succession, as a real time process, is real, if the
vehicle is the same, and the egg of the first part of the tale is the same
as the egg whence comes the chicken, then these real facts, by the
hypothesis of the criterion — yes, this whole real fact, by the same
hypothesis — is known "at once" [OF COURSE, WHEN IT IS KNOWN, I.E.,
REMINISCENTLY BY THE LEARNER, NOT BEFORE]; for only when known

"at once" (though not at any one temporal instant of the series in question), could its assumed relations be known, namely, the sameness, the connectedness of the parts in one time process, and the sameness of the learner. Once more, I am asserting not my theories but the content of your assumptions.

III

Something of a sense of this consequence must beset you when you seem to try to avoid a part of it by insisting, as to the mere time aspects of your world, that, "It is an error to say that any proposition about the chicken is either true or false in advance of his actual presence." [TRUTH, AS I HOLD, BEING A PERFECTLY DEFINITE EXTERNAL RELATION BETWEEN A THOUGHT AND SOMETHING IN WHICH IT "TERMINATES." UNTIL THE TERMINUS EXIST, THE TRUTH IS NOT CONSTRUCTED. THE TERMINUS MAKES THE THOUGHT "TRUE."] Do you mean this only because the chicken is so uncertain and insignificant a thing? But let us pass from chickens to other cases. Do you mean to assert any of the following propositions?

1. An astronomer's present assertion about the eclipses of the year 1900 is neither true nor false until those eclipses occur.

2. It is neither true nor false today that I shall sometime die. (How, then, about life insurance policies? Do they relate to no reality?)

3. A promise made today about the future is neither a true nor a false promise. (How about false lovers, and swindlers, and true souls, and honest pledges? Do they then all alike relate to nothing true or false?)

4. It is neither true nor false that you are to be absent from Harvard during the next year. (What then were we talking about lately? Neither truth nor falsity? Nothing real?)

5. The announcements of next year's courses, when made, are neither true nor false. (I wish Palmer could see that. Then he wouldn't ask me for mine.)

6. If I today say: "The Mississippi River will flow into the Arctic Ocean next year," "The sun will then also rise in the west," "President Eliot will write Shakespeare's plays tomorrow," and "Tomorrow two and two will make four": — if I say these things, each one of my sayings, being about the future, is equally *neither* true nor false. [NEITHER TRUE NOR FALSE, IN THE STRICT SENSE! FOR THE FACTS THAT COULD MAKE THESE HYPOTHESES EITHER TRUE OR FALSE ARE NON-EXISTENT AS YET. OF COURSE WE PRACTICALLY TREAT THEM AS TRUE OR FALSE FOR OURSELVES, SINCE WE COMPARE THEM AS HYPOTHESES WITH EXPECTATIONS OF FULFILMENT OR NON-FULFILMENT THAT OUR MINDS

SUPPLY, AND DENOMINATE THEM ACCORDINGLY.   BUT THIS IS ONLY A
CASE OF POTENTIAL TRUTH, ETC.]

If you mean to make any one of these assertions, you are welcome.
I know, however, in that case, that it is *now* true that you *will,* in
substance, deny them the very next time that you make the least
prediction about the future, or promise or attempt anything whatever.

But a world where future reality is even now an object of assertions
[SUPPOSED TRUE OR FALSE BY US FINITES — I SEE NO OTHER TRUTH IN
THE FIELD] true or false, is a world where the future reality, by the
"criterion," is somehow known "at once" with the assertions about it.
[ALL BY US, NAMELY, PROLEPTICALLY.   OTHERWISE IT IS NOT KNOWN
AT ALL AND HAS AS YET NO TRUTH SAVE WHAT WE GIVE IT.]   "We" do
not so know the future.   But it is, by the "criterion," only as a known
somewhat.   If not so envisaged by "us," what follows?

IV

I have n't at present time to go further into your objections.   The
foregoing attacks the main points.   If you had taken note of them as
I do, I fancy that you would not have written the latter part.   On the
whole the "odd conclusions" about the privative and negative aspects
of reality with which you credit me are not altogether unlike what I
should state as my own.   [I NEVER DOUBTED THIS.   BUT IT DOES SEEM
TO ME ODD ENOUGH TO DRAG IN AN ABSOLUTE BECAUSE FORSOOTH
THERE MUST BE SOMEONE TO THINK ALL THIS RUBBISH THAT WE MAY
FORGET TO THINK OURSELVES.]   Only they are not even "odd," just
as they very certainly are n't especially Hegelian.   They are the mere
commonplaces of logic.   The concept of *zero,* or of *nothing,* in its
countless forms, is familiar both to common sense, and in the sciences.
It is *always,* in some of its aspects, or in some wise, a positive concept.
To say that is simply to report the empirical fact about how men think.
Read Teichmüller's pretty little chapter on the *"Nichts"* in his *Metaphysik,* if you want a very non-Hegelian expression of the same
view. . . .   [page missing]

In the same way, it is not only true, but obvious to the least glance
at countless types of fact, that objects are constantly qualified by their
negatives, that for me merely to mention *A,* and to mention *A* explicitly
as in any sense alone, or as *alone by itself,* may mean for me very
different ways of taking *A.*   As to what follows herefrom I have
shown that elsewhere.   These things are n't disposed of by talking
of "superfætations," but by observing what one means.

J. R.

VI

ROYCE'S CRITICISMS OF "THE MEANING OF THE WORD TRUTH" (1908)

THE following comments by Royce were written in 1908 on a copy of James's leaflet, "The Meaning of the Word Truth" (1907).[1] The page references here given, however, are to *The Meaning of Truth* (1909), where the leaflet was reprinted. James's text is printed in Roman type, Royce's comment in small capitals.

"My account of truth is realistic," p. 217: THIS WORD DOES N'T HELP ONE UNLESS HE KNOWS WHAT YOU MEAN BY REALITY. BUT THAT QUESTION YOU EXPRESSLY POSTPONE.

"You are willing to call my statement true," p. 217: BUT CALLING IT TRUE IS N'T THE WHOLE OF MAKING IT TRUE, OR OF PROVING IT TRUE. MY GENERAL OBJECTION TO YOUR VIEW IS THAT IT IS NOT THE WHOLE TRUTH ABOUT TRUTH. IT LEAVES OUT ESSENTIAL ASPECTS. THIS OBJECTION HAS NEVER BEEN MET OR EVEN TOUCHED IN ANY OF YOUR STATEMENTS. MY DEFINITION OF TRUTH : — A STATEMENT IS TRUE IF THE WHOLE OF THE EXPERIENCE (AND REALITY) TO WHICH THAT STATEMENT BELONGS FULFILS THE PURPOSE WHICH THAT STATEMENT EXPRESSES. THIS DEFINITION INCLUDES YOUR WORKINGS AND MUCH MORE TOO.

"Be they actual or potential," p. 218: A "POTENTIAL" WORKING, THAT IS, A WORKING THAT DOES N'T WORK, HAS EITHER NO BEING, OR ELSE A BEING OF A NON-PRAGMATISTIC TYPE (I.E., OF MY IDEALISTIC TYPE).

"Are thus constituent elements," p. 218: ADMITTED. BUT THERE ARE OTHER CONSTITUENT ELEMENTS. SEE MY DEFINITION OF THEM.

"Without using the notion of the workings," p. 218: I AGREE. BUT I INSIST THAT MORE THAN THESE WORKINGS MUST BE CONSIDERED IN DEFINING THE TRUTH.

"The attitude of belief, the reality-recognizing attitude," p. 219: DOES THIS MEAN THAT THE "BEING" OR "REALITY" OF THINGS IS THE SAME AS OUR BELIEF IN THEM? IF NOT, WHY DO YOU USE THIS EXPRESSION? IF YES, ARE YOU REALISTIC?

[1] *Cf.* above, I, 821.

"Critics . . . call the workings inessential," p. 219: CRITICS OF MY TYPE SAY THAT SOMETHING ELSE IS ALSO ESSENTIAL.

"Functional possibilities . . . give its whole logical content," p. 220: "NECESSARY" OR "INDISPENSABLE" CONDITIONS ARE NOT ALWAYS "SUFFICIENT" CONDITIONS. A TRUE STATEMENT OF COURSE "WORKS." SO MAY A LIE.

"The foregoing statements reproduce the essential content," p. 220: THIS SUMMARY SHOWS THE USUAL TAKING OF A MERE FRAGMENT FOR THE WHOLE. YOU ACCUSE THE OPPONENT OF IGNORING YOUR SCRAP OF A THEORY OF TRUTH. IF THE OPPONENT IS LIKE ME, HE DOES N'T IN THE LEAST IGNORE YOUR SCRAP. HE SAYS THAT IT IS A SCRAP. CONDITIONS NECESSARY TO THE TRUTH OF STATEMENTS YOU NAME. BUT THEY ARE N'T SUFFICIENT CONDITIONS. THAT THEY ARE NOT IS AT ONCE SHOWN BY ANY ASSERTION ABOUT A PAST FACT, WHICH MEANS, FOR ANY ORDINARY MAN, TO POSSESS A TRUTH WHICH NO FUTURE WORKINGS CAN EVER ADEQUATELY OR SUFFICIENTLY EMBODY. BUT THIS IS ONLY ONE OF COUNTLESS INSTANCES. EVERY STATEMENT IMPLIES MORE THAN ITS "WORKINGS" CAN EMBODY. THE CASE OF YOUR OPPONENT IS NOT THAT HE IGNORES YOUR "WORKINGS" AS NEEDED FOR THE TRUTH BUT THAT HE DEMANDS MORE THAN MERE WORKINGS.

VII

FINAL EXAMINATION IN JAMES'S GRADUATE COURSE IN PHYSIOLOGICAL PSYCHOLOGY (PHILOSOPHY 19), 1879–1880 [1]

1. Meaning of "efferent" and "afferent" nerve processes?

2. What are the basal ganglia of the brain?

3. What is probably their function as contrasted with that of the hemispheres?

4. Can actions accompanied by intelligence be conceived under the form of reflex action?

5. What is the present state of the question of localization of functions in the cortex?

6. What were the most characteristic points in your instructor's sketch of space-perception?

7. What proof does there seem to be that the sense of motion is not a synthesis of positions in space occupied in successive moments of time?

8. Why does an ataxic patient walk better with his eyes open? To the disorder of what function do his symptoms essentially seem due?

9. What is the most plausible argument in favor of feelings of efferent innervation? Why is it nugatory?

10. What is muscular effort proper?

11. What is moral or volitional effort proper?

12. It is commonly said that in the phenomenon of effort and there alone, we have a direct transitive relation between the inner and the outer worlds, the outgoing *force* in the former recognizing as its antagonist an equivalent *force* in the latter, which opposes it. And this is said to be our only immediate perception of outward reality. Criticize this doctrine from the point of view of your instructor's opinions.

13. Would the untruth of the "conscious automaton" theory involve the truth of the free will theory?

14. Does the fact that red light and green light combine on the retina into a feeling of yellow prove that our consciousness of yellow is made up of unconscious feelings of red and green? If not, why not?

15. The most important points for and against.

[1] *Cf.* above, 13. This paper, in the handwriting of W.J. and A.H.J., was kindly sent to the author by Francis Almy, Harvard '79, who was a member of the course.

VIII

LETTERS OF CARL STUMPF TO WILLIAM JAMES [1]
(1886–1909)

Sassnitz (auf der Insel Rügen) am 8 Sept., 1886

Lieber James, —

Verzeihung, dass ich Ihren lieben langen Brief vom 1 Januar noch nicht beantwortet! ich verschob es auf die grossen Ferien, nebst so manchem Andern, was liegen geblieben. . . .

Über Lipps denke ich vielleicht nicht ganz so günstig wie Sie; er erscheint mir zwar talentvoll, aber noch recht unreif. Es wäre ihm nützlich wenn er einige Jahre mit Schriftstellern pansirte und nicht seine Studien vor dem Publicum machte. Aber unsere jüngere Generation ist gar ehrgeizig. Die Schrift von Mach hat mir viel Vergnügen bereitet; aber wenn man näher zusieht, löst sich doch Vieles in mehr geistreiche als wahre *Aperçu's* auf. Ich erlaubte mir dies so höflich als möglich in meiner Recension in der *Deutsche Literaturzeitung* anzudeuten und erfuhr zu meiner Freude, dass Mach den Widerspruch nicht übel genommen. Vielmehr sprach er mir seinen Dank aus. Neuerdings habe ich auch Spencer's *Psychology* in derselben *Zeitung* recensirt und bin mir dabei über Spencer's eigentliches Wesen recht Klar geworden; er ist im Grunde ein modernisirter Hegel, scheint's Ihnen nicht auch so? . . .

Diese Einigkeit in den Principien und den Zielen der Forschung wird mir immer wertvoller, je mehr ich sehe, dass Männer, die man früher glaubte der gleichen Richtung und Gesinnung zuzählen zu dürfen, sich von derselben entfernen. Fast scheint es mir zum Beispiel, dass Sully von seinen grossen Talenten nicht mehr ganz den richtigen Gebrauch macht; er scheint mir mehr auf Vielschreiberei und Popularisirung auszugehen. . . . Vielleicht bietet seine Stellung als Examinator dazu die Veranlassung. Aber die Wissenschaft muss trauern, wenn die Studenten lachen. . . .

[Wundt] macht die Studenten und einige andere Leute glauben, dass mit den immer wiederholten Messungen der Reactionszeiten der Anfang zu einer ganz neuen "experimentellen Psychologie" gemacht sei, von welcher aus man nur mit Hohn und Spott auf die alte Psychologie zurückblicken könne. Sehen Sie seine Essays darüber, sehen Sie die

---

[1] *Cf.* above, Ch. LXII.

Äusserungen seiner Schüler im *Literar. Centralblatt*. Als ob aus
jenen Zeitmessungen überhaupt etwas Wichtiges zu folgern wäre, als
ob sie nicht selbst nur durch die innere Beobachtung interpretiert
werden müssten, als ob endlich Zahlen und nicht vielmehr klare
Begriffe die Hauptsache wären! Und welch' schlechtes Beispiel gibt in
Hinsicht des klaren und scharfen Denkens der Lehrer den Schülern!
Wie seine Relativitätslehre, so steckt auch die Apperceptionslehre
und fast alles Allgemeinere voll von Mehrdeutigkeit und Widerspruch. . . . Mein lieber Marty hat in Wundt's eigener *Vierteljahrsschrift* dessen Apperceptionslehre jetzt einer schneidigen Kritik
unterzogen, und dies scheint Wundt so verstimmt zu haben, dass der
Herausgeber Avenarius die Fortsetzung einstweilen sistirt hat. Aber
Wundt wird nichts Triftiges dagegen erwidern können; er wird
versuchen, von oben herab dagegen wieder einige allgemeine Phrasen
in's Feld zu senden, um sich wenigstens bei seinen blinden Verehrern
zu rehabilitiren.

Meine Neigung geht zu wenig auf blosse Polemik, sonst würde ich in
der That einmal das ganze Sündenregister Wundt's zusammenstellen,
und versuchen die Augen wieder auf das wahrhaft Wertvolle in aller
Forschung hinzulenken, über welches die jüngere Generation durch
Wundt vielfach getäuscht wird. Doch wird man von selbst wieder
darauf zurückkommen. Wie oft ist schon die Psychologie in solcher
Weise "exact" gemacht worden, um nachher doch wieder in die alten
Bahnen, in die *psychologische Psychologie* zurückzulenken!

Genug, mein lieber James, der Klagen, ja zu viel davon! Lassen
Sie uns lieber freudig das Erfreuliche hervorsuchen in Welt und
Menschen und es vor allem in uns selbst verwirklichen. Und damit
bleiben Sie gut Ihrem Carl Stumpf, der mit Frau Sie und die Ihrige
von Herzen grüsst.

Halle, 2 Jan., 1887

Lieber James, —

. . . Ihr Urteil über Spencer interessirte mich; da man selten ein
so scharfes Wort über diesen Denker, namentlich von englischen oder
amerikan. Philosophen, aussprechen hört. Jeder von uns beiden sieht
eben die Mängel und die Unsolidität des ihm näher Stehenden deutlicher: Sie diejenigen Spencer's, ich diejenigen Wundt's. . . . Ihr

C. STUMPF

München, 17 Mai, 1893

Lieber James, —

. . . Sie sind ein volles Jahr in Europa — ein Jahr, auf das ich mich
seit 10 Jahren gefreut hatte — : und von diesem Jahr entfallen auf

unser Wiedersehen wenige Stunden, in denen noch dazu Ihr Denken und Fühlen durch dringende Angelegenheiten in Anspruch genommen ist! Ich kann Ihnen dies natürlich nicht zum Vorwurf machen, aber ich bin traurig darüber, und um so trauriger, als ich — um es offen zu sagen — das unbestimmte Gefühl habe, dass Ihre Freundschaft zu mir in den Jahren doch etwas an Lebendigkeit eingebüsst habe, dass Sie vielleicht darin nicht gefunden, was Sie Anfangs sich versprachen, oder dass irgend etwas an mir Ihnen direct befremdlich oder unsympathisch erschien. Etwa das Auftreten gegen Wundt? *Ernster,* viel ernster sind wir ja alle beide seit diesen 10 Jahren geworden; das Leben ist auch so kurz u. die Welt so klein, in der wir leben. Aber nur um so fester möchte ich an denen halten, die ich von Herzen hochschätze und liebe. . . . Ihr getreuer

C. STUMPF

Wengen im Berner Oberland, 8 Sept., 1899

Lieber Freund, —

Allerdings bin ich überrascht durch Ihren Brief, und so sehr ich mich sonst über Ihren Aufenthalt in Deutschland freuen würde — *dieser* Aufenthalt betrübt mich unendlich. Ich setze Vertrauen in die Bäder von Nauheim, die schon manchem Bekannten gut gethan haben, und hoffe, dass Sie neugestärkt daraus hervorgehen. Aber diese Gifford Lectures! . . . Würden Sie nicht besser thun, jetzt in diesem wichtigen, für Ihre weitere Lebenszeit so entscheidenden Moment alles andere gegen die körperliche Kräftigung hintanzusetzen? — Treue Freundschaft und Sorge gibt mir diese Fragen ein. . . .

Nach Paris werde ich 1900 wahrscheinlich *nicht* kommen. Ich bin wohl noch viel weniger als Sie für Congresse geschaffen und würde mir Paris lieber einmal ohne Congress ansehen. Dazu noch das Getümmel einer Weltausstellung — schon der Gedanke macht mich nervös. Was die Franzosen betrifft, so muss ich leider sagen, dass mir die Nation — von Einzelnen natürlich abgesehen — immer weniger Respect einflösst. Wenn auch die Wahrheit über Dreyfus an den Tag kommt — ist es nicht schon über die Massen traurig, dass man ihr solche Hindernisse bereitet? . . . Kann man deutlicher zeigen dass man die Wahrheit nicht *will?*

Darin, lieber James, sind wir bessere Menschen dass wir sie *wollen.* Ob wir sie finden, ist die andere Frage. Und dies sage ich speziell mit Bezug auf eine Gegnerschaft, die zwischen uns beiden entstanden ist, ohne dass Sie, wie es scheint davon wissen. Sie haben wol meine letzte Zusendung "Über den Begriff der Gemütsbewegung" noch nicht bekommen? Da ich darin gegen Ihre Theorie Stellung genommen habe, so wollte ich anfänglich einen Brief als Begleitung mitschicken,

kam aber vor der Abreise nicht mehr dazu und tröstete mich damit dass
Sie mehr als irgendeiner unter den lebenden Philosophen im Stande
sein werden, persönliche Freundschaft mit wissenschaftlicher Gegnerschaft zu vereinigen, u. dass es keiner Worte bedarf, um die Fortdauer
unsres persönlichen Verhältnisses sicher zu stellen. . . .

Merkwürdig ists mir mit Brentano gegangen. Ich dachte, mit ihm
in Hinsicht der Affecte ziemlich einstimmig zu sein und erhalte nun von
ihm einen 7 Bogen langen Brief, worin er sich entschieden für *Ihre*
Auffassung und gegen die meinige erklärt. Eine etwas beschämende
Wirkung meiner Argumentationen! Wenn er einmal an das Veröffentlichen seiner Arbeiten geht, werden Sie an ihm für die Affectlehre eine
nicht zu verachtende Stütze haben. Aber was ist Wahrheit? Das
Eine weiss ich sicher, dass es mir gar keine innere Überwindung
kosten würde, falls ich mich vom Gegenteil überzeuge, mich auch dazu
zu *bekennen* und frühere Ausführungen zu widerrufen, sans phrase,
Ihrem edlen Beispiel in andren Fällen nachfolgend. . . . Seien
Sie . . . herzlich gegrüsst von Ihrem getreuen

Stumpf

Baden-Baden, 26 März, 1904

Mein lieber Freund James, —
Jetzt endlich, fern von Berlin, komme ich zur Beantwortung Ihres
lieben Briefes vom 1 Januar und muss Ihnen vor allem sagen, *wie sehr*
es mich gefreut und gerührt hat, dass Sie in alter treuer Anhänglich-
keit meiner denken. Von mir darf ich es aber auch sagen, dass Bande,
wie sie zwischen uns bestechen, völlig unzerreissbar in meinem Herzen
fortdauern. Es ist wirklich die Hydra der täglichen Arbeiten die mich
so saumselig im Schreiben gemacht hat; mit jedem Jahr scheinen ihr
neue Köpfe zu wachsen, auch ohne dass man die alten abschneidet.
Meine Sehnsucht geht denn auch dieselben Wege wie die Ihrige — das
fernste Thal wäre mir der liebste Aufenthalt. Ich möchte und müsste
endlich auch einmal meine Garben binden — aber ich sehe vorläufig
keine Möglichkeit zu fliehen, ausser in den Ferien, und werde es wohl
so lange auf meinem Posten in Berlin aushalten müssen, als die kör-
perlichen Kräfte reichen.

Münsterberg hatte ich zuerst zugesagt, weil mich das Abenteuer
reizte, aber schon im letzten Sommer schrieb ich ihm wieder ab; meine
Nerven hätten es nicht ausgehalten. Das ganze Unternehmen ist
eigentlich überhaupt nicht erfreulich, es wird nichts herauskommen.
Alle sollen über das Verhältnis ihrer Wissenschaft zu anderen
Wissenschaften reden — man denke sich nun etwa 20 Bände mit
solchen bloss methodologischen Betrachtungen angefüllt!

Nun aber zu Ihrem schönen Buch. Es ist in der That sehr unrecht von mir dass ich Ihnen ausser der Karte, die Sie nicht bekommen haben müssen, nichts darüber geschrieben habe. Verzeihen Sie es dem Vielgeplagten! An Interesse dafür fehlte es mir nicht. Habe ich doch in meiner frühen Jugend jahrelang den Plan gehegt, katholischer Priester zu werden und mich thatsächlich in die Theologie vergraben, bis die inneren Widersprüche der Dogmen mich unter schweren Herzensqualen hinwegtrieben. Was Sie über die Religiösen Erlebnisse berichten, davon habe ich das Meiste am eigenen Leibe erfahren. Freilich bin ich nachher um so strenger in der Beherrschung und Kritik all dieser Gefühle geworden, und so muss ich auch jetzt sagen, dass mir alles Sentimentale, Verzückte, Süssliche, Salbungsvolle in diesen Dingen beim erwachsenen Menschen aufs äusserste zuwider ist und dass mir nur das als wertvoll erscheint was sich in thätige Nächstenliebe umsetzt.

Auch kann ich trotz der Erkenntnis meiner Mängel und Fehler jenes zerknirschte Sündenbewusstsein nicht aufbringen, auf welchem die Religion nach den Frommen ruhen soll. "Something wrong about us" ja freilich aber *ausser* uns ist noch viel mehr schlecht als in uns, und wir brauchen Erlösung nicht bloss von unseren Sünden sondern von all dem unendlich Entsetzlichen in der Welt, die eben *der* Gott geschaffen haben soll, von dem man Erlösung hofft. In allem diesem erscheint mir die Religion der Religiösen verkehrt und unnatürlich.

Aber vollkommen stimme ich dem zu, was Sie über die Religion im weiteren und eigentlichen Sinne sagen (p. 485) und in jedem Augenblick meines Lebens fühle ich diesen Zusammenhang mit dem unsichtbaren Geisterreich das uns umgibt, und die Kraft die von da ausströmt.

Soll ich Ihnen nun auch etwas von meinem "over-belief" sagen? Ich weiss nicht ob ich während meines Lebens jemals solche mich täglich beschäftigende Gedanken zu veröffentlichen mich entschliessen werde. Ihnen aber theile ich sie gern vertraulich mit.

Die persönliche Unsterblichkeit steht mir im Vordergrund. Ihr Satz "if our ideals," p. 524 scheint mir eine Art von innerem Widerspruch zu enthalten. Die Verwirklichung der Ideale *ist* eben nur möglich unter Voraussetzung der individuellen Unsterblichkeit. Psychische Werthe addiren sich nicht. Wenn immer neue Individuen sich ablösen, so mag das folgende besser sein als das frühere, aber es vergeht ebenso in Nichts, und eine Summirung von Werthen, die nur innerhalb einer Persönlichkeit Existenz haben ist absurd. Tritt die Erstarrung der Erde ein, entstehen also keine neuen Individuen mehr, wo bleibt dann die Verwirklichung der Ideale, wenn Geistiges nicht fortdauert? Dies ist für mich die erste Bedingung, wenn das Leben nicht absolut trost-und sinnlos sein soll. Nicht *Egoismus* ist dies;

nicht weil ich es bin, sondern weil es ein Träger von Werthen ist, muss das Geistige dauern; und gewiss ich würde bereit sein auf die Weiter-existenz zu verzichten wenn die des geistig Werthvollen ausser mir an diese Bedingung geknüpft wäre.

Das was von uns fortbesteht wird aber nur das moralisch Werthvolle sein, das, was ein guter Wille in seine Sphäre hineingezogen und da festgehalten hat. In gewissem Sinne wird so allerdings die Indi-vidualität schwinden, nicht bloss die körperliche sondern auch die geistige: wenn anders man die zufälligen Kleinigkeiten, die unsere "Individualpsychologie" als Merkmale benützt, für das Wesen der Individualität ansieht. Wie uns dereinst sein wird, dafür scheint mir die beste Analogie der Zustand während eines hohen Kunstgenusses oder während einer uns ganz erfüllenden ethisch grossen Vorstellung; auch dann ist unser "Ich" vorhanden, aber befreit von jenen zufälligen Kleinigkeiten, in eine höhere Sphäre gehoben und von den beseligendsten Gefühlen des Eins-Seins mit allen guten und hohen Geistern aller Zeiten begleitet. Mir ist es in solchen Augenblicken und Stunden in der That wie eine lebendige Gegenwart meiner Lieben, aller derer die mir vorausgegangen sind; sie scheinen mir in gleicher Weise um mich zu sein und zu meiner Seele zu reden, wie die, welche in empirischer Gegenwart, den gleichen Gefühlen stumm hingegeben, neben mir sitzen.

Dies sind meine zwei Glaubensartikel, die beiden am Schlusse des athanasianischen Credo "Gemeinschaft der Heiligen und ein ewiges Leben" — während alle übrigen Artikel dahin gefallen sind, auch das Dasein des christlichen Gottes. Die fürchterlichen Übel des Natur-laufes und die doch auch dazu gehörige Schlechtigkeit der Menschen schliessen diese Annahme aus. Wollen wir aber einen pantheistischen Gott, so können wir sehr wohl eben diese Gemeinschaft der Seligen dafür einsetzen, die täglich wächst und doch zugleich eine innere Einheit bildet.

Wie ich diese Gedanken mit meinen psychologischen und natur-philosophischen Anschauungen im Einzelnen zusammenreime, will ich Ihnen nicht weiter erklären, Sie werden ja ohnedies auch leicht manche Verbindungslinien mit den kleinen Aufsätzen über Leib und Seele und den Entwicklungsgedanken herausfinden.

Unsere Anschauungen stehen sich hiernach in vieler Beziehung nahe. Selbst Ihr Pluralismus ist mir nicht so fremdartig, wie wohl den meisten Fachgenossen (obschon ich meine, dass Sie den Gefühlswert der "Einheit" des Höchsten unterschätzen). Nur mit dem Unterbewusst-sein möchte ich den Gottesbegriff nicht in Zusammenhang bringen. Was mir darüber bekannt ist, scheint mir nicht nach dieser Richtung zu deuten; eher würde ich glauben, dass diese Zustände zu den mit dem

Körper hinwegfallenden, nicht ewigen, Teilen unseres selbst gehören. . . . Herzliche Grüsse den Ihrigen und Ihnen selbst die treuesten Wünsche Ihres alten

C. STUMPF

Berlin, 8.V.07

Lieber Freund, —

Endlich komme ich dazu, Ihre liebe Karte vom Januar, die immer auf meinem Schreibtisch lag, zu beantworten. Ja es ist wahr "We lead a life of non-communication," und mir tut dies nicht minder leid wie Ihnen. Aber wie soll dies anders werden, solange mich diese Berliner Maschine gefesselt hält? Sie geben Ihre Lehrtätigkeit auf, um ganz der Wissenschaft zu leben. Dazu kann ich mich noch nicht entschliessen. . . .

In unsren Anschauungen, lieber und verehrter Freund, scheint leider eine wachsende Divergenz einzutreten. Ich kann mich mit Pragmatismus und Humanismus nicht befreunden. Die positivistische Erkenntnisstheorie, in der Sie sich mit Mach berühren, scheint mir unmöglich, resp. unfruchtbar. In den beiden Abhandlungen, die Sie etwa zugleich mit diesem Briefe erhalten, versuche ich dies zu begründen. Sie werden dies als einen Standpunkt bezeichnen, den Sie *verlassen* haben; ich stimme mit dem früheren James mehr als mit den heutigen überein. Aber der *Mensch* steht mir dabei innerlich so nahe wie früher, und das, hoffe ich, sagen Sie auch mir gegenüber.

Habe ich Ihnen auch die "Gefühlsempfindungen" geschickt? Diese Abhandlung dürfte eher auf Ihre Zustimmung hoffen können, als die beiden akademischen. . . . Grüssen Sie alle von uns herzlichst und bleiben Sie gut Ihrem treu ergebenen

C. STUMPF

Berlin, 20.V.09

Verehrtester Freund! —

Ich darf nicht länger zögern Ihnen für Ihr letztes Buch den herzlichsten Dank auszusprechen. Es hat mich wieder stark angeregt, u. ich will mich nun auch mit Ihrem Bergson näher befassen. In Bezug auf die "letzten Dinge" glaube ich Ihnen näher zu stehen als in Hinsicht der pragmatischen Wahrheitsbegriffe, obgleich ich Wahres darin auch nicht verkenne. Könnten wir uns nicht einmal wiedersehen? Es ist doch ein zu dürftiger Verkehr mit der Feder, und ich bin ein schlechter Briefschreiber. Meine Frau und ich senden Ihnen beiden u. Ihrem Harry, wenn er sich noch an uns erinnert, beste Grüsse. Ihr getreuer

C. STUMPF

IX

SYLLABUS OF PHILOSOPHY 3 [1]
(1902–1903)

What Philosophy is: an investigation into object-world as well as into subject-world.

"Pragmatism" as our method.

Berkeley's Idealism as an example thereof.

Kant's argument for Idealism.

Post-Kantian Idealism makes experience absolute.

Pluralistic Panpsychism: material objects are "for themselves" also.

Idealism is not necessarily Ideality, for us — even the Absolute may will human frustration.

"Facts," "laws," and ultimate "elements." Elements and laws (the conceived order) have usually been considered to have a deeper reality than facts (the perceived order).

Recent criticism treats them as a subjective short-hand for descriptive purposes: our laws do not preëxist, Nature verifies them only approximately; and our elements (atoms, ether) involve logical absurdities.

The Energy-theory tries to reduce this artificiality and to describe perpetual experiences simply.

Yet "conservation of energy" is also an ideal conception which the facts fit, so Nature does meet our rational demands.

How explain this harmony?

Theistic view: God's design.

Transcendentalist views: Eternal Reason evolving.

Pearson's suggestion: Coevolution of intellect and sense.

Peirce's suggestion: Order results from chance-coming, and survival of the more coherent.

Question of Unity of the World.

Description of world as a multitude of moments of experiences, connected by relations (also experienced) which constitute so many grades of "unity," such as sharing one Space and Time, being of a kind, being

---

[1] *Cf.* above, 373.

known together, interacting, having one origin, etc. Any sort of unity makes a universe of that grade. Our universe is of many grades. It shows, *e.g.*:

Noetic Unity: Complex objects are perceived or conceived; — but there is always some ignorance. The various knowers are not immediately conscious of one another. I only *postulate* your mind, as correlative to what I see your body do.

"Pure Experience" thus agrees with common sense: Our various minds "terminate" at percepts (physical things), which they experience in common.

Objections to this conterminousness of minds:

I. Pluralistic:

a. "Two can't have the same object, because each has its object inside of itself." Pragmatic answer: How can I tell *where* your object is except by your acts? To show where, you point to *my* object with your hand which *I* see. It is only as altering *my* objects that I guess you have a mind. If your object is not where mine is, the objector must show where else it is; he probably introjects it into your head.

b. "Two minds can't have one object because they are two." Answer: A purely verbal objection! The objector should show a *hindrance* to their being one in that point.

c. "Preëstablished harmony is a better theory." Answer: No, for it violates parsimony, precludes eventual increase of conscious union, and involves universal predestination.

II. Monistic objections: They assert that there is no halfway position between absolute unity and absolute disconnection.

a. Royce's argument for Noetic Unity: It assumes self-transcendency of knowing state. Answer by pragmatic description (1) of perceptual knowledge as identity of state and object, and (2) of conceptual knowledge as transition through harmoniously developing intermediary experiences to a terminus (or *towards* such terminus, assumed to be possible if no hindrance appears). On this view knowledge becomes an external relation, and no All-Knower is required.

b. External conjunctions in general are absurd: The conjunctions would have to be conjoined in turn. "Independence" contradicts "connection." *A*, related, is another *A* from *A* not related, etc. — No adventitious union of things is possible, through and through unity is required.

Answer: Such arguments are purely verbal, and even verbally, "partial independence" is an admissible term. Pragmatically, adventitious relations *are* intelligible. Need a space-interval be "linked"? Does *A* "resemble" before its like exists? etc.

Pragmatic discussion of Likeness, Change, Possibility, comes in here.

c. "An absolute Many is absurd on idealistic principles; for then every fact exists only by being known, and if the manyness be a fact, it is established as such by being present to an All-Knower." Answer: If unnoticed, the manyness is (on idealistic principles) no fact. If noted or questioned, it is *we* and not the All-Mind, who make it a fact.

d. "You can't say 'many' without uniting them into a universe of discourse." Answer: But need they for that be a universe of more than discourse?

The constitution of a multiple and additive universe is thus perfectly intelligible after the fact. Questions of *genesis* are more difficult.

Monism affirms one *origin.* Even to get into adventitious relations, things must have been preadapted to the relatedness. In the order of Being, the idea of the whole system had to come first. Block-universe!

Sterility in human hands of the abstract idea of system. It would apply to any universe whatever, after the fact. A chaos has its parts systematically interadapted to that chaotic effect.

No economy of data in one origin: our universe of discourse remains as numerous as if things came singly.

Monists, whenever they study details, have to adopt the pluralistic and empirical method.

All the appearances make for unity being of gradual growth. In concrete experience each step brings new ends into view. "Heterogony of purposes" and substitutability of "fulfilments." The larger systems are only retrospective results.

"Tychism" as an ultimate hypothesis. Some spontaneity is required by every philosophy. As ultimate terms, freedom, chance, necessity, truth, fact, mean one and the same thing — namely *datum* or gift; what (since we find it) we must accept as having *come;* what, for theory, is *taboo.* Is what has actually come incompatible with plural origin?

The details which we find could come in some way or they would not be here; Monism ought to show something to *prevent* their having come piecemeal.

In a world without previous hindering necessity, everything *may* come as a chance; the more stable chance products will accumulate, and if connected, will make a universe which will grow in unity also.

Interaction might also come (hindrance of it would be a case of it). Things instead of interpenetrating and making no difference, might, first, interfere with and *bound* each other, and then grow gregarious, —

associations, habits, and compound units thus accumulating by degrees. What should prevent such variations?

Lotze's proof of Monism by interaction. Purely verbal: *call* them "one," they can, call them "many" they can't, interact. The real question is, What is interaction known as? Whatever it be, it *came,* whether it came with the one, or in the many.

The originals of all that we know as interactions are subjective aspects of experience. Continuity, activity, causality, change, development, help, hindrance, fulfilment, etc., are forms of consciousness of transition.

"Interaction" therefore was realized whenever consciousness of transition came, when boundaries as such became objects, and conterminous experiences were known together. Vast empirical differences in the *spread* of consciousness.

There may, even now, be much more spread than we are aware of. Royce's "time-span" hypothesis. Divine consciousness a question of fact, not of logic.

The wider the span the more is unity realized. "Organic" unity the form of unity most likely to accumulate, if once produced.

Limitless cumulative power of minute variations in conservative direction. Conformably to Science, the increments have been incredibly minute and our universe, now inconceivably old, is already enormously evolved towards order.

Reasons in Tychism's favor.

I. Scientific reasons:

1. No concrete experience ever repeats itself. The usual explanation of concrete variety by permutation of unvarying elements, is, if taken absolutely, only an assumption. Scientific laws express only aggregate results, compatible with individual variation in the elements — recent science abounds in the admission of such variation.

2. We fail to absolutely exclude originality, by assuming that elements only *repeat.* Repeat what? — original models!

3. Our own decisions suggest what "coming into existence" might be like: "Chance" from without, self-sufficing life from within. *What* comes is determined only *when* it comes. *Ab extra* it appears only as a possible gift or "graft."

II. Moral reasons:

1. Absolutely to deny novelty, as Monism does, and to assume that the universe has exhausted its spontaneity in one act, shocks our sense of life.

2. Tychism, essentially pluralistic, goes with empiricism, personalism, democracy, and freedom. It believes that unity is in process of being

genuinely won. In morals it bases obligation on actual demand. Tychism and "external relation" stand or fall together. They mean genuine individuality, something to *respect* in each thing, something sacred from without, *taboo*.

III. Metaphysical reasons:

1. Tychism eliminates the "problem of evil" from theology.

2. It has affinities with common-sense in representing the Divine as finite.

3. It avoids Monism's doubling-up of the world into two editions, the Finite repeating the Absolute in inferior form.

Infinity. — For Tychism, things come in instalments, causing *change*. Continuous change would give us the *completed infinite*.

Zeno's argument conclusive. Continuity is only an ideal construction. In actual experience, there are "threshholds," and change is always by finite increments.

Where the world's elements are represented as standing (space), or as having come already (past time), there seems no incompatibility between their infinity and their actuality.

Kant's antinomies. Fallacy of K.'s argument against infinity. Each condition must indeed be there; but need the "each"-es make an "all" in the sense of a bounded collection? To say so, begs the question. All that logic requires is that no one (distributively taken) must be lacking.

Renouvier's *principe du nombre:* Same fallacy. Real things may be countable *ad infinitum* if each number finds its thing already there.

For the more in these cases is defined as something previous, and not, as in the case of continuous change, as something yet to be produced.

Empirical discussion of infinity of world.

Conclusion. — In any case the "quantity of being" is finite, since, by Tychism, beings have come in successive instalments, each of finite amount, just as our experiences now come. Time and space may be infinite without contradicting logic.

Pragmatically, infinity means that more may come, infinitesimal means that something is lost, has sunk below the pragmatic threshold. "Experience," swinging between the two infinites, is thus most naturally describable in pluralistic or tychistic terms.

The *inanity* of infinite time and space disinclines the mind to their acceptance, and panpsychic idealism, for which infinity no longer forms a problem, seems the most satisfactory theory to adopt.

X

THE MILLER–BODE OBJECTIONS
(1905–1908)

THE following is a selection from the notebook in which James recorded for over two and a half years his attempts to meet certain criticisms of his doctrine of "pure experience" (*cf.* above, 393).

[November 1905] In my psychology I contended that each field of consciousness is entitatively a unit, and that its parts are only different cognitive relations which it may possess with different contexts. But in my doctrine that the same "pen" may be known by two knowers I seem to imply that an identical part can help to *constitute* two fields. Bode and Miller both pick up the contradiction. The fields are . . . decomposable into "parts," one of which, at least, is common to both; and my whole tirade against "composition" in the *Psychology* is belied by my own subsequent doctrine. How can I rescue the situation? Which doctrine must I stand by? . . . In a philosophy of pure experience the terminus must be represented as a possible *terminating experience.* As such it must (whatever it may be actually before we get there) potentially and finally be an experience conterminous to us both. Our two several terminal fields must either stop *at* it, or both run *into* it and include it in such wise that, though *it* is common to us both, the rest of the fields are cut off from each other. So the psychological difficulty recurs. . . . How can our two fields be units if they contain this common part? We must overhaul the whole business of connection, confluence and the like, and do it radically. . . .

Assume two experiences to be originally distinct: — *can* they grow confluent, yet still retain their entitative identity? If so, "composition" is possible in minds. If not, then what grows confluent is not the original terminus, but two substitutes for it, — one which my mind runs into, and another which your mind runs into. The contrast here opens up of the immediate being of things in experience, and the reflective designation of "those same things" by subsequent experience. . . . A thing, we say, *is* self-same, or two things *are* distinct. Yet neither attribution may be explicitly made at the moment it exists, it may only be "recognized" later to have existed. . . . Yet if to be means to be experienced, how can the things be thus or so before the explicit recognition that they are so? . . . I get lost here between the entitative and the functional points of view. If to be is to be experienced, then every thing can be *immediately* only as it is *immediately* experienced. If not immediately experienced *as* the same or *as* other, how can it in its immediacy have been the same? or other? If we meet this by the assumption that things are immediately as they are known to have been, is n't this naïf? Does n't it abrogate the pure-experience principle? . . . This is as far as I can go consecutively today. . . .

November 13 [1905] (Concord). The question is: can the same be in two ways? If to "be" is to be experienced, how can it *be* the same, if experienced in two ways — *i.e.* not *as* the same. . . . The concrete trouble is over the question: can the same terminus be "co" me and "ex" me at the same time? Or can my experience be the same in me and in the world soul, when obviously the world soul's edition of it is so different from mine? . . . Probably the simplest case to handle will be the Fechner or mind-stuff theory, — go right. at it. . . . In the usual cases of knowing-together (those that most struck me when I was writing my psychology) the content is *altered* by the synthesis. Not so with *concepts:* but concepts here are eternal objects, and not psychological contents, or experiences *in concreto.* They are *functions.* Are there any *concrete experiences* that remain unaltered when compared, added, or what not? The parts of space offer themselves, but they are concepts also. . . . In *every* sensational object alteration occurs, and the doctrine of the psychology is true. . . . How then can the pen be the "same" (no difference) if it figures in two minds? The discussion returns, as to its centre, to the question whether an experience that is *co* can be the same as it was when *immediate*, or as it was when *ex*. . . . If the several experiences are successive there would seem to be no trouble, — the doctrine of my psychology apparently will suffice. . . . The hitch comes when we take a single unit of time — *then* can what is immediate be *also co*, and yet can both be pure experience? There is no virtuality here as distinct from the actuality. The *co* must be *constituted* of the several immediates, and if each contains no *co*, how can *all* contain it? Unless it be constituted by an additional express *co-experience?* . . . The difficulty for me here is the same that I lay so much stress on in my criticism of Royce's Absolute, only it is inverted. If the whole is all that is experienced, how can the parts be experienced otherwise than as it experiences them? That is Royce's difficulty. *My* difficulty is the opposite: if the parts are all the experience there is, how can the whole be experienced otherwise than as any of them experiences it? Can we resort to *function* here? For function you must go out of the moment. Function in experience only means leading to a terminus. Can the solution be that pen *schlechthin* leads simply to more pen, whereas pen-*co*-me leads into my life, and pen-*co*-you into your life; and that these two diverse *co's* are constituted by supervening experiences of transition to the diverse termini? At the first blush this sounds rather plausible. . . .

November 22 [1905]. It comes back to the question of identity between "fact of" and "awareness of." Retrospectively, we are aware of fact-without-awareness having been. But the case that concerns us is contemporaneous. The pen is *co* both me and you — that is a fact; and there is also a kind of awareness of it. You and I are at the same time *ex* each other; but of that fact there is no awareness at the moment. It is a much later experience that makes this fact explicit. Thus at the moment under discussion, part of the "fact" is given to consciousness or "experienced" in the full sense, part of it is not. What *happens* here that makes the two *co's* experienced facts, whilst the *ex* of the two minds is a fact but not an experienced one? Will an "Aktionstheorie" help us out? Are things *co* when they *act* together, otherwise not? And is the "event" which I say so much about in my Princeton Address[1] the entrance into one action, so that the pen is consciously *co* my mind whenever it and my mind lead together to a consequence, and *ex* my mind in the opposite case? . . .

When "taken" in my experience, the pen is separated in a sense from . . . other objects. But realistically speaking it bears the same relation to them as before. What curtain, Miller asks, now shuts them off? . . . The difficulty relates . . . to the distinction between fact *per se* and fact as experienced, around which all my present writing has revolved. If you run "fact" consistently, then if object 1 is ever related to 2, 3, 4, it is always so related, and pure experience does n't deny this. Yet how, unless "taking" be different from "fact," does it get "taken" without the relation, or as if unrelated? On the other hand, if you run "experience" consistently, how is object 1 connected with object 2, when not experienced to be so? It is not experienced to be so in my taking of it, therefore *that* object 1 is not connected.

It seems necessary to run fact in part and experience in part, just as common men do. . . . To begin with, you can't get over the retrospective judgment that facts *have* been. Of some facts you can never

---

[1] "The Knowing of Things Together," given before the American Psychological Association at Princeton in Dec. 1894; *C.E.R.*, 383 ff.

say that they have *not* been. Virtualities of experience must then be admitted. What can *never* be experienced as *not* being, *may be;* may virtually be now, in the shape of certain of its constituents or conditions being now. Thus a *many* may be, now; experiences may distributively be, in the shape of eaches, uncollected as yet under the name of many. Separations, or what appear later as such, may thus be, subconsciously as it were; or as previous *grounds* for conscious separation, becoming explicitly experienced a moment later. Assemblages may similarly be, in advance of analytic consciousness that they are conjunctions of parts. . . . Thus "fact" and "experience," so far from being inconsistent, work together beautifully, when the fact and the experience of the fact are not treated as numerically identical. No one treats them as numerically identical when they are successive. But does succession introduce a *logical* difference? Can fact and experience of the fact be discriminated in a contemporaneous content, and the content still retain its identity?

November 26 [1905] . . . In my *Psychology* the real pen figures as a *Grenzbegriff,* for I insist that what the associationist school calls the "same ideas" (*e.g.,* the elements and the compound, or the remembrance and the presence) are different ideas that mean the same objects . . . and so exert the same function. . . . Is the *real* "pen" such a *Grenzbegriff?* . . . Is finite experience a set of Berkeleyan solipsisms . . . while the real pen is . . . the postulate of an absolutely transcendent object, the result of infinite extrapolation of the termini of common sense? Something like this is what Bode and Woodbridge [2] seem to be driving at; yet the statement of so artificial a theory awakens in me deep distrust. Oneness, epistemologically deemed so impossible, is realized *dynamically* all the while, through my actions on *my* objects influencing *yours.* (The dynamic union is perhaps the deeper category to use.) . . . In trying to run things by pure immediacy, as I have done, have we left something vital out? . . . You seem to require *an other than* the immediate to make your world run as it should. Could you possibly treat this other as equivalent to *subconscious* dynamic operations between the parts of experience, distinct from the *conscious* relations which the popular term "experience" exclusively connotes? and which are not dynamic? Would this subconscious realm of operation escape from the definition of experience (on my activity theory, dynamisms have no *esse* other than their *percipi!*), or are they experiences? . . . For my radical empiricism, the realm out of which the changes of experience come would seem to have to be a realm of fact

[2] F. J. E. Woodbridge (Editor of *Journal of Philosophy*), "The Nature of Consciousness," *Jour. of Philos.,* II (1905), 119.

in which experience lies. To make this fact itself reënter experience, so that the all shall be experience, we must endow the bits of experience with immediate *life, i.e.,* not take them statically or immediately, but as Bergson does. So doing, the problem turns into that of what the contents of experience are, not of where experience comes from. . . . The term "experience" overlaps all, and is not overlapped by "fact."

November 30 [1905] . . . In my mind-stuff chapter[3] the criticism was that experience of *a* plus experience of *b* is not experience of *a* and *b*. . . . This looks as if the *fact* of experience was not identical with the *content* thereof. . . . Now my pure-experience theory seems to require a simple identity of content and experience. But "experienced *überhaupt*" is one thing; "experienced singly" another; and "experienced together" a third: yet one content may suffice for these three modes. What is the logical relation here between the one pair of terms *content* and *experience of that content,* and the other pair of terms discussed just now, *fact* and *experience of that fact?* . . . Will the point made in one of my essays serve here? Are the terms coextensive when all are taken abstractly, and coextensive when all are taken concretely, but not coextensive when one is taken concretely and another abstractly? . . . Experience is continually developing and enveloping itself — this is a *fact.* But the fact is *of* experience; and the experience is *of* content; the content in turn may be *that fact* or *those facts* — so you go round in a circle which seems to have no absolute beginning; but which is rather a spiral than a circle. . . . This is obscure groping on my part. . . .

You can't *confine* content. This is the Bergson-Dewey claim. It changes into content witnessed or experience of content. Which is one way of saying *inter alia* that the *witness* thrusts himself in all along the line. . . . This claim is radical empiricism's postulate: "No fact that is not experienced." It should be amended into "no fact that is not conceivable retrospectively as *having been* someone's experience, or prospectively as *ready to be* someone's experience." When talking about fact we must confine it to the sort of fact that does not exclude these possibilities. But these are functional relations between that fact and certain other facts conceived. And the whole realm of *conceivable* fact, contains the notion of facts that might be out of all relation, or out of that kind of relation. Our philosophy would then ignore such facts, and carry on its business with the others. It would not deny them; to deny them it would itself have to experience them abstractly; but that would not contradict its definition of them as what is concretely unexperienced. . . . Revert now to the *Hauptfrage*[1]

[3] *Principles,* Ch. VI.

What does the confluence with me of object 1 mean pragmatically? What does separation of pen from 2, 3, 4, mean pragmatically? Evidently there is an *operative not* in the latter case. There are no such results as would occur from 2, 3, 4, being *co*-me. There is thus a definite kind of *absence*. On the other hand, if object 1 (pen) be *co*-you and also *co*-me, there are two sets of results of the common presence, together with an absence of results that would accrue were the rest of you confluent with me as the pen part of you is, and *vice versa*. . . .

December 1 [1905]. Admit that a transcendent subject and a transcendent object would get rid of all the difficulties : — what do they *mean?* They mean that relations difficult to establish in the train of immediate experience can be established if we draw lines from certain bits of experience to these transcendent terms. Thus the "pen" in experience can be both your pen and my pen if "you" and "I" are transcendent terms, because then *we* severally "take" it, and our taking or knowing in no wise modifies it. Just so, if it is a transcendent "object," its physical relations with other transcendent objects are not interfered with by its being known to the transcendent subject. The world of immediate experience is itself mediatorial between these two transcendencies. The subject's knowing passes clear through it to lay hold on the object *in se*, and any one real object passes round it to influence the other objects *in se* which other parts of experience cover. Since, then, this straightening and simplifying function is that of the transcendencies, the believer in immediacy must ask whether there is no way by which immediate experience can do a similar work. The great law observed in working transcendency is that no change is wrought in anything. . . . One ought therefore to import this postulate into the immediate, in trying to work *that*. No change SHALL take place in the pen when it is *co*-me. Similarly, none when it is *co*-you. Ergo, it SHALL be the same pen. If this won't work in the immediate how can it work in the transcendent? And if it will work in the transcendent, when is the freeing condition there? And can't we get that condition into the immediate and make that work as well? . . .

December 2 [1905] . . . Once for all, transcendentalisms are only *Machtsprüche* that . . . simultaneous *co's* and *ex's shall* come off. They don't cast a ray of light on the how of it. They merely say that the categories of common sense *shall* not be reversed. *Our* quest is to preserve these, if possible, in more intelligible form; or if that be impossible, then to give them up. . . .

December 3 [1905]. The problem is *certainly* soluble. All the materials are in my own hands, being categories . . . belonging to different levels, exercises, or systems of human thinking; and the contradictions met with . . . are contradictions obtaining within our own terms. We certainly ought to be able so to arrange these as to eliminate trouble . . . without bringing in . . . hypothetic terms that have no intrinsic meaning. . . .

December 6 [1905]. (From my reply to Miller) . . . If you allow experience itself to *be,* other things, not "contents" of experience, may also be: — transcendental egos, souls, things-in-themselves, matter, what not — the door being once open. So one must confine being to what is experienced, under penalty of this invasion. Yet I find it not easy to do. Solve it for me!

December 9 [1905] . . . Does the pure-experience principle demand that every bit of experience should function *both* physically and mentally (complete "parallelism")? Or may some bits only function in a mental and others only in a physical context? If the latter were the case, the principle would still mean non-dualism, for the *stuff* would be neutral, and only *per accidens* figure as belonging to either "world," or to both. . . . Calling the stuff "experience" implies that it should either be *witnessed* or be *witnessable;* but what does "witnessable" mean before the actual witnessing? . . . Here . . . the notion of a *being* of "content" logically or ontologically prior to the *experiencing* of it comes upon us; and the fundamental postulate of radical empiricism ("count in being nothing that is not matter of experience, and leave no given matter of experience out") reduces itself to this, that "nothing must get counted that is not definable as positive content." This would rule out such . . . concepts as matter, substance, soul, cause, abstract being. . . . We should apparently revert then to something on the whole more like the world of common sense than is the world described in my essay on "A World of Pure Experience." . . . First of all, it seems as if we gained a more definite basis for saying that things are "virtually" experienceable as so-and-so. The definite entrance into co-relation with a witness would be the complementary condition that turns into an "experience" what till then was only a "content." (Does this also give a more definite notion of what "subconscious" existence may be, or sometimes be?) Schematically, and merely from the point of view of logic, could the entrance of the pen-content into our two consciousnesses be represented as two operations performed *on* it by two external apperceiving selves? . . . Or can the *co* be construed as the mere annulment of isolation? . . . Or . . . will a conjunctive experience, a real "between," additional to the terms, do the business, if brought into play? . . . There seems no way out of it except by analyzing particular cases, one by one. One must obey certain fixed rules in working out any conclusion: — (1) Admit no contentless entities as agents. (2) Don't be satisfied with a harmony of plural solipsisms, discontinuous, whether "preëstablished" or not. The world is *dynamically* continuous, to say the least. (3) Don't violate the principle of non-contradiction. By (1) scholastic common sense seems ruled out; by (2) Berkeley-Millerism; by (3) Royce-Fechnerism. What fourth alternative is there? There seems none. I find that I involuntarily think of *co*-ness under the physical image of a sort of lateral suffusion from one thing into another, like a gas, or warmth, or light. The *places* involved are fixed, but what fills one place radiates and suffuses into the other by . . . "endosmosis." This seems to ally itself with the fact that all consciousness is *positional,* is a "point of view," measures things for a *here,* etc. . . .

December 13 [1905]. There are countless *co's* that are immediately undiscerned as such, unanalyzed: — *e.g.,* the continual *co* of my organic sensations along with my other objects; the coalescence of intensity, extensity, quality and emphasis in all "fields" of experience . . . the sense of the just past, of outlying space, of the background interest, etc., — all these are so ready to be distinctively experienced, that we deem them experienced *subconsciously* all the while. . . . Suppose that total conflux, possible or actual, is really the "bottom" fact, suppose it actual "subconsciously," — then the problem is that of the conditions of insulation. It is the problem of my Ingersoll Lecture, the problem thrown up by Bergson's mind and brain idea. Evidently the *brain* has something to do with it. The pen gets to be *co* my mind through its relations with my brain, and *co* your mind similarly. . . .

December 17 [1905]. Go to a concrete case. Take the *co*-ness of my arm-feeling with the visual arm, whether seen, or imagined. The visual arm, I postulate, is (as a reality) common to me and to you. The felt arm is mine alone, and never becomes common. The *cause* of this difference is physical: the arm physically stimulates your sight apparatus, but only *my* kinæsthetic apparatus. . . . Can other cases of *co* and *ex* be similarly accounted for? . . . Purely on the plane of the analysis of what experience *is,* the *co*-ness of content there is but the intellectual preliminary to *activity*-experience. . . . And this suggests reverting to the Bergson view of the brain as only the point of application of activities. . . . This would formulate consistently the fact that my mind can come into some sort of coöperative contact with the pen and with your visible body, but not with your kinæsthetic and more constant me, — for on my brain *that* part of your body makes no assault whatever. Thus, whatever parts of other real experience assail my brain and prompt it to activity, coalesce with me, while other parts are excluded.   Within the *co*-part, attention can move the threshold back and forth, it being a function of "activity." . . .

June 8, 1906 (Chocorua).   The "cosmic omnibus" around about experience, is the "being" of the experiences and what not *immediately* experienced relations they may stand in.   All these facts are *virtually* experience, or matters of later experience, however. . . .   Not all that an experience virtually *"is"* is content of its immediacy.   But the remainder consists in facts "about" it, which require other experiences related to it and are content of *their* immediacy — often taking retrospective form.   The cosmic omnibus for any given experience would thus seem to be only other correlated experiences.

August 8, 1906 (Cambridge).   One *must* admit a cosmic omnibus of "being" for each "experience," in which what is true *of* it is realized, while *it* realizes only what it is immediately "of." . . .   This idea, worked along with my philosophy of possibility (with absence of hindrance as one kind of "condition") . . . may clear the way for a better discussion than the previous pages have shown with their lamentable groping.   An absence, while it exists, can't be an experience, but only the absence of an experience; yet [as] the condition of a true retrospective experience . . . [it] ought to be treated as a positive object. . . . In itself . . . it is nothing but the negative condition of another object. . . .   No experience can *be* immediately all that it is later experienced as *having been.*   Thus *some* truth must ever be mediated. . . . The later knower about the first piece of experience adds a content which *as* "experience" was not there, and yet which is now true "of" what was there, so that what was there may *always* have been transcendent — in other words, my doctrine may wholly . . . break down.   In what sense can what *was true* be considered as having been in experience?   Or, if out of experience, in what sense can it have *been* at all?

August 14 [1906] . . .   How, in one consolidated fact, can we conceive that the parts should take *themselves* singly or in separation? It is conceivable that that fact should act differently on its environment by its different parts, and that the environmental effects should discriminate or analyze them, as sounds are picked out by a "receiver." But this involves an *other;* and perhaps the best way of stating the whole trouble is something like this: that *ex* and *co* mean analysis of a whole; and that all analysis involves an "other." . . .   A One means that nothing ever or in any respect can be absent, — all being eternally co-present; with a Many, absences . . . are accidents always to be reckoned with. . . .   In this matter of the pen the trouble is not how what is present to the ink can be absent from the mind and *vice versa*

. . . [but] how the pen *in its immediacy* (which is supposed indivisible) can *realize* the one function without the other, and yet not break into two editions of itself. . . .

August 19 [1906] (Swan's Island).   If each part can experience itself without any doubling up, or rather without any "other," if it can be "of" its own content, why then can't the whole, if given at all, do the same? and why is not the being of such a whole exactly tantamount to the being of all its parts?   (Relations between parts ought here to count as parts.)   Acquaintance with each part ought to be equivalent to knowledge of all the parts, if such acquaintance exists. . . . But where does it obtain, if it does exist?   Evidently "taking" must come in, — witnessing!

August 22 [1906].   Remember Lotze's argument for the One, and my criticism on it.   Isn't there some danger that the whole discussion carried on in these present pages may be invalidated by a similar sin of abstraction?   A pen that is defined as *"nothing but ex-*me" can't *as such* be *co-*you.   And a field of consciousness described as *nothing but* a "knowing together" can't know two things "apart." . . .

August 23 [1906].   The essence of the transcendentist contention is that the content of experience is realized *elsewhere* than in the immediate experience of *it*.   It is realized also in what knows the truth *about* it.   This knowledge is often retrospective.   There is thus a sense in which a content (without ceasing to be *that same*) reduplicates, and is saved from being a "flat" datum.   (It is like the phenomenon of "lustre" in stereoscopic vision.) . . . Pragmatically all that is involved is what I stand up for, namely, that further experience in point of fact does offer itself as "of" *the same*. . . .

September 11 [1906] (Chocorua).   Suppose that the immediate is only a name for so much "content" — the potential, or material for all the universes that either con- or dis-junctive relations can weave it into. The question is as to the *simultaneous* application to it of diverse relations — successive application, introducing various "others," seems to offer no logical difficulty.   Allow the immediate, in its potential manyness, to have parts that can come to serve (when explicated or developed) into "me," "you," and pen.   Allow that the connection of pen with you and with me is that of being *apperceived*.   "Me" means my body, here, now; "you," likewise.   The relation is *directed* in each case. The pen is "there."   The "here-there" perspective is, in short, the essence of the pen's entrance into a "consciousness," so far as perception goes.   Can the "takings" of the pen be ascribed to the two different bodies exclusively, all that is different in the two fields remaining external to the pen-part itself?   If so, it might function in both fields without doubling up its immediacy, — only its *co*-me and *co*-you would then have to be treated as external relations, which would seem to violate my psychology.

September 12 [1906] . . . May not my whole trouble be due to the fact that I am still treating what is really a living and dynamic situation by logical and statical categories? If life be anywhere active, and if its activity be an ultimate characteristic, inexplicable by aught lower or simpler, I ought not to be afraid to postulate activity. . . . Over and over again I have been brought up standing, in my account, by finding it run into the notion of "taking," which taking, in turn, seemed most conveniently to reinstate the scholastic self or ego as its agent. Taken in one way, or by one witness or ego, the pen is mine, otherwise, yours; *qua* mine, it makes some connections, or *qua* so connected, it is mine; otherwise, yours, etc. The scholastic self violated the postulate of representability (in radical empiricism), so I always shied away from it in spite of its conveniences. But did n't I at the same time stick to "pen," "me," and "you," and to the relations *"co"* and *"ex,"* in a purely static manner? . . . If I did . . . this, and did it wrongly, would n't the remedy lie in making activity a part of the content itself, or introducing agents, but not leaving them behind the scenes? Vivify the mechanism of change! Make certain parts of *experience* do work upon other parts! Since work gets undeniably done, and "we" feel as if "we" were doing bits of it, why, for Heaven's sake, throw away that *naïf* impression. . . .

September 14 [1906] . . . The radical empiricist deals with the question "of what is experience made?" while the psychological reflector deals with that of "how it comes about." The one takes a static, the other a dynamic point of view. They need not therefore be exactly congruent. . . . Radical empiricism . . . don't forget it — is a theory that arises on the level of analysis. . . . The complete account of cognition, as well as of all else, must arise on the level of history. . . . In my . . . account of knowledge the percept is not the *effect* of the object; it *is* the object. . . . "Seeing" does n't alter, it only extracts aspects. All the aspects make the whole thing. But when the field enters into history the object changes shape and turns into a cause of perception. As such, it is for Bergson a mass of short-rhythm experience; condensed in my long-rhythm mind to what appears, but acting by its short rhythms on my brain. . . .

September 19 [1906]. Omitting Bergson for a moment, the pen-problem and the Fechner-problem are one and the same. They reduce themselves to this: How can any term singly and immediately be both *co* and *ex* another term? The answer is: by "functioning" plurally. But functioning means having relations; and to solve this problem the relations must be external. Yet in the particular cases concerning us, it would seem that they could hardly be external if my chapters on mind-stuff and on the stream of consciousness are correct. . . .

September 20 [1906] . . . When the phenomenon is described in terms of activity, it seems . . . as if the question . . . were answered: a simultaneous plural knowledge of the same is no more self-contradictory than a successive plural knowledge. For in both cases the object is given as entitatively distinct and independent (not consubstantial), and the knowing activity of which it is the terminus *ad quem* offers itself as doing work *on* it from without, and yet as being absolutely *next* it in the conscious field. . . .

September 21 [1906] . . . The delicate problem comes up when a percept ("pen") which at a certain moment unites with the self, is simultaneously supposed to do something else in its quality of a physical thing. The self apperceives and assimilates it, is next to it, yet does n't preclude its relations to other facts that the self does n't similarly include. *"Qua"* in the self, it does n't do these things; *qua* out of it, it does them; how the two *qua's,* unless it somehow doubles? . . . The difficulties come only when for the seen pen is substituted the fixed logical term "pen," and when this is treated as an absolute or indivisible unit that "moveth altogether if it move at all." Then the mare's nest paradoxes begin: *co* and *ex* are contradictories; the same thing can't be both; the pen that is *ex* can't be the pen that is *co;* there must be two pens, one for me, the other for the physical world, etc. . . . We get thus remanded more and more imperatively to a study of what all the talk about union, nextness, separation, distinction, *qua*ness, function, entity, etc., pragmatically *means.* These terms cannot possibly have absolute logical values, irrelevant to and contradictory of the experiences from which they are derived, and within which their consequences actually evolve. They must after all get their meaning interpreted by what they do. . . . The remedy would seem to be this: don't cleave to your physical verbal symbol abstractly and literally, but reinterpret it by your immediate experiential fact. Therefore ask whether the kind of intimate nextness of the pen and the self that experience offers is identical with spatial endosmosis, so that, interpenetration having occurred, *extrication cannot also be.* Obviously an affirmative answer is preposterous. For in the experience as originally given, the pen that the mind sees does extricate itself sufficiently for other relations. . . .

September 22 [1906]. Hereabouts, apparently, is the place to dig:

get close up to what *co*-ness and *ex*-ness concretely and pragmatically are, and the problem will approach or reach its solution.

October 4 [1906] (Cambridge). An object in the outer-world has its relations altogether with the present. In "consciousness" the relations of the same object are with the past and future and timeless, — also with the present *body*. This looks as if Bergson were right in calling the body the mediator between the past and the present. Physical things influence each other only in the present. . . . But acting *through* the body, a present thing also acts *through* the mind, and past and future as such, then coöperate with it and are co-factors of the resultant effect produced. . . .

June 17, 1907 (Chocorua). In a universe à la Bergson, reality being telescopic and endosmotic, and things "through" one another . . . there is no reason why *A* might not be *co*- and *ex-B, i.e.,* continuous in any direction with something else, and be so with *C*, dropping *B*, etc. Nothing, as I understand such a universe, is absolutely cut off from anything else, and nothing is absolutely *solidaire*. The sundry practical relations . . . creep out of the original *A* without shock, constituting its takings. This would seem a view susceptible of expression and defense. . . .

September 19, 1907 (Keene Valley). One can have a succession of differents (tones or colors, *e.g.*), without expressly noting that they are differents. The moment they are noticed from that point of view, however, the moment we say, or someone asks, "Are they or are they not, different?" only one answer is possible, "They are." . . . The *"principle of the raised question"* might be used as a touchstone to decide upon subconscious, virtual, or implicit existence; and the postulate of radical empiricism (that all that is must be experienced) would then have to be modified into this — "must either be experienced immediately, or as soon as the question is asked." The "cosmic omnibus" would then be the *Inbegriff* of all the implicit states in which experiences may be before the question is asked. . . .

January 7, 1908 (Cambridge). Remember the "difference threshold": two weights equal to same, are not equal to each other. . . . A relation may be there, but not *count* (*i.e.*, not be effective) on a certain term, while it does count on another. Not a case of being taken, but of taking, in the sense that smallpox "takes." . . . Is the whole trouble over the fact that connections do obtain, that the logically distinct nevertheless does diffuse, that you can't pen reality in, that its structure is to spread, and *affect,* and that this applies to relations as well as to terms, so that it is impossible to call them absolutely external to each other? The only difficulty in admitting this kind of constitution of reality is our inveterate intellectualism, and its idolatry of the concept. If it were admitted, how would the "compounding" of the psychical occur? . . .

January 11 [1908]. The most general peculiarity of fact is that it consists of things in environments. . . . All living things distinguish, assert, and maintain themselves as against their environment. They actively create the relation. Interactions are grounded in the real. . . . Can the mechanics of psychic fusion be conceived as a sort of interaction among units? Is a self a *vortex?* This would give a direction, a grain, and the total result would be the combined effect of smaller units. . . . From next or next, influence would pass and constitute the insuck, till a critical point was reached, after which the outpour would ensue. Translated into mental terms might this mean diffusion towards a psychic synthesis up to the point of sufficiency, then discharge? The psychic scheme could possibly be made to fit a neural scheme and be treated as its other aspect. Of course ordinary reflex action is a sort of vortex-business at the centre. All terribly vague! . . .

February 10 [1908]. The point is, having given up intellectualism absolutely, and adopted the compenetration view, to see whether the latter admits better of the *con* and *ex* relation being simultaneous, for such simultaneity is the crux that has bothered me so long. Take a Fechner progression *a-M-b,* with the extremes distinguishable, the mean term not distinguished from either. Two terms here, *a* and *b,* are *con* a third term *M,* but *ex* each other. In its turn, *M* is *con a,* and in so far one with *a.* Yet, being *con b,* it is one with what *a* is not one with. Its "oneness" thus is not an inherent attribute of it — it takes it and drops it again. . . . Apply this to the case of mental composition, which has been my crux. The intellectualistic statement is that *esse* and *sentiri* are the same, a state of mind *is* what it is realized as. If *M* is realized as *con a,* then it *is con a,* and to be identical with its own self must always be *con a;* whatever else it may be *con* with, it can never be *ex a.* *That M* must permanently carry *a* along with it.

Is part of the intractability due here to a retention of staticality in the notion of "that" and "is"? According to Bergson . . . what we conceptualize statically as a certain grammatical subject . . . is an active life exhibiting always something new, new by addition and new by default. . . . Does the "active life" character pertain also to the instantaneous constitution of reality? — so that no element of it could be treated as a "piece" or stable grammatical subject . . . implying at bottom that our grammatical forms . . . are inadequate. . . .

February 11 [1908] . . . The problem is to *state* the intuitive or live constitution of it without paradox. One can do so only by approximation, awakening sympathy with it rather than assuming logically to define it; for logic makes all things static. As living, no *it* is a stark numerical unit. They all radiate and coruscate in many directions; and the manyness is due to the plurality round about them. Be the universe as much of a unit as you like, plurality has once for all broken out within it. *Effectively* there are centres of reference and action . . . and these centres disperse each other's rays. . . . They elicit . . . modal possibilities when they interact. . . . A mode is . . . an action; and it takes two to produce an action. . . . The variety in any *M* means the fact that it is a business centre, and that business with *a* does not exclude business with *b,* though they are not one business. The world *is* business . . . but the "agent" (element, substance, subject) which grammar and thought require, can be expressed as the potentiality of residual business. . . . Turning to my own particular puzzle, how shall we translate all this? The "pen," as a living real, is the name of a business centre, a "firm." It has many customers, my mind, *e.g.,* and the physical world. To call it the *same pen* both times would mean that although my mind and the physical world can and may eventually figure in one and the same transaction, they need not do so . . . and that in respect of this particular pen-experience neither *counts* in the transaction which the other is carrying on. Neither *is counted* by the other, neither is *for* the other. All such coming and going and alternation connects with the general notion of being counted, observed, associated, or ignored and left separate. These are essentially psychic expressions so that the constitution of reality which I am making for is of psychic type. . . .

At bottom it seems nothing but this, that "or" is one of the conjunctions of things; that all that is possible is not already effective; that things are, but they are in a world; that a world is, but it is a world of things; that neither world nor things are finished, but in process; and that process means *more's* that are continuous yet novel. This last notion involves the whole paradox of an *it* whose modes are alternate and exclusive of each other, the same and the not-same interpenetrating. Express it as you will, you can't get away from this *sort* of statement when you undertake to describe reality. . . .

February 12 [1908]. Now take a mental "state" and trace the possibility of its being "part" of a wider mental state of which it knows nothing. The *it* here is both *co* and *ex* the same thing. Psychologically we know that such things *do* obtain . . . but how *can* they? With what other facts can we class them so as to formulate them without the appearance of self-contradiction? . . . In general terms the condition in question is only a case of non-reciprocity in relation. That at any rate is the *logic* of it. Experience presents examples of it wherever there is *direction* in the relation. Things are not *mutually* later, higher, between, etc. Remembrance is not mutual. Why need "consciousness" be mutual? If it is not mutual, wherein lies the paradox? Apparently in the principle laid down so stoutly in my *Psychology,* that mental facts are as they appear, and can't "appear" in two ways *to themselves.* . . . [But] a mental *it* . . . is alive enough to carry on more than one business. It can *turn* inside of itself; which means that without ceasing to *be* itself, it can stand in many relations, of which being with the "rest" is only one. Both *ex* and *con!* Yet we should be falling into staticism if we tried to explain this wholly by different *parts* of the *it.* Functions are not parts. . . .

To sum up, mental facts *can* (in spite of my *Principles of Psychology,* I, 158) compound themselves, if you take them concretely and livingly, as possessed of various functions. They can count variously, figure in different constellations, without ceasing to be "themselves.". . . My arm-feelings can *be,* though unnoticed. . . . They can also be noticed, and coöperate with my eye-feelings in a total consciousness of *"my* arm." *Your* arm-feelings can't so coöperate, presumably for lack of neural conditions. . . . To take the pantheistic case, "I" can be, and be known; be, and have another being neXt me; why can't I have another being own and use me, just as I am, for its purposes, without knowing any of those purposes myself?

XI

LETTERS OF É. BOUTROUX TO WILLIAM JAMES[1]
(1907–1909)

Paris, 27 juin, 1907

Très honoré et cher Collègue, —

Je vous remercie bien cordialement de l'envoi de votre volume sur le Pragmatisme. Je viens de le lire d'un trait avec autant de plaisir que de profit. Je crois comme vous que la grande différence est entre ceux qui croient que les choses sont, purement et simplement, et ceux qui pensent qu'elles se font, et que nous sommes au nombre des ouvriers qui contribuent à les faire. Dans le premier cas il n'y a pas d'autre occupation sérieuse que la science; tout le reste est vanité et illusion. On ne voit même pas très bien quelle idée, dans ce cas, nous devons nous faire du travail scientifique, de ses mobiles, de ses vicissitudes, de son progrès. Dans le second cas notre vie tout entière, y compris la vie scientifique, a un sens clair et intéressant. Notre pratique de tous les instants plaide pour cette seconde manière de voir, les raisons qu'on y oppose au nom de la science ne paraissant pas convaincantes. Faisons donc comme si effectivement nous vivions notre vie et comme si elle meritait, par son efficacité, d'être vécue.

Je trouve dans votre ouvrage maint passage d'une clarté et d'une force singulières, et je pense qu'il contribuera, chez nous aussi, à répandre des idées qui certes ont de glorieux antécédents mais contre lesquelles la Scolastique subsistante conserve des préventions. Agréez, je vous prie, très honoré et cher Collègue, l'assurance de ma respectueuse et profonde sympathie.

ÉM. BOUTROUX

Paris, 18 décembre, 1908

Cher Professor James, —

Je vous suis très reconnaissant de votre bon souvenir, et j'ai lu avec un vif intérêt votre article, très net et précis, qui distingue très bien le Pragmatisme du subjectivisme. Ce n'est pas de ce côté là, à mons sens, qu'est la difficulté. Elle gît dans le mot "satisfactorily." Si ce mot veut dire: d'une manière qui réponde à l'attente du sujet, en quoi votre définition de la vérité se distingue-t-elle de l'idée que s'en font les

[1] *Cf.* above, 562, 564-5.

savants, le sens commun, et les intellectualistes eux-mêmes en tant qu'ils se placent au point de vue pratique? Je crains parfois, en lisant certaines définitions, que tout le monde ne soit pragmatiste. Le côté de la doctrine qui me paraît le plus important et le plus distinctif, c'est l'indétermination actuelle du futur, par suite la conception des lois de la nature comme de simples faits contingents. J'adhère, quant à moi, *toto animo* à cette doctrine, que vous soutenez avec tant de force et de clarté. L'intelligence n'y est pas sacrifiée, mais elle est affranchie de l' ἀνάγκη, et fondue avec la vie, l'amour et l'individualité.

Nous nous rappelons toujours avec bonheur, ma femme et moi, les quelques instants passés avec vous à Londres. Je suis comme vous, je trouve que l'abstrait n'est rien devant le concret. Je vous vois, j'entends le son de vos paroles, je goûte la grâce de votre obligeance: quelle description de votre personne pourrait remplacer cette sensation?

J'espère toujours que nous aurons une fois le plaisir de vous posséder ici. En attendant je vous prie de nous accorder de temps en temps une pensée, comme nous aimons à évoquer votre souvenir.

Nous vous offrons ainsi qu'à Mrs. James nos meilleurs vœux pour l'année qui va naître. Je vous prie en particulier d'agréer l'assurance de ma profonde sympathie. Votre bien dévoué

ÉM. BOUTROUX

Paris, 2 mai, 1909

Cher Professor James, —

Je vous remercie bien cordialement de l'envoi de votre nouveau livre. Je le lis, comme tous vos écrits, avec un plaisir particulier, parce que je crois vous entendre, et communiquer avec votre personne autant qu'avec votre philosophie. Celle-ci d'ailleurs m'agrée infiniment. Il me semble que je pose le problème philosophique précisément comme vous le posez p. 76: *either absolute independence or,* etc., et p. 81: *possibly you will yourselves,* etc. Et je voudrais le résoudre comme vous le faites vous-même pp. 324 *sqq: In the each-form, on the contrary,* etc. C'est précisément là ce que j'appelle relation, connexion contingente, entendant exclure par ce terme le hazard pur, aussi bien que la nécessité mécanique ou logique. Je crois que la recherche des meilleures connexions entre choses réellement distinctes et logiquement irréductibles est proprement ce que la langue vulgaire et vivante entend par la raison, et c'est pourquoi je pense qu'une activité peut-être dite raisonnable alors qu'elle n'est pas enchainée, fixée et anéantie par la loi de fer du monism intellectualiste.

Je ne sais si vous avez appris que j'ai reçu et accepté l'invitation de venir faire au printemps prochain à Harvard les Hyde Lectures. Je me propose de traiter précisément ce sujet qui me tient particulièrement à cœur : comment les choses peuvent-elles avoir des rapports les unes avec les autres sans perdre leur réalité, leur individualité, leur spontanéité et leur liberté ? La connexion réelle et vivante, voilà ce que je cherche. Je serais heureux si mon projet avait quelque chance de vous intéresser.

Je n'ai pas besoin de vous dire que ce qui nous séduit particulièrement dans la perspective d'aller à Boston, c'est le plaisir de vous y trouver et de faire la connaissance de Mrs. James.

En attendant cet heureux moment nous vous prions d'agreér nos meilleurs souvenirs et nos meilleurs vœux.

Votre bien cordialement dévoué

ÉM. BOUTROUX

ABBREVIATIONS

I. WORKS OF WILLIAM JAMES

Principles of Psychology, N. Y., 1890	*Principles*
Psychology. Briefer Course, N. Y., 1892	*P. B. C.*
The Will to Believe, and Other Essays in Popular Philosophy, N. Y., 1897	*W. B.*
Human Immortality: Two Supposed Objections to the Doctrine, Boston, 1898	*H. I.*
Talks to Teachers on Psychology: and to Students on Some of Life's Ideals, N. Y., 1899	*T. T.*
The Varieties of Religious Experience: A Study in Human Nature, N. Y., 1902	*V. R. E.*
Pragmatism: A New Name for Some Old Ways of Thinking, N. Y., 1907	*Pragm.*
The Meaning of Truth, A Sequel to "Pragmatism," N. Y., 1909	*M. T.*
A Pluralistic Universe: Hibbert Lectures on the Present Situation in Philosophy, N. Y., 1909	*P. U.*
[1] *Some Problems of Philosophy: A Beginning of an Introduction to Philosophy*, N. Y., 1911	*S. P. P.*
[1] *Memories and Studies*, N. Y., 1911	*M. S.*
[1] *Essays in Radical Empiricism*, N. Y., 1912	*E. R. E.*
[1] *Collected Essays and Reviews*, N. Y., 1920	*C. E. R.*

II. OTHER WORKS, RELATING TO JAMES

Henry James, *A Small Boy and Others*, N. Y., 1913	*S. B. O.*
Henry James, *Notes of a Son and Brother*, N. Y., 1914	*N. S. B.*
Henry James, *Letters of*, edited by Percy Lubbock, N. Y., 1920	*L. H. J.*[2]
William James, *Letters of*, edited by his son Henry James, Boston, 1920	*L. W. J.*
Henry James, *The Literary Remains of the Late*, edited by William James, Boston, 1885	*L.R.H.J.*
R. B. Perry, *Annotated Bibliography of the Writings of William James*, N. Y., 1920	*Bg.*

[1] Posthumous

III. FAMILY NAMES

William James (1842–1910)	W. J.
Henry James (1811–1882), father of W. J.	H. J.[1]
Henry James (1843–1916), brother of W. J.	H. J.[2]
Henry James (1879–), son of W. J.	H. J.[3]
Garth Wilkinson James (1845–1883), brother of W. J.	G. W. J.
Robertson James (1846–1910), brother of W. J.	R. J.
Alice James (1848–1892), sister of W. J.	A. J.
Alice Howe Gibbens James (1849–1922), wife of W. J.	A. H. J.
William James (1882–), son of W. J.	W. J.[2]
Margaret Mary James (1887–), daughter of W. J.	M. M. J.
Alexander Robertson James (1890–), son of W. J.	A. R. J.

INDEX

INDEX

Where a topic appears on several consecutive pages, only the first page is given.

782 INDEX

Mill, J. S., I, 160, 215, 228, 466, 499, 516,
543, 552, 560, 565, 570, 576, 656, 662,
663, 664; II, 5, 78, 262, 295, 447,
457, 490, 641, 703.
Miller, D. S., I, 445, 558, 799; II, 240,
315, 375, 393, 494, 507, 538, 544,
Appendix X.
Letters to: I, 799, 810, 812; II, 240,
399.
Miller, G., I, 238.
Millet, F. D., I, 397.
Mind, I, 597; II, 115.
Mind and Body, I, 460; II, Ch. LIII,
94, 95, 132, 395, 608, 756.
Mitchell, A., II, 629.
Mitchell, Maggie, I, 311.
Modernism, II, 581.
Monism, I, 164, 619, 633, 774, 798, 823;
II, 581, 584, 747.
Montague, W. P., II, 550, 594.
Moore, A. W., II, 375, 519, 521, 524.
Morley, J., I, 344.
Morris, G. S., I, 795.
Morse, Frances R.
Letters to: I, 377; II, 214, 250, 326,
357.
Mott, Lucretia, I, 69.
Müller, G. E., II, 56, 117, 180.
Müller, J., II, 3.
Müller, Max, I. 311.
Münsterberg, H., I, 435, 437, 803, 807;
II, 15, 26, 56, 116, Ch. LX, 170, 177,
180, 186, 187, 190, 191, 195, 200, 201,
270, 342, 376, 469, 470, 620, 700, 741.
Letters from: II, 154, 471.
Letters to: II, 117, 138, 140, 142, 145,
146, 147, 150, 152, 154, 269, 288, 332,
469, 470.
Munthe, A., II, 167.
Mussolini, B., II, 575.
Mussy, G. de, I, 368.
Myers, F. W. H., I, 412, 416, 439, 610,
759; II, 121, 156, 163, 164, 165, 167,
179, 338, 341, 376, 649.
Letters from: II, 157, 163, 166.
Letters to: II, 158, 163, 165, 171, 305.
Myers, J. J., II, 49.
Mysticism, I, 461, 727; II, 225, 334, 338,
349, 351, 355, 556, 582, 632, 650, 658,
676.

Nation, I, 104, 106, 204, 260, 263; II, 104,
290, 296.
Nativism, II, 60, 61, 80, 87.
Naturalism. *See under* Materialism;
Positivism; Science and Religion.
Neilson, L. A., I, 336.
Neuberg, J., I, 65.
New Times, I, 30.
Nichols, H., II, 8, 15.
Nietzsche, II, 575, 577.
Nihilism. *See under* Positivism.
Nominalism, I, 560, 566; II, 407.
North American Review, I, 204, 263.

Norton, C. E., I, 87, 88, 96, 97, 106, 260,
263, 265, 297, 311, 328, 329, 362, 407,
419, 724, 816; II, 283, 314, 696, 702.
Letters from: I, 104, 305, 425; II, 284.
Letters to: I, 426, 607; II, 283, 314,
359.
Norton, Grace, I, 417; II, 283.
Letters to: I, 442, 529, 530; II, 253,
338.
Norton, Jane, I, 106, 293.
Letter to: I, 107.
Norton, R., II, 613.
Nott, E., I, 8; II, 231.
Novelty, II, 656, 664, 666.

Oliphant, E. S., I, 31.
Olney, R., II, 306.
Osborn, H. F., II, 8.
Osgood, J. R., I, 139.
Letter to: I, 117.
Osten-Sacken, C. R., II, 256.
Ostwald, W., I, 492; II, 201, 288, 384,
463, 498, 580.
Owen, George, I, 30.
Oxford University, I, 750, 814; II, 583,
624.

Paige, W., I, 237.
Palladino, Eusapia, II, 164, 170, 566.
Palmer, A. F., II, 295.
Palmer, G. H., I, 330, 404, 405, 590, 596,
674, 712, 743, 755, 764, 787, 789, 790,
795, 797, 804, 807; II, 12, 15, 16, 20,
376, 594, 678.
Letter from: I, 435.
Letters to: I, 437; II, 319.
Panpsychism, I, 492; II, 78, 394, 397,
403, 405, 587.
Papini, G., I, 775; II, 457, 468, 505, 570,
581.
Letters from: II, 572, 573.
Letter to: II, 571.
Parker, T., I, 31, 132.
Parkman, Alice, I, 97.
Pascal, I, 308, 485.
Pasco, J., I, 209.
Pater, Walter, I, 344.
Paulhan, F., I, 702.
Paulsen, F., II, 182, 185.
Peabody, A. P., I, 790; II, 275.
Peabody, Elizabeth, I, 31, 132.
Peabody, F. G., II, 331.
Letters to: II, 269, 301.
Pearson, K., I, 492; II, 390, 463.
Péguy, II, 576.
Peirce, Benj., I, 205.
Peirce, C. S., I, 111, 117, 209, 211, 215,
229, 231, 289, 290, 292, 296, 320, 332,
342, 361, 362, 367, 369, 458, 474, 477,
495, 504, 521, Ch. XXXII, 543, 547,
612, 788, 792; II, 9, 104, 105, 109,
117, 221, 266, 373, 375, Ch. LXX,
Ch. LXXVI, 449, 450, 523, 567, 571,
574, 590, 602, 645, 680.